FrameMaker 7:
The Complete Reference

About the Authors

Sarah S. O'Keefe is founder and president of Scriptorium Publishing Services, Inc. The company provides technical publishing services to high-tech companies, including outsourced documentation solutions, technical training, and consulting. Sarah is an experienced FrameMaker trainer; her background includes technical writing, technical editing, production editing, and extensive online help development with various help authoring tools. Currently, she works as a consultant to assist companies in implementing structured authoring, single-sourcing, and other publishing solutions. Sarah resides in Durham, North Carolina. In her spare time, she likes to cook.

Sheila A. Loring is Senior Technical Consultant for Scriptorium Publishing Services near Research Triangle Park, North Carolina, and an Adobe Certified Expert (ACE) in FrameMaker. She wears several hats at Scriptorium, two of which are writing software documentation exclusively in FrameMaker and designing complex FrameMaker templates. Sheila and Sarah previously collaborated on a WebWorks Publisher book. In her alternate reality, Sheila enjoys gardening and learning to play the mandolin.

FrameMaker 7:
The Complete Reference

Sarah S. O'Keefe
Sheila A. Loring

McGraw-Hill/Osborne
New York   Chicago   San Francisco
Lisbon   London   Madrid   Mexico City
Milan   New Delhi   San Juan
Seoul   Singapore   Sydney   Toronto

McGraw-Hill/Osborne
2600 Tenth Street
Berkeley, California 94710
U.S.A.

To arrange bulk purchase discounts for sales promotions, premiums, or fund-raisers, please contact **McGraw-Hill/Osborne** at the above address. For information on translations or book distributors outside the U.S.A., please see the International Contact Information page immediately following the index of this book.

FrameMaker 7: The Complete Reference

1234567890 CUS CUS 0198765432

ISBN 0-07-222361-8

Publisher
  Brandon A. Nordin

Vice President & Associate Publisher
  Scott Rogers

Acquisitions Editor
  Megg Morin

Senior Project Editor
  Betsy Manini

Acquisitions Coordinator
  Tana Allen

Technical Editor
  Alexia Prendergast

Proofreader
  Stefany Otis

Series Design
  Peter F. Hancik

FrameMaker Composition & Implementation
  Scriptorium Publishing Services, Inc.

This book was written and composed in Adobe® FrameMaker.®

Contents at a Glance

Part VII Structured FrameMaker

Part VIII Appendixes

Contents

Part I

Getting Started with FrameMaker

5   Formatting Text with Paragraph Tags 107

6   Formatting Text with Character Tags 143

Part V

Creating Output

Part VI

Advanced Techniques

Part VIII

Appendixes

Acknowledgments

Although only two names appear on this cover, this book owes its existence to the entire staff at Scriptorium Publishing. When we took on this enormous project, we insisted that the book needed to be created in FrameMaker. As a result, our staff was responsible for writing, editing, production editing, template design, and numerous other tasks. We took this book from proposal to outline to press-ready PDF files—all in a FrameMaker-based workflow.

In particular, we owe thanks to Alan Pringle, who performed the thankless tasks of developmental and copy editing. Alan provided invaluable suggestions and caught numerous errors—some grammatical, some technical. His strong FrameMaker background and low tolerance for vague explanations kept us out of trouble on more than one occasion. Furthermore, he reviewed most of our chapters as early drafts and provided critical feedback on the document organization.

Karen Brown worked days, nights, and weekends (mostly the latter two) to ensure that the indexing could be squeezed into the schedule. Mindy Allport-Settle made technical illustration look easy—and it's not. Pam Castro provided some critical sanity checking, ensuring we remembered that there was light at the end of the 900-page tunnel. The template design and production work was done by the authors and Alan Pringle.

Alexia Prendergast provided an excellent technical edit and identified areas where more information was needed. She also contributed some very useful real-world examples based on her company's workflow.

Megg Morin, our acquisitions editor, was a joy to work with. She helped keep the schedule for this monster book on track and provided moral support when things got a little questionable.

David Fugate of Waterside was instrumental in getting the contract signed, sealed, and delivered. We appreciate his help in getting this project started.

We gratefully acknowledge the assistance of Lee Richardson, Dov Isaacs, Julie Manley, Karl Matthews, Jennifer Brieger, Jo Ann Buckner, Richard Zombeck, and Eve Kosol (all of Adobe Systems, Inc.), who answered technical questions, eliminated red tape, helped us get software, and supported us throughout this insane endeavor.

Finally, the authors wish to acknowledge the inspiration and patience of the men and the dogs in their lives: Mark and Bill, and Ginger and Star. You can find Star living up to her name on pages 310 and 657.

Introduction

Welcome to *FrameMaker 7: The Complete Reference.* Adobe's FrameMaker software is the industry leader in technical publishing, and the release of version 7 continues that tradition. FrameMaker automates mundane but essential tasks, such as maintaining running headers and footers and updating tables of contents. It offers an easy path to producing multiple output formats, including print, Portable Document Format (PDF), and several other online formats. In version 7, FrameMaker lets you import and export Extensible Markup Language (XML) and Standard Generalized Markup Language (SGML) files, and it offers structured authoring features that speed up document creation.

This book will show new users how to use FrameMaker to streamline your publishing workflow and greatly improve efficiency and productivity. For current users, we have provided complete coverage of the new features in version 7—and perhaps some new tips for older features.

In addition to writing about FrameMaker, we practice what we preach. Most of the documents we write are created in FrameMaker. The book you are holding was itself produced in FrameMaker version 6—version 7 wasn't released until this book was almost complete.

What's New in FrameMaker 7

Version 7 contains some significant changes, including the following:

- **Unstructured and structured environments.** FrameMaker 7 represents the merging of the FrameMaker ("unstructured") and the FrameMaker+SGML ("structured") applications. Depending on your document requirements, you can work in the unstructured or structured interface. To switch from one to the other, you change a preference and restart the application.

- **Enhanced support of XML.** FrameMaker 7 gives you the ability to import, export, and roundtrip XML content.

- **WebDAV.** FrameMaker now integrates with WebDAV, so you can use this free content-management system to manage your documents and associated graphics.

- **Automatic assignment of master pages.** You can specify that a particular paragraph or element tag automatically apply a particular master page.

- **Creating PDF files.** You can now create PDF files through the improved FrameMaker Save As feature instead of printing to PostScript and distilling the file separately. You can also control the Acrobat job options from inside FrameMaker before you create the PDF file.

- **Support for Extensible Metadata Platform (XMP).** In version 7, the information you supply as file information is saved as XMP data. This emerging standard for file metadata lets you specify the author, subject, title, keyword, and other information. You can access XMP information without opening the file—and without having access to the application that created the file (in this case, FrameMaker).

Who Should Read This Book

The information in this book will be useful for new and long-time FrameMaker users. For new users, the book provides the first third-party reference that explains FrameMaker from top to bottom, including structured authoring. It details basics, such creating a document, importing formats from one file to another, and applying paragraph tags. In more advanced sections, this reference describes how to create templates, use modular text, insert hypertext commands, and set up an XML round-tripping environment.

If you have used "regular" FrameMaker but not FrameMaker+SGML, this book provides everything you need to get comfortable with the new structured authoring features included in FrameMaker 7. You'll learn how to manipulate elements, create element definition documents (EDD), and find out how structured cross-references, for example, are different from regular cross-references.

In short, there's something in this book for every user. Beginners will find a wealth of information, organized in order of increasing complexity. Advanced users may want to skip the first few parts and focus on the second half of the book. Keep in mind that information about structured FrameMaker is generally included at the end of a chapter; for example, you'll find information about setting up tables in a structured environment at the end of the table chapter.

What's in This Book

This rather large book is divided into several parts to help you find your way around. You'll notice that each part has a handy thumb tab, so that you can easily find the part you need.

Part I, Getting Started with FrameMaker

Part I is intended mainly for new users. It provides an overview of FrameMaker's features and interface. All users should probably read Chapter 2, which describes several different workflows that include FrameMaker.

Part I includes the following chapters:

- Chapter 1, "Why FrameMaker?," offers an overview of FrameMaker's features. It describes some of the features that make FrameMaker unique and explains how you can use them to automate common publishing tasks. This chapter is intended for users who are new to FrameMaker and need an explanation of why FrameMaker makes sense for technical publishing projects.

- Chapter 2, "Establishing a Workflow in FrameMaker," describes the typical publishing workflow and examines how FrameMaker fits into that workflow. It also includes an overview of how to integrate importing and exporting of XML into your workflow and how to set up a single-sourcing workflow that lets you publish to multiple output formats. If you are starting with a clean slate and can configure your workflow however you want, read this chapter to get an idea of the possibilities.

- Chapter 3, "Creating Your First Document," explains how to create a new document and open existing documents. It also describes the document window, toolbars, and status bar. Finally, it explains how to configure preferences to suit your workflow. Read this chapter if you are not familiar with the unstructured FrameMaker interface.

Part II, Creating and Manipulating Text

Part II explains the word processing features of FrameMaker and how to add and manipulate text, tables, and other items in your documents. This part includes basic information, such as how to apply a paragraph tag, but it also covers more advanced topics, such as how to create a paragraph tag and set up autonumbering. New users will want to read at least the first half of each chapter to learn about each feature; more advanced users will probably focus on the latter half of each chapter.

Part II includes the following chapters:

- Chapter 4, "Word-Processing Features," describes how to type text into FrameMaker. It also explains how to import text from other applications. Generally, FrameMaker users write directly in FrameMaker. This chapter will be helpful to new users who are not yet familiar with basic text manipulation in FrameMaker. For more advanced users, the importing section provides detailed information about how to import content from Microsoft Word files successfully.

- Chapter 5, "Formatting Text with Paragraph Tags," begins with an explanation of paragraph-level style sheets and how to apply them. It also provides a detailed explanation of how to create and modify paragraph tags.

- Chapter 6, "Formatting Text with Character Tags," shows you how to apply and create character-level style sheets. In FrameMaker, character-level and paragraph-level style sheets are stored in separate locations. Characters tags are used in several other features, such as cross-references and variables, to provide formatting; this chapter also explains those relationships.

- Chapter 7, "Understanding Table Design," explains how to create tables and modify their formatting. Like paragraphs, tables have style sheets, and this chapter describes how to set up table styles.

- Chapter 8, "Cross-References," describes how to create pointers from one section of a document to another. FrameMaker automatically maintains and updates these references as pagination in the document changes.

- Chapter 9, "Storing Content in Variables," details how to use variables to store and format bits of reused text, such as the title of a book or a product name. It also describes how to use system variables to automate running headers and footers, page numbers, and "continued" labels in tables.

Part III, Controlling Page Layout

The chapters in Part III describe managing blocks of text and positioning them on your pages. This part also includes discussions about importing graphics created in other applications and creating graphics in FrameMaker.

Part III includes the following chapters:

- Chapter 10, "Understanding Text Flows," describes how to create and connect blocks of text, or text flows. This information is especially helpful for template designers, who need to understand how to position text blocks on a page and how text blocks are connected and disconnected.

- Chapter 11, "Understanding Master Pages," explains how to set up master pages to determine the page layout in a file, and it shows how to apply and import page layout definitions.

- Chapter 12, "Importing Graphics," explains anchored frames, which serve as containers for most graphics. It also describes how to import graphics from other applications.

- Chapter 13, "FrameMaker's Graphics Tools," describes how to use FrameMaker's built-in graphics tools to create art.

Part IV, Building Books

You can create a book file to hold a collection of files that make up a larger document. Among these files, you can include automated tables of contents and index files, which are explained in this part.

Part IV includes the following chapters:

- Chapter 14, "Setting Up Book Files," describes how to set up and modify book files. It explains how to control chapter, page, and other numbering from the book and how to perform global (bookwide) updates on your content.

- Chapter 15, "Creating Tables of Contents," explains how you choose items for inclusion in a table of contents and how to format those items.

- Chapter 16, "Creating Indexes," explains how to create the markers that become index entries and how to format the generated index.

- Chapter 17, "Creating Other Generated Files," describes some of the less well-known generated files. You can, for example, create a list of fonts used in a document, or a list of imported graphics. Several variations on the standard index are also available.

Part V, Creating Output

In Part V, you learn how to create print, PDF, and online formats, and you learn about managing color.

Part V includes the following chapters:

- Chapter 18, "Print and PDF Output," provides detailed information about printing FrameMaker files and creating PDF files. It explains how to configure your system for successful PostScript printing and provides some information about Acrobat Distiller settings.

- Chapter 19, "Creating HTML and XML Output," describes the options for creating Hypertext Markup Language (HTML) and XML output *without* using a structure application (structured applications are discussed in Chapter 31). This chapter describes how to use FrameMaker's built-in HTML and XML converters. It also provides an introduction to WebWorks Publisher 7 Standard Edition, a third-party HTML and XML converter that's included with FrameMaker 7.

- Chapter 20, "Color Output," explains how FrameMaker handles color output and describes how to set up colors in your document.

Part VI, Advanced Techniques

Part VI covers a variety of advanced topics, including template design, conditional text, hypertext, and using WebDAV with FrameMaker.

Part VI includes the following chapters:

- Chapter 21, "Setting Up Conditional Text," explains how to create two (or more) versions of a document in a single file. The conditional text feature is an important part of most single-sourcing environments.

- Chapter 22, "Creating Interactive Documents with Hypertext," describes how to link documents, create popups, and insert hotspots into graphics with hypertext commands. Many hypertext commands are translated when you convert to HTML or PDF output.

- Chapter 23, "Writing Equations," tells you how to create and format equations in your documents.

- Chapter 24, "Maker Interchange Format," explains Maker Interchange Format (MIF), which is a text-based markup language that describes FrameMaker files. MIF files can be useful for global changes that aren't easily implemented through the FrameMaker interface. It's also widely used as an intermediate format when converting to and from FrameMaker format.

- Chapter 25, "Creating Modules with Text Insets," provides information about FrameMaker's text importing feature. You can create small text fragments and import them into larger documents to create modular documentation.

- Chapter 26, "Templates," pulls together information about many different features. It describes interactions among different components and provides some tips for designing useful templates.

- Chapter 27, "Sharing and Managing Files Using WebDAV," describes FrameMaker's support for version control and content management through WebDAV. WebDAV software (www.webdav.org) runs on any web server and is accessed via http protocol, so you can store files anywhere and access them over the Internet. This allows you to set up a version control system for authors in many different locations. The "DAV" in WebDAV actually stands for "Distributed Authoring and Versioning."

Part VII, Structured FrameMaker

In version 6, FrameMaker was available in two versions—"regular" FrameMaker and FrameMaker+SGML, or structured FrameMaker. The latter was significantly more expensive. In version 7, Adobe has kept the price of regular FrameMaker but added the functions of FrameMaker+SGML, now called "structured FrameMaker." You can create both structured and unstructured documents in this new version of FrameMaker. Part VII focuses on the structure features now included in FrameMaker. It explains authoring in a structured document, creating structure templates, and converting unstructured documents to structured documents. Finally, this part explains how structured authoring gives you the ability to export, import, and roundtrip tagging language files, such as XML and Standard Generalized Markup Language (SGML).

Part VII includes the following chapters:

- Chapter 28, "Working with Structured Documents," explains how authors use the structure view to create content.

- Chapter 29, "Understanding the Element Definition Document," discusses how template developers create the EDD, which controls the allowable structure in a document. Formatting information is associated with elements in the EDD, so formatting is applied automatically as authors insert elements.

- Chapter 30, "Adding Structure to Unstructured Documents," shows you how to apply structure to unstructured documents. Although you can "wrap" unstructured documents into elements manually, it's a tedious and time-consuming process. FrameMaker offers a mapping feature that automates almost all of the conversion for you—once you set up the mapping.

- Chapter 31, "Importing and Exporting XML/SGML Markup Files," explains how you can create and process XML and SGML markup files with structured FrameMaker. With a properly configured environment, you can successfully "roundtrip" files; that is, you can make changes in FrameMaker, transfer the file to XML, make changes in the XML, and transfer the file back to FrameMaker format, all without losing any formatting or information.

The chapters in this part are not the only ones with information about working in the structured environment—the last pages of several other chapters describe structured documentation. For example, working with variables in a structured document is similar to working with them in unstructured documents, so the end of Chapter 9, "Storing Content in Variables," offers additional information on how variables work in structured documents.

Part VIII, Appendixes

The following appendixes are included:

- Appendix A, "Resources," offers a list of FrameMaker-related resources, including a long list of utilities.
- Appendix B, "Managing Fonts Across Platforms," describes how to transfer font information and manage differences in font handling and font naming across platforms. Read this appendix if you are concerned about mapping fonts from one platform to another.
- Appendix C, "Building Blocks," provides a comprehensive lists of the building blocks you use to create tags and formats in FrameMaker.

Conventions Used in This Book

Some of the text in this book uses special formatting to help indicate emphasis or keystrokes. The text conventions as are follows:

Convention	Example	Meaning
SMALL CAPS	■ press the TAB key ■ ESC O P D ■ ESC SHIFT-F L K	Indicates keystrokes. If a keyboard shortcut (such as ESC O P D) contains no hyphens, press each key individually. When keys are joined by hyphens, press the joined keys at the same time.
Italics	*element document definition*	Indicates a defined term, a book title, a placeholder, or text that requires emphasis.
Bold	if you type **2**	Indicates text you type or terms that are being defined in a list.

Convention	Example	Meaning
Courier	`<$paratext>`	Indicates building block strings or output (for example, Maker Interchange Format output).
Pipe (|)	File | Open	Indicates selecting a menu and menu choice (select the File menu, then select the Open menu choice).

Mistakes Were Made...

We've tried to make this book as accurate as possible, but a feature that changed in the final release of the software might not quite match what's described in this book. There's also the possibility that we were, well, wrong about something. For changes and errata, visit:

`www.scriptorium.com/books/fm7cr/`

The Complete Reference

FrameMaker 7

Part I

Getting Started
with FrameMaker

The
Complete
Reference

Chapter 1

Why FrameMaker?

Adobe Systems Incorporated periodically measures user opinions about its products. In survey after survey, one product is off the charts on customer loyalty: FrameMaker.

Why are the users so enthusiastic? FrameMaker is intended for creating complex documents, especially materials full of technical information, such as:

- Technical documentation—user guides, installation guides, system administration guides, reference guides, and training materials
- Dissertations and other long academic publications
- Nonfiction books, especially third-party documentation (including this book!)
- Legal and financial documents, such as prospectuses

If you're responsible for creating these and similar long, technical documents, your software requirements are quite different from someone who produces short, graphics-intensive documents such as brochures, newsletters, or annual reports. For technical publishing, stability and reliability are critical, especially as documents get longer. Having a document crash because a document exceeds 100 pages or contains too many graphics or cross-references is unacceptable, especially in an environment where books of 200 or 2,000 pages are quite common. FrameMaker provides a stable, reliable environment in which to create and manage these types of documents.

Most likely, though, you're hoping for something more than an application that doesn't crash too often. FrameMaker includes many features that are important for anyone working with long documents in a graphical what-you-see-is-what-you-get (WYSIWYG) environment, shown in Figure 1-1. Highlights include the following:

- **Consistent, repeatable, and maintainable formatting.** FrameMaker's templates make it possible to create different documents with the same look and feel. You use template components to ensure that formatting is consistent from one document to another, and you can quickly copy updates from file to file. Instead of hours of manual reformatting, you apply the template across the document library, and FrameMaker changes formatting and repaginates the documents as necessary.

- **Complex document management.** Equations, variables for text, conditional text, and many other features help you create and maintain complex documents. Imported graphics are updated automatically when you change the referenced file.

- **Stability.** FrameMaker is a stable, reliable application. It does not spontaneously repaginate documents when you change print drivers or perform any of those other maneuvers that can be so frustrating in other applications.

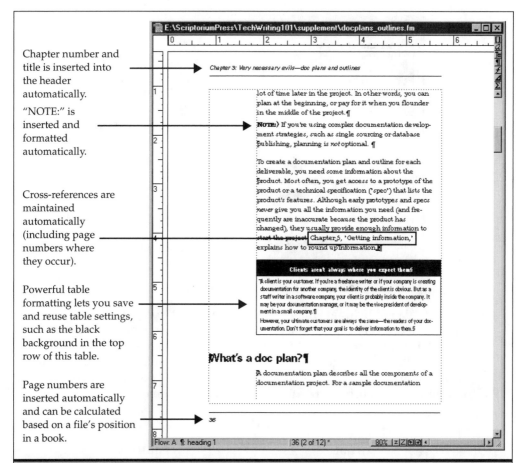

Chapter number and title is inserted into the header automatically.

"NOTE:" is inserted and formatted automatically.

Cross-references are maintained automatically (including page numbers where they occur).

Powerful table formatting lets you save and reuse table settings, such as the black background in the top row of this table.

Page numbers are inserted automatically and can be calculated based on a file's position in a book.

Figure 1-1. *A typical page in FrameMaker*

■ **Long-document management.** FrameMaker provides very strong support for managing pagination, tables of contents, and indexes in books. This lets you process multivolume books, dozens of chapters, and thousands of pages without having to worry about the accuracy of volume, chapter, and page numbering. To rearrange the order of chapters in a book, you drag and drop the files to their new locations, and then update the book. FrameMaker automatically changes the pagination to reflect the new order, changes the chapter numbers as necessary, and updates the table of contents and index.

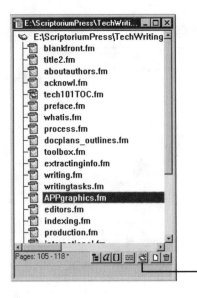

Click the Update button to update tables of contents, indexes, and pagination for the entire book.

■ **Cross-media publishing.** FrameMaker can serve as the engine or as a component of a very sophisticated publishing system, in which you create print, Portable Document Format (PDF), Extensible Markup Language (XML), Hypertext Markup Language (HTML), and various help formats from a single set of documents. This *single-source* publishing makes it possible to write content once and then publish information in several different media.

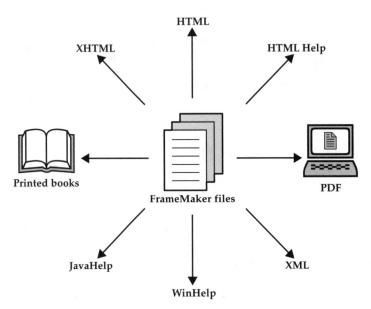

- **Change management.** FrameMaker supports WebDAV, which lets you set up a version control system on a web server. Given a library of very large books, often with multiple authors collaborating on a single document, change management becomes a critical issue.

- **Structured authoring.** FrameMaker lets you create structured documents in which you can see both the regular word processing window and a separate structure view. In the structure view, you have a hierarchical outline of the document and can move information by dragging and dropping elements in the outline. In the past, structured authoring required an upgrade to another, more expensive product, FrameMaker+SGML.

- **XML and SGML support.** You can open XML and Structured Generalized Markup Language (SGML) files directly in FrameMaker, update them in FrameMaker's graphical environment, and save them back to XML or SGML when you're done. You can use XML documents or fragments, and you can integrate the information produced in FrameMaker into various XML-based document repositories.

- **Cross-platform software.** FrameMaker is available for Windows, UNIX, and Macintosh platforms. Files are cross-platform compatible; for example, you can develop a file in FrameMaker for UNIX and open it in FrameMaker for Windows. No conversion is required, and FrameMaker can substitute for any unavailable fonts temporarily or permanently. The user interface is almost identical across platforms, so once you learn how to use FrameMaker for one platform, you can use it on others. Furthermore, a full set of keyboard shortcuts is available that works across platforms.

You'll find many superficial similarities between FrameMaker's feature set and other desktop publishing applications. Only FrameMaker, however, is *designed* for long-document publishing; its document-management features are robust and reliable. In some other applications, those features seem like afterthoughts and don't always work as they should. Highlights of FrameMaker's document-management features include the following:

- **Style sheets.** Most word processors and desktop publishing packages provide style sheets for paragraph formatting, but FrameMaker takes this concept much farther. A FrameMaker file includes style sheets for paragraphs, characters, tables, cross-references, variables, master pages, and several other items. These style sheets, or *tags*, are stored in catalogs, which can be imported from one file to another.

- **Books.** A book is a collection of files (chapters) in a particular sequence. FrameMaker manages the pagination and chapter numbering as information is added to and deleted from the book.

- **Cross-references.** Using cross-references, you create a pointer from one part of the book to another (for example, *see "Widgets" on page 13*). FrameMaker automatically updates the page numbers and heading information when content changes. In PDF and HTML, cross-references are preserved as hyperlinks.

■ **Tables of contents.** You can automatically generate a list of major topics in the document. After making changes to a document, updating the table of contents automatically updates topic lists and page references.

■ **Indexes.** You identify which terms to index by inserting markers in the documents. After that, the index is generated, sorted, and grouped automatically.

■ **Tables.** Table support is very strong and includes the ability to save named table formats with settings for lines and shading.

Table 1-1. Being wired

Not wired	Somewhat wired	Overly wired
Computer	Computer	Computer
Modem	Broadband	Broadband, router, and wireless in-home network
Writes letters	Sends email	Sends email from more than four email accounts per day

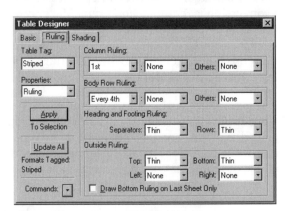

■ **Graphics.** FrameMaker includes a solid set of graphic tools for creating graphics. You can also import external graphics and embed or link them into the document. Linked graphics are automatically updated in the FrameMaker file when the graphic changes.

■ **Conditional text.** Lets you identify information that belongs to a specific version of a document (for example, instructor-only material in a training guide). You can then create document versions that include or exclude the tagged material. Conditional text is an important component of any single-sourcing strategy because it lets you identify information that should be excluded from some output (most commonly, you have "print-only" and "online-only" content).

■ **Metainformation with attributes.** In structured documents, you can set up attributes for a particular element. This lets you embed information about an element, such as the author, revision date, classification level, and so on. These attributes are preserved when you export to XML and can be used there to control how sections of a document are processed.

■ **Variables.** Useful for items that can change frequently. For example, you can create a variable called ProductName and use it throughout the document wherever the product name is needed. If the product name changes, you change the value of the variable, which automatically changes every occurrence of the variable throughout the document.

■ **Modular text.** You can create small files that contain chunks of content, and then assemble the chunks into larger documents. Modular text lets you reuse chunks in different documents and maintain the information for both documents in a single file.

■ **Equations.** FrameMaker includes an equation editor, which lets you create complex mathematical expressions.

■ **Templates.** FrameMaker lets you save named style sheets as a template. In most desktop publishing applications, templates are limited to paragraph style sheets and master pages, but in FrameMaker, template items include paragraph tags, character tags (for formatting inside paragraphs, such as italics), tables, master pages, cross-reference formats, variable names and definitions, conditional text tag names, custom elements for equations, and more.

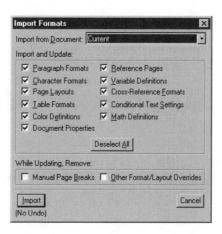

It's possible to use FrameMaker to create highly designed documents, such as annual reports and newsletters, where the layout changes on every page, and FrameMaker is also capable of handling full-color publications. However, FrameMaker's document-management features are much more useful in enforcing consistency across hundreds (or thousands) of pages.

FrameMaker is very good at...	FrameMaker isn't ideal for...
■ Enforcing consistency throughout documents ■ Handling long documents ■ Enforcing structure ■ Providing stability ■ Managing books, tables of contents, and indexes ■ Single sourcing/converting to other formats ■ Formatting tables ■ Importing and maintaining graphics ■ Creating graphics ■ Providing cross-platform compatibility	■ Easy word processing ■ Working in an environment with users who don't believe in using structure or templates in their documents ■ Creating artistic typography ■ Setting up complex, "one-off" layouts

FrameMaker won't solve all of your problems, but if you're looking for a reliable, industrial-strength publishing tool that produces consistent output, it is the software for you.

The Complete Reference

FrameMaker 7

Chapter 2

Establishing a Workflow in FrameMaker

S etting up a publishing workflow requires you to organize the publishing process (which many have compared to the inner workings of a sausage factory—you *really* don't want to know the details) into discrete tasks. Fortunately, the high-level process is fairly standard:

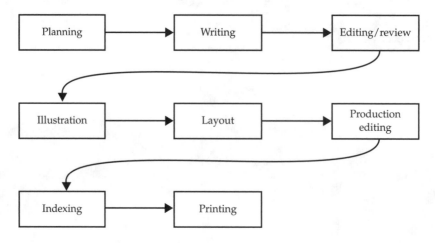

In many cases, the initial work is done in a word processor, and information is transferred from a word processor into a desktop publishing tool. Illustration is done in a separate graphics program. The index may be created in the desktop publishing tool ("embedded") or as a stand-alone file:

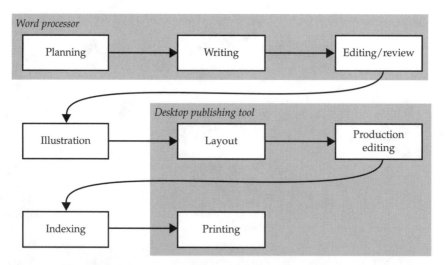

Many desktop publishing applications have rather limited word processing capabilities, so it's more efficient to have the writers work in a separate tool. This approach, however, means that a conversion step is required to go from the word processor to the publishing package. Several features do not transfer well, so it's likely that the layout step will require cleaning up several of the following problems:

- Bullets disappear from bulleted lists or don't convert correctly.
- Numbers in numbered lists don't convert correctly.
- Special characters (such as curly quotes and em dashes) may not convert correctly.
- Cross-references do not convert from one application to another, so they are either hard-coded (that is, typed in), or must be re-created in the desktop publishing application.
- Tables often do not convert properly or must be reformatted.
- Graphics must be inserted after conversion to the desktop publishing tool.

Before computers and desktop publishing were available, writers were expected to generate a manuscript, which contained text and placeholders for graphics, and the design and layout functions were performed by typesetting specialists. A workflow that uses a word processor and a separate publishing tool tends to preserve the separation between writers and formatters.

Note *It's unlikely that this book will resolve the long-standing debate over the proper role of the writer. Some people argue that writers should never have responsibility for formatting documents; they should "just write." Others believe that writing and presentation go hand in hand and that the person developing the information should have some idea what the end result will look like. In a FrameMaker workflow, an author can see approximately what the final document will look like while writing.*

FrameMaker eliminates the need for a separate authoring tool by providing a comprehensive set of word processing tools. Most formatting is handled by applying paragraph styles, which writers can master fairly easily. Creating content directly in FrameMaker eliminates the layout step from your workflow because layout is done automatically as the author creates information. A production editor can review the files to finalize pagination, but the vast majority of the layout work is done by the time the file reaches the production stage.

As authors create information, they can add illustrations or other graphic elements. These might be created by a graphic artist, but there's no need to wait until after the manuscript review to insert them. This makes it possible for editors and reviewers to see text and graphics on the same page, just as the reader will in the final printed version.

Note *It's possible to create content in an external word processor and then import information into FrameMaker, but the time and effort required to convert content makes it a less efficient option than doing all the development in FrameMaker.*

The following illustration shows a typical FrameMaker-based workflow:

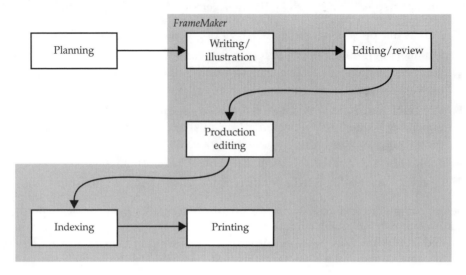

Planning

Given a tight deadline and limited resources, planning is often the first thing to go. However, a minimal amount of time invested at the beginning of the project will make the whole project much more efficient. For short, simple documents, the only thing required in planning may be to create a document template (or identify an existing template that will be used). There are three items that should be created during planning:

- Document templates (if they do not exist already)
- Document outline
- Documentation plan, which includes resources required, a preliminary schedule, a high-level description of the document to be created, and related project-management information

More complex projects make planning more critical—failing to address issues before development begins invariably results in more work (and rework) later. When the following factors are present in a project, even more up-front planning is required:

- **Cross-media publishing/single sourcing.** If the content being developed needs to be delivered in several different media (print, online, and so on), detailed planning is required to analyze the documents and map out how information is presented in each medium.
- **Structured authoring.** Creating templates for structured authoring requires detailed document analysis.

- **Complex document libraries.** If your document library will contain thousands (as opposed to hundreds) of pages of content, planning helps you to avoid redundancy and ensures that all needed topics are covered.

- **Multiple authors.** If multiple authors are working on different books (or portions of the same book), you need to coordinate to make sure that the finished product looks like a single book and not a collection of disjointed sections with different voices.

- **Modular documentation.** Setting up documents with "chunks" of content lets you reuse information instead of writing multiple versions of the same information. It does, however, require careful planning of the document structure, storage and retrieval of the modules, and authoring to ensure that modules are consistent.

- **Distributed or "virtual" workgroup.** A group of authors and editors in a single physical location can communicate informally (by shouting over cubicle walls). When content creators are in different locations all over the world, more formal communication is necessary.

Writing

In a FrameMaker workflow, authors write in FrameMaker, not in a separate word processor. Authors should be given a template and some instructions on how to use it. They should also be able to use certain FrameMaker features, such as cross-references, variables, and markers.

To ensure that writers can succeed in a new FrameMaker environment, it's important to provide some information about the new environment. Working in FrameMaker, with its emphasis on structure, templates, and tagging, is quite different from working in a word processor or desktop publishing tool. It's important that authors understand why tagging is so critical.

Some writers believe, "I'm a writer, not a publisher." Typically, this translates into disinterest or outright hostility toward templates, structure, and formatting rules. In a FrameMaker workflow, following the template is a requirement. Writers who cannot or will not follow templates create documents that will probably print adequately (because they look correct on screen), but the document cannot be reused or processed to produce other output in a single-sourcing environment. If your group includes such a writer, your options are as follows:

- **Education.** Explain to the writer why following the template is necessary. Show what happens when the template is not followed and how this completely destroys the automated workflow and the ability to produce other formats (such as HTML, XML, or help files) from the FrameMaker files.

- **Persuasion/coercion.** Ensure that there are consequences for not following the template. This approach could include requiring the writer to fix any errors that occur in the final output. Keep in mind, though, that a software-averse writer may not have the skills to correct problems, so additional training might be needed.

■ **Cleaning up.** As a last resort, evaluate the writer's value to the organization. Is this person a particularly talented writer with specific knowledge that no one else shares? In that case, it may be worthwhile to assign a person to clean up the writer's files so that they conform to the template.

It's been our experience that up to 10 percent of the writers moving from a word processing environment to a single-sourcing or structured workflow will be unwilling or unable to follow strict template rules.

Illustration

Some authors create their own illustrations and other graphic elements, but most work with a graphic artist or technical illustrator. FrameMaker provides a basic set of graphic tools, which are adequate for simple line art or small flowcharts. To create more complex graphics, use a dedicated graphic package (such as Illustrator, FreeHand, or Visio) and then import the graphic into FrameMaker. FrameMaker supports a wide variety of graphic formats, including EPS, TIFF, and GIF. When importing graphics, you can either create a link to the graphic (import by reference) or embed the graphic in the FrameMaker file (copying into the document). Although most organizations use the import-by-reference feature, each has advantages and disadvantages. These are discussed in detail in "Importing a Graphic" on page 304.

Editing/Reviewing

Instead of distributing FrameMaker files, which would require the reviewers to have access to FrameMaker, most organizations generate PDF files from the FrameMaker source files and use the PDF files for review. Reviewers can mark up changes on a paper copy or use Acrobat's online annotation tools.

The inability for reviewers to edit files directly is a double-edged sword. Some reviewers will complain that they would prefer to go into the source files and make changes, but restricting access to these files makes it easier for authors to keep track of changes and control the information in the files. Furthermore, correcting their own errors makes it more likely that authors will learn from their mistakes and improve their writing over time. Finally, there is the issue of reviewer accuracy. More than one well-intentioned reviewer has "corrected" information by sprinkling commas at random throughout a document. Using PDF files prevents these types of mishaps.

Technical editing and copy editing can be done directly in the FrameMaker files, perhaps with change bars turned on, or on paper copies, which provide much better audit trails for tracking changes.

Production Editing

During the production edit, the document is checked to ensure that each page is copyfitted; that is, the pages are filled with consistent amounts of text and graphics. Production editors also look for awkward line and page breaks, and verify that headers and footers, cross-references, tables of contents and indexes, and front and back matter are set up correctly. Because FrameMaker automates many of these tasks, the main task of the production editor is to verify that the template was applied correctly—overrides to template formatting often cause problems elsewhere. For example, applying the wrong paragraph tag to a heading causes that heading to disappear from the table of contents.

Indexing

When indexing a book, there are two workflow options:

- **Embedded indexing.** The index is generated from markers that are inserted (embedded) into the document files.
- **Stand-alone indexing.** The index is generated in dedicated indexing software, and the resulting text is inserted into the document.

If you plan to make frequent, incremental updates to the content, creating an embedded index is probably the right choice because you can reuse markers and reduce the amount of work required to update the index. If the book is a one-time project, you may want to create a stand-alone index, especially if you plan to use a freelance indexer. In technical writing groups, embedded indexes are the standard; in publishing environments, stand-alone indexes are more common. Table 2-1 on page 18 lists the advantages and disadvantages of each approach.

Printing

You can print documents from FrameMaker directly to a printer (such as your office laser printer), but most professional output is done by creating an intermediate PostScript or PDF file, which is sent to a print vendor. In most cases, there's no need to give the print vendor your FrameMaker source files.

Printing and other output are described in detail in Part V, "Creating Output."

Embedded	Stand-Alone
Pro	**Pro**
■ Page numbers are automatically updated when content moves, including text expansion during translation.	■ Faster development of the index.
	■ Powerful editing capabilities. You can make changes directly in the index and make global changes quickly.
■ You can reuse index markers when a document is revised, which can make revisions much faster.	■ Sort options are adequate and easy to use.
■ Using the built-in indexing feature eliminates the cost of a separate tool.	■ Cross-references (see and see also) are verified automatically.
■ Easier to learn than stand-alone indexing software.	■ Different view options are available for the index: standard alphabetical order, primary headings only, page order, chronological order (the order in which you created the index entries), and entries that contain specific keywords only.
Con	
■ Creating markers is time consuming.	
■ The indexer must have access to source files.	**Con**
■ Editing the index is difficult and tedious. Global changes are very time consuming.	■ The document must be very close to finished before it can be indexed.
■ You cannot change the index perspective; only an alphabetical list is available.	■ The indexer must type in all the page numbers, so they are hard-coded in the index. Hand-typed page numbers are subject to human error.
■ Cross-references in the index (see and see also references) are not verified.	■ Dedicated software is expensive and has a significant learning curve.
■ Sort options are limited.	■ Updated or translated documents usually have to be reindexed from scratch.

Thanks to Dick Evans of Infodex Indexing Services (infodex@mindspring.com) for his assistance in creating this list.

Table 2-1. *Comparing Embedded and Stand-Alone Indexing*

Adding Structured Authoring to Your Workflow

In previous versions, the structured and unstructured versions of FrameMaker were sold separately. FrameMaker+SGML (and its predecessor, FrameBuilder) are equivalent to structured FrameMaker, and unstructured FrameMaker is "regular" FrameMaker in earlier versions. In version 7, both unstructured and structured FrameMaker are delivered in a single product.

The single FrameMaker product now gives you the choice of working in a structured or unstructured authoring environment. Unstructured authoring means that you use paragraph and character tags to control formatting. With structured authoring, you define an allowable structure for your document, and FrameMaker automatically handles formatting based on the structure. In the structured authoring environment, you can create both structured and unstructured documents. In unstructured FrameMaker, though, you can create only unstructured documents.

Because you can enforce structure rules, structured FrameMaker gives a template designer more control over the author's workflow. However, setting up a structured FrameMaker template is significantly more challenging and more time consuming than creating an unstructured FrameMaker template. In the unstructured version, the template designer creates paragraph tags and other components that control the appearance of the document. For the structured version, the template designer must create a document that describes the structure of the document and then attach formatting information to each element in the structure.

Understanding Structured Documents

Structured and unstructured documents look identical in print. There are major differences, however, in how you create, edit, and format information. In unstructured documents, you apply paragraph tags and other formatting to control the appearance of the document. FrameMaker sees the document as a sequence of paragraphs, which have various styles applied to them.

Heading1 ———— **Herding Your Cats**

Body ———— Here are some reasons why you should never herd your cats:

Bullet ———— • Painful scratches

Bullet ———— • Loud meowing

Bullet ———— • Intense frustration

Bullet ———— • Complete futility

Structured documents can look just like the unstructured version, but they contain additional information. In a structured document, information is organized with elements. Elements contain paragraphs, tables, graphics, and other types of information. Elements can also contain other elements. This allows you to create a document in which a Section element contains a heading and several paragraphs of information.

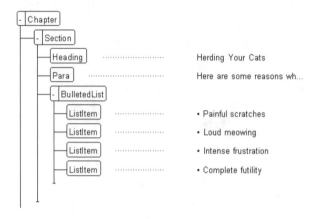

Choosing Between Structured and Unstructured Documents

All of the features available in unstructured FrameMaker are also present in structured FrameMaker, but structured FrameMaker provides additional capabilities beyond what's in regular, unstructured FrameMaker.

There are some advantages and disadvantages to each type of document:

- **Unstructured documents.** If you are starting from scratch, getting started in unstructured FrameMaker is faster and easier than working in structured FrameMaker. Unstructured documents are less restrictive for authors than structured documents.

- **Structured documents.** If you need the ability to convert to and from XML, structured documents are a must. The guidance that structured documents provide to authors becomes more and more important in larger workgroups. Structured FrameMaker (or FrameMaker+SGML) is common in large organizations, especially in the aerospace and telecommunications industries and in government organizations.

Table 2-2 summarizes the differences between structured and unstructured FrameMaker.

	Unstructured	Structured
Authoring	Document authors must remember to follow certain formatting rules (for example, "a heading must be followed by a lead-in paragraph"). Authors must apply paragraph tags and often have multiple tags, such as Note, TableNote, and NoteContinued. Authors must learn which paragraph tag to use in which context.	The template enforces structuring rules. Authors are guided through the available elements. Authors choose elements; the template controls what formatting is applied, sometimes applying different formatting to the same element based on the context of the element.
Template design	Creating templates is easier in unstructured FrameMaker because you do not have to set up structured templates.	Creating structured document templates is quite challenging.
Single-source publishing	You can export unstructured documents to other formats through a number of third-party tools.	You can publish to other formats through third-party tools, or use the SGML/XML conversion features and process that output.
Learning curve	Moderate for document authors; high for template designers.	Low to moderate for document authors; very high for template designers.
Workflow	Works well in small groups; more difficult to manage in large groups.	Requires additional up-front planning, but works well for large groups.
XML conversion	Export only. No element hierarchy.	Import and export. Element hierarchy is preserved.

Table 2-2. *Structured vs. Unstructured FrameMaker*

How Structure Changes Your Workflow

If your writing group's workflow is based on a word processing or desktop publishing application, you generally write content and apply formatting style sheets (or tags) to get the look and feel you want for the document. But the word processor–based approach has some serious limitations. Most importantly, the writer does not have any information about or control over the structure of the document other than by remembering to follow your organization's "rules." Learning those rules could take a significant amount of time. For example, your style guidelines might include the following items:

- A heading cannot be immediately followed by another heading. You must have at least one paragraph of body text after each heading.
- A step list must have at least two steps.
- A bulleted list must have at least two bullets.
- The first bullet in a list should have some extra space above it; the last bullet in a list should have some extra space below.

You can ask writers to remember to follow these rules in unstructured FrameMaker. However, structured FrameMaker lets you create a template that *requires* you to follow these rules. This makes it much easier for new writers to learn the rules because the document itself enforces them!

Creating a template that contains a significant amount of logic (including rules such as those in the preceding list) removes the burden of remembering these rules from the writers, but it shifts the work to the template designer, who must write the code that implements these rules.

In unstructured FrameMaker, any document can be a template, which contains paragraph tags, character tags, master pages, and other formatting elements.

In structured FrameMaker, you still have a formatting template, but there is also a second, structured template, the element definition document (EDD). (In some cases, the formatting information is embedded in the EDD.) The EDD describes the elements that are allowed in a document, their relationship to each other, and what formats they use. For details about EDDs and structured authoring, see Part VII, "Structured FrameMaker."

Authoring in a Structured Environment

Working in structured FrameMaker simplifies the authoring process. Instead of choosing from a long list of paragraph tags, structured FrameMaker can show you only the elements that are permitted at that point in the structure. For example, if the structure requires that a heading is always followed by body text, the list of available elements would show just the body text element.

By changing what elements are available based on the location in the document's structure, the EDD provides guidance to authors and reduces the number of choices they have to make at each point. This, in turn, helps the authors work more efficiently. Formatting is applied automatically based on each element's position in the hierarchy and can change on the fly when authors move elements.

FrameMaker's Role in Single Sourcing

The term *single sourcing* refers to creating multiple outputs (for example, print, PDF, and online help) or multiple documents (for example, a user's guide and an administrator's guide) from one set of files. Single-sourcing implementation can be simple; for example, a FrameMaker file sent to print and converted to PDF. A more complex setup might involve a content repository from which you extract relevant information by keyword searches and then assemble and format it for print or online help.

The basic premise of single sourcing is that you "write once, publish many." Because you write content once and then use automated tools to process the information for different output media, you save time and money.

Note   *Adobe defines network publishing as "making visually rich, personalized content available anytime, anywhere on any device." A single-sourcing workflow can give you the ability to perform network publishing, so the two concepts are closely related.*

For a single-sourcing project, the planning stage is absolutely essential. Each piece of content can be presented differently in each medium, and understanding these relationships before beginning the writing process is critical. To ensure that single sourcing succeeds, content must conform to templates—overrides and "custom" formatting are usually lost when converting from one format to another.

Aside from the increased emphasis on planning and standards, workflow is modified because additional output is generated in the last stage of the project. A number of FrameMaker add-on tools are available that convert your source files into other output media. The most important ones are as follows:

- **Adobe Acrobat.** Acrobat Distiller creates PDF files from PostScript files. Distiller ships with FrameMaker.
- **WebWorks Publisher.** Creates HTML and various flavors of online help from FrameMaker files.
- **MIF2GO.** Creates HTML and various flavors of online help from FrameMaker files. Also provides a very good FrameMaker-to-Word filter.

Evaluating Workflow Options

Before embarking on a single-sourcing project, it can be helpful to review the pros and cons of different workflow options. If you need to deliver the same information in different media (for example, procedures in both a user's guide and in the online help), single sourcing will probably be the most efficient approach, but there are other options.

Parallel Development

In a parallel development process, all deliverables are created simultaneously. For example, one writer might create a user's guide in FrameMaker while another writer creates online help in a help authoring tool.

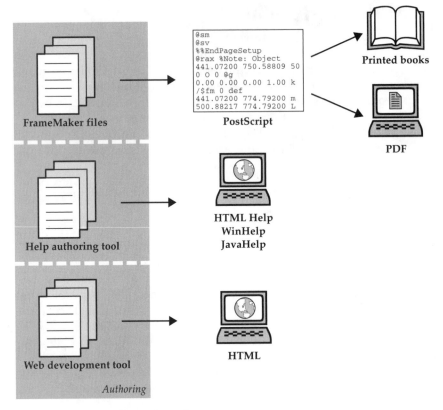

Parallel development has a few advantages:

- Both deliverables are ready at the same time.
- Writers can specialize in print or online work and optimize the information for each deliverable.

Parallel development can be a good choice if the information in the two deliverables is different. If, however, there is content overlap between the deliverables, there are a number of problems with this workflow:

- Because the same information is being created twice, the workflow is very labor-intensive.
- Maintenance is problematic, and differences in terminology or even outright contradictions often creep into the documents. This confuses the readers.
- Transferring information from one tool to another is time consuming. Formatting is often lost, so you spend a lot of time cleaning up after conversion.

Parallel development makes sense when the information in the print and the online help does not overlap. But when there is significant overlap, parallel development is time consuming and inefficient.

Serial Development

Serial development could be considered a type of single sourcing. You write the information once and then convert it from one format to another. However, serial development typically involves copying the information from one format (for example, the print development tool) to another format (the help authoring tool) and then reworking the information to add formatting.

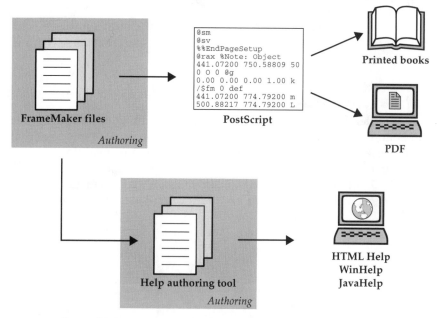

You could also create the help first and then move the information to FrameMaker to create the print and PDF versions.

Serial development has some advantages:

- ■ Because the information is written once, information is consistent across all deliverables.

- ■ The second deliverable is not created until the first deliverable is completed, so the information is finalized.

- ■ Maintenance is simplified because you only convert once per release and do not have to maintain two sets of documentation.

- ■ One writer can create the print output and then the help, so it's less expensive than having two writers working in parallel.

But there are some serious disadvantages:

■ Serial development means that one deliverable will lag significantly behind the other. For example, the printed version might be ready three or four weeks before the online help. This leads to scheduling problems before a release because you have to build in several weeks for the conversion and reformatting process.

■ Often, the print tool and the online help tool do not work well together, so formatting is lost when you transfer information from one tool to the other. The cleanup that's done in the second version must be repeated for each release (unless you keep the files and only put in the changes, in which case you've switched to a parallel development process).

Serial development can be viable if you need to transfer only a small amount of content from one deliverable to another. But large-scale manual conversion is incredibly tedious, and better options are available.

Modular Development

Single sourcing often focuses on creating multiple deliverables in different media, such as print and online help, from a single set of files. Modular development has a slightly different emphasis—creating multiple deliverables in the same medium and reusing overlapping content. For example, if two products share several features, it would be helpful to write about those features only once and reuse the information in both books. Modular development lets you separate out the information that both products share so you can reuse that information.

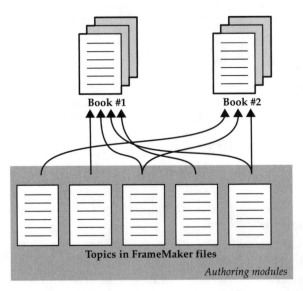

Book #1   Book #2

Topics in FrameMaker files

Authoring modules

To implement modular development in FrameMaker, you typically use text insets, which are discussed in Chapter 25, "Creating Modules with Text Insets."

When you reuse modules, you create multiple deliverables (books) from a single set of source files, but modular development does not necessarily include delivery of information in multiple media. Many (but not all) technical publishers use the term single sourcing only when they are producing different media from a single set of source files.

Database Publishing

Database publishing is used most often for directories or other highly structured content. The information that needs to be published is already stored as records in a database, so you extract information from the database, tag it as appropriate to format it, and create a FrameMaker file. A number of third-party applications, such as Miramo, PatternStream, and UniMerge, can create FrameMaker or MIF files from database content.

Database publishing is best suited for working with highly structured information that's already in a database. Information that's output in a particular sequence (for example, alphabetical order for a list of doctors) works well in this environment. Documents that have a well-defined sequence and structure (for example, a programmer's reference with an alphabetical list of commands) can also work well in this environment. Less structured documents, such as user's guides, tutorials, and the like, do not work well in database publishing.

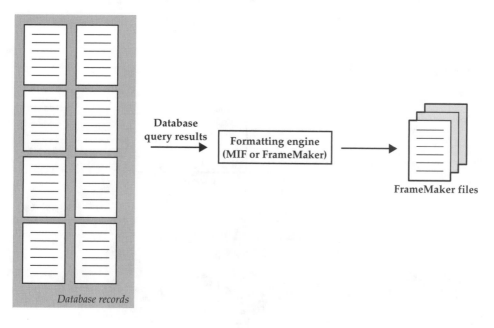

The database serves as the content repository, so you make changes to the information only in the database. The generated FrameMaker files may need formatting tweaks, but any changes you make in them are lost the next time you export from the database.

Single-Sourcing Workflows

If you are required to deliver the same content in multiple media, you should consider a single-sourcing approach. In this environment, FrameMaker can be used either as an authoring tool and content repository or solely as a print and PDF creation engine.

If you plan to use FrameMaker for authoring, you can export to other formats either via XML or by using third-party tools to convert from FrameMaker directly to the required format (such as WinHelp). FrameMaker also provides a built-in HTML converter, but it does not offer enough control for anything but the most basic conversions of short documents.

Structured Authoring with XML Import and Export   With structured files, you can import and export XML ("round-tripping"). This lets you author content either in FrameMaker or in XML. From the FrameMaker files, you can produce PostScript, printed books, and PDF as usual. From the XML files, you can use Extensible Stylesheet Language Transform (XSLT) files to process the XML and produce HTML and online help formats.

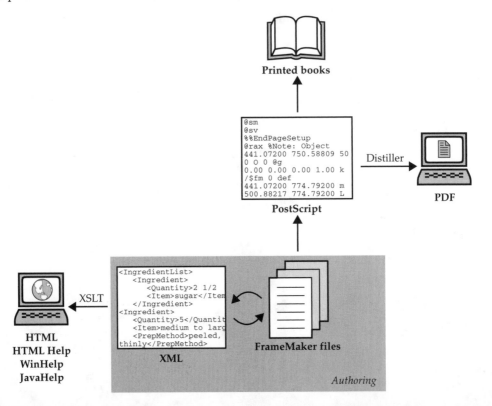

Creating HTML and Help with Third-Party Tools Two very good third-party tools are available to create HTML and various help formats (JavaHelp, WinHelp, HTML Help, and so on) from FrameMaker files. They are MIF2GO and WebWorks Publisher Professional Edition. Although the tools have very different interfaces, they are conceptually similar: they read the tagging information in the FrameMaker files and replace it with HTML, RTF, or other markup.

Both tools are highly customizable; in fact, they function as scripting environments, in which you can create exact specifications for your output.

Note	*WebWorks Publisher Standard Edition is a stripped-down version of WebWorks Publisher Professional Edition. Customization options are highly limited in the Standard Edition (which is free and ships with FrameMaker). For example, you can only use predefined, provided styles for mapping; you cannot create any new styles.*

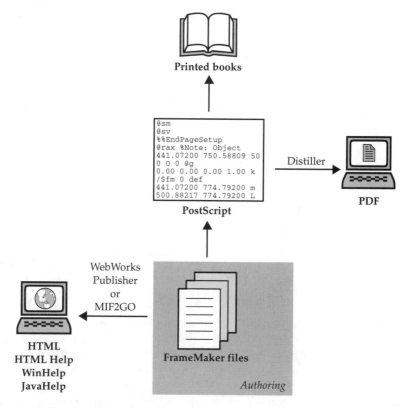

XML-Based Authoring Instead of using FrameMaker files as your content repository, you could store information in XML. Given a structured authoring environment, you can then open files in FrameMaker, edit them, and then save them back to XML. You could also use XML editors to modify the XML files and pull information into FrameMaker when you need to print or create a PDF file. The latter case that you use

FrameMaker as a print rendering engine only, not as a content-development tool. Given FrameMaker's maturity and powerful features, especially compared to the available XML editors, this does not appear to be the best choice today.

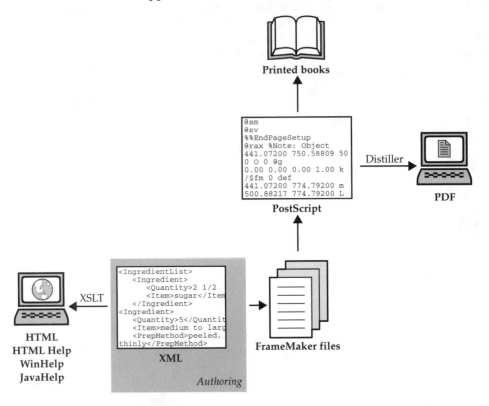

Transferring Information Between SGML/XML and FrameMaker

Creating an EDD and a formatting template allows you to create structured documents. If you want to import and export XML, some additional configuration is required in a *structured application.* The application controls how structured FrameMaker documents are transformed into SGML or XML and vice versa. For example, the application specifies which DTD is used in SGML or XML content, and how the structure of the DTD and the EDD match up. You set up an application by defining settings for your conversions in a special (structured) FrameMaker file. FrameMaker reads this file to identify the available applications for a given FrameMaker installation. Structured applications are discussed in detail in Chapter 31, "Importing and Exporting XML/SGML Markup Files."

FrameMaker

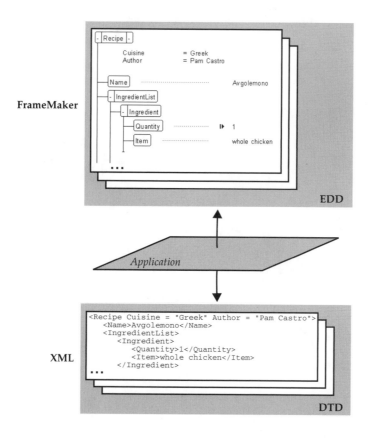

The
Complete
Reference

Chapter 3

Creating Your
First Document

T̲o start working, you launch FrameMaker and either create a new document or open an existing document. Once you do that, you can start learning how to get around in the FrameMaker interface. This chapter explains how to start FrameMaker, create documents, and open them.

Starting FrameMaker

The process of starting FrameMaker varies by platform.

Operating System	Instructions
Windows	A shortcut for FrameMaker is installed in the Start menu after installation. Assuming that you installed FrameMaker in the default location, select Start | Programs | Adobe | FrameMaker 7.0 | Adobe FrameMaker 7.0 to start the program.
UNIX	The exact location of FrameMaker will depend on your system's configuration. If your system administrator installed everything properly and set the proper paths, you can launch FrameMaker from a terminal window by typing: `maker &` If this doesn't work, locate the FrameMaker installation directory and launch FrameMaker from there.
Macintosh	Locate the FrameMaker installation directory and double-click the FrameMaker icon. By default, the installation directory is Adobe FrameMaker 7.0 at the top level of your main hard drive partition (that is, the hard drive that your System folder resides in).

The first time you launch FrameMaker, you are prompted to register the product. Next, you are prompted to select an interface.

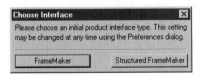

FrameMaker provides you with two operating modes: structured and unstructured. You can change this selection later if you need to.

Choose one of the following options:

- **FrameMaker** (unstructured): Starts the "vanilla," unstructured version of FrameMaker. Lets you work on unstructured documents without the structure features getting in the way. (Unstructured FrameMaker is equivalent to regular FrameMaker in version 6.)
- **Structured FrameMaker:** Starts the structured version of FrameMaker. Lets you create structured documents, import and export SGML and XML, and see the structure view. (In version 6, structured FrameMaker was a separate product called FrameMaker+SGML.)

Tip   *In structured FrameMaker, you can create both structured and unstructured documents, so if you're comfortable with that interface, use it even when creating unstructured documents. Structured FrameMaker is a superset of unstructured FrameMaker; the structured version provides all the same features as the unstructured version and adds to them. Unstructured FrameMaker may be a little less overwhelming if you're new to FrameMaker because it doesn't have quite as many menus and features. You can open unstructured documents in structured FrameMaker, but opening structured documents in unstructured FrameMaker will strip the structure information. FrameMaker warns you if you attempt to do this.*

When you launch FrameMaker, it does not automatically create a blank document. Instead, the Windows and Mac versions display the menu bar and no document. To begin working, you need to either create a new document or open an existing one.

Under UNIX, launching FrameMaker displays a set of buttons.

The buttons give you the following choices:

- **New:** Creates a new document. Equivalent to selecting File | New | Document inside FrameMaker.
- **Open:** Opens an existing document. Equivalent to selecting File | Open.
- **Help:** Displays the online help. Equivalent to selecting Help | Help Topics.
- **Info:** Displays information about FrameMaker licenses. See "Understanding UNIX Licensing" on page 39 for details.
- **Exit:** Closes the button bar and shuts down FrameMaker. Equivalent to selecting File | Exit (Windows and UNIX) or File | Quit (Mac).

Setting Up a New Document

When you create a new document, FrameMaker names the file Untitled1.fm (additional documents are named Untitled2.fm, Untitled3.fm, and so on). You can save the document with a more informative name.

There are several ways to create a new document:

- Exploring the standard templates, then choosing one of those templates
- Using a file as a template
- Creating a blank document
- Saving an existing file under a new name

Exploring the Standard (Unstructured) Templates

For each of the default templates, FrameMaker includes a preview and a feature summary. This information helps you determine whether a particular template will meet your needs.

To examine the unstructured templates, follow these steps:

1. Select File | New | Document, press CTRL-N (Windows) or COMMAND-N (Mac), or click the New File button on the Quick Access Bar. The New dialog box is displayed (Figure 3-1).

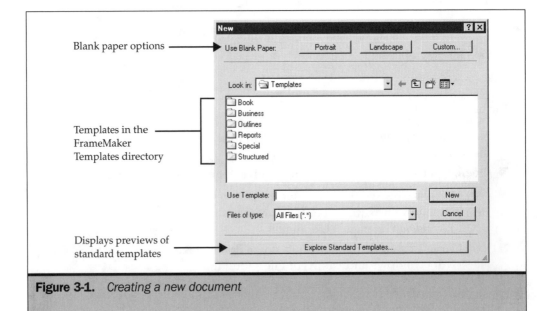

Figure 3-1. *Creating a new document*

2. Click the Explore Standard Templates button. A list of templates is displayed with previews.

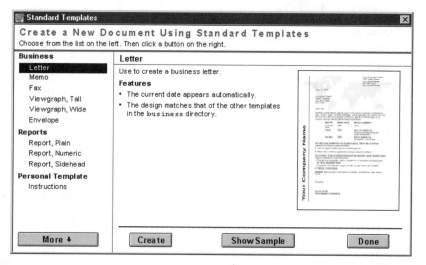

3. Click an item in the template list on the left to display a feature summary and preview for that template on the right. To see a sample document with placeholder text, click the Show Sample button.

4. To use a particular template, click the Create button. FrameMaker creates a new, untitled document by making a copy of the template file.

You can now save the document with an appropriate name and begin working.

Using a File as a Template

In addition to the standard templates, you can use any FrameMaker file as a template. To use a file as a template, follow these steps:

1. Select File | New | Document, press CTRL-N (Windows) or COMMAND-N (Mac), or click the New File button on the Quick Access Bar. The New dialog box is displayed (Figure 3-1 on page 36).

2. Select the template by doing one of the following:

   ■ To find a standard FrameMaker template, double-click a folder in the Look In window and then double-click the template. You can display a preview of FrameMaker's standard templates by clicking the Explore Standard Templates button.

If you save a file in FrameMaker's template directory, that file will be displayed along with the standard FrameMaker templates. It will not, however, be listed when you explore templates.

■ To use another file as a template, navigate to the directory that contains the file and double-click the file.

The new document is displayed.

When you create a new document from a template, FrameMaker makes a complete copy of the file. Any content in the original file is included in the new, untitled document. For documents that contain a lot of standard information (such as contracts), you can use this feature to your advantage. Create a template file that includes standard information, perhaps with variables where information will change:

SCRIPTORIUM
p u b l i s h i n g   s e r v i c e s

P.O. Box 12761, Research Triangle Park, NC 27709
voice: 919-481-2701   fax: 919-481-4641
http://www.scriptorium.com
training@scriptorium.com

March 5, 2002

Ms. ???contact_name
???Job Title
???client_full_name
???address
City, state, zip

Dear Ms. ???client_last_name:

This letter of agreement outlines the training services that Scriptorium Publishing
Services, Inc. will provide to ???client_full_name (???client_short_name). Scriptorium
Publishing will deliver ???days of ???classtype training for up to ???#ofstudents
???client_short_name employees. The instructor for this class will be ??? with ??? and ???
available as backup instructors.

Understanding UNIX Licensing

On UNIX machines, FrameMaker installs a license server. To run FrameMaker,
your machine must get a license from the license server. Two types of licenses are
available:

- **Personal:** A personal license is assigned to a specific individual. If you have a
  personal license, that license is available to you whenever you request it.
  Nobody else can use your personal license.

- **Shared:** A shared license is available to anyone who requests it. If all shared
  licenses are in use when you request a license, you will not receive one and
  must wait until someone else finishes working and gives up a license.

When purchasing FrameMaker licenses, personal licenses require that you
purchase one license per user. With shared licenses, you only need one license per
concurrent user. As a result, shared licenses are usually more cost-effective.

Click the Info button to display information about your FrameMaker software,
then click the License button to get licensing information.

Creating a Blank Document

When you create a blank document, you can use a default portrait or landscape page, or you can create a custom page size.

To create a blank portrait or landscape document, follow these steps:

1. Select File | New | Document, press CTRL-N (Windows) or COMMAND-N (Mac), or click the New button (UNIX). The New dialog box is displayed (Figure 3-1 on page 36).

2. In the Use Blank Paper section, click the Portrait or Landscape button. The new document is displayed.

To create a document that uses a custom paper size, follow these steps:

1. Select File | New | Document, press CTRL-N (Windows) or COMMAND-N (Mac), or click the New button (UNIX). The New dialog box is displayed (Figure 3-1 on page 36).

2. In the Use Blank Paper section, click the Custom button. The Custom Blank Paper dialog box is displayed.

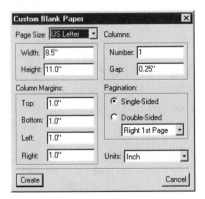

3. Click a paper size in the Page Size drop-down list:
   - **Custom:** You specify the page width and height.
   - **US Letter:** 8.5 inches wide by 11 inches tall
   - **US Legal:** 8.5 inches wide by 14 inches tall
   - **Tabloid:** 11 inches wide by 17 inches tall
   - **A3 Tabloid:** 29.7 cm wide by 42 cm tall
   - **A4 Letter:** 21 cm wide by 29.7 cm tall
   - **A5 Letter:** 14.8 cm wide by 21 cm tall
   - **B5 Letter:** 17.6 cm wide by 25 cm tall

To change the measurement units (for example, from inches to picas), select a measurement unit in the Units drop-down list at the bottom right. FrameMaker automatically converts the current measurements into the new units.

4. Modify the margins as appropriate. Margins are measured from the edge of the page to the edge of the text area.

5. To create a document with equal-sized columns, specify the number of columns you want in the Columns area. The default is 1. The Gap measurement determines the amount of space between the columns. After you specify the columns and gap value, FrameMaker automatically creates even columns.

6. Set the pagination. Most books use double-sided pagination and start with a right first page. If you specify single-sided pagination, only one master page is created (called Right); if you specify double-sided pagination, two master pages are created (Left and Right). For details, see "Switching from Single- to Double-Sided Pages" on page 267.

7. Click the Create button. Your new document is displayed.

Using an Existing File

Instead of using a document as a template and creating a new file, you can save the template file with a new name to make a copy. To use an existing file, follow these steps:

1. Open a file that has the correct formats.

2. *(optional)* To delete the content in the file, highlight all the information in the file by selecting Edit | Select All in Flow, then press the DELETE key.

3. Select File | Save As and save the file with a new name.

You now have a new file and can begin editing it.

Opening, Saving, Closing, and Printing Documents

FrameMaker includes standard open, save, close, and printing commands:

■ To open a file, select File | Open, then locate the file you want.

■ To close a file, select File | Close.

■ To save a file, select File | Save, or select File | Save As to save the file with a different name.

■ To print a file, select File | Print.

Files created in earlier versions of FrameMaker open in newer versions; for example, a file created in FrameMaker 6 opens in FrameMaker 7. However, you cannot open a version 7 FrameMaker file in earlier versions of FrameMaker. To move a file "back" to an earlier version of FrameMaker, save the file as Maker Interchange Format (MIF), then open the MIF file in the older version. You will lose features that are not supported in the older versions, but the files usually open cleanly.

FrameMaker 7 also provides a Save As FrameMaker 6 feature, which lets you save files in FrameMaker 6 format directly instead of using MIF as an intermediate format. This feature could be very useful if you are working in a mixed version 6/version 7 environment.

Understanding the Document Window

You view and edit your document in the document window. A dotted line indicates the area in which you can insert content. (If you do not see the dotted line, select View | Borders to display it.)

Indicates the border of the text area. Click anywhere inside this area to position the cursor at the top of the text area, and then type in text.

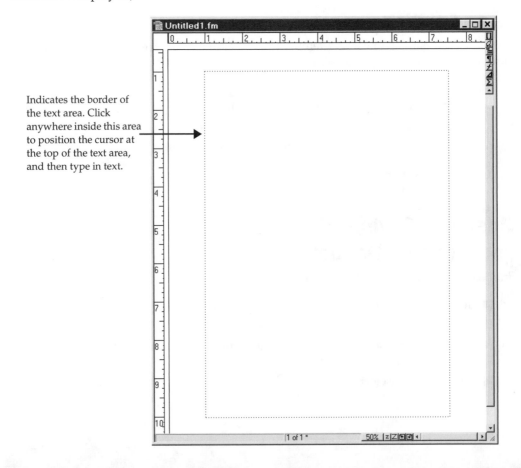

At the bottom of the document window, a status bar displays information about the the current document. By looking at the status bar, you can find out the following information:

- Flow tag, paragraph tag, character tag, and conditional text tag for the currently selected item. (In structured documents, the element name is listed instead of the paragraph and character tags.)
- Current page number and total page count.
- Whether the file has been modified since you last saved it.
- The current percentage zoom at which the file is being displayed.

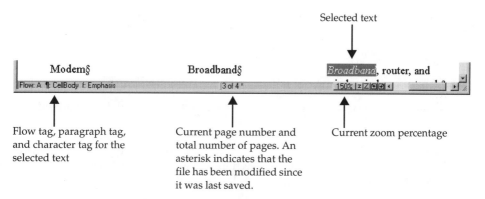

Selected text

Flow tag, paragraph tag, and character tag for the selected text

Current page number and total number of pages. An asterisk indicates that the file has been modified since it was last saved.

Current zoom percentage

Changing the Zoom Settings

To change the size at which a document is displayed, you can zoom in or zoom out. The big and little Zs on the status bar let you zoom in or out one step at a time.

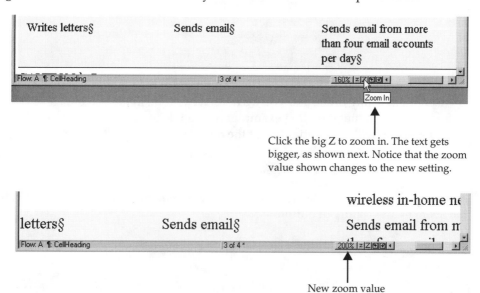

Click the big Z to zoom in. The text gets bigger, as shown next. Notice that the zoom value shown changes to the new setting.

New zoom value

You can also use the zoom pop-up menu to change to a specific setting immediately. To change the zoom level through this menu, follow these steps:

1. Click on the zoom percentage to display the zoom pop-up menu.

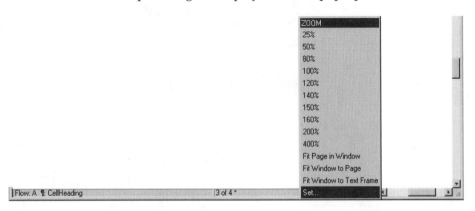

2. Click the zoom setting you want. The document is immediately changed to that zoom level.

FrameMaker provides ten zoom settings. You cannot add more settings, but you can change the provided settings to values anywhere between 25% and 1600%.
To change the available zoom settings, follow these steps:

1. Click on the zoom percentage to display the zoom pop-up menu.
2. Click the Set button. The Zoom Menu Options dialog box is displayed.

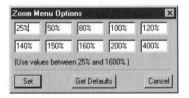

3. To change a setting, delete the existing number and type in a new one. You can insert them in any order, and you do not have to type in the percentage sign. For instance, in the preceding example, you can delete 25% and type in 250. FrameMaker will automatically put the new 250% setting in the correct order.
4. Click the Set button to save your changes. To revert back to FrameMaker's default zoom settings, click the Get Defaults button.

The new settings are immediately shown in the zoom menu and are used when you click the zoom in and zoom out buttons.

Displaying Nonprinting Items in the Document Window

You can turn on and off the display of several items in the document window. They are as follows:

- **Borders.** With borders on, the edge of text frames, table cells, and the like are indicated with dotted lines.
- **Text Symbols.** With text symbols on, tabs, end-of-paragraph symbols, markers, and other nonprinting characters are displayed on screen.
- **Rulers.** With rulers on, measurements are shown on the top and right of the document window.
- **Grid Lines.** With grid lines on, a grid pattern is shown to help you align objects on the page.

The commands to toggle each of these options are in the View menu.

Note *In structured FrameMaker, you can also toggle element boundaries. See Chapter 28, "Working with Structured Documents," for details.*

Borders, Text Symbols, Rulers, and Grid Lines off.

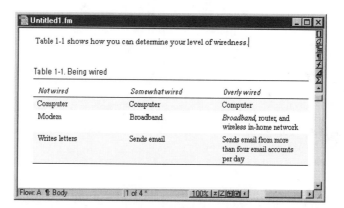

Borders on.
The dotted lines indicate the edge of the text area and the table cell boundaries.
Select View | Borders to toggle borders.

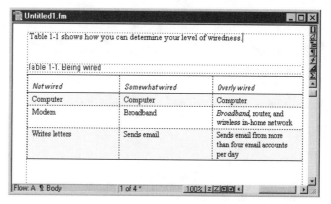

Borders and Text Symbols on.
When text symbols are on,
non-printing symbols, such as tabs
and end-of-paragraph symbols,
are displayed. See Table 3-1 on
page 47 for a list of text symbols.

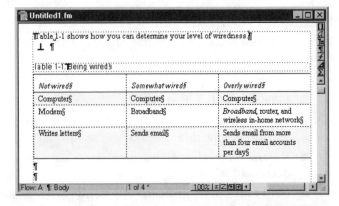

Rulers on.
Select View | Rulers to toggle
rulers. The measurement units
used are determined by the view
options you set. See "Changing
View Options" on page 48.

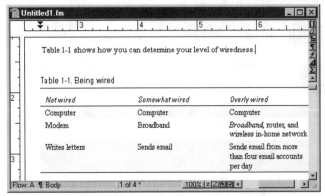

Grid Lines on.
Grid lines can help with aligning
graphics or other elements.
Select View | Grid Lines to toggle
grid lines.

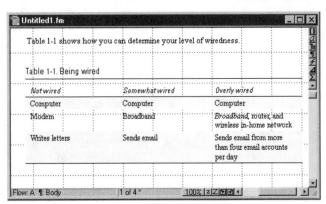

FrameMaker uses many different nonprinting symbols. Table 3-1 lists them.

Symbol	Description
〉	**Tab.** Indicates a tab character. Keep in mind that tabs do not move text unless a tab stop is defined for that paragraph. For details, see "Setting Tab Stops" on page 115.
¶	**End of paragraph symbol.** Indicates the end of a paragraph. When you press ENTER to end a paragraph, FrameMaker inserts this symbol.
§	**End of flow symbol.** Indicates the end of the content in the current flow. As you add more content, the end of flow symbol always stays at the end of the text. You cannot remove this symbol.
〈	**Forced return.** Indicates a forced line break. Press SHIFT-ENTER to insert a forced return.
⌴	**Hard space.** Indicates a nonbreaking space (inserted by pressing CTRL-SPACE), which does not allow a line break to occur at that location.
⊤	**Discretionary hyphen.** Indicates a location at which the word can be hyphenated if necessary, in addition to the hyphenation points defined in the dictionary. Press ESC HYPHEN SHIFT-D to insert a discretionary hyphen. Discretionary hyphens are shown above the text: <div align="center">dete͞rmine</div>
—	**Suppress hyphen.** Indicates a location at which the word cannot be hyphenated, even if the dictionary allows hyphenation there. Press ESC N S to suppress hyphenation for a word and insert a suppress hyphen symbol. The suppress hyphenation symbol appears under the text: <div align="center">w̲ire</div>
⊥	**Anchor for table or anchored frame.** Indicates the location at which a table or anchored frame is anchored to a paragraph.

Table 3-1.   *Text Symbols*

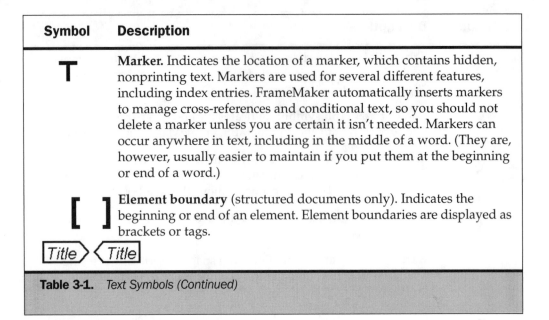

Symbol	Description
T	**Marker.** Indicates the location of a marker, which contains hidden, nonprinting text. Markers are used for several different features, including index entries. FrameMaker automatically inserts markers to manage cross-references and conditional text, so you should not delete a marker unless you are certain it isn't needed. Markers can occur anywhere in text, including in the middle of a word. (They are, however, usually easier to maintain if you put them at the beginning or end of a word.)
[ ] Title⟩ ⟨Title	**Element boundary** (structured documents only). Indicates the beginning or end of an element. Element boundaries are displayed as brackets or tags.

Table 3-1.   *Text Symbols (Continued)*

Changing View Options

The view options let you set measurement units, page options, and more.
To change your view options, follow these steps:

1. Select View | Options. The View Options dialog box is displayed.

2. Set the page scrolling you want. Your choices are as follows:

- **Vertical:** In the document window, pages scroll vertically. (This is standard behavior in most word processing and publishing applications.)

- **Horizontal:** Pages scroll horizontally.

- **Facing Pages:** Pages are displayed in spreads, with the left and right pages displayed in the document window together.

- **Variable:** Pages are displayed depending on how the document is zoomed. If facing pages fit in the window, they are displayed; if not, pages scroll vertically.

3. Set the display units with the Display Units and Font Units drop-down lists. The font units are used for font size, leading, and space above and below paragraph. Display units are used for all other items.

Refer to Chapter 13, "FrameMaker's Graphics Tools," for information about the grid and snap options.

4. In the Display section, check the items you want to display. Unchecking the Graphics check box results in all of your graphics turning into gray boxes temporarily. This can help speed up display of your file.

5. Click the Set button to save and apply your changes.

Button List

At the top-right corner of the document window, FrameMaker displays a series of buttons in a vertical column.

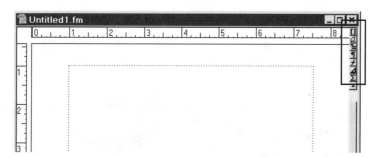

These buttons provide shortcuts to frequently used windows, such as the paragraph and element catalogs. The top three buttons are displayed only in the structured FrameMaker interface.

Button	Function
[I]	**Element Catalog:** Displays the element catalog, which lets you insert, change, and wrap elements. For details, see Chapter 28, "Working with Structured Documents."
a	**Attributes Editor:** Lets you view and edit attribute values for an element. For details, see Chapter 28, "Working with Structured Documents."
≡	**Structure View:** Lets you view and modify the structure of a document. For details, see Chapter 28, "Working with Structured Documents."
¶	**Paragraph Catalog:** Displays the paragraph catalog, which lets you apply paragraph tags to your content. For details, see Chapter 5, "Formatting Text with Paragraph Tags."
f	**Character Catalog:** Lets you apply formatting within a paragraph. For details, see Chapter 6, "Formatting Text with Character Tags."
◢	**Graphic Toolbar:** Lets you create graphics with FrameMaker's graphics tools. For details, see Chapter 13, "FrameMaker's Graphics Tools."
Σ	**Equation Editor:** Lets you create and modify equations. For details, see Chapter 23, "Writing Equations."

Toolbars

FrameMaker provides two toolbars at the top of the main window: the Quick Access Bar and the Formatting Bar. To toggle display of the toolbars, select View | QuickAccess Bar and View | Formatting Bar.

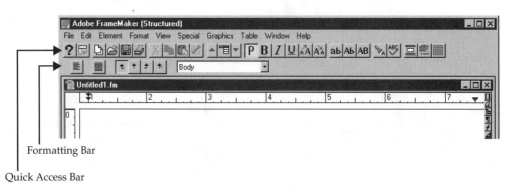

Formatting Bar

Quick Access Bar

The Quick Access Bar is really four toolbars in one. The left side of the Quick Access Bar is always the same, but the information shown on the right changes when you click the up and down arrows in the middle of the bar. Table 3-2 lists the buttons on the bar.

 The Plain, Bold, Italics, Underline, and Increase/Decrease Font Size buttons introduce untagged formatting. In general, you should avoid these buttons; use character tags instead. For details on character tags, see Chapter 6, "Formatting Text with Character Tags."

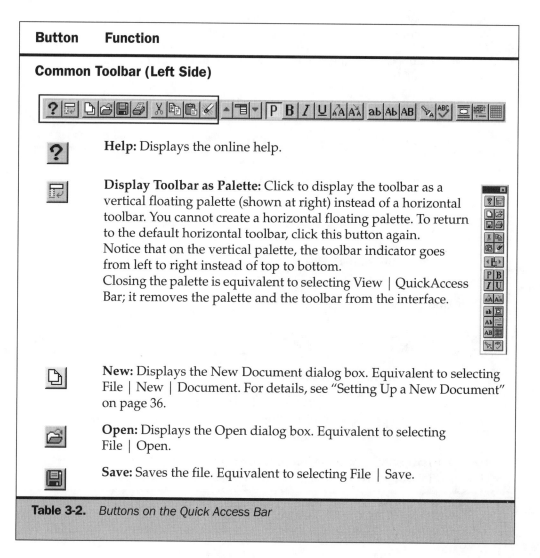

Button	Function
Common Toolbar (Left Side)	
	![toolbar]
?	**Help:** Displays the online help.
	Display Toolbar as Palette: Click to display the toolbar as a vertical floating palette (shown at right) instead of a horizontal toolbar. You cannot create a horizontal floating palette. To return to the default horizontal toolbar, click this button again. Notice that on the vertical palette, the toolbar indicator goes from left to right instead of top to bottom. Closing the palette is equivalent to selecting View | QuickAccess Bar; it removes the palette and the toolbar from the interface.
	New: Displays the New Document dialog box. Equivalent to selecting File | New | Document. For details, see "Setting Up a New Document" on page 36.
	Open: Displays the Open dialog box. Equivalent to selecting File | Open.
	Save: Saves the file. Equivalent to selecting File | Save.

Table 3-2. *Buttons on the Quick Access Bar*

Button	Function
	Print: Displays the Print dialog box. Equivalent to selecting File | Print.
	Cut: Deletes the selected content and puts it on the clipboard. Equivalent to selecting Edit | Cut.
	Copy: Puts a copy of the selected content on the clipboard. Equivalent to selecting Edit | Copy.
	Paste: Retrieves the information on the clipboard and inserts it into the document. Equivalent to selecting Edit | Paste.
	Undo: Undoes the last action. Multiple undo functions are *not* available.

Toolbar Navigation

	Next Toolbar: Displays the next set of toolbar buttons.
	Toolbar Indicator: Shows which of the four toolbars is currently being displayed.
	Previous Toolbar: Displays the previous set of toolbar buttons.

Toolbar One (Formatting Items)

P	**Plain:** Removes any bold, italic, or underlining from the selected text. Use character tags instead to avoid formatting overrides.
B	**Bold:** Applies bold formatting to the selected text. Use character tags instead to avoid formatting overrides.
I	**Italics:** Applies italic formatting to the selected text. Use character tags instead to avoid formatting overrides.

Table 3-2.   *Buttons on the Quick Access Bar (Continued)*

Button	Function
U	**Underline:** Adds underlining to the selected text. Use character tags instead to avoid formatting overrides.
AA	**Increase Font Size:** Increases the font size of the selected text. Use character tags instead to avoid formatting overrides.
AA	**Decrease Font Size:** Decreases the font size of the selected text. Use character tags instead to avoid formatting overrides.
ab	**Lowercase:** Changes the selected text to lowercase.
Ab	**Initial Capital:** Changes the selected text to Initial Capitals (that is, first letter of each word is uppercase; the remainder is lowercase).
AB	**Uppercase:** Changes the selected text to UPPERCASE.
	Thesaurus: Displays the thesaurus. For details about the thesaurus, see page 84.
ABC	**Check Spelling:** Displays the spell-checker. For details about spell-checking, see page 75.
	Anchored Frame: Inserts an anchored frame, which is used to place graphics. For details about anchored frames, see page 303.
	Footnote: Inserts a footnote. For details about footnotes, see page 104.
	Table: Inserts a table. For details, see Chapter 7, "Understanding Table Design."

Toolbar Two (Graphics)

Button	Function
	Group: Groups the selected objects. For details about grouping and ungrouping, see "Grouping" on page 353.
	Ungroup: Ungroups the selected objects. For details about grouping and ungrouping, see "Grouping" on page 353.

Table 3-2. *Buttons on the Quick Access Bar (Continued)*

Button	Function
	Bring to Front: Puts the selected object on top of the object stack. For details about stacking, see "Layering Objects" on page 355.
	Send to Back: Puts the selected object at the bottom of the object stack. For details about stacking, see "Layering Objects" on page 355.
	Distribute: Lets you space objects evenly. For details about distributing, see page 351.
	Reshape: Provides selection handles so that you can change the shape (not just the size) of the selected object. For details, see page 344.
	Smooth: Makes corners in the selected object curvy rather than sharp. For details, see page 345.
	Unsmooth: Makes corners in the selected object sharp rather than curvy. For details, see page 345.
	Flip Vertically: Flips the selected object vertically. For details, see page 357.
	Flip Horizontally: Flips the selected object horizontally. For details, see page 357.
	Scale: Displays the Scale dialog box, where you can change the size of the selected object. For details about scaling, see "Resizing" on page 341.
	Object Properties: Displays the Object Properties dialog box, which provides information about the selected object, such as the height, width, location, and border. For details, see "Modifying Objects" on page 336.
	Snap: If selected, objects you move are snapped to a grid. For details, see "Working with Grids" on page 334.
	Gravity: If selected, objects are attracted to each other, which makes it easier to align them. For details, see page 341.

Table 3-2. *Buttons on the Quick Access Bar (Continued)*

GETTING STARTED
WITH FRAMEMAKER

Button	Function

Toolbar Three (More Graphics)

Move Up: Nudges the selected object up. Equivalent to ALT-UP ARROW.

Move Down: Nudges the selected object down. Equivalent to ALT-DOWN ARROW.

Move Left: Nudges the selected object to the left. Equivalent to ALT-LEFT ARROW.

Move Right: Nudges the selected object to the right. Equivalent to ALT-RIGHT ARROW.

Align Top: Aligns the selected objects to the top edge of the last-selected object. For details about alignment, see page 350.

Align Middle: Aligns the selected objects to the middle of the last-selected object. For details about alignment, see page 350.

Align Bottom: Aligns the selected objects to the bottom edge of the last-selected object. For details about alignment, see page 350.

Align Left: Aligns the selected objects to the left edge of the last-selected object. For details about alignment, see page 350.

Align Center: Aligns the selected objects to the center of the last-selected object. For details about alignment, see page 350.

Align Right: Aligns the selected objects to the right edge of the last-selected object. For details about alignment, see page 350.

Rotate Clockwise: Rotates the selected object clockwise in 15-degree increments. For details about rotating objects, see page 356.

Rotate Counterclockwise: Rotates the selected object counterclockwise in 15-degree increments. For details about rotating objects, see page 356.

Table 3-2. *Buttons on the Quick Access Bar (Continued)*

Button	Function
	Set Solid Line: Sets a solid line for lines and object borders.
	Set Dashed Line: Sets a dashed line for lines and object borders.

Toolbar Four (Tables)

Button	Function
	Select Row: Selects the current table row.
	Select Column: Selects the current column, including any heading rows.
	Select Column Body Cells: Selects the current column, but not any of the heading rows.
	Select Table: Selects the entire table.
	Move Insertion Point to Top Left Cell: Positions the cursor in the top left cell of the table.
	Add Row Below: Adds a row below the current row.
	Add Column to Right: Adds a column to the right of the current column.
	Remove Row or Column: If an entire row or column is selected, that row or column is deleted. If only a few cells in a row or column are selected, nothing is deleted.
	Align Top: Aligns the contents of the current cell to the top of the cell.
	Align Middle: Aligns the contents of the current cell to the middle of the cell.
	Align Bottom: Aligns the contents of the current cell to the bottom of the cell.

Table 3-2.   *Buttons on the Quick Access Bar (Continued)*

Button	Function
	**Straddle:** If two or more cells are selected, they are straddled (merged) into a single cell.
	Shrink-wrap Column Width: The current column is adjusted to the width of its contents.
	Custom Ruling and Shading: Displays the Custom Ruling & Shading dialog box. For details about applying custom ruling and shading, see page 175.

Table 3-2.   *Buttons on the Quick Access Bar (Continued)*

Importing Text from Other Applications

FrameMaker provides filters that let you convert text from many applications into FrameMaker. (Importing graphic files is discussed separately; see Chapter 12, "Importing Graphics.") Depending on the source format, you may have several different options available for pulling text into FrameMaker, including the following:

- **Copying and pasting.** For some applications, you can open the source document, copy the information you want, then switch to FrameMaker and paste it in. From Microsoft Word, select Edit | Paste Special and select RTF or unformatted text. Otherwise, text is imported as an OLE object (Windows only).

- **Opening the source document.** In FrameMaker, try selecting File | Open and then opening the source document (such as a Word file). FrameMaker will filter the document and open it as a FrameMaker document. If FrameMaker does not automatically identify the file type, you are prompted to identify it:

Unknown File Type

File:
E:\Marketing\sarahclass-1

Convert From:

Microsoft Word97/98/2000
MIF
MML
RTF Japanese
RTF Ver1.6
SGML
Text

Convert   Cancel

> **Tip**
>
> *The filters are different on each platform; that is, the Word import filter for Windows is different from the Word import filter for Macintosh. If you are having trouble importing a file, try opening it in FrameMaker on a different platform; sometimes, you may have better results with a different set of filters. Keep in mind, too, that it's possible to exclude filters from the installation (although they are all installed by default). If you appear to be lacking filters, check to see whether you can install more.*

■ **Creating an intermediate file.** For some applications, such as QuarkXPress and PageMaker, direct import is not available. In most cases, though, you can export the file to an intermediate format (for example, PageMaker offers RTF export), and import the intermediate file into FrameMaker. The resulting FrameMaker file usually requires major clean-up.

Microsoft Word

Importing content from Microsoft Word is a relatively smooth process. Text usually converts reasonably well, and paragraph styles applied in Word show up in FrameMaker.

Feature	Conversion Result
Text	Text is imported with minimal problems. Be sure to accept any revisions in Word *before* importing the document; otherwise, revisions may be displayed as FrameMaker conditional text.
Index entries	Converted as FrameMaker index markers.
Cross-references	Converted as text.
Tables	Converted, but Word formatting is applied as overrides. Cleanup is required. Reapply a table format in FrameMaker and remove custom formatting. See Chapter 7, "Understanding Table Design," for details.
Graphics	Converted, but results are not usable. Remove graphics before conversion, and import the graphics directly into FrameMaker instead of attempting to convert them through the filter. If source files are unavailable, try saving the Word file as HTML and using the resulting GIF, JPEG, or PNG files, which are usually higher quality than the graphics that are produced during Word-to-FrameMaker conversion.

Feature	Conversion Result
Headers and footers	Master pages are produced with garbage headers and footers. Cleanup is required.
Master documents	Not converted.

Adobe PageMaker

No direct import from PageMaker is available. Instead, you must export from PageMaker to RTF. Each story in PageMaker becomes a separate file; you may need to reassemble these into a single flow in FrameMaker. RTF export from PageMaker is adequate, but graphics are not converted in this workflow. You must reimport the graphics from the source files.

QuarkXPress

To import QuarkXPress content, you must export the Quark file to RTF, and then import the RTF information.

Interleaf, Ventura Publisher, and Other File Formats

For a detailed list of all available filters, check the *Using Filters* online manual. You will find this manual, delivered as a PDF file, in the OnlineManuals folder in your FrameMaker installation folder. In addition to FrameMaker's built-in filters, a few third-party vendors make import filters. See Appendix A, "Resources," for a list.

Understanding File Configuration and Preferences

Under Windows and UNIX, FrameMaker files normally use the .fm extension. FrameMaker book files (more on those in Chapter 14, "Setting Up Book Files") normally use .book or .bk. On the Macintosh, file extensions are not normally used.

A FrameMaker document file is self-contained; it includes all of the formatting or structure information needed to display and print the content. Unlike some other applications, FrameMaker files do not refer to a separate template file; the template information is embedded in each individual document file.

When you add graphics to a document, you can either link or embed the graphic. When you link (import by reference) a graphic, you insert a pointer from the FrameMaker file to the graphic. This pointer is basically just a file name and path, so it's very small. If you embed (copy into document) a graphic, you insert the entire graphic into the FrameMaker file, so the FrameMaker file grows accordingly.

To prevent two people from working on the same file simultaneously, FrameMaker provides a feature called network file locking. If network file locking is active, opening a file creates a .lck file ("lock" file, *not* "ick" file). If a second person attempts to open the locked file, FrameMaker displays an error message:

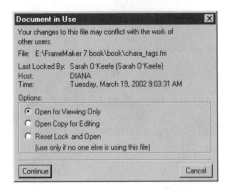

You have three choices:

- **Open for Viewing Only:** Opens a read-only version of the file. You cannot make any changes to this file.
- **Open Copy for Editing:** Creates an untitled copy of the file. You can make changes in this file.
- **Reset Lock and Open:** Removes the lock and lets you edit the file. Use this option only when you are certain that nobody else is using the file (for example, if your computer crashed and left incorrect locking information on the server).

To activate network file locking, follow these steps:

1. Select File | Preferences | General. The Preferences dialog box is displayed (Figure 3-2).
2. Check the Network File Locking check box.
3. Click the Set button to save your change.

Network file locking is turned on by default when you install FrameMaker. Keep in mind, though, that each user must have network file locking activated in their copy of FrameMaker.

In a larger group, the basic file security provided by file locking may not suffice. If this is the case, you have a number of other options:

- **WebDAV.** FrameMaker supports file check-in and check-out on a WebDAV server. See Chapter 27, "Sharing and Managing Files Using WebDAV," for details.

Figure 3-2. *Use the Preferences dialog box to set file locking, backup settings, and other options.*

■ **Other version control systems.** FrameMaker provides support for Open Document Management Architecture (ODMA). You can also use source control systems to manage FrameMaker files.

Handling Missing Font Problems

To display text, FrameMaker uses fonts that are installed on your system. When you open a file, any missing fonts are identified and listed in the console window. By default, FrameMaker performs only a temporary font replacement. This makes sense, especially in a multiplatform environment. You might have a situation where authors working on the Windows platform are missing several fonts that are required to print the document correctly. The final production, however, is done on Macintosh machines. In this scenario, you want FrameMaker to keep track of the missing fonts and replace them only while the file is being edited on the Windows side. When the file is transferred back to a Mac with the appropriate fonts, it will open and display the correct formatting.

In some cases, though, you may want permanent font substitution. You might, for example, receive a file from another company, which uses fonts that you do not have and don't plan to install. In that case, you'd probably want to get rid of the fonts so that you don't get the annoying missing fonts message every time you open the file.

To toggle your missing font setting, follow these steps:

1. Select File | Preferences | General. The Preferences dialog box is displayed (Figure 3-2).

2. Check or uncheck the Remember Missing Font Names check box.

3. Click the Set button to save your change.

To remove missing fonts from a file, follow these steps:

1. In the Preferences dialog box, turn off Remember Missing Font Names as described in the preceding steps.

2. Open the problem file.

3. Save the file.

4. *(optional, but recommended)* Return to the Preferences dialog box and turn on Remember Missing Font Names.

The fonts are now removed from the file.

Organizing Directories and Files

Although many companies establish rules about how to store files and set up directories to manage content, a surprising number do not. If you need to set up a new structure for your documentation library, this section provides some suggestions on how best to manage the files.

The first principle of organizing documents is that a book should have its own directory. Moving the directory (and any associated subdirectories) should move all of the contents of the book. For instance, you can set up a directory structure for a book that includes the book file, chapter files, and graphics in a simple structure:

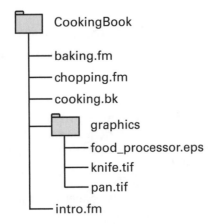

We recommend against naming chapters by their numbers; for example, chap01.fm, chap02.fm, and so on. If you move chapters around, you will either have chapters whose file names doesn't match their numbers or a big renaming job. Instead, name chapters by subject: production_editing.fm, workflow.fm, and so on.

Putting referenced graphics in a subdirectory makes it easier to keep track of them and to separate the graphics from the FrameMaker content files. Creating subdirectories for each chapter can be appealing when you have lots and lots of graphics, but again, avoid naming these directories by chapter number because of the naming mismatch that will occur if you rearrange chapters. For longer books, consider using a prefix for each chapter so that the graphics sort nicely into chapter groups.

Files that are reused across chapters and especially across books present a problem. Consider creating a special "shared" folder in the book folder or one level up from the book folder if you want to share across different books. Keep in mind, though, that you must remember to send the shared folder in addition to the book folder if you ship the files to someone who cannot access them from your network.

File Naming Conventions

You can open a FrameMaker file created on one platform's version of FrameMaker in any of the other platforms. For example, if you create a file in FrameMaker for UNIX, you can open that file in Mac or Windows FrameMaker without any trouble.

The version numbers have to match; you cannot open a FrameMaker 7 file in FrameMaker 6 unless you go through Maker Interchange Format (MIF) or save to FrameMaker 6 format—see page 41.

To ensure that files transfer seamlessly from one platform to another, you need to use file names that work on all platforms. Here are some common tips that will help you create well-behaved file names (the platform that requires the limitation is listed in parentheses):

- Do not use spaces in file names (UNIX).
- Do not use colons in file names (Mac).
- Do not use slashes or backslashes in file names (UNIX, Windows).
- Limit the total file name, including any extension (and the dot in the extension), to 32 characters or less (Mac).
- Use a file-name extension (.fm or .book) to ensure files are recognized by the application and the operating system (Windows).

FrameMaker provides a preferences setting to help you create compatible file names. If you attempt to create a file with a name that will not work on the target platform, a warning message is displayed.

To set cross-platform file naming, follow these steps:

1. Select File | Preferences | General. The Preferences dialog box is displayed (Figure 3-2 on page 61).

2. In the Cross-Platform File Naming drop-down list, click the platform to which you plan to send the files. For example, if you're working under Windows but will need to use the files on a Macintosh, click Macintosh.

3. Click the Set button to save your change.

The next time you save a file, FrameMaker will check the file name for compatibility with the platform specified in the preferences. If any problems are detected, an error message is displayed:

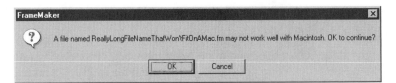

Click the OK button to save the file with the incompatible name. Click the Cancel button to return to the Save dialog box and specify a different name.

Saving File Information with XMP

You can save file information, such as the author, keywords, and title, along with your file. This information is saved as *metadata*, or information about the document. The file information you save is stored in a special format called Extensible Metadata Platform, or XMP. XMP allows you to view metadata without opening the file. You could, for example, define some file information and save your FrameMaker file. An XMP-compatible application or browser can access the XMP data stored for your FrameMaker file, even if the FrameMaker application is not available.

To set up file information, follow these steps:

1. Open the file or book for which you want to save file information.

2. Select File | File Info. The File Info dialog box is displayed.

3. Type in the information you want to save. You can fill in any or all of the available fields.

4. Click the Set button to save your changes with this file.

After setting file information, the data you provided is included as XMP metadata when you save the file.

For more details about XMP, consult Adobe's web site. A search on XMP will yield useful white papers and frequently asked questions about XMP.

Setting Automatic Backup and Save Features

FrameMaker provides two complementary features that save files automatically:

■ **Automatic save.** While you work in FrameMaker, a backup file (.save) is created periodically. If you exit FrameMaker normally, the file is deleted. However, if your system crashes (which means you didn't close FrameMaker properly), the file is preserved. When you reopen the file you were working on, FrameMaker offers to open the .save file, which may contain more recent information.

■ **Automatic backup.** When you save the working file, a .backup.fm file is created. Backup files reside in the same directory as the working file.

To set your file backup options, follow these steps:

1. Select File | Preferences | General. The Preferences dialog box is displayed (Figure 3-2 on page 61).

2. To set automatic backup, check the Automatic Backup on Save check box.

3. To set automatic saving, check the Automatic Save check box, then specify the interval at which you want the file saved. (The default is 5 minutes.)

4. Click the Set button to save your changes.

Sometimes, FrameMaker saves a crash recovery file (.recover) when a crash occurs. That file may contain more up-to-date information than the .save file. We recommend that you inspect both the .recover and the .save files to identify which one is most current.

Switching Between Structured and Unstructured Interfaces

To switch between structured and unstructured FrameMaker, you must choose the new interface, close FrameMaker, and reopen it.

To change interfaces, follow these steps:

1. Select File | Preferences | General. The Preferences dialog box is displayed (Figure 3-2 on page 61).

2. In the Product Interface drop-down list, select the interface you want to switch to.

3. Save all your open files.

4. Exit FrameMaker.

5. Restart FrameMaker. The product is launched and displays the interface you selected.

The Complete Reference

FrameMaker 7

Part II

Creating and Manipulating Text

The
Complete
Reference

FrameMaker 7

Chapter 4

Word-Processing Features

69

FrameMaker includes some of the same features you find in word-processing programs. Many features, such as search and replace, are fairly standard, but they integrate FrameMaker-specific options, such as searching for paragraph tags or cross-references.

In structured and unstructured documents, most FrameMaker word-processing features work the same. For example, the structure of a document doesn't affect tracking changes or looking up a word in the Thesaurus. There are a few additional features in structured documents, such as the ability to search for an element and replace it with another element. You can narrow the search by including an attribute name or value, and then update the attributes as well. Inserting footnotes is also slightly different. You can insert footnotes the standard way—through the Special menu—or by inserting a footnote element. If you need to insert an unstructured footnote, however, you must use the Special menu.

Standard Word-Processing Features

FrameMaker's word-processing features work much like those found in typical word-processing programs. Using the Find/Change feature, you can find and replace words, paragraph tags, and other components. The Spelling Checker locates misspelled words, extra spaces, unusual punctuation, and other irregularities. The Thesaurus helps you find synonyms, antonyms, and other information about specific words.

Searching and Replacing

The Find/Change feature lets you search for text strings, paragraph tags, variable names, broken cross-references, and other items. You can search selected text, the current document, or an entire book. Suppose that you create a variable for your document title after you typed the title in several places. You can search for the places where you typed the document title and replace the title with the variable.

There are several ways to customize your search:

- **Consider Case:** Finds text capitalized like the search item. If you search for *island*, FrameMaker skips the capitalized word *Island*.
- **Whole Word:** Finds the exact words and skips all instances where the text is part of a larger word. If you search for *object*, FrameMaker finds *object* and skips *objective*, *objects*, and *objectification*.
- **Use Wildcards:** Lets you use special characters in place of one or more unspecified characters. Table 4-1 describes how to use each wildcard.
- **Find Backward:** Searches the selection, document, or book starting with the location of the cursor towards the beginning of the document.
- **Clone Case:** Matches the case of the original item in the replacement. For example, if you type "President" in the search field and "leader" in the replace

Wildcard	Description	Example
*	Placeholder for zero or more characters.	s*n finds *sin, son, soon,* and *sullen.*
?	Placeholder for any single character except for spaces and punctuation.	s?n finds *sin, sun,* and *sandle.*
|	Placeholder for one or more spaces and punctuation characters.	gh | the | wo finds *through the woods.*
[ ]	Placeholder for one or more characters you type between the square brackets.	s[ai]ng finds *sang* and *sing.*
[^]	Excludes the characters in brackets from the search.	s[^i]ng finds *sang, song,* and *sung,* but not *sing.*
^	Placeholder for the beginning of a line. Not applicable with the Whole Word option.	^si finds *sing* and *single* only at the beginning of a line.
$	Placeholder for the end of a line. Not applicable with the Whole Word option.	is$ finds *Paris* and *paralysis* at the end of a line. If you search for $is, FrameMaker finds the end of a line followed by *is* on the next line.

Table 4-1.   *Using Wildcards in a Search*

field and do not check Clone Case, then FrameMaker replaces "President" with "leader." With Clone Case checked, "President" is replaced with "Leader."

■ **Look in:** Searches the current document, selected text, or an entire book. To search a book, the book file must be opened in the background.

FrameMaker provides a list of search criteria and replace items. You pick an item to search for—marker text, for example—and replace it with text or an item you copy and paste. In structured documents, you can search and replace elements and attributes.

Searching for an Item

To find and change an item in an unstructured document, follow these steps:

1. You can search a book, a document, or selected text. Do one of the following:

   ■ To search a document, click anywhere in the document's text.

- To search a specific section of text, select that text.
- To search a book, open the book. You can start your search from the book window or inside a file that belongs to that book. To search only specific files in the book, select them by CTRL-clicking (Windows and UNIX) or COMMAND-clicking (Mac) the files you want.

2. Select Edit | Find/Change. The Find/Change dialog box is displayed (Figure 4-1).

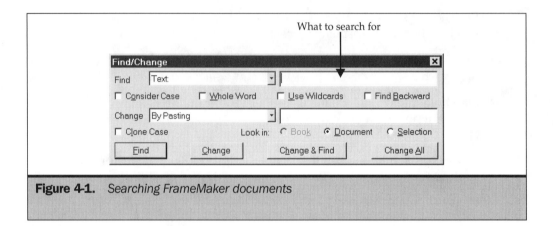

Figure 4-1. *Searching FrameMaker documents*

3. In the Find drop-down list, click the item you want to find. Items followed by ellipses (...) will display a dialog box in which you select additional options. Items followed by colons (:) require that you type in additional search information in the Find field. Table 4-2 describes the search options.

4. *(optional)* To limit the search, check any of the Consider Case, Whole Word, Use Wildcards (only if searching for text), or Find Backward check boxes.

5. To indicate the scope of the search, click the Book, Document, or Selection radio button in the Look in section. (If the book file is displayed, and you have two chapters selected, choose Selection, not Book.)

6. Click the Find button or press ENTER to begin the search. FrameMaker highlights the first match in your document, book, or selection.

7. Click the Find button to search for the next occurrence.

Don't press ENTER to search for the next occurrence. FrameMaker positions the cursor on the page, so you'll insert a carriage return if you do so.

Search for...	To find...
Text:	Text you type in the Find field.
Element...	An element. You can specify the element name, an attribute, and a value for the attribute. See "Searching for Elements" on page 103 for details.
Character Format...	Text that uses the specified character formatting. When you select Character Format, the Find Character Format dialog box is displayed, which lets you specify which formatting properties you want to search for.

FrameMaker will
find italicized
characters, including →
those italicized by a
character tag.

When you click As Is in the Size drop-down list, the setting defaults to the size of the font at the insertion point. To remove the setting, you must delete the font size or click As Is in the drop-down list. To set the Spread and Stretch properties to As Is, delete the information shown in the fields. To set the pair kerning to As Is, check the Pair Kern check box once. The gray check mark, as shown in the preceding example, indicates the As Is setting.

Paragraph Tag:	The paragraph tag name you specify in the Find field.
Character Tag:	The character tag name you specify in the Find field.
Any Marker	Any type of marker, such as hypertext markers, index markers, cross-reference markers, and so on.
Marker of Type:	Markers of the type you specify in the Find field.

Table 4-2.   *Search Criteria*

Search for...	To find...
Marker Text:	Markers of any type that contain the text you specify in the Find field.
Any Cross-Reference	Any cross-reference.
Cross-Reference of Format:	Cross-references that use the cross-reference format you specify in the Find field.
Unresolved Cross-Reference	Unresolved (broken) cross-references.
Any Text Inset	Any text inset.
Unresolved Text Inset	Unresolved (broken) text insets.
Any Publisher	Links to Macintosh text publishers. (See "Platform-Specific Import Features" on page 321 for details.)
Any Variable	Any variable.
Variable of Name:	A variable that matches the name you specify in the Find field.
Any Rubi	Rubi characters. Rubi are pronunciation cues for Japanese characters.
Anchored Frame	Any anchored frame.
Footnote	Any footnote.
Any Table	Any table.
Table Tag:	Tables that use the table tag you specify in the Find field.
Conditional Text:	Conditional text. When you choose this option, the Find Conditional Text dialog box is displayed. Set the condition tags to match the conditional text you want to find, then click the Set button.

Table 4-2.   *Search Criteria (Continued)*

Search for...	To find...
Automatic Hyphen	Hyphens inserted by FrameMaker's hyphenation utility.
Text & Character Formats on Clipboard	Text or character formatting you've copied from the FrameMaker document.

Table 4-2.   *Search Criteria (Continued)*

Replacing an Item

To replace the item you've found, follow these steps:

1. Click a replacement method in the Change drop-down list.

   - **To Text:** Replaces the found item with the text you type in the Change field.

   - **To Character Format:** Displays the Change to Character Format dialog box, which looks similar to the Character Designer. Click the properties you want in the drop-down lists, then click the Set button.

   - **By Pasting:** Replaces the found item with the contents of the clipboard.

2. After FrameMaker finds the item you searched for, do one of the following to replace the item:

   - To change only the first match, click the Change button.

   - To change the first match and find the next one, click the Change & Find button.

   - To change all matches, click the Change All button. A confirmation dialog box is displayed warning that you cannot undo the changes. Click the OK button to replace all matches. If you searched across a book, the item is replaced throughout the book.

For details on searching for elements in structured documents, see "Searching for Elements" on page 103.

Spell-Checking

FrameMaker spell-checks using four dictionaries:

- **Main dictionary.** The primary dictionary installed with the program. FrameMaker provides main dictionaries in several languages. You pick the language in paragraph and character tags. For example, users often set the language in a Code paragraph tag to None to skip spell-checking computer code.

- **Personal dictionary.** The dictionary of words added during a spell-check. You click the Learn button to add words to this dictionary. FrameMaker also lets you create additional personal dictionaries to use, for example, in different types of documents—a financial dictionary for annual reports or a computer dictionary for user's guides. Coworkers can merge your personal dictionary with their personal dictionaries.

- **Document dictionary.** The dictionary embedded in the document. You add words that are correct in the current document but not in other contexts by clicking the Allow in Document button. This dictionary is part of the FrameMaker document, not a separate file like the other dictionaries. As a result, anyone who spell-checks the document has access to the same dictionary, even if the document is opened on another computer. You can write this dictionary to a separate file and clear the dictionary.

- **Site dictionary.** A dictionary containing terms specific to your company, for example, and generally maintained by a system administrator.

When you spell-check, FrameMaker looks for misspelled words and items you select in the Spelling Checker options. Extra spaces, straight quotes, repeated words, and unusual punctuation are among the options you can choose. See "Spelling Checker Options" on page 78 for details.

To spell-check, follow these steps:

1. Display the item you want to spell-check by doing one of the following:

   - Position your cursor in the page or document you want to spell-check.

   - Display the book file you want to spell-check. To spell-check specific chapters, CTRL-click (Windows and UNIX) or COMMAND-click (Mac) each chapter.

2. Select Edit | Spelling Checker. The Spelling Checker dialog box is displayed (Figure 4-2).

3. In the Check section, indicate the item you want to search by doing one of the following:

   - In a book file, click the Book or Selection radio button. (The Document radio button is grayed out at the book level.)

   - In a document, click the Book, Document, or Current Page radio button. (The Book radio button is grayed out if the book file isn't open.)

4. To start spell-checking, click the Start Checking button, or press ENTER. When FrameMaker finds a misspelled word, possible corrections are displayed. The closest match is displayed in the Correction field. The remaining possibilities are displayed in the list beneath the Correction field.

Note   *If no misspellings are found, "Spelling OK" is displayed in the upper-left corner of the Spelling Checker dialog box.*

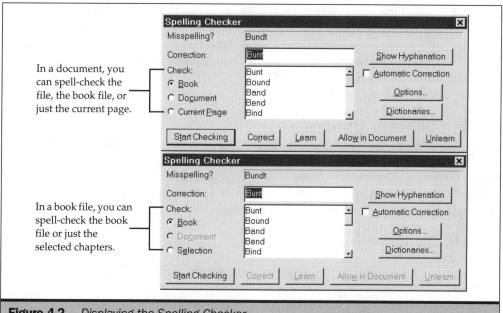

In a document, you can spell-check the file, the book file, or just the current page.

In a book file, you can spell-check the book file or just the selected chapters.

Figure 4-2. *Displaying the Spelling Checker*

5. Do one of the following:

■ To correct the word, either click the Correct button to accept the first suggested word, double-click another word in the list, or type in the correct word in the Correction field, then click the Correct button. The word on the page is updated.

■ To add the word to the current document dictionary, click the Allow in Document button. The word won't be flagged again in the current document.

■ To add the word to your personal dictionary, click the Learn button. The word won't be flagged again in any document you spell-check. See "Modifying Your Personal Dictionary" on page 79 for details.

Tip

When the correct spelling is displayed in the Correction field, check the Automatic Correction check box to replace the word automatically as you spell-check. FrameMaker won't prompt you each time the Spelling Checker finds the word. You can undo the automatic corrections by clicking the Dictionaries button in the Spelling Checker, clicking the Clear Automatic Corrections check box, and then clicking the OK button.

■ To skip the word, click the Start Checking button or press ENTER. You can't add the spell-check options (extra spaces, straight quotes, repeated words, and so on) to the dictionary, so you should skip a straight quote if you need it in the document. FrameMaker will find skipped items, however, each time you spell-check the document.

Spelling Checker Options

The Spelling Checker options let you include additional items in a spell-check. By default, FrameMaker checks for repeated words, two consecutive punctuation marks of several types, straight quotes, extra spaces, and spaces before and after specific characters. Single words, all uppercase words, words containing a period, and words with digits are ignored. You can modify the defaults by clicking the Options button in the Spelling Checker and changing the settings in the Spelling Checker Options dialog box. Table 4-3 describes the options.

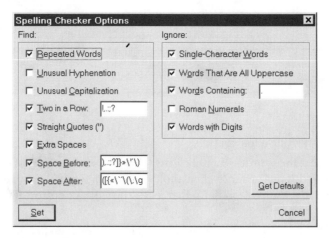

After you modify the Spelling Checker options, you can spell-check the document using the new guidelines. To do so, click the Dictionaries button in the Spelling Checker, click the Mark All Paragraphs for Rechecking check box, and click the OK button.

You cannot add items to the dictionary that the Spelling Checker looks for, such as repeated words or extra spaces. If you want to skip these items, modify the Spelling Checker options and spell-check again.

Item	Example
Find	
Repeated Words	the the
Unusual Hyphenation	un-usual
Unusual Capitalization	cRazY
Two in a Row	Why??
Straight Quotes	"happy"
Extra Spaces	party time
Spaces Before and Spaces After	(howling)
Ignore	
Single-Character Words	a
Words That Are All Uppercase	OLE
Words Containing	7.0 (ignores period)
Roman Numerals	ii
Words with Digits	555-TIME

Table 4-3. *Spell-Check Options*

Modifying Your Personal Dictionary

FrameMaker updates your personal dictionary when you click the Learn and Unlearn buttons. You can also create new personal dictionaries, merge another dictionary into yours, save unknown words to a separate file, and stop using your personal dictionary.

To modify your personal dictionary or create a new one, follow these steps:

1. Click the Dictionaries button in the Spelling Checker dialog box. The Dictionary Functions dialog box is displayed (Figure 4-3 on page 80).

2. In the Personal Dictionary drop-down list, do one of the following:

   ■ To export your personal dictionary to a text file, click Write to File, then click the OK button. The Write Personal Dictionary to File dialog box is displayed. Type the name of the dictionary in the File name field, then click the Save button. The text file is created.

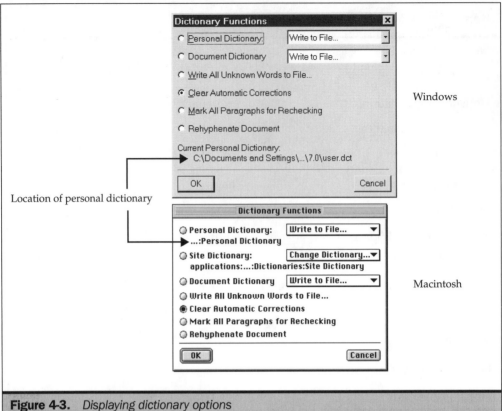

Location of personal dictionary

Windows

Macintosh

Figure 4-3.   *Displaying dictionary options*

■ To switch personal dictionaries, click Change Dictionary, then click the OK button. The Use File for Personal Dictionary dialog box is displayed. Click the file you want to use, then click the Use button. The name of the new personal dictionary is displayed.

■ To add entries from another dictionary to your dictionary, click Merge from File, then click the OK button. The Merge File into Personal Dictionary dialog box is displayed. Click the file you want to merge into your dictionary, then click the Merge button. The dictionaries are merged.

■ To stop using your personal dictionary, click Set to None, then click the OK button. The name of your current personal dictionary is no longer displayed in the Dictionary Functions dialog box. (If you click the Learn or Unlearn button without a personal dictionary selected, FrameMaker warns that you need to select the personal dictionary and try again.)

Modifying the Document Dictionary

FrameMaker updates the document dictionary when you click the Allow in Document button during a spell-check. You can also remove entries, merge another document dictionary into the current one, and save the dictionary to a separate file.

 To edit the document dictionary by hand, save your FrameMaker document as a Maker Interchange Format (MIF) file, and then open the MIF file in a text editor. The words you allowed in the document are in the Dictionary section. See Chapter 24, "Maker Interchange Format," for details about MIF files.

To modify the document dictionary, follow these steps:

1. Click the Dictionaries button in the Spelling Checker dialog box. The Dictionary Functions dialog box is displayed (Figure 4-3).

2. In the Document Dictionary drop-down list, do one of the following:

   ■ To remove all entries from the document dictionary, click Clear, then click the OK button. The words are removed from the document dictionary.

   ■ To merge another FrameMaker file with the current document dictionary, click Merge from File, then click the OK button. The Merge File into Document Dictionary dialog box is displayed. Click the FrameMaker file you want to merge with your dictionary, then click the Merge button. The files are merged.

   ■ To save the document dictionary in a separate text file, click Write to File, then click the OK button. The Write Document Dictionary to File dialog box is displayed. Type the name of the dictionary in the File name field, then click the Save button. The dictionary file is created.

 You can merge the exported document dictionary with your personal dictionary. See "Modifying Your Personal Dictionary" on page 79 for details.

Customizing Hyphenation

Dictionaries don't just contain lists of words; they also show how words are hyphenated. FrameMaker shows the hyphenation points when you click the Show Hyphenation button in the Spelling Checker. For example, the following dictionary entries suggest hyphenation for three words:

```
fire-wall
gray-scale
hy-per-link
```

When you install FrameMaker, dictionaries for different languages and the corresponding hyphenation files are also installed. For example, the *hyphens.itl* file contains hyphenation points for popular Italian words. If you don't like the hyphenation, you correct the hyphenation in the Spelling Checker and click the Learn button. The main dictionary is updated.

Paragraph tags also determine how words are hyphenated:

■ **Language:** On the Default Font sheet of the Paragraph Designer, you select a language for the paragraph tag, and FrameMaker uses the corresponding hyphenation file.

■ **Hyphenation parameters:** On the Paragraph Designer's Advanced sheet, you turn hyphenation off or on and specify how words are broken across lines. For example, the CellBody paragraph style shown in the following screen shot limits the shortest prefix and suffix to three characters each. See "Advanced Sheet" on page 126 for details.

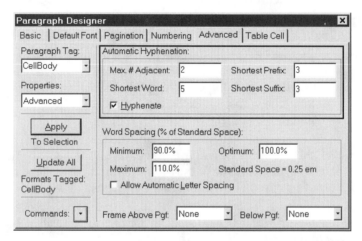

The paragraph tag hyphenation settings take precedence over the hyphenation points. For example, suppose the word *paper* is hyphenated as *pa-per*. According to the predefined hyphenation, the word breaks after the two-letter prefix *pa-*. If the paragraph tag requires at least a three-character prefix, *paper* moves to the next line, and FrameMaker doesn't use the predefined hyphenation.

Paragraph tag allows a two-character prefix at the end of the line. ──────▶ We subscribe to the local pa-per, *The News and Observer.*

Paragraph tag requires a three-character prefix, so the hyphenated word moves to the next line. ──────▶ We subscribe to the local paper, *The News and Observer.*

To display and modify hyphenation, follow these steps:

1. Select Edit | Spelling Checker. The Spelling Checker is displayed (Figure 4-2 on page 77).

2. Type a word in the Correction field, then click the Show Hyphenation button. The hyphenation points are displayed.

3. To change the hyphenation, modify the word in the Correction field, then click the Learn button. (To remove all hyphenation from a word, type a hyphen before the word, as in **-paper**.) The hyphenation points are updated in your personal dictionary.

4. *(optional)* To update hyphenation throughout the document after you correct hyphenation points, follow these steps:

   a. Click the Dictionaries button in the Spelling Checker. The Dictionary Functions dialog box is displayed (Figure 4-3 on page 80).

   b. Click the Rehyphenate Document radio button.

   c. Click the OK button. The hyphenation in your document is updated.

To edit hyphenation by hand, open your personal dictionary in a text editor and type the hyphens where you want them.

Hyphenation Shortcuts

In addition to using the Spelling Checker and paragraph tags to control hyphenation, you can insert symbols in specific words.

- **Prevent hyphenation.** To prevent a word from hyphenating, insert the suppress hyphenation symbol where the word breaks. Press ESC N S to insert the symbol. In a variable or cross-reference format, type \+ where you want to prevent hyphenation.

- **Prevent hyphenation at the end of the line.** To prevent a word from hyphenating at the end of a line, insert a nonbreaking hyphen before the hyphen at the end of the line. Press ESC hyphen H to insert the symbol.

- **Force hyphenation.** To force a hyphen to display in a specific location, insert a discretionary hyphen where you want the word to break. Press ESC HYPHEN SHIFT-D.

Suppressed hyphen	Non-breaking hyphen	Discretionary hyphen
This year, we're celebrating in Costa Rica and you're all invited!	Bring film. Our little hide-a-way is near the edge of the rain forest.	This year, we're cele- brating in Costa Rica, and you're all invited!

Thesaurus

FrameMaker's Thesaurus identifies the part of speech, synonyms, antonyms, and related words for the selected word or phrase. The Thesaurus isn't as comprehensive as a traditional printed thesaurus. You may not find an entire word, but you can try to find the root word.

To use the Thesaurus, follow these steps:

1. Do one of the following:

   - If the word doesn't occur in the document or you haven't selected it, select Edit | Thesaurus. The Thesaurus Look Up dialog box is displayed. Type the word in the Word field, then click the Look Up button. You can also search for the word in a different language by clicking an item in the Language drop-down list.

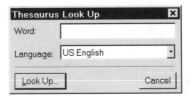

   - To look up a word in the document, select the word, then select Edit | Thesaurus.

   The word, definition, and corresponding entries are displayed in the Thesaurus dialog box.

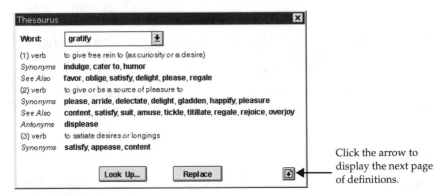

Click the arrow to display the next page of definitions.

2. Click a word in the Synonyms, Antonyms, or See Also sections to explore its meaning. The last ten words you look up are displayed in the Word drop-down list.

3. Click the Replace button to substitute the word in the Word drop-down list for the highlighted word in your document. (The word must be highlighted, or you'll insert the new word where you inserted the cursor.)

Configuring Default Text Options

Though paragraph tags determine most of the formatting, FrameMaker lets you specify document defaults to fine-tune the display of text. For example, the Smart Spaces option allows only one consecutive space in the document. Smart Quotes turn straight quotes into curly quotes. You can also prevent line breaks after certain characters and specify size and spacing for superscript, subscript, and small caps characters.

You modify text options in an individual file or book file. Because FrameMaker considers the default text options part of the document properties, you can also import the document properties into another FrameMaker file, and the text options are updated. Select Format | Document | Text Options to display and change these default text options (Figure 4-4).

CREATING AND MANIPULATING TEXT

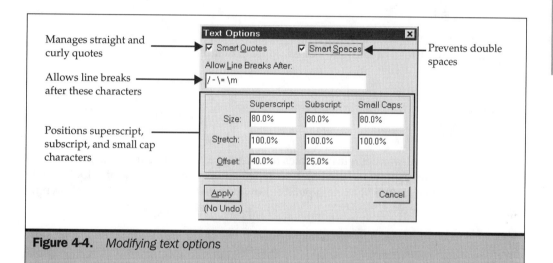

Manages straight and curly quotes

Allows line breaks after these characters

Positions superscript, subscript, and small cap characters

Prevents double spaces

Figure 4-4. *Modifying text options*

Smart Spaces

Smart Spaces prevent you from typing more than one space in a row. This feature provides consistent spacing throughout a document. Although the Smart Spaces text option isn't enabled by default, the spell-checker's Extra Spaces is enabled by default. That means that FrameMaker automatically searches for extra spaces during a spell-check, which is especially handy when you import documents of other formats into FrameMaker. For example, an imported Microsoft Word document may have extra spaces after periods. Extra spaces may also have been inserted instead of tabs to position words. When you spell-check the document, FrameMaker finds the extra spaces and replaces them with a single space.

To enable Smart Spaces, follow these steps:

1. In an individual file or book file, select Format | Document | Text Options. The Text Options dialog box is displayed (Figure 4-4 on page 85).

2. Check the Smart Spaces check box, then click the Apply button. In any new text, you are prevented from typing two spaces in a row. To remove extra spaces from the existing information, you need to spell-check with the Extra Spaces option checked.

If you turn off Smart Spaces, you need to modify the Spelling Checker options to disable checking for extra spaces. See "Spelling Checker Options" on page 78 for more information.

Smart Quotes

When you type single and double quotes, the Smart Quotes option ensures that the quotes are curly instead of straight. For example, instead of typing

' and "

you type

' and "

In some typeface families, curly quotes are more curved than curly. The previous example shows curly quotes in the Palatino typeface. Notice that the quotes look more angled than curved. In the Veljovic typeface, however, the quotes are curly, as shown in the following sentence:

"Hurry up," cried the impatient customer.

The Spelling Checker can find straight quotes and replace them with curly quotes. This feature is particularly helpful when you import another type of file into FrameMaker. For example, in an imported Microsoft Word document, you need to run the Spelling Checker to find and correct straight quotes. Though FrameMaker catches most of the straight double quotes, it skips over some of the straight single quotes. You need to find and correct the skipped quotes by hand.

Smart Quotes are enabled by default. To turn off smart quotes, follow these steps:

1. In an individual file or book file, select Format | Document | Text Options. The Text Options dialog box is displayed (Figure 4-4 on page 85).

2. Uncheck the Smart Quotes check box, then click the Apply button. Your changes are saved in the document.

When Smart Quotes are enabled, you still type straight quotes, but you must use the keyboard shortcuts shown in Table 4-4.

Platform	Single Quote	Double Quote
Windows	ESC CTRL-'	ESC SHIFT-'
Mac	CTRL-'	CTRL-SHIFT-'
UNIX	ESC CTRL-'	ESC SHIFT-'

Table 4-4. *Keyboard Shortcuts for Straight Quotes*

Restricting Line Breaks

You can force special characters and spaces to move to the next line or prevent them from doing so. By default, line breaks are permitted after the following characters:

- **Forward slash.** /
- **Dash.** -
- **En dash.** \=
- **Em dash.** \m

These characters are displayed in the Allow Line Breaks After field of the Text Options dialog box (Figure 4-4 on page 85). When you modify characters in the field, FrameMaker instantly updates line breaks in the document.

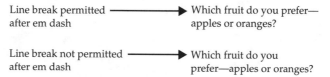

Line break permitted after em dash ——————▶ Which fruit do you prefer— apples or oranges?

Line break not permitted after em dash ——————▶ Which fruit do you prefer—apples or oranges?

In dialog boxes, you type special characters, such as the en and em dash, differently depending on your computer platform. Table 4-5 on page 88 describes the distinctions.

To configure line breaks, follow these steps:

1. In an individual file or book file, select Format | Document | Text Options. The Text Options dialog box is displayed (Figure 4-4 on page 85).

2. Modify characters in the Allow Line Breaks After field, then click the Apply button. Your changes are applied to the document.

Platform	Description
Windows	Type a shortcut or hexadecimal code and *escape out* the characters with a backslash. This prevents FrameMaker from processing the text as literal characters. For instance, you type an en space as \x13 or \sn. (The hex code is replaced with the alphabetic version when you close and reopen the dialog box.) For more information on typing special characters in dialog boxes and a list of specific hex codes, refer to the *Character Sets* online manual. You'll find it in the FrameMaker installation directory's OnlineManuals folder.
Macintosh	Type the actual character.
UNIX	Type the actual character. After you close the dialog box and open it again, the character is replaced with the escaped version.

Table 4-5. *Typing in Dialog Boxes*

Formatting Superscripts, Subscripts, and Small Caps

The document text options largely determine the size, offset, and width for superscript, subscript, and small caps characters. When you change the defaults, FrameMaker updates paragraph tags, character tags, footnotes, variables, and other components that include these characters. These settings apply to the entire document.

You can change the following properties:

■ **Size.** The superscript, subscript, and small caps characters are a certain percentage smaller than the default paragraph or character formatting. To change the size of the characters throughout a document, you modify the percentage in the appropriate Size fields of the Text Options dialog box.

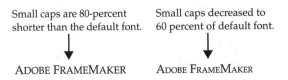

■ **Offset.** Superscript and subscript characters are displayed a certain percentage above or below the current line. To increase the offset, you increase the percentages in the Offset fields. To decrease the offset, you decrease the percentage as shown in the following example:

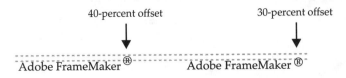

■ **Width.** You can change the width of superscript, subscript, and small caps characters by modifying the Stretch fields. In the following example, the registration mark is displayed with a 100-percent stretch (the same size as the paragraph tag) and with an 80-percent stretch:

In the document text options, the stretch value applies only to superscript, subscript, and small caps characters. You can set the stretch in paragraph and character tags, but those settings are unrelated to the text options.

To change the superscript, subscript, and small caps settings, follow these steps:

1. In an individual file or book file, select Format | Document | Text Options. The Text Options dialog box is displayed (Figure 4-4 on page 85).

2. Do any of the following:

   ■ To change the size, stretch, or offset of superscript and subscript characters, type new percentages in the Size, Stretch, or Offset fields.

   ■ To change the size or stretch of small caps characters, type new percentages in the Small Caps fields.

3. Click the Apply button. The new settings are applied to the document.

Tracking Changes

You can keep track of changes to some degree in FrameMaker. The basic word count tells you the number of words in the document. You might compare this number to the number of words in a previous version of the document. To show modified text on the page, you turn on automatic change bars, which are displayed in the margin of the document when any change is made. For more specific information, you can compare two versions of the same document or book.

Displaying the Word Count

FrameMaker's Word Count feature shows the number of words in a document. You might run a word count in conjunction with comparing documents to show the degree to which content has been modified. Running a word count may also help you meet a specific word quota.

In the word count, items such as variables and cross-references are included; paragraph autonumbers (step or footnote numbers, for instance) and hidden conditional text are excluded.

To run a word count, follow these steps:

1. Select File | Utilities | Document Reports. The Document Reports dialog box is displayed.

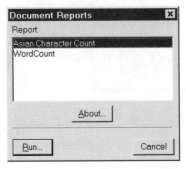

2. In the Report list, click Word Count, then click the Run button. The results are displayed.

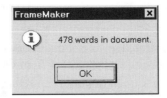

3. Click the OK button to close the dialog box.

For Asian language documents, run an Asian Character Count instead of a word count. The number of single- and double-byte characters is displayed.

Using Change Bars

Change bars help readers locate new material. When you modify a document, change bars are displayed in the margin on the line containing the change, even when you only insert a space. As a result, it's often difficult to decipher exactly what was changed. For instance, the following example shows change bars next to modified lines, but the exact changes are not apparent. You can determine only that information changed in lines 1, 2, and 4; but not in line 3.

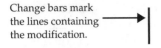

Change bars mark the lines containing the modification. → | Remove broth from pot and cool.

In a mixing bowl, beat the egg whites until foamy, then add egg yolks and lemon juice. Add slowly to rice mixture, stirring gently.

| Return reserved broth to the pot. Serve immediately.

You can customize the color, position, and thickness of automatic change bars and their distance from the text column. These settings apply to the entire document, and you cannot define change bars for individual users. Character tags have a change bar option, but you must mark changes manually. You're also still limited to one change bar style.

FrameMaker does not have a revision-tracking feature. You can, however, compare two versions of a document. See "Comparing Documents and Books" on page 92.

To toggle and customize automatic change bars, follow these steps:

1. Select Format | Document | Change Bars. The Change Bar Properties dialog box is displayed.

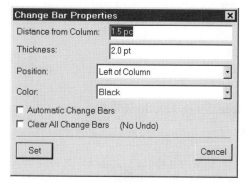

2. To change the space between the change bar and text column, type a new number in the Distance from Column field.

3. To change the size of the change bar, type a new width in the Thickness field.

4. To modify the change bar location, click a location in the Position drop-down list:

   ■ **Left of Column** *(single-sided document)*: Change bar is displayed in the left margin.

   ■ **Right of Column** *(single-sided document)*: Change bar is displayed in the right margin.

   ■ **Side Closer to Page Edge** *(double-sided document)*: Change bar is displayed in the left margin on a left page or in the right margin on a right page.

   ■ **Side Farther from Page Edge** *(double-sided document)*: Change bar is displayed in the right margin on a left page or in the left margin on a right page.

5. To change the color, click a color in the Color drop-down list. The colors defined in your document are displayed in the list, but you can create new colors. See Chapter 20, "Color Output," for details.

CREATING AND
MANIPULATING TEXT

6. To remove all change bars from your document, check the Clear All Change Bars check box. All change bars are cleared from the document once you click the Set button.

Clearing change bars also removes those applied by character tags. You cannot undo this command once change bars are removed. To be safe, save your document before you clear change bars, and you can revert to the saved file if necessary.

7. Check the Automatic Change Bars check box, then click the Set button.

Comparing Documents and Books

The Compare Documents feature lets you compare two versions of the same document or book to see what's changed. In a document comparison, FrameMaker analyzes the contents of identical flows and reports changes to items including the following:

- Text
- Variable definitions
- Marker contents
- Cross-reference formats and the location of cross-reference links
- Anchored frames
- Tables

In a book comparison, FrameMaker lists the modified book components in addition to the document components. For example, the modified items in each file are displayed, along with which files were inserted, modified, or deleted in the book.

There are two types of document comparison reports. In the *composite report*, a marked-up version of the newer document is displayed. The changes are marked with condition tags or special characters—you choose the style before running the report. The *summary report* is only a list of changes. FrameMaker lets you run just a summary report or both the composite and summary reports. You can also print and save the reports. The structure of a document is excluded from the comparison.

Figure 4-5 shows samples of the reports.

Summary document →

Composite document →

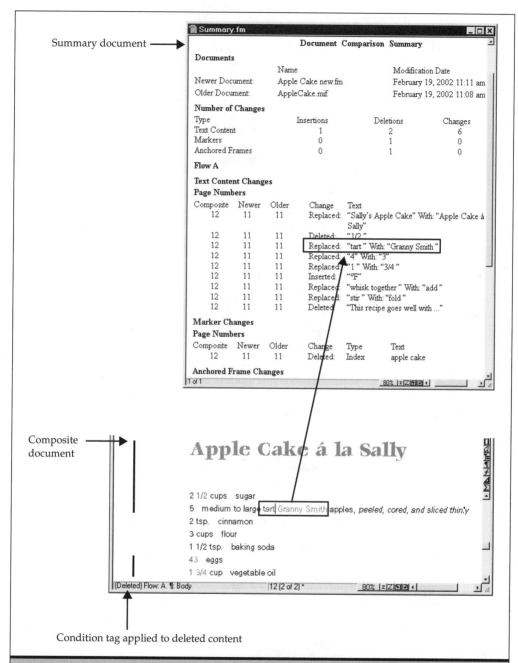

Condition tag applied to deleted content

CREATING AND MANIPULATING TEXT

Figure 4-5. *The summary and composite document comparison reports*

To compare two versions of the same document, follow these steps:

1. Open the old version of the document you want to compare.
2. Open the new version of the document.
3. From the new document, select File | Utilities | Compare Documents. The Compare Documents dialog box is displayed.

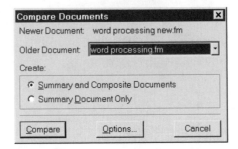

4. If several documents are open, click the name of the document you want to compare in the Older Document drop-down list.

Comparing two completely different documents is possible, but it's usually pointless. You compare documents to pinpoint the changes, and FrameMaker doesn't find changes in disparate documents!

5. Do one of the following:
   - Click the Summary and Composite Documents radio button to create both a summary of changes and the marked document.
   - Click the Summary Document Only radio button to create a list of changes.
6. *(optional)* Click the Options button to change the mark-up methods. The Comparison Options dialog box is displayed.

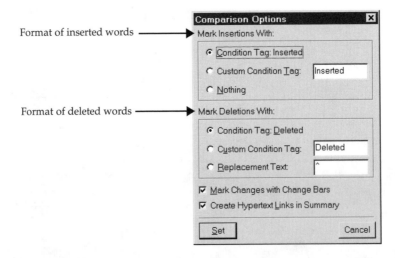

- In the Mark Insertions With section, click one of the radio buttons to specify formatting for the inserted characters. The default setting applies a condition tag called Inserted, but you can type a new or existing condition in the Custom Condition Tag field or click the Nothing radio button to avoid marking insertions.

- In the Mark Deletions With section, click one of the radio buttons to customize formatting for the deleted characters. You can assign the Deleted condition, specify a different condition, or replace the deletion with text, such as "Deleted Text."

- To display change bars in the margin, check the Mark Changes with Change Bars check box.

- To link the changes in the summary document to the original document, check the Create Hypertext Links in Summary check box. You can CTRL-ALT-click (Windows) or COMMAND-OPTION-click (Mac) a hyperlink to display the referenced document. In UNIX, press CTRL and right-click the link.

7. Click the Compare button. The document reports you chose are displayed.

To compare two versions of the same book file, follow these steps:

1. Open the old and new versions of the book file. The two book files must have identical names, and only chapter files with the same names are compared.

2. From the new book file, select File | Utilities | Compare Books. The Compare Books dialog box is displayed.

3. Click the name of the old book file in the Older Book drop-down list.

4. Click the Compare button. The documents you chose are displayed.

Working with Footnotes

Footnotes include ancillary information at the bottom of the text column or below a table. Three factors affect the format and structure of footnotes:

- **Numbering properties.** In the footnote properties of a book or stand-alone document, you set up the footnote number position, prefix or suffix, paragraph tag applied to the footnote, and maximum height. There are separate properties for main footnotes and table footnotes. If the document is in a book, you select the two properties in the book setup—the footnote format and the numbering options. The footnote format can be numeric, uppercase or lowercase alphabetic, uppercase or lowercase Roman numerals, or a custom format. Numbering options let you specify whether you want the footnote numbering to start over on each page, continue from previous number, or read the footnote number from the file. You can also specify the starting footnote number for each document in the book. See "Managing Numbering" on page 373 for more information.

- **Footnote paragraph tag.** FrameMaker applies the paragraph tag you specify in the footnote properties to the footnote paragraph. The paragraph uses the Footnote border on the reference page as the frame above the paragraph. You might need to change the height of the frame to adjust spacing. You can also change the properties of the footnote border—for example, modify the line width or color. See "Placing Graphics Above and Below the Paragraph" on page 322 for more information on reference page graphics. Table footnotes and main footnotes can use different paragraph tags.

- **Paragraph tag for main text.** The paragraph tag applied at the location of the footnote number formats the number. If the main paragraph has a serif font, the footnote number is displayed in a serif font.

Figure 4-6 shows the pieces of a footnote.

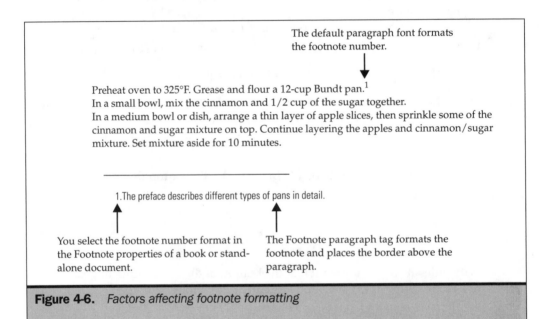

Figure 4-6. *Factors affecting footnote formatting*

Inserting Footnotes

When you insert a footnote, the number is displayed at the insertion point. Your cursor appears in a new footnote paragraph, which is located at the bottom of the text column (if your cursor is in the body text) or below the table (if your cursor is in a table).

Footnotes are displayed by their position in the body text or table, not by the order in which you insert the footnotes. For example, if you insert a footnote in the first paragraph and the third paragraph, and then insert one in the second paragraph, FrameMaker renumbers the footnote paragraphs.

FrameMaker does not split footnotes between two pages. For example, if there isn't enough room for the footnote paragraph on the current page, the entire paragraph moves to the next page. You can prevent this problem by manually adjusting the text frame so the footnote fits on the current page or by changing the maximum height of the footnote paragraph. See "Customizing Footnote Properties" on page 99 for details on increasing the maximum height.

The footnote paragraph can be displayed in the column or side head space, across all columns, or across all columns and side heads. If you're working in a multicolumn document, you must adjust the pagination settings in the footnote paragraph tag accordingly. See "Modifying Paragraph Tags" on page 112 for details.

To insert a footnote, follow these steps:

1. Position the cursor where you want the footnote number to be displayed, then select Special | Footnote. The footnote number is displayed in the main text, and your cursor is displayed in the new footnote paragraph at the bottom of the column or below the table, depending on the type of footnote.

2. Type your footnote. The footnote is displayed in the document.

Using the Same Number for Several Footnotes

When you need to refer to the same footnote number in several places, you insert a cross-reference to the existing footnote. The following example shows the initial footnote in the first line and the cross-referenced footnote in the second line. The two references look the same because the footnote number in the second line uses a cross-reference format that applies the superscript automatically.

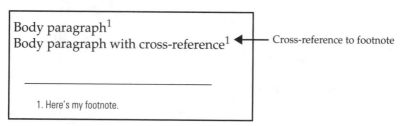

Body paragraph[1]
Body paragraph with cross-reference[1] ◄——— Cross-reference to footnote

_____

1. Here's my footnote.

The font properties for the footnote number and cross-reference number are determined by the paragraph tag. For instance, if the footnote paragraph has a serif font and the cross-reference number is in a sans-serif paragraph, the two numbers won't match.

The following example shows the serif footnote number and a sans-serif number for the cross-reference:

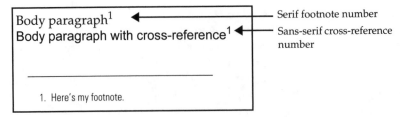

You can prevent this problem by creating a character tag for the cross-reference that specifies the font you want to use for the imitation footnotes. The character tag should also include a subscript or superscript property to match the style of the existing footnote. In the cross-reference format, you insert the character tag before the <$paranumonly> building block. The cross-reference format looks something like this:

```
<footnote><$paranumonly><Default Para Font>
```

To create a cross-reference to an existing footnote, follow these steps:

1. Create a character tag that matches the footnote paragraph tag's font properties and the style of the footnote number (superscript or subscript).

2. Create a cross-reference format that includes the character tag and <$paranumonly> building block.

3. Position the cursor where you want the cross-reference, then select Special | Cross-Reference. The Cross-Reference dialog box is displayed.

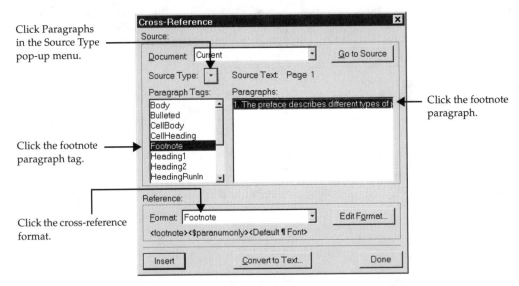

4. Click Paragraphs in the Source Type pop-up menu to display the paragraph tags.

5. In the Paragraph Tags section, click the footnote paragraph tag. The footnote paragraph is displayed in the Paragraphs section.

6. In the Paragraphs section, click the footnote paragraph.

7. In the Format drop-down list, click the footnote cross-reference format you created.

8. Click the Insert button. The cross-reference number is displayed in the text.

For more information on creating cross-reference formats, see "Setting Up Cross-Reference Formats" on page 198. See "Creating Character Tags" on page 149 for details on setting up a character tag.

Customizing Footnote Properties

FrameMaker lets you customize footnote formatting and numbering properties. The formatting properties, which you configure in individual files, consist of the footnote prefix or suffix, position of the number, paragraph tag applied to the footnote, and maximum height. The numbering properties determine how footnotes are numbered in a book (or document) and the type of alphanumeric footnote character. If the document is in a book file, you set the number format in the book file setup. If not, you can change the number format in the document's numbering properties.

Modifying Footnote Formatting

To customize footnote formatting, follow these steps:

1. Open the file or book file you want to modify, then select Format | Document | Footnote Properties. The Footnote Properties dialog box is displayed.

Click the sheet (Windows only) or drop-down list for the type of footnote you want to edit.

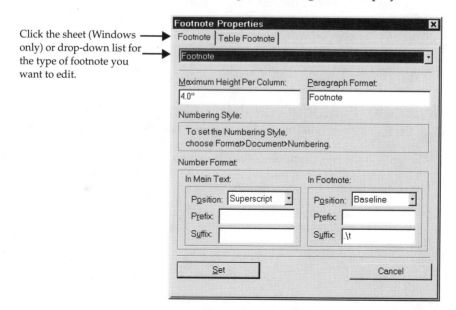

2. Click the Footnote or Table Footnote sheet, depending on which type of footnote you need to modify. You can also click Footnote or Table Footnote in the drop-down list at the top.

3. *(standard footnote only)* To limit the height of the Footnote paragraph, type a number in the Maximum Height Per Column field. (The unit of measure is specified in the document's view options. Select View | Options to display the setting.)

4. To change the paragraph tag applied to new footnotes, type the tag name in the Paragraph Format field. This setting does not change existing footnotes.

 If you misspell the paragraph tag name, FrameMaker applies the paragraph tag to new footnotes and considers the paragraph tag an override. In the status bar, the asterisk next to the misspelled paragraph tag indicates the override. You can either correct the paragraph tag in the footnote properties or create a new paragraph tag.

5. To change the format of the footnote character in the main text, do any of the following in the In Main Text section (or the In Cell section of table footnotes):

   ■ Click a position in the Position drop-down list. (Baseline aligns the character with the main text.)

   ■ To precede the footnote character with a specific character, type the character in the Prefix field. You can type special characters such as an em space (\sm) or en space (\sn).

   ■ To display a specific character after the footnote character, type the character in the Suffix field.

6. To change the format of the footnote character in the actual footnote, change settings in the In Footnote section. See the previous step for descriptions of each option.

7. Click the Set button. Your changes are applied to existing footnotes, except for the maximum height and paragraph tag settings, which are only applied to future footnotes.

Modifying the Footnote Numbering Properties in the Book File

To change the footnote numbering properties in a book file, follow these steps:

1. Open the book file, then select the files whose footnote properties you want to change. Press CTRL-A (Windows and UNIX) or COMMAND-A (Mac) to select all files in the book; CTRL-click (Windows and UNIX) or COMMAND-click (Mac) specific files.

2. Select Format | Document | Numbering. The Numbering Properties dialog box is displayed.

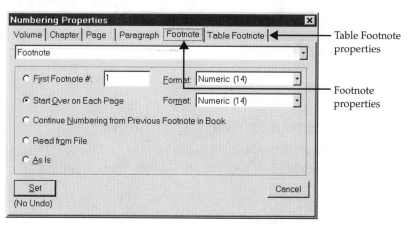

3. Click the Footnote or Table Footnote sheet (Windows only) or click a choice in the drop-down list, depending on the type of footnote you need to modify.

4. Do any of the following:

- To specify the number of the first footnote in each file, type the number in the First Footnote # field.

- To change the format of the first footnote, click an item in the Format drop-down list that is displayed next to the First Footnote # field. If you click Custom, the Custom Numbering dialog box is displayed. You change the numbering pattern for the footnotes here. According to the following example, FrameMaker assigns the asterisk to the first footnote, the dagger to the second footnote, and the double dagger to the third footnote in the document or book. These symbols are repeated if you have more than three footnotes. For more information on typing special characters in dialog boxes, refer to the *Character Sets* online manual. You'll find it in the FrameMaker installation directory's OnlineManuals folder.

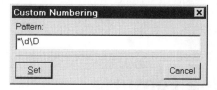

- To restart footnote numbering on each page, click the Start Over on Each Page radio button, then click the numbering style from the Format drop-down list.

- To continue numbering from the previous footnote, click the Continue Numbering from Previous Footnote in Book radio button.

- To use the footnote numbering properties set up in the file, click the Read from File radio button.

Caution   *If the file- and book-level footnote properties differ, FrameMaker displays an Inconsistent Numbering Properties warning when you update the book. The warning explains that file-level numbering properties are ignored during the update.*

5. Click the Set button. Your changes are applied to the selected files in the book.

Modifying the Footnote Numbering Properties in Stand-Alone Documents

To modify footnote numbering in individual documents, follow these steps:

1. Select Format | Document | Numbering. The Numbering Properties dialog box is displayed.

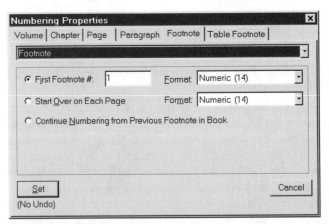

2. Click the Footnote or Table Footnote sheet (or item in the drop-down list), depending on the properties you need to edit.

3. Change the properties as described in "Modifying the Footnote Numbering Properties in the Book File" on page 100, then click the Set button. Your changes are applied to the file.

Word-Processing Features in Structured Documents

Most word-processing features are identical in structured and unstructured documents. There are two variations in structured documents. You can search for elements and replace them with another element, or you can change the attribute name or value. Inserting footnotes also differs because you can insert an element to create a footnote.

Searching for Elements

FrameMaker lets you search for elements in structured documents. You can search the document or the structure view. When FrameMaker finds a match, the element bubble is highlighted in the structure view, and the element is highlighted on the page.

You cannot search exclusively for attributes, but you can include an attribute name or value in an element search. For example, you might search for a Frame element tag with a Floating attribute name. You then have the option of replacing the element tag, attribute name, or attribute value with the specified item.

To search for an element, complete these steps:

1. You can search a book, a document, or selected text. Do one of the following:

   ■ To search a document, click anywhere in the document's text.

   ■ To search a specific section of text, select that text.

   ■ To search a book, open the book. You can start your search from the book window or inside a file that belongs to that book. To search only specific files in the book, select them by CTRL-clicking (Windows and UNIX) or COMMAND-clicking (Mac) the files you want.

2. Select Edit | Find/Change. The Find/Change dialog box is displayed (Figure 4-1 on page 72).

3. In the Find drop-down list, click Element. The Find Element dialog box is displayed.

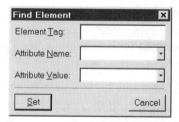

4. Type the name of the element you want to search for in the Element Tag field.

5. *(optional)* To search for the attribute name, click the name in the Attribute Name drop-down list. Only attributes defined for the selected element tag are displayed.

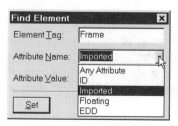

6. *(optional)* To search for an attribute value, click the value in the Attribute Value drop-down list.

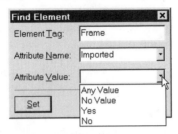

7. Click the Set button. The Find/Change dialog box is displayed again.

8. To replace the item, click one of the following items in the Change drop-down list.

   - **Element Tag To:** Lets you replace the element with a different element. Type the new element name in the Change field.

   - **Attribute Name To:** Lets you replace the attribute with a different attribute. Type the new attribute name in the Change field.

   - **Attribute Value To:** Lets you change the value of the attribute. Type the new attribute value in the Change field.

9. To indicate the scope of the search, click the Book, Document, or Selection radio button in the Look in section. (If the book file is displayed, and you have two chapters selected, choose Selection, not Book.)

10. Click the Find button or press ENTER to begin the search. FrameMaker highlights the first match in your document, book, or selection.

11. Do one of the following to replace the item:

    - To change only the first match, click the Change button.

    - To change the first match and find the next one, click the Change & Find button.

    - To change all matches, click the Change All button. A confirmation dialog box is displayed warning that you cannot undo the changes. Click the OK button to replace all matches.

Inserting Footnotes

To insert a footnote in a structured document, you pick an element from the element catalog or select Special | Footnote. Generally, you use the element catalog. If you use the Special menu, the result depends on whether a footnote element is defined for the document or not. If a footnote element is available, then selecting Special | Footnote inserts a footnote element; it's no different from selecting the footnote element in the element catalog. If no footnote element is available, then selecting Special | Footnote inserts an invalid footnote.

Figure 4-7 on page 106 shows the valid and invalid elements in the structure view. You'll find more information on footnote elements in "Footnotes" on page 688.

To insert a footnote in a structured document, follow these steps:

1. Insert your cursor where you want the footnote.

2. Do one of the following:

   ■ Select Element | Element Catalog to display the elements catalog, click the footnote element, and then click the Insert button.

Click the footnote element. ——▶

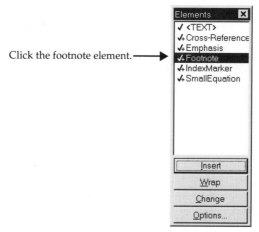

   ■ Select Special | Footnote.

The footnote is inserted, your cursor is displayed in the new footnote paragraph, and a footnote element bubble is displayed in the structure view. For invalid footnotes, FrameMaker creates an element called FOOTNOTE and assigns the default Footnote paragraph tag. If the Footnote paragraph tag wasn't defined in the document (that is, FrameMaker created it for this footnote), an asterisk is displayed in the status bar next to the tag name. You'll need to open the Paragraph Designer and add the tag to the catalog. See "Creating Paragraph Tags" on page 128 for details.

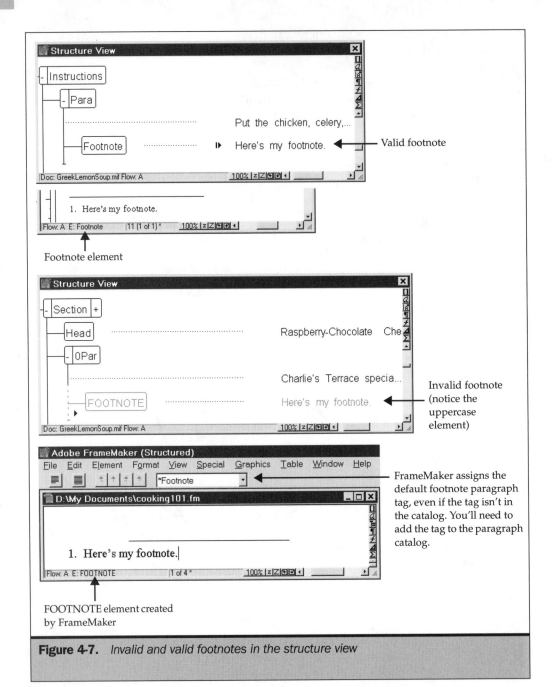

Figure 4-7. *Invalid and valid footnotes in the structure view*

Chapter 5

Formatting Text with Paragraph Tags

FrameMaker provides several different ways to format text. *Paragraph tags* (equivalent to style sheets in other applications) let you save a group of formatting choices and apply them in one step. In a single, named paragraph tag (for example, "Body" or "ChapterTitle"), you can store information including font name and size, tabs, indents, lines above or below, and hyphenation settings. When you apply the Body paragraph tag to a paragraph, all of the stored settings are applied, which is much more efficient than assigning each item individually.

Efficiency, however, is only half the story. Using paragraph tags ensures that formatting is consistent across an entire document. Every time you apply a body tag, FrameMaker assigns the same formatting. The result is that all of your body paragraphs use identical settings. In a two-page document, this is nice. In a 200-page document, it's critical. When you update the body tag's settings, FrameMaker immediately updates every body paragraph in the document.

When you assign a paragraph tag, it's applied to the paragraph where the cursor is located or to the paragraph with selected text. (You do not have to select the entire paragraph.) Unlike some other applications, FrameMaker *will not* apply a paragraph tag to a portion of a paragraph (a few words or characters); paragraph tags are always applied to the entire paragraph. If you need to assign special formatting to a few words or characters within the paragraph, use character tags. These are discussed in Chapter 6, "Formatting Text with Character Tags."

In structured FrameMaker, the elements you apply can have underlying paragraph tags, use a separate formatting approach called Format Change Lists, or specify all formatting as overrides. Refer to "Adding Formatting Information to the EDD" on page 732 for detailed information about implementing paragraph formatting in structured documents.

Applying Paragraph Tags

Paragraph tags are listed in the paragraph catalog. To display it, click the paragraph catalog button in the upper-right corner of your document.

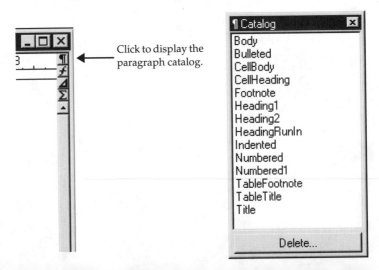

Click to display the paragraph catalog.

¶ Catalog

Body
Bulleted
CellBody
CellHeading
Footnote
Heading1
Heading2
HeadingRunIn
Indented
Numbered
Numbered1
TableFootnote
TableTitle
Title

Delete...

Using the Paragraph Catalog to Apply a Tag

To apply a paragraph tag using the paragraph catalog, follow these steps:

1. In the text, click in a paragraph or select a portion of the paragraph.

2. In the paragraph catalog, click a paragraph tag. The selected tag is applied to the current paragraph. The lower-left corner of the status bar shows the paragraph tag name.

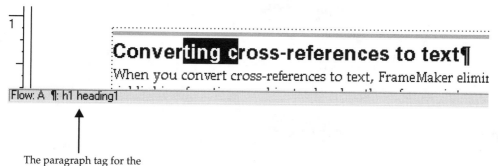

The paragraph tag for the selected paragraph is shown in the status bar.

FrameMaker provides other ways to apply paragraph tags, including:

- Using the Formatting Bar
- Selecting a menu choice
- Using the right-click pop-up menu
- Using keyboard shortcuts

Note   *You can also use the Paragraph Designer to apply paragraph tags, but because you could inadvertently change the paragraph tag definition, this approach is not recommended.*

Using the Formatting Bar

You can use the drop-down list on the Formatting Bar to apply paragraph tags. The list of tags is identical to the list in the paragraph catalog.

To apply paragraph tags using the Formatting Bar, follow these steps:

1. If the formatting toolbar is not visible, select View | Formatting Bar to display it.

2. In the text, click in a paragraph.

3. In the Formatting Bar, click a paragraph tag in the drop-down list.

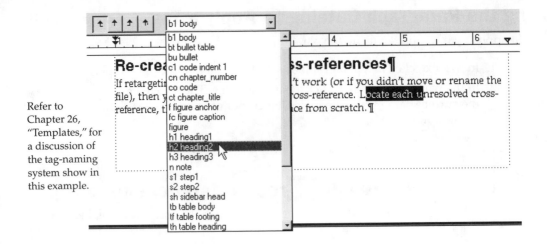

Refer to Chapter 26, "Templates," for a discussion of the tag-naming system show in this example.

Selecting a Menu Choice

To apply paragraph tags using a menu choice, follow these steps:

1. In the text, click in a paragraph.
2. Select Format | Paragraphs, then select a paragraph tag from the list that is displayed in the submenu.

Using the Right-Click Pop-Up Menu

The pop-up menu displayed when you right-click also gives you a way to access the paragraph catalog. Follow these steps:

1. In the text, click in a paragraph.
2. Right-click to display the pop-up menu, select Paragraphs, then select a tag from the list that's displayed.

Using Keyboard Shortcuts

You can use keyboard shortcuts to assign paragraph tags. To do so, follow these steps:

1. In the text, click in a paragraph.
2. Press F9 (Windows or UNIX) or CTRL-9 (all platforms). Notice that the left side of the status bar changes color.

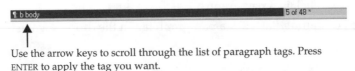

Use the arrow keys to scroll through the list of paragraph tags. Press ENTER to apply the tag you want.

3. Display the tag you want by doing any of the following:
   - Use the arrow keys to scroll through the list of available tags.
   - Type a letter to jump to that section of the paragraph catalog.
   - Type the first few letters of the tag name.
4. Press ENTER.

Avoiding Formatting Overrides and Empty Paragraphs

FrameMaker's paragraph tagging gives you complete control over the appearance of the text in your document. When you change paragraph tag settings, FrameMaker automatically applies those changes to every instance of that paragraph in the entire the document.

Formatting overrides occur when the tag settings are changed for a single paragraph. Overrides cause inconsistency in the document and make it much more difficult to maintain. When a paragraph has an override, the status bar usually indicates this with a star in front of the tag name.

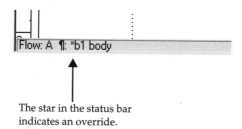

The star in the status bar
indicates an override.

The fastest way to remove overrides is to reapply your template and tell FrameMaker to remove all formatting overrides (see Chapter 26, "Templates").

A better approach is not to introduce overrides at all. As long as you apply paragraph tags from the paragraph catalog, you won't have any overrides. Problems occur when you go into the Paragraph Designer and make changes "just this once" to customize the paragraph for a special formatting requirement. Applying font, font size, or font style attributes from the Format menu is an override; avoid these if at all possible. Similarly, assigning tabs by dropping them on the ruler creates overrides; you can make tabs part of the tag definition by setting the tab in the ruler and then clicking the Update All button in the Paragraph Designer. The Bold, Italics, and Underline buttons on the Formatting Bar are also overrides; use character tagging instead.

Modifying Paragraph Tags

Applying paragraph tags is useful, but it probably won't be long before you need to modify the tags. You can make changes in the Paragraph Designer.

Caution   *In many companies, templates are set up and maintained by a standards group or template guru (some have less complimentary names for this person). If you have an official template, you're probably not supposed to make changes to it—unless, of course, you are the template guru.*

To make changes to an existing tag, follow these steps:

1. Display the Paragraph Designer by selecting Format | Paragraph | Designer or by pressing CTRL-M (Windows), COMMAND-M (Mac), or ESC O P D (all platforms) (Figure 5-1). You can also CTRL-click on a paragraph tag in the paragraph catalog to display the Paragraph Designer for that tag.

2. For each of the six property sheets, change the properties as needed, then click the Update All button. You can move from sheet to sheet using the tabs at the top of the window (Windows and UNIX) or the Properties drop-down list (all).

   The Update All button applies your change to all of the existing paragraphs that use the current tag. It also saves the changes into the paragraph catalog, so that any paragraphs you create in the future will use the same formatting.

Note   *Clicking the Apply button instead of the Update All button creates an override, which is not recommended.*

The following sections describe each setting in the Paragraph Designer.

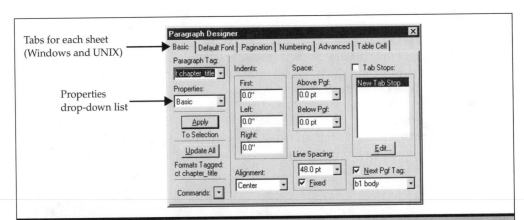

Figure 5-1.   *Paragraph Designer, Basic properties*

Paragraph Designer Settings

Tag settings are stored in the Paragraph Designer's six property sheets. To navigate from one sheet to the next, click the tab at the top of the dialog box (Windows or UNIX), or select from the Properties drop-down list. The sheets are as follows:

- Basic
- Default Font
- Pagination
- Numbering
- Advanced
- Table Cell

Options Available on Every Sheet

The items on the left side of the Paragraph Designer are displayed on every sheet. Table 5-1 lists these properties.

Item	Description
Paragraph Tag drop-down list	Lists the paragraph tags defined in the catalog.
Properties drop-down list	Lists the paragraph properties (or sheets). On Windows and UNIX, you can also access the properties using the tabs across the top of the Paragraph Designer dialog box.
Apply button	Applies the changes you've made to the current selection. Use the Apply button only when you want to create an override.
Update All button	Applies the changes you've made to all paragraphs that use the current tag and updates the paragraph catalog. Use the Update All button whenever you want to make a global change.
Commands pop-up menu	Provides advanced commands, such as global updates (see page 131).

Table 5-1.   *Paragraph Designer Common Properties*

Basic Sheet

The options on the Basic sheet (Figure 5-1 on page 112) let you control the paragraph's positioning, such as indents and space above and below the paragraph. You'll find additional positioning choices on the Pagination sheet. Table 5-2 describes the items on the Basic sheet.

Item	Description
Indents	All indents are measured from the edge of the text frame, not from the edge of the paper. (The text frame is represented by a dotted line surrounding the "live" area where you can insert text.) ■ **First:** Sets a left indent for the first line of the paragraph. ■ **Left:** Sets a left indent for the second and subsequent lines of the paragraph. This indent does not affect the first line. ■ **Right:** Sets the right indent for each line of the paragraph.
Alignment	Sets the alignment—left, center, right, or justified—for the paragraph.
Space Above Pgf	Sets the amount of white space between the current paragraph and the preceding paragraph. To determine spacing between paragraphs, FrameMaker uses the larger of the space above the current paragraph or the space below the previous paragraph. They are *not* added together. The Space Above setting is ignored for a paragraph at the top of a page. If you need to move a paragraph down from the top of the page, either move the text frame down or use a graphic frame to provide spacing (see "Table Cell Sheet" on page 128 for details).
Space Below Pgf	Sets the space below the paragraph.
Line Spacing	Sets the *leading*—the vertical space between lines inside the paragraph. When you change the font size (on the Default Font properties), the leading automatically changes (to about 15 percent more than the font size value) so set the font size before setting the line spacing.

Table 5-2.   *Basic Sheet*

Item	Description
Fixed	When checked, this option sets line spacing from baseline to baseline. (The *baseline* is the bottom of a line of text, not including characters that drop below this invisible line. The letters g, p, q, and y are all *descenders;* they extend below the baseline.) If not checked, line spacing is adjusted to accommodate superscripts and subscripts. Compare the following two paragraphs: ■ This bullet uses fixed line spacing. Superscripts don't have much[1] of an effect. ■ In this bullet, line spacing is not fixed. The superscript does make a[1] difference here.
Tab Stops	Lets you set tab stops for the paragraph. In FrameMaker, paragraphs do not have tab stops by default. Until you add tab stops, pressing the TAB key in a paragraph has no effect. See the following section, "Setting Tab Stops," for details on how to control the tab settings.
Next Pgf Tag	Sets the default tag for the next paragraph tag. When you press ENTER to start a new paragraph, this choice determines what paragraph tag is set by default. For example, a Heading tag could default to Body as the next tag. You can change the Body tag to something else later. If you do not specify a setting for the next paragraph tag, FrameMaker uses the same tag as the current paragraph.

Table 5-2.   *Basic Sheet (Continued)*

> **Note** *You can change the display units (points, picas, and the like) in the View Options dialog box (View | Options). See "Changing View Options" on page 48 for details.*

Setting Tab Stops   FrameMaker's tab stops are measured from the edge of the text frame, not the edge of the page. By default, paragraphs do not have any tab stops defined; until you create them, pressing the TAB key doesn't have any effect. (There are anecdotes about people replacing their keyboards to correct this problem because they didn't realize they needed to make a change in FrameMaker.)

To set up tab stops, follow these steps:

1. In the Paragraph Designer's Basic sheet, make sure that New Tab Stop is selected in the Tab Stops section. (If a specific tab location is selected, the following steps will change its position.)

2. Click the Edit button in the Tab Stops section to display the Edit Tab Stop dialog box.

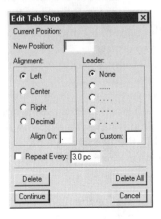

3. In the New Position field, type the position you want to use for the new tab stop.

4. In the Alignment section, specify one of the following:

   - **Left:** Text after the tab is left-aligned starting at the tab's position.
   - **Center:** Text after the tab is centered at the tab's position.
   - **Right:** Text after the tab is right-justified from the tab's position.
   - **Decimal:** Text after the tab is aligned so that the decimal point (a period by default in the English version) is aligned on the tab. To align based on a different character, type that character in the Align On field.

5. In the Leader section, specify whether you want any character preceding the tab. Most often, you use "dot leaders" in tables of contents. To create a different leader, type the character or symbol in the Custom field.

6. If you want to create several tabs at once, specify at what increments you want to repeat the tab in the Repeat Every field.

7. Click the Continue button to set up the new tabs and return to the Paragraph Designer. If you made a mistake, double-click the tab, then click the Delete button in the Edit Tab Stop dialog box. (Or, click the Delete All button to delete every tab that's defined for this paragraph and start over.)

8. Click the Update All button to save your changes in the paragraph definition.

Note   *If you prefer to use the ruler to create tabs, set up the tab in the ruler at the top of the window (click and drag to position a tab on the ruler), then display the Paragraph Designer and click the Update All button to save the tab in the paragraph definition.*

Setting Up Indentation   Getting your indents positioned correctly can be confusing because FrameMaker calculates indentation differently from most other applications. All indents are calculated from the edge of the text frame (not the edge of the page). The Left indent setting is applied only to the second and subsequent lines of a paragraph, never to the first paragraph—it uses the First indent setting. The following illustration shows a few examples of the interaction between the First and Left indent settings.

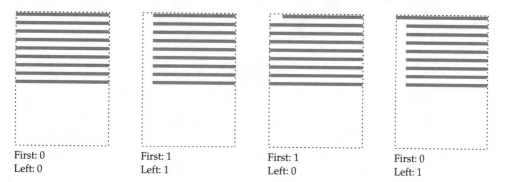

First: 0   First: 1   First: 1   First: 0
Left: 0   Left: 1   Left: 0   Left: 1

The Right indent always applies to all lines in the paragraph and is measured from the right side of the text frame.

Default Font Sheet

The Default Font sheet lets you specify font, font size, and other typographical controls. Table 5-3 lists the Default Font sheet items.

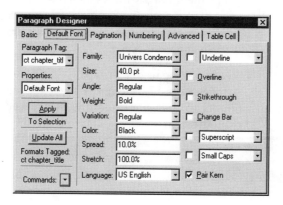

Item	Description
Family	Sets the overall typeface, such as Garamond, Palatino, Helvetica, or Times.
Size	Sets the size of the type. The smallest allowed value is 2 points.
Angle	Sets the angle, such as Italic or Oblique.
Weight	Sets the weight, such as Bold, Black, Medium, or Light.
Variation	Some fonts have variations available. These might be choices such as Small Caps or Expert Numbers.
Color	Sets the color of the text. The choices come from the color catalog. See Chapter 20, "Color Output," for information about how to add colors to the color catalog.
Spread	Adjusts the space between letters. The default is 0%. Increasing this value increases the space between letters; a negative value reduces the space between letters. Spread is similar to tracking in other applications.
Stretch	Adjusts the shape of the letters to the specified percentage. The default is 100% (normal shape). A stretch of 200% results in letters that are twice their normal width. *A condensed or expanded font is usually a better choice than using the Stretch attribute.*
Language	Sets the language of the current paragraph. This determines which dictionary is used when the paragraph is hyphenated or spell-checked. To prevent spell-checking, set the Language to None. This is useful for paragraphs that contain code samples.
Underline Double Underline Numeric Underline	Applies a line under the text. Applies a double line under the text. Similar to a regular underline, but spaced a little farther from the text.

Table 5-3.   *Default Font Sheet*

Item	Description
Overline	Applies a line over the text.
Strikethrough	Applies a strikethrough line (a line through the middle of the text).
Change Bar	Applies a vertical line in the margin of the document. You can create automatic change bars; for details, see "Using Change Bars" on page 90.
Superscript Subscript	Sets text above the baseline. Sets text below the baseline.
Small Caps Lowercase Uppercase	All of the capitalization choices change the appearance of the text but preserve the capitalization of the underlying text. For example, you can display the text as ALL CAPS, but a cross-reference would pick up the underlying Regular Capitalization (whatever the user typed). ■ **Small Caps:** Sets the text in capital letters that fit in the normal *x-height* of the typeface. (The x-height is the size of the lowercase letter x in a particular font.) ■ **Lowercase:** Sets the text in lowercase letters. ■ **Uppercase:** Sets the text in uppercase letters.
Pair Kern	Adjusts the spacing between each pair of letters to improve readability. In general, Pair Kern should be turned on for most paragraphs with the exception of paragraphs that use monospaced fonts (such as code examples).

Table 5-3.   *Default Font Sheet (Continued)*

CREATING AND
MANIPULATING TEXT

Pagination Sheet

The Pagination sheet sets the paragraph's position on the page. For example, you can set a particular paragraph to start at the top of a page. Table 5-4 lists the Pagination sheet items.

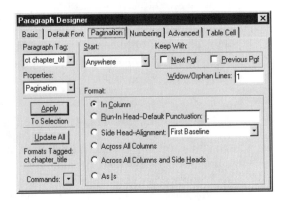

Item	Description
Start	Lets you set where on the page the paragraph begins. ■ **Anywhere:** Starts in the next available space, subject to the space above and below settings on the Basic sheet and any restrictions from *widow/orphan lines* or *keep with* settings (described in the text that follows). ■ **Top of Column:** Starts at the top of the next column. (In a single-column document, this is the same as Top of Page.) ■ **Top of Page:** Starts at the top of the next page. ■ **Top of Left Page:** Starts at the top of the next left page. ■ **Top of Right Page:** Starts at the top of the next right page. (This setting is very common for chapter titles, which are often required to be on a right page.)

Table 5-4.   *Pagination Sheet*

Item	Description
Keep With	Controls how the paragraph interacts with the preceding and following paragraphs. ■ **Next Pgf:** If checked, the current paragraph is attached to the next paragraph. Use this for headings that you want to keep on the same page as their introductory paragraphs. The Keep With setting forces at least the number of lines specified in the Widow/Orphan Lines setting to be placed on the same page as the next paragraph. ■ **Previous Pgf:** If checked, the current paragraph is attached to the previous paragraph.
Widow/Orphan Lines	Sets the number of lines that can appear at the top or bottom of a page. For example, if you type **2**, the paragraph must always have at least two lines at the bottom of the page or at the top of the page.
Format	See Figure 5-2 for examples of each Format option. ■ **In Column:** Positions the paragraph in the main text column. ■ **Run-In Head:** Positions the paragraph so that the next paragraph starts on the same line. This is very useful for glossary entries and to save space for lower-level headings. In the Default Punctuation field, you can specify any default punctuation you want after the heading, such as a period. In this book, the fourth-level headings (such as "Setting Tab Stops" on page 115) use a run-in heading. The punctuation is set as an em space. ■ **Side Head:** Positions the paragraph so that it is on the same line as the following paragraph, in a separate column. You must define a side head area (discussed in Chapter 11, "Understanding Master Pages"). ■ **Across All Columns:** Positions the paragraph to span all text columns (but not the side head area). ■ **Across All Columns and Side Heads:** Positions the paragraph to span all available columns and the side head area. ■ **As Is:** The paragraph inherits the setting that was previously applied. This setting is useful only when you are performing global updates ("Setting Properties Across the Entire Paragraph Catalog" on page 130).

Table 5-4. *Pagination Sheet (Continued)*

CREATING AND
MANIPULATING TEXT

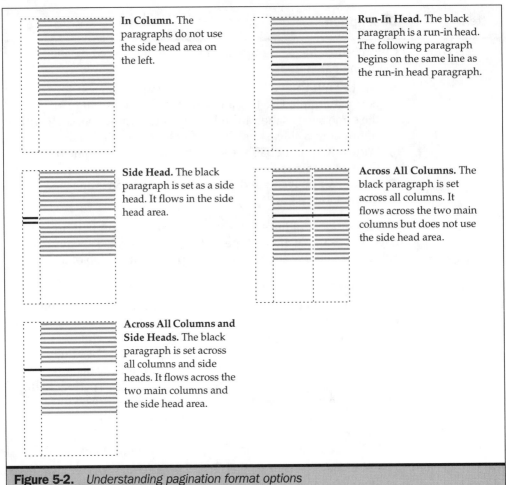

In Column. The paragraphs do not use the side head area on the left.

Run-In Head. The black paragraph is a run-in head. The following paragraph begins on the same line as the run-in head paragraph.

Side Head. The black paragraph is set as a side head. It flows in the side head area.

Across All Columns. The black paragraph is set across all columns. It flows across the two main columns but does not use the side head area.

Across All Columns and Side Heads. The black paragraph is set across all columns and side heads. It flows across the two main columns and the side head area.

Figure 5-2. *Understanding pagination format options*

Numbering Sheet

The Numbering sheet lets you set up automatic numbering for your paragraph. This includes step numbers, chapter numbers, bullets, and repeated words, such as "Note:", at the beginning of a paragraph.

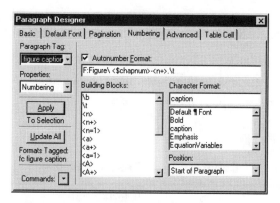

Table 5-5 describes the Numbering sheet items. Table 5-6 lists the building blocks you can use in the Autonumber Format field.

Item	Description
Autonumber Format	Sets the definition of the numbering for the paragraph. See page 134 for a full discussion.
Building Blocks	Provides a list of building blocks that you can select to insert in the Autonumber Format field. See Table 5-6 for a description of each building block. You can also type the building blocks instead of selecting them from the list.
Character Format	Provides a list of character tags. The selected character tag is applied only to the autonumber for the paragraph. If the style you want isn't available, you must create a character tag to add it to the list. See Chapter 6, "Formatting Text with Character Tags," for details.
Position	Determines whether the autonumber occurs at the beginning or the end of the paragraph. Steps, bullets, and the like are normally at the beginning of the paragraph. You might use the end of paragraph position for a graphic "bug" that marks the end of a section. The autonumber is always right-aligned when positioned at the end of a paragraph.

Table 5-5. *Numbering Sheet*

Using counters, you can create several different types of numbering—numeric, alphabetic, and Roman. The counters come in groups of three:

■ Display current value (for example, <n> or <a>)

■ Increment counter and display new value (for example, <r+> or <A+>)

■ Set counter (for example, <n=1> or <a=6>)

Name/Function	Counter	Description
Bullet	• or \b	Inserts a bullet.
Tab	\t	Inserts a tab. (You cannot use the TAB key inside a dialog box.) In the Basic sheet of the Paragraph Designer, specify tab position, type and leader, and the hanging indent.
Hard space	\	Type backslash-space to insert a nonbreaking space.
Displays the current value	<n> <a> <A> <r> <R>	Numeric value (1, 2, 3) Lowercase alphabetic value (a, b, c) Uppercase alphabetic value (A, B, C) Lowercase Roman value (i, ii, iii) Uppercase Roman value (I, II, III)
Increments by 1 and displays the new value	<n+> <a+> <A+> <r+> <R+>	Numeric value (1, 2, 3) Lowercase alphabetic value (a, b, c) Uppercase alphabetic value (A, B, C) Lowercase Roman value (i, ii, iii) Uppercase Roman value (I, II, III)

Table 5-6.   *Building Blocks for Autonumbering*

Name/Function	Counter	Description
Sets to the specified value and displays that value	`<n=1>` `<a=1>` `<A=1>` `<r=1>` `<R=1>`	Numeric value (1, 2, 3) Lowercase alphabetic value (a, b, c) Uppercase alphabetic value (A, B, C) Lowercase Roman value (i, ii, iii) Uppercase Roman value (I, II, III)
Volume number	`<$volnum>`	Displays the current value of the volume number.
Chapter number	`<$chapnum>`	Displays the current value of the chapter number.
Placeholder counters	`< >`	Suppresses display of a counter but does not change its value. This building block has a space between the angle brackets. This counter was in common use in numbering series developed in version 5.5 or earlier.
Reset	`< =0>`	Suppresses display of a counter and resets counter to zero. This counter isn't listed as a building block; you have to type it in the Autonumber Format field. (A space precedes the equals sign.)

Table 5-6.   *Building Blocks for Autonumbering (Continued)*

See "Autonumbering Details" on page 134 for several examples of autonumbering.

CREATING AND
MANIPULATING TEXT

Advanced Sheet

The Advanced sheet lets you set hyphenation controls, justification, and lines above or below the paragraph.

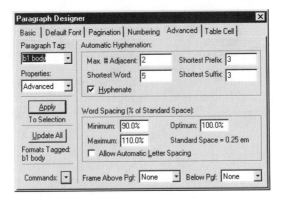

Table 5-7 lists the Advanced sheet items.

Item	Description
Max. # Adjacent	Sets the number of hyphens that can occur in consecutive lines in the paragraph. For example, 2 means that if you have two lines with hyphens at the end, the next line cannot be hyphenated.
Shortest Prefix	Sets the minimum number of letters for a hyphenated beginning fragment. For example, 3 means that the prefix must have at least three letters—"pre-fix" could be hyphenated but "re-create" could not.
Shortest Word	Sets the minimum length of a hyphenated word. For example, 8 means that FrameMaker cannot hyphenate "pre-view."
Shortest Suffix	Sets the minimum number of letters for a hyphenated end fragment. For example, 5 means that FrameMaker cannot hyphenate "pre-tend."

Table 5-7.   *Advanced Sheet*

Item	Description
Hyphenate	If checked, the paragraph is hyphenated. That is, if a word doesn't quite fit at the end of a line, FrameMaker may break it with a hyphen (for example, "acro-batic"). The locations where hyphens are allowed are called hyphenation points. Each language dictionary stores hyphenation points for its words, so if you check hyphenation, the processing is based on the language that's selected on the Default Font sheet for this paragraph. If no language is selected, the paragraph is not hyphenated.
Word Spacing	Word Spacing controls the changes FrameMaker can make when justifying text in a paragraph. ■ **Minimum:** Sets the minimum amount of word spacing that's allowed when justifying text and avoiding hyphenation. For example, 90% means that each space between words must be no smaller than 90 percent of a normal space. ■ **Optimum:** Sets the target amount of word spacing. The default is normally 100%. ■ **Maximum:** Sets the maximum amount of word spacing allowed.
Allow Automatic Letter Spacing	If checked, FrameMaker adds space between characters (not just words) when justifying text.
Frame Above Pgf	Lets you specify a graphic frame that's inserted above this paragraph. The graphic frames are stored on the reference pages. See "Placing Graphics Above and Below the Paragraph" on page 322 for details.
Below Pgf	Lets you specify a graphic frame that's inserted below this paragraph.

Table 5-7.   *Advanced Sheet (Continued)*

CREATING AND
MANIPULATING TEXT

Table Cell Sheet

The Table Cell sheet sets properties for paragraphs inside tables (Table 5-8). The cell margin properties interact with the default cell margins set in the Table Designer. You can either add to (or subtract from) the default margins in the Table Designer, or you can override the Table Designer's margins entirely with the settings in these paragraphs.

These properties do not have any effect unless the paragraph is in a table. Furthermore, the Top setting is ignored except for the first paragraph in a cell. The Bottom setting is ignored except for the last paragraph in a cell. The Left and Right settings are used for every paragraph.

Item	Description
Cell Vertical Alignment	Sets the vertical position of the paragraph in the table cell.
Cell Margins (Top, Bottom, Left, Right)	Sets the cell margins when this paragraph is the first paragraph in the cell. You can add to the default margins (From Table Format, Plus) or you can completely ignore the default margins (Custom).

Table 5-8. *Table Cell Sheet*

Creating Paragraph Tags

The easiest way to create a new paragraph tag is to start with a tag that's close to what you need. If, for example, you want to create an indented paragraph, you could start with the Body tag—Body and Indent are probably identical except for the first and left indent settings.

To create a new paragraph tag, follow these steps:

1. Click in a paragraph that is similar to what you need. (For example, the Body paragraph in my example.)

2. Display the Paragraph Designer.

3. Click the Commands button, then select New Format from the pop-up menu. The New Format dialog box is displayed.

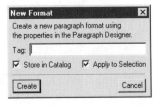

4. In the Tag field, type a name for the new paragraph tag (such as Indented). Verify that the Store in Catalog and Apply to Selection check boxes are checked.

5. Click the Create button. FrameMaker creates a new paragraph tag. At this point, the tag's definition is identical to the tag you started with.

6. In each sheet of the Paragraph Designer, make the needed changes. Click the Update All button before moving from one sheet to the next. If you forget, a dialog box is displayed.

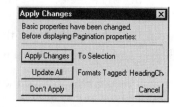

If the dialog box is displayed, do one of the following:

- Click the Update All button to update the paragraph definition and all of the tags that use it.

- Click the Don't Apply button to throw away your changes and go to the next sheet.

- Click the Apply Changes button to apply your changes to the current selection only. *This creates a formatting override.*

- Click the Cancel button to discard your changes and go back to the current sheet.

7. When you are finished, close the Paragraph Designer. The new paragraph tag is now available in the paragraph catalog.

If you want to rename the current paragraph, you can use a slightly faster approach. In the Paragraph Designer, type the new tag name in the Tag Name field. Click the Apply button to display the New Format dialog box, then click the Create button. (If you click the Update All button, you rename the existing tag.)

Renaming Paragraph Tags

You can rename any paragraph tag. When you rename a paragraph tag, FrameMaker does the following:

- The original tag name (A) is changed to the new tag name (B).

- Tag A is removed from the Paragraph Catalog. Tag B appears in the paragraph catalog.

- All paragraphs that use tag A now use tag B.

You can also make a copy of an existing paragraph tag. In this case, the old tag is retained in the paragraph catalog. For details, see "Creating Paragraph Tags" on page 128.

To rename a paragraph tag, follow these steps:

1. Display the Paragraph Designer.
2. In the Paragraph Tag drop-down list, select the paragraph tag you want to rename.
3. In the Paragraph Tag field, type the new name of the paragraph tag.
4. Click the Update All button and confirm that you want to rename the tag.

All the paragraph tags are renamed for you. Notice that the old tag name is no longer available in the paragraph catalog.

 The Global Update Options dialog box lets you accomplish the same thing, but it takes more steps.

Setting Properties Across the Entire Paragraph Catalog

Changing properties for a single paragraph tag is fairly quick, but if you need to make the same change for all of your paragraph tags, then changing them one by one is tedious.

FrameMaker gives you a way of making global changes within your paragraph tags. For example, assume that your original files use GimzelFlopper as the official font, so all of your paragraph tags use GimzelFlopper. But now, the new corporate guidelines dictate that GimzelFlopper is no longer allowed. Instead, you need to switch to the new, official font MegaCorpo.

You could make this change by displaying each paragraph tag in turn, changing the font, and selecting the Update All button. But you can also do this with a global change, even though your paragraph tags use all sorts of different settings.

 This is not for the faint of heart. You might want to back up your file before trying this.

To change a paragraph property for all the tags in your document, follow these steps:

1. Display the Paragraph Designer. It doesn't matter which paragraph tag is selected.
2. Display the Default Font properties.

3. Click the Commands button, then select Set Window to As Is from the pop-up menu. This sets all of the properties in the Default Font sheet to "use what's there." This is useful when you're trying to preserve conflicting settings in different paragraphs.

4. In the Family field, select MegaCorpo as your new font.

5. Click the Commands button, then select Global Update Options from the pop-up menus. The Global Update Options dialog box is displayed (Figure 5-3).

6. In the Use Properties in the Paragraph Designer section, click the Default Font Properties Only radio button (this option changes depending on which sheet you started on).

7. In the Update Paragraph Formats section, click the All Paragraphs and Catalog Entries radio button.

8. Click the Update button. Every paragraph tag in your document now uses the new font.

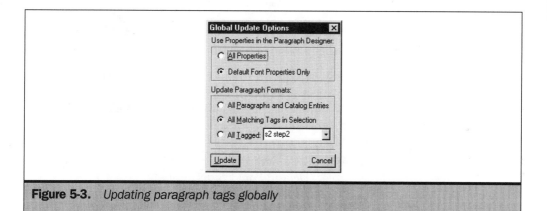

Figure 5-3.   *Updating paragraph tags globally*

Updating Selected Paragraphs Globally

Instead of modifying all of the tags in the paragraph catalog, you can change specific paragraphs. To update several tags at once, use the All Matching Tags in Selection radio button in the Global Update Options dialog box (see Figure 5-3). Before you begin, set up several paragraphs in a row, and apply a paragraph tag you want to change to each paragraph. (The paragraphs can be empty.) Then, follow these steps to modify the tags globally:

1. Select the paragraphs you created. Every paragraph tag in this text will be changed, so you select only tags you want to change.

2. Display the Paragraph Designer. Notice that where the various paragraph tag settings conflict, the As Is setting is used.

Because the fonts are different for the selected paragraphs, the font family is set to As Is. Color and size are also As Is.

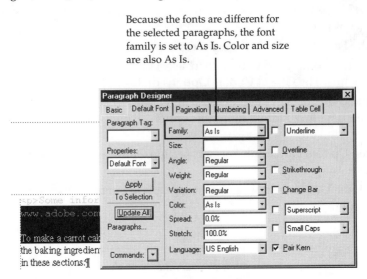

3. For each sheet of the Paragraph Designer, follow these steps to make changes:

   a. Modify the sheet as needed. If you want the paragraphs to retain different settings for an item, leave the As Is setting intact.

   b. Click the Commands button, then select Global Update Options from the pop-up list. This displays the Global Update Options dialog box, shown in Figure 5-3 on page 131.

   c. In the Use Properties in the Paragraph Designer section, select the current sheet only (for example, "Default Font Properties only").

   d. In the Update Paragraph Formats section, click the All Matching Tags in Selection radio button.

   e. Click the Update button.

Deleting Paragraph Tags

You can remove paragraph tags from the catalog. Those tags are no longer available for you to apply to new paragraphs. But any paragraph that uses the tag you delete still has that tag applied to it—but now it's considered an override. Once you delete the tag, apply a different tag to the left-over paragraphs. Alternatively, you can reassign a new tag to the paragraphs that use the tag you plan to delete. It's usually more efficient to apply the new tag before you delete a paragraph tag.

To delete paragraph tags, follow these steps:

1. Display the Paragraph Catalog.

2. Click the Delete button at the bottom of the paragraph catalog. The Delete Formats from Catalog dialog box is displayed.

3. For each tag you want to delete, select the style, then click the Delete button. To delete all of the tags, press and hold ALT-E (Windows only) until all of the tags are gone.

 If you make a mistake, you must click the Cancel button and start over. There is no Apply button.

4. When you are finished, click the Done button.

Creating New Formats

Every once in a while (and we hope this is a rare occurrence), you will inherit bad FrameMaker files. The files will be riddled with overrides; in fact, the paragraph and character override may be the rule and not the exception. In this case, you may want to identify all the overrides. FrameMaker provides a way to do this—select File | Utilities | Create & Apply Formats.

The Create & Apply Formats feature does the following for paragraph and character tags:

- If a tag is used by a paragraph or character but doesn't appear in the appropriate catalog, Create & Apply Formats adds it to the catalog.
- If a paragraph or character uses a tag that's in the catalog, but the tag is used with an override, Create & Apply Formats creates a new tag for that item and adds it to the catalog. The tag name is based on the original name, so if the tag was Code, then any new tags would be Code1, Code2, and so on.

Once you create the new tags, you can rename them or apply the correct tag globally to remove the overrides.

When you delete paragraph tags from the paragraph catalog, the tags are not stripped from the paragraphs. As a result, you can have paragraphs that use tags that are no longer available in the paragraph catalog. However, these tags are now considered overrides (because they use a paragraph tag that's not available in the paragraph catalog). After removing the paragraph tag, you'll probably want to assign new names to those paragraphs (see sidebar).

A number of third-party tools are available to help you find those overrides. In particular, you might want to look into the aptly named HuntOverrides. See Appendix A, "Resources," for more details about these and other add-on tools.

Autonumbering Details

FrameMaker's autonumbering lets you set up automated numbering, such as step numbers and chapter numbers. But you can also use autonumbering for repeated *text*, such as "Note:", "Caution:", and bullets, at the beginning or end of the paragraph. It's much more efficient to define a paragraph tag that automatically inserts these items because you don't have to type in the text over and over again or keep track of the last number used.

To strip off an autonumbering, you must apply a different (non-autonumbered) paragraph tag. You cannot select an autonumber or backspace to delete it.

This section describes how to set up autonumbers with varying degrees of complexity. In some cases, the autonumbering in different paragraph tags interacts, so you have to set up several paragraph tags to get the effect you want.

Some of the examples build on concepts introduced in the early examples, so we recommend that you read this entire section through the first time.

Basic Autonumbering

As mentioned in "Numbering Sheet" on page 122, you use automated numbering for bullets and text-based formats, such as notes, cautions, and warnings. To set up these autonumbers, you insert the text you need in the Autonumbering Format field. When you apply the paragraph tag, the text is inserted automatically.

Bullets

FrameMaker includes a building block, \b, for inserting bullets. You can also use other characters, such as hyphens, em dashes, or wingdings, to create bullets.

To create a basic bullet, insert the following code in the Autonumbering Format field:

```
\b\t
```

Next, set up the Basic properties to allow for the tab and a left indent. The definition and the result are shown in the following illustration.

Inside dialog boxes, Windows and UNIX will not allow you to use the "normal" commands for special characters. An em dash, for example, is created by pressing CTRL-Q SHIFT-Q in text, but this command doesn't work inside the dialog box. Instead, you must use a special set of commands that's available for use inside dialog boxes. For example, the command for the em dash is **\md**. These are listed in the online manual entitled Character Sets, found in the OnlineManuals directory in your FrameMaker installation directory. On the Mac, you can use most of the built-in Mac commands (such as SHIFT-OPTION-hyphen for an em dash) inside the dialog boxes.

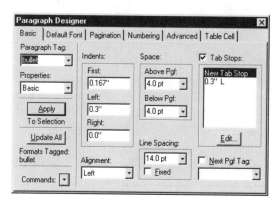

Typical information in a spec includes:

The bullets are indented according to the settings on the Basic sheet. ——————
- Lists of menus and menu choices (software)
- Mock-ups of the interface (software)
- Illustrations of components (hardware)

Another way to set up bullets involves taking advantage of the character formatting that's available. You can, for example, create a character format that applies Zapf Dingbats or Wingdings font, and then use one of the dingbats or wingdings to make a special bullet (such as diamonds or pointing hands).

Notes, Cautions, and Warnings

You can set up notes and similar formats with autonumbering. For example, consider the following note format:

Note: This is a note. It uses autonumbering so that you don't have to type in the word "Note:" and apply bold formatting every time you need a note.

It uses the following autonumbering format:

```
Note:\t
```

To add the bold formatting, apply a Bold character format.

After setting the autonumbering, you'll need to set the appropriate indents for your note.

Numbered Steps (1, 2, 3 and a, b, c)

When you create step formats, you must tell FrameMaker when to increment (or count) steps, and when to reset them to restart at 1. There are two ways of doing this:

- You can create two step formats: StepFirst and StepNext. StepFirst resets your steps to start at 1 and is always used for the first step in a series. StepNext is used for all subsequent steps.
- You can create a single step format, Step. In this approach, you must use another format, such as Body or Heading, to reset your step series.

Working with the Two-Step Format

The advantage of using StepFirst and StepNext is that you explicitly control how the steps are reset. The disadvantage is that you have to remember to reset the step list. And if you rearrange the steps, you may have to change the paragraph tag assignments to ensure that StepFirst is applied to only the first paragraph in the list of steps.

Paragraph Tag	Definition
StepFirst	S:<n=1>
StepNext	S:<n+>

The S: is called a series label. It tells FrameMaker that the counters in the two paragraph tags are interdependent. You can use any letter for a series label, but each series must have a unique series label. (For example, S for steps and F for figures.) Because of the series label, the <n=1> and <n+> counters affect each other. The result looks like this:

Paragraph Tag	Autonumber	Result
StepFirst	S:<n=1>	1
StepNext	S:<n+>	2
StepNext	S:<n+>	3
StepNext	S:<n+>	4
StepNext	S:<n+>	5
StepNext	S:<n+>	6
StepFirst	S:<n=1>	1
StepNext	S:<n+>	2

If you need second-level steps (a, b, c) in addition to the first-level numbered steps, you can set up two more tags, StepLetterA and StepLetterNext. Make sure that the new tags use a different series label.

Paragraph Tag	Definition
StepFirst	S:<n=1>
StepNext	S:<n+>
StepLetterA	T:<a=1>
StepLetterNext	T:<a+>

To set up similar numbering with Roman numerals, use the <r> and <R> building blocks for lowercase and uppercase Roman numerals.

Working with a Single Step Format

If you want to minimize the number of paragraph tags in your document, you can use a single step format. In this case, you need to use another paragraph tag to reset your steps. The disadvantage to this approach is that you must always have the separator paragraph (Body in the example) between your step lists. If this doesn't happen, the numbering won't work properly. Set up the paragraphs as shown here:

Paragraph Tag	Definition
Step	S:<n+>
Body	S:

Here, the Step tag is set to <n+>, increasing each time you use it. But the Body tag uses an empty autonumber definition with just a series label. This lets you take advantage of a little-known autonumbering feature: *When a counter is not listed in the definition, it is reset to zero.* If you prefer you can write out the "reset to zero" for Body:

```
S:< =0>
```

The single-step approach relies on the fact that you do not plan to have two step lists without an intervening Body paragraph tag. You could use a similar approach for your substeps, but you would probably assign the reset function to the first-level steps.

Paragraph Tag	Definition
Step	`S:<n+>`
Body	`S:`
StepA	`S:< ><a+>`

To ensure that the Step tag resets the StepA tag, you must use the same series label for those tags. But at the same time, the StepA tag should not interact with the Step's numbering, so you have to insert a blank counter < > (with a space between the brackets) at the first position. This tells FrameMaker not to display a counter at that position, but also to preserve the value of that counter.

Incorporating Chapter and Volume Numbers

In FrameMaker version 6, Adobe introduced two new building blocks: <$chapnum> and <$volnum>. These are a departure from paragraph-based autonumbering. In effect, <$chapnum> and <$volnum> are *global* building blocks—they are available in autonumbers, cross-references, variables, and several other places. Within an autonumber, <$chapnum> returns the current value of the chapter number and <$volnum> returns the value of the volume or part number. These are normally set in your book file (see "Managing Numbering" on page 373 for details).

Unlike most other building blocks, you cannot change the value of <$chapnum> or <$volnum> (for example, <$chapnum+> doesn't work). Furthermore, you can use them in several different autonumbering definitions that are *not* tied together with a series label.

If you need to reference the chapter number (for example, in your chapter title paragraph tag), you can use the following autonumber definition:

```
<$chapnum>
```

This will retrieve the value of <$chapnum>. The formatting (such as numeric or Roman) is determined at the book level in the Numbering dialog box (Format | Document | Numbering) in the Chapter sheet. You can change this inside the file, but the book overrides the value set in the file. The rules for <$volnum> are the same; it uses the Volume sheet on the Numbering dialog box.

The example that follows shows how you can take advantage of <$chapnum> to set up independent figure, table, and example numbering that uses the chapter number.

This is a major change from earlier versions of FrameMaker (5.5.6 and earlier), which required all of these items to be in a single numbering series and led to very complicated numbering schemes.

Paragraph Tag	Definition	Result
ChapterTitle	`<$chapnum>`	1, 2, 3
FigureTitle	`F:Figure\ <$chapnum>\+<n+>`	Figure 1-1, Figure 1-2, Figure 1-3
TableTitle	`U:Table\ <$chapnum>\+<n+>`	Table 1-1, Table 1-2, Table 1-3
ExampleTitle	`E:Example\ <$chapnum>\+<n+>`	Example 1-1, Example 1-2, Example 1-3

The backslash-space sequence produces a nonbreaking space; backslash-plus produces a nonbreaking hyphen. Using these special characters prevents unattractive line breaks. The nonbreaking spaces and hyphens are also picked up by any cross-references to these items.

Creating Numbered Headings

Some documents require that you number your headings and perhaps even the body paragraphs. FrameMaker autonumbering can handle this situation for you. You use the higher-level headings to restart the lower-level headings. The following example shows a typical setup.

Paragraph Tag	Definition	Result
ChapterTitle	`H:<$chapnum>`	1, 2, 3
Heading1	`H:<$chapnum>.<n+>`	1.1, 1.2, 1.3, 1.4
Heading2	`H:<$chapnum>.<n>.<n+>`	1.1.1, 1.1.2, 1.1.3, 1.1.4
Body	`H:<$chapnum>.<n>.<a+>`	1.1.1.a, 1.1.1.b, 1.1.1.c, 1.1.1.d, 1.1.1.e

In this example, the ChapterTitle tag carries a series label because it resets the second counter in the Heading1 format to zero.

You might also want to set up numbered headings for an outline.

Paragraph Tag	Definition	Result
Heading1	H:<R+>	I, II, III, IV
Heading2	H:<R>.<A+>	I.A, I.B, I.C, I.D
Heading3	H:<R>.<A>.<r+>	I.A.i, I.A.ii, I.A.iii, I.A.iv
Heading4	H:<R>.<A>.<r>.<n+>	I.A.i.1, I.A.i.2, I.A.i.3, I.A.i.4

Marking the End of a Story

In many magazines, the end of a story is indicated by a small graphic "bug," which gives the reader a visual indication that the article is done. This is very helpful when the story jumps over pages of advertisements and the like. You can automate the insertion of this graphic by setting up a special paragraph tag for it. You might, for instance, create a paragraph tag called BodyEnd. In it, you could set up the autonumbering format to insert the graphic. You may need to apply a character format to use a font such as Zapf Dingbats.

The BodyEnd style uses a small box to indicate the end of the story. ■

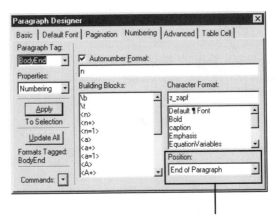

The autonumber is positioned at the end of the paragraph.

Paragraph Formatting in Structured FrameMaker

In structured FrameMaker, you generally apply elements instead of paragraph tags. The elements can have paragraph tags associated with them. Conveniently, these associated paragraph tags are context-sensitive. You can, for instance, set up a List element that contains ListItems. Within the list, you could specify that the first ListItem uses the

ListItemFirst paragraph tag, the last ListItem uses the ListItemLast paragraph tag, and all other list items use the ListItem paragraph tag. If you rearrange the elements, FrameMaker automatically changes the paragraph tag assignments for you. This is a big improvement over the paragraph-based (unstructured approach), where you have to remember to change the paragraph tags manually.

Instead of using paragraph tags, you can use Format Change Lists or override the paragraph definition inside the element definition. Refer to Chapter 29, "Understanding the Element Definition Document," for details on how to do this.

Formatting Ideas for Paragraph Tags

FrameMaker's Paragraph Designer offers some standard formatting and interesting customization options. Here are some ideas:

- **Inserting lines above or below a paragraph.** On the Advanced sheet, use the Frame Above and Frame Below settings to set lines or other graphics above or below your headings. If you don't like the provided lines, go to the reference pages and create your own graphic frames (see "Placing Graphics Above and Below the Paragraph" on page 322 for details).

- **Forcing headings to the top of a page.** On the Pagination sheet, use the Start drop-down list to specify that a particular heading must always start at the top of the page.

- **Formatting your glossary with run-in headings.** Use run-in headings (set on the Pagination sheet) for glossary terms; body text for the definitions. Set the glossary term in bold. (This also makes it easier to cross-reference the glossary later because the term is in its own paragraph. If you use a single paragraph tag and bold the glossary term, you cannot pick up just the term in a cross-reference.)

- **Eliminating spell-checking.** For paragraphs that should not be spell-checked (such as code listings), set the Language to None on the Default Font sheet.

- **Stacking lines with negative line spacing.** On the Basic sheet, if you set the space below paragraph one to a negative number and the space above paragraph two to a negative number, you can force FrameMaker to write two paragraphs in the same location. You can use this to create some interesting effects, such as white text in a black box.

- **Invisible autonumbers.** Include an autonumber at the end of your paragraph, but set the autonumber on the Numbering sheet to be white text and tiny (2 points) using a character tag. When you reference the paragraph in a variable, cross-reference, or generated file, you can take advantage of the hidden autonumber to accomplish some interesting effects. (This is helpful if you have generated a table of contents and need to refer to an autonumber that isn't normally defined in the paragraph you're working with.)

- **Change bars.** For typing comments in a file, create a comment paragraph tag with the Change Bar property selected on the Default Font sheet.

The Complete Reference

FrameMaker 7

Chapter 6

Formatting Text with Character Tags

In many desktop publishing applications, you use a single style sheet for both paragraph and character formatting. If you select a word, the style is applied just to that word. If you select a paragraph (or just click in the paragraph), the style is applied to the entire paragraph.

FrameMaker, by contrast, makes a distinction between paragraph-level and character-level formatting. Paragraph tags always format an entire paragraph. *Character tags* provide a way to format one or more characters inside the paragraph. For example, you can create formats for italicized, underlined, or bold text.

By applying character tags, you can quickly format text, but more importantly, you maintain consistency and make it easy to update your document. For example, suppose your new corporate style department bans boldface text from product documentation. The Menu Item character tag formats menu items in boldface text, so you change the weight property of the Menu Item character tag and update the tag's definition globally in the book. If you had used the Format menu (or B button) to emphasize menu items, you would have to scan your book for each bold menu item and manually remove the bold formatting.

Character tags also act as formatting building blocks for other FrameMaker features. Using character tags, you can assign color or other formatting to a portion of a cross-reference or a variable.

In structured documents, text range elements can use character tags for their formatting. Character tags also format specific portions of an element, such as prefixes or suffixes.

Applying Character Tags

 The *character catalog* lists the character tags in a document. To display the catalog, click the character catalog button in the upper-right corner of the FrameMaker window.

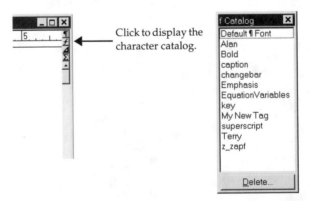

Click to display the character catalog.

Although you can apply multiple character tags to achieve formatting effects, FrameMaker recognizes just the last tag. If, for example, you apply an italicized character tag and then apply a boldface tag, the text will most likely display as boldface, italicized text. FrameMaker, however, recognizes only the last character tag you applied. A better approach is to create a single character tag that combines both properties.

Using the Character Catalog to Apply a Tag

To apply a character tag through the character catalog, follow these steps:

1. Select the text you want to format.
2. In the character catalog, click a character tag. The character tag is applied to the selected text. In the status bar, the character tag name indicates that you applied the tag.

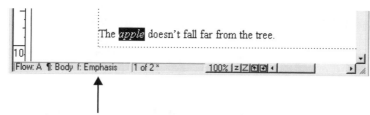

Name of character tag applied to selected text

FrameMaker provides other ways to apply a character tag, including:

■ Selecting a menu choice
■ Using the right-click pop-up menu
■ Using keyboard shortcuts

Note *You can also apply character tags by using the Character Designer, but this isn't recommended because you could accidentally modify the character tag definition.*

Selecting a Menu Choice

To apply a character tag through a menu choice, follow these steps:

1. Select the text you want to format.
2. Select Format | Characters, then select a character tag from the submenu.

Using the Right-Click Pop-Up Menu

The pop-up menu displayed when you right-click (Windows) or CTRL-click (Mac) also gives you a way to apply a character tag. Follow these steps:

1. Select the text you want to format.
2. Right-click (Windows) or CTRL-click (Mac) to display the pop-up menu, select Characters, and then select a tag from the list that's displayed.

Using Keyboard Shortcuts

To apply a character tag using a keyboard shortcut, follow these steps:

1. Select the text you want to format.
2. Press F8 (Windows or UNIX) or CTRL-8 (all platforms). The bottom-left of the status bar is highlighted.

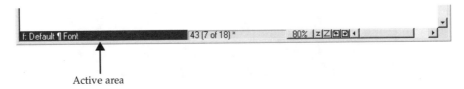

Active area

3. Display the character tag you want by doing any of the following:
   - Use the arrow keys to scroll through the list of available tags.
   - Type a letter to jump to that section of the character catalog.
   - Type the first few letters of the character tag name.
4. Press ENTER.

Some of the keys on your computer may be specially programmed. If so, one or more keyboard shortcuts may not work as described. Consult your system documentation for help.

Modifying Character Tags

In the Character Designer, you modify character tag properties, such as font size, color, and angle. When you save your changes, you update all character tags in the document at once. Content formatted by the updated character tag is automatically reformatted.

The Character Designer consists of the same choices as the Paragraph Designer's Default Font sheet. For a description of each item, see "Default Font Sheet" on page 117. The commands on the left side of the Character Designer also work very much like the commands in the Paragraph Designer.

To modify a character tag, follow these steps:

1. Display the Character Designer by selecting Format | Designer or by pressing CTRL-D (Windows or UNIX) or ESC O C D (all platforms).
2. Click the character tag you want to modify in the Character Tag drop-down list.

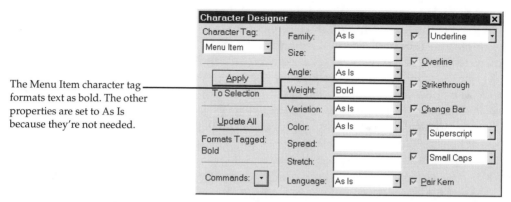

The Menu Item character tag formats text as bold. The other properties are set to As Is because they're not needed.

3. Click As Is for the properties you want determined by the paragraph tag. Font size is a good example. In some templates, the body and table cell paragraph tags have different font sizes. If you want to emphasize something in a body paragraph and in a table cell, you don't want the character tag to control the font size. This would make the table cell text as large as the body paragraph text. For this reason, it's best to set font size to As Is. See the following section, "As Is Character Properties," for details.

4. Use the other drop-down lists to change the properties you need.

Note

If the color you need isn't listed, modify your document's color definitions (select View | Color | Definitions), and the new color will be displayed in the Character Designer. For details, see Chapter 20, "Color Output."

5. Click the Apply button. Your changes are displayed on the selected text.

6. Click the Update All button to modify all instances of the character tag in your document. If you don't click the Update All button, you create an override. See "Avoiding Character Tag Overrides" on page 148 for more information.

As Is Character Properties

When you create a character tag, you don't use many properties in the Character Designer. For example, in an Emphasis character tag, you change the angle setting to Italics (or Oblique, depending on the font). The remaining properties—font family, font size, weight, variation, color, word spread, underline, and so on—come from the paragraph tag applied to the current paragraph. Using the As Is setting for the other properties saves time and helps you build character tags that format content properly.

Figure 6-1 illustrates the benefit of using As Is properties. Most properties have been modified in the first example, which improperly formats the text. In the second example, most properties except weight are set to As Is, so the text is formatted correctly. Most of the check boxes are grayed out, and the Size drop-down list is blank. This indicates that those properties have been set to As Is. You set check box properties to As Is by double-clicking the check box (if the check box is originally clear). When you click As Is in the Size drop-down list, the field is cleared. See the sidebar "Understanding Check Boxes in FrameMaker" on page 151 for more information.

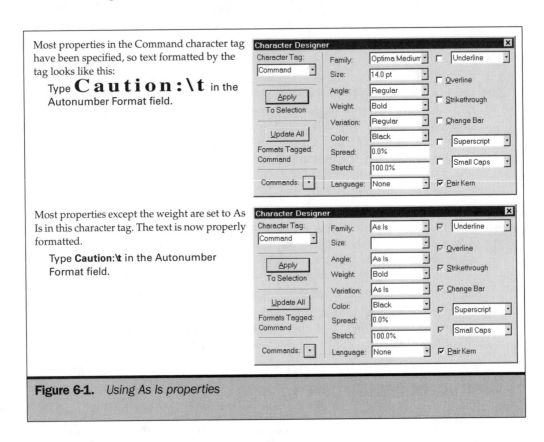

Figure 6-1. Using As Is properties

Avoiding Character Tag Overrides

When you modify a tag in the Character Designer and click the Apply button instead of clicking the Update All button, you create an override. A star is displayed next to the character tag name in the status bar. You also create an override by applying a character tag to an entire paragraph. Typically, if you need to change the style of the entire paragraph, you should create a new paragraph tag instead of applying a character tag.

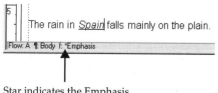

Star indicates the Emphasis
character tag has been modified.

Star indicates the Emphasis character
tag overrides the Body paragraph tag.

You remove character tag overrides by importing the template with the Remove Format Overrides option checked or by reapplying the character tag. To remove a paragraph tag override, apply the Default Paragraph Font character tag and reapply the paragraph tag. In a structured document, you need to reapply the original element.

Overrides defeat the goal of maintaining consistently formatted and structured documents. Though FrameMaker provides ways to remove overrides, you should avoid creating them in the first place.

Creating Character Tags

In addition to modifying tags in the Character Designer, you also create them. When you create a character tag, it's best to follow a specific naming convention. Typically, you should name character tags based on their function rather than their style properties. For example, your template may include a character tag that formats computer commands with the Courier font. Instead of naming the tag Courier, you name it Command. If you decide later to format commands in bold, you can update the Command character tag without changing the tag name. If you had named the tag Bold, the character tag name would not describe the new property.

To create a character tag, follow these steps:

1. Display the Character Designer. The settings of the currently selected text (or of the text at the insertion point) are displayed.

Caution   *When you position the cursor in text formatted with a character tag, the Character Designer displays that character tag's name. However, the properties shown in the Character Designer are not necessarily that character tag's properties. Many character tags have items set to As Is, and those will not be reflected when you first display the Character Designer. Instead, you see the setting of the underlying paragraph tag. To see the actual settings, click the tag name again in the Character Tag drop-down list.*

2. Click the Commands button, then select Set Window to As Is from the pop-up menu to reset the character properties. This crucial step is discussed in more detail in "As Is Character Properties" on page 147.

CREATING AND
MANIPULATING TEXT

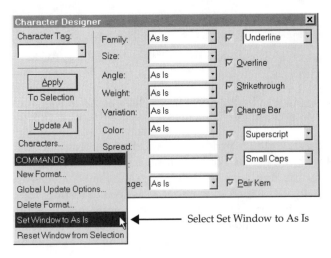

Select Set Window to As Is

3. Click the Commands button and select New Format from the pop-up menu. The New Format dialog box is displayed.

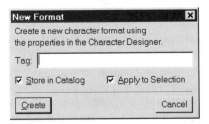

4. Type the name of your new tag in the Tag field, then click the Create button. The new tag is displayed in the character catalog.

By default, the Store in Catalog and Apply to Selection check boxes are checked. The latter is irrelevant unless you selected text before creating the tag. Do make sure that Store in Catalog is checked, or the tag will not be displayed in the character catalog.

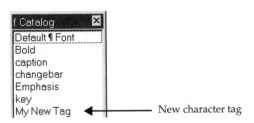

New character tag

5. Change the properties as needed, then click the Update All button to save your changes. Notice that all of the As Is settings disappear again. To verify that the tag is set correctly, click its name in the Character Tag drop-down list again.

Understanding Check Boxes in FrameMaker

FrameMaker check boxes confuse many users. Most programs have only two settings for a check box—checked or unchecked. In FrameMaker, there are three values—checked, unchecked, and As Is. As you see in the following examples, the check boxes look different on the Mac, Windows, and UNIX platforms.

	Checked	Unchecked	As Is
Windows	☑	☐	☑
Mac	☑	☐	⊟
UNIX	◪	◪	▨

Check boxes set to As Is are particularly confusing, but you change the value of check boxes the same way on all three platforms. To clear the As Is setting, check the box once. To change the value from As Is to checked, check the box twice.

Renaming Character Tags

FrameMaker makes it easy to change the name of a character tag you've already created. For example, you may need to rename the Emphasis character tag Strong. After you rename Emphasis, the character tag name will change to Strong where you've applied it, and the previous tag name will no longer be displayed in the character catalog.

Renaming character tags also lets you globally assign a new character tag to text formatted by a deleted tag. When you select the formatted text, the deleted character tag name is still displayed in the status bar. You can "rename" the deleted tag in the Character Designer. This applies the new character tag where the deleted tag is applied in your document.

When you rename a character tag, FrameMaker updates the catalog definition and the locations where you applied the tag; however, references to the old tag name (for example, in variables and cross-references) are not updated. You'll need to search for the old tag name in these components and change the name yourself.

To rename a character tag, follow these steps:

1. Display the Character Designer.
2. Click the tag you plan to rename from the Character Tag drop-down list. If you're renaming a deleted tag, select the text that was previously formatted by the tag. (The deleted tag name is marked in the status bar with a star.)

CREATING AND
MANIPULATING TEXT

3. In the Character Tag field, type the new name over the name.

4. Click the Update All button. A confirmation dialog box is displayed.

5. Click the OK button. The renamed character tag is applied in your document and listed in the character catalog in place of the initial tag.

The Global Update Options dialog box also lets you rename a tag, but the method involves more steps. See the next section for details.

Updating Character Properties Globally

FrameMaker's global update feature provides several ways to modify more than one character tag at once. For example, you can replace all instances of magenta text with black text, apply a different character tag in place of the old one throughout the document, and more.

There are three global update options:

- **All Characters and Catalog Entries:** You can update specific properties in all character tags, paragraph tags, and text lines. Use this option if, for instance, you need to change the default font size in all tag definitions and text lines.

- **All Matching Tags in Selection:** You can modify character tags that have been applied to different words in a paragraph. For example, suppose the Menu Item character tag is applied to one word and the Command character tag is applied to a different word in the same paragraph. You can select the paragraph and remove bold formatting from both character tags.

- **All Tagged:** Applies a new character tag in place of the selected tag. For example, you can use this option to apply the Hyperlink character tag instead of the Underline character tag in an entire document.

Changing Specific Properties

You can instantly modify specific character properties in a document, whether the properties are in character tags, paragraph tags, or text lines. This is handy for removing color from all characters or only from selected character tags and changing the default font.

To modify selected properties, follow these steps:

1. Display the Character Designer.

2. Click the Commands button, then select Set Window to As Is from the pop-up menu. This resets all character properties.

3. Click the properties you want to update from the drop-down lists, click the Commands button, then select Global Update Options from the pop-up menu. The Global Update Options dialog box is displayed.

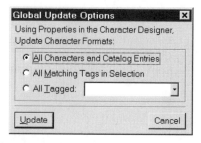

4. Do *one* of the following:

   ■ To update specific properties in *all* character tags, paragraph tags, and text lines, click the All Characters and Catalog Entries radio button. If you selected a tag name before performing this step, FrameMaker gives you the option to apply the tag to all characters in the document. Typically, you want to avoid this, so click the No button to update only the properties you changed.

   ■ To update specific properties in character tags applied to *selected text*, click the All Matching Tags in Selection radio button.

5. Click the Update button. FrameMaker globally makes the appropriate changes.

Reassigning a Character Tag Globally

FrameMaker provides a way to assign a new character tag in place of the selected tag. For example, you can swap each instance of the Button character tag with the Key character tag.

To reassign a character tag globally, follow these steps:

1. Display the Character Designer.

2. In the Character Tag drop-down list, click the tag name you want to apply.

3. Click the Commands button, then select Global Update Options from the pop-up menu. The Global Update Options dialog box is displayed.

4. Click the All Tagged radio button, then click the tag you want to replace from the drop-down list.

5. Click the Update button. A confirmation dialog box is displayed.

6. Click the OK button to update the tag.

Removing Character Tag Formatting

After you apply a character tag, you can remove the tag by selecting text and applying the Default Paragraph Font character tag. The text will be reformatted with the paragraph tag properties. If a character tag has been applied to an entire paragraph, you need to remove the character tag formatting and reapply the paragraph tag (or for structured documents, reapply the original element).

To remove character tag formatting from selected text, follow these steps:

1. Display the character catalog.

2. Select the text you want to reformat.

3. In the character catalog, click Default Paragraph Font. The text is reformatted with the original paragraph style. In the left status bar, the character tag name is no longer displayed. A star displayed next to the paragraph tag name indicates an override. See "Avoiding Character Tag Overrides" on page 148 for more information.

Instead of using the character catalog, you can press F8 (Windows or UNIX) or CTRL-8 (all platforms) to activate the status bar and select Default Paragraph Font to remove the character formatting.

Deleting Character Tags

All character tags can be deleted from the character catalog except the Default Paragraph Font. When you delete a tag, the catalog is updated, but variables, cross-references, and other components can still refer to the deleted tag name. Deleting a tag also does not remove the character format from text. The name of the deleted character tag is still displayed in the status bar, along with a star to indicate that it's an override. To prevent the override, globally replace each instance of the character tag you plan to delete with another tag. See "Reassigning a Character Tag Globally" on page 153 for details.

If you delete the tag without globally applying another one, you can select the text formatted by the deleted tag and assign a new one in its place. For more information, see "Renaming Character Tags" on page 151.

To delete a character tag from the character catalog, follow these steps:

1. Display the character catalog.

2. Click the Delete button to display the Delete Formats from Catalog dialog box. You can also display the dialog box by clicking the Commands button in the Character Designer and selecting Delete Format from the pop-up menu.

3. Click the tag you want to delete, then click the Delete button. To delete all character tags, press and hold ALT-E (Windows only). This method quickly deletes the tags. You can delete tags from the paragraph catalog the same way.

If you make a mistake, you must click the Cancel button and start over. There is no Apply button.

Click the tag you want to delete. ⟶

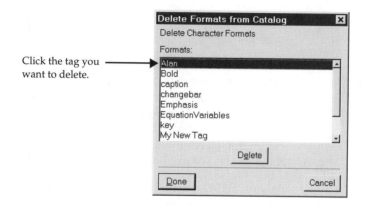

4. Click the Done button. The character tag you deleted is no longer displayed in the character catalog.

Additional Character Tags Tips

This chapter has covered applying character tags to text directly, but you can also format text in variables, cross references, autonumbered paragraphs, markers, and other FrameMaker components. Table 6-1 describes more advanced uses for character tags. You'll read more about each component in the corresponding chapter (for example, cross-references formats are discussed in the cross-reference chapter).

Item	Description
Variable	Create a book title variable and include a character tag to italicize the title. See Chapter 9, "Storing Content in Variables."
Autonumbered paragraph	Create a bullet character tag that uses the Wingdings font and use the character tag in the autonumber format of a bulleted paragraph tag. See "Autonumbering Details" on page 134.
Cross-reference format	Format cross-references as blue in a PDF by inserting a blue character tag in the cross-reference format. Before you create a PDF file for printing, set the color in the blue tag to As Is. See "Formatting Cross-References" on page 200. You can achieve the same result by printing spot color to black, except that *all* color would print as black. Read more about spot color in Chapter 20, "Color Output."
Marker	Italicize *See Also* in an index entry by including a character tag in the index marker. See Chapter 16, "Creating Indexes."
Text line	Draw a text line using the Text Line feature in the Tools Palette and format the text with an italicized character tag. See Chapter 13, "FrameMaker's Graphics Tools."
Spell checker	Skip spell checking for specific words by setting their language to "None" in a character format. See Chapter 4, "Word-Processing Features."
Change bar	Mark text you modify with a change bar character tag instead of or in addition to relying on automatic change bars. See Chapter 4, "Word-Processing Features."
Reference page	Create highlighted page numbers for TOC entries in a PDF file by applying a blue character tag to <$pagenum> building blocks on the TOC reference page. See Chapter 15, "Creating Tables of Contents."
Hyperlink	Create a character tag with all properties set to As Is and apply to hyperlinks. The format marks the beginning and end of the hyperlink without modifying the character properties. See Chapter 22, "Creating Interactive Documents with Hypertext."

Table 6-1. *Character Tag Tips*

The Complete Reference

Chapter 7

Understanding Table Design

FrameMaker lets you define preformatted table structures using *table tags*. The table tags store formatting such as alignment, spacing, cell margins, pagination, ruling, shading, and the default number of columns and rows. When you need a table, you select a table tag and insert the table in your document. Table tags also store paragraph formatting, so when you insert a new table, the paragraph tags for text in the table are already applied to the table title and cells.

Table 7: Results of Annual Tri-City Dog Show

Ribbon	Dog Name	Breed
Red	Charlie Chan's Revival	Toy Poodle
Blue	Trixie the Trotter	Pomeranian
Purple	Island Girl Blanc	Maltese
Yellow	Jake's Nine Lives	Pointer

Judge R.C. Smith presided.

The biggest advantage of table tags is that they help maintain consistency. If the corporate style guide changes or your department decides to redesign tables, you update the FrameMaker template and import the new table style into your document. Tables tagged with the modified table style are updated instantly. Some properties, however, do not change until you insert a new table. For example, if you update a table tag's default column width or number of rows, existing tables are not affected; the changes apply only to new tables.

Table tags store many of the same properties as paragraph tags. Both table and paragraph tags provide default formatting for the underlying content. To emphasize text in a paragraph, you apply a character tag. This reformats the selected text without changing the paragraph tag. Similarly, you can modify a table without changing the default table design. Adding rows and columns, inserting a table title, shading specific cells, merging cells, modifying borders, and other reformatting can be done on a table-by-table basis. Some of these changes, such as adding rows and columns, can be saved in the table tag; others apply only to the selected table. For example, you can't save merged table cells or irregular ruling patterns in a table tag.

In a structured document, some changes are easier to make in the structure view. For instance, you can move table cells by dragging them to a new location. The table on the body page is updated as you modify the table in the structure view.

Inserting Tables

Tables consist of three basic components—heading rows, body rows, and footing rows. When you insert a table into your document, you specify the number and types of rows, the number of columns, and the table tag. You can make many modifications to the table—both inside and outside the Table Designer.

To insert a table, follow these steps:

1. Position your cursor where you want to put the table.
2. Select Table | Insert Table. The Insert Table dialog box is displayed.

Click a table tag here. 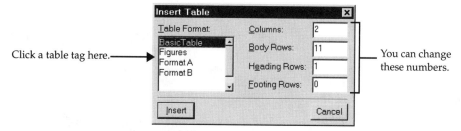 You can change these numbers.

3. Click a table tag in the Table Format list.
4. In the fields on the right, type the number of rows and columns you want for the table. You can add three kinds of rows to a table:
   - **Heading row.** Contains the names of each column and repeats when the table breaks to the next page.
   - **Body row.** Displays main content.
   - **Footing row.** Includes text that repeats at the bottom of multipage tables.
5. Click the Insert button. The table is displayed in your document.

With the FrameMaker text symbols displayed, you'll see an upside-down T (or table anchor) above the table. The anchor locks the table to the paragraph. As the paragraph fills the page, the table moves down. (Floating tables are a bit different. See "Basic Sheet" on page 164.)

The table is anchored to this paragraph. ⊥ ¶ —— Anchor symbol
(Select View | Text Symbols to display symbols.)

Table 1: §

§	§	§
§	§	§
§	§	§
§	§	§

After you insert a table, you type text in the table cells and press the TAB key to move the cursor from cell to cell. The cursor moves horizontally to the end of the row and then to the first cell in the next row until reaching the end of the table. In some word processing programs, you can press the TAB key at the end of the table to add a row. In FrameMaker, when the cursor reaches the last cell in the last row, the cursor jumps to the table title (if the table has one) or the first cell of the table.

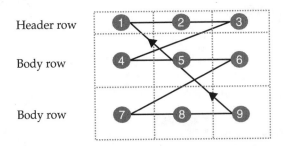

Inserting a tab in a table cell is also different. To insert a tab, position your cursor in the cell and press ESC TAB. The paragraph tag applied to the table cell must include a tab stop, or this will not work.

Selecting Cells

Double-clicking a table cell selects the contents of the cell, not the actual table cell. The quickest way to select a table cell is by CTRL-clicking (Windows) or OPTION-CTRL (Mac) the cell you want to select. While you press CTRL, the cursor displays as perpendicular arrows. A small square, or *handle*, is displayed on the right border. You select and drag a handle to resize the selected column manually.

Macintosh users should substitute OPTION *for* CTRL *in this section.*

You can also select a cell by using the Object pointer in the Tools Palette or by pressing the mouse button and dragging the cursor over the table cells.

Equipment§	Aisle Number§	Stock Number§
Lantern§	3D§	730-439H93§
Portable Stove§	5A§	072-321C85§

Perpendicular arrows are displayed while you CTRL-click cells.

Equipment§	Aisle Number§	Stock Number§
Lantern§	3D§	730-439H93§
Portable stove§	5A§	072-321C85§

Drag the handle to resize the column manually.

To select a row or column, you CTRL-click twice in a specific location. Typically, the border closer to your cursor before you select the cells determines whether the row or column is selected. If the cursor is closer to the left or right cell border, you select the row. If the cursor is closer to the top or bottom cell border, you select the column. Adding to the confusion, CTRL-click twice in the *middle* of the cell also selects the column.

CTRL-click near the left or right border to select the cell.

CTRL-click near the left or right border twice to select the row.

CTRL-click near the top or bottom border twice to select the column.

English Setter	Sporting
Beagle	Hound
Poodle	Toy

English Setter	Sporting
Beagle	Hound
Poodle	Toy

English Setter	Sporting
Beagle	Hound
Poodle	Toy

English Setter	Sporting
Beagle	Hound
Poodle	Toy

English Setter	Sporting
Beagle	Hound
Poodle	Toy

English Setter	Sporting
Beagle	Hound
Poodle	Toy

Moving and Deleting Tables

You can move and delete tables by selecting the table anchor or selecting the table itself and then pressing the DELETE key. The document symbols must be displayed for you to see anchors (select View | Text Symbols), and anchors can be difficult to select. If there are two adjacent tables, the anchors may be stacked on top of one another on the same line. Cutting and pasting is easier, but both methods are described here.

If you don't select the entire table before cutting and pasting or selecting the anchor, a warning dialog box is displayed with the choice to leave the cells empty or to remove the cells. Click the Cancel button and start over.

To cut and paste a table to another paragraph, follow these steps:

1. Position your cursor in the table you want to move.
2. CTRL-click three times to select the table.
3. Press CTRL-X (Windows) or COMMAND-X (Mac). The table is no longer displayed.
4. Position the cursor where you want the table and press CTRL-V (Windows) or COMMAND-V (Mac). The table is displayed in the new location.

To select the anchor to move the table, follow these steps:

1. Position your cursor next to the anchor. You might have to change the page magnification rate to 150 or 200 percent to see the anchor.
2. Press the LEFT ARROW or RIGHT ARROW key to select the anchor until the table is highlighted. Keep in mind the following tips:
   - If you're moving a table that is above other tables, the two anchors may be stacked. They're on the same line but are displayed as one anchor. You'll

need to position your cursor in the middle of the anchor, press the RIGHT ARROW key, and then press the SPACEBAR until the two anchors are separated.

Cursor in middle of
stacked anchors

Separated anchors

■ If you don't select the end of flow symbol with the table anchor, you'll leave an empty paragraph.

3. Press CTRL-X (Windows) or COMMAND-X (Mac). The table is no longer displayed.

4. Position the cursor where you want the table and press CTRL-V (Windows) or COMMAND-V (Mac). The table is displayed in the new location.

To delete a table, follow these steps:

1. Select the table.

2. Press the DELETE key, or select Edit | Clear. The table is deleted from the document.

Changing the Assigned Table Tag

You can apply table tags to existing tables. This lets you reformat the selected table with a different table tag. Unlike the paragraph and character catalogs, which can be displayed in separate palettes, the table catalog has no palette. Table tag names are displayed only in the Table Designer and when you insert a table.

To apply a table tag, follow these steps:

1. Place your cursor inside a table.

2. Display the Table Designer by pressing CTRL-T (Windows), OPTION-COMMAND-T (Mac), or ESC-SHIFT-F I T (all).

3. Click the new tag in the Table Tag drop-down list, then click the Apply button.

If the table doesn't appear to be formatted by the table tag—the borders or colors are wrong, for instance—check the table's current settings, remove all custom formatting, and reapply the tag. See "Displaying and Removing Custom Ruling and Shading" on page 178 for details.

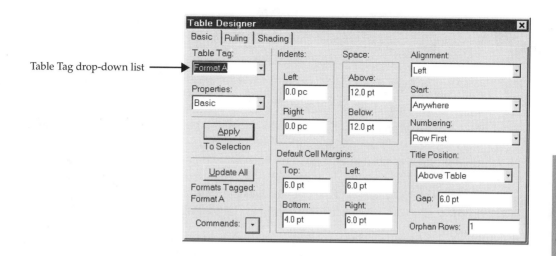

Table Tag drop-down list

Modifying a Table Tag

Most table tag properties are configured in the Table Designer. When you make changes in the Table Designer and click the Update All button, two things happen—all tables of that type document are updated where you inserted them, and new tables of that type have the new formatting. When you modify a table definition outside the Table Designer, the changes aren't applied throughout the document; they only apply to the selected table and those you insert in the future using the modified tag.

In the Table Designer, you can change the following properties:

- Indents
- Space above and below
- Cell margins
- Vertical and horizontal table alignment
- Autonumber direction
- Title position and gap
- Number of orphan rows
- Borders
- Shading

Outside the Table Designer, you can modify the following properties:

- Column width
- Number of columns and rows
- Types of columns (heading, body, footing)
- Paragraph tags applied to the table

If you make changes outside the Table Designer and don't click the Update All button in the Table Designer, those changes only apply to the selected table.

To modify a table tag in the Table Designer, follow these steps:

1. Insert a table and display the Table Designer.
2. Make changes on one of the sheets, then click the Update All button. Repeat for the other sheets. Your changes are saved in the table tag and applied to all existing tables of the same type.

 Clicking the Apply button instead of the Update All button creates a formatting override. This isn't recommended because your changes are saved only in the current table, not in the table tag.

The following sections describe each setting in the Table Designer. For details on changing table tags outside the Table Designer, see "Customizing Tables Outside the Table Designer" on page 170.

Changing Table Designer Settings

The Table Designer has three property sheets. To view a sheet, click its tab (Windows and UNIX), or click the sheet in the Properties drop-down list (all). This section describes the sheets.

Basic Sheet

On the Basic sheet, you change spacing, pagination, numbering, orphan rows, and other properties. Table 7-1 describes the options.

Item	Description
Indents	Adds space between the left or right edge of the text frame and the table.
Spacing	Determines the room above the table title and below the last row. The paragraphs above and below the table also include spacing properties, so FrameMaker uses the larger of the two spaces; the sizes aren't added. For example, the space above a table (12 points) takes precedence over the space below the previous paragraph (3 points).

Table 7-1. *Table Designer, Basic Sheet*

Item	Description
Default Cell Margins	Adds space inside each table cell. Interacts with settings in the Paragraph Designer Table Cell sheet, where you can customize table cell margins and alignment for a paragraph tag. (See "Table Cell Sheet" on page 128 for details.)
Alignment	Horizontal position of table under the previous paragraph. Interacts with the paragraph's pagination settings. For example, in a paragraph that begins within the side head, a left-aligned table also stays in the side head. ■ **Left:** Aligns the table with the left side of the column. ■ **Right:** Aligns the table with the right side of the column. ■ **Center:** Places the table in the center of the text area. ■ **Side Closer to Binding:** Aligns the table closer to the bound edge of the page. ■ **Side Farther from Binding:** Aligns the table farther from the bound edge of the page.
Start	Positions the table vertically on the page. ■ **Anywhere:** Places the table wherever it fits on the page; table moves down with the anchored paragraph. ■ **Top of Column:** Places the table at the top of the text column; same as Top of Page in one-column documents. ■ **Top of Page:** Moves the table to the top of the page. ■ **Top of Left Page:** Places the table at the top of the next left page in a double-sided document. ■ **Top of Right Page:** Places the table at the top of the next right page in a double-sided document. ■ **Float:** Moves the table to the first text column that has room for the entire table. If you type text above the table and the table can't fit on the current page, it floats to the next page.

Table 7-1. *Table Designer, Basic Sheet (Continued)*

CREATING AND MANIPULATING TEXT

Item	Description

Numbering	Organizes autonumbered paragraph either horizontally or vertically:
	■ **Row First:** Numbers paragraphs horizontally, as in:
	
	    1. Go 2. Yield 3. Stop
	
	■ **Column First:** Numbers paragraph vertically, as in:
	
	    1. Go
	    2. Yield
	    3. Stop

Title Position and Gap	Positions the table title. ■ **No Title:** Indicates the table has no title. ■ **Above Table:** Displays the title above the table. ■ **Below Table:** Places the title below the table. The gap is the space between the table and the table title. (Spacing in the table title paragraph itself does not apply.)
Orphan Rows	Indicates the number of table rows that must stay together when the table breaks across a page. To force the entire table to fit on the same page (as in a floating table), specify up to 255 rows.

Table 7-1.   *Table Designer, Basic Sheet (Continued)*

Ruling Sheet

The Ruling sheet contains border styles for rows, columns, heading and footing rows, and the outside edges of the table. You can arrange borders in a variety of patterns. For example, the second column has a thick border, and the other columns have a thin border or no border at all. In rows, a medium ruling may separate every fifth row, and thin rulings may be used for the rest. The five default ruling styles—double, medium, thick, thin, and very thin—are defined in the custom ruling and shading properties of a document and are also displayed in the Table Designer. For details on creating, editing, and deleting ruling styles, see "Changing Ruling Options" on page 177. Table 7-2 describes the Ruling sheet.

Item	Description
Column Ruling	Specifies a unique border for the nth column and a repeating border for the remaining columns. Useful if the table cell headings are vertical instead of horizontal. The following table has a single ruling for the first column and no ruling for the others.

Ribbon	Dog Name	Breed
Red	Charlie Chan's Revival	Standard Poodle
Blue	Trixie the Trotter	Pomeranian
Purple	Island Girl Blanc	Maltese
Yellow	Jake's Nine Lives	Pointer

First column has thin ruling.

Basset hound Blaze Star Vega missed winning last place because she was too busy napping.

Judge Ken Smith presided.

Item	Description
Body Row Ruling	Specifies a repeating border for every nth body row and the same border for the remaining body rows. The previous table has a thin border for every second body row and no border for the others.
Heading and Footing Ruling	Separates heading and footing rows from the table and provides border for multiple heading and footing rows. The previous table has a thin border for the separator and a thin border for the footing row.
Outside Ruling	Specifies the outside border with an option to draw the bottom border only on the last sheet of a table (for tables that break across pages). The previous table has a medium top border, a thin bottom border, and no left or right borders.

Table 7-2. *Table Designer, Ruling Sheet*

Shading Sheet

On the Shading sheet, you choose the color and shading amount for heading and footing rows and the body cells. For example, your table can have a 30 percent blue heading row and alternate 10 percent yellow and white body rows. The fill percentages—3, 10, 30, 50, 70, 90, and 100—are defaults and cannot be modified. You *can* set up additional colors in the document's color definitions, and the color itself can have a tint. See Chapter 20, "Color Output," for details. Table 7-3 describes the Shading sheet.

Item	Description
Heading and Footing Shading	Applies fill percentage and color to *both* the heading and footing rows. The heading row of the following table shows a 100 percent black fill. If the table had a footing row, the row would have the same shading.
Body Shading	Applies fill percentage and color to *either* the rows or the columns and lets you define alternate shading for each row or column. The previous table is shaded by column with a 10 percent black fill.

Table 7-3. *Table Designer, Shading Sheet*

Globally Updating Table Tags

You can update table tag properties across the entire table catalog, just as you do with the paragraph and character tags. For example, you can change the body row ruling in all table definitions to None, and all tables in the document will be updated.

The ruling and shading options differ depending on which Table Designer sheet is displayed. If you clicked the Ruling sheet before displaying the Global Update Options dialog box, you have the option to change just the ruling properties. With the Shading sheet displayed, you have the option to change only the shading properties.

For more information about global updating, see "Setting Properties Across the Entire Paragraph Catalog" on page 130.

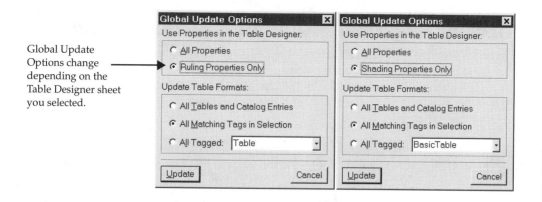

Global Update Options change depending on the Table Designer sheet you selected.

Creating a Table Tag

New table tags are based on existing tags—you must insert a table before creating a new tag. While most table properties come from the Table Designer, there are a few properties that you configure outside the Table Designer. For a list, see "Modifying a Table Tag" on page 163.

To create a table tag, follow these steps:

1. Insert a table with the tag that looks closest to the table you want to create.
2. Display the Table Designer, then type a new name in the Table Tag field.
3. Click the Apply button. The New Format dialog box is displayed.
4. Verify the name you typed, then click the Create button. Your table format is displayed in the Table Designer.

Caution *By default, the Store in Catalog and Apply to Selection check boxes are checked. Most of the time, you don't uncheck the Store in Catalog check box unless you don't want to use the new table format for other tables. Uncheck the Apply to Selection check box only if your cursor is in a table, but you don't want to apply the new tag to it.*

5. Make changes on one of the Table Designer sheets, then click the Update All button to save your changes. Repeat for remaining sheets. (If you click the Apply button, the table definition is not updated. This creates a formatting override.)
6. Be sure to click the Update All button in the Table Designer when you're finished.

Customizing Tables Outside the Table Designer

You can customize a table outside the Table Designer by applying paragraph tags to the text in the cells, adding and deleting columns or rows, and resizing columns. If you make such changes in a table and click the Update All button in the Table Designer, your changes are made to the current table and become the default properties for all future tables of that type.

Unlike changes you make in the Table Designer, changes you make to a table outside the Table Designer are not applied to existing tables of that type in the document except for the current table. If you click the Update All button in the Table Designer, however, the changes are applied to tables you insert in the future using the modified tag.

Adding and Deleting Rows and Columns

When your cursor is in a table and you click the Update All button, the table tag uses the number and location of rows and columns in that table as the default the next time you add a table of the same type. For example, if the current table consists of one heading row, five body rows, and two columns, those defaults are stored in the updated tag. When you insert a new table using the updated tag, the default row and column settings are included unless you change them in the Insert Table dialog box. You can, however, add rows and columns to an existing table and save your changes as the new defaults for that tag.

While there's only one type of column, there are three types of rows:

- **Heading row.** Repeats column headings.
- **Body row.** Contains main content.
- **Footing row.** Repeats text at the bottom of the table.

Table on page 1

Genre	Artist
Opera	Maria Callas
Bluegrass	Ralph Stanley
Folk	Emmylou Harris
Country	Johnny Cash
Rock	Rolling Stones
Source: Guide for Music Aficionados, Franklin Press	

◄────── Heading row

◄────── Footing row

Table continued on page 2

Genre	Artist
Jazz	Sarah Vaughan
Blues	Albert King
Pop	Michael Jackson
Punk	The Ramones
Source: Guide for Music Aficionados, Franklin Press	

To change the number of rows and columns in a table, follow these steps:

1. Place your cursor in a table formatted by the tag you want to modify.
2. Select Table | Add Rows or Columns. The Add Rows or Columns dialog box is displayed.

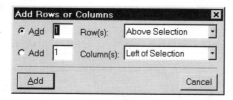

3. To add rows, type the number of rows in the Add field, then click the row location in the Row(s) drop-down list. You can also add a row below the current row by pressing CTRL-ENTER (Windows and UNIX) or CTRL-RETURN (Mac).
4. To add columns, type the number of columns in the Add field and click the column location in the Column(s) drop-down list.
5. Click the Add button. You can click the Cancel button if you change your mind.
6. *(optional)* To update the table tag, keep your cursor in the table, display the Table Designer, and click the Update All button.

To delete rows and columns, do the following:

1. Select the row or column you want to delete. If you select only one cell, you'll delete the contents of the cell, not the cell itself.
2. Press the DELETE key. The Clear Table Cells dialog box is displayed.

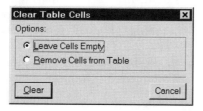

3. Click the Remove Cells from Table radio button to delete the cells, then click the Clear button. The row or column is removed from the table.

  If you click the Leave Cells Empty radio button, the contents of the row or column are deleted, not the row or column.

4. *(optional)* Click the Update All button in the Table Designer to save your changes in the table tag. The selected table is modified, and all new tables inserted using the modified tag will have the new number of rows and columns.

Resizing Columns

Table tags store default column widths. Each time you insert a particular table style, the columns are the same size from table to table. You can resize table columns either manually or by specifying a width. When you resize one column, the other columns remain the same size. This differs in other word processing programs, where table columns adjust to maintain the table width. To maintain the table width when you manually resize a column in FrameMaker, press SHIFT. The width of the column on the right is automatically adjusted to maintain the original table width.

Original column widths

Equipment	Aisle	Stock Number
Lantern	3B	730-439H93

Column 2 is resized while maintaining the table width.

Equipment	Aisle	Stock Number
Lantern	3B	730-439H93

The table widens when column 2 is resized without maintaining the table width.

Equipment	Aisle	Stock Number
Lantern	3B	730-439H93

After resizing a table, you can update the table tag to save the new default column widths. This updates the table tag but not tables already in the document.

Manually Resizing Columns

You can resize table columns manually and use the FrameMaker ruler as a guide. As you drag the column border, the ruler marking moves. If you turn on FrameMaker's snap feature, the border moves to the nearest ruler marking. This helps you precisely resize the columns. To drag the column border between markings, you need to turn snap off. Select Graphics | Snap to toggle the snap feature. See "Working with Grids" on page 334 for details.

As you resize a table column, the width displayed in the status bar also changes. The dimensions reflect the width of all selected columns.

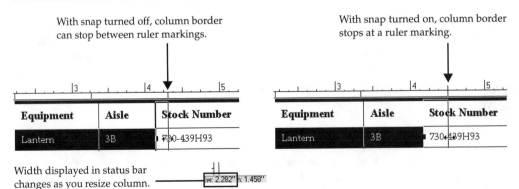

With snap turned off, column border can stop between ruler markings.

With snap turned on, column border stops at a ruler marking.

Width displayed in status bar changes as you resize column.

w: 2.282" h: 1.458"

To resize columns manually, do the following:

1. In the column you want to resize, either CTRL-click twice to highlight the column or select a few cells in the column. Both methods end in the same result. The sizing arrow and handles are displayed.

Table 1-1. *Original format*

Group	Breeds
Working Dogs	St. Bernard
	German Shepherd
Hounds	Basset Hound
	English Foxhound

When you select cells, the arrow
and handles are displayed.

2. Select one of the handles and drag the column to the left or right. When the column is adjusted to the correct width, let go of the cell handles. The new column width is displayed.

3. *(optional)* To update the table tag, keep your cursor in the table, display the Table Designer, and click the Update All button. The selected table is modified, and all new tables inserted using the modified tag will have the new column widths.

Specifying the Column Width

Instead of manually resizing table columns, you can choose a specific resizing method and value in the Resize Selected Columns dialog box. The choices are as follows:

- **To Width:** Type the column width. If you select two columns, each column is resized to the specified width.

- **By Scaling:** Change the width by a specific percentage. For example, you can scale the selected column 200 percent to double the width.

- **To Width of Column Number:** Match the column width to the specified column.

- **To Equal Widths Totalling:** Resize two or more columns to equal a specific width.

- **By Scaling to Widths Totalling:** Resize two or more columns a specific percentage while maintaining the original column proportions.

- **To Width of Selected Cells' Contents:** Resize the cell to fit its contents.

Note

The display units (inches, picas, and the like) in the Resize Selected Columns dialog box are determined by the document viewing options. You can change the setting by selecting View | Options and selecting another display unit. For details on the display units, see "Changing View Options" on page 48.

To specify the column width, follow these steps:

1. Select the column or columns you want to resize.

2. Select Table | Resize Columns. The Resize Selected Columns dialog box is displayed.

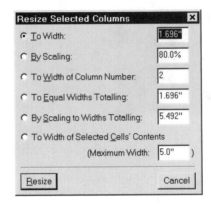

3. Type the appropriate measurement next to the method you want to use.

4. Click the Resize button. The selected table columns are updated.

5. *(optional)* To update the table tag, keep your cursor in the table, display the Table Designer, and click the Update All button. The selected table is modified, and all new tables inserted using the modified tag will have the new column widths.

Applying Paragraph Tags

Paragraph tags format the text in each table cell and in the table title. The typical FrameMaker template includes paragraph tags such as TableTitle, CellBody, CellHeading, and TableFooting. When you apply these tags to cells in the table and update the table tag, you don't have to apply the tags manually after inserting a new table.

The paragraph tags applied to the first row of each row type—heading, body, and footing row—are stored in the table tag. You cannot apply a different paragraph tag to each cell in a table and save the table tag. For example, the following table on the left is consistently formatted—CellHeading is applied to the heading row, CellBody is applied to all body rows, and TableFooting is applied to the footing row. The table on the right is formatted inconsistently. Even though the CellBullet paragraph tags are applied in the second body row, these tags won't be saved in the table tag; the tags applied in the *first* body row are saved.

To apply paragraph tags to cells in a table, follow these steps:

1. Put your cursor in a cell, or select several cells and apply a paragraph tag.

Formatting overrides (indicated by the star displayed in the status bar by the paragraph tag name) are saved with the table tag. If you modify a paragraph tag in the table, be sure you avoid overrides by updating the paragraph tag definition.

2. *(optional)* To save the paragraph formatting in the table tag, display the Table Designer, then click the Update All button. The paragraph formatting is saved in the table tag.

Consistent application of paragraph tags

Inconsistent CellBullet tags aren't saved in the table tag.

Table 6: Table Title

CellHeading	CellHeading	CellHeading
CellBody	CellBody	CellBody
CellBody	CellBody	CellBody
CellBody	CellBody	CellBody
TableFooting		

Table 6: Table Title

CellHeading	CellHeading	CellHeading
CellBody	CellBody	CellBody
• CellBullet	• CellBullet	CellBody
CellBody	CellBody	CellBody
TableFooting		

Customizing Cell Ruling and Shading

FrameMaker's custom ruling and shading feature lets you apply ruling and shading to particular cells in a table, providing more flexibility than the Table Designer properties. You apply the formatting only when you need it (for example, to highlight important content). The following table cells have been reformatted with a 10 percent black fill and a medium border.

By applying custom ruling and shading to table cells, you create a formatting override. Typically, you can remove overrides by reimporting the template with the Remove Layout/Format Overrides setting checked. To strip custom ruling and shading, however, you'll need to remove the formatting manually. Modifying tables outside the table tag makes it difficult to maintain consistency, so you should customize tables sparingly.

To apply custom ruling and shading, follow these steps:

1. Highlight the cell(s) you want to format.
2. Select Table | Custom Ruling & Shading. The Custom Ruling and Shading dialog box is displayed.

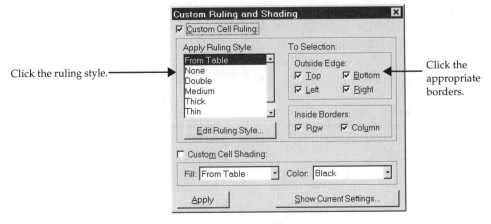

Click the ruling style.

Click the appropriate borders.

3. To apply custom ruling, complete the following:

a. Uncheck the Custom Cell Shading check box, then click a border style in the Apply Ruling Style list.

> **Note**
>
> *You can modify cell ruling and shading at the same time by checking both the Custom Cell Ruling and Custom Cell Shading check boxes and then making your changes.*

b. Click the cell borders you want to reformat in the To Selection section. The border types are displayed in the following table.

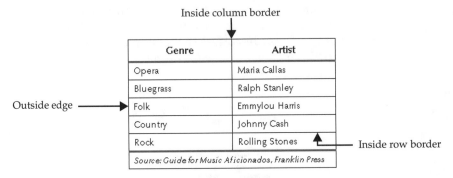

4. To apply custom shading to selected cells, do the following:

a. Uncheck the Custom Cell Ruling check box, then click the type of shading in the Fill drop-down list. You can choose specific percentages or solid white.

b. Click a color in the Color drop-down list (unless you set the fill to Solid White, None, or As Is).

5. Click the Apply button. Your changes are made to the selected table cell or cells.

Changing Ruling Options

You can edit, create, and delete ruling styles, and the changes will be displayed in the Custom Ruling and Shading dialog box and the Table Designer.

To edit and create ruling styles, follow these steps:

1. *(optional)* Select the cells you need to format.
2. Select Table | Custom Ruling & Shading. The Custom Ruling and Shading dialog box is displayed.
3. In the Apply Ruling Style list, click the style you want to edit or base the new style on, then click the Edit Ruling Style button. The Edit Ruling Style dialog box is displayed.

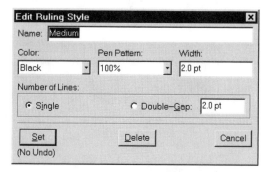

4. Change the appropriate properties:
   - Click a color in the Color drop-down list.
   - Click a fill percentage (or solid white) in the Pen Pattern drop-down list.
   - Type a new line width from .015 to 360 points in the Width field.
   - Click the Double-Gap radio button to create a double line and type the space between the lines (from .015 to 360 points).
5. If you're creating a new style, type a new name in the Name window.
6. Click the Set button. The ruling style is updated in the selected cells.

To delete a ruling style, follow these steps:

1. Display the Custom Ruling and Shading dialog box.
2. Click the style you want to delete, then click the Edit Ruling Style button.
3. Click the Delete button. If the ruling style is used in the document, a warning is displayed.
4. Click the OK button to confirm the change. The ruling style is removed from the Custom Ruling and Shading dialog box and from table cells to which you applied the border.

Displaying and Removing Custom Ruling and Shading

In addition to customizing table cells, you can also display and remove formatting properties for selected table cells. Showing the current settings indicates whether cells are formatted by the table tag or the custom ruling and shading properties. If table tag properties aren't displaying correctly in a particular table, you can show the current settings through the Custom Ruling and Shading dialog box and reset the properties.

To display current table settings, follow these steps:

1. Select specific table cells to view their settings, or select the entire table to view all settings.

2. Display the Custom Ruling and Shading dialog box, then click the Show Current Settings button. The Current Selection's Settings dialog box is displayed.

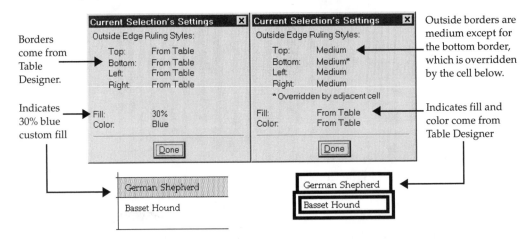

3. Click the Done button.

To restore table tag defaults, do the following:

1. Make sure the table cells are still selected, then display the Custom Ruling and Shading dialog box.

2. Check the Custom Cell Shading and Custom Cell Ruling check boxes.

3. In the Apply Ruling Style list, click From Table, then check all check boxes in the To Selection section.

4. In the Fill and Color drop-down lists under the Custom Cell Shading check box, click From Table.

5. Click the Apply button. The default borders and shading are restored.

Merging Table Cells

You merge, or *straddle*, table cells to create one cell across two or more rows or columns. By straddling cells, you can modify the table design to display content more clearly. For instance, the following tables list two dog groups—working dogs and hounds—and two breeds for each group. Unless you know your dog breeds, the two blank cells in the Group column of Table A are confusing. Should the blank cells contain content or remain empty?

Table B (on the right) divides the space more efficiently. In the first column, the first and second body cells—and then the third and fourth body cells—have been straddled. Now it's evident that two breeds belong to each dog group.

Note *Straddled table cells cannot break across pages. This can cause unsightly page breaks. When a straddled cell fills with text, the entire row moves to the next available page or text column. If you have this problem, it's easier to use a different table design.*

Table A

Group	Breeds
Working dogs	St. Bernard
	German Shepherd
Hounds	Basset Hound
	English Foxhound

Table B

Group	Breeds
Working dogs	St. Bernard
	German Shepherd
Hounds	Basset Hound
	English Foxhound

Displaying document borders make it easier to see straddled cells.

Before straddling table cells, consider the following:

■ You can straddle two or more heading rows, body rows, footing rows, and vertical cells; however, you cannot straddle across different types of rows—a body row with a footing row, for instance.

■ In a table with straddled cells, you can sort by column, but you cannot sort the rows. For example, the breeds in Table B cannot be alphabetized until you unstraddle the rows in the Group column. You can, however, alphabetize the columns, which would place the Breeds column before the Group column.

■ Display the document borders before straddling table cells (select View | Borders). It's easier to see which cells you've selected.

■ You cannot save straddled table cells in a table definition.

Note *Though you can select Edit | Undo to take back the previous action, save the file before you straddle table cells. If the results are not what you expected, you can select File | Revert to Saved to restore the file to its previous state.*

CREATING AND MANIPULATING TEXT

To straddle table cells, follow these steps:

1. Select the table cells you want to join.
2. Select Table | Straddle. The straddled table cells appear as one cell.

Group	Breeds
Working dogs (two breeds are provided as examples)	St. Bernard
	German Shepherd

To unstraddle table cells, follow these steps:

1. Select the merged table cells.
2. Select Table | Unstraddle. The merged cells appear in their original state. Notice that the cell expands to accommodate the text.

The first unstraddled cell expands to accommodate the text.

Group	Breeds
Working dogs (two breeds are provided as examples)	St. Bernard
	German Shepherd

Rotating Table Cells

You can rotate table cells to change the direction in which content is displayed. For example, to prevent text in the heading row from wrapping, you rotate the text vertically. The table cell expands vertically to display the line of text. The width of the rotated table cell, however, does not change. It is still determined by the column width.

FrameMaker rotates table cells in 90° increments. In the following Table A, the heading cells were rotated counterclockwise 90° to prevent text from wrapping.

Table A

Table 6: The Sweet Shack Inventory of Desserts

	Wareho use A	Wareho use B	Wareho use C
Strawberry Pie	54	29	3
Angel Food Cake	32	94	43
Chocolate Mousse	5	23	382

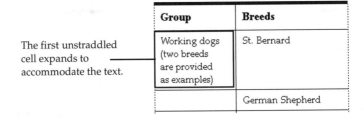

Table B

Table 6: The Sweet Shack Inventory of Desserts

	Warehouse A	Warehouse B	Warehouse C
Strawberry Pie	54	29	3
Angel Food Cake	32	94	43
Chocolate Mousse	5	23	382

To rotate a table cell, follow these steps:

1. Select the cell or cells you want to rotate.

2. Select Graphics | Rotate. The Rotate Table Cells dialog box is displayed.

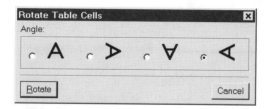

3. Click one of the radio buttons to indicate the direction you want to rotate the cell. To rotate text counterclockwise 90°, as shown in the previous table, click the last radio button.

4. Click the Rotate button. The text appears in the new orientation. If you make a mistake, you can select Edit | Undo.

Note   *You can rotate only table cells this way; tables themselves are reoriented by applying a rotated master page. For details, see Chapter 11, "Understanding Master Pages."*

Sorting Table Data

FrameMaker can sort table data in a number of ways:

- **By row or column.** Sorted vertically (by row) or horizontally (by column). When sorting by row, you can sort specific rows or all rows in the table.

- **In ascending or descending alphanumeric order.** Sorted from A to Z and 1 to 9 (ascending), or Z to A and 9 to 1 (descending).

- **Considering case sensitivity.** If capitalization is considered, *snake* is sorted before *Snake*.

- **Second- and third-level sorting.** After sorting the table by the initial criteria, FrameMaker performs the second and third sorts. For example, FrameMaker can sort a table of university departments and courses in which departments are sorted first and then each course within the department is sorted.

Caution   *You cannot undo a table sort, so save the file before you begin. You can select File | Revert to Saved to restore the original file.*

To sort a table, follow these steps:

1. Click in the table you want to sort.

2. To sort only part of the table, select those rows. If you do not select anything in the table, the entire table is sorted.

3. Select Table | Sort. The Sort Table dialog box is displayed.

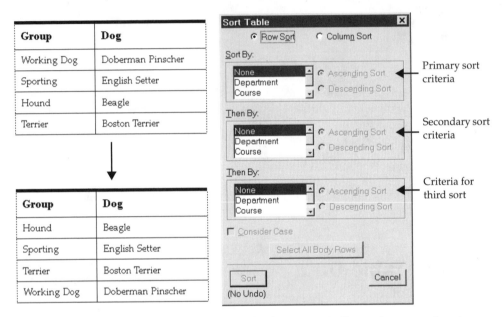

4. Click the Row Sort or Column Sort radio button to indicate the type of sort you want.

5. In the Sort By window, click the appropriate column or row you want to use to sort by.

   ■ To rearrange data by rows, specify the column to be sorted. In the preceding table, FrameMaker alphabetized the table rows by the Group column.

   ■ For a column sort, specify a row to sort on. If row one is empty, for example, specify row two.

6. Indicate whether the sort should be in ascending or descending order by clicking the appropriate radio button.

7. *(optional)* For secondary and tertiary sorting, change settings in the Then By sections. In the following table, rows in the first column were sorted first, followed by rows in the second column, then rows in the third column. For the secondary sort, courses within each department are alphabetized. For the tertiary sort, course numbers in the third row were alphabetized within each department.

If you click the None setting for the primary sort, you cannot change the secondary and tertiary sort options.

Table A

Department	Course	Number
Art History	Rothko	GT4901-F
Art History	Rothko	DS2031-S
English	Film Noir 101	AT8032-E
English	French Poetry	Z87322-N

For the secondary sort, courses within each department were sorted.

Table B

Department	Course	Number
Art History	Rothko	DS2031-S
Art History	Rothko	GT4901-F
English	Film Noir 101	AT8032-E
English	French Poetry	Z87322-N

For the tertiary sort, course numbers for the identical Rothko courses were sorted.

8. To consider the capitalization of words during the sort, check the Consider Case check box.

9. *(optional)* If you selected specific rows to sort and change your mind, click the Select All Body Rows button to highlight all rows in the table. This option is grayed out if you clicked in one cell instead of selecting rows.

10. Click the Sort button. The table data is rearranged to your specifications.

Deleting Table Tags

You can delete table tags in the Table Designer. Existing tables, however, are still formatted by the deleted tags. This is considered an override—the tables aren't actually tagged and they can't be updated. Before deleting a table tag, you can assign a different tag to the tables globally, just as you can with paragraph and character tags. "Reassigning a Character Tag Globally" on page 153 describes the process.

If you do find a table still formatted by a deleted tag, you can globally "rename" the deleted tag. This applies the new table tag where the deleted tag is applied in your document. "Renaming Character Tags" on page 151 describes the process.

To delete a table tag, follow these steps:

1. Display the Table Designer.

2. Click the Commands button, then select Delete Format from the pop-up menu. The Delete Formats from Catalog dialog box is displayed.

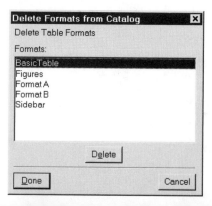

3. Click the tag you want to delete, then click the Delete button. To delete all table tags quickly, press and hold ALT-E (Windows).

4. Click the Done button. The tags are removed from the table catalog. If you click in a table still formatted by a deleted tag, the tag name is displayed in the Table Tag field but not in the drop-down list.

Creating Tables from Text

Instead of inserting an empty table and typing text into the cells, you can convert imported text files or existing text to tables. The pieces of text must be separated by one of the following:

- Tabs
- Two or more spaces
- Commas or another specific character
- Paragraphs

The following illustration shows text separated by all four methods and the table created by converting the data. The converted data is displayed identically despite the differences in the original structure.

After you convert text to a table, you can convert it back to paragraph format. This option lets you undo a table conversion or format text to import into other applications. See "Converting a Table to Text" on page 186 for details.

Caution   *Table conversion can be tricky, so be sure to save your file or create a backup copy before the table conversion. Though you can undo any mess you might create, it's safer not to rely on FrameMaker's single undo feature.*

Tabs	Spaces	Commas	Paragraphs
Fruit Color¶	Fruit Color¶	Fruit,Color¶	Fruit¶
Pear Green¶	Pear Green¶	Pear,Green¶	Color¶
Apple Red¶	Apple Red¶	Apple,Red¶	Pear¶
Pomegranate Purple¶	Pomegranate Purple¶	Pomegranate,Purple¶	Green¶
Banana Yellow¶	Banana Yellow¶	Banana,Yellow¶	Apple¶
			Red¶
			Pomegranate¶
			Purple¶
			Banana¶
			Yellow§

Fruit	Color
Pear	Green
Apple	Red
Pomegranate	Purple
Banana	Yellow

To create a table from text, follow these steps:

1. Set up the text using one of the four methods.

2. Select the text, then select Table | Convert to Table. The Convert to Table dialog box is displayed.

In a structured document, you click an element tag in the Element Tag drop-down list.

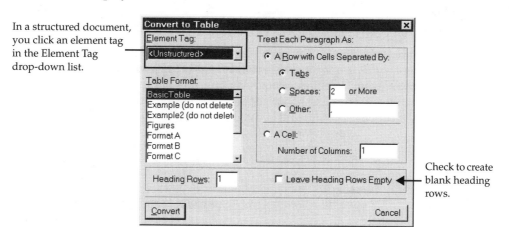

Check to create blank heading rows.

3. *(Structured table only)* To assign an element to the table, click a tag in the Element Tag drop-down list.

4. In the Table Format list, click a format for the table.

5. Click the radio button that describes how your text is currently formatted.

   ■ For text separated by tabs, click the Tabs radio button.

   ■ For text separated by spaces, click the Spaces radio button and type the number of spaces (not applicable when the document uses smart spaces). See Chapter 4, "Word-Processing Features."

   ■ If another character (such as a comma) separates the text, click the Other radio button and type the character.

   ■ If the text is in paragraphs, click the A Cell radio button and type the number of columns you want in the table.

6. Define the heading row.

   ■ To type the column headings after the table is created, check the Leave Heading Rows Empty check box and type the number of heading rows you want in the Heading Rows field.

   ■ To convert existing text to column headings, type the number of heading rows and clear the check box.

   ■ To create a table with no heading, type **0** in the Heading Rows field. You can add a heading row later if you change your mind. See "Customizing Tables Outside the Table Designer" on page 170 for details.

CREATING AND
MANIPULATING TEXT

7. Click the Convert button. The text is formatted with the selected table tag. Converting data takes practice, so don't worry if your table doesn't convert correctly the first time. Undo your changes, or open the duplicate file you created and verify the text formatting.

Converting a Table to Text

When you convert a table to text, the table content (including the title) is converted to separate paragraphs. The original paragraph tags are still applied to each paragraph. To convert a table to text, you specify conversion by row or column. Tables that read across must be converted by rows to display correctly in paragraph format. Tables that read down must be converted by columns. The following table was converted using both methods.

Dog	Group
English Setter	Sporting
Beagle	Hound
Boston Terrier	Terrier

Converted by rows

Dog
Group
English Setter
Sporting
Beagle
Hound
Boston Terrier
Terrier

Converted by columns

Dog
English Setter
Beagle
Boston Terrier
Group
Sporting
Hound
Terrier

To convert a table to text, follow these steps:

1. Select the table, then select Table | Convert to Paragraphs. The Convert to Paragraphs dialog box is displayed.

2. Do one of the following:
   - ■ To convert text horizontally, click the Row by Row radio button.
   - ■ To convert text vertically, click the Column by Column radio button.
3. Click the Convert button. The table appears in the selected format. If necessary, you can undo the conversion by selecting Edit | Undo.

Reformatting Word Tables

Converting Microsoft Word tables to FrameMaker can be tedious. When you open a Word document, FrameMaker assigns the table tag called Format A to all tables in the document. Because the table retains its original Word formatting, table tag properties such as border ruling are not displayed correctly.

In addition, Word tables lack typical FrameMaker table components. For example, the repeating table rows in Word don't convert into FrameMaker heading rows.

You'll need to clean up imported Word tables by doing the following:

- **Adding a heading row.** Heading rows in a Word document convert to body rows. You need to add a heading row to the table, copy or type the column headings into the heading row, and delete the former Word heading row.

- **Adding a table title.** In Word tables, the table title is a standard paragraph above the table; it isn't part of the table format. If your Word table has a title, you'll need to copy and paste the title above the converted table into the table title paragraph. If necessary, remove the title from the current table or assign a table tag that doesn't include a title.

- **Removing border and shading.** The Word table colors and ruling are converted in FrameMaker. After you convert the table, the ruling and shading properties must be reset to their defaults.

- **Assigning paragraph tags.** FrameMaker assigns paragraph tags from the Format A table tag to the converted Word table. If the paragraph tags contain overrides or don't exist in the document, you need to reapply the paragraph tags.

A third-party FrameMaker plug-in called Table Cleaner automates these functions. The program adds heading rows to tables and automates many other functions, such as applying paragraph tags and removing custom ruling and shading. For details, see Appendix A, "Resources."

FrameMaker may choke if you try to convert a document with table footnotes. An error dialog box displays the message "The filter encountered an error and could not complete the conversion." To prevent this problem, type the table footnote as regular text below the Word table and hard-code the footnote number in the table cell. You can create a real table footnote in the FrameMaker table after conversion.

Creating Structured Tables

In a structured document, elements are defined for each piece of the table—the heading row cells, body cells, table title, and so on. When you insert a table, there is an element inserted for each table component defined by the table tag (heading row, body row, and footing row). The elements format the table according to rules in the EDD.

Using the structure view can make some table operations easier. For example, you can drag and drop rows and cells (but not columns) in the structure view to move them. The table in the following illustration has two rows (indicated by the TableRow element) and three columns (formatted by the TableCell element). To move a row, select the TableRow element bubble and drag the row above or below another TableRow element. When you move the elements to a valid location, a check mark is displayed in the TableRow element bubble, and an arrow points to the valid location.

Title	Publisher	ISBN
FrameMaker 7: The Complete Reference	McGraw-Hill/Osborne	0072223618
Technical Writing 101	Scriptorium Press	0970473303

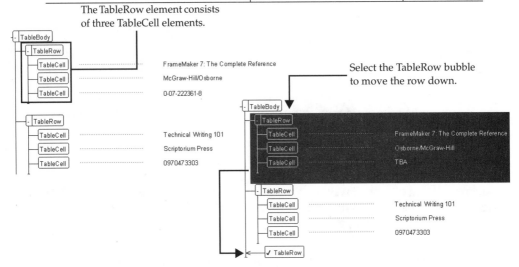

For more information on working with structured documents, see Chapter 28, "Working with Structured Documents."

Handy Table Tags

Most FrameMaker documents include table tags with basic features such as heading rows and cell ruling. You can, however, use tables for other reasons, such as for displaying lists of interface buttons and labels, creating a warning paragraph with the graphic displayed, and more.

- **List of icons.** Insert a two-column borderless table with narrow cell margins. You apply paragraph tags and save them in the table tag. After inserting the table in your document, you can import the icons in the first column and type the icon names in the other column (as shown on the right).

   Text Frame

   Rectangle

- **Warning paragraph.** Create a two-column, one-row table with the graphic inserted in the left column, and the warning paragraph tag applied to the right column. Add the warning graphic on the Reference page in a graphic frame named something like *Warning icon*. Create a 2-point font paragraph tag and specify *Warning icon* as the Frame Above Paragraph drop-down list. See "Placing Graphics Above and Below the Paragraph" on page 322 for details.

- **Figure table.** Insert an invisible one-cell table into which you import screen shots and graphics. Apply a figure caption paragraph tag to the table title section. Use this table to keep a floating graphic with the caption (otherwise, the graphic floats away from the graphic, which is a bad thing).

- **Shaded sidebar.** Create the two-column, one-row table used for this sidebar. For the borders, set the first column ruling to Medium and the other columns to None. Set the outside ruling to Thin. For the shading, specify a 30 percent black fill for the first column.

Chapter 8

Cross-References

FrameMaker's cross-references let you refer readers to other parts of a document. Often, cross-references start with "see" or "refer to"; for example:

```
see page 217
refer to "All About Chocolate" on page 82
```

You could type these references, but setting them up with cross-references lets FrameMaker update the page numbers and referenced text for you automatically. This is much more efficient than checking all the references manually after the pagination is finally set for your document.

Another major advantage to using cross-references is that they become live hyperlinks when you convert the FrameMaker file to PDF, HTML, or other online formats. They are also live links in view-only FrameMaker documents.

When you set up a cross-reference, you create a pointer from the cross-reference to the target location (Figure 8-1). FrameMaker calls this the "source"—the place where the information is coming from.

Once you insert a cross-reference, the text is formatted as part of the current paragraph. Several default cross-references formats are provided, and you can create additional ones as necessary.

Cross-references look like the surrounding text, but they are treated differently in some cases:

- **You cannot edit cross-references as part of the text.** You can't even click inside the cross-reference text. When you click on text that's part of a cross-reference, FrameMaker selects the entire cross-reference. To change it, you must edit the cross-reference inside the Cross-Reference dialog box. This feature is very useful when you want to verify that a page reference is actually a cross-reference. Just click on it and see whether the entire reference is selected. If you can position the cursor in the text, then it's regular text. If the reference is selected as a block, then it's a cross-reference.

A real cross-reference is selected as a single block.

"How to consume chocolate truffles" on page 88

Regular text

"How to consume chocolate truffles" on page 88

- **When searching for text, cross-references are ignored.** If, for example, you search for the word "page," none of the occurrences inside cross-references will match. The Find/Change dialog box does, however, give you the option of searching for cross-references, unresolved cross-references, or cross-references that use a specific format.

- **You can use cross-references as hyperlinks inside a regular FrameMaker document.** On Windows, CTRL-ALT-click on the cross-reference, and it will take you to the cross-reference's source. On the Mac platform, use COMMAND-OPTION-click; on UNIX, it's CTRL-right-click.

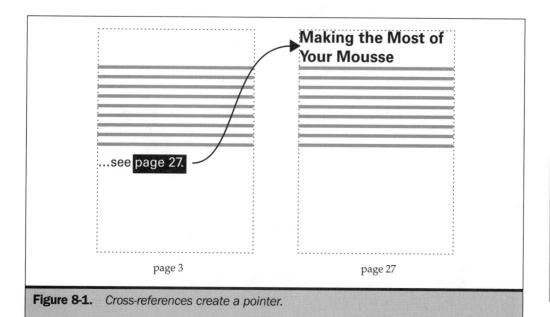

Figure 8-1.   *Cross-references create a pointer.*

By default, cross-references are updated when you update a book file, open a file, save, or print. They are not, however, updated immediately when the file changes. For example, if you create a cross-reference to an item on page 17, then rearrange your file so that the referenced information moves to page 23, FrameMaker does *not* immediately update the reference to page 17. When you perform an update, however, the page number changes.

How Cross-References Really Work

When you create a cross-reference, FrameMaker inserts a marker (or an ID attribute in structured FrameMaker) at the destination. The cross-reference itself points to the unique identifier in the destination paragraph or element.

Inserting Cross-References

When you insert a cross-reference, you must define the link's destination and specify the formatting. In unstructured FrameMaker, paragraph-based cross-references are the most common; another alternative is spot cross-references. In structured FrameMaker, you can also link to elements or IDs.

Creating Paragraph-Based Cross-References

To create a paragraph-based cross-reference, follow these steps:

1. Open the file that contains the target paragraph. (Not necessary if you're creating a cross-reference within a single file.)

2. Locate the target paragraph (the paragraph you want to point to). Make a note of its paragraph tag and what file it's in.

3. Position your cursor where you want to insert the cross-reference.

4. Select Special | Cross-Reference. The Cross-Reference dialog box is displayed (Figure 8-2).

5. In the Document drop-down list, click the file that you are linking to. Notice that only currently open files are available in this list. If your file isn't open, click the Cancel button to exit this dialog box, open the file, and start over.

6. Select the Source Type button, then select Paragraphs from the pop-up menu.

7. In the Paragraph Tags list, click the paragraph tag you want. The right side of the dialog box displays the first few words of each occurrence of that paragraph tag.

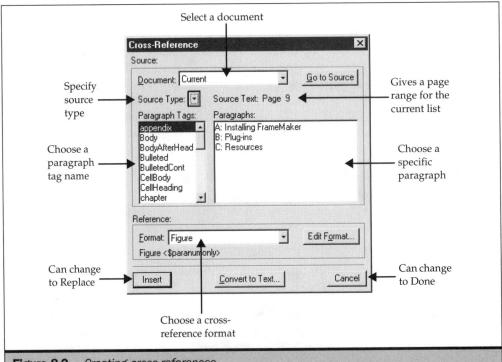

Figure 8-2. *Creating cross-references*

8. In the Paragraphs list, select the specific paragraph you want. To help you locate the correct paragraph, an approximate page range for the items is displayed above the list.

9. In the Format drop-down list, click a cross-reference format. If the format you want isn't available, you can create a new one. See "Setting Up Cross-Reference Formats" on page 198.

10. Click the Insert button to insert the cross-reference.

 If you selected some text or are modifying an existing cross-reference, you see a Replace button instead of an Insert button.

After inserting a cross-reference, you can double-click it to display the Cross-Reference dialog box and make changes (such as choosing a different format).

Creating Spot Cross-References

Spot cross-references let you point to a particular line in a paragraph. Paragraph references always point to the beginning of the paragraph, and when the paragraph is lengthy, the information you're referencing might end up on a different page. To ensure that you point to the exact location where the information occurs, you can use a spot cross-reference. You create a marker and link the cross-reference to that marker.

To create a spot cross-reference, follow these steps:

1. Locate the spot that you want to link to and position your cursor there.

2. Select Special | Marker. The Marker dialog box is displayed.

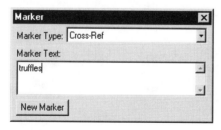

3. In the Marker Type drop-down list, click Cross-Ref.

4. In the Marker Text field, type a unique label for this cross-reference. The label should be short and descriptive.

5. Click the New Marker button to save your changes. If you have text symbols turned on (View | Text Symbols), you will see a marker symbol.

6. Leave the destination document open and go to the document in which you want to create the cross-reference.

7. Position your cursor where you want to insert the reference.

8. Select Special | Cross-Reference. The Cross-Reference dialog box is displayed (Figure 8-2 on page 194).

9. In the Document drop-down list, click the file that you are linking to.

10. In the Source Type pop-up menu, click Cross-Reference Markers.

11. In the Cross-Reference Markers list, select the marker you created.

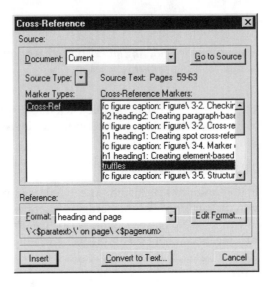

Whenever you create a paragraph-based cross-reference, FrameMaker automatically inserts Cross-Ref markers. You will see these in the cross-reference marker list. However, those markers usually include the paragraph tag name and the text of the paragraph; yours is shorter.

12. In the Format drop-down list, click a cross-reference format.

For spot cross-references, you usually want a page-based reference instead of pulling in the entire paragraph.

13. Click the Insert button to insert the cross-reference.

Creating Cross-References in Structured Documents

In structured documents, both paragraph and spot cross-references will work correctly. But these two options insert unstructured information into the document. To create a structured cross-reference, you must set up a reference to an element or to an element attribute. Only structured cross-references will convert correctly when you export to SGML or XML.

Note	*If you are using Format Change Lists (instead of paragraph tags) to apply paragraph formatting in structured documents, using paragraph cross-references will be tedious because almost all of your paragraphs will be listed under a single paragraph tag (most likely, Body).*

Element cross-references are very similar to paragraph references. Instead of specifying a paragraph tag and a specific paragraph, you specify an element and a specific instance of that element.

To create an element cross-reference, follow the instructions for paragraph-based cross-references (page 194). Instead of selecting paragraphs, select one of the following options from the Source Type pop-up menu:

- **Elements Listed in Order:** If you list elements in order, the right side of the Cross-Reference dialog box displays the first few words of each element. Within each element name, the items are listed in the order they occur in the document.

- **Elements Sorted by ID:** In structured FrameMaker, some elements have an associated ID attribute. The ID attribute identifies that element uniquely and is for linking and identifying the elements when you convert to SGML or XML. If you sort elements by ID, the right side of the Cross-Reference dialog box displays the ID for the element, followed by the first few words of the element. This lets you more easily locate elements by their ID.

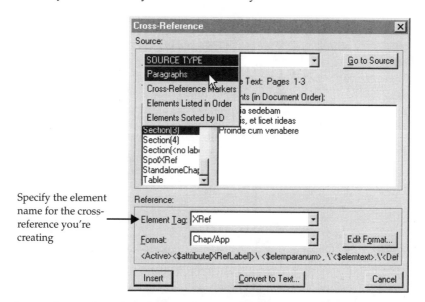

Specify the element
name for the cross-
reference you're
creating

You choose from a list of elements on the left and a list of specific element instances on the right. In structured FrameMaker, you must also specify the element tag you want to use for the cross-reference.

Note   *In the Element Tag drop-down list, only elements that are defined as cross-reference elements in the current element definition document (EDD) are listed. See Chapter 29, "Understanding the Element Definition Document," for more information about how elements are defined.*

You can see the cross-reference's components in the structure view. They are as follows:

- **ID attribute:** FrameMaker assigns an ID attribute with a unique value to the target of the cross-reference (the destination element).

- **XRef element:** The cross-reference itself has an element. By default, this element is named XRef, but your structured documents may have several different elements available for cross-references.

- **IDRef attribute:** The cross-reference element has an IDRef attribute with a unique value. This value matches the ID attribute of the target.

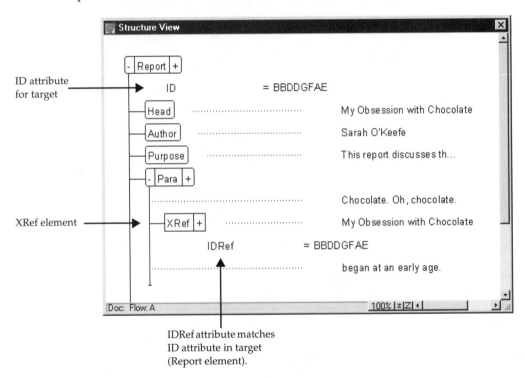

Setting Up Cross-Reference Formats

FrameMaker provides some default cross-reference formats, but you can create your own new formats. To do so, you assemble a combination of text, character tags, and building blocks to create a cross-reference format. *Building blocks* are placeholders; they change for each cross-reference. For example, a cross-reference definition might read:

```
see page <$pagenum>
```

<$pagenum> is a building block; it is replaced with the page number of the target paragraph. The rest of the definition is text that doesn't change.

To create a new cross-reference format, follow these steps:

1. Select Special | Cross-Reference. The Cross-Reference dialog box is displayed (Figure 8-2 on page 194).

2. Click the Edit Format button. The Edit Cross-Reference Format dialog box is displayed (Figure 8-3).

3. You can change an existing format or create a new one:

   ■ To change an existing format, click that format in the Formats list.

   ■ To create a new format, type the name for the new format in the Name field. The name is what you see when you're selecting a format for a new cross-reference (in the Format drop-down list; see Figure 8-2 on page 194), so the name should be descriptive. If you're creating a new Chapter cross-reference format, you might call it:

   ```
   Chapter "title"
   ```

4. In the Definition field, modify the existing definition as needed or create a new definition.

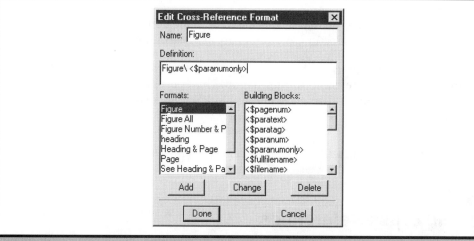

Figure 8-3. *Modifying cross-reference formats*

Cross-references usually contain text (such as the word "page") and building blocks. You can select the building blocks from the list or type them in. You can also apply character formatting by inserting character tags, which are available at the bottom of the building block list. Except for character tags, all building blocks start with a dollar sign ($).

Refer to Table 8-1 on page 202 for a list of available building blocks. For the new Chapter cross-reference, the definition could look like this:

```
Chapter\ <$chapnum>, \'<$paratext>\'
```

A backslash followed by a space creates a nonbreaking space. A backslash followed by a backtick creates an opening curly quote. A backslash followed by a regular straight quote creates a closing curly quote. On the Macintosh, you can use regular keyboard shortcuts to create those special characters, but on Windows and UNIX, you need to use the characters shown in the preceding example.

5. To create a new format, click the Add button. To modify an existing format, click the Change button.

If you select the Change button instead of Add, the original format is replaced with the one you just created. This means you renamed and redefined the cross-reference format you started with.

6. Click the Done button to return to the Cross-Reference dialog box. If the format you modified is already in use in your document, FrameMaker prompts you to update the existing cross-references. Click the OK button to update your cross-references.

7. In the Cross-Reference dialog box, click the Done button to close the dialog box and return to your document. (It appears in place of the Cancel button.)

Occasionally, you'll notice that the building block appears in your text instead of being replacing with the referenced information. This is usually caused by a typo in your definition; for example, using a building block with a missing bracket:

```
$paratext>
```

To correct the problem, add the opening bracket in the format's definition. The building block should then be replaced with the correct information.

Formatting Cross-References

Inside the cross-reference definition, you can use character tags to create special formatting. By default, the cross-reference will match the format of the surrounding paragraph.

One very common requirement is to create a cross-reference that is blue and underlined for hyperlinks. When you convert the FrameMaker file to PDF, readers of the PDF file can easily see where the links occur.

To create a blue, underlined cross-reference, follow these steps:

1. Create a character tag called Hyperlink that applies blue and an underline. (For information on creating character tags, see page 149.)

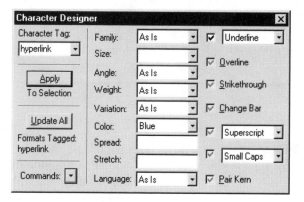

2. Select Special | Cross-Reference. The Cross-Reference dialog box is displayed (Figure 8-2 on page 194).

3. Click the Edit Format button. The Edit Cross-Reference Format dialog box is displayed (Figure 8-3 on page 199).

4. In the Name field, type a name for the cross-reference format; for example:

   `HeadingPDF`

5. In the Definition field, insert the definition for the cross-reference format; for example:

   `<Hyperlink><$paratext><Default Para Font>`

6. Click the Add button to add the new format.

7. Click the Done button.

8. In the Cross-Reference dialog box, click the Done button. (It appears in place of the Cancel button.)

Cross-Reference Building Blocks

FrameMaker provides several building blocks for creating cross-reference formats. A very basic cross-reference looks like this:

`<$paratext> on page <$pagenum>`

It tells FrameMaker to insert the contents of the destination paragraph (<$paratext>) followed by a space, the words "on page," and another space. Then, it inserts the page number of the destination paragraph. The result would look something like this:

```
Chocolate Mousse Pie on page 27
```

Table 8-1 lists the available building blocks. They are grouped by function; all of the building blocks that display paragraph or element text are in one group, all building blocks that display paragraph numbers are in another group, and so on.

Building Block	Description
Text	
`<$paratext>`	Displays the text of the linked paragraph.
`<$paratext[paratag]>`	Works from the linked paragraph toward the beginning of the document to locate a paragraph that uses the specified paragraph tag. Displays the text of that paragraph. If no paragraph in the document matches, nothing is displayed.

`<$paratext[tag1,tag2,`
`tag3]>`
(not shown in the dialog box)
	Displays the first instance of tag1, tag2, or tag3, whichever occurs first. Useful when you're not sure where a building block might be used. For example:
	
	`<$paranumonly[ChapterTitle,`
	`AppendixTitle]>`

`<$paratext[+,paratag]>` *(not shown in the dialog box)*	Searches for the last paragraph on the page instead of the first. (This building block is also available in running header/footer variables, where it's often used for dictionary or directory headers.)
`<$elemtext>`	Inserts the first paragraph of the source element, including any prefixes or suffixes. The autonumber is not included.
`<$elemtext[elemtag]>`	Works from the linked element toward the beginning of the document to locate an element that uses the specified element tag. Displays the first paragraph of that element. If no element in the document matches, nothing is displayed.

Table 8-1. *Cross-Reference Building Blocks Grouped by Function—Not in FrameMaker Order*

Building Block	Description
`<$elemtextonly>`	Inserts the first paragraph of the source element, without any prefixes or suffixes. (Prefixes or suffixes of child elements *are* included.) The autonumber is not included.
`<$elemtextonly [elemtag] >`	Works from the linked element toward the beginning of the document to locate an element that uses the specified element tag. Displays the first paragraph of that element, without any prefixes or suffixes. If no element in the document matches, nothing is displayed.
Paragraph number	
`<$paranum>`	Displays the paragraph number of the linked paragraph.
`<$paranum[paratag] >`	Works from the linked paragraph toward the beginning of the document to locate a paragraph that uses the specified paragraph tag. Displays the paragraph number of that paragraph. If no paragraph in the document matches, nothing is displayed.
`<$paranumonly>`	Displays the numeric portion of the linked paragraph's paragraph number. For example, if the paragraph number is "Figure 17," this building block displays "17." Chapter and volume numbers are considered numeric. The <$paranumonly> building block includes everything from the first building block to the last in the autonumber definition, including any embedded text. If the autonumber definition is Figure <$chapnum>\+<n+>, this building block returns 1-4 (or whatever the current figure number is). Notice that the nonbreaking hyphen between the numbers is included.

Table 8-1. *Cross-Reference Building Blocks Grouped by Function—Not in FrameMaker Order (Continued)*

Building Block	Description
`<$paranumonly[paratag]>`	Works from the linked paragraph toward the beginning of the document to locate a paragraph that uses the specified paragraph tag. Displays the numeric portion of that paragraph's number. If no paragraph in the document matches, nothing is displayed.
`<$elemparanum>`	Displays the autonumber of the linked element.
`<$elemparanum[elemtag]>`	Works from the linked element toward the beginning of the document to locate an element that uses the specified element tag. Displays the text of that element. If no element in the document matches, nothing is displayed.
`<$elemparanumonly>`	Displays the numeric portion of the linked element's paragraph number.
`<$elemparanumonly [elemtag]>`	Works from the linked element toward the beginning of the document to locate an element that uses the specified element tag. Displays the numeric portion of that element's paragraph number. If no element in the document matches, nothing is displayed.
Page numbers	
`<$pagenum>`	Displays the page number of the linked paragraph.
`<$pagenum[paratag]>`	Works from the linked paragraph toward the beginning of the document to locate a paragraph that uses the specified paragraph tag. Displays the page number of that paragraph. If no paragraph in the document matches, nothing is displayed.
`<$elempagenum>`	Displays the page number of the linked element.
`<$elempagenum[elemtag]>`	Displays the page number on which the specified element occurs.

Table 8-1.   *Cross-Reference Building Blocks Grouped by Function— Not in FrameMaker Order (Continued)*

Building Block	Description
`<$chapnum>`	Displays the current chapter number.
`<$volnum>`	Displays the current volume number.
Tag names	
`<$paratag>`	Displays the name of the linked paragraph tag.
`<$elemtag>`	Displays the name of the linked element.
`<$elemtag[elemtag]>`	Displays the name of the specified element tag.
Other	
`<$filename>`	Displays the file name of the linked file.
`<$fullfilename>`	Displays the path and file name of the linked file.
`<$attribute[attrname]>`	Displays the value of the specified attribute for the linked element.
`<character_tag>`	Applies the specified character tag to the items that follow in the cross-reference definition. Note that this building block does not begin with a dollar sign ($).
`<Default Para Font>` or `</>`	Removes any character formatting and returns to the regular paragraph formatting of the parent paragraph.

Table 8-1. *Cross-Reference Building Blocks Grouped by Function— Not in FrameMaker Order (Continued)*

Cross-Reference Examples

Table 8-2 shows cross-reference formats you might need to create. The exact code depends on your paragraph tag, character tag, and element names; the names are italicized in the table.

Deleting Cross-Reference Formats

FrameMaker gives you the ability to delete cross-reference formats from your document. When you do this, any cross-references that use the format are converted to text (see page 212 for details).

To delete a cross-reference format, follow these steps:

1. Select Special | Cross-Reference. The Cross-Reference dialog box is displayed (Figure 8-2 on page 194).
2. Click the Edit Format button. The Edit Cross-Reference Format dialog box is displayed (Figure 8-3 on page 199).

Result	Definition
see page 3-17	`see page\ <$chapnum>\+<$pagenum>`
see Volume II, Chapter 7	`see Volume\ <$volnum>,` `Chapter\ <$chapnum>`
Chapter 7, "The Glories of Chocolate"	`Chapter\ <$chapnum>,` `\'<$paratext>\'`

see "Tempering chocolate" in Chapter 7, "The Glories of Chocolate"	`see \'<$paratext>\' in`
	`Chapter\ <$chapnum>,`
	`\'<$paratext[ChapterTitle]>\'`

see *Tempering chocolate* in Chapter 7, "The Glories of Chocolate"	`see <Emphasis>\'<$paratext>\'`
	`<Default Para Font> in`
	`Chapter\ <$chapnum>,`
	`\'<$paratext[ChapterTitle]>\'`

see "Baking chocolate" in the "Types of chocolate" section	`see \'<$elemtext>\' in the`
	`\'<$elemtext[SectionHead]>`
	`section\'`

The file name is **E:/scriptorium/data/ projects/chocolate.fm**.	`The file name is` `<Bold><$fullfilename></>.`

Table 8-2. *Cross-Reference Sample Definitions*

3. In the list on the left, click the format you want to delete.

4. Click the Delete button.

Note *You can delete multiple cross-reference formats by clicking each format in turn and clicking the Delete button (you cannot SHIFT-click to select several at once).*

5. Click the Done button. If the cross-reference format is used in the document, FrameMaker prompts you to confirm that you want to convert the cross-references to text. You are prompted separately for each cross-reference format that's in use. Click the OK button to delete the cross-reference format and convert it to text; click the Cancel button to retain the cross-references that use the specified format.

6. In the Cross-Reference dialog box, click the Done button to close the dialog box. (It appears in place of the Cancel button.)

Updating Cross-References

FrameMaker generally does a good job of updating cross-references and keeping them in sync. Occasionally, you may need to force an update. This section describes when updates occur and how to manage them.

By default, FrameMaker updates your cross-references when any of the following actions occur:

- Opening a file
- Saving a file
- Printing a file
- Updating a book file (cross-references are updated for all files in the book)

If you need to update a single cross-reference, the fastest way to do it is to double-click the reference to display the Cross-Reference dialog box, then click the Replace button. This works well for one or two references, but if you need to update all the references in a document (or book), the techniques described in this section are more efficient.

Automatic Updating Problems

When FrameMaker performs an automatic update, it checks each cross-reference to ensure that the paragraph, marker, element, or ID specified in the cross-reference still exists. For references within a single file, this works perfectly. You can run into problems, though, when the reference is one file to another. To verify the cross-reference's destination, FrameMaker opens the target file and looks for the target item. If FrameMaker cannot open the target file for some reason, the resolve process fails. The most common cause of this failure is that the target file uses fonts that are not installed on your system. The "missing fonts" message that's displayed when you open the file causes the cross-reference verification process to fail. FrameMaker reports that you have unresolved cross-references when in fact you merely have a cross-reference to a file that FrameMaker couldn't open. To prevent this problem, open all of the files that the current file points to, and see whether that removes the unresolved message.

Updating Cross-References in a Book

If you are working in a document that's part of a book, then whenever you update the book file, FrameMaker will update the cross-references for you. To update the book file, go to the book window, then click the Update Book icon at the bottom of the window.

This process is described in detail in "Updating the Book" on page 369.

Forcing a Cross-Reference Update

Occasionally, you'll want to force FrameMaker to perform a cross-reference update. To do this, follow these steps:

1. Select Edit | Update References. The Update References dialog box is displayed (Figure 8-4).
2. Check the All Cross-References check box, then click the Update button.

FrameMaker updates all of the cross-references in the current document.

Note   *The update works only if FrameMaker can open all of the target documents.*

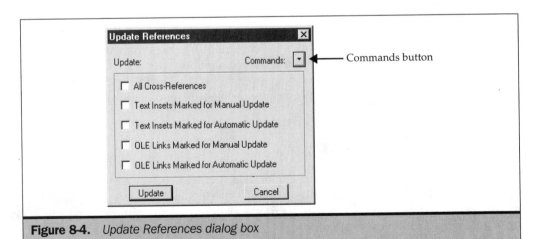

Figure 8-4.   *Update References dialog box*

Preventing Automatic Updates

In some cases, you may need to prevent FrameMaker from updating the cross-references automatically; for example, if your FrameMaker files are in a version control system and you've only checked out one file.

To prevent FrameMaker from trying to update your cross-references inside a file, follow these steps:

1. Select Edit | Update References. The Update References dialog box is displayed (Figure 8-4).

2. Click the Commands button and select Suppress Automatic Reference Updating from the pop-up menu. This displays the Suppress Automatic Reference Updating dialog box.

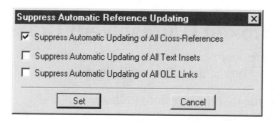

3. Check the Suppress Automatic Updating of All Cross-References check box.

4. Click the Set button.

5. In the Update References dialog box, click the Done button. (It appears in place of the Cancel button.)

You can perform the same action for an entire book by selecting Edit | Suppress Automatic Updating when the book is the active window.

To turn automatic updating back on, repeat this procedure and uncheck the check box.

Renaming Files Without Breaking Cross-References

If you rename a file from inside the book file, FrameMaker will update the cross-references (also text insets and hypertext links) to that file.

FrameMaker checks only the files in the current book. If the file you're renaming is used in another book, references in that book are not updated.

To rename a file in a book file, follow these steps:

1. *(optional)* Open all the files in the book by selecting SHIFT-File | Open All Files in Book. This ensures that the update will work even if you have missing fonts in some of the files.

2. In the book window, click on the file you want to rename.

3. Click the file name again to make it editable. Type in the new name for the file, then press ENTER.

4. FrameMaker notifies you that it is going to update cross-references, hypertext links, and other items within the book file. Click the OK button to continue.

FrameMaker makes the needed updates and changes the file name.

Correcting Broken (Unresolved) Cross-References

Cross-references can break or become *unresolved*. Most often, unresolved cross-references are caused by one of the following actions:

- Renaming the file that the reference points to
- Deleting the paragraph or element that the reference is linked to
- Linking to text insets (for details on text insets, see Chapter 25, "Creating Modules with Text Insets")
- Deleting the cross-reference marker at the target location

Unresolved cross-references are not flagged with any special formatting. When you open a FrameMaker file, cross-references are checked. If any are unresolved, an error message is displayed.

 If you suppress automatic updating, FrameMaker does not check for unresolved references when you open the file.

Cross-references are also updated when you update your book file. The book error report lists the unresolved cross-references. You can click each entry to go directly to that cross-reference so that you can fix it. (For details about the book error log, see "Troubleshooting Book Updates" on page 371.)

You can correct unresolved cross-references in two different ways:

- By changing the file that the reference points to
- By re-creating the cross-reference

You may see "bogus" unresolved cross-reference messages. To verify references, FrameMaker attempts to open the target file. If the file-opening process fails, you get an unresolved cross-reference error. To ensure that your unresolved cross-references are not because of a file-opening error, open the target file before opening the file in which the cross-reference occurs. If this approach eliminates the message, the cross-reference is in fact resolved. The most common cause of this problem is missing fonts in the target file (which causes the automatic open to fail).

Changing the Referenced File

If the cross-reference is broken because the file it's pointing to has been renamed or changed, FrameMaker provides you with a very useful way of retargeting the references to the new file name. This actually works for all of the references that are using the old file name.

To update the file name that references are pointing to, follow these steps:

1. Select Edit | Update References. The Update References dialog box is displayed (Figure 8-4 on page 208).
2. Click the Commands button, then select Update Unresolved Cross-References from the pop-up menu. The Update Unresolved Cross-References dialog box is displayed (Figure 8-5).

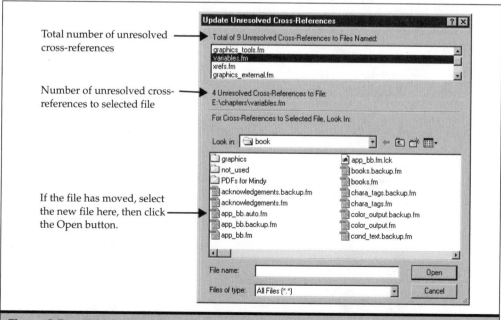

Figure 8-5. *Fixing unresolved cross-references*

At the top, this dialog box lists the total number of unresolved references in this file. Click on a file name in the list to see how many references to that file are unresolved.

3. For each renamed file, select the old name of the file at the top, then use the bottom half of the dialog box to locate the new file name. Click the file, then click the Open button.

The numbers at the top of the dialog box are updated.

4. When you are finished updating file locations, click the Cancel button to close the dialog box.

Re-Creating Broken Cross-References

If retargeting the new file name doesn't work (or if you didn't move or rename the file), you'll need to rebuild the cross-reference. Locate each unresolved cross-reference (use Edit | Find and select Unresolved Cross-References in the Find drop-down list), double-click it to display the Cross-Reference dialog box, and re-create the reference.

Converting Cross-References to Text

When you convert cross-references to text, FrameMaker eliminates all of the special linking functions and changes the reference into ordinary editable text.

Caution *If you change your mind about converting to text, you will have to re-create the cross-references. This action cannot be undone.*

Changing cross-references to text means that they are no longer live links and will not appear as such in any output. It destroys the link between the cross-reference and the targeted paragraph or element. *It is very rarely a good idea.* (You might consider it if for some reason you do *not* want live hyperlinks in your PDF files.)

If you need to convert some or all of your cross-references to text, follow these steps:

1. *(optional)* If you want to convert a single cross-reference to text, select it.

2. Select Special | Cross-Reference. The Cross-Reference dialog box is displayed (Figure 8-2 on page 194).

3. Select the Convert to Text button. The Convert Cross-References to Text dialog box is displayed.

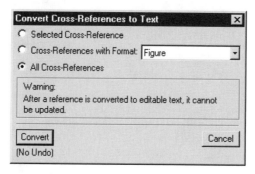

4. Specify which cross-references you want to convert:

- To convert just the selected cross-reference, click the Selected Cross-Reference radio button.

- To convert all cross-references of a specified format, click the Cross-References with Format radio button and, in the drop-down list, click the format you want to convert to text. All cross-references in the document that use the specified format will be converted to text.

- To convert all cross-references in the document, click the All Cross-References radio button.

Caution

Once you convert the cross-references to text, you cannot undo this action.

5. Click the Convert button to convert the specified cross-references to text. FrameMaker converts the specified formats to regular, editable text.

Chapter 9

Storing Content in Variables

Variables store system-generated information, frequently used words, and terms that often change. Instead of typing a term in your document, you insert a variable. By using a variable, you save time typing and don't have to remember the correct spelling or capitalization.

More importantly, variables make it easy to update your documents. If your company merges with another company and the name changes, you can change the Company Name variable in your template instead of searching for and replacing the name. You might also need to display your document's file name in the footer. By inserting the Filename variable, you won't need to type the file name or modify the footer when the file name changes. The variable is automatically updated.

The two types of variables are as follows:

- **System variables.** Display information updated by your computer. Many system variables relate to the time and date. The Current Date variable displays the month, date, and year. Other system variables apply specifically to the current file. For example, the Chapter Number variable displays a chapter number based on the location of the file in a book. As you add documents to a book file, the chapter number is updated in each file containing the variable. Though you cannot create or delete system variables, you can edit them.

- **User variables.** Provide more flexibility than system variables because you can create, edit, and delete them. A user variable can contain words that you use often, such as a book name, rough draft statement, and text for a watermark. You can also store terms that might change, such as a company or product name. Unlike system variables, which change values when you open, save, or page up and down in a document, user variables are static. You must edit a user variable definition yourself to change its value.

Variables consist of building blocks, character tags, and text. *Building blocks* (pieces of code that display a specific value) do much of the work. For example, the <$paratext> building block displays text from a specific paragraph, such as a section heading. If the section heading changes, the <$paratext> building block displays the updated text.

Character tags let you format the variable. This means you don't need to apply a character tag to the variable after you insert it in the document. For instance, you can include an italicized character tag in a book title variable, and the book title will be italicized when you insert it.

In structured documents, you can insert system variables with or without a variable element. If you use the variable element, formatting rules from the EDD are automatically applied to the variable text, and the number of valid variables may be limited. Without the variable element, you can insert system variables as you would in an unstructured document, and the paragraph tag will format the variable definition. There is no variable element for user variables, so they can be inserted in any text frame.

Inserting Variables

Variables are displayed in the Variable dialog box (Figure 9-1). System variables are at the top of the list (note that they're capitalized), and user variables are toward the end. The definition for a highlighted variable is displayed below the list of variables.

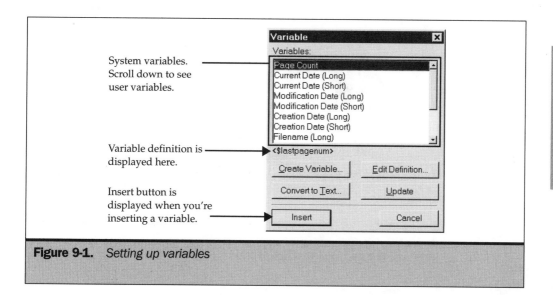

Figure 9-1. *Setting up variables*

Variables look like standard text on the page until you try to click in the text. Clicking highlights the entire variable. Because variable information is not actually part of the text, FrameMaker doesn't spell-check variables. If you misspell the variable definition, you can, however, correct the spelling in the variable, and each instance of the variable in your document is updated.

You can't edit the selected text
because it's a variable.

Be sure to press SHIFT while resizing the EPS, or you'll distort the graphic.

Be sure to press SHIFT while resizing the EPS, or you'll distort the graphic.

Regular text isn't highlighted.

Some system variables are available only on the master pages. For example, the twelve running header/footer variables display information such as chapter and section headings in the header or footer, so you insert them on the master pages. The Current

Page Number variable inserts the page number on the master page. These variables are not available when you display the Variable dialog box on a body page.

Running H/F variables are available only on master pages.

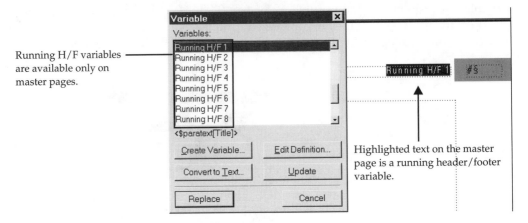

Highlighted text on the master page is a running header/footer variable.

FrameMaker provides three ways to insert a variable:

- Using the menu
- Using the right-click pop-up menu
- Using a keyboard shortcut

In the Variable dialog box, the Replace button is displayed if text or a variable is selected on the page (for example, if you double-clicked a variable to display the Variable dialog box). If no text or variable is selected, the Insert button is displayed instead.

Using the Menu

To insert a variable using the Special menu, follow these steps:

1. Position the cursor on the page.
2. Select Special | Variable. The Variable dialog box is displayed (Figure 9-1 on page 217).
3. Click the variable name and then click the Insert button.

Using the Right-Click Pop-Up Menu

You can use the pop-up menu that is displayed when you right-click (Windows) or CTRL-click (Mac) to insert a variable. To use the pop-up menu to insert a variable, follow these steps:

1. Position the cursor on the page.

2. Right-click (Windows) or CTRL-click (Mac) to display the pop-up menu, then select Variables.

3. Click the variable name, then click the Insert button.

Using a Keyboard Shortcut

To insert a variable using a keyboard shortcut, follow these steps:

1. Position the cursor on the page.

2. Press CTRL-0 (all platforms). The bottom-left status bar is highlighted.

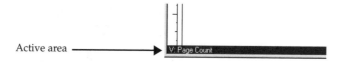

Active area ⎯⎯⎯⎯⎯⎯▶ V: Page Count

3. Display the variable you want by doing any of the following:

   ■ Use the arrow keys to scroll through the list of available variables.

   ■ Type a letter to jump to that section of the variables.

   ■ Type the first few letters of the variable name.

4. Press ENTER.

Note *Some of the keys on your computer may be specially programmed. If so, one or more keyboard shortcuts may not work as described. Consult your system documentation for assistance.*

Modifying System Variable Definitions

When you modify a system variable, a list of building blocks is displayed based on the function of the variable. For example, FrameMaker provides several building blocks that return the value of the current month, such as <$monthname> and <$monthnum>. The date building blocks are valid only in variables that display the date. If you type them in unrelated variables—the Filename variable, for example—an error is displayed.

System variables may not be available on all types of pages. Table 9-1 shows the locations in which system variables are valid.

To modify a system variable, follow these steps:

1. Do one of the following:

   ■ In your document, double-click the variable that you want to modify.

   ■ Select Special | Variable.

   The Variable dialog box is displayed (Figure 9-1 on page 217).

2. Click the variable you want to edit (if it's not already highlighted), then click the Edit Definition button. The Edit System Variable dialog box is displayed (Figure 9-2 on page 221).

Location	Available System Variables
Any text frame (body, master, or reference page)	
	Page Count
	Current Date, long or short
	Modification Date, long or short
	Creation Date, long or short
	Filename, long or short
	Volume Number
	Chapter Number
Table title, heading, and footing rows	
	Table Continuation
	Table Sheet
Master pages only, in text frames with no flow tag	
	Current Page #
	Running H/F 1, 2, 3, 4…12

Table 9-1. *Valid Locations for System Variables*

3. To add a building block or character style to the definition, click it in the Building Blocks list. You can also type building blocks, character tags, or text in the Definition field. If you use a character tag, include the <Default Para Font> character tag where the character formatting should end, as shown in the following example:

```
<Bold>Volume <$volnum>:<Default Para Font> Complete Classics
```

This variable definition displays the following formatting:

Volume IX: Complete Classics

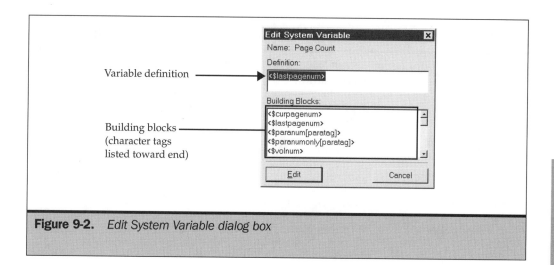

Variable definition

Building blocks
(character tags
listed toward end)

Figure 9-2.   *Edit System Variable dialog box*

4. Click the Edit button to save your changes, then click the Done button. The
    variable definition is modified, and the variable is updated where you've
    inserted it in the document.

Date and Time Variables

FrameMaker provides system variables that display the month, day, and year in long
and abbreviated formats. You can access the following time variables in any text frame:

- **Creation Date:** Displays the month, date, and year when you created the file,
  such as November 14, 2001 or 11/14/01.

- **Modification Date:** Displays the month, date, year, and time the document was
  last opened or saved, such as May 24, 2002 12:13 pm or 5/24/02. Updated when
  you open or save the file.

- **Current Date:** Displays the current month, date, and year, such as May 24, 2002
  or 5/24/02. Updated when you change the page magnification or display a
  different page.

The date variables consist of building blocks that display different aspects of the
date and time. You can change the building blocks in each variable, but you cannot
change the function of the variable. For example, you can add seconds to the
Modification Date variable by inserting the <$second> building block. However, you
cannot force the Modification Date variable to display the *creation* date because
FrameMaker predefines the function of system variables. Table 9-2 on page 222
describes the building blocks used in date variables.

Building Block	Description	Example
<$ampm>	Lowercase morning or evening abbreviation	am or pm
<$AMPM>	Uppercase morning or evening abbreviation	AM or PM
<$dayname>	Name of the day	Monday
<$shortdayname>	Abbreviated name of the day	Mon
<$daynum>	Number of the day	20
<$daynum01>	Number of the day with leading zero	09
<$hour>	Hour	1
<$hour01>	Hour with leading zero	01
<$hour24>	Hour in military format	13
<$minute>	Minute	5
<$minute00>	Minute with leading zero	05
<$monthname>	Name of the month	September
<$shortmonthname>	Abbreviated name of the month	Sept
<$monthnum>	Number of the month	9
<$second>	Seconds	8
<$second00>	Seconds with leading zero	08
<$shortyear>	Abbreviated year	30
<$year>	Year	2030

Table 9-2.   *Building Blocks for Date Variables*

Numerical Variables

The numerical system variables display page, volume, and chapter numbers that are automatically updated when you open or save the file. You can insert a numerical variable in any text frame with the exception of the Current Page Number variable, which is available only on master pages. The following are numerical variables:

- **Current Page Number:** Displays the number of the current page.
- **Page Count:** Displays the number of the last page in the file.
- **Volume Number:** Displays the file's volume number.
- **Chapter Number:** Displays the chapter number for the file.

The format of the page, volume, and chapter numbers depend on settings in the document or book file. You can specify uppercase and lowercase Roman, alphabetic, or text-based numerals, along with standard arabic numerals. For details, see "Managing Numbering" on page 373.

Table 9-3 describes the building blocks used in numerical variables.

Building Block	Description	Example
<$curpagenum>	Page number (only available on master pages)	735
<$lastpagenum>	Last page number in the document	758
<$paranum>	Value of autonumber field in paragraph tag	Step 2.
<$paranumonly>	Numerical value of the autonumber field (excludes punctuation and text)	2
<$chapnum>	Chapter number	9
<$volnum>	Volume number	II

Table 9-3. *Building Blocks for Numerical Variables*

Filename Variables

Two system variables display your document's file name. You can use the following Filename variables in any text frame:

- **Filename (Long):** Displays the full file name, including the entire path, in a platform-dependent format.
- **Filename (Short):** Displays only the file name.

Table 9-4 describes the building blocks used in Filename variables.

Building Block	Description	Example
<$fullfilename>	Displays the document's entire file name, including the path.	c:\Book\widget.fm *(Windows)* Book:widget *(Mac)* /var/Book/widget.fm *(UNIX)*
<$filename>	Displays the document's file name without the path.	widget.fm *(Windows)* widget *(Mac)* widget.fm *(UNIX)*

Table 9-4.   *Building Blocks for Filename Variables*

Table Variables

The following system variables are available only in tables:

- **Table Continuation:** Displays the definition of the variable on subsequent sheets of a table when inserted into a table's title, heading, or footing row. By default, the Table Continuation variable displays "(Continued)," but you can change the text. When you insert the Table Continuation variable, a bracket (or hard space) is displayed. You must have the document text symbols turned on to see the character.

Table 1: Books for Technical Communicator §₎ —— Bracket indicates Table Continuation variable is inserted.

- **Table Sheet:** Displays the sheet number and the total number of sheets. By default, the variable displays "(Sheet # of #)," but you can edit the definition.

Table 1: Books for Technical Communicators (Sheet 1 of 2)§

No building blocks are available in the Table Continuation variable except for character tags. Table 9-5 describes the building blocks used in the Table Sheet variable.

Building Block	Description	Example
<$tblsheetnum>	Displays the sheet number.	1
<$tblsheetcount>	Displays the total number of sheets in the table.	2

Table 9-5. *Building Blocks for Table Variables*

Running Header/Footer Variables

Twelve Running H/F system variables are available on the master pages of your document. You can use these variables to insert headers and footers in your document. For example, they can display the text or autonumbering from a specific paragraph tag on the right pages of a document and the book title on the left pages. In this book, the right header consists of the Running H/F 1 variable. Here's the variable definition:

```
Chapter <$paranumonly[Chapter_Number]>: <$paratext[Chapter_Title]>
```

In this example, the <$paranumonly> building block displays the value of the Chapter_Number paragraph tag, and the <$paratext> building block displays the value of the Chapter_Title tag (for example, Chapter 25: Cleaning Your Widget).

Most building blocks in Running H/F variables point to the first instance of the specified paragraph tag on the page. If the variable points to the Heading3 paragraph tag, and the page has two Heading3s, FrameMaker displays text from the first occurrence. If the page lacks a Heading3, the running/header footer is blank.

To prevent this problem, include an alternate paragraph tag in the variable definition, such as the Heading2 paragraph in the following example:

```
<$paratext[Heading3,Heading2]>
```

This variable directs FrameMaker to display text from the first Heading3 paragraph on the page. In the absence of a Heading3 paragraph, text from the first Heading2 on the page will be displayed.

The following three running header/footer building blocks have special functions:

■ **<$marker1> and <$marker2>:** Display text from a marker instead of a long header or footer. For details, see the next section.

■ **<$paratext[+,paratag]>:** Displays the last instance of the specified paragraph tag. See "Displaying Dictionary-Style Headings" on page 229 for details.

■ **<$condtag[hitag,...lotag,nomatch]>:** Searches for one or two condition tags on a page and displays the highest match. For details, see "Displaying Condition Tags" on page 230.

Table 9-6 lists the building blocks used in both structured and unstructured Running H/F variables. For more information on the element and attribute building blocks, see "Using Variables in Structured Documents" on page 236.

Displaying Text from a Marker

Instead of using the Running H/F variables to display text from a paragraph, you can display text from a marker. This technique is useful for displaying abbreviated headings or information that is not available in a paragraph. In the following example, the heading on the body page won't fit in the running header/footer text frame. You can type an alternate heading in a special Header/Footer marker and refer to that marker in the Running H/F variable with the appropriate building block. The abbreviated heading from the marker is displayed instead of the long heading.

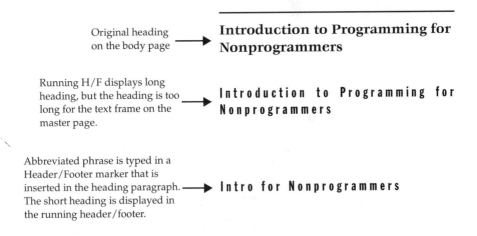

Original heading on the body page → **Introduction to Programming for Nonprogrammers**

Running H/F displays long heading, but the heading is too long for the text frame on the master page. → **Introduction to Programming for Nonprogrammers**

Abbreviated phrase is typed in a Header/Footer marker that is inserted in the heading paragraph. The short heading is displayed in the running header/footer. → **Intro for Nonprogrammers**

Building Block	Description
Text	
`<$paratext[paratag]>`	Displays text from the specified paragraph tag.
`<$paratext[+,paratag]>`	Displays the last instance of the specified paragraph tag on the page. Often used to display dictionary-style headings. (See "Displaying Dictionary-Style Headings" on page 229 for an example.)

Table 9-6.   *Building Blocks for Running Header/Footers*

Building Block	Description
`<$paratag[paratag]>`	Displays the paragraph tag rather than contents of the paragraph.
`<$condtag[hitag,...` `lotag,nomatch]>`	Displays the specified condition tag or alternate text, if the condition is not found.
`<$marker1>`	Displays text from the Header/Footer $1 marker in the document.
`<$marker2>`	Displays text from the Header/Footer $2 marker in the document.
Paragraph numbers	
`<$paranum[paratag]>`	Displays the autonumbering from the referenced paragraph, including punctuation.
`<$paranumonly[paratag]>`	Displays only the numeric portion of the referenced paragraph's autonumber.
Unstructured	
`<$elemtext[elemtag]>`	Inserts the first paragraph of the source element, including any prefixes or suffixes. The autonumber is not included.
`<$elemtextonly[elemtag]>`	Inserts the first paragraph of the source element, excluding prefixes, suffixes, and autonumbers. (Prefixes or suffixes of child elements *are* included.)
`<$lowchoice[attrname]>`	Displays the lowest value on the current page of the specified attribute.
`<$highchoice[attrname]>`	Displays the highest value on the current page of the specified attribute.
`<$attribute[attrname]>`	Displays the value of the first specified attribute on the page.

Table 9-6. *Building Blocks for Running Header/Footers (Continued)*

FrameMaker provides two building blocks and matching markers to display marker text in a running header/footer. The <$marker1> building block displays the definition of Header/Footer $1 markers; <$marker2> displays the definition of Header/Footer $2 markers. You cannot create additional Header/Footer markers as you can with most custom markers.

To display text from a marker, follow these steps:

1. Create the marker by doing the following:

   a. Position your cursor where you want the marker (for example, in the paragraph of a long heading).

   b. Select Special | Marker.

   The Marker dialog box is displayed.

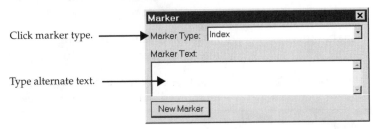

2. Click Header/Footer $1 or Header/Footer $2 in the Marker Type drop-down list.

3. In the Marker Text field, type the alternate text that you want displayed. The limit is 255 characters.

4. Click the New Marker button. The marker is inserted in the paragraph.

5. Do one of the following:

   ■ In your document, double-click the variable that you want to modify.

   ■ Position your cursor where you want the variable and select Special | Variable.

   The Variable dialog box is displayed (Figure 9-1 on page 217).

6. Click the Running H/F variable you want to edit (if it's not already highlighted), then click the Edit Definition button. The Edit System Variable dialog box is displayed (Figure 9-2 on page 221).

7. Type either **<$marker1>** or **<$marker2>** in the Definition field, depending on which Header/Footer marker you inserted.

8. Click the Edit button, then click the Insert button (or the Replace button if the variable was already on the master page).

When you display the body page, the marker text will be displayed in the running header/footer.

Displaying Dictionary-Style Headings

While many building blocks display the first instance of a paragraph tag on the page, you can also use a variable to display the value of the last specified paragraph tag on the page. In the following example, the word at the top of the second column is also the last dictionary term on the page. The <$paratext[+,paratag]> building block in the running header refers to the Term paragraph tag.

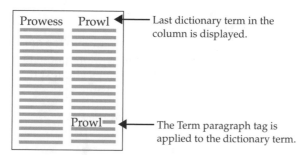

Last dictionary term in the column is displayed.

The Term paragraph tag is applied to the dictionary term.

To create a dictionary-style running header/footer, follow these steps:

1. Do one of the following:

   ■ In your document, double-click the variable that you want to modify.

   ■ Position your cursor where you want the variable and select Special | Variable.

   The Variable dialog box is displayed (Figure 9-1 on page 217).

2. Click the running header/footer variable you want to edit (if it's not already highlighted), then click the Edit Definition button. The Edit System Variable dialog box is displayed.

3. Type **<$paratext[+,paratag]>** in the Definition field. (This building block is not displayed in the list of building blocks, so you must type it in.)

4. Replace **paratag** with the appropriate paragraph tag.

5. Click the Edit button, then click the Insert button (or the Replace button if the variable was already on the master page).

When you display the body page, text from the last paragraph tag you specified is displayed in the running header/footer.

Displaying Condition Tags

In your running header/footer, you can display a condition tag applied to text on the current page. To do so, you use the <$condtag[hitag,...lotag,nomatch]> building block. This building block includes one or more condition tags and text that is displayed when the page has no condition tags, as in the following example:

```
<$condtag[Print,Online,No Conditional Text]>
```

Here, FrameMaker first searches the page for the Print condition tag. If found, "Print" is displayed in the running header/footer. If not found, FrameMaker looks for the Online condition tag and displays it, if found. If it is not found, the last value is displayed. This can be either a phrase, such as "No Conditional Text," or a blank space (if you use a nonbreaking space for the last value).

The ellipsis in the <$condtag[hitag,...lotag,nomatch]> building block indicates that you can provide additional condition tags, and FrameMaker will also search for them. It's essential, however, to indicate what FrameMaker should display if no condition tags are found. Without the nomatch value, FrameMaker displays the last condition tag in the building block ("Online," in this example), even if the condition tag isn't actually on the page.

To set up a condition tag variable, follow these steps:

1. Do one of the following:

   ■ On the master page, double-click the variable that you want to modify.

   ■ Position your cursor where you want the variable and select Special | Variable.

   The Variable dialog box is displayed (Figure 9-1 on page 217).

2. Click the variable you want to edit (if it's not already highlighted), then click the Edit Definition button. The Edit System Variable dialog box is displayed (Figure 9-2 on page 221).

3. Click the <$condtag[hitag,...lotag,nomatch]> building block to add it to the variable definition, or type it in the Definition field.

4. In place of **hitag,...lotag**, type the condition tags you want to display, for example, "Print,Online."

5. In place of **nomatch**, type one of the following:

   ■ The text you want displayed if no match is found, such as "No Conditional Text."

   ■ A nonbreaking space to display nothing if no match is found. In Windows and UNIX, type \ followed by a space. On the Mac, press OPTION-SPACE.

6. Click the Edit button, then click the Insert button (or the Replace button if the variable was already on the master page).

7. Display the body page. The variable text is updated.

Updating System Variables

System variables don't automatically update their content; they must be updated by you or the system. For example, if you insert a current date variable that includes the hour, minute, and seconds, it will not be updated automatically as the time changes. The content is updated when you open or save the document. You can also force an update of the variables to update without saving the file.

Controlling Time Display with Building Blocks

As mentioned in "Date and Time Variables" on page 221, you can insert the creation, current, or modification date and time in a document. FrameMaker 7 provides three new building blocks that help display time in other system variables and in running header/footer variables. The new building blocks don't do anything when used alone; instead, they work with the other time building blocks to display time. For example, the <$currenttime> building block is inserted with other time building blocks in the following running header/footer variable definition:

```
<$currenttime><$hour>:<$minute> <$AMPM>
```

This variable displays the following text:

```
11:53 AM
```

The three building blocks can be used in system variables that are unrelated to time, such as Filename, but they're mostly used in running header/footer variables to create a custom header or footer. The new building blocks are as follows:

■ **<$creationtime>:** Causes any following time building block to display the creation time.

■ **<$currenttime>:** Causes any following time building block to display the current time.

■ **<$modificationtime>:** Causes any following time building block to display the time the file was last opened or saved.

To update system variables, follow these steps:

1. Select Special | Variable to display the Variable dialog box (Figure 9-1 on page 217).
2. Click the Update button. FrameMaker displays a confirmation dialog box.
3. Click the OK button to update the variables.

Creating User Variables

User variables provide a way to store common terms and update words that change often. One example is a Product Name variable. During the development process, a software program may have an alias, such as Orion. If you save the alias in a Product Name variable and use the variable in your document, you can modify the variable when the product is finally named. The term will be updated in each place you've inserted the variable. To update the term in an entire book, you import the variables into the book file.

When you create user variables, assign your variable names so that you can easily remember which variable to insert. The variable name and definition might be the same, but it's better to use general terms for the names. For example, suppose you create a variable containing the name of a book's author—Shakespeare. If the author changes to Jack Smith, you'll need to change both the variable name and definition. The variable name should be something generic, such as Author.

In some cases, the variable name and definition may be similar. If you create a variable for every product your company develops, don't use generic names, such as Product1, Product2, and so on. The variables will be easier to identify if they're named after the product.

FrameMaker doesn't spell-check variables, so make sure you spell the definition correctly.

To create a new user variable, follow these steps:

1. Select Special | Variable. The Variable dialog box is displayed (Figure 9-1 on page 217).
2. Click the Create Variable button. The Edit User Variable dialog box is displayed (Figure 9-3).
3. In the Name field, type a name for the new variable.
4. In the Definition field, type a definition for the variable. This text is displayed in the document. In addition to regular text, you can use character tags in the variable definition by clicking the tags in the Character Formats list or by typing the tags in the Definition field. The definition cannot exceed 255 characters.

Include the <Default Para Font> character tag where the character formatting should end, as shown in the following example:

```
<SmallCaps>shift<Default Para Font> key
```

This variable is used in the following sentence to format "shift" in small caps:

Press the SHIFT key, then select File | Save All Open Files.

5. Click the Add button to add the variable to your list of user variables.

6. Click the Done button to close the Edit User Variable dialog box and return to the Variable dialog box.

7. Click the Done button to close the Variable dialog box. You can also insert the variable by clicking the Insert button.

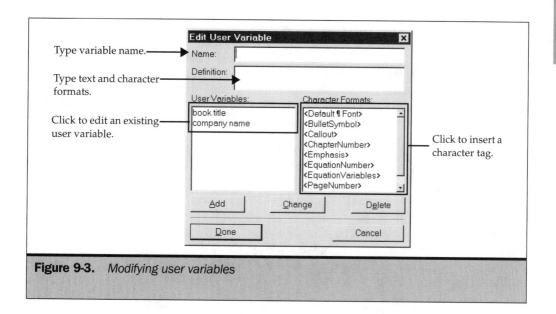

Figure 9-3.   *Modifying user variables*

Modifying User Variable Definitions

After you create a user variable, you can modify the definition by changing the text or adding character tags. The modified variable is automatically updated when you open or save the document.

To change the name or definition of an existing variable, follow these steps:

1. Do one of the following:

   ■ In your document, double-click the variable that you want to modify.

   ■ Select Special | Variable.

   The Variable dialog box is displayed (Figure 9-1 on page 217).

2. Click the variable you want to edit (if it's not already highlighted), then click the Edit Definition button. The Edit User Variable dialog box is displayed (Figure 9-3 on page 233).

3. Change the name and definition of the variable as needed.

4. To save your changes and modify another user variable, click the Change button.

5. When you're finished modifying user variables, click the Done button.

6. In the Variable dialog box, click the Done button. The variable definition is modified, and the variable is updated where you've inserted it in the document.

In the Variable dialog box, the Replace button is displayed if text or a variable is selected on the page (for example, if you double-clicked a variable to display the Variable dialog box). If no text or variable is selected, the Insert button is displayed instead.

Converting User Variables to Text

You can convert user variables to standard text. For example, you might insert a term as a variable and decide later that the term doesn't need to be in a variable. When you convert the variable to text, character tags in the variable are applied to the converted term. For example, the Legacy Product variable is formatted by the Emphasis character tag. After converting the variable, FrameMaker applies the Emphasis character tag to the text on the page.

```
<Emphasis>Widget<Default Para Font>
```
↓
Widget

The converted variable can be edited and spell-checked; however, it can't be updated. For this reason, converting variables typically isn't a good idea unless you're cleaning up a template and see variables that shouldn't be there.

To convert a variable to text, follow these steps:

1. *(optional)* On the page, select the variable you want to convert.

2. Select Special | Variable. The Variable dialog box is displayed (Figure 9-1 on page 217).

3. Click the Convert to Text button. The Convert Variables to Text dialog box is displayed.

In an unstructured document   In a structured document

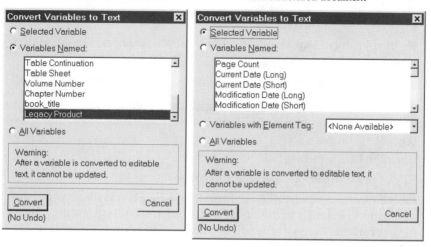

4. Do any of the following:

■   Click the Selected Variable radio button if you only want to convert the
    selected variable.

■   Click the Variables Named radio button, then click the name of the variable
    you want to delete. You can't click multiple variables.

■   *(structured only)* Click an element in the Variables with Element Tag drop-
    down list if an element is assigned to the variable.

■   Click the All Variables radio button to convert all variables in the document
    to text.

Caution   *At this point, you can change your mind and click the Cancel button. If you proceed to
                the next step, however, you cannot undo the conversion.*

5. Click the Convert button, then click the Done button. The variable definition is
    converted to text. If you click the word, it's no longer highlighted like a variable,
    and character tags that were in the variable are applied to the converted text.

Deleting User Variables

You cannot delete system variables, but you can remove user variables from your
document. If the variable is in use, FrameMaker displays a warning, and you choose to
convert the variable to standard text or cancel the action. If you're unsure whether a
specific variable has been inserted in the document, search for the variable before you
try to delete it. You can insert another variable in its place and then delete the variable.
For details on searching for FrameMaker components, see "Searching and Replacing"
on page 70.

To delete a user variable, follow these steps:

1. Do one of the following:
   - In your document, double-click the variable that you want to delete.
   - Select Special | Variable.

   The Variable dialog box is displayed (Figure 9-1 on page 217).

2. Click the variable you want to delete (if it's not already highlighted), then click the Edit Definition button. The Edit User Variable dialog box is displayed (Figure 9-3 on page 233).

3. Click the Delete button.

4. Click the Done button to save your changes.

5. *(Skip if variable isn't in use)* A confirmation dialog box is displayed if the variable you want to delete is in the document. Click the OK button, and every instance of that variable in the document is converted to regular, editable text.

FrameMaker warns that the variable you're trying to delete is in the document.

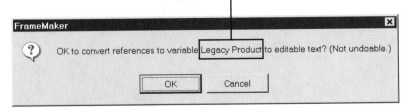

The Variable dialog box is displayed again.

6. *(Skip if variable isn't in use)* Click the Done button to close the dialog box.

Using Variables in Structured Documents

You can insert a system variable into a structured document with or without a variable element. The variable element defines formatting for the variable and may limit available variables based on the parent element. For instance, in the following rule, the long version of the Filename variable is valid only if the parent element is DocID. The short Filename variable is valid in all other cases.

Element (System Variable): Filename
    System variable format rule
        1.   **If context is: DocID**
            Use system variable: Filename (Long)

            Else
                Use system variable: Filename (Short)

Tips for Variables

You can create your own variables to store frequently used words or phrases that often change. The variables may include character tags to format the text. Some uses of variables are as follows:

- **Software Release.** Type the software release number, as in "7.0."
- **Product Name.** Type the name of the product. During the development phase, your product might have an internal code name, such as "Pegasus." When the name is finalized, you update the variable definition. You could include the product name in the Software Release variable, but the Product Name variable can be used in several different ways with just the name.
- **Menu Item Separator.** Insert a Wingdings character tag in the variable and type \xd8 as the variable definition. (Don't forget to include the <Default Para Font> character tag after the variable definition to return the formatting to the paragraph tag settings.) Separate menu items by inserting the variable, as in Special ➤ Paragraphs ➤ Designer. The Wingdings typeface must be installed on the computer displaying the document. Wingdings is installed by default with Microsoft Windows and Microsoft Office. If you're concerned about cross-platform compatibility, consider using OpenType fonts. For details, see Appendix B, "Managing Fonts Across Platforms."
- **Copyright.** Type a copyright statement. When the copyright year changes, you update the variable instead of searching for the year.
- **Company Name Long and Short.** Create two company variables: one with the full name of your company (Acme Brothers Limited Liability Company), and the other with an abbreviated name (Acme). These variables are especially useful if your company is sold to another corporation and the name changes.
- **Manual Version.** Type "First Draft" or "Second Draft" to indicate the version of your document.

In the running header/footer variables of structured documents, many of the building blocks are based on elements or attributes instead of on paragraph tags. For example, the <$elemtext[elemtag]> building block functions like the standard <$paratext[paratag]> building block, but it displays text from the linked element tag rather than the paragraph tag. The following running header/footer variable displays the first sibling Section element in the document header:

```
<$elemtext[Section(1)]>
```

In the structure view, you can see the first sibling Section element. If you change the section order in the document, the new sibling Section heading is displayed in the header. As with standard running header/footers, the header is also automatically updated if you modify the name of the section.

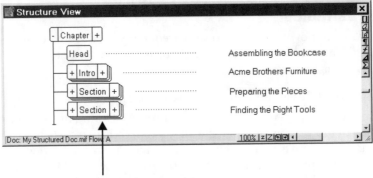

First sibling Section element to the
"Preparing the Pieces" Section element

FrameMaker can also display an attribute in the running header/footer. The <$lowchoice> and <$highchoice> building blocks are used to display the lowest or highest value of a particular attribute. The highest value of an attribute is displayed at the bottom of the Attribute Value Choices drop-down list.

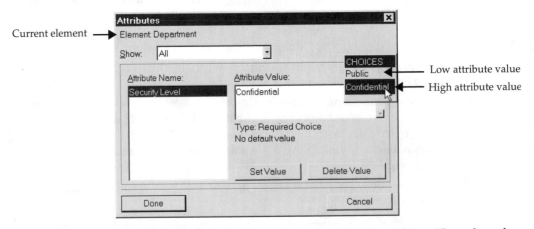

Suppose that all of your documents include a Security Level attribute. The value of the Security Level attribute is either Public or Confidential. To quickly identify confidential information, you can insert the following building block in the running header/footer:

```
<$highchoice[Security Level]>
```

FrameMaker will display "Confidential" in the running header/footer if that attribute value is on the page. If the Confidential attribute value is not found, and the highest value on the page is Public, then "Public" is displayed.

The Security Level attribute may be used in more than one element—for instance, in the Department and Type of Bulletin attributes. To specify the element FrameMaker should search for, you include the element name after the attribute name:

```
<$highchoice[Security Level:Department]>
```

The other unique running header/footer element displays the first referenced attribute value on the page, whether it's the highest or lowest value. With the following building block, the first Security Level attribute value on the page is displayed:

```
<$attribute[Security Level]>
```

User variables aren't nearly as complicated as system variables. They don't require variable elements, so you can insert a user variable anywhere in the text frame. See "Inserting Variables" on page 217 for more information.

The
Complete
Reference

FrameMaker 7

Part III

Controlling Page Layout

The Complete Reference

FrameMaker 7

Chapter 10

Understanding Text Flows

In FrameMaker, you create page layouts by placing text frames and graphics on the master pages. Content on the body pages flows through the document according to the structure of the master pages. For example, if you create a two-column text frame on the master page, the text on a body page formatted by that master page is displayed in two columns.

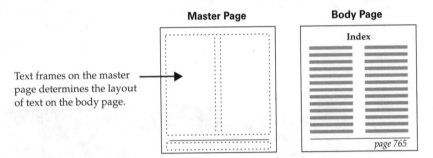

Master Page   **Body Page**

Text frames on the master page determines the layout of text on the body page.

Most text frames are associated with *flow tags*. Flow tags control how text fills the frames. When the first text frame in flow A gets full, FrameMaker generates a new page. This means you don't need to insert new pages manually. You can define more than one flow in a document to create custom layouts, and text in each flow is displayed independently throughout the document. Take, for example, a newsletter in which the front-page article continues on page three. For this layout, you create a text flow that begins on page one and continues on page three. The article will flow automatically through from page one to page three, skipping page two, which is in another flow.

In a structured document, you set up one or more structured flows and define at least one container to be valid as the highest element in a particular flow. For example, you can define the Book element to be valid at the highest level in the flow and then fill the flow with descendants of the Book element.

Understanding Text Flows

You define text flows on the master pages by drawing text frames and assigning a flow tag. By default, your documents have only one flow tag—A. As you type text, FrameMaker automatically adds new pages and allows the text to flow onto those pages. A symbol marks the end of the flow, indicating that FrameMaker will add a new page if you add content right before the symbol.

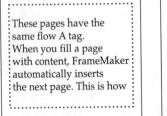

These pages have the same flow A tag. When you fill a page with content, FrameMaker automatically inserts the next page. This is how

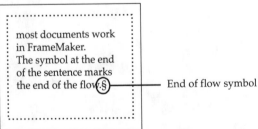

most documents work in FrameMaker. The symbol at the end of the sentence marks the end of the flow.§   ——— End of flow symbol

The document shown in the following example has two text flows. The text with flow tag A goes into the A columns, and the B text flow goes into the B columns. One common use for multiple flows is in creating newsletters. You can easily "jump" a story from the front page to an inside page by creating custom text flows and connecting them.

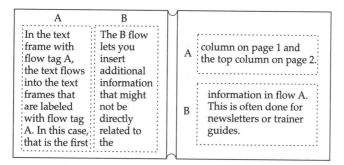

The flow tag for a text frame is displayed in the status bar next to the paragraph tag or element name. For example, the First master page displayed in the following example is in Flow A.

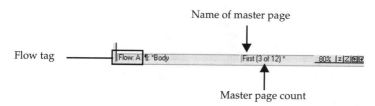

Reference pages also have text flows. These special flows help generate the index, table of contents, list of tables, and list of figures, and they contain master page mapping, graphics, and so on. See Chapter 17, "Creating Other Generated Files," for details.

Understanding Text Frame Properties

The characteristics of each text frame in a document are displayed in the text frame properties. You select the frame and select Graphic | Object Properties to display the properties. (You can select Format | Customize Page Layout | Customize Text Frame to display the same properties, but using the Graphics menu is quicker.) You can modify the flow tag, text frame size, side head space, columns, and other items in the text frame properties, shown in Figure 10-1.

If you change the text frame properties on a body page, only the selected text frame is modified. On the master page, editing a text frame updates all body pages that use that master page.

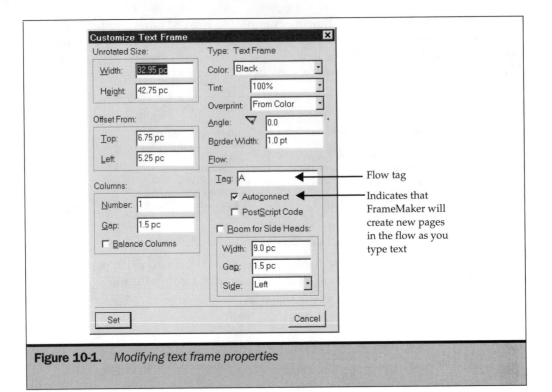

Figure 10-1. *Modifying text frame properties*

Table 10-1 describes the text frame properties. You can modify many graphic-related aspects, such as setting the color, tint, and border, in the Tools palette. For details, see "Drawing Basic Shapes" on page 328.

Property	Description
Unrotated Size	Sets the width and height of the text frame. If the text frame is rotated on the master page, the dimensions displayed are the opposite of those you see on the page.
Offset From	Indicates the space between the text frame and the top and left edge of the page or graphic frame.
Columns	Divides the text frame into columns and defines the space between columns. Check the Balance Columns check box if you want to distribute text evenly in columns that don't have a lot of text. The text will end on or near the same horizontal axis in all columns.

Table 10-1. *Text Frame Properties*

Property	Description
Color	Assigns a color for the fill and pen (or outline) pattern. You must select the fill and pen *style* (for example, crosshatch or solid, in the Tools palette.
Tint	Lightens the text frame color by a specific percentage. You select from 0–100 percent in 5-percent increments, or you can type another percentage in that range. For the tint to be displayed, you must select the fill style in the Tools palette.
Overprint	Indicates how FrameMaker prints the colors of an overlapping text frame and object. ■ **Knock Out:** FrameMaker does not print the overlapped portion of the text frame and object. ■ **Overprint:** FrameMaker prints the overlapped portion. ■ **From Color:** FrameMaker prints color from the color definition. It's easier to use the Tools palette to set the color, tint, and overprint because you need to select the fill there anyway.
Angle	Indicates the number of degrees the text frame is rotated.
Border Width	Specifies a border between .015 and 360 points. You must select the border (or pen) style in the Tools palette.
Flow	Associates a flow tag with the text frame and specifies the flow properties. Options are as follows: ■ **Tag:** Name of the flow tag. ■ **Autoconnect:** Indicates whether FrameMaker adds new pages to the flow automatically. If turned off, you have to add a page manually as the page fills with content and connect it with the previous page. ■ **PostScript Code:** Indicates code that a PostScript printer processes, for example, commands to create watermarks in PDF files, print an image, or print a document in landscape orientation. Embedding PostScript code is an alternative to physically altering the page. ■ **Room for Side Heads:** Creates a side head area, for which you specify the width, the gap between the side head area and in-column content, and the side head location.

Table 10-1. *Text Frame Properties (Continued)*

Adding Text Flows to Master Pages

On master pages, text frames provide structure for foreground and background elements. Text frames for foreground elements have an associated flow tag, identifying which text frames are related. Text frames for background elements, such as headers and footers, have no flow tag.

When you draw a text frame on the master page, you connect it to an existing flow on the page, or you assign a new flow tag. If the text frame is connected to an existing flow, text on the body page will flow into the new text frame. If you create a new flow, existing text will not be displayed in the new flow; you need to type new text on the body page. See "Connecting Text Flows" on page 254 for more information.

Some text frames on the master page aren't part of a flow. For example, the header and footer text frames, which contain repeated information, are considered background elements. They don't need flow tags because they're not connected and don't generate new pages as foreground text frames do.

To draw a text frame on the master page, follow these steps:

1. Select View | Master Pages to display the master pages, then page up or down to find the page you want to modify.

2. Select Graphics | Tools to display the Tools palette, then click the Text Frame icon.

3. Drag the cursor across the page to draw a text frame. (To draw a square, press SHIFT while you draw the frame.) The Add New Text Frame dialog box is displayed.

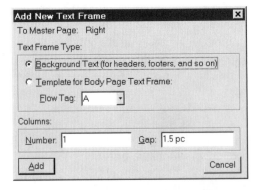

4. Do one of the following:

   ■ To create background text, click the Background Text radio button.

   ■ To create a frame for the body page, click the Template for Body Page Text Frame radio button and assign a flow tag. Though flow A is appropriate for most text frames, you can type another tag name in the Flow Tag field or change the tag later if the text frame belongs in a new flow.

5. *(optional)* To create a multicolumn text frame, type the number of columns in the Number field, then type the measurement between the columns in the Gap field. See "Adding Columns" on page 258 for more information.

6. Click the Add button. The new text frame is displayed.

7. When changes are complete, select View | Body Pages. Your changes are displayed on the page formatted by the modified master page.

If you want to change the dimensions of the text frame, you can resize the text frame manually, using the FrameMaker rulers as a guide. You can also edit the text frame properties to assign precise dimensions. For details, see "Understanding Text Flows" on page 244.

If the document has multiple flows, text frames within each flow are connected. You create a new flow by creating the text frame first and then changing the assigned flow tag. For details, see "Changing the Flow Tag" on page 266.

Drawing Text Frames on the Body Page

Text frames added to the body pages don't belong to a flow. You can connect the text frames to a flow later, and content will fill the first frame and then flow to the second frame. If you want to reuse the layout on another page, however, you should modify the master page instead of the body page.

To draw a text frame on the body page, follow these steps:

1. Display the body page you want to modify.

2. Select Graphics | Tools to display the Tools palette, then click the Text Frame icon.

3. Drag the cursor across the page to draw a text frame. (To draw a square, press SHIFT while you draw the frame.) The Create New Text Frame dialog box is displayed.

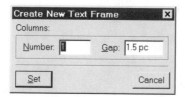

4. Type the number of columns. For multiple columns, type the space between each column in the Gap field.

In FrameMaker, you can specify the unit of measure used throughout the document—in paragraph tags, text frame properties, table tags, and so on. To change the unit of measure, select View | Options and click a different item in the Display Unit drop-down list.

5. Click the Set button. The text frame is displayed on the page. You can position the cursor in the frame, add content, apply a paragraph tag, and modify other properties discussed in this chapter.

Selecting Text Frames

You select a text frame by CTRL-clicking (Windows and UNIX) or OPTION-clicking (Mac) the edge of the frame. Handles are displayed on the edge of the frame, indicating that the text frame is selected. You can also select objects with the Object Pointer in the Tools palette, but you'll need to select the Smart Select pointer button again to type text.

There are three ways to select several frames:

- Drag the cursor across the frames as if you're drawing a box. An outline is displayed around the frames as you press the mouse button. When you take your finger off the mouse button, the outline disappears, and the frames are selected.

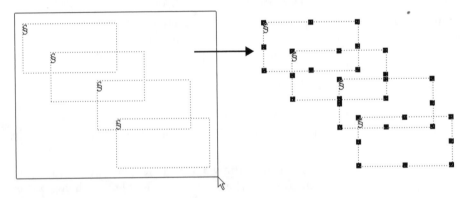

- CTRL-click (Windows and UNIX) or COMMAND-click (Mac) the first frame, then the second frame, and so on.

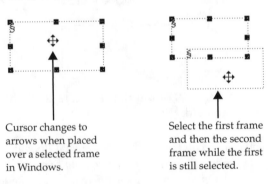

Cursor changes to arrows when placed over a selected frame in Windows.

Select the first frame and then the second frame while the first is still selected.

■ Click outside the main text frame and press CTRL-A (Windows and UNIX) or COMMAND-A (Mac). This selects all objects on the page, and you can CTRL-click or COMMAND-click the objects you don't want selected. Typically, you use this option if the text frames are in an anchored frame or on a page with few objects. (If your cursor is inside the text frame when you press CTRL-A or COMMAND-A, the text in the flow is highlighted instead.)

Resizing Text Frames

When you resize text frames on the master pages, the body pages formatted by those master pages are updated, and text reflows to fit the new frames. On the body page, you can resize a specific text frame, and only that body page is updated; the text frame on the master page remains unchanged. For example, you can force a line of text or a particular paragraph to move to the next page by resizing the text frame until the text is displayed on the next page.

Note *Adjusting a text frame on the body page (instead of on the master page) creates an override. You'll get an error message when switching from the master page to body page, but you can click the Keep Overrides radio button to preserve your changes. Generally, you should avoid overrides. Adjusting text frames to copyfit text, however, is often necessary. See "Removing Master Page Overrides" on page 290 for more information.*

There are two ways to resize a text frame. You select the text frame and then drag the handles, or you change the dimensions in the text frame properties. Typically, you manually resize text frames when copyfitting a page or modifying simple items, such as figure callouts. If you need to place the text frame at a specific place on the page, you modify the height and width in the text frame properties.

To resize a text frame manually, follow these steps:

1. Display the body page or master page containing the text frame you want to modify, then select the frame. The handles are displayed on the edges of the text frame.

2. Do one of the following to resize the frame:

   ■ To change the height, drag one of the middle handles on the top or bottom edge.

   ■ To change the width, drag one of the middle handles on the left or right edge.

   ■ To change the width and height at the same time, drag a corner handle.

   You can use the FrameMaker ruler or the dimensions in the left corner of the status bar as a guide. As you drag the edge of the text frame, FrameMaker updates the dimensions displayed in the status bar, and the ruler marking moves.

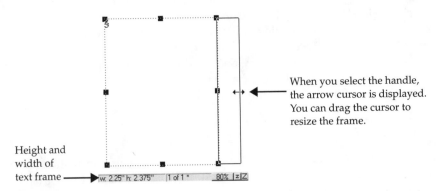

When you select the handle, the arrow cursor is displayed. You can drag the cursor to resize the frame.

Height and width of text frame

To modify the height and width of the text frame in the text frame properties, follow these steps:

1. Display the body page or master page containing the text frame you want to modify, then select the frame. The handles are displayed on the edges of the text frame.

2. Select Graphics | Object Properties to display the text frame properties (Figure 10-1 on page 246), then change the measurements in the Height and Width fields.

3. Click the Set button. The text frame is resized.

   Notice that the top and left offset don't change when you modify the height and width of the text frame. For example, after the following text frame is resized, the left and top offsets are both still 1 inch.

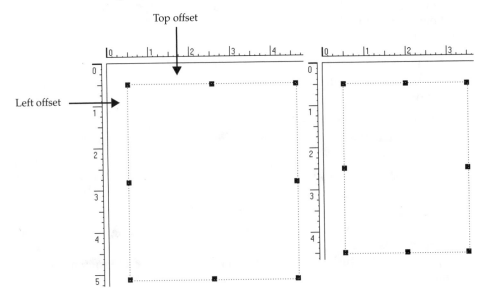

Moving and Copying Text Frames

You move and copy a text frame by dragging it on the page. To move the frame, CTRL-click (Windows and UNIX) or OPTION-click (Mac) the edge of the text frame and then drag and drop the frame. To copy the frame, select the frame, press CTRL (Windows and UNIX) or OPTION (Mac) and then drag and drop the frame. You can copy and paste a text frame, but the new frame is displayed on top of the original frame, making the new frame difficult to see. It's easier to use the keyboard shortcuts and mouse to copy the frame.

> **Note** *Don't select the text frame handles when you move or copy a text frame. The handles are for resizing the frame. If you try to drag the handle, you'll resize the text frame.*

With FrameMaker's snap feature turned on, the edge of the text frame moves to the nearest ruler marking. In the following example, the text frame was moved to the 6-inch ruler marking. If you turn snap off, you can move the text frame between ruler markings. For details, see "Working with Grids" on page 334.

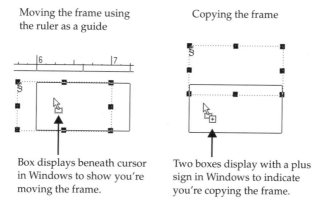

Moving the frame using the ruler as a guide

Copying the frame

Box displays beneath cursor in Windows to show you're moving the frame.

Two boxes display with a plus sign in Windows to indicate you're copying the frame.

To move a text frame to a specific place on the page, you edit the top and left offset in the text frame properties. If you're moving the text frame for a figure callout, modifying these properties probably won't help—it's easier to drag the frame where you need it; however, to move the frame to a specific place, editing the text frame offset gives you more precise control over the location of the frame.

Deleting Text Frames

After you select one or more text frames, you can delete the frames by pressing the DELETE key or selecting Edit | Clear. If a frame contains text that's in an autoconnected flow, FrameMaker won't delete the content but warns you that a new page may be generated to hold the displaced content.

Customizing Text Flows

You can customize text flows by adding columns and side head space, splitting text frames to create multiple flows, and disconnecting flows. When you modify a flow on the master page, text on the body pages formatted by that master page reflows into the new layout. You can also fine-tune the display of text in columns by balancing columns, feathering text across columns, and aligning baselines. This feature comes in handy for formatting documents such as newsletters. The following sections describe how to use these methods to modify text flows.

Connecting Text Flows

A master page might have two or more text frames that are in different flows. The text frames either have different flow tags, or one of them may have no flow tag. You can connect a text frame to the previous text frame, and they'll be in the same flow. To connect more than one frame to the current flow, you must connect the first text frame you want in the flow to the second frame, then connect the second frame to the third frame, and so on.

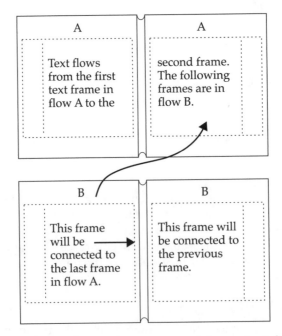

When you run out of room for text in an untagged frame, text disappears below a line, and the end of flow symbol is not displayed (shown in the next illustration). In the following example, the line on the bottom edge of the second frame indicates that the frame should be resized to make room for the underlying text. To find out what's in the same flow, position the cursor in the top frame, and select Edit | Select All in Flow. All content in the current flow is highlighted.

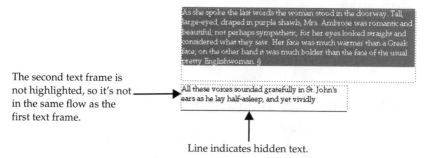

The second text frame is not highlighted, so it's not in the same flow as the first text frame.

Line indicates hidden text.

A disconnected flow can be connected to a flow that extends over more than one page. For example, suppose flow A in the next illustration is displayed on pages 1 and 2, and the disconnected flow is last on page 1. When you connect the disconnected flow to flow A, the autoconnect feature is turned off throughout flow A. This means that FrameMaker doesn't generate new pages when the existing frames fill with content. After you connect the frames, you need to turn on autoconnect in the first text frame in the flow.

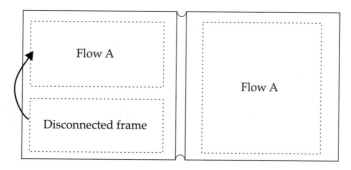

To connect text flows, follow these steps:

1. Display the body page containing the flow you want to modify.

2. Select the first frame you want in the flow, then select the second frame. If the frames are on different pages, the frames aren't displayed as selected at the same time, but FrameMaker remembers which frame you selected first and makes it the first in the flow.

3. Select Format | Customize Layout | Connect Text Frames. One of the following occurs:

   ■ If you're connecting an untagged flow to a tagged flow, FrameMaker connects the frames.

   ■ If you're connecting two different flows, a confirmation dialog box is displayed. Click the OK button to connect the frames.

■ If one of the frames isn't visible—for example, it's on a page that's not displayed—a confirmation dialog box is displayed. Click the OK button to connect the frames.

Reapply the master page to return the page layout to its original design. Text is displayed according to the master page layout; it will not be deleted.

Creating Room for Side Heads

A side head area provides white space for text or graphics. You set up side head space on the master page, and the extra space is displayed on all body pages in that flow. The side head space may be on the left side, right side, side closer to binding, or side farther from binding. Figure 10-2 shows the four side head positions.

After you set up side head space, you create paragraph tags to stay in the main column or flow into the side head space. For example, text in Figure 10-2 stays within the column. In the following illustration, the headings paginate across the side head space and the main column. The document borders are displayed only for paragraphs other than side heads, and when the document borders are turned off, you won't see any borders. For more information on changing the pagination settings in a paragraph tag, see "Pagination Sheet" on page 120.

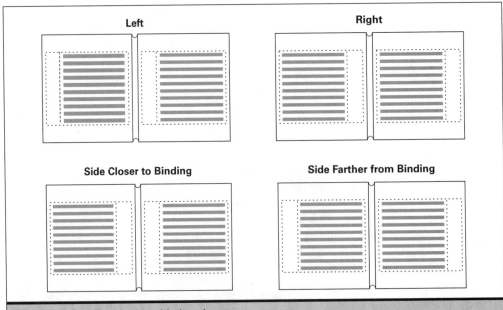

Figure 10-2. *Positioning side head space*

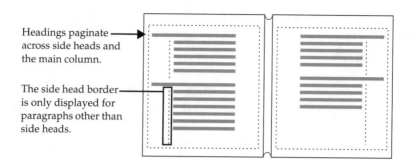

Headings paginate across side heads and the main column.

The side head border is only displayed for paragraphs other than side heads.

Note

If you add side head space to the master page of an existing document, your changes aren't displayed on the body pages. The same thing happens when you remove side head space from the master pages. You'll need to update the column layout for the entire flow. See "Removing Master Page Overrides" on page 290 for details.

To create space for side heads in a new document or template, follow these steps:

1. Select View | Master Pages to display the master pages, then page up or down to find the page you want to modify.

2. Select the text frame, then select Graphics | Object Properties. The Customize Text Frame dialog box is displayed (Figure 10-1 on page 246).

3. In the Flow section, check the Room for Side Heads check box.

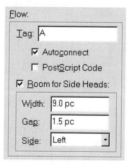

4. In the Width field, type the width of the side head area.

5. In the Gap field, type the width between the side head area and the main text.

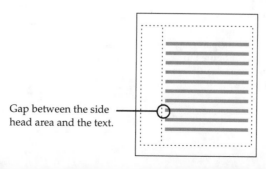

Gap between the side head area and the text.

6. In the Side drop-down list, click the location of the side head:

- **Left:** Places the side head area on the left side of the page.
- **Right:** Places the side head area on the right side of the page.
- **Side Closer to Binding:** Alternates the side head area in a double-sided document. On a left page, the side head area is on the right side of the page. On a right page, the side head area is on the left side of the page. See Figure 10-2 on page 256.
- **Side Farther from Binding:** Alternates the side head area in a double-sided document. On a left page, the side head area is on the left side of the page. On a right page, the side head area is on the right side of the page.

7. Click the Set button. The master page layout is updated.

Adding Columns

You can add columns to a text flow and specify the gap between each column. The columns may be balanced so that text ends on or near the same line across all columns on the page. For details, see "Balancing Columns" on page 260.

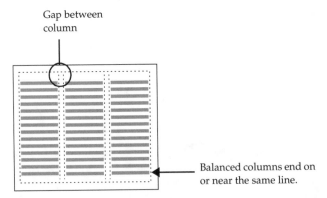

Gap between column

Balanced columns end on or near the same line.

In a document with columns, you must set up paragraph tags to display text across all columns or in column. For example, if the Heading1 paragraph is displayed across all columns, and the next column contains text, the heading covers that text. You'll need to modify the paragraph tag to stay in column. See "Pagination Sheet" on page 120 for details.

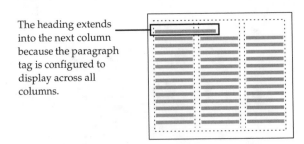

The heading extends into the next column because the paragraph tag is configured to display across all columns.

To create columns, follow these steps:

1. Select View | Master Pages to display the master pages, then page up or down to find the page you want to modify.
2. Select the text frame, then select Graphics | Object Properties. The Customize Text Frame dialog box is displayed (Figure 10-1 on page 246).
3. In the Columns section, type the number of columns. Thirty columns is the limit.

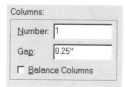

4. In the Gap field, type the space between the columns.
5. Check the Balance Columns check box for the text in all columns to end near the same horizontal line.

If you set up balanced columns on the master page, all pages formatted by the master page are affected. This gives you less control over layout on specific pages, and the results can be unattractive.

6. Click the Set button. The master page and body pages formatted by the master page are updated.

Aligning Text Across Columns

There are three ways to align text across columns:

- **Balancing columns.** Moves the baseline of each column on the page so that text ends on or near the same horizontal axis. Does not change the amount of space between lines of text.
- **Feathering text.** Adds space between lines of text and paragraphs so that text in a column ends near the baseline. You set the maximum amount of space.
- **Synchronizing baselines.** Lines up text across columns. You specify the line spacing of the paragraphs you want to align, and you can limit how headings are aligned at the top of columns.

Though you can set up balanced columns, feathered text, and synchronized baselines on the master pages, you usually align text to copyfit specific body pages.

CONTROLLING PAGE LAYOUT

Balancing Columns

To balance text across columns, FrameMaker changes the line breaks so that the baseline in each column is on or near the same line. By balancing columns on a specific body page, you modify only the selected page.

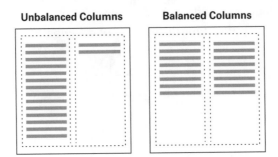

To balance columns on a body page, follow these steps:

1. Display the body page you want to modify, then select the text frame.
2. Select Graphics | Object Properties. The Customize Text Frame dialog box is displayed (Figure 10-1 on page 246).
3. Check the Balance Columns check box, then click the Set button. Text on the body page reflows to balance across both columns.

Feathering Text

When you feather text, FrameMaker adds space, or padding, between lines of text and paragraphs to fill each page in the flow with text. You specify the maximum amount of space FrameMaker can add. There are two types of padding:

- **Interline:** FrameMaker changes the amount of line spacing displayed on the page.
- **Interparagraph:** FrameMaker adjusts the space displayed above and below paragraphs.

Feathering doesn't modify the line spacing or space above and below settings in the paragraph tags; only the appearance of text on the page looks different. Though feathering is considered an override, it's the kind of override that's sometimes necessary to copyfit a page.

In Figure 10-3, the original unfeathered page is at the top. The bottom-left page shows interline padding. The bottom-right page shows interparagraph padding. Notice that adding space between lines creates more even spacing than adding space between paragraphs. In the last column, the extra padding between the bulleted paragraphs looks awkward.

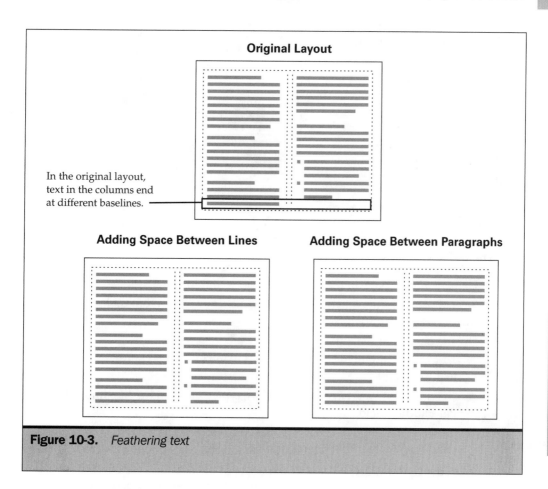

In the original layout, text in the columns end at different baselines.

Figure 10-3. *Feathering text*

Note *Unlike balancing columns, which changes only the selected body page, feathering text affects all pages in the selected flow.*

You can combine interline and interparagraph padding to get the look you want, but you should add as little space as possible so that paragraph tags control the spacing. It's also best to feather text after you're sure that the line spacing and space above and below settings in the paragraph tags won't change. For example, suppose you configure interline padding and then decrease line spacing in the Body paragraph tag. The text will move up on the page, and you might need to change the interline padding again.

Before modifying the Body paragraph tag, the feather settings control line spacing.

After modifying line spacing in the Body paragraph tag, the paragraphs move up on the page.

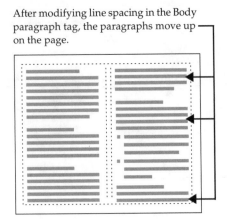

To feather text, follow these steps:

1. Display a body page in the flow you want to modify, then select the text frame.

2. Select Format | Page Layout | Line Layout. The Line Layout dialog box is displayed (Figure 10-4).

3. Do one or both of the following:

   ■ To add padding between lines, type a value in the Maximum Interline Padding field.

   ■ To add padding between paragraphs, type a value in the Maximum Inter-Pgf Padding field.

   If you select both options, FrameMaker feathers the text between paragraphs first and then feathers between lines if necessary.

4. Click the Update Flow button. The spacing in the flow is updated. If the spacing doesn't change on the page, experiment with increasing the padding.

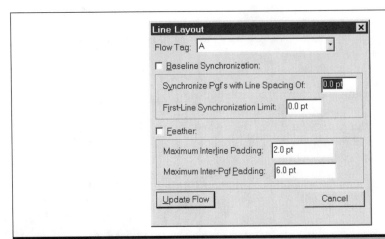

Figure 10-4. *Modifying the line layout*

To experiment with settings, turn on feathering, display the page and then select Edit | Undo.

Synchronizing Baselines

To align baselines across columns, you specify the line spacing of the paragraphs you want to align, and FrameMaker snaps the text to an imaginary grid. In the following example, the body paragraphs have 12-point line spacing, so the paragraph synchronization is set to 12 points. Paragraphs that have different line spacing, such as the headings, are not aligned.

You can also limit the alignment of headings when they appear at the top of the column. For example, you might want all headings up to 12 points aligned. The headings are actually displayed above the text column, as shown in the next illustration.

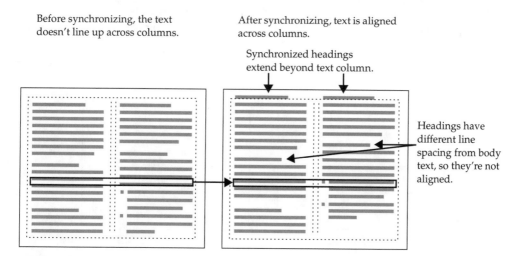

Before synchronizing, the text doesn't line up across columns.

After synchronizing, text is aligned across columns.

Synchronized headings extend beyond text column.

Headings have different line spacing from body text, so they're not aligned.

Note *Unlike balancing columns, which changes only the selected body page, synchronizing baselines affects all pages in the selected flow.*

Synchronizing baselines is most useful when you're working with newsletters or magazine articles because the paragraphs must line up to form a pleasing layout. In technical documentation, you typically don't use this feature unless you're working with a highly customized layout.

To synchronize baselines, follow these steps:

1. Display a body page in the flow you want to modify, then select the text frame.
2. Select Format | Page Layout | Line Layout. The Line Layout dialog box is displayed (Figure 10-4).
3. Uncheck Feather if it's checked, or synchronization will not work.

4. Do one or both of the following:

- To specify the line spacing for paragraphs, type a value in the Synchronize Pgf's with Line Spacing Of field.

- To specify the limit for synchronizing headings at the top of a column, type the heading size in the First-Line Synchronization Limit field.

5. Click the Update Flow button. The text in the flow is updated.

To compare the synchronized and unsynchronized layouts, turn on synchronization, display the page and then select Edit | Undo.

Splitting Text Frames

You can split a text frame on the master or body pages. Content continues from the first text frame to the second frame because they're in the same flow. The insertion point determines where FrameMaker splits the frame. In the following example, the cursor is at the end of the first paragraph, so the frame is split below that line.

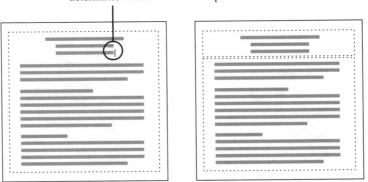

The location of the insertion point determines where the frame is split.

On a page with two text frames, you can make the last text frame the first in the flow by splitting and resizing the top frame and deleting the last frame.

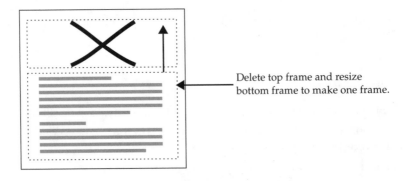

Delete top frame and resize bottom frame to make one frame.

If you split text frames on the body page and decide you don't need the split layout, you can reapply the master page, and the page will be reformatted by the master page.

The space below the paragraph tag at the insertion point determines the initial height of the split frame. The more space, the higher the frame. After you split a text frame, you can adjust its dimensions in the text frame properties.

To split a text frame, follow these steps:

1. Display the body or master page you want to modify.
2. Position your cursor in the paragraph above the line where the frame will be split.
3. Select Format | Customize Layout | Split Text Frames. The text frame is divided into two frames. You can resize the frames to get the layout you want. See "Resizing Text Frames" on page 251 for details.

Disconnecting Text Frames

You disconnect text frames to separate content from the rest of the document. If the frames are on the same page, FrameMaker converts them to two untagged flows. If the frames are on different pages, the pages are also considered disconnected, even though they still have the same flow tag. The autoconnect feature is turned off in the frame on the first page to prevent new pages from generating. In the second text frame, autoconnect is still on, so FrameMaker adds a new page when the second page is filled.

Avoid disconnecting pages unless it's absolutely necessary (for example, when creating a complex layout). A disconnected page prevents autonumbered paragraphs from incrementing correctly.

Existing text remains unchanged when you disconnect text frames. You can cut and paste the text into a different text frame, but when you add new text to the disconnected frame, the text disappears under the bottom edge of the frame. To make room for the text, you resize the bottom edge of the frame. See "Resizing Text Frames" on page 251 for details.

To find disconnected text frames in a document, place your cursor in a text frame and select Edit | Select All in Flow. Text in the same flow is highlighted. You might need to decrease the document magnification to 25 percent or 50 percent to see the entire flow.

Headers and footers aren't in a flow, so they're not selected.

Text in the flow is highlighted.

This text isn't in the previous flow.

CONTROLLING
PAGE LAYOUT

To disconnect text frames, follow these steps:

1. Display the body page you want to modify, then select one of the text frames you want to disconnect.

2. Select Format | Customize Layout and click one of the following in the pop-up menu that is displayed:

   - To disconnect the preceding text frame, select Disconnect Previous.
   - To disconnect the following text frame, select Disconnect Next.
   - To disconnect both text frames on the page, select Disconnect Both.

   One of the following occurs:

   - If the text frames are on the same page, a confirmation dialog box is displayed. Click OK to disconnect the text frames and remove them from the flow.

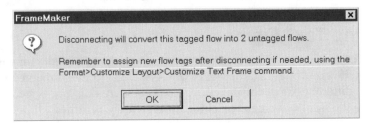

   - If the text frames are on different pages, FrameMaker disconnects the frames without warning and turns off autoconnect on the first disconnected flow.

Changing the Flow Tag

After you create a flow, you can change the flow tag. FrameMaker lets you assign a flow tag to the current frame only or to all frames in the current flow. Text on the body pages will reflow according to your changes.

To change the flow tag, follow these steps:

1. Select View | Master Pages to display the master pages, then page up or down to find the page you want to modify.

2. Select the text frame, then select Graphics | Object Properties. The Customize Text Frame dialog box is displayed (Figure 10-1 on page 246).

3. In the Tag field, type in a new flow tag.

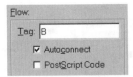

The convention is to use A, B, C, and so on for flow tags, but you can also create meaningful flow tag names. For example, a front-page newsletter article may be in the LeadStory flow and the organizational logo in the Masthead flow. You also want to keep the flow tag name short because a long flow tag name takes up more room in the status bar.

4. If you want FrameMaker to automatically create new pages when necessary, check the Autoconnect check box.

5. Click the Set button. If the text frame previously had no flow tag, the master page is updated, and you can skip the remaining steps. If you're changing the tag assigned to the text frame, the Rename Flow dialog box is displayed.

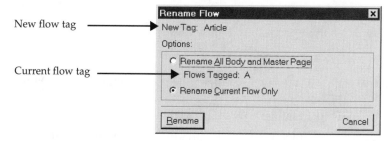

6. Do one of the following:

   ■ To rename all flows assigned to the current flow tag, click the Rename All Body and Master Page radio button. This doesn't create a new flow; it renames all of the existing flows with the current flow tag.

   ■ To rename just the current flow, click the Rename Current Flow Only radio button. This creates a new flow in the document.

7. Click the Rename button to rename the text flow.

Switching from Single- to Double-Sided Pages

The template you use to create a new document determines whether the document is single- or double-sided. For a single-sided document, FrameMaker creates a Right master page and applies it to every page. For a double-sided document, FrameMaker creates default Left and Right master pages. The Left master page is applied to the even pages, and the Right master page is applied to the odd pages by default. You can create additional master pages and apply them to create different layouts. See Chapter 11, "Understanding Master Pages," for details.

You may decide to switch a document from single- to double-sided or vice versa. Instead of creating and applying master pages manually, FrameMaker instantly adjusts the page layouts. For example, when you change a document to double-sided, FrameMaker creates a Left master page and applies it to the even pages. When you switch the document back to single-sided, FrameMaker applies the Right master page to all pages.

You can also control the page count in a document or book. For instance, in a double-sided book, you can force an even page count so that chapters always begin on the right page. FrameMaker can delete empty pages automatically. This is particularly handy for Portable Document Format (PDF) output if you don't want to convert the empty pages in your FrameMaker book.

If your document is part of a book file, you need to set the pagination for the entire book, because FrameMaker overrides pagination settings in individual files when you generate the book.

To modify pagination properties, follow these steps:

1. Do one of the following:

   - Display the book file, then CTRL-click to highlight each file you want to modify.
   - Display the document you want to modify.

2. Select Format | Page Layout | Pagination. The Pagination dialog box is displayed.

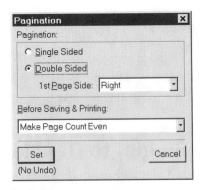

3. Set the pagination. The choices are as follows:

   - **Single-sided:** Creates a single-sided document with one master page called Right and applies it to all pages by default.

- **Double-sided:** Creates a double-sided document with a Left and Right master page and applies them to the even and odd pages, respectively. You also specify which type of page the document begins with.

    - **Right:** The first page is a right page (unless you've applied a custom master page to the first page).

    - **Left:** The first page is a left page (unless you've applied a custom master page to the first page).

    - **Read from File:** Begins document with the page specified in the file. Typically, you don't use this option unless you want to preserve a special layout in one document of the book. Otherwise, it can cause pagination problems.

    - **Next Available:** Begins document with the next available page and deletes the empty pages. For example, if Chapter 1 ends on the right page, Chapter 2 will begin on the left page, despite how you've configured the page count settings. (FrameMaker changes the page count to Delete Empty Pages.)

Last Page of Chapter 1	First Page of Chapter 2	Second Page of Chapter 2

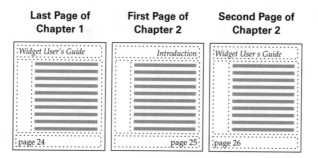

4. To set up the page count, follow these steps:

    - **Make Page Count Even:** Adds an empty page to files that have an odd page count. In a book file, for example, you may want to force an even page count so that all chapters begin on the right page and end on the left page.

    - **Make Page Count Odd:** Adds an empty page to files that have an even page count.

    - **Delete Empty Pages:** Automatically removes empty pages from the end of each file. You might want to do this before converting a book to PDF. The printed book, for instance, can have an even page count. When you make a PDF of the book, you can change the pagination to prevent empty pages from printing at the end of chapters. This only applies to left or right pages; pages formatted by custom master pages are unchanged.

    - **Don't Change Page Count:** Doesn't change the page count. If the document has several blank pages at the end, those pages are not deleted.

5. Click the Set button. The page layout is updated.

For more information on setting up numbering in book files, see "Managing Numbering" on page 373.

Structured Flows

In a structured document, you create and modify flows as you do in standard documents; however, the element definition document (EDD) must specify at least one container in each flow as valid at the highest level. For example, the Chapter element is valid at the highest level using the following rule:

Element (Container): Chapter
> **General rule:** Intro, (Process | Task | Concept | Context | Reference)+, Summar
> **Valid as the highest-level element.**

If your document has multiple flows, you might name elements based on the flow. For example, in a trainer's guide, the Chapter element could be the highest-level element followed by either the Student element (inserted if you're typing in the Student flow) or the Trainer element (inserted if you're typing in the Trainer flow). In the Student element, only the Concept, Task, and Tip elements are valid. In the Trainer element, the Overview, Concept, Task, Tip, and Comment elements are valid.

In a structured document, you can split text frames, add text frames, align text, and modify text frame properties, but you cannot change the way text frames are connected. For instance, if you split a text frame, you cannot disconnect it from the rest of the flow. Typically, you don't encounter this problem because you want the structured document to conform to the master page layout.

The Complete Reference

FrameMaker 7

Chapter 11

Understanding Master Pages

FrameMaker files are made up of body pages and master pages. A master page defines the size and shape of items—such as the default text frames and headers—that appear on the body page. In the following illustration, the Left master page creates a one-column layout for content on the body page and displays a header and footer.

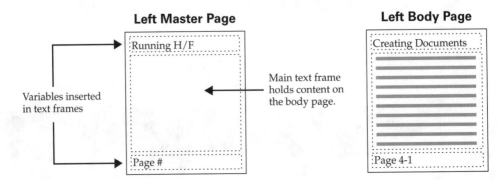

Many page layout properties, such as margin widths or the number of columns, can be modified on either the body or master page. If you update the master page, *all* body pages formatted by the master page are updated. If you update the body page, only that page changes; you modify the body page layout if you need to customize only one page.

In a structured document, you can create, apply, and modify master pages as you do in standard FrameMaker documents. The main difference is the building blocks in the running headers and footers. Because elements format the structured document instead of paragraph tags, the variables in building blocks refer to elements instead of paragraphs. For example, you use the <$elempagenum> to display a page number instead of the <$pagenum> building block. If you use the standard building blocks, the header and footer information is not displayed.

Applying a Master Page

For every body page, the underlying master page defines the location of headers and footers, background graphics, page numbers, and other items. Master pages let you create a consistent look and feel for your pages. All body pages formatted by the Left master page, for example, will have the same layout, and you can define a different layout for body pages formatted by the Right master page. Examples are displayed in the next illustration.

When you add content to your FrameMaker document, the new pages are automatically set to Right (for a single-sided document) or alternating Left and Right (for a double-sided document). You can, however, change the layout by applying a different master page to one or more body pages.

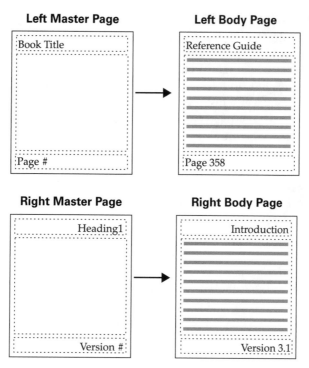

To apply a master page, follow these steps:

1. Display the body page you want to format.
2. Select Format | Page Layout | Master Page Usage. The Master Page Usage dialog box is displayed.

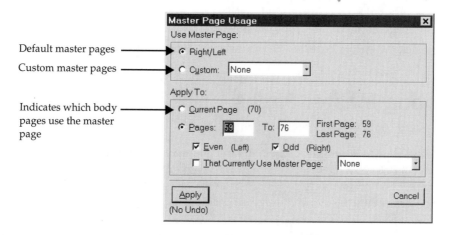

3. In the Use Master Page section, click the master page you want to apply:

   ■ To apply the default master page, click the Right radio button (in a single-sided document) or the Right/Left radio button (in a double-sided document). In a single-sided document, this applies the Right master page to all pages. In a double-sided document, this applies the Left master page to the even pages and the Right master page to the odd pages.

   ■ To apply a master page you created, click that page in the Custom drop-down list.

Caution *Avoid setting the master page to None. The body page will no longer be formatted by a master page even though it still looks like the previously applied master page. If the Right master page was applied before you set the custom master page to None, and you modify the Right master page, those changes are not displayed on the body page.*

4. In the Apply To section, do one of the following:

   ■ To apply the master page to the current body page, click the Current Page radio button. Verify that the page number displayed next to Current Page is correct. For example, if your cursor is on page 3 and the bottom of page 4 is displayed, the current page is page 4.

   ■ To apply the master page to a range of pages, type the page numbers in the Pages fields.

   ■ To apply the master page to even or odd pages, check the Even or Odd check box.

   ■ To apply the master page to all pages in the document, type the page range in the Pages section and check both the Even and Odd check boxes.

   ■ To apply the master page to pages that currently use a specific master page, check the That Currently Use Master Page check box and click the master page name in the drop-down list.

5. Click the Apply button. The master page is applied to the specified pages.

Creating Master Pages

Master pages contain two types of items:

■ **Foreground elements.** Containers for the main text of the document. Many master pages have just one foreground element—the text frame in which you insert text on the body pages. Chapter 10, "Understanding Text Flows," describes how to modify foreground elements, such as adding columns and room for side heads.

■ **Background elements.** Headers, footers, background graphics, page numbers, and other information that is repeated on the body pages. This chapter deals with background elements.

To create foreground and background elements, you place text frames, graphic frames, and graphics on the master pages. When you draw a *text frame*, you are prompted to specify whether the frame is for background elements or for body page information. Each foreground text frame has a *flow tag*, which controls how text fills the text frames. As you type text, FrameMaker automatically adds new pages and allows the text to flow onto those pages. (See "Understanding Text Flows" on page 244.) When you place a *graphic frame* or a graphic on the master page, it automatically becomes a background element. Background elements are not part of a flow.

One type of background element—running header and footers—repeats information on each body page. You can type content in the running header/footers or insert variables to display the page number, book title, file name, heading, and so on. The value of a variable is automatically updated when you open or save the file or generate the book file. For details, see "Inserting Variables" on page 217.

Creating Default Left and Right Master Pages

When you create a new document, FrameMaker creates default master pages for you— Right in a single-sided document, and Left and Right in a double-sided document. If you switch a single-sided document to double-sided, FrameMaker automatically creates the Left master page. You can modify the layout of default master pages, but you cannot rename, reorder, or delete them. For more information on changing the pagination of a document, see "Switching from Single- to Double-Sided Pages" on page 267.

Creating Custom Master Pages

In a typical double-sided book, you use Left and Right for regular pages, and then create custom master pages for cover, title, landscape, rotated, and other special page layouts. You can create up to 100 master pages. All master pages in a document must be the same size. You can change the paper size for an entire document, but to create a master page with different dimensions, you need to create a new document and define the size. See "Creating a Blank Document" on page 40 for details.

You can create a master page while you're viewing a body page, but if you create a new master page while viewing the master pages, you have more design options. On the master pages, you can copy the layout of any master page or create an empty page. On the body pages, you're limited to copying the master page applied to the current page.

To create a master page based on the current body page layout, follow these steps:

1. Display the body page that looks similar to the master page you want to create.
2. Select Format | Page Layout | New Master Page. The New Master Page dialog box is displayed.

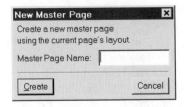

3. Type the name of the new master page in the Master Page Name field, then click the Create button. A confirmation is displayed, explaining how to apply and edit the new master page.

4. Click the OK button. The new master page is displayed.

To copy the layout of any master page or to create an empty master page, follow these steps:

1. Display any master page, then select Special | Add Master Page. The Add Master Page dialog box is displayed.

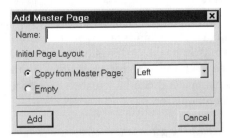

2. In the Name field, type a name for the new master page. Remember that the master page name is case sensitive.

3. Do one of the following:

■ Make a copy of an existing page by clicking the page from the Copy from Master Page drop-down list. Select this option if an existing page resembles the page you want to create. (The new master page will belong to the same flow as the copied page.)

■ Create a blank page by clicking the Empty radio button. Select this option if none of the existing master pages resembles the page you want to create. (The new master page will belong to flow A.)

4. Click the Add button. The new master page is displayed.

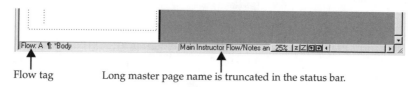

Flow tag   Long master page name is truncated in the status bar.

Renaming Master Pages

When you rename a custom master page, the body pages that use the renamed master page are not affected. To rename a master page, follow these steps:

1. Select View | Master Pages to display the master pages.
2. Page up or down to find the page you want to rename.
3. Click the name of the master page in the status bar. The Master Page Name dialog box is displayed.

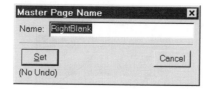

4. Type the new master page name over the highlighted name, then click the Set button. The master page is renamed. Body pages that use the master page are still formatted by the renamed page.

Rearranging Master Pages

Initially, master pages are displayed in the order you create them, shown in the following example. In FrameMaker 7, you can rearrange custom master pages to display them in a different order in drop-down lists and in the master page view. You might prefer placing frequently used master pages at the top for easier access.

The order of the master pages cannot be imported into other FrameMaker files; you'll need to rearrange them in each file. In addition, you cannot move the default master pages. They're always displayed first.

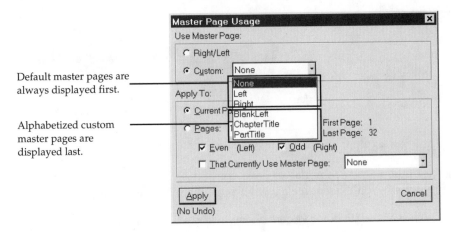

Default master pages are always displayed first.

Alphabetized custom master pages are displayed last.

To rearrange the master pages, follow these steps:

1. Select View | Master Pages to display the master pages.

2. Select Format | Page Layout | Reorder Custom Master Pages. The Reorder Custom Master Pages dialog box is displayed.

3. Click the master page you want to move, then click the Move Up or Move Down button.

4. Click the Set button. The custom master pages are rearranged.

Modifying Master Pages

There are a number of ways to customize master pages. You can create multiple flows to separate text on the body pages, set up running headers and footers, and add a watermark. When you modify a master page that's already been applied, the master page layout is displayed on the body page, and text reflows into the new layout, if necessary.

Adding Text Flows

Most master page text frames are associated with flow tags, which control how text fills text frames. In documents with more than one flow, text in each flow is displayed independently from the other flow. Newsletters often have multiple flows that continue a story from page 2, for example, to page 4. Many documents only have the default flow A, but you can add new flows. For details, see "Adding Text Flows to Master Pages" on page 248.

Setting Up Headers and Footers

Running headers and footers repeat information on body pages, such as the page number, book title, modification date, or content from a heading. Typically, you insert variables to display this information because they're easier to update than text. For example, if you type the book title instead of inserting a variable, and the name of the book changes, you'll need to change the book title wherever you typed it on the master pages. Using a variable, you update the variable once, and the book title is updated throughout the document. See Chapter 9, "Storing Content in Variables," for more information.

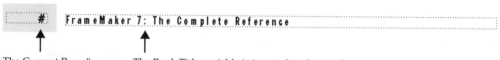

The Current Page #
variable is inserted
in the text frame.

The Book Title variable is inserted in the text frame

FrameMaker provides twelve running header/footer variables that can display information, usually the text or paragraph number of a specific paragraph or element. The values of these running header/footer variables are updated when content on the body page changes. For example, if the variable displays the first second-level heading on the page, and the heading changes, the new heading is displayed where you inserted the variable. For more information on running header/footer variables, see "Running Header/Footer Variables" on page 225.

FrameMaker includes running headers and footers in new documents by default. If you delete the default running header/footer or add an empty master page, you might need to add a new running header/footer.

To create a running header/footer, follow these steps:

1. Select View | Master Pages to display the master pages.
2. Page up or down to find the page you want to modify.
3. Draw the text frame where you want it on the master page. The Add New Text Frame dialog box is displayed.

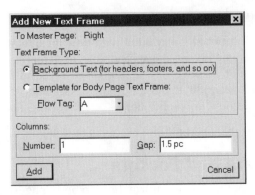

4. Click the Background Text radio button, then click the Add button. The text frame is displayed on the master page.

5. Place your cursor in the text frame, then select Special | Variable. The Variable dialog box is displayed.

6. Click the running header/footer variable you want to insert, then click the Insert button. The variable is displayed in the text frame.

Setting Up a Watermark

You can place a watermark on the master pages that is displayed on the body pages. The watermark can contain a rough draft statement, a graphic, or another message. Some printer drivers also let you set up a watermark. You configure the watermark in the printer details and print the watermark only when you need to.

To create a watermark in FrameMaker, you type text on the page, in a paragraph tag's autonumber, or in a variable. You can also insert a graphic. Paragraph tags and variables are updated more easily than if you type text on the page—you update the watermark in the tag or variable, and each instance of the watermark is updated automatically. You can't, however, apply a condition to the autonumbered watermark. Conditions only work with text you can select.

To set up a graphic watermark, you create the graphic and import it onto the master page. If you have a specific watermark design that's difficult to set up in FrameMaker, the graphic watermark is a good alternative to text. As long as the graphic is imported by reference and not embedded, the file size doesn't increase.

You need to experiment with the watermark color and tint, because optimum settings depend largely on your printer driver and paper. Most watermarks use a 10 percent to 25 percent gray tint. Be sure to print a page in the document to verify the color before you print the whole document. If you plan to distribute a PDF of the document, create a test PDF to make sure the color isn't too dark on screen.

In Windows 95, 98, and Millennium Edition, Adobe Acrobat 5 lets you define a watermark in the Acrobat Distiller printer options before you convert the FrameMaker file to PDF. Refer to the Acrobat help for details.

Creating a Text Watermark in FrameMaker

To create a text watermark in FrameMaker, follow these steps:

1. Create a paragraph tag to format the text. For example, you can create a paragraph tag that formats the watermark with a 15-percent gray sans-serif font set to 48 points. Be sure to print the document to make sure the color prints dark enough without reducing document readability.

Rough Draft

2. Select View | Master Pages to display the master pages.

3. Page up or down to find the page you want to modify.

4. Select Graphics | Tools to display the Tools palette, then click the Text Frame icon.

5. Draw a background text frame where you want the watermark. The text frame is displayed on the page.

6. Position your cursor in the text frame and do one of the following:

   ■ To store the watermark in a paragraph tag, create a paragraph tag or display an existing tag in the Paragraph Designer, then type the watermark text in the Autonumbering Format field of the Numbering sheet.

   ■ To store the watermark in a variable, create a variable, type the watermark text in the variable, and insert the variable.

   ■ To type the watermark on the page, click in the text frame and type.

   The watermark is displayed on the master page.

7. *(optional)* Resize the text frame to remove white space between the watermark and text frame.

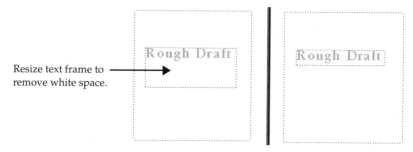

Resize text frame to remove white space.

Next, you can rotate and align the watermark. See Chapter 13, "FrameMaker's Graphics Tools," for details.

If you typed the watermark text or inserted a variable, you can apply a condition tag. When you need to hide the watermark, change the Show/Hide settings for the condition tag, and the condition is updated on all body and master pages. For details, see Chapter 21, "Setting Up Conditional Text."

Using a Watermark Graphic

When you create a watermark graphic, you should make sure the color of the watermark is light enough to display behind the main content without reducing readability. As mentioned in the previous procedure, you might start with 15-percent gray. To angle the graphic on the page, rotate the watermark in your graphics program. This saves you the step of rotating the graphic after you insert it in the document.

You can embed a watermark graphic onto the master page or import the file by reference. To minimize the size of your document, import the watermark graphic by reference. In addition, you can modify the watermark more quickly if you import the file by reference. However, embedding the graphic also has advantages. If you need to send the FrameMaker document to your client or print vendor, for example, you don't need to worry about losing the graphics because they're in the file. For more information on embedding and importing graphics, see Chapter 12, "Importing Graphics."

To use a graphic as a watermark, follow these steps:

1. Select View | Master Pages to display the master pages.

2. Page up or down to find the page you want to modify.

3. Click outside the main text frame so your cursor isn't in the text frame, then select File | Import | File. The Import dialog box is displayed. (If the cursor is in the text frame, the graphic will import inside an anchored frame. This is unnecessary on the master page because you're not anchoring the graphic to text.)

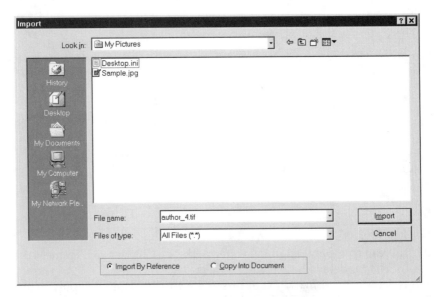

4. Import the watermark graphic as you would other graphics. The graphic is displayed in the main text frame. See "Graphic Formats" on page 317 for details on importing different types of graphics.

If the graphic isn't displayed, click the main text frame and select Graphics | Send to Back. This moves the text frame behind the graphic.

Creating a Landscape Master Page

You can create pages that have portrait and landscape orientation in a single file. (You cannot, however, use different page sizes in a single file.) Basically, you create a new master page, rotate the page, and then adjust the main text frame dimensions. To create landscape-style headers or footers, you rotate the running header/footer text frames along with the page. To create portrait-style headers or footers, you delete the existing running header/footer text frames *before* rotating the page, then add them back to the master page. In the following illustration, the original portrait-style pages included footers, so when the pages were rotated, the footers rotated to the landscape view.

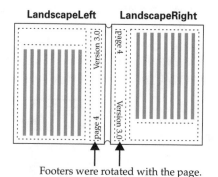

Footers were rotated with the page.

In contrast, the original portrait-style page in the next illustration was rotated counterclockwise (to create the LandscapeLeft master page) and clockwise (to create the LandscapeRight master page). After the landscape pages were rotated, the footer text frames were added to create portrait-style footers.

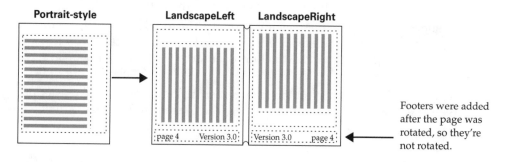

Footers were added after the page was rotated, so they're not rotated.

CONTROLLING
PAGE LAYOUT

To decide which direction the headers and footers on landscape pages should face, consider the following factors:

- **Rotated header/footer.** The header and footer information is harder to read from the vertical perspective, and the book binding could cut off the text. However, in a section with several landscape pages, you can rotate the headers and footers so they all match within the group.

- **Unrotated header/footer.** The headers and footers on landscape pages match those found on portrait-style pages and can be read quickly while scanning the book. Typically, this option makes more sense in terms of document readability.

You should apply a landscape master page after you've added most of the content to the page. Otherwise, you'll either have to type sideways or rotate the main text frame to its original position, add your content, and then rotate the frame back to the landscape position. For more information on rotating text frames, see "Rotating" on page 356.

To create a landscape master page, follow these steps:

1. Create a new master page with a name such as LandscapeLeft or LandscapeRight.

2. *(Portrait-style running headers/footers only)* To prevent running headers and footers from rotating, delete their text frames.

3. On the new master page, select the main text frame, then select Graphics | Object Properties. The Customize Text Frame dialog box is displayed. (The Unrotated Size and Offset From settings are displayed here.)

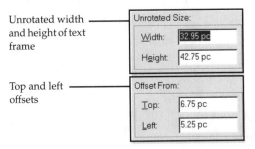

Unrotated width and height of text frame

Top and left offsets

4. Write down the width and height of the main text frame, along with the top and left offset. You'll need these numbers after you rotate the page.

5. Rotate the master page by selecting Format | Customize Layout | Rotate Page Clockwise (for a right master page) or Rotate Page Counterclockwise (for a left master page). The entire page (including headers, footers, and the main text frame) is rotated.

6. If not already selected, select the main text frame on the landscape master page, then select Graphics | Object Properties. The Customize Text Frame dialog box is displayed.

7. Refer back to the settings you wrote down in step 3 and adjust the text frame dimensions, as follows.

   a. In the Unrotated Size section, type the original height in the Width field, and type the original width in the Height field.

   b. In the Offset From section, type the original left offset in the Top field, and type the original top offset in the Left field. You might need to adjust these values.

8. Click the Set button. The landscape master page is displayed.

9. *(Portrait-style running headers/footers only)* Draw new text frames for the running headers and footers.

Creating Bleeding Tabs

Thumb tabs help a reader find information in a book. They can contain the chapter heading, chapter number, or other descriptive text. *Bleeding thumb tabs* are printed on the edge of the page so that the reader can easily identify section breaks while flipping through the book. In this book, all thumb tabs are stored on the Right master page. During the production edit, the unnecessary tabs were deleted, and the variable definition was updated. For example, in Part 1, all thumb tabs were deleted except for the first one. In Part 2, all thumb tabs were deleted except for the second one.

Figure 11-1 shows the page layout before and after removing tabs and updating the variable. The thumb tabs appear to be one long graphic, but they're actually several overlapping graphics. The overlap prevents gaps from printing between sections on the outside edge of the page.

Thumb tabs have four components:

■ **Shaded rectangle.** The tabs are rectangles with a solid fill.

■ **Text frame.** Drawn on each tab to hold the content.

■ **Variable.** Inserted into the text frames displays the content.

■ **Paragraph tag.** Formats the content in a color that displays clearly against the solid background. The tag may also center-align the text.

Consider the following factors when you plan thumb tabs:

■ **Size.** How much text will be displayed on the tabs? For the chapter number and title, you'll need to create a longer tab and text frame than for just the chapter number.

Your print vendor may trim the paper to reduce the finished book size. If so, you need to know which edges of the page will be cut off. If all four edges are trimmed, you need to adjust the top offset of the first and last tab on the page in addition to adjusting the left offset for all tabs. If the bottom edge of the page isn't trimmed, you don't need to adjust the top offset of the last tab.

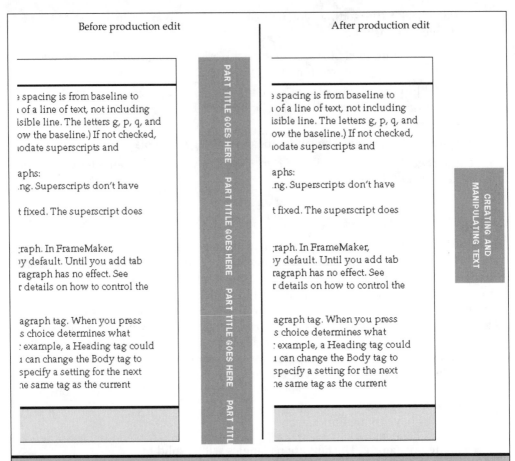

Figure 11-1. *Deleting thumb tabs from the master page*

■ **Formatting.** How will you format the text? The font face, size, and color should display clearly against the thumb tab. The amount of content on the tab affects the font size. The more text, the smaller the font.

■ **Placement.** Will the paper be trimmed? To create bleeding tabs, the tabs must be large enough for the text, and the text frames must be placed closer to the left edge of the tab so the content isn't trimmed off.

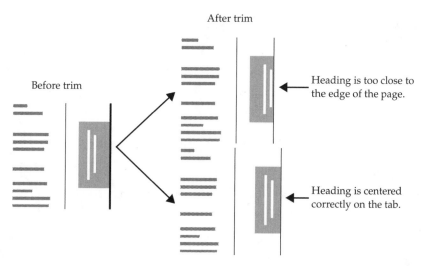

After trim

Before trim

Heading is too close to
the edge of the page.

Heading is centered
correctly on the tab.

■ **Master page setup.** Some users create one page for all thumb tabs, while others prefer creating a master page for each part or chapter (depending on your thumb tab setup) with the thumb tab in the correct position for that section. Creating separate thumb tab master pages saves you the step of deleting extra tabs in every section, but it also multiplies the number of master pages in your template. If your book doesn't have many parts or chapters, this may not be an issue.

The following procedure describes how to add thumb tabs to one master page.

Drawing the Thumb Tab

Creating thumb tabs involves several stages. First, you need to draw a rectangle for the tab. To do so, follow these steps:

1. Select View | Master Pages to display the master pages.

2. Page up or down to find the page you want to modify.

3. Select Graphics | Tools to display the Tools palette, then click the Rectangle icon.

4. Draw a rectangle against the right edge of the page. The blank rectangle is displayed. Don't worry about the position. You'll calculate the bleed and distribute the tabs later.

5. With the rectangle selected, click the Fill Pattern icon, then click the shading pattern (such as *solid*) from the Fill pop-up menu. The pattern is displayed on the tab.

CONTROLLING
PAGE LAYOUT

The shaded thumb tab is displayed on the master page.

Adding the Text Frame

After you draw the thumb tab, you need to add the text frame. To do so, follow these steps:

1. Draw a small background text frame over the thumb tab. It shouldn't be the size of the final text frame. You're going to rotate the frame, so it will change dimensions. The background text frame is displayed on the shaded tab.

2. With the text frame selected, rotate it 90 degrees clockwise. See "Rotating" on page 356 for details.

3. Lengthen the text frame and move it closer to the left edge of the tab. This helps prevent the text from being trimmed off. You can either drag the borders of the text frame to resize it or change the size in the text frame properties.

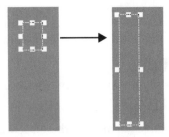

4. Insert a variable in the text frame and apply a paragraph tag. The variable is displayed on the tab, and the paragraph tag formatting is applied.

To shorten long headings so they fit on the tab, you can insert a Header/Footer marker in the heading paragraph, type the shortened heading in the marker, and cross-reference that marker in the variable. For details, see "Displaying Text from a Marker" on page 226.

5. Select View | Body Pages to display the body pages.

6. Apply the thumb tab master page to the correct body pages, and check the position of the thumb tab text. If the paragraph is too long, you can resize the text frame or change the font size.

Creating Additional Thumb Tabs

To place additional thumb tabs down the edge of the master page and align them, follow these steps:

1. Select View | Master Pages and page up or down to find the thumb tab page.

2. Select the thumb tab rectangle and text frame, then select Graphics | Group. The text frame and thumb tab are grouped.

3. Copy the tab, then paste it down the edge of the page.

4. Select all tabs, then left align them. See "Aligning" on page 350 for details.

You should wait to delete extra thumb tabs and modify any thumb tab variables until production. If you reimport the page layout properties and variable definitions from your template, the original thumb tabs are displayed, and you'll have to modify the thumb tabs and variables again.

Creating the Bleed

To make sure that the thumb tab prints to the edge of the page, follow these steps:

1. Select one of the thumb tabs, then select Graphics | Object Properties. The Object Properties dialog box is displayed. The Offset From section is shown here.

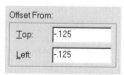

CONTROLLING
PAGE LAYOUT

2. Change the offset values, which are different for the first and last tab. If the top or bottom edge will not be trimmed, you only need to follow step b.

   a. *(first tab only)* Type a value between **-0.125** and **-0.25** inches in the Offset From Top field.

   b. *(all tabs)* To calculate the Offset From Left value, subtract the tab width from the page width and add between 0.125 and 0.25 inches. Type the value in the Offset From Left field.

   c. *(last tab only)* To calculate the Offset From Top value, subtract the tab height from the page height, add between 0.125 and 0.25 inches. Type the value in the Offset From Top field.

To check the page size, select Format | Page Layout | Page Size. The page width and height are displayed.

3. Click the Set button to save your changes. You'll need to experiment with the offset values and then trim the page to find the best location. After changing the offset, you can widen the tab to make room for text.

4. After you place all tabs on the page, you need to distribute them evenly. See "Distributing" on page 351 for details.

Once you've set up the tabs on the master page, you can import the page layouts into other files, apply the thumb tab master page, and delete the unnecessary tabs.

Removing Master Page Overrides

You create overrides to the master page by modifying text frame properties on the body page. For instance, when you adjust the size of the text frame to copyfit a body page, you create an override. FrameMaker warns you about the overrides when you switch from the master page to body page view. If you remove the override, FrameMaker removes all master page overrides—not just the overrides on the current page—so that the body pages match the master pages again. If you keep the override, the customized body pages are no longer formatted by the master page.

Click to remove master page overrides.

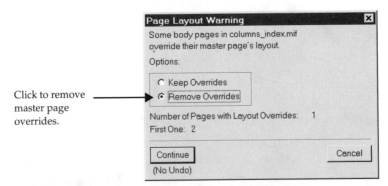

Reapplying Master Pages Globally

FrameMaker 7 lets you map paragraph and element tags to master pages. When you reapply all master pages, FrameMaker scans pages for the specified paragraph tags and assigns the correct master pages. For example, you might map the ChapTitle paragraph tag to the First master page. Instead of manually applying the master page, you apply all master pages in the document with the Apply Master Pages menu choice, which is new in FrameMaker 7. The First master page is instantly applied to the page containing the ChapTitle paragraph tag. This feature also removes all page layout overrides in the document at once.

Mapping Tags to Master Pages

On the MasterPageMaps reference page, you map paragraph and element tags to master pages. For each mapped paragraph or element, you must specify the master page to apply to all right body pages. This page is applied to left body pages if you don't assign a master page to the left pages.

You have the option of assigning a page range for each master page. For example, the master page might be applied to a single page, a page range, or until you specify another master page. You can also provide comments so that other writers understand the mapping. Sample mappings for an unstructured document are displayed in the following example.

UnstructMasterPageMaps
Book Update (Yes or No): Yes

Paragraph Tag Name	Right-Handed Master Page (or Single-Sided Master Page)	Left-Handed Master Page	Range Indicator (Single, Span pages, Until changed)	Comments
Heading1	RightSL	LeftSL	Until changed	
ChapTitle	ChapTitle	ChapTitle	Until changed	
Intro	RightNonum	LeftNonum	Until changed	
Notes	NotesRight	NotesLeft	Single	

Note *When more than one mapped paragraph or element tag is on the same page, FrameMaker applies the master page for the first tag.*

In a structured document, the StructMasterPageMaps table has the same features, but you can map either elements or paragraphs. The "E:" prefix indicates an element; the "P:" prefix indicates a paragraph. You can also qualify the elements with attribute names, values, and context labels. Using the following entries, FrameMaker scans the page for a Head element with a Type attribute value of "Section" and the context label "Level 1." Sample mappings are displayed in the following example.

CONTROLLING
PAGE LAYOUT

StructMasterPageMaps
Book Update (Yes or No): Yes

Element/ Paragraph Tag Name	Right-Handed Master Page (or Single-Sided Master Page)	Left-Handed Master Page	Attribute Name	Attribute Value	Context	Range Indicator (Single, Span pages, Until changed)	Comments
E:Head	RightSL	LeftSL	Type	Section	Level 1	Until changed	

In both structured and unstructured documents, you can turn on book-level master pages updates. This lets you reapply all master pages at the book level. If the Book Update indicator above the mapping table is blank, FrameMaker uses the default value "Yes."

Be sure to map at least the right master page, or FrameMaker will set the master page to None when you reapply the master pages. Though the body page still looks like the previously applied master page, the None setting means the page layout isn't determined by the master page—an override you want to avoid.

Table 11-1 describes all mapping options.

Field	Description
Required Fields	
Element/Paragraph Tag Name	Paragraph or element to which the master page is automatically applied. Must be spelled and capitalized correctly, or FrameMaker ignores the setting and applies the default master page.
Right-Handed Master Page (or Single-Sided Master Page)	Master page applied to right body pages (in a double-sided document) or all body pages (in a single-sided document). Must be spelled and capitalized correctly, or FrameMaker displays an error when you reapply master pages and stops the process. If blank, the master page is set to None.
Optional Fields	
Left-Handed Master Page	Master page applied to left body pages. If blank, FrameMaker applies the master page mapped to the right body pages.

Table 11-1.   *Mapping Paragraph Tags to Master Pages*

Field	Description
Attribute Name (*structured only*)	Element must include the specified attribute.
Attribute Value (*structured only*)	Attribute must include the specified value.
Context (*structured only*)	Element must occur under the specified context. For example, the entry "Head(First Level)" means that the mapped master page is applied only if the Head element occurs at the first level. If the Head element has the context label "Second Level," the master page isn't applied.
Range Indicator	Pages to which the master page is applied. Options are as follows: ■ **Single:** Applied only to the page with the specified tag. ■ **Span pages:** Applied to pages within the range, beginning with the specified paragraph tag. ■ **Until changed:** Applied to all pages until FrameMaker finds another mapped paragraph tag. For instance, according to the previous example, the RightSL and LeftSL master pages are applied until another mapped paragraph tag is found. If blank, FrameMaker applies the master page to a single page.
Comments	Notes on the mapping.

Table 11-1. *Mapping Paragraph Tags to Master Pages (Continued)*

If you're working in a pre-FrameMaker 7 document, you need to complete the following procedure before you can map master pages. FrameMaker will add the MasterPageMaps reference page and the unstructured or structured mapping table, depending on your document. In a book file, you must generate the reference page for one file, then you can import the reference pages from the updated file into the rest of the book. See "Importing Settings from a Template File" on page 617 for details.

Processing the Master Page Mappings

To reapply master pages you've mapped to paragraph or element tags, follow these steps:

1. Do one of the following:
   - *(book file)* Select Page Layout | Apply Master Pages.
   - *(single file)* Select Format | Page Layout | Apply Master Pages.

   A confirmation dialog box is displayed.

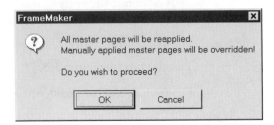

2. Click the OK button. The master pages are reapplied.

At the book level, an error is displayed if one of the chapters doesn't have a MasterPageMaps reference page. You must repeat the preceding procedure for one file in the book, which generates the reference page automatically, then you can map master pages from the book file.

Eliminating Page Layout Overrides

After you modify the text frame on a body page, you can update the master page applied to that page, or you can update the entire flow. When you update the master pages, all body pages to which you've applied the master page are reformatted. For example, suppose you experiment with different side head widths on a body page to see how text appears in the new layout. If you like the new size and want to modify all pages in the flow to match the current body page, you update the column layout, and FrameMaker changes the master pages in the flow according to your specifications.

Removing All Layout Overrides

To remove all layout overrides by displaying the master pages, follow these steps:

1. Select View | Master Pages to display the master pages, then select View | Body Pages. The Page Layout Warning dialog box is displayed (Figure 11-2).
2. Click the Remove Overrides radio button, then click the Continue button. All page layout overrides are removed.

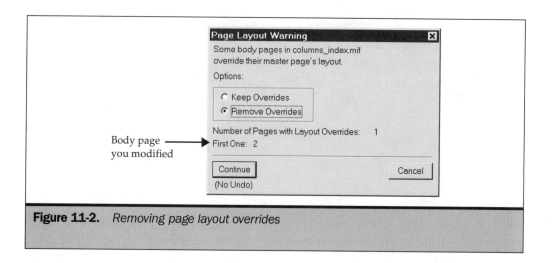

Figure 11-2.   *Removing page layout overrides*

Updating Master Pages and Body Pages Simultaneously

To update default master pages and body pages in the same flow all at once, follow these steps:

1. Display either the master pages or the body pages. (You're updating both layouts at the same time, so the type of page displayed doesn't matter.)

2. Select Format | Page Layout | Column Layout. If the left and master pages have different layouts, a warning is displayed. Click the OK button.

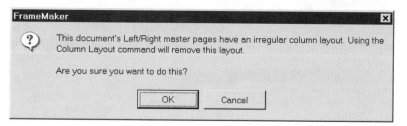

The Column Layout dialog box is displayed.

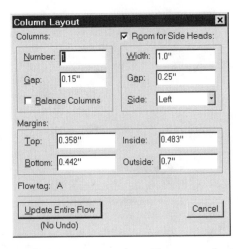

3. Change the settings you want to update. For example, to remove the side head area, uncheck the Room for Side Heads check box.

4. Click the Update Entire Flow button. The master page and body page layouts are updated.

Only the default master pages are updated. You'll need to update custom master pages individually.

Updating One Master Page

To update the master page applied to the current body page, follow these steps:

1. Display the customized body page, then select Format | Page Layout | Update Column Layout. The Update Column Layout dialog box is displayed.

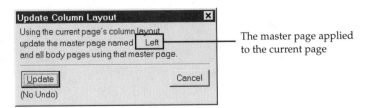

The master page applied to the current page

2. Click the Update button. The master page applied to the current body page is updated.

Deleting Master Pages

While you can delete several body pages at a time, you must delete master pages individually. You can delete only the master pages you create; default master pages (Left and Right in a double-sided document and Right in a single-sided document) cannot be removed.

Before you delete a master page that has been applied to a body page, you must apply another master page to all pages that use that master page. FrameMaker warns if the master page is in use, so there's no way to delete a master page you've applied to a body page. See "Applying a Master Page" on page 272 for details.

To delete a master page, follow these steps:

1. Display the master page you want to delete.

2. Select Special | Delete Page "*master page name.*" A confirmation dialog box is displayed. If the master page is applied to a body page, an error is displayed. You'll need to display the body page, apply a different master page in its place, and then repeat this procedure.

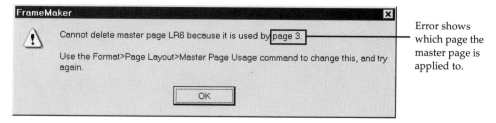

Error shows which page the master page is applied to.

3. On the confirmation dialog box, click the OK button. The master page is no longer in the document.

Master Pages in Structured Documents

In structured documents, you create and apply master pages as you do in unstructured documents. The only difference involves defining running header/footers, which you insert on the master page to display content from a specific tag in a structured document. For instance, the Section element is displayed in the header using the following variable definition:

```
<$elemtext[Section]>
```

The <$elemtext> building block displays the contents of the first Section element on the page. There are several other building blocks unique to structured documents. Though you use them to build running header/footer variables, the building blocks are also included in cross-reference formats. For a list of building blocks for structured documents, see "Cross-Reference Building Blocks" on page 201.

Chapter 12

Importing Graphics

FrameMaker supports line art (vector graphics) and bitmap graphics in many formats. Most graphics are displayed in frames. On body pages, most graphics are in anchored frames. An anchored frame attaches the graphic to a paragraph. When the paragraph moves up or down on the page, the anchored frame moves with the anchoring paragraph. This lets you control the graphic alignment and position. For example, the following illustration shows a graphic anchored to the previous paragraph.

The graphic is anchored to this line.

You can crop graphics with anchored frames by sizing the frame around the part of the graphic you need to crop. Graphic frames also let you mask graphics, but they're used primarily on reference and master pages. On reference pages, you store frequently used objects, such as icons or borders.

In structured documents, you insert a graphic element to import graphics. The element can insert the anchored frame first or let you choose the graphic, then import the graphic into an anchored frame automatically.

Anchoring Graphics

When you import a graphic into a text frame, the graphic is automatically inserted in an anchored frame centered below the current line. The anchor, which looks like an upside-down T, appears on the line where you position your cursor. Alternatively, you can insert the anchored frame first, with the alignment and position you want, and then import the graphic into the frame. Inserting the frame first lets you select the alignment and position. However, importing the graphic directly into the document saves you the step of inserting the empty frame.

You can change the default anchored frame properties by installing a third-party FrameMaker plug-in called ImpGraph. The plug-in saves you the step of repositioning the anchored frame each time you import a graphic. For details, see Appendix A, "Resources."

There are seven anchored frame positions. Each position has specific alignment options. Some frames can be inserted outside the text column or text frame to display, for instance, an icon in the margin. Other frames are displayed in different positions inside a text frame. Table 12-1 describes the anchored frame options.

Position	Description
Below Current Line 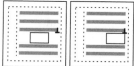 Closer Farther to Binding from Binding 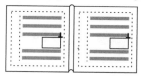 Side head area crops — the frame. 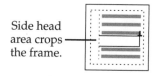 Frame floats where it fits. 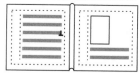	Places the anchored frame below the line containing the insertion point. Select the position of the frame: ■ **Left:** Left aligns the frame in the text column unless the anchoring paragraph extends across the side head and columns. In that case, the graphic aligns under the anchoring paragraph. ■ **Center:** Centers the frame in the text column or across the columns and side head. ■ **Right:** Aligns the frame at the right edge of the column or across the columns and side head. ■ **Side Closer to Binding:** In a single-sided document, aligns the frame with the left side of all pages; in a double-sided document, aligns the frame with the right side of even-numbered pages or the left side of odd-numbered pages. ■ **Side Farther from Binding:** In a single-sided document, aligns the frame on the left side of all pages; in a double-sided document, aligns the frame with the left side of even-numbered pages or the right side of odd-numbered pages. You can apply two additional properties: ■ **Cropped:** Fits the anchored frame within the text column (or side head area, if one exists). Cropped anchored frames are cut off by the borders of the text frame or the side head area. Uncropped anchored frames extend into the side head or margins. ■ **Floating:** Moves the anchored frame to the top of the next column without moving the anchor when there is not enough space for the anchored frame in the current column.
At Top of Column 	Places the anchored frame at the top of the column containing the insertion point. Has the same alignment and options as the Below the Current Line setting.

Table 12-1. *Anchored Frame Options*

CONTROLLING
PAGE LAYOUT

Position	Description
At Bottom of Column	Places the anchored frame at the bottom of the column containing the insertion point. Has the same alignment and options as the Below the Current Line setting.
At Insertion Point	Aligns the anchored frame vertically with the bottom of the current line. The anchor is not displayed. The Distance Above Baseline option adds space between the anchored frame and the current line. For example, the illustration on the left shows a graphic placed -0.5 inches from the baseline.
Outside Column	Places the anchored frame in the side head space outside the text column. Select where the frame is displayed: ■ **Left, Right, Side Closer to Binding,** or **Side Farther from Binding:** See alignment options for "Below Current Line" on page 301. ■ **Side Closer to Page Edge:** Aligns the frame closer to the edge of the page in single-sided documents. Same as Side Farther from Binding in double-sided documents. ■ **Side Farther from Page Edge:** Aligns the frame farther from the edge of the page in single-sided documents. Same as Side Closer to Binding in double-sided documents. You can also change the vertical and horizontal spacing: ■ **Distance above Baseline:** Space above or below the anchored frame. A negative setting extends the anchored frame below the baseline. ■ **Distance from Text Column:** Space to the left or right of the anchored frame.
Outside Text Frame	Places the anchored frame in the margin of the document outside the main text column. In a single-column document, shown in the illustration on the left, this position is the same as the Outside Column position. See alignment and spacing options for outside column earlier in this table.

Table 12-1.   *Anchored Frame Options (Continued)*

Position	Description
Run into Paragraph 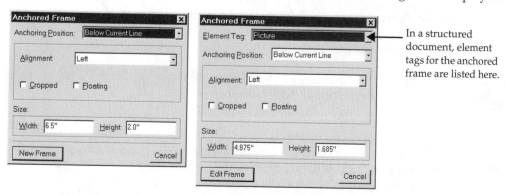	Places the anchored frame in the text column with the paragraph. Text is displayed around one side of the anchored frame. To adjust the space between the text and frame, you modify the gap setting in the anchored frame properties. Alignment options are the same for "Below Current Line" on page 301, except the center alignment is unavailable.

Table 12-1.   *Anchored Frame Options (Continued)*

Inserting an Anchored Frame

You can insert an anchored frame in a document, then import a graphic or place objects in the frame. Although this adds a step to the import process, it lets you position and align the frame.

To insert an empty anchored frame, follow these steps:

1. Select Special | Anchored Frame. The Anchored Frame dialog box is displayed.

In a structured document, element tags for the anchored frame are listed here.

2. *(optional)* In a structured document, click an element in the Element Tag drop-down list. If no graphic elements are defined in the element catalog, "<NONE AVAILABLE>" is displayed.

3. Click the anchored frame position in the Anchoring Position drop-down list.

4. Click the anchored frame alignment in the Alignment drop-down list. The available choices depend on the anchoring position. See Table 12-1 on page 301 for details.

5. Complete additional fields that are displayed for the alignment you selected. Table 12-1 also describes these fields.

6. Type the size of the anchored frame in the Width and Height fields.

7. Click the New Frame button. The empty frame is inserted on the page. You can click it to import a graphic, or you can draw objects inside the frame. For details on drawing objects, see "Drawing Basic Shapes" on page 328.

You can format anchored frames as you do other objects in FrameMaker. If you need a border around the imported graphic, for instance, you can add a border to the anchored frame. See "Modifying Objects" on page 336.

Importing a Graphic

When you import a graphic into a text frame, the graphic is inserted into an anchored frame. You can either copy the graphic directly into the document or import the file by reference, which creates a link to the source graphic. You and your coworkers need to weigh the pros and cons before deciding which method to use. Generally, you should import graphics by reference to minimize the size of your files and make organizing the graphics easier; however, if you're concerned more about losing graphics, copy them into the document. Table 12-2 describes the pros and cons of importing graphics by reference.

FrameMaker supports both bitmap and vector graphics. When you import bitmap graphics, which consist of pixels, you must specify the DPI (dots per inch) setting. The DPI indicates the number of pixels per inch in the imported graphic. The higher the DPI, the smaller the dimensions of the graphic. The DPI setting is crucial because it controls the image resolution. If you resize a bitmap image by dragging one of its corners, the DPI no longer determines the resolution, and the image may become distorted.

You can resize vector images, such as EPS files, by pressing SHIFT *while dragging the corner or using the Graphics | Scale command.*

For consistency's sake, you usually decide on one or two DPI settings to use in a single book. If you use different DPIs when importing screen shots of dialog boxes, for instance, the reader can't judge the true size of the images.

Most vector graphics don't have DPI settings because they consist of lines, not pixels. You do, however, need to set the DPI when you import Scalable Vector Graphics (SVGs). FrameMaker converts SVGs to bitmaps (or rasterizes them) for display in your document. The rasterizing doesn't change printing or converting the graphic; it's only for FrameMaker's display of the SVG. You can even import an animated SVG, and the animation will be displayed when you export the file to HTML or XML.

To display SVG files in a browser, you might need to download an SVG viewer plug-in. Some browsers give you this option; others may require you to download and install the viewer yourself. For SVG resources, see Appendix A, "Resources."

	Advantages	Disadvantages
Organizing	■ You maintain a central repository of graphics for your documentation, which lets coworkers insert the same graphic in multiple documents. ■ Because you can reuse the graphic, you save storage space.	■ You must organize graphics clearly so that others can find what they need. ■ Anyone who opens a document with referenced graphics must have access to the location of the graphics. If the graphics are on your hard drive and the drive isn't shared, the graphics are not displayed. ■ The link to the referenced graphic will break if the graphic is renamed, moved to another directory, or deleted. ■ If cross-platform compatibility is an issue, you need to follow file naming and graphic format guidelines. See "Cross-Platform Images" on page 320 for details.
Updating	■ To modify a graphic, you edit the file and save it with the original name. All FrameMaker files that reference the graphic are updated when you open or save the files. ■ The name of the referenced graphic is displayed in the object properties. The file name isn't displayed with copied graphics.	You and a coworker might try to update the same graphic simultaneously.
Archiving	Your archives are smaller because the same graphic isn't placed in multiple documents.	You must be careful archiving a document with graphics that are used in other documents. To avoid breaking links in current documentation, you can generate a report of imported graphics in FrameMaker to see which graphics need to be archived.
Minimizing File Size	Files are smaller when they contain links to graphics and not the graphics themselves. Large FrameMaker files can cause memory problems, even on the most powerful computers.	None!

Table 12-2.   *Pros and Cons of Importing Graphics by Reference*

CONTROLLING
PAGE LAYOUT

Importing a Vector Graphic

To import a vector graphic (other than an SVG), follow these steps:

1. Position the insertion point in the paragraph where you want to display a graphic.
2. Select File | Import | File. The Import dialog box is displayed.

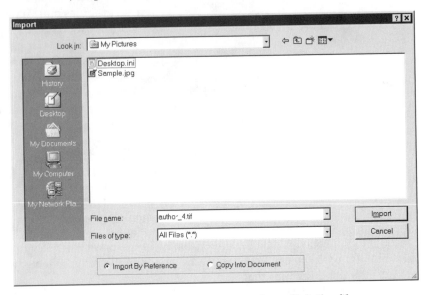

3. Browse to find the file you want to import, then click the file name.
4. Do one of the following:
   - Click the Import By Reference radio button to create a link to the graphic.
   - Click the Copy Into Document radio button to embed the graphic in the FrameMaker file.

   The next time you import a graphic, FrameMaker defaults to the setting you choose.
5. Click the Import button. The file is displayed in the document.

Importing an SVG File

To import an SVG file, follow these steps:

1. Follow the previous procedure for importing a vector graphic. After you click the Import button, the Unknown File Type dialog box is displayed.

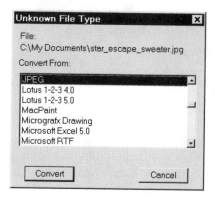

2. Click SVG in the filter list, then click the Convert button. The Import SVG dialog box is displayed.

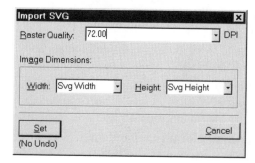

3. Do one of the following:

   ■ To set the DPI, click a DPI in the Raster Quality drop-down list. This resizes the graphic proportionately. (The current DPI for the graphic is displayed in this list by default.)

   ■ To change the specific dimensions, click a width in the Width drop-down list and a height in the Height drop-down list. This option may distort the image because you're not sizing the image proportionately.

Caution

For the best results, resize SVGs in a graphics program. The SVG must have a viewBox attribute in the top-level element, and the units of measure must be specified in the file for the graphic to resize correctly when imported into FrameMaker. In Adobe Illustrator version 10, SVGs are automatically saved with these attributes. Check your graphics program documentation for more information.

4. Click the Set button. The image is converted to a bitmap and displayed in the document.

Note

When you convert a document to HTML or XML, you have the choice of converting SVG files to GIF, JPEG, or PNG, or you can pass them through in their native format.

Advice on Organizing Graphic Files

It's important to plan how you'll name and store graphics that are imported by reference. Lack of planning can cause organizational and computer resource problems. You might also need to follow cross-platform guidelines. Consider the following tips:

- **Decide how to organize your files.** You might group screen shots by the product or feature they depict. It's generally not a good idea to store graphics in folders named after particular chapters in a book—if you move a graphic into a different chapter, you'll have to move the graphic to the corresponding directory. To resolve missing graphics that are in different directories, you'll have to select the directory for each graphic, which is time-consuming. If graphics are in one directory, you point FrameMaker to that directory for the first graphic you're relinking, then the rest of the graphics in the directory are automatically relinked.

- **Consider a document management system.** Large corporations often use a document management system to organize files. Such systems not only track the location of files, but they also can track who modifies the files.

- **Use short folder and file names.** The Object Properties dialog box truncates long path names, so the file name of the imported graphic is sometimes not displayed. Short file names are also easier to remember.

- **Make file names platform-independent.** If your document is viewed on multiple platforms, file names should conform to the following conventions:

    - Include file name extensions. Windows identifies files by their extensions.

    - Keep file names short. The Mac truncates file names over 32 characters.

    - Use lowercase file names. UNIX is case sensitive.

    - Exclude spaces, asterisks, quotes, slashes, question marks, colons, and other special characters from file names. Many special characters are reserved for specific functions on the Windows, UNIX, and Mac platforms. You can, however, use underscores, hyphens, tildes, dollar signs, parentheses, exclamation points, pound signs, and apostrophes.

For details on cross-platform graphic formats, see "Cross-Platform Images" on page 320.

Importing a Bitmap Graphic

To import a bitmap graphic, follow these steps:

1. Follow the steps for importing a vector graphic. (See "Importing a Vector Graphic" on page 306.) When you click the Import button, one of the following results occurs:

- If FrameMaker can't detect the graphic format, the Unknown File Type dialog box is displayed. Click the format that matches the graphic and then click the Convert button. The Imported Graphic Scaling dialog box is displayed. Continue to step 2.

- If FrameMaker can pick the correct graphics filter, the Imported Graphic Scaling dialog box is displayed.

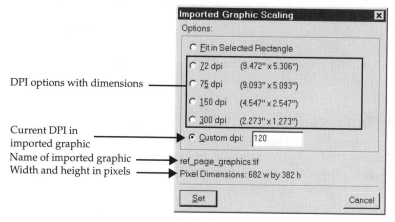

DPI options with dimensions

Current DPI in imported graphic

Name of imported graphic

Width and height in pixels

2. Select the size of the graphic:

- To use the DPI from the graphic, don't change the setting in the Custom dpi field. The number that is displayed is the DPI of the imported graphic.

- To change the size of the graphic, click a different radio button for the DPI, or type another number in the Custom dpi field. To protect the quality of the image, avoid the Fit in Selected Rectangle option. This setting resizes the object to fit inside the selected anchored or graphic frame, setting the DPI to Unknown and usually distorting the graphic in the process.

3. Click the Set button. The graphic is displayed in an anchored frame. (The following anchored frame has a border, so you can see the space between the graphic and frame.)

After you import a graphic, you can remove all white space between the graphic and anchored frame by shrink-wrapping the frame. See "Shrink-Wrapping an Anchored Frame" on page 311 for details.

Understanding Graphic Filters

During the FrameMaker installation, you install filters by default. Some filters convert text to a format FrameMaker understands; other filters are for importing graphics. When you import a graphic, FrameMaker either detects the file type automatically or requires you to pick the correct filter. For example, FrameMaker can't read the file types of PNG or SVG files, so you must select the correct filter when you import the graphic. For most graphics, however, FrameMaker chooses the filter automatically. All you do is set the DPI.

If you select the filter and an error is displayed during conversion, the file might be corrupt, or your computer might not have the correct filter installed. For more information on filters, refer to the FrameMaker online manual called *Filters.* You'll find the document in the FrameMaker installation directory's OnlineManuals folder.

Resizing Imported Graphics

For the best results, you resize an imported bitmap by changing the DPI. Imported graphics print well when you can evenly divide the DPI of your printer by the graphic's DPI. For instance, suppose you've set the printer driver DPI to 600. Graphics could be imported at 100, 120, 150, 300 DPI, and so on. You should experiment with your printer to find the best DPI values.

You should avoid dragging the corner of a graphic to resize it. Doing so often distorts the graphic, as shown in the following example. Though you can resize objects and vector graphics proportionately by pressing SHIFT while dragging a corner, using this method on bitmaps resets the DPI to "Unknown." As a result, the graphic may not print or export properly.

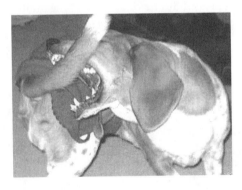

72-DPI graphic was imported at 150 DPI to decrease the dimensions of the displayed image.

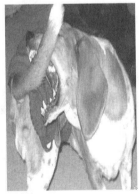

150-DPI graphic was resized by dragging a corner.

The DPI of the imported graphic is displayed in the object properties, which you display by selecting Graphics | Object Properties. Next to the DPI, the scaling value shows the percentage by which the graphic was scaled when imported. For example, a 72-DPI graphic imported at 150 DPI is scaled 47.99 percent.

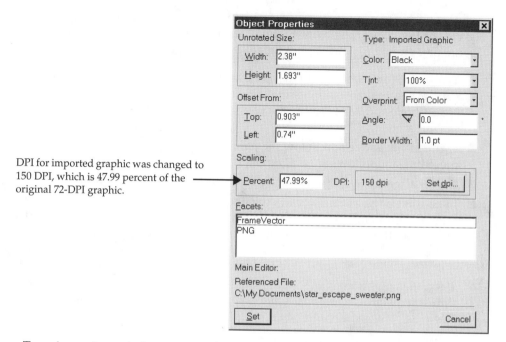

DPI for imported graphic was changed to 150 DPI, which is 47.99 percent of the original 72-DPI graphic.

To resize an imported vector graphic, you can either scale the graphic (select Graphics | Scale and type a percentage) or press SHIFT and drag a corner of the graphic. Be sure to press SHIFT while resizing the graphic manually to maintain proportions.

Shrink-Wrapping an Anchored Frame

You shrink-wrap an anchored frame to remove the spacing between the imported graphic and its frame. Shrink-wrapping makes the anchored frame just large enough for its contents, changes the anchoring position to At Insertion Point, and displays the frame 0 points above the baseline of the text. If the anchored frame is on the same line as text, the 0-point baseline causes a problem—the graphic covers the text on the preceding lines. To prevent the problem, import a graphic on a blank line. The shrink-wrapped object doesn't cover text on blank lines. The following illustration shows the difference between inserting and shrink-wrapping an anchored frame in text and on a line by itself.

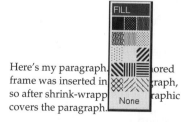

Here's my paragraph. ored frame was inserted in raph, so after shrink-wrapp raphic covers the paragraph.

Here's my paragraph. The anchored frame is on a blank line.

When you import a graphic on a blank line, you can customize the paragraph tag applied to the line. The graphics in this book are inserted on a blank line formatted by the Figure paragraph tag. This tag has the following properties:

- **Two-point font.** Works with the space above and below the paragraph to control vertical spacing. You use the smallest supported font in FrameMaker so that the space above and below settings actually position the figure. The font family doesn't matter.

- **Eight points above and below the paragraph.** Separates the figure from the preceding and following paragraphs.

- **Center alignment.** Displays the figure in the center of the text column.

- **In-column pagination.** Displays the figure in the text column so that the figure is aligned consistently with in-column text. As a result, anchored frames that are wider than the column overlap the right margin, except for cropped anchored frames, which are clipped by the borders of the text frame or the side head area.

Tip   *If you often have wide figures, create a separate paragraph tag that displays content across all columns and side heads and apply the tag to the paragraph containing the figure. See "Pagination Sheet" on page 120 for details.*

Side head area

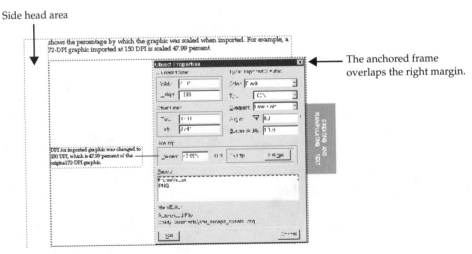

To shrink-wrap an anchored frame in an empty paragraph, follow these steps:

1. Click the anchored frame or the contents of the frame.

2. *(optional)* If the anchored frame contains several objects, select Graphics | Group to group them.

3. Press ESC M P. The anchored frame is shrunk or expanded to fit the contents and is positioned according to the paragraph pagination settings.

Relinking Missing Imported Graphics

Missing graphics show up as gray boxes in your document. The link to the graphic breaks if the graphic is renamed, moved, or deleted. When you open a document with a missing graphic, FrameMaker prompts you to find the graphic. You can either browse to find the file on your computer, or you can skip the search and worry about it later.

The name of the missing graphic is also displayed in the object properties. You can use this information to reimport the graphic if you find missing images while working on a document.

Note

Gray boxes can indicate missing graphics, but they are also displayed when the computer platform doesn't support the graphic and preview formats. You can tell the difference by looking at the facets in the object properties. The Facets field shows the graphic format and preview format (for graphics not supported on the platform). If there are no facets, the graphic is missing. If there are facets, the formats are not supported on the computer. For details, see "Image Facets" on page 320.

To relink a missing graphic when opening a document, follow these steps:

1. After you open the document with the missing graphic, the Missing File dialog box is displayed.

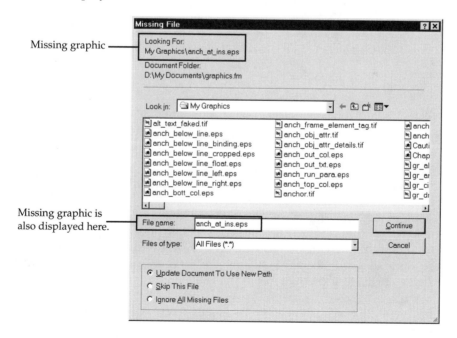

2. Do one of the following:

   ■ To relink the graphic, browse to find the file. Make sure the Update Document To Use New Path radio button is selected.

   ■ To skip the graphic, click the Skip This File radio button.

   ■ To skip all missing graphics, click the Ignore All Missing Files radio button.

3. Click the Continue button. The document is displayed along with the missing graphic (if you chose to relink the graphic).

Setting Anchored Frame Object Properties

In the anchored frame object properties, you can describe the contents of the frame by including the following information:

■ **Alternate text.** Displayed when you place your cursor over a graphic in a browser or when the display device isn't downloading graphics. Alternate text is exported only from structured documents to XML, SGML, and tagged PDF. The document type definition (DTD) must permit the export. If you define alternate text in the DTD *and* the anchored frame object properties, FrameMaker processes only the alternate text. In tagged PDF, the alternate text converts to an attribute of the anchored frame element.

■ **Actual text.** Describes characters in the anchored frame (as opposed to graphics); exported only to *tagged PDF*. In tagged PDF, elements and attributes are displayed in a logical tree structure. This structure is read more reliably by screen readers than standard PDF and helps export PDF accurately to Rich Text Format (RTF) in Acrobat 5. In the next example, the "H" is placed in an anchored frame at the beginning of the sentence. The actual text in the anchored frame object properties is "H." When the sentence is exported to tagged PDF, the actual text is displayed in the tree structure. Without the actual text, the incomplete sentence shown on the right is displayed. For more information, see "Generating Tagged PDF Files" on page 474.

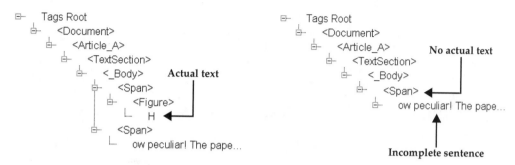

■ **Attributes.** The attributes you define in the anchored frame object properties are not the same as attributes displayed in the structure view, and they're not exported to XML, SGML, or tagged PDF. Third-party applications may process the anchored frame attributes, or you may use them for your own benefit.

When you define both alternate and actual text, only the alternate text is converted.

To define anchored frame object properties, follow these steps:

1. Click the anchored frame, then select Graphics | Object Properties. The Object Properties dialog box is displayed.

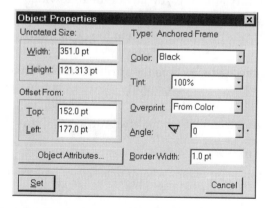

2. Click the Object Attributes button. The Object Attributes dialog box is displayed.

CONTROLLING
PAGE LAYOUT

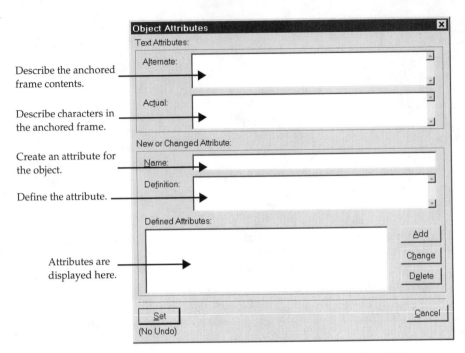

Describe the anchored frame contents.

Describe characters in the anchored frame.

Create an attribute for the object.

Define the attribute.

Attributes are displayed here.

3. To describe the anchored frame contents for display in XML, SGML, or tagged PDF, type text in the Alternate field.

4. To describe characters in the anchored frame for display in tagged PDF, type text in the Actual Text field.

5. To add and modify attributes, do any of the following:

   ■ To create an attribute to describe the object, type the attribute in the Name field, type the attribute definition in the Definition field, then click the Add button.

   ■ To change the attribute, type the attribute in the Name field of the New or Changed Attribute section, modify the definition in the Definition field, then click the Change button.

   ■ To delete an attribute, click the attribute in the Defined Attributes section, then click the Delete button.

Remember   *The attributes you define in the anchored frame object properties are not displayed in the structure view.*

6. Click the Set button to return to the Object Properties dialog box, then click the Set button to save your changes. (If you click the Cancel button, your changes aren't saved.)

When you export the document, the alternate text or actual text is converted. For more information on exporting FrameMaker documents to SGML, XHTML, or XML, see Chapter 19, "Creating HTML and XML Output," or Chapter 31, "Importing and Exporting XML/SGML Markup Files." For more information on creating PDFs, see Chapter 18, "Print and PDF Output."

Graphic Formats

There are two types of images—vector, which consist of lines, and bitmap, which consist of pixels. FrameMaker supports many file formats in each category. The format you choose depends largely on the final output of your document and your computer platform.

Choosing the Best Graphics Format

Your computer platform and the final output of your document determine which graphic formats you can use. Some image formats are more compatible with printed documents, while others work well in both printed and online documentation. For example, if you plan to print the document and convert a FrameMaker file to PDF, Encapsulated PostScript (EPS) graphics are a good choice because they have sharp resolution. For HTML or XML, screen shots are best displayed as Graphics Interchange Format (GIF), Portable Network Graphic (PNG), or SVG files. For HTMLHelp, GIFs work well.

Though FrameMaker supports many types of graphics, Table 12-3 lists the supported graphic formats for different kinds of output.

Vector Graphics

A vector graphic consists of mathematical formulas that describe the drawing. EPS, SVG, CorelDRAW, and Computer Graphics Metafile are popular vector formats. If you open a vector graphic in a text editor such as TextPad or EditPlus, you'll see code like this:

```
%AI3_DocumentPreview: PC_TIFF
%AI5_ArtSize: 424.8 792
%AI5_RulerUnits: 0
%AI5_ArtFlags: 0 0 0 1 0 0 1 0 0
%AI5_TargetResolution: 800
%AI5_NumLayers: 1
```

You can decipher some of the code, but most of it is incomprehensible by any entity other than a printer. The main advantage of vector graphics is their resolution—they can be scaled drastically while maintaining sharp resolution. The files are also smaller than

Graphic Format	Print	PDF	HTML and XML	HTMLHelp 2	WinHelp	RTF
					Final Output	
Bitmap (BMP)				✔	✔	✔
CorelDRAW (CDR)	✔	✔				
Computer Graphics Metafile (CGM)	✔	✔	✔			
Enhanced Metafile (EMF)						✔
Encapsulated PostScript (EPS)	✔	✔				
Graphics Interchange Format (GIF)	✔	✔	✔	✔	✔	✔
Joint Photography Experts Group (JPEG)	✔	✔	✔	✔	✔	✔
Portable Network Graphic (PNG)	✔	✔	✔	✔		✔
Scalable Vector Graphic (SVG)	✔	✔	✔	✔		✔
Tagged Image File Format (TIFF)	✔	✔				✔
Windows Metafile (WMF)					✔	✔

Table 12-3. *Choosing Graphic Formats*

bitmap images. The following illustration shows an original EPS graphic and another version scaled 300 percent, which looks just as crisp as the original.

Original EPS graphic

Graphic was scaled 300 percent without losing resolution.

What Are Those Gray Boxes?

Imported graphics may be displayed as gray boxes for several reasons:

- The image is missing. The referenced file might have been renamed, moved, or deleted. When you open a file with a missing image, FrameMaker prompts you to find the correct path, skip the file, or skip all missing files. Skipping the file causes the gray box to be displayed. See "Relinking Missing Imported Graphics" on page 313 for details.

- The preview format may not be supported on the current platform, or there may be no preview at all. Windows machines cannot display an EPS with a Mac preview, for instance. Graphics with PC previews, however, are displayed on the Mac, Windows, and UNIX platforms.

- The file format isn't supported on your platform. For example, the Mac platform does not support WMF graphics.

To prevent the gray boxes, you should follow guidelines for cross-platform graphics (if applicable) and make sure referenced graphics are not moved, renamed, or deleted.

Some vector graphics have bitmap previews that are saved with the graphic in their native application. FrameMaker considers the preview image a *facet*, or a separate version of the same image. For example, if you save an EPS with a TIFF preview, you can view the EPS on a computer that supports TIFFs but doesn't have a PostScript printer driver.

FrameMaker 7 supports CorelDRAW (CDR) graphics up to version 7. You can, however, save the CDR graphic as a FrameVector Image (FMV) file. The FMV file can be imported directly into a FrameMaker document.

Bitmap Graphics

Colored dots, or pixels, are arranged to create bitmap images. Bitmaps have a fixed number of pixels, and each pixel expands as you enlarge the image. The result can be a fuzzy, distorted graphic. Bitmaps in general are larger than vector graphics. FrameMaker supports GIF, JPEG, BMP, EMF, PNG, TIFF, PDF, WMF, and several other bitmap formats.

For some file types, FrameMaker uses a filter to import the file. You select the appropriate filter when importing the graphic, then you set the DPI. See "Understanding Graphic Filters" on page 310 for more information.

Image Facets

Many graphics include more than one image, though only one image is displayed. FrameMaker considers each image a *facet*, or a separate format of the same image. Facets make graphics formats compatible across computer platforms and monitors. For example, a Macintosh PICT image might have a WMF facet that lets Windows users view the graphic. With an EPS graphic, the TIFF facet is displayed as a preview of the graphic. The facets are listed in the imported graphic's object properties.

FrameMaker added the FrameImage facet to the SVG during import.

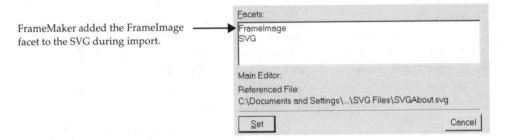

Cross-Platform Images

FrameMaker supports cross-platform graphics. This feature lets you view graphics on more than one platform. Some graphic formats, such as the WMF and PICT, are displayed only on their native platforms. To view the image on non-native platforms, you copy the graphics into your document and set the FrameMaker preferences to create FrameImage facets (for bitmaps) and FrameVector facets (for vector graphics) when you save the document. The facet is displayed when a Macintosh user, for example, views a document containing a WMF graphic. Without the facet, the WMF is displayed as a gray box on the Macintosh and UNIX platforms.

FrameImages are saved along with the copied graphic, so the file size increases, especially with graphics-intensive documents. As a result, you might run into the following problems with FrameImages:

- If your computer doesn't have enough free memory, FrameMaker may not be able to save the document.
- Lack of free memory slows down the display of images, so scrolling through the document can take longer.
- The inflated file size can cause printing errors and problems converting the document to another format.

FrameImages are primarily for viewing the document. If you plan to do anything other than view the document, you're better off converting the graphics to a compatible format and importing them by reference.

To save FrameImage or FrameVector facets, follow these steps:

1. Select File | Preferences | General. The Preferences dialog box is displayed.

2. In the Compatibility Preferences section, check the Save FrameImage with Imported Graphics check box.

3. Click the Set button. The FrameImage or FrameVector will be saved in all documents that contain copied graphics until you change the preferences again.

Platform-Specific Import Features

FrameMaker provides the following platform-specific features for importing graphics:

■ **Object linking and embedding (OLE).** In Windows, you can use OLE to embed objects while maintaining the object's association with its native program. When you double-click a Visio graphic, for instance, the Visio interface appears inside FrameMaker. You can edit the graphic inside the FrameMaker window instead of leaving FrameMaker and opening Visio. You can also create a number of different objects inside FrameMaker without opening the appropriate program or saving the object as a separate file. OLE has some major drawbacks. The technology is not supported on UNIX and the Mac, so documents with OLE items must be saved with the FrameImage facet, or a gray box is displayed. In addition, documents are large because the OLE items are embedded, not referenced. Those who open your document must have the same version of software you used to create an OLE graphic (or a higher version). It's difficult to resize an OLE object—you can't set the DPI, and scaling the object often results in a distorted or pixelated image.

■ **Publish and Subscribe.** On the Mac, publishing and subscribing is similar to importing by reference except that you insert a link to a *copy* of the graphic, not the actual graphic. First, you draw the image in a program that supports Publish and Subscribe, then you publish the image to create a separate edition. In your FrameMaker document, you subscribe to the edition, which places a copy of the edition on the page. The image in the FrameMaker file is updated when the original image changes. Windows and UNIX do not support Publish and Subscribe, but a preview image can be displayed, if available.

■ **Graphic insets.** In UNIX, you create graphic insets in an inset editing application. As an inset, the graphic can be edited inside FrameMaker, similar to OLE objects in Windows. Graphic insets are displayed on Windows and Mac computers if the graphic inset preview image is a TIFF or EPS.

OLE items, subscribed images, and graphic insets are compatible on non-native platforms if the platform supports the file format or if the item has a bitmap preview. To avoid cross-platform problems, however, create graphic objects in a graphics program and import the files. For more information, see "Importing a Graphic" on page 304 and "Cross-Platform Images" on page 320.

Placing Graphics on the Reference Pages

You can store frequently used objects, such as logos or borders, on the reference pages. Some FrameMaker users maintain a library of objects on the reference pages so they can copy an object on the reference page and paste it on a body page when they need it. By default, FrameMaker provides four line styles on the reference pages—Footnote, TableFootnote, SingleLine, and DoubleLine. You can use the line styles in paragraph tags to create a border above or below the paragraph.

Objects are displayed in graphic frames on the reference pages. Each graphic frame has a name. You can either copy graphics or import them by reference into the graphic frame. If you copy graphics, keep in mind that the graphics increase the size of the file. Most of the time, you'll import the graphics by reference to make updating the graphics throughout the book easier. See "Importing a Graphic" on page 304 for more details.

Note   *Reference pages also store definitions for the table of contents and other generated files, and HTML conversion information. See "Creating Paragraph-Based and Element-Based Lists" on page 428 for details.*

Placing Graphics Above and Below the Paragraph

You can set up a paragraph that always has a line or other graphics above or below it. FrameMaker provides a few graphics; you can also create your own. For example, the notes, tips, and caution paragraphs in this book are inserted in two-column, one-row invisible tables. The TipGraphic paragraph tag is applied in the left column. This tag inserts the Tip icon above the paragraph.

The Tip icon is displayed on the reference page. The label *tip_graphic* describes the image; the name of the actual graphic frame, which is displayed in the status bar, may differ. In the Advanced tab of the Paragraph Designer, graphic frame names are listed in the Frame Above Pgf and Frame Below Pgf drop-down lists.

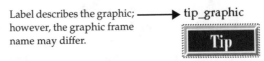

In this book, the gray bar and icon for the first-level headings is a grouped object on the reference page. When you apply the H1_graphic paragraph tag, the object is displayed above the paragraph.

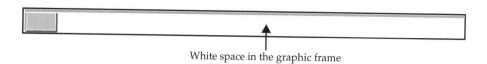

White space in the graphic frame

Typically, the white space in the graphic frame is displayed when you apply the paragraph tag. To display text directly over the object, however, you set the space above the paragraph tag to a negative number. For example, the Heading1 paragraph tag has -36 points above the paragraph. You'll need to adjust the spacing based on the size of the font and the graphic.

The graphic frame may appear to crop a line on the reference page, but the true dimensions of the line are displayed on master and body pages. To shorten a line, edit the object properties.

To set up a graphic to precede or follow your paragraph, follow these steps:

1. *(optional)* If you don't like any of the default FrameMaker graphics, you can create your own. Follow these steps:

    a. Select View | Reference Pages to display the reference pages. The default FrameMaker graphics are included on the first reference page, which happens to be called "Reference."

     b. Click the Graphic Frame icon in the Graphics toolbar.

    c. Click and drag to create a new frame. The location doesn't matter. When you release the cursor, FrameMaker prompts you to name the frame.

Name displayed in the ⟶ Paragraph Designer

    d. In the Name field, type a name for the frame, then click the Set button. This is the name you will select later in the Paragraph Designer.

    e. Put the graphic elements you want inside the graphic frame. You can use FrameMaker's drawing tools, import an external graphic, or both.

    f. Above the frame, insert a text label (you can copy, paste, and then edit one of the existing ones) with the name of the graphic frame. This name is for identification purposes only; it's not associated with the graphic frame name.

    g. Select View | Body Pages to return to the body pages. In the Paragraph Designer, the new frame is now available in the Frame Above and Frame Below drop-down lists on the Advanced tab.

2. Display the Paragraph Designer, then click the tag that you want to add a graphic to.

3. Click the Advanced sheet.

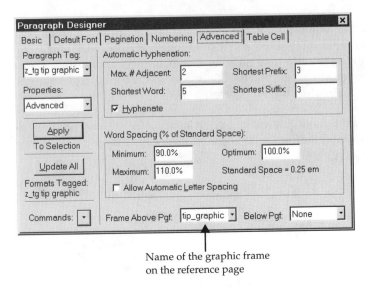

Name of the graphic frame
on the reference page

4. In the Frame Above Pgf or Frame Below Pgf drop-down list, click the frame you want to use.

5. Click the Update All button to save your changes. The new graphic is displayed in each paragraph formatted by the tag.

Changing the Name of a Graphic Frame

When you add a graphic frame to the reference pages, you name the frame. You can change this name later, and the new graphic frame name will be displayed in the Frame Above Pgf and Frame Below Pgf paragraph tags.

Don't rename graphic frames that are already referenced in paragraph tags, or you'll remove the object from the paragraph tag definition. FrameMaker doesn't provide a warning, so be sure the graphic frame isn't in use.

To change the graphic frame name, follow these steps:

1. Select View | Reference Pages to display the reference pages.

2. Click the graphic frame, then do one of the following:

   ■ Click the name in the status bar. The Frame Name dialog box is displayed.

   ■ Select Graphic | Object Properties. The Object Properties dialog box is displayed.

Select graphic frame.

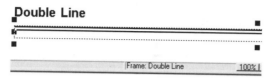

Click status bar.   **OR**   Select Graphic | Object Properties.

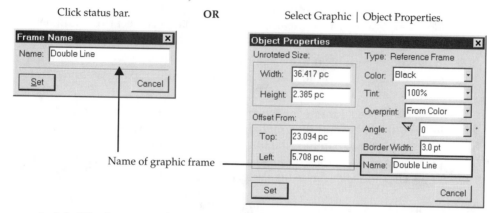

Name of graphic frame

3. Modify the text in the Name field, then click the Set button. The new graphic frame name is displayed in the status bar, object properties, and paragraph tags.

CONTROLLING PAGE LAYOUT

Importing Graphics on a Master Page

Graphics are often placed on master pages to create special designs. Most of the time, you don't need a frame for the graphic—you just import the graphic onto the page outside the main text flow, using a graphic frame to crop the graphic, if necessary. For many graphics on the master page, you don't need an anchored frame because there's no text to displace the graphic. More importantly, if you import the graphic into the main text flow, the graphic isn't displayed on the body pages.

In this book, the title page of each chapter has two graphics—one graphic for the background image and one for the FrameMaker seal. Both graphics were imported outside the text frame on the ChapterTitle master page. The background image is slightly larger than the paper and offset from the left -0.174 inches to make sure the design prints to the edge of the page. Because the graphics are each over 1MB, they're imported by reference. This also makes updating the images easier than if they were copied into the document.

Note   *Objects on the master pages aren't exported to HTML or XML.*

To import a graphic on the master page, follow these steps:

1. Select View | Master Pages to display the master pages.

2. Scroll to the master page you want to edit, or select Special | Add Master Page to create a new one.

3. Do one of the following:

   - To import the graphic into a graphic frame, click the Graphic Frame button in the Tools palette and draw the graphic frame, then click the frame and import the graphic. You can also copy and paste the object (from another master page, for instance) into the frame.

   - To import the graphic into a background element, place your cursor in the text frame and import the graphic. You can shrink-wrap the anchored frame to remove extra space.

   - If you don't need a frame for the graphic, click outside the text frame to deselect it, then import the graphic. The graphic is centered on the page. We used this method to import the title page graphic onto the Title master page. If you need to select the graphic, but the graphic is displayed behind the text frame, click the text frame, then select Graphics | Send to Back.

After you import the graphic, you can adjust the frame or offsets to create the design you need. For details on cropping images with graphic frames, see "Cropping and Masking Graphics" on page 348.

Graphics in Structured Documents

To import a graphic into a structured document, you insert a graphic element. The graphic element either inserts an anchored frame first and lets you set the anchored frame properties, or the element lets you select the graphic you want to import and inserts it into a centered anchored frame. For details, see "Graphic Elements" on page 715 for details.

The object properties of anchored frames may include attributes. These attributes are not displayed in the structure view. See "Setting Anchored Frame Object Properties" on page 314 for more information.

Chapter 13

FrameMaker's Graphics Tools

F rameMaker includes drawing tools similar to those found in basic graphics programs. They let you draw a number of different shapes and combine them to create objects, such as those shown in the following examples. You can change the colors and borders, apply shading, resize, rotate, layer, align, and so forth. The tools aren't appropriate for designing sophisticated magazine or book covers, but they provide most of the features you need for illustrations in reference guides, newsletters, training manuals, or simple brochures.

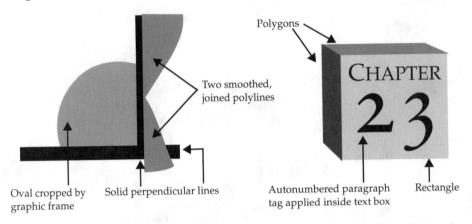

You can draw objects directly on the page, or you can place them in a frame. An *anchored frame* attaches the object to a paragraph. When the paragraph moves, the anchored frame moves as well. *Graphic frames* can crop or mask objects. They also store frequently used items on the reference pages.

In structured FrameMaker documents, objects aren't part of the structure, but you can insert a graphic element to create an anchored frame, then draw objects inside the anchored frame and import graphics.

Note   *You can place imported graphics and drawn objects in the same anchored or graphic frame. In this book, for example, we imported the graphics, drew small text frames inside the anchored frame for callout text, then drew the callout arrows.*

Drawing Basic Shapes

You draw most objects by clicking a button on the Tools palette and then dragging the cursor across the page. As you draw an object, an outline appears on the page. This outline is the *path* of the object—an imaginary line that bisects the object border. When you let go of the cursor, the object border is displayed on the page, and the object is selected.

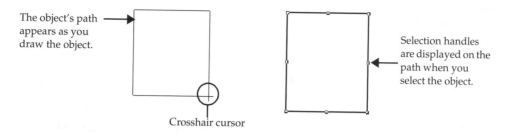

The object's path appears as you draw the object.

Crosshair cursor

Selection handles are displayed on the path when you select the object.

Most graphic tools are available in the Tools palette. You can format objects with a color, pattern, border, and other properties. To display the tools, select Graphics | Tools or click the Tools palette button in the upper-right corner of your document.

The Tools palette looks slightly different on the Windows, Mac, and UNIX platforms (Figure 13-1). The Mac and UNIX platforms provide two views of the palette—compact, as shown in Windows, and expanded, which also shows commands from the Graphics menu. The expanded view is shown in Figure 13-2. To display the expanded view on the Mac, click the button in the upper-right corner of the palette. In UNIX, click the button in the lower left corner of the palette.

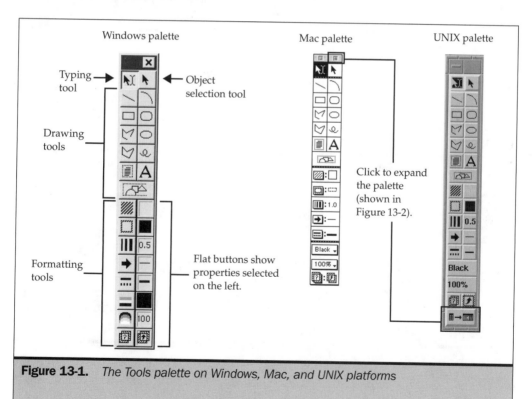

Figure 13-1. *The Tools palette on Windows, Mac, and UNIX platforms*

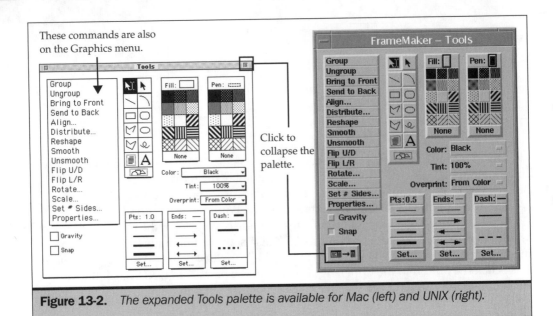

Figure 13-2. *The expanded Tools palette is available for Mac (left) and UNIX (right).*

Table 13-1 summarizes the features on the Tools palette.

Button	Description
	Smart Select. For selecting text or objects. Press CTRL (Windows and UNIX) or OPTION (Mac) to force selection of an object.
	Select Object. For selecting an object but not text.
	Line. For drawing a straight line. To draw a line at a 45-degree angle, press SHIFT when drawing the line.
	Arc. For drawing a curved line. To draw one-fourth of a circle, press SHIFT when drawing the segment.

Table 13-1. *Tools Palette Buttons*

Button	Description
	Rectangle. For drawing a rectangle. To draw a square, press SHIFT when drawing the shape.
	Rounded Rectangle. For drawing a rectangle with rounded corners. To draw a square with rounded corners, press SHIFT when drawing the shape.
	Polyline. For drawing a line with several segments. To draw a polyline, click at each segment point and then double-click at the end of the line.
	Oval. For drawing ovals and circles. To draw a circle, press SHIFT when drawing the shape.
	Polygon. For drawing a closed shape composed of several line segments. To draw a polygon, click at each corner, then double-click at the end point.
	Freehand Curve. For drawing a smoothed polyline. To draw a freehand curve, click and drag the cursor.
	Text Frame. For drawing a text frame on any page in a document, including master and reference pages.
	Text Line. For typing lines of text. To type several lines of text, click where the text begins, type the text, and press ENTER to type another line. (Text lines don't wrap, so you must press ENTER where you want the line to break.) Each text line is a separate object that you click and move on the page. The previous insertion point determines the default font properties. For example, if your cursor was previously in a paragraph with a 24-point blue font, the text line has the same properties. You can change the text line font properties using the Format menu, object properties, character tags, or the Color button in the Tools palette. You cannot apply a paragraph tag to text lines.
	Graphic Frame. For drawing a frame to crop or mask objects. Also used on the reference pages to hold frequently used objects, such as note icons and borders.

Table 13-1.   *Tools Palette Buttons (Continued)*

Button	Description
	Fill Pattern. For choosing a fill pattern for the selected object. Some striped fill and pen patterns don't display accurately in PDF. If you plan to convert your document to PDF, you should create a test PDF before using a particular pattern. (If you click the fill pattern, pen pattern, or line width buttons when your cursor is in a table, the Custom Ruling and Shading dialog box is displayed.)
	Pen Pattern. For choosing a pen pattern, or border style, for the selected object. As is the case with fill patterns, you should create a test PDF before using a particular pen pattern if you plan to distribute the document as a PDF.
	Line Width. For choosing from four preset line widths or changing the default widths.
	Line End Style. For selecting from four plain or arrowhead line ends. You can also choose from eight additional arrow styles, specify a custom arrow style, and select the shape for line ends.
	Dashed Line Pattern. For selecting plain or dashed line patterns. You can also choose from eight additional line patterns.
	Color. For setting the color of selected objects. Select from the eight basic colors, plus any custom colors that you have defined. See "Managing Color Definitions" on page 518 for details.
	Tint. For setting the tint of a previously selected color in 5-percent increments from 0 percent to 100 percent. You can also type in a specific tint between zero and one hundred percent. The tint is reset to 100 percent when you apply a different color to the object.
	Overprint. Indicates how FrameMaker prints the colors of an overlapping text frame and object. When you change the color of an object, the overprint is reset to From Color. ■ **Knock Out:** FrameMaker prints only the color of the top object. ■ **Overprint:** FrameMaker prints both colors from the overlapped portion of the objects. ■ **From Color:** FrameMaker prints the color defined for each object. See Chapter 20, "Color Output," for more information on color.

Table 13-1. *Tools Palette Buttons (Continued)*

To draw an object, follow these steps:

1. *(optional)* Insert one of the following:
   - An anchored frame to lock the graphic to a specific paragraph.
   - A graphic frame to crop or mask the graphic or to draw the graphic on the reference page. (See "Placing Graphics on the Reference Pages" on page 322 for more information.)

2. Select Graphics | Tools. The Tools palette is displayed (Figure 13-1 on page 329).

3. Click the button for the object you want to draw.

4. Click where you want the object.

5. Draw the object according to descriptions in Table 13-1. For example, to draw a freehand curve, click at the starting point and drag your cursor to form the line. To draw a rectangle, rounded rectangle, or oval, click at the starting point and drag to the opposite corner or edge. To draw a polygon, click at the first point, click at the midpoints, and then double-click at the end point.

Tip   *To judge the size of the object as you draw, use the FrameMaker rulers or status bar dimensions as guides. The ruler markings show the size of the object as you draw, as do the dimensions displayed in the status bar. Select View | Rulers to toggle the ruler display.*

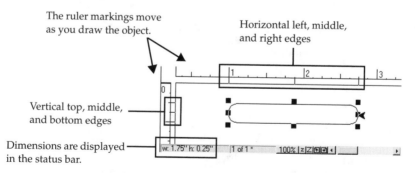

The ruler markings move as you draw the object.

Horizontal left, middle, and right edges

Vertical top, middle, and bottom edges

Dimensions are displayed in the status bar.

For more information on anchored frames, see "Anchoring Graphics" on page 300. See "Cropping and Masking Graphics" on page 348 for details on graphic frames.

Working with Grids

There are two types of grids in FrameMaker.

- **Snap grid.** Lets you specify spacing for an imaginary grid. Typically, you can draw, move, copy, or resize an object and drop the edge of the object at any point on the page. When snap is turned on, the edge of the object "snaps" to the imaginary grid. Snap also applies when you reshape, rotate, and align objects. To toggle the snap grid, select Graphics | Snap.

- **Grid Lines.** Displays grid lines on the page, which may have different dimensions from the snap grid. The following example shows 0.5-inch grid lines, and the snap grid is set to 0.25 inches. When the square is resized, it snaps to the closest 0.25-inch mark on the ruler.

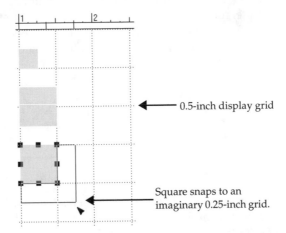

0.5-inch display grid

Square snaps to an
imaginary 0.25-inch grid.

To toggle the grid lines, select View | Grid Lines. To change the spacing for snap grid and grid lines, follow these steps:

1. Select View | Options. The View Options dialog box is displayed (Figure 13-3).
2. To change the snap grid spacing, type a number in the Grid Spacing field.

Tip   *To change the unit of measure for snap, click a different item in the Display Units drop-down list.*

3. *(optional)* To apply snap to objects that you rotate manually, type the degree of rotation in the Rotation field. (Note that the setting is not in degrees proper— you type a decimal point before the number.) For instance, the following illustration shows objects rotated manually on a 45-degree snap grid. See "Rotating" on page 356 for details.

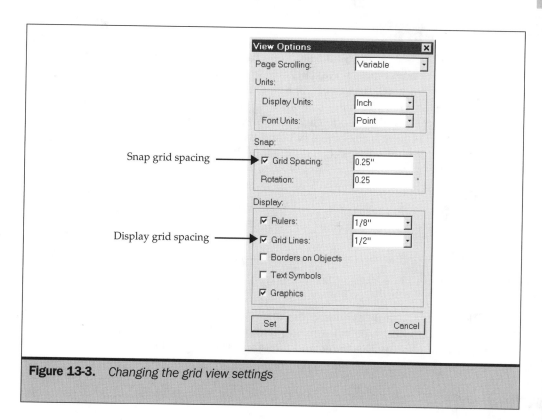

Figure 13-3. *Changing the grid view settings*

4. To change the display grid spacing, click a measurement in the Grid Lines drop-down list.

After you change the grid line spacing, the Grid Lines check box is automatically checked. This means the grid lines will be displayed when you save your changes. You can uncheck the check box if you don't want to display the grid lines yet.

5. Click the Set button to save your changes.

Selecting Objects

You can select objects with the Smart Select pointer, which is displayed when you edit text, or the Object Pointer, which you click in the Tools palette to select objects. Using the Smart Select pointer, you select an object by CTRL-clicking (Windows and UNIX) or OPTION-clicking (Mac) the object or border. Using the Object Pointer, you can just click the object to select it. You'll need to click the Smart Select pointer button in the Tools palette to type text again. If the object has a fill pattern, you can click anywhere in the object to select it; for hollow objects, you must click the border.

When an object is selected, square selection handles are displayed on the path of the object. You drag a handle to manually resize the object. See "Resizing" on page 341 for details.

To select several objects at once, press CTRL (Windows and UNIX) or COMMAND (Mac) while you click each object. You can also select all objects inside an anchored or graphic frame by clicking the frame and pressing CTRL-A (Windows and UNIX) or COMMAND-A (Mac).

Pressing CTRL-A or COMMAND-A with your cursor in the main flow selects all content in the flow instead of the objects.

Deleting Objects

To delete one object, select the object and press the DELETE key. To delete several objects, do one of the following:

- Select only the objects you want to delete.
- Select all objects, press CTRL (Windows and UNIX) or COMMAND (Mac), and click the objects you *don't* want to delete. Only the objects you want to delete are selected.

Press the DELETE key to remove the selected objects.

Modifying Objects

You change basic properties such as color, tint, pattern, and border attributes in the object properties or the Tools palette. For a single object, you can use either method. To format several objects, select properties in the Tools palette. Typically, using the Tools palette is quicker; however, the object dimensions, offsets from the left and top of the page, and angle must be changed in the object properties. The following example shows the color, tint, and border width properties that are displayed in both the object properties and the Tools palette.

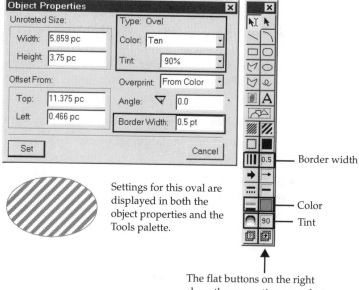

Settings for this oval are displayed in both the object properties and the Tools palette.

Border width

Color

Tint

The flat buttons on the right show the properties you select.

CONTROLLING PAGE LAYOUT

After you select a property in the Tools palette, that property is displayed until you change it or close FrameMaker. For example, the object in the preceding example has a 0.5-point border. This border width is displayed on the flat Line Width button until you select another line width. The property is also displayed when no objects are selected. To apply the same border to other objects, select the objects, then click the flat Line Width button.

To display the properties of any object in the Tools palette, select the object, press SHIFT, and then select Graphics | Pick up Object Properties. The formatting is displayed on the flat buttons.

To format an object using the Tools palette, follow these steps:

1. Select the object or objects you want to format, then select Graphics | Tools. The Tools palette is displayed (Figure 13-1 on page 329).
2. Click the button for the property you need to change, then click an item in the pop-up menu. The properties are described in Table 13-1 on page 330. Your changes are displayed on the object, and the flat buttons on the Tools palette show the selected properties.

To format an item through the object properties, follow these steps:

1. Select the object you want to format, then select Graphics | Object Properties. The Object Properties dialog box is displayed (see the previous illustration).

2. Do any of the following:

   ■ To change the size of the object, type different dimensions in the Width and Height fields. (The unrotated size of the object doesn't change after rotating an object.)

   ■ To change the distance from the top and left edges of the page or graphic frame, type different offsets in the Top and Left fields.

   ■ To change the color, click a color in the Color drop-down list.

   ■ To lighten or darken the color, click a percentage in the Tint drop-down list.

   ■ To control how colors print on overlapping objects, click an option in the Overprint drop-down list.

   ■ To modify the orientation of the object, type the degrees in the Angle field.

   ■ To change the border, type the new width in the Border Width field.

3. Click the Set button. Your changes are applied.

Redefining Line Widths

In the Tools palette, you can change the four predefined line widths. The new line widths may be applied to objects, but they're not automatically updated in existing objects. For example, if you change the thinnest default line to 1 point, the 0.5-point lines in your document aren't instantly updated. You have to apply the new line width to objects manually.

Unlike other properties, custom line widths don't change when you close FrameMaker; the values are saved until you change them. The chosen line width, however, defaults to the thinnest value when you close and reopen FrameMaker. So if you want the default line width to be 1 point, modify the predefined line widths to include a 1-point line as the thinnest line.

To change the default line widths, follow these steps:

1. Select Graphics | Tools. The Tools palette is displayed (Figure 13-1 on page 329).

2. Click the Line Width button. The Line Widths pop-up menu is displayed.

3. Click Set. The Line Width Options dialog box is displayed.

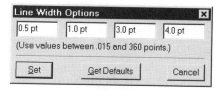

4. Type new point values in the fields, then click the Set button. The values are mapped to lines in the Line Widths pop-up menu.

Note *You can apply a border to an individual object in the Object Properties dialog box, and the border doesn't have to be defined in the default line widths. For example, you might need a 12-point border in a diagram, but the default line widths only go up to 8 points. You can type the border width in the object properties. This value is displayed on the Tools palette as the selected line width until you change it or close FrameMaker.*

Changing the Default Arrowhead

FrameMaker provides eight predefined arrowheads. If you don't like the predefined arrowheads, you can create your own by specifying the base angle, tip angle, and length. The following example shows the settings for a custom arrowhead.

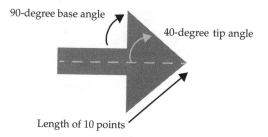

You can select a predefined or custom arrow style as the default. FrameMaker's default arrow style looks like the following:

When you close and reopen FrameMaker, the arrow style reverts to FrameMaker's default style. If you use a different arrow style in your documentation, you'll need to select it again in the Tools palette after reopening FrameMaker. Alternatively, you can click an existing arrow, press SHIFT, and then select Graphics | Pick up Object Properties. The arrow style is selected and displayed on the flat Line End Style button in the Tools palette.

To change the default arrow style in a document, follow these steps:

1. Select Graphics | Tools. The Tools palette is displayed (Figure 13-1 on page 329).
2. Click the Line End Style button. The Line Ends pop-up menu is displayed.

3. Click Set. The Line End Options dialog box is displayed.

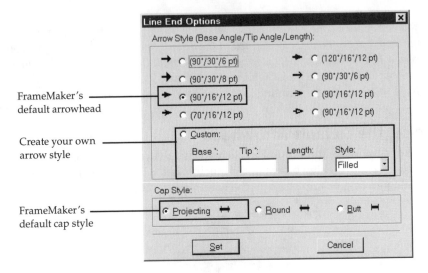

The third arrowhead on the left is FrameMaker's default arrow style.

Note

4. Do one of the following:

   ■ Click a radio button for the arrow you like.

   ■ Click the Custom radio button, then type the base and tip angle in degrees and the length in points. Click the arrowhead style in the Style drop-down list. (The tip angle must be at least 5 degrees smaller than the base angle.)

5. To change the end of the arrowhead, click one of the radio buttons in the Cap Style section. The default is a projecting cap.

6. Click the Set button. The default arrow style is updated and can be applied to new and existing objects. (Existing objects are not automatically updated.)

Modifying the Default Dashed Line

FrameMaker provides eight default dashed lines. You can set one as the default; however, when you close and reopen FrameMaker, the line style reverts to FrameMaker's default style.

To modify the default dashed line, follow these steps:

1. Select Graphics | Tools. The Tools palette is displayed (Figure 13-1 on page 329).
2. Click the Dashed Line Pattern button. The Line Styles pop-up menu is displayed.

3. Click Set. The Dashed Line Options dialog box is displayed.

FrameMaker's default dashed line ──────→

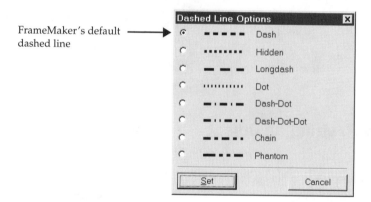

4. Click the radio button for the line you like, then click the Set button. The default dashed line is updated and can be applied to new and existing objects. (Existing objects are not automatically updated.)

Resizing

You resize objects by dragging the edge or corner of the object or providing specific dimensions. If you know the approximate size for an object, it's quicker to resize the object manually and use the FrameMaker rulers as a guide. The ruler markings are updated as you resize the object, as are the dimensions displayed in the status bar. To change the specific height or width, you need to type new dimensions in the object properties or scaling properties.

FrameMaker has a handy feature called *gravity* that snaps objects together. As you resize, reshape, or draw an object, the path or corner of the object meets the closest path or corner of the adjacent object. The centers of ovals and rectangles also have gravity. The following illustration shows how the paths of two objects meet as you resize the gray rectangle toward the hollow rectangle. To toggle gravity, select Graphics | Gravity.

Manually Resizing an Object

To resize an object using the mouse, follow these steps:

1. Click one of the object selection handles. The cursor changes to an arrow.
2. Drag the handle to form the shape you need. The object is resized.

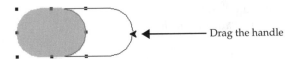

Drag the handle

Typing a Specific Height or Width

To type a specific height or width, do one of the following:

■ Select the object, then select Graphics | Scale. The Scale dialog box is displayed. Type new dimensions in the Width or Height fields, then click the Scale button. The object is resized from the center.

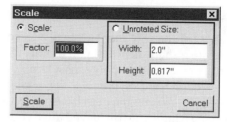

Scaled object is resized
from the middle.

■ Select the object, then select Graphics | Object Properties. The Object Properties
dialog box is displayed. Type new dimensions in the Width or Height fields,
then click the Set button. The object is resized from the top-left corner.

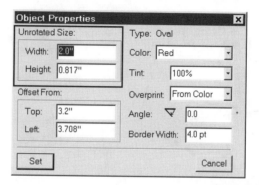

Modifying the object
properties resizes from
the top-left corner.

 *When you rotate an object, the width and height in the Object Properties don't change to
reflect the rotated width and height.*

Resizing Proportionately

To resize an object proportionately, do one of the following:

■ Click a selection handle and press SHIFT while you drag the handle.
■ Click the graphic, then select Graphics | Scale. The Scale dialog box is displayed.
Type a percentage in the Factor field, then click the Scale button.

The object is resized proportionately.

 *To resize several objects without grouping them, select them all and then use the
Scale command.*

Reshaping

You can alter the shape of many objects instead of redrawing them. By adding, moving, or deleting the reshape handles, you modify the direction, angle, and shape of freehand curves, arcs, polylines, and polygons. On polylines and polygons, the reshape handles look like selection handles, but they are displayed only on the corners of the object. Display them by clicking the object, then selecting Graphics | Reshape. On the freehand curve, reshape handles are displayed after you draw the object and it's still selected. The freehand curve also has control points that let you change the direction and shape of the line.

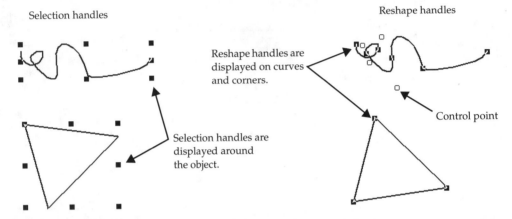

To alter the shape of a freehand curve, arc, polyline, or polygon, follow these steps:

1. Select the object, then select Graphics | Reshape. The reshape handles are displayed.

2. Do any of the following:

   ■ To change the bow of a freehand curve, drag a control point or reshape handle until a solid line appears, then change the length and direction of the line. The crosshair pointer marks the location of the control point as you move it. Lengthen the line and change the direction of the line until you like the shape.

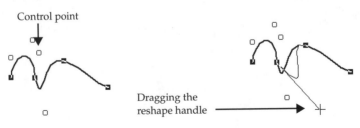

■ To add a reshape handle to a freehand curve, polyline, or polygon, CTRL-click (Windows and UNIX) or OPTION-COMMAND-click (Mac) the border where you want the handle. The new handle is displayed on the object.

Original object   New handle

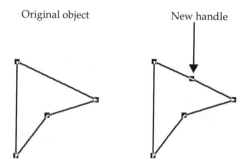

■ To remove a reshape handle, CTRL-click (Windows and UNIX) or OPTION-COMMAND-click (Mac) an existing handle. The handle is no longer displayed.

Smoothing Corners

On rectangles, polylines, and polygons, you can convert the corners to curves. To smooth an object, select the object, then select Graphics | Smooth. The corners of the object are displayed as rounded edges, and the object type is updated in the object properties. To revert to the original shape, select Graphics | Unsmooth.

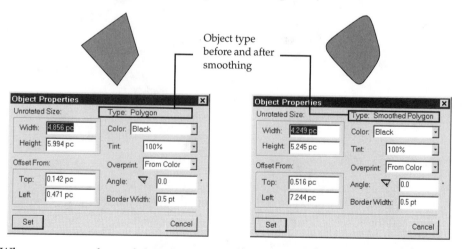

Object type before and after smoothing

When you smooth a polyline or polygon, FrameMaker adds control points to the object. You change the curvature of the object by dragging a control point. For details on modifying a curve, see "Reshaping" on page 344.

Changing the Number of Sides

You can draw multisided objects, such as octagons and hexagons, using a polyline or polygon; however, it's quicker to draw an oval or rectangle and then change the number of sides. To configure the orientation of the object, you change the angle of the first side. For example, the following illustration shows an oval converted to an octagon with a 22-degree start angle.

The object properties also show the angle of an object, but this angle is different from the start angle. The start angle is the degree at which the first side of the object is displayed; the angle in the object properties is the degree to which the object is rotated. If you rotate an object that has a start angle, the object is rotated from the start angle. The following illustration shows the hexagon rotated 25 degrees.

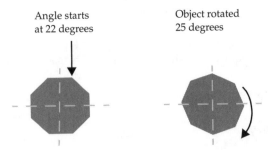

You can change the number of sides on multiple objects by selecting them all at once, but a grouped or smoothed object's sides cannot be modified.

To change the number of sides on an object, follow these steps:

1. Select the oval or rectangle (not the rounded rectangle) you want to reshape, then select Graphics | Set # Sides. The Set Number of Sides dialog box is displayed.

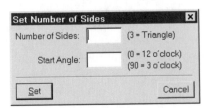

2. Type a number (3 or higher) in the Number of Sides field. For example, to convert a circle to a hexagon, type **5**.

3. To change the angle of the first side, type the number of degrees in the Start Angle field.

4. Click the Set button. The object is reshaped.

Joining Lines

You can join two or more lines (straight lines, arcs, freehand curves, and polylines) to form a single object. This feature lets you create a shape from several kinds of lines.

When you join lines with different weights, FrameMaker assigns the width of the last selected line. The following illustration compares the result of selecting the thin line last with selecting the thick line last and then joining the lines.

Original lines

Thin line
selected last

Thick line
selected last

FrameMaker's gravity feature helps "attract" the ends of two lines so you can join them. As you draw, resize, or reshape a line near another line, the closest paths or corners of the two lines meet. Gravity doesn't apply when you *move* a line near another line; it only works when you draw, resize, or reshape a line. If you need to move two lines together before joining them, try aligning them, then moving the lines until the edges meet. See "Aligning" on page 350 for details. To toggle gravity, select Graphics | Gravity.

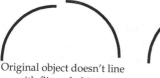
Original object doesn't line
up with flipped object.

Bottom edges
are aligned.

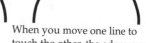
When you move one line to
touch the other, the edges meet.

Caution *There is no "unjoin" command. You must press CTRL-Z (Windows and UNIX) or COMMAND-Z (Mac) to undo the joined lines immediately after you join them.*

To join lines, follow these steps:

1. Drag one line toward the end of the line you want to join until the ends meet. The ends of the lines (not the paths) must touch for you to connect them.
2. Select both lines, then select Graphics | Join. The lines form one object. If the lines weren't touching, an error is displayed. Align the objects, then try to join them again.

To create a symmetrical shape, follow these steps:

1. Draw a line that's half of the shape you need.
2. With the line selected, press SHIFT, then press CTRL (Windows and UNIX) or COMMAND (Mac) and drag the line to copy it. (Pressing SHIFT while you copy a line keeps the alignment.)
3. Flip the copied line.
4. Move the flipped line toward the original line until the ends meet.
5. Select both lines, then select Graphics | Join. The lines form one object unless they weren't really close enough to touch. If necessary, align the objects, then try to join them again.

Draw Copy Flip   Move one line to touch   Apply a fill, set the pen
                     the other line and then   pattern (the border), then
                     join the lines.   scale the object 50 percent.

After you create the symmetrical shape, you can format the object and, if necessary, scale the object. It's easier to create small items, such as the candle flame in the preceding example, by scaling a large joined object rather than trying to work with small lines.

Cropping and Masking Graphics

Graphic frames are handy for cropping or masking objects. In the following illustration, the graphic frame on the left is placed behind the sun. This crops the bottom-right edge of the sun to fit inside the windowpane. On the right, the graphic frame is placed over the clock to mask the object and create white space. Though the graphic frame has a white background by default, you can apply a color and tint to the frame to create special effects.

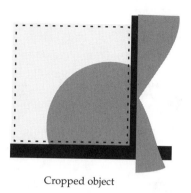

Cropped object

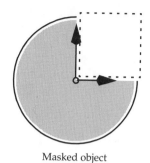

Masked object

To crop an object, follow these steps:

1. Click the Graphic Frame icon in the Tools palette and draw the frame.
2. Do one of the following:
   - Draw the object you're cropping inside the graphic frame and move the frame to crop the object.
   - Drag an existing object into the graphic frame and then adjust the frame to crop the object.

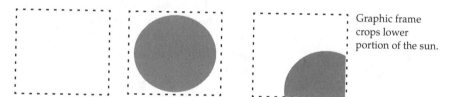

Graphic frame crops lower portion of the sun.

3. *(optional)* To apply a fill pattern and color to the graphic frame, select the frame and then click a fill pattern and color on the Tools palette.

To mask an object, follow these steps:

1. Click the Graphic frame icon in the Tools palette.
2. Draw a graphic frame over the area of the object you want to mask. For a graphic consisting of several objects, you might need to force one of the objects to be displayed over the graphic frame. For example, when the graphic frame was placed over the following clock, the frame covered the clock hands. To display the hands on top of the frame, click the hands, then select Graphics | Bring to Front.

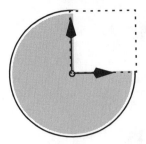

For more information on working with layered objects, see "Layering Objects" on page 355.

Rearranging Objects

Besides dragging and dropping objects to rearrange them, you can arrange objects by aligning, distributing, or moving them to the foreground or background.

Aligning

FrameMaker aligns objects along their paths. As mentioned in "Drawing Basic Shapes" on page 328, the path of an object runs through the middle of the object border, not the center of the object. In an object with a narrow border, such as the triangle in the following example, the path is displayed near the edge of the object; however, in an object with a thick border, such as the 12-point line, the path runs through the middle of the object.

Path runs through the middle of the 12-point line.

Path is displayed near the edge of the oval, which has a 0.5-point border.

Alignment is based on the position of the last object you select. Suppose you want to align the tops of the line and triangle. If you select the line and then the triangle, the line moves down to align with the triangle. If you select the triangle first, the triangle moves up to align with the line.

Original arrangement

Line selected first

Triangle selected first

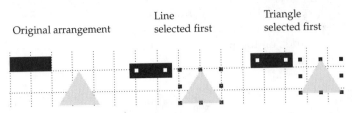

To align objects, follow these steps:

1. Select the objects you want to align.

2. Select Graphics | Align. The Align dialog box is displayed. (If you previously aligned objects, the settings you used are displayed.)

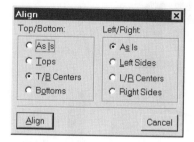

3. Do any of the following:

    ■ To align graphics vertically, click the appropriate radio button in the Top/Bottom section.

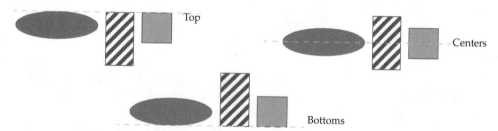

    ■ To align shapes horizontally, click the appropriate radio button in the Left/Right section.

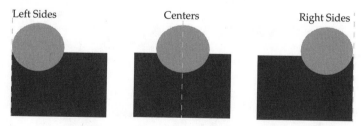

4. Click the Align button. The objects are aligned.

Distributing

You change the space among objects by distributing them. Distributing objects adds an equal amount of space vertically or horizontally, depending on your choice. For example, if you specify a horizontal gap of 0.05 inches, FrameMaker adds 0.05 inches of space between each object horizontally.

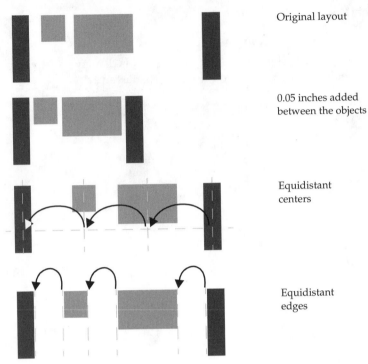

Original layout

0.05 inches added
between the objects

Equidistant
centers

Equidistant
edges

Unlike aligning, which lines up objects with the last selected object, distributing objects doesn't move the left and right objects (in horizontal distribution) or top and bottom objects (in vertical distribution); only the objects in the middle move to distribute the space. The only exception occurs when you type in the amount of space between the objects. When aligned horizontally, the objects move from the right to the left. When aligned vertically, the objects move from the bottom up.

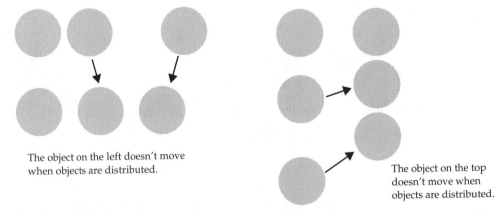

The object on the left doesn't move
when objects are distributed.

The object on the top
doesn't move when
objects are distributed.

To distribute spacing among objects, follow these steps:

1. Select the objects you want to distribute.
2. Select Graphics | Distribute. The Distribute dialog box is displayed.

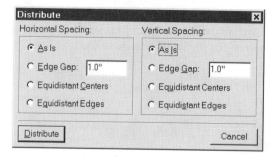

3. Do either of the following:
   - To align the objects horizontally, click the appropriate radio button in the Horizontal Spacing section.
   - To align the objects vertically, click the appropriate radio button in the Vertical Spacing section.
4. Click the Distribute button. The objects are distributed.

Grouping

Grouping is useful for creating one object from several shapes or for preventing objects from accidentally being moved on the page. You select the objects and then select Graphics | Group to group them. Once objects are grouped, you can modify, copy, move, or delete the group as one unit. For example, you can format all grouped objects with a solid fill and 5-point border. You can also flip, scale, rotate, reshape, and smooth or unsmooth; you cannot, however, change the number of sides. To ungroup a selected object, select Graphics | Ungroup.

Original grouped objects

Flipped, rotated, smoothed, scaled, and formatted with striped fill pattern

Note *The Ungroup command is grayed out in the Graphics menu when you try to ungroup an object consisting of joined lines. See "Joining Lines" on page 347 for details.*

Running Text Around an Object

You control how text is displayed around an adjacent object by configuring the object's runaround properties. The text is either displayed around the object's contour or an imaginary box. You can also set the gap between the text and object. In the following illustration, the first object shows text running around the contour of the pyramid. The second object shows text that goes around an imaginary bounding box. Runaround properties aren't configured for the third object, so the text runs behind the object.

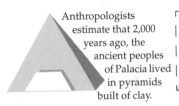

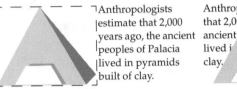

Text runs around the
contour of the object.

Text runs around an imaginary box
(represented by the dotted line).

Text does not run
around the object.

You can set runaround properties for more than one object at a time by selecting all objects first and then changing the properties.

To configure runaround properties, follow these steps:

1. Select the object or objects, then select Graphics | Runaround Properties. The Runaround Properties dialog box is displayed.

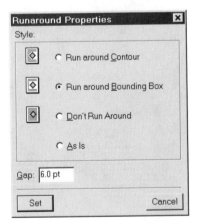

2. Do one of the following:
   - To flow text around the edge of the object, click the Run around Contour radio button.

- To flow text around an imaginary box, click the Run around Bounding Box radio button.

- To avoid running text around the adjacent object, click the Don't Run Around radio button.

3. *(optional)* Type the number of points between the text and object in the Gap field. The default is 6 points. You cannot change the unit of measurement as you can with the default display unit.

4. Click the Set button. The text is displayed around the object as you specified.

Layering Objects

To change the order in which layered objects are displayed, you send an object to the foreground or background. Some graphics programs let you send objects forward or backward one layer at a time, which is handy when you have several layers of objects. In FrameMaker, you have two options—to move the object to the front or the back.

Objects are layered in the order you draw them. For example, in a drawing with three layers, the object you draw first is displayed on the back layer, the second object is displayed in the middle layer, and the last object is displayed on the top layer. To display the top layer in the middle, you need to bring the middle layer to the front, as shown in the following illustration.

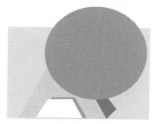

The sky is drawn first, the pyramid is drawn next, and the sun is drawn last.

To display the sun behind the pyramid, the pyramid is sent to the front.

To rearrange layers, do any of the following:

- To display an object as the back layer, click the object and select Graphics | Send to Back. The object is displayed in back.

- To display an object on the top layer, click the object and select Graphics | Bring to Front. The object is displayed in front.

- To display an object on a middle layer, do one of the following:

  - Click the object you want on top, then select Graphics | Bring to Front.

  - If you can't select the middle object, click the top layer, then select Graphics | Send to Back. For example, the rounded rectangle in the following illustration was previously on the back layer. When the top layer is sent to the back, the rounded rectangle is displayed in the middle layer.

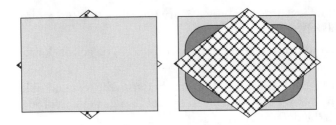

Changing the Orientation

You change the orientation of objects by rotating or flipping them. Rotating an object modifies the angle of the object; flipping creates a mirror image of the object.

Rotating

There are two ways to rotate an object. You use the mouse to rotate the object, or you specify the degree of rotation. When you drag a corner to rotate the object with the graphics snap on, the degree to which you can rotate the object might be limited by the snap rotation in the View Options. For instance, a 25-degree snap rotation means that the object will snap to an imaginary grid every 25 degrees when you manually rotate the object. See "Working with Grids" on page 334 for details.

To rotate an object, follow these steps:

1. Select the object you want to rotate.

2. Do one of the following:

   ■ To rotate the object clockwise or counterclockwise, select Graphics | Rotate. The Rotate Selected Objects dialog box is displayed. Type the degree in the Rotate By dialog box, click the Clockwise or Counterclockwise radio button, then click the Rotate button. The object is rotated.

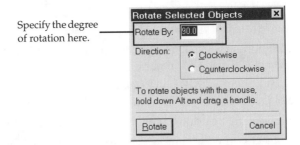

Specify the degree of rotation here.

   ■ To rotate the object in only the clockwise direction, select Graphics | Object Properties. The Object Properties dialog box is displayed. Type the degree of the angle in the Angle field, then click the Set button. The object is rotated.

The width and height don't change
when you rotate an object.

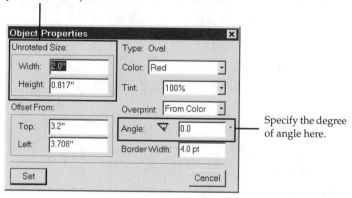

Specify the degree
of angle here.

■ ALT-click (Windows and UNIX) or COMMAND-click (Mac) a corner of the
object. The rotation arrow is displayed. Drag the corner to a new orientation.
(If the rotation arrow isn't displayed, you'll reshape the object instead of
rotating it. Try deselecting the object and then ALT-click or COMMAND-click
the corner again.)

Rotation arrow is displayed
when you press ALT.

Drag the corner to
rotate the object.

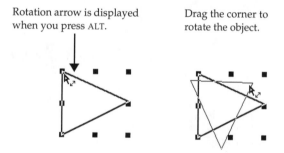

Flipping Horizontally or Vertically

When you flip an object, FrameMaker creates a mirror image of the object along an
imaginary line. The object is flipped left-to-right (horizontally) or up-and-down
(vertically).

Flipped horizontally   Flipped vertically

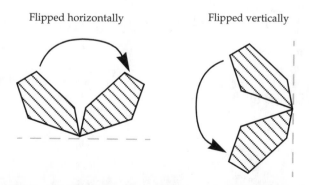

Text lines inside the object are not flipped; only the alignment point of the text changes. In the following illustration, each text line is left aligned. After flipping the objects horizontally, the grouped text lines are right aligned. If you ungroup the text lines and view the object properties, you'll see that the alignment has changed from left to right.

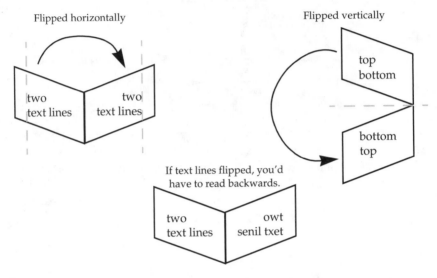

Note   *Flipping an object with a text frame does not change the text alignment because the paragraph tag applied inside the frame controls the alignment of the text.*

To flip an object, follow these steps:

1. Select the object or objects you want to flip.
2. Do one of the following:
   - To flip the object horizontally, select Graphics | Flip Left/Right.
   - To flip the object vertically, select Graphics | Flip Up/Down.

The object is flipped as you specified.

Drawing Objects in Structured Documents

Drawn objects themselves are not part of a document's structure. You can draw objects directly on the page, or attach them to the preceding paragraph by inserting a graphic element. This displays the Anchored Frame dialog box, where you set the alignment, anchored frame size, and other options. Then you draw the objects and import graphics into the anchored frame. For more information, see "Graphics in Structured Documents" on page 326.

The Complete Reference

Part IV

Building Books

The
Complete
Reference

Chapter 14

Setting Up Book Files

FrameMaker does a good job of handling short, structured documents, but it really shines with long, complex documents. One example of this is FrameMaker's book feature, which lets you group related documents. Once you put a collection of documents in a book, you can control pagination and create generated files, such as tables of contents, for the entire book. You can also perform many actions on the book instead of on individual files. For example, you can use the book to change conditional text settings across all the files in the book in a single step.

Creating a book file does not affect the component files; the book file is little more than a file list. Opening a file by double-clicking its icon in the book is exactly the same as using the File | Open command. The book file contains pointers to the files—FrameMaker does not embed copies of the files in the book file.

Book files work reliably for small and large books; books with thousands of pages and hundreds of component files are not unusual. During updating, FrameMaker opens and scans each file in the book, so updating a very large book can take some time. If you have a computer with plenty of system resources, you can speed things up by opening all the files before updating.

In unstructured FrameMaker, books consist of a list of files. In structured FrameMaker, you can also create structured books, in which each file is an element in the top-level Book element.

To adjust pagination, you must update the book file. This tells FrameMaker to scan the book file and update everything. The book file does not update pagination automatically when you add a new file to the book or when you modify a component file; you must explicitly tell FrameMaker to update the files.

Creating a Book File

Before you can take advantage of all the handy management features that the book offers, you need to create a book file that contains all of your files. To create an unstructured book file, follow these steps:

1. *(optional)* Open a file that belongs in the book file.
2. Select File | New | Book. If you opened a file in step 1 (or started from any open file), FrameMaker asks you whether you want to add that file to the book. Click the Yes button to include the file or the No button to create the book file without it. FrameMaker creates the book and displays it.

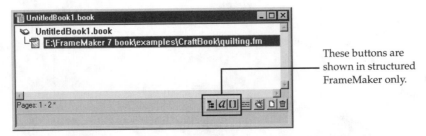

These buttons are shown in structured FrameMaker only.

3. Save the book file.

When you save your book file, notice that the book file name is listed with a complete path. The component file is now listed with the path relative to the book file (in the example shown, the book file and the content file are in the same directory).

What the Book Window Tells You

FrameMaker packs a lot of information about your files into the book window (Figure 14-1).

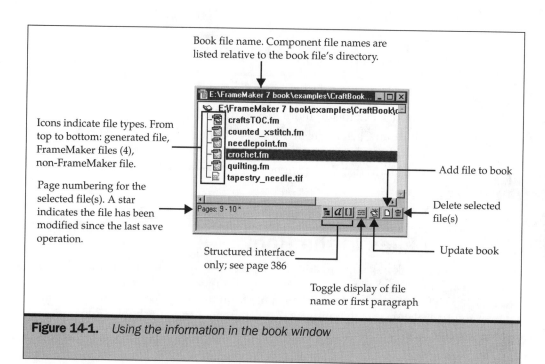

Figure 14-1.   *Using the information in the book window*

BUILDING BOOKS

The following items are available:

■ **File icons:** The icons preceding the file name tell you whether a file is a regular FrameMaker file, a generated file, or a non-FrameMaker file. (Non-FrameMaker files use their native icons.)

■ **Page numbering:** Select a file to see the current page numbers for that file in the status bar. If you select several files, FrameMaker lists the pagination for all of them in the status bar. A star following the page numbers indicates that the file needs to be saved.

■ **File name/paragraph text toggle (Display Filenames button):** Click this button to display the first paragraph of text from each document instead of the file name. Click it again to return to the file name. This is especially helpful if you must use cryptic file names, such as ch01-rev3.fm.

■ **Update Book button:** Click to update the book.

■ **Add File button:** Click to add more files to the book.

■ **Delete File button:** Click to delete the selected file or files from the book.

 In structured FrameMaker, three additional buttons are available. See page 386 for details.

Managing Files in the Book

Once you create a book file, you can add files to it, delete files that are listed in the book, change the order of files, and rename files. Except for renaming, these features do not affect the actual files; for example, deleting a file from the book *does not* delete it from your computer. Deleting merely removes that component from the book. (Renaming a file does rename it on the system as well as in the book file.)

Adding Files

FrameMaker makes a distinction between adding "regular" content files and adding generated files. Generated files are created from information in the book; they include the table of contents, index, and other less common files, such as lists of figures, lists of imported graphics, and subject indexes.

Generated files do not exist until you instruct the book file to create them. Regular files already have information in them and are added to the book so that you can control pagination and the like. Chapter 15, "Creating Tables of Contents," Chapter 16, "Creating Indexes," and Chapter 17, "Creating Other Generated Files," describe how to add generated files to your book. This chapter focuses exclusively on managing regular files.

To add a content file (such as a chapter or appendix file), you must tell FrameMaker where the file is located and position it in the book file, as described in the following steps:

1. Make sure the book window is the active window.

By default, files are added after the selected file. It's easy to rearrange files, though, so you may want to add your files and worry about their order later.

2. Select Add | Files (or click the Add Files icon at the bottom of the window). The Add Files dialog box is displayed.

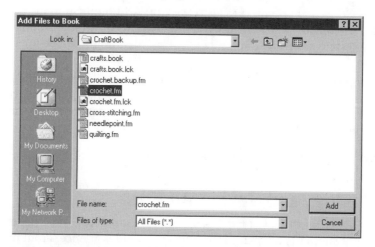

3. Locate the file you want to add and select it. To add several files, CTRL-click them (Windows and UNIX) or SHIFT-click them (Mac).
4. Click the Add button. The file is added to the book file.

BUILDING BOOKS

If the files are not in the right order, you can move them around. See "Rearranging Files" on page 367 for details.

You can also drag and drop files from the Desktop or Explorer (Windows) or Finder (Mac) onto the book window to add them.

Adding Non-FrameMaker Files

You can include non-FrameMaker files in your book file. Only FrameMaker files are counted in the book's pagination or numbering; however, adding a non-FrameMaker file does provide you with a few useful features, including the following:

- **Keeping track of related files.** While working on a book, you'll have many ancillary files that you need to keep track of. Adding them to the book helps to keep those files organized. Files you might want to add to the book file include outlines, style guidelines, and other "extras" that might not be in FrameMaker format.

- **Opening from the book file.** You can open the non-FrameMaker files from the book file. FrameMaker prompts you to specify whether you want to open them in FrameMaker (which probably means a conversion) or in the native application (such as Acrobat Reader for a PDF file).

When you print the book, only the FrameMaker files are printed.

Opening, Closing, and Saving All Files

Opening each file in the book is a tedious process. Fortunately, FrameMaker provides a convenient set of shortcuts to open, close, and save all files at once. From the book file, hold down the SHIFT key, then select the File menu to see the global commands:

- Open All Files in Book
- Close All Files in Book
- Save All Files in Book

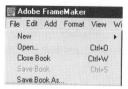

Regular File menu

SHIFT-File menu

Removing Files

Removing a file from the book file does not delete the file itself from the computer; it only removes the reference to the file from the book file.

To remove a file from the book, follow these steps:

1. In the book file, select the file or files you want to remove.
2. Select Edit | Delete File from Book or click the Delete icon in the lower-right corner of the book window. The file disappears from the book window. There is no confirmation prompt.

 The file is still available on your system.

Rearranging Files

When you first add files to the book, they may not appear in the order that you want them. To correct this, you can drag and drop icons in the book window to rearrange the files. To rearrange files, follow these steps:

1. Select the file you need to move.
2. Click and drag to reposition the file. A bar shows you where the file will end up.

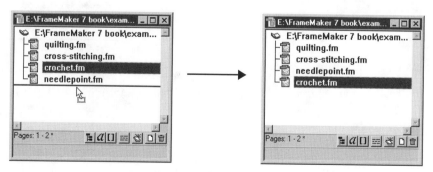

3. Release the mouse button to drop the file in its new location.

Renaming Files

Starting with version 6, you have the ability to rename files from within the book file. When you rename a file, FrameMaker updates references to that file throughout the book.

Caution   *FrameMaker updates only references within the current book file when you rename. If you rename a file that is referenced **by files outside the current book**, those references will be broken by the renaming process. For example, assume that you have a file called apple.fm. There are a number of cross-references from pie.fm and from horse_favorites.fm that point to apple.fm. The apple.fm and pie.fm files are in the book called baking.book. The horse_favorites.fm file is not part of this book. If you use the book-level renaming feature from baking.book, references between apple.fm and pie.fm will be updated correctly. However, the links from horse_favorites.fm will be broken.*

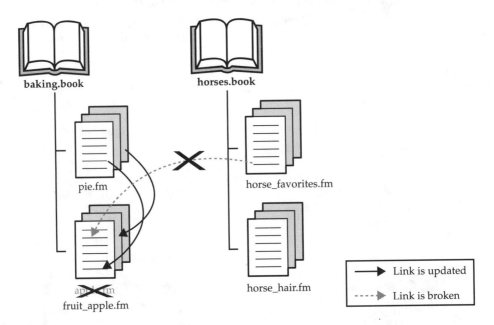

To rename a file, follow these steps:

1. *(optional, but recommended)* Open all files in the book (SHIFT-File | Open). Opening all files speeds up the process and also ensures that any missing font problems are avoided.

Caution   *If you do not open all files, missing fonts or other opening errors (such as files in an earlier version of FrameMaker) will cause the renaming operation to fail.*

2. Make sure that file names are displayed in the book window. If they are not, click the Display Filenames button to see them.

3. *(required for Windows and UNIX but not Mac)* Click the file you want to rename.

4. Click in the file name to make it editable.

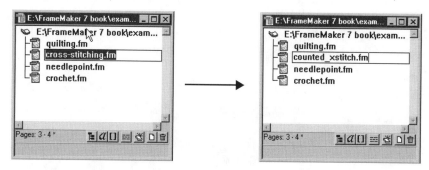

5. Type the new file name and press ENTER.

   FrameMaker prompts you to confirm that you want to rename ("move") the file and update all references to that file with the new name.

6. Click the OK button. FrameMaker scans all of the files in the book for cross-references, hypertext links, and text insets that refer to the old file name and updates them.

After completing the updating process, FrameMaker notifies you that it has updated the files.

Updating the Book

To manage your book file, you need to instruct FrameMaker to update the book. During updating, FrameMaker modifies the following items:

- **Numbering.** Chapter numbers, volume numbers, and paragraph-based numbering (autonumbers) are updated.

- **Pagination.** Page numbers are updated based on the settings in the book.

- **Cross-references.** The reference page numbers and text are updated to reflect any changes.

- **Text insets.** If imported-by-reference FrameMaker files have been updated, the insets are refreshed (see Chapter 25, "Creating Modules with Text Insets").

- **OLE links (Windows only).** Any OLE links are refreshed.

- **Generated files.** The entire book is scanned and generated files are replaced with new versions.

- **Master pages.** Any master pages applied based on paragraph tags are updated.

To update your book, follow these steps:

1. Display the book file.

2. *(optional)* To speed up the generation process, and to ensure that it works even if you have missing fonts in some of the files, open all of the files in the book (SHIFT-File | Open All Files in Book).

3. Select Edit | Update Book or click the Update icon at the bottom of the book window. The Update Book dialog box is displayed (Figure 14-2).

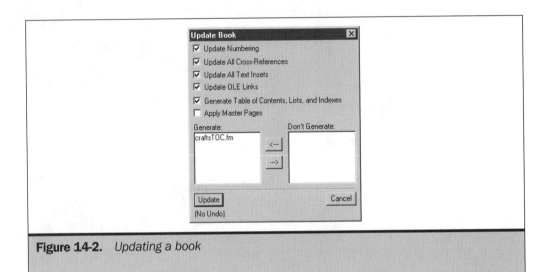

Figure 14-2. *Updating a book*

4. Check each of the items that you want to update. (Generally, it's a good idea to check everything except Apply Master Pages.) Your choices are as follows:

   ■ **Update Numbering:** If checked, all page, chapter, volume, and paragraph numbering is updated.

   ■ **Update All Cross-References:** If checked, all cross-references are updated.

   ■ **Update All Text Insets:** If checked, all text insets are updated.

   ■ **Update OLE Links** (Windows only): If checked, all files that are imported with OLE links are updated.

   ■ **Generate Table of Contents, Lists, and Indexes:** If checked, FrameMaker generates the files that are listed in the Generate list. Only tables of contents, indexes, and similar generated files are available to generate or not generate.

   ■ **Apply Master Pages:** If checked, FrameMaker updates master page assignments. For details, see "Reapplying Master Pages Globally" on page 291.

Creating generated files is the most time-consuming part of an update. If your book is very large or your system resources are limited, you can save some time by not generating tables of contents and the like. Be sure, though, to update them before you finalize the book to ensure that the most current information appears in generated files.

Troubleshooting Book Updates

When you update your book, FrameMaker reports any problems in the book error log (Figure 14-3).

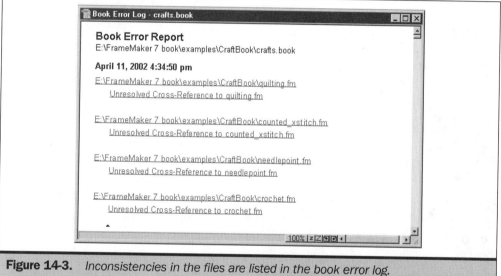

Figure 14-3.   *Inconsistencies in the files are listed in the book error log.*

The following issues can cause the update process to fail:

- Missing fonts
- FrameMaker files from an earlier version of FrameMaker
- FrameMaker files in use
- Read/write permissions on the files

Other generation problems do not cause the process to fail, but are reported in the book error log. They include the following:

- Unresolved cross-references
- Inconsistent conditional text settings

- Inconsistent color settings
- Inconsistent numbering properties

The following sections explain how to correct these problems.

Missing Fonts   A missing fonts message indicates that when FrameMaker attempted to open a file, the file called for fonts that are not installed on the current system. The missing font message causes the file-opening process to fail, which in turn causes the entire book update to fail. To correct the missing fonts problem, you have three choices:

- **Install the missing fonts on your system.** This is an operating system task. Refer to your system documentation for more information. (Depending on your operating system, you might also need software such as Adobe Type Manager.)
- **Remove the missing fonts from the document.** You can change the FrameMaker preferences so that missing fonts are permanently replaced. Refer to "Handling Missing Font Problems" on page 61 for instructions.
- **Open all files before updating the book.** If the files are open, then FrameMaker doesn't have to open them during the update, so you avoid this error.

FrameMaker Files from an Earlier Version of FrameMaker   Before updating the book, open all of the files and save them in the latest version of FrameMaker. That will eliminate this message. FrameMaker will not update a book that contains files from earlier versions of FrameMaker.

FrameMaker Files in Use   This message indicates that one of the files has been opened by another user. If you attempt to open the file directly, FrameMaker will tell the machine name or user name that has locked the file. Have the other user close the file so that you can update the book.

Read/Write Permissions on the Files   To open the files, FrameMaker needs read permissions. To save them, FrameMaker needs write permissions. Make sure that you have the appropriate permissions on the files. Files that are set to be read-only will not update properly. (This often happens with files that are copied from a CD.) You can also create view-only files inside FrameMaker; these will not update, either. To correct the latter problem, open the view-only file and press ESC SHIFT-F L K.

Unresolved Cross-References   This message indicates that FrameMaker has been unable to resolve cross-references in the book. The listed cross-references are hyperlinked, so click the error to jump to an unresolved cross-reference. This message can occur because of problems opening the file due to missing fonts in the target file or because of actual unresolved cross-references. You need to fix the broken cross-references to eliminate this message or open the files in the book before updating again.

Inconsistent Conditional Text Settings   This message indicates that a particular conditional text tag is set to be shown in one file and hidden in another. The message is informational; if you need to have your files set up this way, you can ignore it (for one or all files). If the conditional text settings should be consistent across the entire book, select all the files in the book, select View | Show/Hide Conditional Text and choose the settings you want for all the files.

Inconsistent Color Settings This message indicates that color definitions or color print settings are inconsistent. To correct the problem, apply consistent settings across the entire book (see Chapter 20, "Color Output"). You can safely ignore this message if your files do not actually use the inconsistent color.

Inconsistent Numbering Properties Indicates that the numbering set in the file conflicts with the numbering in the book. To correct this, assign consistent numbering, as described in the next section.

Managing Numbering

FrameMaker uses the order of files in the book and information you provide about numbering to control the numbering sequence for your book. You can, for example, specify that the files in the book should be numbered sequentially. When you make changes to the files, FrameMaker manages the pagination to keep everything in sequence, as shown in the following example:

After you add information to the documents, the new sequence is this:

Another numbering setup might require that each chapter's page numbering restarts at 1. The page numbering would look something like this example:

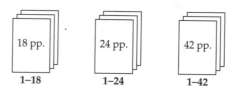

All numbering is controlled in the Numbering Properties dialog box (Format | Document | Numbering, shown in Figure 14-4), which provides sheets for volume, chapter, page, paragraph, footnote, and table footnote numbering.

On the Mac, no tabs are available; you navigate from sheet to sheet using the drop-down list.

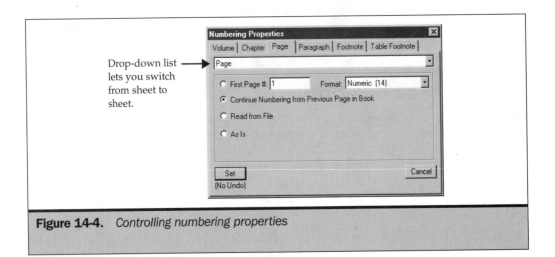

Drop-down list lets you switch from sheet to sheet.

Figure 14-4.   *Controlling numbering properties*

One major point of confusion is the Continue Numbering option, which is available in most tabs. Selecting this option causes the numbering to increase by one from the previous file. To keep the same number as the previous file, choose the Use Same Number option. In other words, "Continue" means that if the first file ends on page 57, the next file will begin on page 58.

Because FrameMaker's numbering is calculated by the file sequence, a missing file will throw off the numbering. You can eliminate this problem by assigning fixed values to a chapter (instead of letting FrameMaker calculate the value that should be there). This can make life difficult later, though, if you need to move chapters around because the hard-coded chapter number interferes with FrameMaker's ability to calculate the correct chapter numbers by position. We recommend that you resign yourself to having incorrect numbers until all of the chapters have been created. If this is unacceptable, consider creating dummy (empty) chapters and adding them to the book until the real file is ready.

Format Choices for Numbers

The Format drop-down list, available in several of the numbering tabs, lets you specify the type of numbering you want to use. Your choices are:

- Numeric (14). Creates a numeric sequence: 1, 2, 3, …
- roman (xiv). Creates lowercase Roman numerals: i, ii, iii, …
- ROMAN (XIV). Creates uppercase Roman numerals: I, II, III, …
- alphabetic (n). Creates lowercase letters: a, b, c, …
- ALPHABETIC (N). Creates uppercase letters: A, B, C, …
- Text (volume and chapter only). Creates a custom label. If you select text, you must specify the label you want for each item. You could, for example, have a volume number of Read Me.
- Custom (footnote only). Creates a custom footnote sequence.

Each example shows the result for the number 14 in parentheses, presumably because it shows the differences clearly.

The following sections explain how to set up numbering for each of the numbering types available in FrameMaker:

- **Pages.** Controls the value of the <$pagenum> building block inside the files. Page numbers increase from page to page within a file.
- **Chapters.** Controls the value of the <$chapnum> building block inside the files. You cannot have two different values for the chapter number inside a single file; the chapter number is always the same value across the entire document. (In other words, you cannot embed both chapter 1 and chapter 2 in a single file if you want to use <$chapnum> to control the chapter numbering.)
- **Volumes.** A volume usually contains several files. Controls the value of the <$volnum> building block inside the files. Like <$chapnum>, <$volnum> can have only one value inside a file.
- **Paragraphs.** Controls whether counters in the numbering properties for the Paragraph Designer are reset or not.
- **Footnotes.** Controls the value of the footnotes.
- **Table footnotes.** Controls the value of the table footnotes.

Page Numbers

FrameMaker provides three options for page numbering. The numbering can begin on a specified page (with a specified format), can continue whatever numbering was specified in the previous file, or start on the page specified in the file-level numbering properties (Read from File). To set up numbering that works properly, you want the page numbers to continue from the previous document whenever possible.

Consider the numbering example shown in the following table. The first few files in the book (table of contents, preface, and other front matter) use Roman numerals. After that, the first chapter starts with a numeric 1. All other documents are numbered straight through.

Document	Page Numbers	Setting Needed
Title page	i–ii	Start at: 1 roman (xiv)
Table of contents	iii–vi	Continue
Preface	vii–x	Continue
Chapter 1	1–16	Start at: 1 Numeric (14)
Chapter 2	17–28	Continue
Chapter 3	29–34	Continue
Chapter 4	35–46	Continue

To match this numbering, you need to set most of the files to "continue numbering." The files will pick up the last number in the previous file and increment by 1 to continue. Set the first file in the book to start at 1 and use Roman numerals. The first chapter file needs to restart at 1 and use numerics. To set up this numbering, follow these steps:

1. Select all of the files in the book window (click in the book window and press CTRL-A (Windows), ESC E A (all platforms), or COMMAND-A (Mac) to select all the files).

2. Select Format | Document | Numbering to display the numbering properties.

3. Click the Page tab to display the page numbering properties.

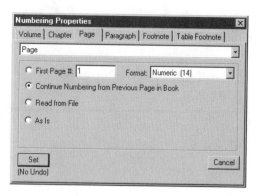

4. Click the Continue Numbering from Previous Page in Book radio button and click the Set button. FrameMaker applies the specified numbering scheme to every file in the book.

5. Now, set the numbering exceptions. Select the table of contents file only and display the Page tab in the Numbering dialog box again. In the First Page # field, type **1**. In the Format drop-down list, click roman (xiv). Click the Set button.

6. Select the first chapter file. Display the Page tab. In the First Page # field, type **1**. In the Format drop-down list, click Numeric (14). Click the Set button.

7. Update the book. Your new settings are applied throughout the book.

To set up page numbers that restart with every chapter, select all the files and set the first page number as 1 for each file. Separately, you'll need to set the chapter numbering to continue. The result will be the correct sequence:

```
1-1, 1-2, 1-3, ..., 2-1, 2-2, 2-3, ..., 3-1, 3-2, 3-3, ...
```

You'll also need to set up the generated files and the master pages to use the chapter numbers.

Chapter Numbers

For chapter numbers, FrameMaker provides the same "restart" and "continue" settings as for page numbers. In addition, you also have the option of retaining the same chapter number as for the previous file. This allows you to split a large chapter into two files and assign the same chapter number to both files.

By default, each file in the book (including generated files such as the table of contents) is assigned a chapter number, starting with 1. The fourth file would be chapter 4. You can reference the current chapter number in a document using the <$chapnum> building block.

You will probably need to customize the numbering to ensure that you get the correct numbers in your book. Consider the book shown in the following table. Because each file initially is assigned a chapter number, you end up with the table of contents, preface, and other front matter incrementing the chapter number.

Document	Default Chapter Number	Correct Chapter Number	Setting Needed
Title page	1	N/A	Doesn't matter
Table of contents	2	N/A	Doesn't matter
Preface	3	N/A	Doesn't matter
Chapter 1	4	1	Start at: 1 Numeric (14)
Chapter 2	5	2	Continue
Chapter 3	6	3	Continue
Chapter 4	7	4	Continue

To correct this, you need to set the chapter numbering properties so that the first chapter file starts at 1. Follow these steps:

1. Select all of the files in the book window.
2. Select Format | Document | Numbering to display the numbering properties.
3. Click the Chapter tab to display the chapter numbering properties.

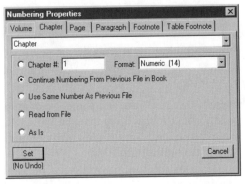

4. Select the Continue Numbering from Previous File in Book radio button and click the Set button. FrameMaker now assigns an incrementing chapter number to each file in the book.

Managing Numbering for Multifile Chapters

You may need to set up some chapters that are split across two or more files; often, because the chapters are very large or to accommodate custom master pages in the middle of a document. (If you need to assign a special master page—for example, a landscape page in a portrait document—it's helpful to split the document so that the landscape page is the first page in a file. Otherwise, you'll have to reassign master pages every time you add new information before the landscape page.)

A multifile chapter requires you to customize the book's chapter numbering handling. Make sure that the second and subsequent pieces of a chapter are set to use the same chapter number as the previous file.

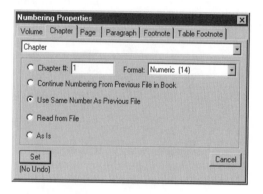

Note *This is the default setting for chapter numbers, but it's a good idea to reset them to ensure that any custom numbering is stripped.*

5. Select only the first chapter file. Display the Chapter tab again. In the Chapter # field, type **1**, and in the Format drop-down list, select Numeric (14). Click the Set button.

6. Update the book. Your new settings are applied throughout the book. Inside the files, every reference to <$chapnum> is also updated.

The chapter number in the front matter is still incorrect, but because the front matter doesn't normally use the chapter number, you can ignore this issue.

Volume Numbers

For volume numbers, FrameMaker provides the same options as for chapter numbers. FrameMaker assumes that your volumes would typically contain multiple chapters (files). To accommodate this, each file in the book defaults to using the same volume number as the preceding file (the chapter numbers increment by default).

You can reference the current volume number in a document using the <$volnum> building block.

If your book uses volume (or part) numbers, you need to customize the numbering to set the volume numbers. Consider the book shown in the following table. The book defaults to a single volume number for each file, but you need the volume number to increment with each part of the book.

Document	Volume Number	Setting Needed
Title page		Doesn't matter
Table of contents		Doesn't matter
Preface		Doesn't matter
Part I title page	I	Start at: 1 ROMAN (XIV)
Chapter 1	I	Same As Previous File
Chapter 2	I	Same As Previous File
Part II title page	II	Continue
Chapter 3	II	Same As Previous File
Chapter 4	II	Same As Previous File
Part III title page	III	Continue
Chapter 5	III	Same As Previous File
Chapter 6	III	Same As Previous File

To set the volume numbering properties, follow these steps:

1. Select all of the files in the book window.
2. Select Format | Document | Numbering to display the numbering properties.
3. Click the Volume tab to display the volume numbering properties.

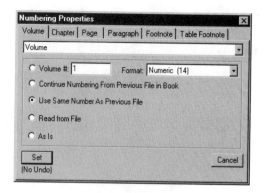

4. Select the Use Same Number As Previous File radio button, and click the Set button. FrameMaker now assigns the same volume number (1) to each file in the book.

Note   *This is the default setting for volume numbers, but it's a good idea to reset them to ensure that any custom numbering is stripped.*

5. Select only the first file in the first part. Display the Volume tab again. In the Volume # field, type **1**, and in the Format drop-down list, select ROMAN (XIV). Click the Set button.

6. Select the first file in the second part. Display the Volume tab. Select the Continue Numbering from Previous File in Book radio button, and click the Set button.

7. Repeat step 6 for each additional part.

8. Update the book. Your new settings are applied throughout the book.

Inside the files, every reference to <$volnum> is also updated.

Paragraph Numbers

The paragraph numbering properties determine whether autonumbering continues or restarts from one file to the next. The setting you choose here matters only if you have a numbering stream that carries over from one chapter to the next. If, for example, you have figure or table numbers that carry through the entire book (1, 2, 3, …, 57, 58, 59, …), make sure that paragraph numbering is set to Continue. The paragraph numbering properties control the values of the autonumbering counters.

For paragraph numbering, you have the following choices:

■ **Restart Paragraph Numbering:** All counters are reset to zero at the beginning of the selected file.

- **Continue Numbering from Previous Paragraph in Book:** Counter values are carried over from the previous file.
- **Read from File:** Counter values are picked up from the current file.

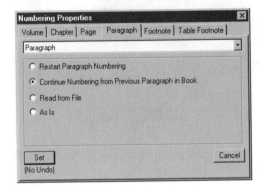

Footnote Numbers

FrameMaker's footnote numbering gives you three alternatives. Footnotes can:

- Increment through the entire book (which means there would be only one footnote number 3 in the entire book).
- Increment starting with every chapter (footnotes would start with 1, 2, 3 in each chapter, meaning you could have several footnotes labeled 3—one per chapter).
- Restart on every page (footnotes would start with 1, 2, 3 on each page, so you could theoretically have a footnote number 3 on each page in the file).

To set up footnote numbering properties for all of the files in your book, follow these steps:

1. Select all of the files in the book window.
2. Select Format | Document | Numbering to display the numbering properties.
3. Click the Footnote tab to display the footnote numbering properties.

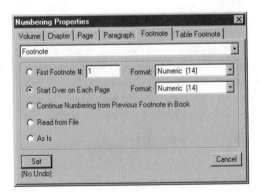

4. Select the pagination option you want:

   ■ To start the footnotes with a particular number (usually 1) for each file, select First Footnote, type in the number, and select a format from the drop-down list.

   ■ To restart footnotes on every page, select Start Over on Each Page and select a format from the drop-down list.

   ■ To number footnotes consecutively through the book, select Continue Numbering from Previous Footnote in Book. (If you do this, you should also set the first file to start footnotes at 1. The file *should* default to this setting, but it's safer to apply it explicitly.)

5. Click the Set button.

6. Update the book. Your new settings are applied throughout the book.

Table Footnote Numbers

Table footnotes are footnotes that are created for text inside a table. You cannot change the numbering for table footnotes; they always restart for each table. You can, however, set the format of the number at the book level.

To set the formatting for table footnotes, follow these steps:

1. Select all of the files in the book window.

2. Select Format | Document | Numbering to display the numbering properties.

3. Click the Table Footnote tab to display the table footnote numbering properties.

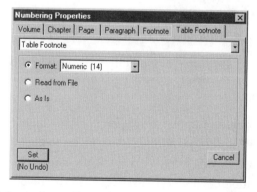

4. In the Format drop-down list, select the option you want. Click the Set button.

5. Update the book. Your new settings are applied throughout the book.

BUILDING BOOKS

Printing a Book

From the book file, selecting File | Print Book results in printing all the files in the book. But if you need to print just a portion of the book, you have that option, too. To print specific files in a book, follow these steps:

1. In the book window, select the files you want to print by CTRL-clicking (Windows and UNIX) or SHIFT-clicking (Mac) each file.

2. Select File | Print Selected Files.

3. Proceed as usual in selecting your print options.

4. Click the Print button to print the selected files.

Modifying Files from the Book

From the book window, FrameMaker provides a subset of the regular FrameMaker commands on the menus. These include spell-checking, find/change, conditional text settings, and more. Using these commands is equivalent to opening each file in the book and issuing the command there. The book file can save you lots of time because FrameMaker takes care of opening each file, making the change, and then saving and closing the file.

With the exception of the spell-checking and the find/change utility, the book-level commands are reversible. You can, for example, change your view settings for all the files in the book, but that change is easy to undo.

Spell-Checking and Finding/Changing Items

When you display the spell-checker or the Find/Change window from the book file, the utility begins working on the first file in the book and works through every file in order. To spell-check at the book level, follow these steps:

1. Select Edit | Spelling Checker to display the Spelling Checker dialog box.

2. Verify that the Book radio button is selected on the left.

3. Click the Start Checking button to begin checking spelling.

   FrameMaker attempts to open each document in the book and spell-check its contents. If FrameMaker cannot open a file, an entry is made in the book error log and the spell-checker continues with the next file. After completing spell-checking in a file, that file is saved and closed and FrameMaker moves on to the next file.

4. Use the spell-checking options as normal. See page 75 for details.

5. When FrameMaker reaches the end of the book, the spell-check is complete.

The Find/Change utility works the same way as the spell-checker. See page 70 for details.

 You can start the spell-checker or find/change process at a specific location by opening that file, displaying the utility you want, and then selecting the Book radio button to ensure that the operation is performed for all the files in the book. This works only if the book file is open when you go to a component file; otherwise, the Book option is grayed out.

Choosing Files When Performing Other Book-Level Features

For most book-level features, you can select which files the operation is performed on. If you want to make a change to all of the files in the book, you must select all of the files in the book before applying the command.

To apply a book-level command, follow these steps:

1. In the book window, select the files that you want to make changes to.

2. Select the command you want from the menus. For example, to toggle the display of document borders, select View | Show Borders (or Hide Borders). FrameMaker opens each file in turn and makes the change in the file.

Note *If you open all your files before making changes, then remember to save them (SHIFT-File | Save All Open Files).*

Book Features Available Inside Files

Although most book features are available only from the book window, a few things change inside the files. To use these features, the book file must be open in FrameMaker while you're working inside the component file.

You can perform book-level spell-checking and find/change operations from inside the file by clicking the Book radio button in the dialog boxes for those functions.

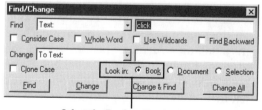

Select the Book option to start a global find/change operation.

BUILDING BOOKS

Paging Through Files in a Book

If you are working in a file that belongs to a book (and that book is open), FrameMaker understands that the current file is part of a sequence. When you scroll down through a file and reach the end of a file, you can press PAGE DOWN to go to the next file in the book. If the file is already open, FrameMaker displays the next file automatically (which can be quite disconcerting). If the file is not open, FrameMaker offers to open it.

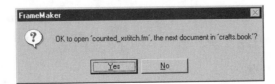

Pressing PAGE UP at the beginning of a file produces a similar result.

Structured Books

In structured FrameMaker, you'll notice that a few additional buttons are available in the book window.

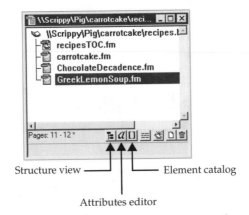

Structure view ⎯⎯⎯⎯⎯⎯⎯⎯ ⎯⎯⎯ Element catalog

Attributes editor

You can display and manipulate a structure view for the book, just as you have a structure view for regular document files. When you create a book from unstructured files, FrameMaker assigns a default structure. The top-level element is NoName, and each of the book files is assigned the BOOK-COMPONENT element.

When you create a book from structured files, the book's structure view shows the top-level element for each file:

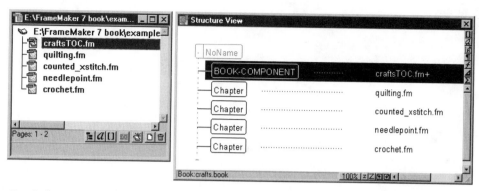

By default, generated files, such as the table of contents shown in the previous example, are not structured. You can open the table of contents file, wrap a top-level element around the document, and then regenerate the book file to see the new structured element in place of BOOK-COMPONENT:

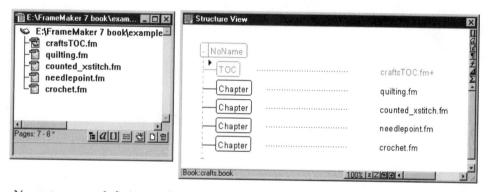

Your structure definitions should also include a top-level element for the book itself, often "Book." Change the default NoName element to a Book element, and the resulting structure looks like this:

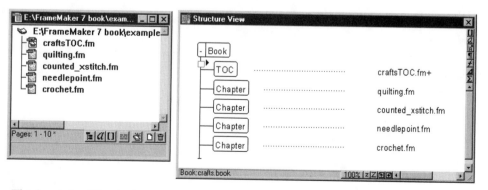

The book is still missing a required FrontMatter element, but the TOC and Chapter elements are in place.

Chapter 15

Creating Tables
of Contents

Y ou can automatically create and maintain tables of contents in FrameMaker. When you set up a table of contents, you specify which paragraphs or elements should be included. FrameMaker takes care of the rest; it scans the documents to locate every instance of those paragraphs (or elements), and then lists them in the table of contents along with their page number (Figure 15-1).

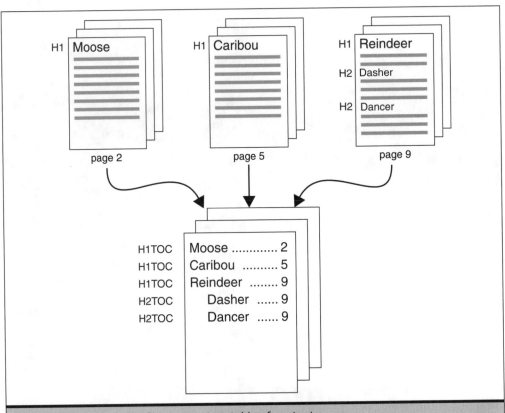

Figure 15-1. *Scanning files to create a table of contents*

Setting Up the Table of Contents File

When you create a table of contents, you must specify which paragraph tags (or elements) you want to include in the document. This is an all-or-nothing operation—if you include the Heading1 paragraph tag, every Heading1 in the book will be included in the generated table of contents.

Tip	*If you want to eliminate a few headings, you must create two paragraph tags (with identical settings): Heading1 and Heading1NoTOCEntry. Tag the paragraphs as appropriate and include only the Heading1 items in your generated list.* *For example, if you want to exclude the "Caribou" entry in Figure 15-1, you would tag Moose and Reindeer as Heading1s and tag Caribou as Heading1NoTOCEntry. This lets you exclude Caribou, even though it looks just like the other first-level headings.*

To set up a table of contents, follow these steps:

1. Open the book file.

2. *(optional)* To add the table of contents at a particular location, select the file immediately before or after where you want the table of contents. Because you can move the table of contents after creating it, this is not a critical step.

3. Select Add | Table of Contents. The Set Up Table of Contents dialog box is displayed.

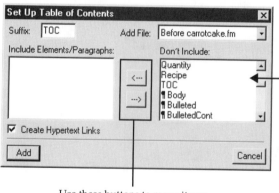

In structured FrameMaker (shown), th list includes elements and paragraphs. Elements are first, then paragraphs (shown with the paragraph symbol). In unstructured FrameMaker, this list includes only paragraphs, with no special label.

Use these buttons to move items from one list to the other.

4. The default file name suffix for the table of contents is TOC. You can change it if you want to. If you create several tables of contents, the suffix increments (TOC, TOC2, TOC3, and so on).

5. *(optional)* In the Add File drop-down list, specify whether you want the table of contents before or after the file you selected in step 2.

6. Move the items that you want to include to the Include list on the left.

   In unstructured FrameMaker, only paragraph tags are available for inclusion. In structured FrameMaker, you can use elements or paragraph tags. The elements are listed first, followed by the paragraph tags. To distinguish elements from paragraph tags, the paragraph tags have a paragraph symbol prefix (structured FrameMaker only).

You can move items by doing any of the following:

- Select an item, then click the left or right arrow button to move it from one list to another.
- Select an item, then double-click it to move it to the other list.
- To move all the items from one list to another, press and hold SHIFT, then click the appropriate arrow button.

7. Make sure that the Create Hypertext Links check box is checked. This activates hyperlinks for each entry in the table of contents. It also ensures that if you convert to other formats (PDF or HTML), the links in the table of contents are preserved. If you are absolutely sure that you do not want hyperlinks, you can uncheck this box.

8. Click the Add button. FrameMaker offers to update the book immediately.

Note *The file name of the table of contents file is based on the book file name. If your book file is foo.book, the table of contents file will be fooTOC.fm.*

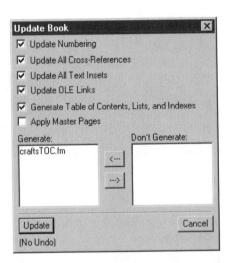

9. Click the Update button to create the table of contents. (See page 369 for a detailed discussion of updates.) The table of contents file now appears in the book; you can move it just like any regular file; see "Rearranging Files" on page 367.

To change the items included in the table of contents, select the table of contents file, and select Edit | Set Up Table of Contents to display the setup dialog box again.

Embedding the Table of Contents in a File

The automatic table of contents feature always creates a separate table of contents file. This presents a problem if you want to create a table of contents that's embedded on a page; for example, a list of topics at the beginning of a chapter.

You can accomplish this in at least two different ways:

- Generate a table of contents file and then use a text inset (Chapter 25, "Creating Modules with Text Insets") to embed the information in the file.

- Create cross-references (Chapter 8, "Cross-References") or hypertext links (Chapter 22, "Creating Interactive Documents with Hypertext") that point to the relevant headings.

Each approach has advantages and disadvantages. Creating a table of contents as a text inset is appealing because you update the table of contents and then update the text insets to automatically get any new information in the list. If you use cross-references or hyperlinks, you must add or delete the entries yourself.

However, cross-references or hyperlinks have the advantage of being self-contained in the file—you don't have to create a separate table of contents file and then import it back into the source file, which is inelegant at best.

If your headings change frequently or you have a long list in each chapter, you'll probably want to use the more automated approach (inset table of contents). If you're working with shorter, more manageable lists that don't change often, the cross-reference or hyperlink approach can work well.

The Initial Table of Contents File

After creating the table of contents, you can double-click it in the book file to display it. The exact formatting of this initial table of contents depends on the TOC formatting set up in the first file in the book. If you used a default template, your table of contents will look something like Figure 15-2.

FrameMaker uses reference pages and paragraph tags to determine the appearance of the table of contents. When you create the table of contents, FrameMaker uses the first file in the book as the template for the table of contents file. If that file is set up with all the needed table of contents settings (that is, if the reference pages and paragraph tags contain the needed definitions), your work may be done. It's likely, though, that you'll want to make some changes.

If you have a table of contents template, you can import formats from that template into the table of contents file and update the book again. You should then have a table of contents that's formatted correctly.

The rest of this chapter describes how to set up the formatting in the TOC file.

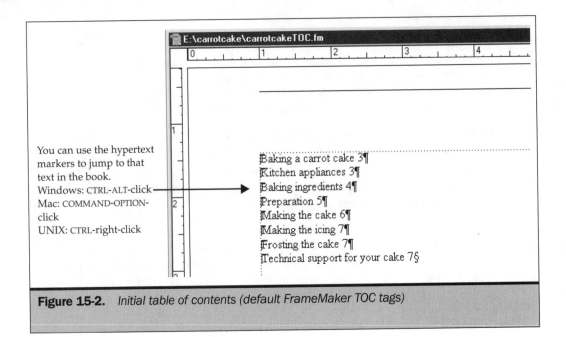

You can use the hypertext markers to jump to that text in the book.
Windows: CTRL-ALT-click
Mac: COMMAND-OPTION-click
UNIX: CTRL-right-click

Baking a carrot cake 3¶
Kitchen appliances 3¶
Baking ingredients 4¶
Preparation 5¶
Making the cake 6¶
Making the icing 7¶
Frosting the cake 7¶
Technical support for your cake 7§

Figure 15-2. *Initial table of contents (default FrameMaker TOC tags)*

You can insert a title of the table of contents (such as "Contents") and apply a Title paragraph tag to it. If you do, make sure that the title is positioned before any of the generated text and before the first hypertext marker. Any information that follows the first hypertext marker in the generated file is deleted when you regenerate the file.

A Sneaky Way of Avoiding Formatting Work

If you have a template file that contains the table of contents settings you need, you can save yourself some time. Instead of generating the table of contents and then importing from the template file, try this:

1. Copy the template file to the book directory.
2. Rename the template file to match the name that FrameMaker assigns to the table of contents. For example, if your book is named long.book, the table of contents name will be longTOC.fm.
3. Open the book file and add the table of contents file as usual.
4. Update the book. FrameMaker automatically uses the file that you've snuck into the book's directory and picks up all the formatting from that file.

Fine-Tuning the Table of Contents

After creating the initial file, you have several ways to customize the table of contents. You can do any of the following:

- Include or exclude paragraphs and elements when you set up the table of contents.

- Specify what information is included for each item (for example, paragraph text, paragraph autonumber, page number, or chapter number).

- Formatting the included information.

The latter two bullets require you to modify the reference pages and the paragraph tags in the table of contents file.

The information you set up on the reference pages depends on the paragraph tag settings, so often you have to go back and forth to get everything exactly right. You also need to update the book every time you make changes on the reference pages.

Because the table of contents picks up specific paragraphs or elements, it's important (once again) to tag your document consistently. One common problem is using blank paragraphs to provide vertical white space in a document. If the blank paragraphs use a tag that's included in the table of contents, you will see empty entries in the table of contents.

To remove them, go to the source file and delete the empty paragraph. Use the space above and space below settings in the Paragraph Designer instead (see "Avoiding Formatting Overrides and Empty Paragraphs" on page 111 for details).

Locating the TOC Reference Flow

The information that's displayed for each paragraph or element is controlled by the reference pages of the generated file. For the table of contents, the reference pages contain a reference page called TOC. On that TOC page, you will find a text frame with a TOC flow (Figure 15-3).

FrameMaker has three types of pages: body pages (which are printed), master pages (which provide the templates for the body pages with headers and footers), and reference pages. Reference pages store information used ("referenced") by other parts of the document.

Each paragraph or element that you have included in the table of contents will have its own entry in the reference pages. This entry determines what information is displayed for each item.

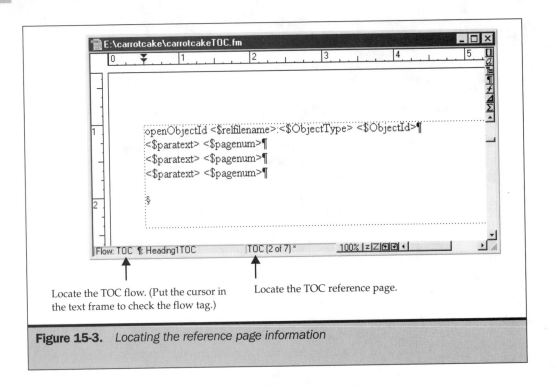

Locate the TOC flow. (Put the cursor in the text frame to check the flow tag.)

Locate the TOC reference page.

Figure 15-3. *Locating the reference page information*

Caution *If you have two TOC flows in the file, FrameMaker uses the one that comes first in its internal sort order. If you repeatedly update the TOC flow but do not see any results when you update the book, check the reference pages for an extra TOC flow. FrameMaker might be using the other flow instead of the one you're modifying. Sort order is not necessarily the same as the page order of the reference pages, so a flow that occurs later in the document could be considered the "first" TOC flow. Check every text frame's flow tag to verify that only one text frame in the reference pages is labeled TOC. Keep in mind that the renegade extra flow might be in a very small text frame. If you do find an extra TOC flow, we recommend that you copy the information in your good flow and then delete **both** flows and regenerate. FrameMaker re-creates a TOC text frame, and you can paste the good information into this new text frame.*

To locate the TOC flow on the reference pages, follow these steps:

1. Display the reference pages by selecting View | Reference Pages.
2. Find the TOC reference page. Notice that the status bar tells you the name of each page along with the number of pages as you move from page to page (as shown in Figure 15-3).

Book vs. Stand-Alone Table of Contents

Most of the information in this chapter focuses on tables of contents for a book. You can, however, also create a table of contents for a single file. FrameMaker calls this a *stand-alone* table of contents (presumably because the file stands alone instead of being part of a book).

Without a book file, you can't update from the book. Instead, you select Special | Table of Contents to create a stand-alone table of contents. Once you create the file, selecting Special | Table of Contents again will update the file. Any changes you made to the list of included tags, the paragraph formats, or the reference pages in the generated file are preserved.

On the TOC reference page, locate the TOC flow. Click inside the flow, and check the status bar to verify that you are in the TOC flow.

 After changing the reference pages, you must update the book before your changes are shown in the table of contents entries.

Understanding the TOC Flow Entries

In the TOC flow, you will find an entry for each of the tags you've included in the table of contents. You can determine which paragraph belongs to an included item based on the paragraph tag. For example, if you included ChapterTitle in your table of contents, you will find a ChapterTitleTOC paragraph in the TOC flow.

 FrameMaker does not delete entries from the TOC flow. If you added a paragraph tag and later removed it from the setup dialog box, you will still see an entry here. You can safely remove that line if you want to.

Each entry in the TOC flow determines what information is included for a specific paragraph or element. For instance, you might have an entry such as the following with a paragraph tag of Heading1TOC:

```
<$paratext> <$pagenum>
```

For each Heading1, FrameMaker will pick up the contents of the paragraph (<$paratext>), followed by a space, followed by the page number of the paragraph (<$pagenum>).

You can customize the entries using various building blocks, but you must type in the building blocks from scratch. Table 15-1 lists the available building blocks.

Most TOC flow definitions consist of a mixture of text and building blocks. For instance, you could use the following definition for a chapter title:

```
Chapter <$chapnum>: <$paratext>\t<$pagenum>
```

Building Block	Description
`<$paratext>`	Inserts the text of the source paragraph (for example, "Reindeer" or "Caribou" from the example in Figure 15-1 on page 390).
`<$paranum>`	Inserts the entire autonumber (if any) of the source paragraph.
`<$paranumonly>`	Inserts the numeric portion of the autonumber from the source paragraph.
`<$pagenum>`	Inserts the page number on which the source paragraph occurs.
`<$chapnum>`	Inserts the chapter number of the source paragraph's file.
`<$volnum>`	Inserts the volume number of the source paragraph's file.
`<$elemtext>`	Inserts the first paragraph of the source element, including any prefixes or suffixes. The autonumber is not included.
`<$elemtextonly>`	Inserts the first paragraph of the source element, without any prefixes or suffixes assigned to the source element. (Prefixes or suffixes of child elements within the first paragraph *are* included.) The autonumber is not included.
`<char_tag>`	Applies the specified character tag to the text that follows in the paragraph.
`<Default Para Font>` or `</>`	Removes any character tagging and returns to the paragraph's formatting.
`\t`	Inserts a tab.

Table 15-1. *Building Blocks for the TOC Entries*

In the chapter title tag, the word "Chapter," the colon, and the various spaces are regular, literal text. The <$chapnum>, <$paratext>, and <$pagenum> building blocks are processed every time this entry is used to determine the current values for those items. Typing in \t inserts a tab character.

Several FrameMaker features—such as cross-references and variables—use building blocks. The building blocks for the table of contents are special in a few ways:

- FrameMaker does not provide you with a way to insert building blocks by choosing them from a list. Instead, you must type the building block.

- In the table of contents definitions, you cannot use building blocks that call other paragraph tags, such as:

  ```
  <$paratext[some_other_para]>
  ```

  FrameMaker can pick up information only from the paragraph that's currently being processed.

- Because you are typing in a text frame and not a dialog box, you can use the normal keyboard shortcuts for special characters.

Autonumbering in the Table of Contents

Autonumbering is available for the paragraph tags in the table of contents, just like any regular document. However, we advise you not to use autonumbering in the table of contents paragraph definitions.

Using autonumbering lets you, for example, create a ChapterTitleTOC entry that uses only:

```
<$paratext> <$pagenum>
```

The chapter number is inserted by paragraph numbering set for ChapterTitleTOC (in the Numbering sheet of the Paragraph Designer):

```
S:Chapter <n+>
```

You cannot use <$chapnum> because FrameMaker will pick up the chapter number of the *current* file (that is, the table of contents) when <$chapnum> is used in the autonumber definition.

We recommend against this technique because the autonumbering stream is completely unrelated to the actual chapter number. Using autonumbering hides any possible problems with the chapter numbering sequence because you do not see the true chapter number; you see only the autonumber. Instead, we recommend that you use the following definition in the TOC flow on the reference page:

```
Chapter <$chapnum>: <$paratext> <$pagenum>
```

BUILDING BOOKS

Formatting the Table of Contents

For each tag you include in the table of contents, FrameMaker automatically creates a paragraph tag. The tag name is the name of the source tag with "TOC" appended. If, for example, you include Heading1 in your table of contents, all of the Heading1 entries will use the Heading1TOC paragraph tag. To format the table of contents, you modify these tag definitions in the table of contents. Refer to Chapter 5, "Formatting Text with Paragraph Tags," for details on how to format the paragraph tags.

Because of FrameMaker's convention of appending TOC, it's probably a good idea not to create any tag names for your regular content that end in TOC. In fact, this recommendation is for all generated files. The default file name suffix of the generated file is used for the paragraph tags that control the formatting in the generated file. (For example, in the index, the tag names end with IX; in lists of references, they end with LOR.)

Using Character-Level Formatting

If you want to format a portion of a table of contents entry differently from the rest of the paragraph, you use character tags as building blocks. For example, to make only the page number boldface, you would do something like this:

```
<$paratext> <Bold><$pagenum><Default Para Font>
```

The character tag you use must be defined in the character catalog of the table of contents file.

Formatting Examples

Many users are intimidated by the process of getting a table of contents to look just right. The trouble is that you have to make changes in two different places—the reference pages and the paragraph tags. Reference-page changes don't take effect until you update the book, but paragraph tag changes are immediate. In this section, you'll find explanations of two common formatting problems:

- Dot leaders
- Putting two paragraphs on a single line

Creating Entries with Dot Leaders

Setting up table of contents entries with dot leaders is a common requirement. FrameMaker can handle these automatically, but setting them up can be a bit disconcerting.

To create a table of contents entry with dot leaders, follow these steps:

1. Go to the reference pages (View | Reference Pages) and locate the TOC flow.

2. Modify the TOC definition as follows for each paragraph that should have a dot leader:

   ```
   <$paratext>TAB<$pagenum>
   ```

   That is, put a TAB character between the <$paratext> and <$pagenum> building blocks. (You can also use \t.) If you are using chapter numbers, your definition might look more like this:

   ```
   <$paratext>TAB<$chapnum>-<$pagenum>
   ```

   The effect (or rather lack thereof) on the reference page is shown in the following example:

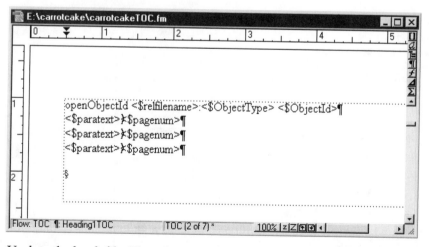

3. Update the book file. The tabs now appear in your table of contents entries, but they probably aren't working yet.

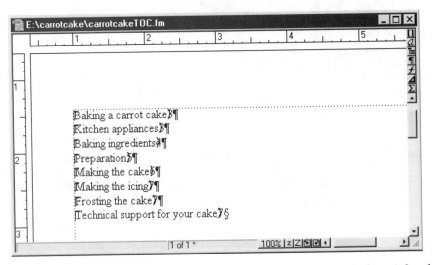

4. Modify the paragraph tags in the table of contents file to include a right-aligned tab stop with a dot leader. The following illustration shows a sample paragraph tag with the appropriate settings. You need to make this change in every TOC paragraph tag that includes a tab.

Note *Remember to click the Update All button to save your changes for each paragraph tag you change.*

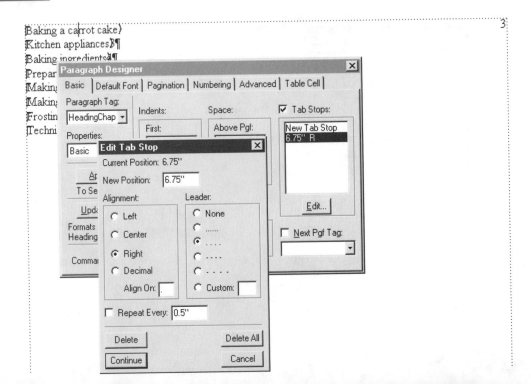

Your table of contents entries should now line up correctly.

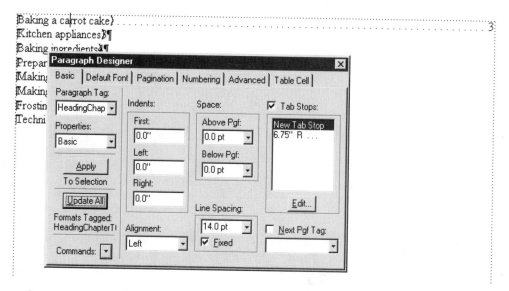

Once you set up the dot leaders for each paragraph, FrameMaker generates them every time you update the table of contents.

Putting Two Paragraphs on a Single Line

A common technique used in cross-references and variables is not available inside the table of contents. In cross-references and variables, you can use building blocks that call a particular paragraph tag or element, such as these:

```
<$paratext[ChapTitle]>
<$elemtext[DocumentTitle]>
```

These options are not available inside the table of contents definition. While generating the table of contents, FrameMaker can pick up information only from the current paragraph.

This presents a problem when, for example, your chapter number and chapter title are stored in two separate paragraphs. In the table of contents, you want something like this:

Chapter 7: Important Information

But in the document, you have two paragraphs:

- chap_number: Chapter 7
- chap_title: Important Information

Managing Line Breaks in the Table of Contents

After generating the table of contents, you'll probably have a few lines that break in interesting and unfortunate ways. It's tempting to correct them by inserting forced returns (SHIFT-ENTER), but those changes are lost when you regenerate. A better strategy is to use hard spaces in the source paragraph to "glue together" the relevant pieces so that they break properly in the generated table of contents.

If the paragraphs are in sequence, you can use a run-in heading format in the table of contents. If the chapter_numberTOC paragraph uses a run-in heading, the chapter number and title will appear on the same line.

Structured Tables of Contents

Generated lists, such as tables of contents and indexes, are always unstructured when you first create them. You can add structure to them so that the final book reflects the structure you want. However, every time you update the book, the structure you've added to the generated file disappears. Therefore, it's best to wait until you are completely done with your book before you add structure to the generated files. Often, you can apply a top-level TOC or Index element and leave the remainder of the document unstructured.

Chapter 16

Creating Indexes

M any readers of technical books consider the index to be the most important part of the book. A complete index lets readers locate information quickly. You can create indexes for your FrameMaker books (or files). An index, like a table of contents, is a generated file. Creating indexes, however, takes more work than creating a table of contents. Before you can generate the index, you must insert index markers (hidden text with index information) throughout the document to identify terms that should appear in the index. Markers can be structured or unstructured.

FrameMaker doesn't automatically create index entries for you, but it does provide automatic sorting and concatenation of index entries (see Figure 16-1). Specifically, FrameMaker takes your index markers and does the following:

- Alphabetizes entries
- Inserts group titles (A, B, C, D, and so on)
- Groups identical entries into a single entry with multiple page numbers
- Groups secondary entries under their parent entry
- Inserts the correct page number for each entry (based on the marker location)

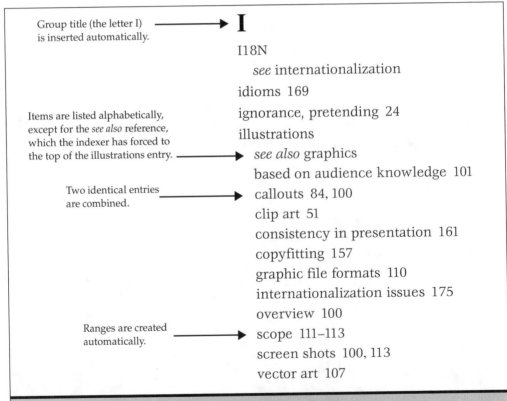

Figure 16-1. *Most indexing functions are done automatically.*

Creating the Index File

To create an index, you must insert index markers into the document files to create content in the index.

To create an index file, follow these steps:

1. Open the book file.
2. *(optional)* Click the file that will be immediately before or after the index.
3. Select Add | Standard Index. The Set Up Standard Index dialog box is displayed (Figure 16-2).

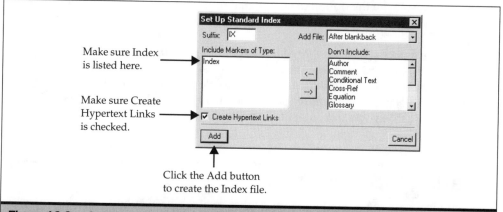

Figure 16-2. *Setting up the index file*

4. *(optional)* In the Add File drop-down list, choose whether you want the index before or after the file you selected in step 2.
5. Verify that the Index marker is in the Include Markers of Type list.
6. Make sure that the Create Hypertext Links check box is checked. This feature creates the index entries as hyperlinks. It also ensures that if you convert to other formats (PDF or HTML), the links in the index are preserved.

If you are generating indexes with a very large number of entries (more than 50,000 or so), don't check the Create Hypertext Links check box. With the links, the index will either take a very long time to generate or fail to generate.

7. Click the Add button. The Update Book dialog box (Figure 14-2 on page 370) is displayed. The index you're creating is shown in the generated files list.

8. Make sure that the index is in the Generate list (and not the Don't Generate list), then click the Update button. The file name of the index file is based on the book file name. If your book file is foo.book, the index file will be fooIX.fm.

   The index file now appears in the book; you can move it just like any regular file (see "Rearranging Files" on page 367).

File-Level (Stand-Alone) Indexes

Although you'll probably create most indexes for a collection of files (that is, a book), you also have the option of creating an index for a single file. FrameMaker calls this a *stand-alone* index because the index stands on its own and is not part of a book.

If you're working on a very large index, consider creating a stand-alone index for each chapter as you're inserting the index markers. This lets you check the index entries chapter by chapter (instead of having to plow through the entire index).

To create a stand-alone index, open a document, then select Special | Standard Index. Specify that you want to create a stand-alone index.

Creating Index Entries

When you insert an index marker, FrameMaker creates a corresponding index entry. The page number that appears in the index matches the page on which the index marker occurs. In addition to basic index markers, FrameMaker provides a variety of building blocks and commands that let you create secondary entries, entries with character formatting, and the like. Table 16-1 provides a quick reference for indexing commands; the sections that follow explain the commands in more detail.

Command	Marker Text Example	Result
: colon Creates a secondary reference	`apple:pie`	**A** apple pie 7

Table 16-1. *Indexing Command Examples*

Command	Marker Text Example	Result

	`apple:pie:a la mode`	**A**
		apple
		  pie
		    a la mode 7

`;` semicolon Creates two entries in a single marker	`apple;banana`	**A** apple 7 **B** banana 7

	`pie:apple;cream pie:banana`	**C**
		cream pie
		  banana 7
		P
		pie
		  apple 7

`<$nopage>` Suppresses display of the page number	`torte, see cake<$nopage>`	**T** torte, see pie
`<character_tag>` Assigns the specified character tag to the marker text that follows	`torte, <Emphasis>see<Default Para Font> pie<$nopage>`	**T** torte, *see* pie

`[sort_order]`
Sorts the entry as if it used the text shown in brackets
	`pie:<Emphasis>see also<Default Para Font>cream pie<$nopage>[pie:aa]`	**P**
		pie
		  see also cream pie
		  apple 7

`<$startrange>`
`<$endrange>`
Lets you create entries with ranges
	On page 8: `pear<$startrange>`
	On page 12: `pear<$endrange>`
		P
		pear 8–12

Table 16-1. *Indexing Command Examples (Continued)*

Basic Entries

To create a basic index entry, follow these steps:

1. Position the cursor where the relevant information occurs in the document.

2. *(optional)* Select the term you want to index before displaying the Marker dialog box. FrameMaker automatically puts the selected text in the marker text field.

3. Select Special | Marker. The Marker dialog box is displayed.

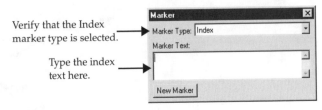

4. In the Marker Type drop-down list, make sure that Index is selected.

The marker type defaults to whatever type was last used, so if you just inserted a hypertext marker, you'll need to change the marker type from Hypertext back to Index.

5. In the Marker Text field, type the text you want in the index. For example, to create an entry under A for apple on page 7, go to page 7, insert a marker in the apple-related content, and type in:

```
apple
```

Caution *There is a 255-character limit (including spaces) on marker text. If you type in more than 255 characters, FrameMaker displays an error message when you attempt to create the marker. To eliminate the problem, you must cut down the text in each marker to no more than 255 characters. You can create two markers at the same location and divide up the information into two markers.*

To insert a command character (such as colon, semicolon, or brackets) as a literal, precede it with a backslash. For example:

```
\<HTML\>
```

6. Click the New Marker button to insert the marker. A marker symbol is displayed in your text. It looks like a boldface T, but it does not print.

Index marker symbol

7. To see the result in your index, update the book file. The new index entry appears in the generated index.

A

apple 7

The letter A and the page number are automatically inserted. You provide only the actual index entry text.

If the entry you want appears in the text, you can insert a blank index marker immediately to the left of the relevant word. If the index marker is blank, it picks up the word to the right of the index marker during generation. However, we do not recommend this method because it makes index maintenance more difficult. You cannot search for index text; instead, you must locate the blank index markers and then check the words next to them.

Editing and Deleting Index Entries

To edit an existing marker, select the marker (or select a block of text that includes the marker). Then, select Special | Marker to display the Marker dialog box, make your changes, and click the Edit Marker button to save them.

Tip

If you are planning to do a lot of indexing, we highly recommend that you get the IXgen plug-in, which helps automate a lot of index maintenance.

To delete an index entry, delete the marker. However, locating index markers for editing or deleting can be tedious. Here are some tips for finding index markers:

- Use the Find command and specify that you want to locate marker text or a marker of type Index.

- Take advantage of the hypertext links in the index. When you CTRL-ALT-click (Windows), COMMAND-OPTION-click (Mac), or CTRL-right-click (UNIX) on a page entry, FrameMaker opens the appropriate file, locates the index marker, and selects it.

- Leave the Marker dialog box open. When you select a marker, the marker text is displayed in the Marker dialog box automatically.

Creating Subentries

To create a subentry, separate the primary and secondary entry with a colon. For example, type the following:

```
soup:chicken noodle
```

The entry will look like this:

S
soup
   chicken noodle 27

Stacking Multiple Entries in a Single Index Marker

Use a semicolon to separate multiple, independent entries in a single index marker. For example:

```
food;drink
```

D
drink 36
F
food 36

This is equivalent to creating two separate markers, each of which contains one entry.

Creating Ranges

Page ranges in indexes tell the reader that there is a significant amount of information available about a particular topic. You indicate the beginning and the end of the range with separate, matching markers. A range looks like this:

G
gluttony 121–135

There are two ways to create ranges—you can use index markers that define ranges, or you can use the <$autorange> command. This section discusses how to create ranges with index markers; refer to page 421 for details on the <$autorange> command, which is inserted in the IX reference page flow.

To create an index entry with a range of pages, follow these steps:

1. On the first page of the range, insert an index marker with the relevant text and the <$startrange> command:

```
gluttony<$startrange>
```

A Few Words About Good Indexing

The index provides readers with *information access points*—a way to locate the content that's of interest. Creating a detailed, useful index is critical to the success of your document. The longer the document, the more important the index becomes to the reader. A complete discussion of indexing is beyond the scope of this book, but here are a few pointers:

- Index terms where they are defined and when important information about the term is provided. Do not index every occurrence of a term (unless you're creating a specialized concordance index).

- Index actions by the action (gerund) and the item (noun). For example, for information about steeping tea, put an entry under "steeping tea" and another under "tea, steeping."

- If you have more than two or three page entries for a particular item, modify the entries to create secondary entries under the primary entry.

- Use ranges to cue readers that a detailed discussion of a topic is available.

- Provide synonyms ("see" references) to help readers locate the information they want even if they don't know your terminology.

Refer to Appendix A, "Resources," for books about indexing. If you do not want to create the index yourself, consider hiring a professional indexer. The American Society of Indexers (www.asi.org) is a good place to start.

2. On the last page of the range, insert a matching index marker with the <$endrange> command:

```
gluttony<$endrange>
```

FrameMaker matches the <$startrange> and <$endrange> commands and puts a single index entry in the index.

The marker text must match exactly (other than the range command); otherwise, FrameMaker cannot resolve the markers. If FrameMaker cannot match the two ends of the range, you see question marks in the index:

G

gluttony ??–135

To correct this problem, make sure that every <$startrange> marker has a corresponding <$endrange> marker and that the marker text matches in those entries. A common mistake is to create one singular and one plural entry:

```
apple<$startrange>
apples<$endrange>
```

The result in the index is two entries, each with half a range:

A
apple 40–??
apples ??–46

When you insert a range command, the command is applied to the current index entry in the marker and all that follow to the right in that marker. For example, assume you have the following two markers:

```
land<$startrange>
sea;land<$endrange>
```

In this case, the "land" range resolves correctly, and you see a single page entry under "sea." However, the following will cause problems:

```
land<$startrange>
land<$endrange>;sea
```

The <$endrange> command is applied to the "land" entry and also to the "sea" entry, so the result is a broken range because you do not have a sea<$startrange> entry anywhere.

L
land 2–10

S
sea ??–10

To prevent this problem, which is hard to track down and correct, we recommend that you put all range commands in individual markers instead of stacking them with other entries in a single marker.

Creating References to Synonyms ("see")

In an index, *see* references or synonyms are very helpful because they point the reader in the right direction. For example, a reader might find something like this:

G
Granny Smith, *see* apple

These references are inserted just like regular index markers, except that you need to suppress the page number. For this, you need the <$nopage> command:

```
Granny Smith, see apple<$nopage>
```

If you want to italicize the word *see,* use a character tag inside the index marker and the <Default Para Font> tag to turn off the character tagging:

```
Granny Smith, <Emphasis>see <Default Para Font>apple<$nopage>
```

*The character tag you specify must be available in the index file's character catalog. It does **not** have to be available in the file where you insert the marker.*

Like the range commands, <$nopage> applies to all the text that follows in the marker. You can restart pagination with the <$singlepage> building block, but it's usually easier to separate the <$nopage> entries into individual markers.

Changing Sorting Order for a Single Entry

The *see also* reference is a variation on *see* references. You generally use *see* references when you need to point readers to a different location in a document. By contrast, *see also* references are used when the current entry has some information, but there is also another relevant possibility. In Figure 16-1 on page 406, for example, the index includes a *see also* reference (illustrations, see also graphics) and a *see* reference (I18N, see internationalization).

The problem with *see also* references is that, by default, FrameMaker sorts them under S in the subentry. Instead, you probably want them to appear at the top of the list. You accomplish this by modifying the alphabetization of that entry. Instead of using the actual text of the entry, you provide alternate text that's used when sorting the entry.

The see also entry in Figure 16-1 uses the following syntax:

```
illustrations:<Emphasis>see also<Default Para Font>
graphics<$nopage>[illustrations:aa]
```

The text in brackets at the end of the entry controls where the information is sorted in the index. In the preceding example, the aa text ensures that the entry is sorted to the top of the illustrations subentries.

The text in brackets is only for the current entry in the marker. For example, consider the following:

```
Korean War;'50s[Fifties]
```

The Korean War entry appears under K, but the '50s entry shows up under F.

Formatting the Index

To format the index, you modify the index paragraph tags and the reference pages. The paragraph tags are as follows:

- **GroupTitlesIX** is applied to the lettered headings (A, B, C, and so on) that separate the alphabetical groupings in the index.
- **Level1IX** is applied to the first-level index entries.
- **Level2IX** is applied to the second-level index entries.
- If you have deeper index levels, FrameMaker creates the appropriate **Level3IX**, **Level4IX**, and so on.

You can change these paragraph tags inside the index file to create the look you want.

When you generate the index, FrameMaker replaces the entire generated flow in the index. If you want to insert text preceding the index (such as the title "Index"), type this text into the index file before the generated text. Be sure that the first marker in the flow is after the title. FrameMaker will not delete any text that precedes the generated flow.

In addition to the paragraph tags, some formatting information is controlled by the IX flow on the reference pages (View | Reference Pages). Figure 16-3 shows a sample IX flow.

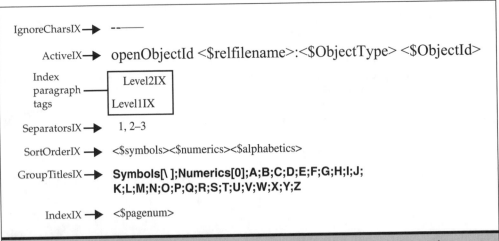

Figure 16-3. *The IX flow on the reference pages controls some of the index settings.*

Table 16-2 describes the function of each paragraph in the flow.

Most likely, you'll make fewer changes in the IX reference flow than you do in the TOC reference flow. The most common change that's needed is to control the formatting of the index page number (see page 420).

Paragraph Tag on Reference Page	Text in Flow	Function
IgnoreCharsIX	` ---- ` (hyphen, minus sign, en dash, em dash)	Lists the characters that are ignored when FrameMaker sorts index entries

ActiveIX	`open ObjectId`
	`<$relfilename>:`
	`<$ObjectType>`
	`<$ObjectId>`
		Inserts the hypertext markers needed to make the index markers into links

Level3IX, Level2IX, Level1IX	`Level3IX`
	`Level2IX`
	`Level1IX`
		Lists the levels of index

SeparatorsIX	`1, 2-3`	Lists the characters that separate index entries and page references.
SortOrderIX	`<$symbols><$numerics>` `<$alphabetics>`	Determines the order in which symbol entries, numeric entries, and alphabetic entries are presented

GroupTitlesIX	`Symbols[\ ];Numerics`
	`[0];A;B;C;D;E;F;G;H;I`
	`;J;K;L;M;N;O;P;Q;R;S;`
	`T;U;V;W;X;Y;Z`
		Lists the group titles (usually A, B, C, and so on)

IndexIX	`<$pagenum>`	Controls the formatting of the page numbers in the index

Table 16-2. *IX Reference Flow Paragraphs*

BUILDING BOOKS

Ignoring Characters While Sorting

The IgnoreCharsIX paragraph in the IX flow controls which characters are ignored for alphabetization purposes when the index is sorted. By default, the IgnoreCharsIX contains these characters:

    - - - -

The characters are hyphen, minus sign, en dash, and em dash.

To change which characters are considered (or not) when sorting the index, modify the items in the list. For example, to eliminate the forward slash (/) from consideration during sorting, add it to the IgnoreCharsIX line, like this:

    - - - -/

When you regenerate the index, FrameMaker ignores any forward slashes while sorting index entries. The slashes and other characters listed here are still printed as part of the index entry.

By default, FrameMaker sorts index entries word-by-word. That is, the spaces between words are taken into account when sorting. To change your sort to letter-by-letter, where spaces are ignored, add a space to the IgnoreCharIX paragraph.

Modifying Page Separators

An index entry has several different components that control the overall format. The SeparatorsIX entry in the IX reference flow sets three following parameters:

- The separator between the index entry text and the first page number
- The separator between multiple page numbers
- The separator in a range

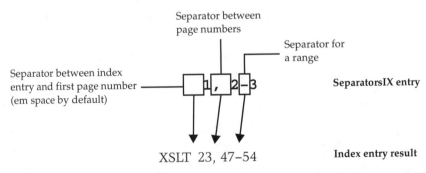

The default SeparatorsIX entry looks like this:

    1, 2-3

Its settings are as follows:

- An em space between the index entry and first page number
- A comma followed by a space between separate page entries
- An en dash in ranges

To change the separators, you change the items in this line.

If you need to change the formatting of the page number, you need to modify the IndexIX entry. See "Formatting the Page Number" on page 420.

Changing the Sort Order

The SortOrderIX entry in the reference flow determines how entries are sorted. By default, it contains the following building blocks:

```
<$symbols><$numerics><$alphabetics>
```

The building blocks are placeholders for the following characters:

<$symbols>	All characters not listed under <$numerics> or <$alphabetics>, sorted by ASCII value
<$numerics>	0 1 2 3 4 5 6 7 8 9
<$alphabetics>	AÁÀÂÄÃÅaáàâäãåªBb CÇcçDdEÉÈÊËeéèêëF fƒGgHhIÍÌÎÏiíìîïJjKk LlMmNÑnñOÓÒÔÖÕØ oóòôöõø° PpQqRrSsTtUÚÙÛÜuúùûüVvWw XxYŸyÿZz This is the sort order for the U.S. English interface; other languages are slightly different. You can find the specifics for other languages in the localized help.

To put the symbol characters last in the index, change the building block order:

```
<$numerics><$alphabetics><$symbols>
```

If you need finer control over the sort order, you can replace the building blocks with an expanded list. Assume, for instance, that you have a number of index entries that start with pound signs (#98). Normally, those would be sorted in the <$symbols> sections, but you want them to appear in the <$numerics> section. You can remove the <$numerics> building block and replace it with a list of characters:

```
<$symbols>0 1 2 3 4 5 6 7 8 9 #<$alphabetics>
```

The result will be that the entries that begin with a pound sign (#) are sorted after the number nine and appear in the Numerics section.

BUILDING BOOKS

Changing the Group Titles

When you generate the index, the alphabetic group titles are inserted automatically. For sorting purposes, the titles are treated just like regular index entries; however, they use the GroupTitlesIX paragraph tag instead of one of the Level*n*IX tags. The most common modification of the group titles is consolidating entries. For example, you might have an index that contains only two or three entries under X, Y, and Z. Instead of listing them separately, you could combine them under an X–Z group title.

X
X-ray 44

Y

Yeti 36

Z

zebra 7

→

X–Z
X-ray 44
Yeti 36
zebra 7

The default GroupTitlesIX entry looks like this:

```
Symbols[\ ];Numerics[0];A;B;C;D;E;F;G;H;I;J;K;L;M;N;O;P;Q;R;S;T;U;V;
W;X;Y;Z
```

To consolidate titles, you must make two changes:

- Group the letters you want to combine.
- Force that title to appear at the beginning of the first letter (by customizing the alphabetization of that item).

To create an X–Z group title, modify GroupTitlesIX to look like this:

```
Symbols[\ ];Numerics[0];A;B;C;D;E;F;G;H;I;J;K;L;M;N;O;P;Q;R;S;T;U;V;
W;X-Z[X]
```

Formatting the Page Number

The information presented in the page number is set by the IndexIX entry in the IX reference flow. By default, it is set to:

```
<$pagenum>
```

If you want to include a chapter number in your index page references, modify IndexIX to include the chapter number:

```
<$chapnum>-<$pagenum>
```

Use a nonbreaking hyphen (ESC HYPHEN H) instead of a regular hyphen to prevent unattractive line breaks in the index.

You can also add the volume number (<$volnum>) and the paragraph number (<$paranum> or <$paranumonly>).

The formatting of the IndexIX paragraph tag controls the appearance of page numbers in the generated files, even though the page numbers end up being part of the Level*n*IX paragraphs. If, for example, you want the page number to be italic while the index entry is regular text, you would define the Level1IX paragraph tag with the regular font and the IndexIX paragraph tag with the italic font.

Creating Ranges Automatically

FrameMaker has a little-known option called autorange. Instead of creating matching startrange and endrange markers for each of your ranges (see page 412), you can let FrameMaker create the ranges automatically.

With autoranging activated, FrameMaker scans index entries for matching entries. When an entry occurs on two or more pages in sequence, a range is created in the index.

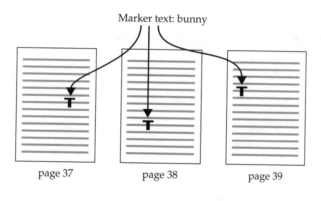

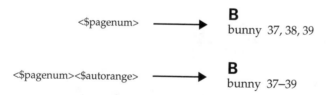

To activate autoranging, modify the IndexIX paragraph in the IX reference flow to contain the <$autorange> command:

```
<$pagenum><$autorange>
```

Autorange lets you avoid creating startrange and endrange markers. The disadvantage of autorange is that you must insert identical index markers on every page in the sequence. If the range is more than two or three pages, inserting all those markers will become quite tedious. Inserting just a startrange and an endrange command is suddenly much more appealing.

Eliminating Unwanted Chapter Numbers

Including the <$chapnum> building block in the IndexIX definition is much faster than the old way of setting up page numbers, which involved using chapter prefixes that had to be set individually for each chapter. There is, however, a problem with the new feature if your files are set up as follows:

- The main body text has multipart page numbers with chapter and page number (3-1, 3-2, and so on).

- The front matter (or back matter) uses a different numbering scheme without a chapter number (for example, i, ii, iii, iv, and so on).

If you insert index entries into both numbering streams, you end up with the following numbers for the front matter entries: 1-iv, 1-x, and so on.

The problem occurs because the reference page flow requires a <$chapnum> building block to be inserted for every index entry. There are two solutions for this problem:

- Eliminate index entries from the front matter (this is known as "avoidance").

- Use a special marker type (for example, IndexRoman) for all of the index entries in the front matter.

To set up the special entries, follow these steps:

1. In the files that use Roman numerals, create an IndexRoman marker type by following these steps:

   a. Select Special | Marker. The Marker dialog box is displayed.

   b. In the Marker Type drop-down list, click Edit. The Edit Custom Marker Type dialog box is displayed.

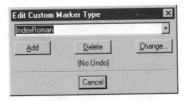

c. In the marker type field, type in **IndexRoman**, the name of the new marker.

d. Click the Add button.

e. Click the Done button to close the Edit Custom Marker Type dialog box and return to the Marker dialog box. The new marker type is now shown in the Marker Type list.

Custom marker definitions are stored as part of the document properties, so you can import formats from one file to another to copy over the new marker type.

2. Make sure that all of the index entries in the front matter use the IndexRoman marker type.

Note

If you're using structured FrameMaker, you can do this with a context rule for your IndexEntry element. See Chapter 29, "Understanding the Element Definition Document," for details about context rules.

3. Go to your book file, click the index, then select Edit | Set Up Standard Index.

4. Add IndexRoman to the list of markers that are included when this file is generated.

5. Update the book.

6. Open the index and go to the reference pages. Locate the IndexRomanIX entry in the IX flow and make sure it includes only the page number:

   `<$pagenum>`

7. Update the book again to see the results.

Creating Structured Index Markers

As with the table of contents and other generated files, the index itself is normally not structured. You can, however, create structured index markers if your EDD is set up for it.

To create a structured index marker, follow these steps:

1. Select Special | Marker. The Marker dialog box is displayed. Notice the Element Tag drop-down list, which is available only in structured FrameMaker.

Element Tag drop-down list
lets you set the element for ⟶
the marker.

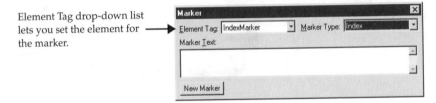

2. In the Element Tag drop-down list, click an available element. In the example shown here, an IndexMarker element is available. Based on the selected element tag, the marker type may change.

3. Verify that the correct marker type (usually Index) is selected.

4. Create the marker text as described on page 410.

Once you insert the marker, it appears in the structure view.

Chapter 17

Creating Other Generated Files

Tables of contents and indexes—discussed in Chapters 15 and 16, respectively—are the most common generated files, but you can also generate several other types of files. They are divided into generated lists and generated indexes.

Broadly, generated lists list information in the order that it occurs in the document; indexes list information in alphabetical order with separators (or "group titles") for each letter in the alphabet. (Just to confuse matters further, two lists are available in page order or alphabetical order.) Figure 17-1 shows how the same information is organized differently in a generated list and a generated index.

Like indexes and tables of contents, you can customize other generated lists by controlling the formatting and by using reference page flows to determine what information is included.

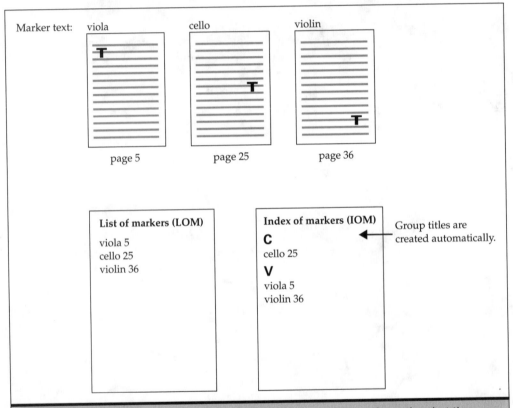

Figure 17-1.   Generated lists and indexes can include the same information, but they organize it differently.

Each generated file has a unique suffix, which is used for the file name, the paragraphs tags in the generated file, and the reference page flow tag. For example, a list of markers uses the LOM suffix by default. If the book file you start from is named foo.book, the list of markers file will be fooLOM.fm, and the reference page flow tag is LOM. The paragraphs tags in the generated file will end with LOM (for example, if you include Cross-Ref markers, they will be formatted by the Cross-RefLOM paragraph tag).

Generated File	Suffix
List of figures	LOF
List of tables	LOT
List of paragraphs and elements	LOP
Alphabetical list of paragraphs and elements	APL
List of markers	LOM
Alphabetical list of markers	AML
List of references	LOR
Index of authors	AIX
Index of subjects	SIX
Index of markers	IOM
Index of references	IOR

The steps you follow to create a generated list or index are basically the same for each type of generated file.

To create a generated list or index, follow these steps:

1. Select the book or file for which you want to create a list.

2. Select Special | List Of *or* Index Of | and the appropriate item. A setup dialog box is displayed for the list or index.

3. Make sure that the Create Hypertext Links check box is checked. This creates a hyperlinked generated list. If you do not want the list to be linked, or if you do not need links in any PDF or HTML you might create, you can uncheck this option.

4. Choose the settings you want for the generated file, then click the Set button to create it.

If the item you want does not appear in the list, try updating the book.

5. *(for file-level generated files)* Confirm that you want to create a file-level, stand-alone generated file.

6. *(for book-level generated files)* Click the Update button to create the new file.

The following sections discuss how to set up and customize each type of generated file.

Creating Paragraph-Based and Element-Based Lists

Several of the generated lists are based on selecting items from a list of available paragraphs (or elements). They are as follows:

- List of figures
- List of tables
- List of paragraphs (called list of paragraphs and elements in structured FrameMaker)
- Table of contents

There is no functional difference between these four lists. In each case, you select various paragraph tags (or elements), and FrameMaker generates a list of those items in the order they occur in the documents.

Chapter 15, "Creating Tables of Contents," describes in detail how to set up table of contents files. You can apply the information provided there to the list of figures, list of tables, and list of paragraphs and elements.

Keep in mind that you can use the list of figures and list of tables for generated lists other than those implied by the titles. You could, for example, generate a list of syntax examples by including the CodeExampleTitle tag instead of the FigureTitle tag for a so-called "list of figures."

List of Figures

When you create a list of figures, the Set Up List of Figures dialog box provides a list of paragraphs (and elements) to choose from, as shown in Figure 17-2.

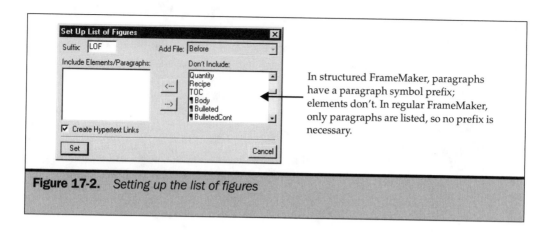

In structured FrameMaker, paragraphs have a paragraph symbol prefix; elements don't. In regular FrameMaker, only paragraphs are listed, so no prefix is necessary.

Figure 17-2. *Setting up the list of figures*

To create a simple list of figures, select your figure caption paragraph tag (for example, Caption) and generate the list. To display the figure number along with the caption, format the CaptionLOF entry in the reference page flow similar to this example:

```
Figure <$paranumonly>: <$paratext>\t<$pagenum>
```

You must define a tab stop in the Paragraph Designer so that the page number is aligned correctly.

List of Tables

When you create a list of tables, the Set Up List of Tables dialog box provides a list of paragraphs and elements to choose from. The dialog box is identical to the Set Up List of Figures dialog box (shown in Figure 17-2), except for the window title and the default suffix.

To create a list of tables, select your table title paragraph tag (for example, TableTitle) and generate the list. To display the table number along with the caption, format the TableTitleLOT entry in the reference page flow similar to this example:

```
Table <$paranumonly>: <$paratext>\t<$pagenum>
```

You must define a tab stop in the Paragraph Designer so that the page number is aligned correctly.

List of Paragraphs

The list of paragraphs works just like the table of contents. The Set Up List of Paragraphs (& Elements) dialog box provides a list of paragraphs (and elements) to choose from. Except for the window title and the default suffix, the dialog box is identical to the Set Up List of Figures dialog box shown in Figure 17-2.

To create a list of paragraphs, choose the items you want to include and generate the list. The reference page LOP flow will provide entries for each included item, which you can format just like table of contents entries.

The list of paragraphs is very useful for review comments. If you have a review comment paragraph tag, you can generate a hyperlinked list of all review comments in the file or book.

Alphabetical List of Paragraphs

The alphabetical list of paragraphs contains the same information as the regular list of paragraphs, but instead of listing the items in the order they occur in the book, they are listed in alphabetical order. To set up the list of paragraphs, specify the paragraphs you want to include in the Set Up Alphabetical Paragraph List dialog box. Except for the dialog box name and the default suffix, the dialog box is identical to the Set Up List of Figures dialog box shown in Figure 17-2.

Creating Lists of Other Items

In addition to the paragraph- and element-based lists, you can create lists of markers and of references. Within the list of references, you can choose from several items, including imported graphics, conditional text tags, and fonts.

List of Markers

The generated list of markers lets you create a page-by-page list of markers that occur in the document. When you set up the list of markers, you can include one or all of the marker types, including custom markers, as shown in Figure 17-3.

For each marker you select, the LOM flow on the reference page will contain a corresponding entry. For example, if you include the Index marker type, the LOM flow will contain an IndexLOM entry.

By default, the definition for each entry is:

```
<$markertext> <$pagenum>
```

The <$markertext> building block picks up the information in the marker text field for each marker.

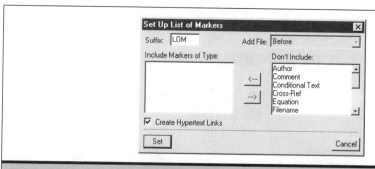

Figure 17-3.   *The list of markers lets you select any or all marker types, including any custom markers you've created.*

Alphabetical List of Markers

Like the list of markers, the alphabetical list of markers lets you select which marker types you want to include. Except for the dialog box name and the default suffix, the dialog box is identical to the Set Up List of Markers dialog box shown in Figure 17-3.

The resulting list, however, is sorted alphabetically by marker text rather than in page order.

The only difference between the alphabetical list of markers and an index is how the entries are organized. The index provides group titles along with primary and secondary entries. See Figure 17-1 on page 426 for an example.

List of References

The list of references feature lets you create generated lists that include the following items:

- Condition tags
- External cross-references (that is, cross-references that point to information in a different file)
- Fonts
- Imported graphics
- Text insets
- Unresolved cross-references
- Unresolved text insets

BUILDING BOOKS

When you set up the list of references, you can choose to include any or all of these items in the Set Up List of References dialog box:

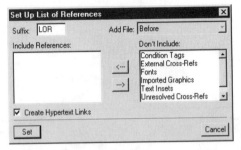

For each item, FrameMaker creates an entry in the LOR flow on the reference pages. The entry's name is the included item with an LOR suffix; for example, Text InsetsLOR. The same building blocks are used for each item:

```
<$referencename> <$pagenum>
```

The <$referencename> building block, however, results in different information for each type of reference.

Condition Tags

Select condition tags to create a list of every occurrence of *shown* conditional text in the document. FrameMaker will ignore any conditional text that is currently hidden. The generated file lists the name of the condition tag and the page on which it is used, such as:

```
Comment 47
Draft 58
```

If you need a list of all conditional text, show all the conditional text tags before you create this list.

External Cross-References

Select external cross-references to create a list of references from the current file to other files. If you create this list for a book, the list will include references from one file in the book to another as well as references to files outside the current book. The resulting list will show the name of the referenced file (including any path name that FrameMaker has stored) and the text of the Cross-Reference marker or attribute ID that identifies the cross-reference's target. For example:

```
toc.fm (cn chapter_number: Chapter 5) 214
index.fm (cn chapter_number: Chapter 9) 214
```

Lists of external cross-references are very useful for locating cross-references that point to local files instead of network files and the like.

Fonts

Select Fonts to create a list of all the fonts that occur in the document. FrameMaker lists the font, the font size, and the page on which the font occurs. The font list is based on the fonts that occur on each page, so you'll see the same font listed multiple times. The following is a short excerpt from a generated list of fonts.

```
Univers 57 Condensed @ 12.0 pt 213
Palatino Linotype @ 75.0 pt 213
Univers Condensed @ 40.0 pt 213
Univers 57 Condensed @ 10.0 pt 214
Univers 57 Condensed @ 12.0 pt 214
Times @ 12.0 pt 214
```

To create an alphabetical list of fonts, convert the listings to a table (each paragraph should be a cell) and sort the table. Better yet, generate an index of references for your fonts, which will automatically create one entry per font. See page 436.

Imported Graphics

The list of imported graphics lists only graphics that are imported by reference, not graphics that were copied (or embedded) into the document. For each graphic, FrameMaker lists the file path, the DPI setting being used (bitmaps only), and the page number on which the graphic occurs, as shown in the example that follows:

```
graphics/para_cat_button.tif @ 48 dpi 6
graphics/status_bar_para.tif @ 96 dpi 7
graphics/formatting_bar.tif @ 125 dpi 8
graphics/override_para.tif @ 96 dpi 10
graphics/para_des.tif @ 125 dpi 11
graphics/para_des_pagination.tif @ 125 dpi 12
graphics/tabs.tif @ 125 dpi 15
graphics/no_indent.eps 16
graphics/all_indent.eps 16
```

The list of imported graphics is useful for verifying any or all of the following items for a file:

- Checking DPI settings to ensure that graphics are sized consistently.
- Verifying file locations to ensure graphics are in the correct directory. (In the preceding example, all graphics are stored in a graphics subdirectory; an entry that doesn't begin with `graphics/` would indicate a graphic that needs to be moved.)

- Checking file names to ensure that they follow naming conventions established by your company or client.
- Verifying that all graphics are copied instead of embedded. (If all graphics are copied in, the generated list of imported graphics should be empty.)

Text Insets

Generating a list of text insets has a similar purpose as generating lists of imported graphics; it lets you verify that external files are being imported properly. For each text inset, the generated file lists the file name and path, and the page number on which it begins, as shown in the following example:

```
segment1.fm 222
segment2.fm 255
```

The list of text insets lets you quickly review a list of files that are being imported into the book or file you generated from.

Unresolved Cross-References and Text Insets

When you generate a book file, the book error log creates a list of unresolved cross-references and text insets that occur in the documents. When you use the list of references to create a list of unresolved cross-references or text insets, you get the same information. If you created the list with hyperlinks (highly recommended), you can use the generated list to jump directly to the unresolved item and fix it.

Generated Indexes

The various "other" indexes are all quite similar to the standard index (IX) discussed in Chapter 15, "Creating Tables of Contents." In addition to the standard index, the following indexes are available:

- Index of authors
- Index of subjects
- Index of markers
- Index of references

Each index creates an alphabetical list of entries, with matching entries grouped into a single index entry with multiple page numbers.

Although the standard index defaults to using only the Index marker type, you can use other (or additional markers) in the standard index. The index of authors and index of subjects default to including the matching index markers to create the index, but you can choose to include other marker types instead (or in addition to the default Author and Subject markers).

Index of Authors

The index of authors creates an index of the various Author markers in the documents. The index lets the reader look up information based on the original author. To set up an index of this type, you would first go through your document and identify the sections where different authors are involved. For each entry you want to create, set up an Author marker by following these steps:

1. Click in the text where the author's material occurs.
2. Create an Author marker (Special | Marker; make sure that Author is selected in the Marker Type drop-down list).

Note   *For detailed instructions on inserting markers, see "Creating Index Entries" on page 408.*

3. In the marker text field, type in the author's name. For example:

```
Sayers, Dorothy
```

Repeat this process for every item that you want to mark for a particular author. Then, generate the index of authors to see the result:

J
James, P.D. 35

M
Marsh, Ngaio 22
Maron, Margaret 45

R
Reichs, Kathy 12

S
Sayers, Dorothy 100

Index of Subjects

By default, the index of subjects creates an index from all of the Subject markers in the documents. You can customize them just like any other index entries.

Index of Markers

The index of markers lets you create an index of any marker type. You might, for instance, create an index of hypertext markers to verify that the syntax and path names are correct for each. If you use spot cross-references extensively in a document, you could use an index of Cross-Reference markers to verify that each marker's text is unique.

BUILDING BOOKS

Index of References

The index of references lets you create an index for each of the items that are available for the list of references. Instead of sorting items by page number, an index sorts them alphabetically, and matching items are grouped. That can make the index version much more manageable and usable than the list version. The index of fonts, for example, would look something like the following example:

```
Courier @ 9.0 pt 185-189, 192
Palatino Linotype @ 10.0 pt 178-193
Palatino Linotype @ 4.0 pt 178-180, 182-187, 189, 191-193
Palatino Linotype @ 75.0 pt 177
Palatino Linotype @ 8.0 pt 179, 182, 184
Times New Roman @ 2.0 pt 178-182, 184, 189-192
Univers @ 10.0 pt 178-180, 182, 184, 186, 189, 191
Univers @ 11.0 pt 186
Univers @ 16.0 pt 178, 181-183, 185, 187-188, 193
Univers 57 Condensed @ 10.0 pt 178-194
Univers 57 Condensed @ 12.0 pt 177-194
Univers Condensed @ 40.0 pt 177
ZapfDingbats @ 10.0 pt 180-181, 183, 187-188
```

You can quickly scan this list to determine whether any renegade fonts have snuck into your document.

The
Complete
Reference

FrameMaker 7

Part V

Creating Output

The Complete Reference

FrameMaker 7

Chapter 18

Print and PDF Output

Y ou can create many kinds of output from FrameMaker documents. The most common output formats are print and Portable Document Format (PDF). Readers who follow procedures in a guide might prefer to read a printed document rather than an online PDF file; however, if the reader only occasionally refers to the document, the PDF file often suffices.

The print and PDF formats both have advantages. The advantages to printed documents are as follows:

- Readers who don't work at a computer station—for example, when repairing equipment at a customer's office—can read the document and write notes.

- When the reader is installing software, the installation often covers the entire screen. In many cases, the installer will not permit other applications to run, so the reader cannot read a file online. (Furthermore, the online books or online help are often not available because they haven't been installed yet.) Installation documents need to be available separately.

- Many readers (and salespeople) consider printed documentation an integral part of a product. The documentation helps them understand the product and also enhances the quality of their experience with the product.

- Many readers don't want to use their own paper to print a document.

- You choose the size of the printed document and the binding method. This increases the usability of the document. For example, it's quicker to flip through a small spiral-bound document than a PDF file the reader prints on letter-sized paper.

- Printed screen shots are clearer than those displayed in PDF files, so readability is better.

- Some readers can locate printed documents more quickly than browsing their computers or a web site for the PDF file.

The main advantages of PDF files are as follows:

- The PDF file preserves formatting from the FrameMaker file, unlike online formats such as HTML and XML.

- Many companies post PDF versions of their documentation on an intranet or on the Internet, which gives users and employees easy access to the information.

- PDF files save you the step of converting the document to an online format.

- The reader can search the PDF file in Acrobat. In print, you have to rely on a comprehensive index and table of contents to find information.

- The reader can print only the pages he or she needs, which conserves paper.

- Compared to the printing and packaging costs of a book, PDF files are far less expensive.

- Producing PDF files is quicker than printing a book. This gives you more time before a product release to complete the documentation because you don't have to send the documentation to a print vendor.

- The PDF file can be updated more easily and economically than printed documents, which require you to print change pages or reprint the entire book.

- You can create tagged PDF files, which lets you repurpose the document for screen readers and small displays. You can also export PDF to Rich Text Format (RTF) more reliably.

Your company or documentation group usually decides which format works best for you or your customers. Based on the situation, you might choose print versus PDF or produce both formats.

In this chapter, the terms "print vendor" and "printer" have different meanings. A print vendor is a commercial printer that prints books on offset or digital presses. The print vendor may bind the books, or the binding may be outsourced to an external bindery. The term "printer" refers to a physical printer, such as the one in your office or home.

Printing Your Documents

FrameMaker provides numerous printing options. Many of the basic word-processing features, such as printing page ranges or printing several copies, come in handy daily. Other options, such as printing registration marks and creating PostScript files, are used primarily in preparing your document for final printing. You can print a single document, specific chapters in a book file, or an entire book. The print options for document files and book files are nearly the same. The printer you select provides additional features, such as support for special paper sizes, sophisticated color matching, and high print resolutions. You should make sure the printer is set up correctly before printing. See "Configuring Your Printer" on page 451 for details on printer drivers.

Printing an Individual Document

To print a single document outside the book window, follow these steps:

1. Open the document you want to print, then select File | Print. The print dialog box is displayed (Figure 18-1).

The term "print dialog box" refers to the main print dialog box on all three platforms at the document or book level and therefore isn't capitalized in this chapter.

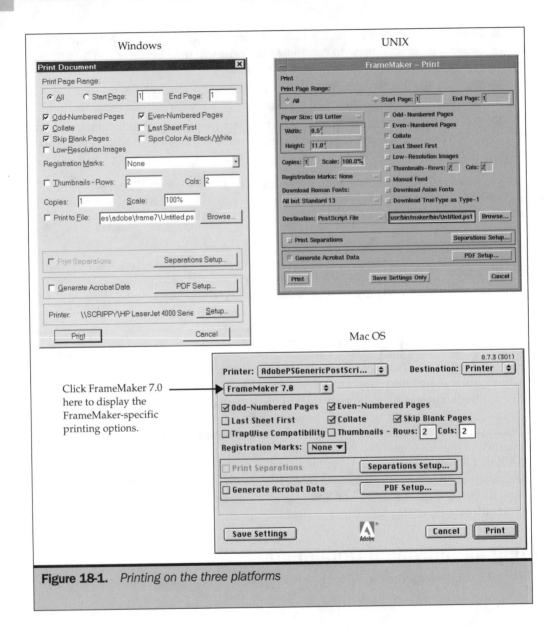

Figure 18-1. Printing on the three platforms

2. *(Mac OS)* Click FrameMaker 7.0 in the printer options drop-down list (below the Printer drop-down list). The printer options are displayed. Additional options are displayed when you click General (Figure 18-2).

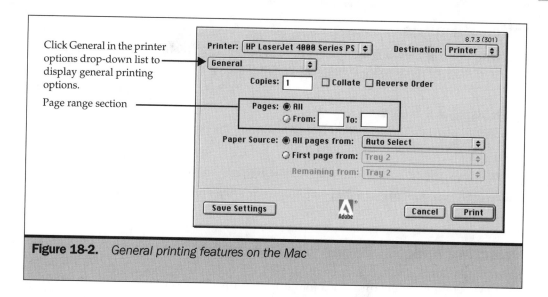

Click General in the printer options drop-down list to display general printing options.

Page range section

Figure 18-2.   *General printing features on the Mac*

Note   *For the Mac OS, all procedures in this chapter refer to options displayed in the print dialog box when FrameMaker 7.0 is selected in the drop-down list (unless otherwise noted).*

3. Change the printer options based on the following sections, then click the Print button. Your document prints.

Printing from the Book File

In a book file, you can print one file, specific pages in the book, or the entire book. To print from the book file, follow these steps:

1. Open the book file, then specify the file or files you want to print by doing one of the following:

   ■ To print the entire book, select File | Print Book. The Print Book dialog box is displayed. The book and standard print dialog boxes are identical. See Figure 18-1 on page 442.

   ■ To print specific chapters in a book, CTRL-click (Windows and UNIX) or COMMAND-click (Mac) the files in the book window, then select File | Print Selected Files. The Print Selected Files dialog box is displayed.

2. Change the printer options based on the following sections, then click the Print button. The book or selected documents are printed.

Specifying Pages

You can print one page, a range of pages, or the entire document. This section describes how to specify the pages you want to print in a document or book.

Selecting All Pages

To select all pages in the document or book, display the print dialog box (Figure 18-1 on page 442), and follow the directions for your platform:

- *(Windows and UNIX)* Click the All radio button in the Print Page Range section.
- *(Mac)* Click General in the printer options drop-down list, and click the All radio button (Figure 18-2 on page 443).

Selecting Specific Pages in a Document

To select specific pages in a document, display the print dialog box (Figure 18-1 on page 442), and follow the directions for your platform:

- *(Windows and UNIX)* In the Print Page Range section, type the first page in the Start Page field and type the last page in the End Page field. Click the Print button to print the selected range. (The current page number is displayed in both fields by default.) Note that you cannot specify multiple ranges in one step.
- *(Mac)* Click General in the printer options drop-down list, then type the first page in the From field and the last page in the To field (Figure 18-2 on page 443). (The From and To fields are blank by default.)

If Your Document Doesn't Print

There are several reasons why a document might not print. Before reprinting, verify the following:

- You could have inadvertently printed the document to file. In the print dialog box, make sure the Print to File check box is unchecked (Windows) or click the Printer option (not File or PostScript File) in the Destination drop-down list (Mac and UNIX) before printing.
- If the document is long or graphics-intensive, check the print job dialog box to see if the document is displayed. The document might still be spooling to the printer.
- There could also be a problem with the printer. Check for a paper jam or an empty paper tray.

See your network administrator for additional assistance.

Selecting Specific Pages in a Book

To select specific pages in a book, display the print dialog box (Figure 18-1 on page 442), and follow the directions for your platform:

- *(Windows and UNIX)* CTRL-click the file or files in which the pages occur, select File | Print Selected Files, and then type the first and last page in the Start Page and End Page fields, respectively.

- *(Mac)* SHIFT-click the file or files in which the pages occur, select File | Print Selected Files, click General in the printer options drop-down list, and then type the first and last page in the From and To fields, respectively.

Printing Several Copies

You can print several copies of one page, a range of pages, or the entire document, and you can print the copies one set at time. To specify copies, follow these steps:

1. Display the print dialog box (Figure 18-1 on page 442), then indicate the pages you want to print. See "Specifying Pages" on page 444 for details.

2. Indicate the number of copies to print by following the directions for your platform:

   - *(Windows and UNIX)* In the Copies field, type the number of copies to print.

   - *(Mac)* Click General in the printer options drop-down list, then type the number of copies to print in the Copies field (Figure 18-2 on page 443).

3. To print one set at a time (for example, pages 1–15) instead of all copies of page 1, all copies of page 2, and so on, check the Collate check box.

4. If your printer places the printed page face-up, check the Last Sheet First check box.

Changing the Paper Size

You can change the paper size in your printer driver (Windows and Mac) or in FrameMaker (UNIX). You might print a document on a larger paper size to make room for registration marks. FrameMaker displays a warning if the paper isn't large enough for the text or registration marks to print completely.

To change the paper size, follow the directions for your platform:

- *(Windows)* Display the print dialog box, then click the Setup button. Depending on your printer driver, the paper options might be displayed in this dialog box. If not, click the Properties button, then click the Advanced button. Click a different paper size in the Paper Size drop-down list.

- *(Mac)* Select File | Page Setup to display the Page Setup dialog box, click Page Attributes, and then click an item in the Paper drop-down list.

- *(UNIX)* Display the print dialog box (Figure 18-1 on page 442), then click a size in the Paper Size drop-down list. If your paper size isn't listed, type the dimensions in the Width and Height fields.

Printing Double-Sided Documents

Some printers have duplexing units that automatically print odd pages on one side of the paper and even pages on the reverse side. You can print a double-sided document on a printer that only prints single-sided by printing all odd pages first, flipping the paper in the printer, and printing the even pages. Before you print an entire document this way, test a few pages to make sure the paper is in the right direction. After printing one side of the document, you might need to print the other side in reverse order depending on your printer. Refer to your printer documentation for instructions on feeding the paper correctly.

To print a double-sided document, follow these steps:

1. Display the print dialog box (Figure 18-1 on page 442), then check the Odd-Numbered Pages check box and uncheck the Even-Numbered Pages check box.

2. Click the Print button. The odd-numbered pages (1, 3, 5, 7...) are printed.

3. Flip over the paper in the paper tray. If you're printing to the manual feed paper tray in the Windows or Mac OS, change the paper setting in your printer driver. In UNIX, check the Manual Feed check box in the FrameMaker printer dialog box.

4. Select File | Print to display the print dialog box again, then uncheck the Odd-Numbered Pages check box and check the Even-Numbered Pages check box.

5. If your printer requires it, check the Last Sheet First check box to print the other side in order.

6. Click the Print button. The even-numbered pages (2, 4, 6, 8...) are printed on the back of the odd-numbered pages.

Skipping Blank Pages

You can skip printing blank pages on the Windows and Mac platforms. This is handy for printing a double-sided document as a single-sided document. Many double-sided documents have blank pages to force chapters to begin on a right page. When you print rough drafts, you can save paper by skipping the blank pages.

To avoid printing blank pages, display the print dialog box (Figure 18-1 on page 442), and check the Skip Blank Pages check box. Another way to avoid printing blank pages is to convert a double-sided document to single-sided before you print, and then convert it back to double-sided. See "Switching from Single- to Double-Sided Pages" on page 267 for more information.

 A page is considered blank if the main text flow is empty. The running headers and footers and other background elements don't count.

Printing Thumbnails

You can print several pages as mini-images on a single page. This option is useful for checking the pagination of an entire document. You indicate the number of rows and columns you want printed (for instance, the 2-row by 4-column layout shown in the following illustration). The document is double-sided, so the thumbnails begin with the first right page.

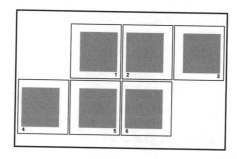

 Some printers don't support thumbnails. Refer to your printer documentation for details.

To print thumbnails, follow these steps:

1. Display the print dialog box (Figure 18-1 on page 442), then check the Thumbnails check box.

2. In the Cols field, type the number of columns to print. Keep in mind the orientation of the paper. You can print more thumbnails on a landscape page than a portrait page. Refer to your printer documentation for details on specifying landscape pages.

3. In the Rows field, type the number of rows to print across the page.

4. Click the Print button.

Printing Spot Color in Black and White

You can save color ink by printing *spot color* as black and white. Spot color is premixed before the printing process and printed on one printing plate. *Process color* mixes shades of cyan, magenta, yellow, and black (CMYK), with each color printing on a different plate. To see which colors in your document are spot colors, select View | Color | Definitions, then click a color in the Name drop-down list. The setting is displayed in the Print As drop-down list. For more information, see Chapter 20, "Color Output."

To print spot color in black and white, follow the directions for your platform:

- *(Windows)* Display the print dialog box (Figure 18-1 on page 442), then check the Spot Color as Black/White check box.

- *(Mac)* Display the print dialog box, then click Color Matching in the printer options drop-down list, and then click Black and White in the Print Color drop-down list.

- *(UNIX)* In the $FMHOME/fminit directory, open ps_prolog.ps and substitute "true" for "false" in the following line:

```
/FMPrintAllColorsAsBlack false def
```

(If you don't see the file, it might be hidden. See your UNIX documentation for directions on showing all files in a directory.)

 To avoid changing settings for other users in UNIX, save the file as ~/fminit/ps_prolog. The file will save to your home directory.

Printing Low-Resolution Images

You can speed up the printing of graphic-intensive documents by printing the images in low resolutions. In Windows, the images print as gray boxes. In UNIX, the graphics print at a low resolution. Though this feature isn't provided on the Mac, you can turn off the display of images before printing by selecting View | Options and unchecking the Graphics check box.

To turn on low-resolution printing, display the print dialog box (Figure 18-1 on page 442), and check the Low-Resolution Images check box.

Printing Registration Marks

Registration marks provide instructions for printing color separations—the individual pages that describe how to mix color for four-color printing. Information about the document is also displayed outside the registration marks—the date, time, file name, and page number. When you print registration marks in FrameMaker, *crop marks* also print in each corner of the page to indicate where to trim the paper after the book is printed. Registration marks are automatically added to color separations, and the color and halftone information is displayed outside the registration marks.

Caution *To provide room for registration marks, you must print on paper that is at least one inch taller and wider than the paper size. If, for example, your document is 7 inches wide by 9 inches tall, you must use paper that's at least 8 inches wide by 10 inches tall to ensure that registration marks are displayed. In practice, this means that if your page size is a standard letter size (US Letter or A4), you cannot print registration marks for your document—unless you output the pages onto larger paper.*

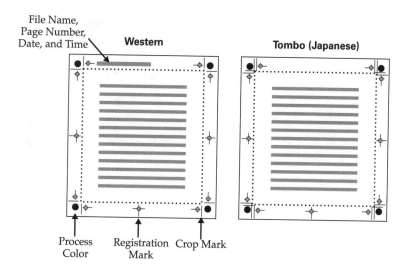

Many print vendors require registration marks in the PostScript or PDF file, but some printers add registration crop marks automatically. Be sure to consult with your print vendor. Most of the time, you'll choose Western registration marks; however, when printing Japanese text, you'll probably use the Tombo (Japanese) registration marks.

To select registration marks, display the print dialog box (Figure 18-1 on page 442), and click Western or Tombo in the Registration Marks drop-down list.

Caution *To print registration marks in a PDF file, you must increase the page size in the PDF setup because Acrobat Distiller crops the page. See "Setting Up Registration Marks in a PDF File" on page 474 for details.*

Changing the Printer

Initially, the printer displayed in the print dialog box is the default printer for your system. You can, however, change the printer used in FrameMaker without changing the default printer. Many times, you need to switch to the Acrobat Distiller printer to create a PostScript file for conversion to PDF format. You also need to switch to a PostScript printer for documents that have Encapsulated PostScript (EPS) images, or bitmap versions of the images print instead. See "Vector Graphics" on page 317 for more information.

When you switch printers in Windows, a warning is displayed, indicating that the fonts for your system have changed. These fonts are the *printer-resident fonts* (described in "Printing Fonts Accurately" on page 462). If the required fonts are installed on your computer, the document should print correctly.

Don't change drivers after you copyfit a book because the line breaks might change. If you do need to change the printer, you'll need to skim the pages for bad page and line breaks and regenerate the book file to update cross-references and generated files.

In Windows

To change the printer in Windows, follow these steps:

1. In the Printer section of the print dialog box, click the Setup button. The Print Setup dialog box is displayed.

2. Click a printer in the Name drop-down list, then click the OK button. The new printer is displayed. (If the resident fonts change, a warning is displayed. Click the OK button.)

On the Mac

To change the printer on the Mac, click another printer in the Printer drop-down list. The new printer is displayed.

In UNIX

To change the printer in UNIX, open a command prompt and type **setenv PRINTER** *printer*, where *printer* is the new printer name.

Creating PostScript Files

PostScript is a complex programming language created by Adobe that describes the contents of a page. The code contains directions for printing the correct page orientation, margin widths, graphics, and other document settings. Unless you're a programming prodigy, you'll probably find PostScript code cryptic. In a text editor, PostScript looks something like the following:

```
%%BeginResource: file Pscript_WinNT_ErrorHandler 5.0 0 /
currentpacking where{pop/oldpack currentpacking def/setpacking
where{pop false setpacking}if}if/$brkpage 64 dict def $brkpage begin/
prnt{dup type/stringtype ne{=string cvs}if dup length 6 mul/tx exch
def/ty 10 def currentpoint/toy exch
```

When you print a document or book to file using a PostScript printer driver, these printing instructions are saved in a PostScript file instead of actually printing. You can send the PostScript file to a print vendor rather than sending individual chapter and book files. This method has the following advantages:

- Print vendors don't need FrameMaker to open your files.
- You don't need to send graphics imported by reference or worry about broken links because the graphics are embedded in the PostScript file.
- You avoid font problems—either the printer not owning the fonts you need or owning a different version.
- Line breaks might shift if the print vendor opens your files on a computer that has a different printer driver than yours. Text in small text frames might also expand. In a PostScript file, line breaks and the display of text don't change.
- It's easier to send one PostScript file than a lot of FrameMaker, graphic, and font files.

Print vendors often provide a list of printer drivers they consider reliable, or they might require you to use the driver made for their printer. Be sure to ask the print vendor which driver they prefer before copyfitting and preparing your final document.

Configuring Your Printer

Before you create a PostScript file, you need to install and configure the driver. A printer driver provides device settings—the default paper tray, job timeout setting, print spool parameters, and so on. The PostScript Printer Definition (PPD) file associated with the printer contains additional options, such as default printer fonts, supported paper sizes, image resolution, and PostScript levels. Some PPD files support colors and high-resolution images. The Acrobat Distiller PPD file, for example, supports CMYK color and resolutions up to 4000 DPI (or dots per inch). In contrast, the default Windows PostScript PPD doesn't support color and only prints up to 300 DPI. Without the PPD, you wouldn't have such options.

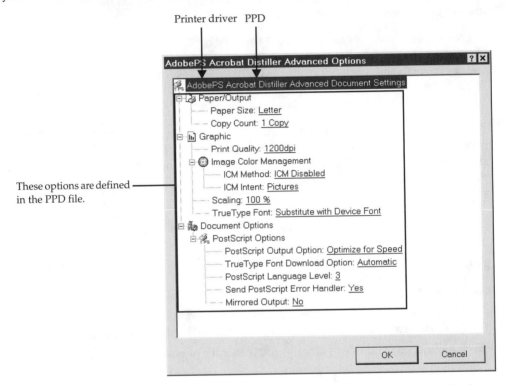

When you install a printer driver in Windows (or *after* installation on the Mac), you associate the driver with the PPD file. Unless your print vendor requires a specific driver, the Adobe PostScript driver is your best choice. You can install the driver with FrameMaker, or you can download it later for free at www.adobe.com/products/printerdrivers/main.html. This driver should use the Acrobat Distiller PPD to print high-resolution, color PostScript files. During the FrameMaker installation, this PPD is copied into the Acrobat Distiller directory.

Setting Up the Windows Adobe PostScript Driver

If your computer is on a network, you've probably already installed the shared network printer. To set up the Adobe PostScript driver, you'll add a printer instance to your computer and associate it with the Acrobat Distiller PPD. The term printer instance refers to the fact that you're not installing a physical printer; you're only setting up the driver and PPD file.

To install and configure the Adobe PostScript driver in Windows, follow these steps:

1. Follow the onscreen instructions for installing the Adobe PostScript driver. When the Printer Connection Type dialog box is displayed, click the Local Printer radio button, then click the Next button. The Local Port Selection dialog box is displayed.

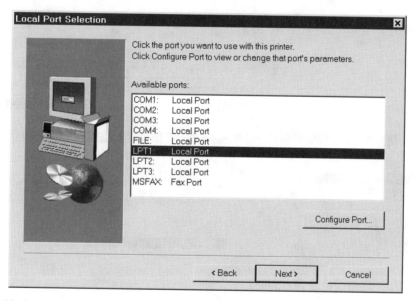

2. Click LPT1: Local Port, then click the Next button. The Select Printer Model dialog box is displayed.

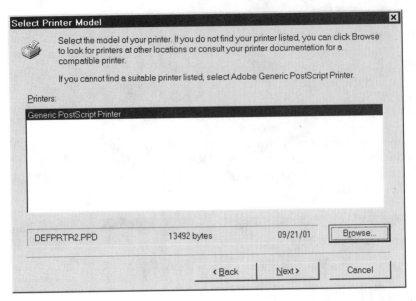

3. Click the Browse button. The Browse for Printer dialog box is displayed.

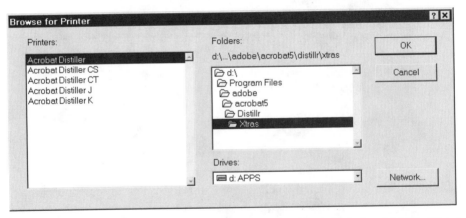

4. Display the Acrobat X\Distillr\Xtras directory, then click Acrobat Distiller in the Printers section. The PPD for more than one language may be displayed—Standard Chinese, Traditional Chinese, Japanese, or Korean. If you need support for one of these languages, click the corresponding file.

5. Click the OK button and finish the installation. The Acrobat Distiller printer will be displayed in your Printers folder. (When you're prompted to configure the device options, click the No radio button. These options are for the physical printer, not the document settings.)

Setting Up the Mac Adobe PostScript Driver

To install and configure the Adobe PostScript driver on a Mac, follow these steps:

1. Follow the on-screen instructions for installing the Adobe PostScript driver.

2. After you're finished, select Apple | Chooser. The Chooser is displayed.

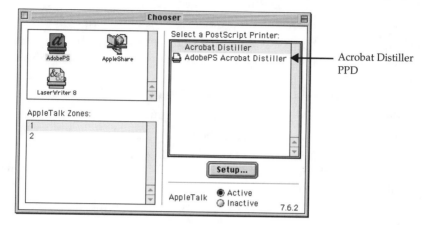

Acrobat Distiller PPD

3. *(optional)* If your network has AppleTalk zones, click the zone for your printer in the AppleTalk Zones field. The AdobePS icon is displayed in the upper-left corner.

4. Click the AdobePS icon, then click the Setup button. The PPD files are displayed. They're located in the System:Extensions:Printer Descriptions folder by default.

5. Click the Acrobat Distiller PPD file, then click the OK button to display the Chooser again. The Adobe PostScript driver is configured with the Distiller PPD.

Printing to a PostScript File

After you set up the printer, you're ready to create the PostScript file. If you plan to send the PostScript file to a print vendor, ask the vendor which driver to use and whether they require registration marks. They might use the marks to trim the edges of the page or line up color separations. If you create the PostScript file solely to convert to PDF, you usually don't need registration marks unless you plan to trim the paper.

When printing a book, open all files in the book to prevent missing font and other error messages from stopping the process. The file will also print more quickly because FrameMaker doesn't have to open each file in the book. You should also regenerate the book to update the cross-references, page numbers, autonumbering, text insets, OLE links, generated files (the table of contents, list of figures, and list of tables). For more information, see "Printing a Book" on page 384.

To create a PostScript file, follow these steps:

1. Display the print dialog box (Figure 18-1 on page 442), then do the following based on your platform:

   ■ *(Windows)* Check the Print to File check box.

   ■ *(Mac)* In the Destination drop-down list, click File.

   ■ *(UNIX)* In the Destination drop-down list, click PostScript File.

2. *(Windows and UNIX)* In the path field, the current directory and file name are displayed. Change the path to save the PostScript file in a different directory, and change the file name, if necessary.

3. To change the printer driver, do the following based on your platform:

   ■ *(Windows)* Click the Setup button in the Printer section.

   ■ *(Mac)* Click the correct printer in the Printer drop-down list.

   ■ *(UNIX)* Click a printer in the Destination drop-down list. If the printer isn't displayed, click Other Printer in the drop-down list and type the printer parameters in the field that is displayed.

4. *(Windows and UNIX)* Determine which fonts should be embedded. See "Printing Fonts Accurately" on page 462 for details.

5. *(optional)* To print color separations, check the Print Separations check box, then click the Separations Setup button. The Set Print Separations dialog box is displayed. See "Printing Color Separations" on page 457 for details on setting up color separations.

6. *(optional)* To generate bookmarks and other Acrobat data, check the Generate Acrobat Data check box, then click the PDF Setup button. The PDF Setup dialog box is displayed. (You must print the entire document or book to file when generating Acrobat data. If you're printing only the current page or a range of pages and set up the Acrobat data, the Print Page Range setting will default to All.) See "Customizing the PDF File" on page 468 for details on setting up the Acrobat options.

Don't generate Acrobat data for PostScript files you send to the printer. The data could cause errors and increases the size of the PostScript file. You also shouldn't generate Acrobat data if you're printing registration marks. The marks will get cropped out of the PDF file.

7. To save the file, do the following based on your platform:

   ■ *(Windows and UNIX)* Click the Print button.

   ■ *(Mac)* Click the Save button, then click the directory you want to save the file in, and then click the Save button. Rename the file if necessary.

FrameMaker creates the PostScript file in the directory you indicated. Large books, long documents, or documents with lots of graphics take more time to convert to PostScript than a simple document.

You can compress PostScript files before sending them to the print vendor.

Printing Color Separations

In documents with four-process color, you create color separations when preparing the final PostScript file for a print vendor. For a page with CMYK color, there are four separations—one each for cyan, magenta, yellow, and black. If registration marks are turned on, the name of the color prints on each separation along with the page number on which that color occurs.

Process color is printed using *halftones*—grids of dots overlapped to form a pattern. The more dots, the darker the color. The frequency of the dots and the angle of the grid make up a *halftone screen*. Screen angles must be precise, or the halftones will print in a checkerboard (or moire) pattern. Though the initial halftone screen settings are determined by the selected printer driver, you should consult with your print vendor or printer documentation before setting up the halftone screens for final printing. See "Understanding Process Color" on page 514 for more information.

To view the color separations before you send the file to the printer, convert the PostScript file to PDF. See "Distilling a PostScript File" on page 465 for details.

Setting Up Separations

To set up color separations, follow these steps:

1. Display the print dialog box (Figure 18-1 on page 442).

2. To print all separations for one page before printing all separations for the following page, check the Collate check box in the print dialog box. On the Mac, click the General drop-down list to find this option. If unchecked, the separations print by color—all cyan separations in the document, all magenta separations, and so on.

3. Verify that the correct color PostScript printer is displayed.

4. Click the Separations Setup button. The Set Print Separations dialog box is displayed (Figure 18-3 on page 458). Don't worry if the Print Separations check box is grayed out. After you configure the separations, the check box is checked by default.

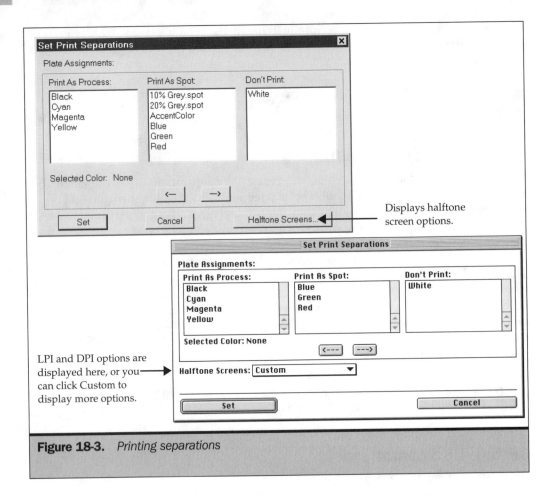

Figure 18-3.   *Printing separations*

5. To set up the separations, click a color, then click the left or right arrows as follows:

   ■ To print separations for a process color, make sure that the color is displayed in the Print As Process section. CMYK colors should already be there.

   ■ To print separations for a spot color, verify that the color is displayed in the Print As Spot section.

   ■ Move the colors you don't want to print into the Don't Print section.

Note   *The Print As Process section is not displayed if the selected printer doesn't support color separations. You'll need to select another printer, and then set up the separations.*

6. Click the Set button. Depending on the selected printer, you might need to specify halftone screens. In this case, a warning is displayed, and you must set up the screens before saving the color separation settings.

Configuring Halftones

To configure halftone screens, follow the directions for your platform:

Windows   Follow these steps to configure halftone screens for Windows:

1. In the Set Print Separations dialog box (Figure 18-3 on page 458), click the Halftone Screens button. The Halftone Screens dialog box is displayed.

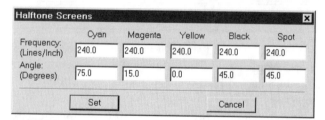

2. To configure the accuracy of the halftone, increase or decrease the line per inch (LPI) values in the Frequency section. The higher the LPI, the more accurate the halftone.

3. To change the angle at which the halftone is printed, change the value in the appropriate Angle field.

4. Click the Set button. The Set Print Separations dialog box is displayed.

5. Click the Set button, then print the PostScript file. See "Printing to a PostScript File" on page 455 for details.

Mac   Follow these steps to configure halftone screens for Windows:

1. In the Set Print Separations dialog box (Figure 18-3 on page 458), do one of the following:

   ■ In the Halftone Screens drop-down list, click one of the predefined settings to indicate LPI and DPI, then click the Set button.

   ■ In the Halftone Screens drop-down list, click Custom. The Halftone Screens dialog box is displayed.

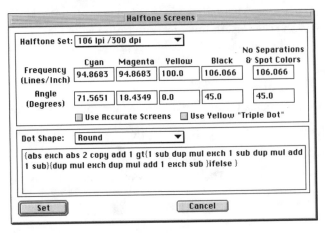

2. To change the frequency and angle of the halftones, type new values in the Frequency and Angle fields. The values in the Frequency and Angle fields are based on the selected Halftone Set. Your print vendor can help you with these settings.

3. Do one of the following: To print more accurate yellows, check the Use Yellow "Triple Dot" check box; to print all colors more accurately, check the Use Accurate Screens check box.

4. Click the Set button to display the Set Print Separations dialog box again, then click the Set button.

After setting up the Windows or Mac options, print the PostScript file. See "Printing to a PostScript File" on page 455 for details.

UNIX   In the $FMHOME/fminit directory, open ps_prolog.ps. There are many settings for halftone screens that you might need to change. Refer to your printer documentation for more information. (If you don't see the file, it might be hidden. See your UNIX documentation for directions on showing all files in a directory.)

To avoid changing halftone settings for other users, save the file as ~/fminit/ps_prolog. The file will be saved in your home directory.

Creating a TrapWise PostScript File

On the Mac, FrameMaker lets you create a PostScript file that can be edited in TrapWise software. If your document has colors that print close together or overlap, you may need to use the software to create traps, which prevent white space from printing between the colors. To print a PostScript file for TrapWise software, check the TrapWise Compatibility check box, click File in the Destination drop-down list, and click the Save button.

Symbols in Windows 2000 and Windows XP

The Zapf Dingbat font is displayed as a Wingding in Windows 2000 and Windows XP when the font is defined in the PPD file. For example, the ✔ Zapf Dingbat is displayed as the 📄 Wingding in your FrameMaker document. This problem occurs because Windows 2000 and XP try to match the Base 35 fonts, which are PostScript fonts, to TrueType fonts.

In the font mapping table, each font belongs to a particular character set, and each character in the font has a code. The ✔ Zapf Dingbat is mapped to Unicode value 34 in the Unicode character set, and the 📄 Wingding is mapped to hexadecimal 34 in the Windows character set. To display the Zapf Dingbat character, Windows finds the closest value in the Windows character set, which is the 📄 Wingding.

Until Adobe or Microsoft find a solution to the problem, you can modify your PPD files to force Windows to use the fonts on your computer instead of the printer fonts. To do so, follow these steps:

1. Close all applications.
2. Log in to Windows as an Administrator or using an ID that has administrative privileges.
3. Find the c:\WINNT\system32\spool\drivers\w32x86\3 directory.
4. Copy the PPD files to another directory so you'll have backups.
5. Open a PPD in a text editor and find the fonts section. In the Acrobat Distiller PPD, the fonts section and Zapf Dingbats definition are as follows:

```
*% Base fonts
*Font ZapfDingbats: Special "(002.000)" Special ROM
```

6. Type % between the asterisk and "Font." The line should read:

```
*%Font ZapfDingbats: Special "(002.000)" Special ROM
```

7. Save and close the file, and repeat for the remaining PPDs.
8. Delete all binary printer description (BPD) files in the directory. Each PPD file has a BPD file, which Windows creates by converting the PPD file to a binary format. Windows regenerates the BPD file every time the PPD file is modified.

Open your document in FrameMaker, and the Zapf Dingbat should be displayed correctly. Thanks to Dov Isaacs, Principal Scientist at Adobe Systems, and an authority on print, PostScript, and PDF issues, for this work-around.

Printing Fonts Accurately

You should embed fonts in your PostScript files to avoid font substitution problems. By embedding fonts, you can be sure that the print vendor has all of the fonts used in the document. Typically, when you print a document from your computer, the printer uses printer-resident fonts (fonts kept in the printer memory) or downloads the fonts from your computer (if the fonts aren't in memory). Suppose you use the Veljovic font in your document. Because Veljovic is not a printer-resident font, the printer downloads it from your computer. However, if a print vendor processes your PostScript file and does not have Veljovic, another font will be substituted.

There are two groups of printer-resident fonts—the Standard 13 and the Base 35. The PPD file associated with your printer specifies the printer fonts. The two groups consist of the following fonts:

- **Standard 13.** Courier, Symbol, and Zapf Dingbats. Most printers include these fonts.
- **Base 35.** Avant Garde, Bookman, Courier, Helvetica, New Century Schoolbook, Palatino, Symbol, Times, Zapf Chancery Medium Italic, and Zapf Dingbats. Many PostScript printers include these fonts.

The Standard 13 and Base 35 fonts have different angles and weights for each font, (for example, Courier, Courier Bold, and Courier Bold Oblique, and Courier Oblique).

In Windows, you don't need to configure FrameMaker to embed fonts when you print a FrameMaker document. The nonresident fonts (those not listed in the PPD) are automatically embedded with all print jobs. In UNIX and Mac OS, you choose which fonts to embed in the FrameMaker print setup. When a nonresident font is excluded from the print job, the default font prints instead. For example, if you don't embed the nonresident font Optima, and the Distiller PPD selected, the default font Courier is printed in place of Optima.

Embed all fonts to be safe, or ask your print vendor which fonts to embed.

To embed fonts in your PostScript file in UNIX and Mac OS, follow these steps:

1. Display the print dialog box (Figure 18-1 on page 442), then click one of the following in the Download Roman Fonts drop-down list (UNIX) or the Font Inclusion drop-down list of the PostScript Settings (Mac):
   - **All:** All fonts are sent to the printer (which slows down the print job).
   - **All but Standard 13:** All fonts but the Standard 13 are sent to the printer.
   - **All but Base 35:** All fonts but the Base 35 are sent to the printer.
2. *(UNIX)* To download Asian fonts, check the Download Asian Fonts check box. If not checked, printer fonts will be substituted for the Asian fonts in your document.

3. *(UNIX)* When you're printing TrueType fonts on a Level 1 PostScript printer, check the Download TrueType as Type-1 check box.

4. Print the PostScript file. See "Printing to a PostScript File" on page 455 for details.

What Are My Printer-Resident Fonts?

Most PostScript printers have the Base 35 fonts. To see which fonts your printer uses, you need to open the PPD file associated with the printer in a text editor.

In Windows, the easiest way to tell which PPD file your printer uses is to print a test page. To do so, follow these steps:

1. Select Start | Settings | Printers. The Printers dialog box is displayed.
2. Right-click the printer, and select Properties from the pop-up menu.
3. Click the Print Test Page button on the General tab. The test page is printed.
4. Check for the name of the PPD file. You'll find the file in WINNT\system32\spool\drivers\w32x86\3 (Windows 2000) or Windows\system (Windows 98).

To find out which PPD file your printer uses on the Mac, follow these steps:

1. Select Apple | Chooser. The Chooser dialog box is displayed.
2. Click the printer, then click the Setup button. The current PPD file is displayed. (If the PPD hasn't been selected, the Create button is displayed instead, and you'll need to select a PPD file.) You'll find the file in the System:Preferences:Printing Pref folder.

Creating PDF Files

You create a PDF file by saving the FrameMaker document as PDF or by creating a PostScript file and converting the file with Acrobat Distiller. In previous versions of FrameMaker, you had to set up Acrobat Distiller with the options you wanted before saving the file as PDF. Distilling PostScript files produced the most reliable PDF files; however, it involved two steps—creating the PostScript file and distilling the file.

In FrameMaker 7, you can create high-quality PDF files by saving the document as PDF. Distiller must be set up with the correct job options before you save the document as PDF because you choose the job option profile in FrameMaker. If you need to change the job options, such as color conversion or font embedding settings, change them in Distiller before saving the document as PDF or converting the file to PostScript and distilling the file separately.

Note   *In Windows, a Distiller printer instance is created when you install Distiller (which is included with the FrameMaker installation.) In Mac OS, a printer instance called FrameMakerPDFWriter is created when you select File | Print for the first time in FrameMaker 7. In UNIX, the distillation process is built into the operating system.*

Using the Save As Menu Choice

To save a FrameMaker file as PDF, follow these steps:

1. Select File | Save As. The Save Document dialog box is displayed.

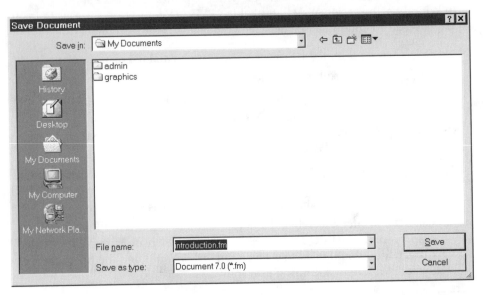

2. In the Save As Type drop-down list, click PDF.

3. In the File Name field, change the file name extension to **.PDF**. You must manually change the file extension, or a warning is displayed, asking whether you want to save the file with the .PDF extension.

4. Click the Save button. The PDF Setup dialog box is displayed. The same options are displayed by selecting Format | Document | PDF Setup.

5. Set up your PDF options and click the Set button. You must click the Set button even if you don't customize the settings at this point. See "Customizing the PDF File" on page 468 for details.

FrameMaker creates a PostScript file, launches Acrobat Distiller (you'll see it minimized in the Windows taskbar), and converts the file to PDF.

Distilling a PostScript File

Once you've created a PostScript file, you can double-click the file or open the file in Acrobat Distiller to convert it to PDF. The PDF file is saved in the same folder as the PostScript file and has the same name as the original file (except for the file extension). To generate a PDF file with a different name (if you don't want to rename it after distilling) or save it in another folder, you should open the PostScript file inside Acrobat Distiller. This also gives you the opportunity to change job options or security settings.

It's often quicker, though, to double-click the PostScript file to create the PDF file. On most computers, the .PS extension is associated with Acrobat Distiller upon installation. If your system is configured another way, you'll either need to change the configuration, open the PostScript file in Acrobat Distiller, or drag the PostScript file from the computer window to Acrobat Distiller in Windows and Mac OS. In UNIX, you distill the PostScript file from the command line.

If you try to distill a PostScript file and a PDF file by the same name is open in Acrobat, Distiller displays an error. You'll need to click the OK button on the warning dialog box, close the PDF file, and then try distilling again.

How to Avoid Fuzzy Screen Shots in PDF Files

Acrobat Distiller comes with predefined job option profiles based on how the PDF file will be used. For example, the Screen job options are theoretically optimized for viewing PDF files online. Many users find, however, that the Screen job option creates fuzzy screen shots in PDF files. Images are compressed using downsampling, which decreases the number of pixels in an image to reduce the size of the PDF file. To avoid this problem, you need to turn off downsampling, set the compression method to 8-bit Zip, and save the profile with a different name, such as Best Screen Shots. If your document includes JPEGs, set the compression to JPEG or Automatic. (With automatic compression, Distiller uses JPEG compression on photographic images—those with blended, continuous color—and Zip compression on images with sharp changes in color.

Double-Clicking the File

To distill a PostScript file by double-clicking, find the PostScript file and double-click it. Acrobat Distiller is displayed (Figure 18-4 on page 466), and the PostScript file is converted to PDF.

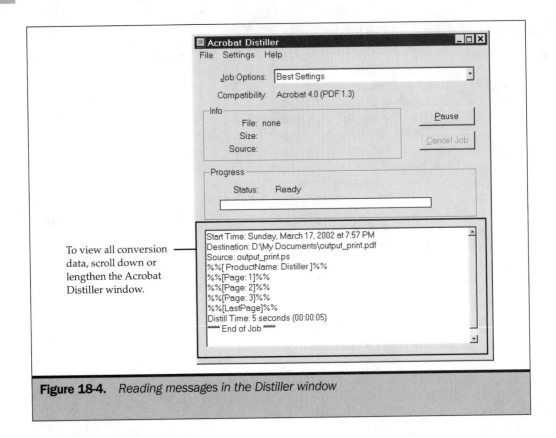

To view all conversion
data, scroll down or
lengthen the Acrobat
Distiller window.

Figure 18-4.   *Reading messages in the Distiller window*

Opening the File in Acrobat Distiller

To convert the PostScript file by opening it in Acrobat Distiller, follow these steps:

1. Open Acrobat Distiller if it's not already open.
2. Select the job option profile you want, or select Settings and modify the current options. Refer to Acrobat Distiller documentation for details.
3. Select File | Open. The Open PostScript dialog box is displayed.

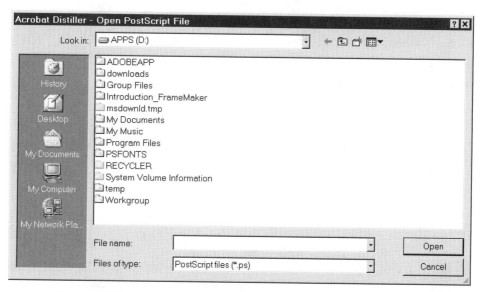

4. Browse to find the PostScript file you want to convert to PDF and click the Open button. The Specify PDF File Name dialog box is displayed.

5. In the File name field, type the name of the final PDF file and change the location, if necessary.

6. Click the Save button. The PostScript file is converted to PDF.

From the Command Line (UNIX)

To convert a PostScript file to PDF in UNIX, follow these steps:

1. From the command prompt, switch to the directory that contains the PostScript file.

2. Type **distill** *filename*, substituting the name of the PostScript file for *filename*. The PostScript file is converted to PDF.

For more information on distill commands, type **distill -help** from the command line.

Preventing PDF Conversion Errors

When the PostScript file is being converted, information such as the following is displayed in the Acrobat Distiller window:

```
Start Time: Wednesday, March 20, 2002 at 3:50 PM
Destination: D:\My Documents\test docs\My Structured Doc.pdf
Source: My Structured Doc.ps
%%[ ProductName: Distiller ]%%
%%[Page: 1]%%
%%[Page: 2]%%
%%[Page: 3]%%
%%[Page: 4]%%
%%[LastPage]%%
Distill Time: 12 seconds (00:00:12)
**** End of Job ****
```

Conversion errors are displayed and also are saved in a log file in the same directory as the PDF file. For example, the following error occurs when you create the print file with a non-PostScript driver:

```
%%[ Flushing: rest of job (to end-of-file) will be ignored ]%%
%%[ Warning: PostScript error. No PDF file produced. ]%%
```

Missing fonts also cause problems. The Findfont error occurs when Distiller can't find the fonts used in the PostScript file—either the fonts weren't saved with the PostScript file, or Distiller can't find the font on your computer. To prevent the problem, specify the locations of fonts on your computer under Settings | Font Locations in Distiller, and include the fonts in the PostScript file. See "Printing Fonts Accurately" on page 462 for details on embedding fonts in PostScript files.

For more information on other error messages, you can search the Adobe online support database at www.adobe.com/support/main.html.

You don't need the log file when the PostScript file converts successfully, so you can configure the Acrobat Distiller Preferences to delete the file automatically.

Customizing the PDF File

You need to set up many PDF characteristics inside FrameMaker before you create a PostScript file (if you're generating Acrobat data) or save the document or book as PDF. Other Acrobat features can be configured only in Distiller. Table 18-1 shows where you set up many popular features.

To set up Distiller options, you select Settings | Job Options, make changes, and save the profile under a new name. The new profile is displayed in the PDF Setup dialog box in FrameMaker, shown in Figure 18-5 on page 470.

Item	FrameMaker	Acrobat Distiller
Elements or paragraph tags to convert to bookmarks	✔	
Color management, including halftone, overprint, CMYK, and RGB profiles		✔
Gradients converted to smooth shades		✔
Fonts embedded in PDF file		✔
Named destinations for hyperlinks	✔	
Page displayed first when you open the PDF file	✔	
Page size	✔	✔
Password		✔
Print and PDF modifications permissions		✔
Registration marks	✔	
Image resolution		✔
Structure for tagged PDF file	✔	
Thumbnails		✔
Zoom level	✔	

Table 18-1. *Changing PDF Options*

Generating Bookmarks

A *bookmark* is text from an element or paragraph displayed in the left pane of the Acrobat window. The reader can click the bookmark to view a specific topic. In FrameMaker, you choose the element or paragraph tags and indicate a hierarchy for the bookmarks. Top-level bookmarks are displayed flush left. The second-level bookmarks are indented once, the third-level bookmarks are indented twice, and so on. See Figure 18-6 on page 470.

See Figure 18-6 on page 470.

CREATING OUTPUT

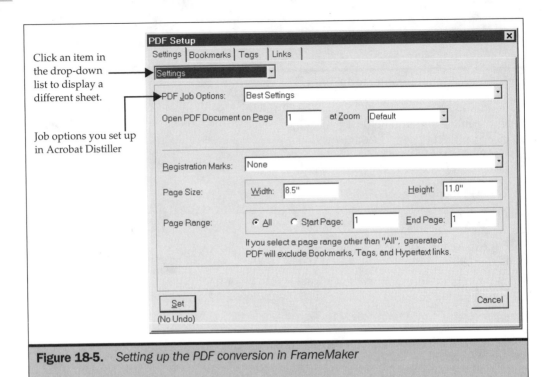

Click an item in the drop-down list to display a different sheet.

Job options you set up in Acrobat Distiller

Figure 18-5. *Setting up the PDF conversion in FrameMaker*

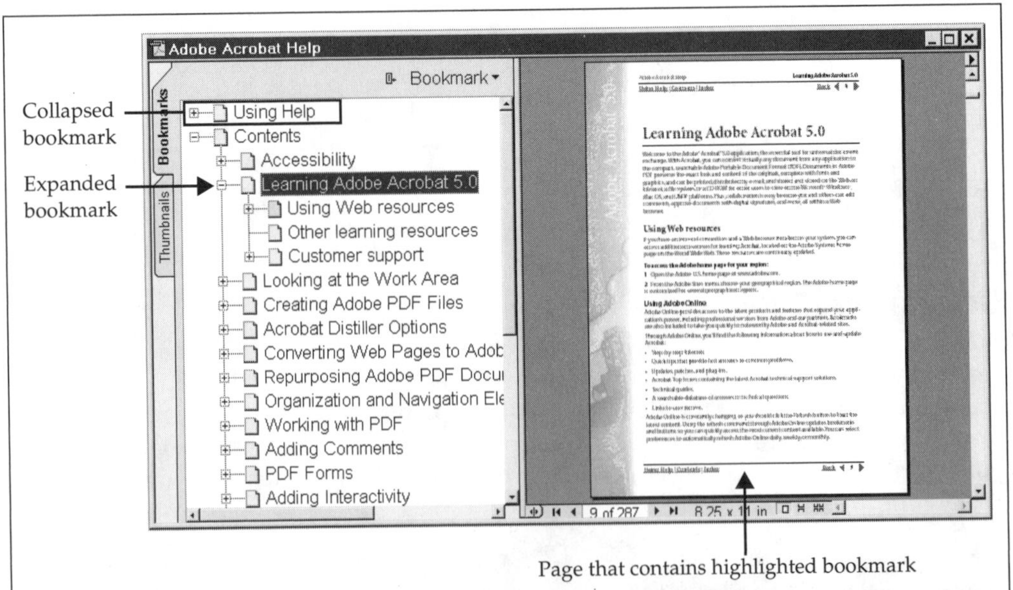

Collapsed bookmark

Expanded bookmark

Page that contains highlighted bookmark

Figure 18-6. *Acrobat bookmarks helps readers navigate through the PDF file.*

In the bookmark setup, you decide whether the bookmarks are expanded or collapsed by default when the reader opens the PDF file. If all bookmarks are expanded, the reader doesn't need to click each collapsed bookmark to display the list. But if the document has many bookmarks, and they're all expanded, the reader will have to scroll down to search through all of the bookmarks.

Setting up bookmarks in structured and unstructured documents works a bit differently. In a structured document, the bookmarks are based on elements instead of paragraphs. See "Printing and Converting Structured Documents to PDF Files" on page 476 for more information.

To specify the tags you want to convert to bookmarks in an unstructured document, follow these steps:

1. Display the print dialog box, then click the PDF Setup button. The PDF Setup dialog box is displayed (Figure 18-5 on page 470).

2. Click the Bookmarks sheet, or click Bookmarks in the drop-down list. The Bookmarks sheet is displayed.

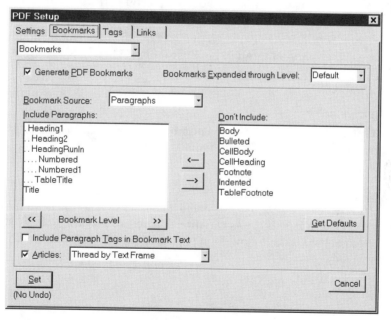

3. Make sure the Generate PDF Bookmarks check box is checked.

4. Specify the tags you want to bookmark by doing the following:

    ■ In the Bookmark Source drop-down list, click Paragraphs to indicate the basis of the bookmarks.

    ■ To include a paragraph, click the item in the Don't Include Paragraphs column, then click the left arrow button. The tag is displayed in the Include Paragraphs column.

■ To exclude a paragraph, click the item in the Include Paragraphs column, then click the right arrow button. The tag is displayed in the Don't Include Paragraphs column.

Tip   *To move all tags at once, press* SHIFT *while clicking the left arrow or right arrow button.*

5. To specify the hierarchy of the bookmarks, click the tag in the Include Paragraphs column, then click the Bookmark Level (<< and >>) buttons until the tag is indented correctly. A dot is displayed next to the tag to indicate the level of indentation—one dot indicates the first indented paragraph tag, two dots indicates the second indented paragraph tag, up to the sixth level. After the sixth level, a number is displayed instead of the dots. (Most readers don't use bookmarks after the third or fourth level, so keep the hierarchy to a minimum.)

6. To include the paragraph tag name in the bookmark, check the Include Tags in Bookmark Text check box. This option helps you verify bookmark levels in draft PDF files.

7. To expand or collapse bookmarks in the PDF file, do one of the following in the Bookmarks Expanded through Level drop-down list:

   ■ Click None to collapse all bookmarks.

   ■ Click All to expand all bookmarks. A maximum of 25 bookmarks can be expanded.

   ■ Type a number to indicate the number of levels to expand. For example, to expand three levels of bookmarks, type **3**.

Threading Articles

Documents such as newsletters and magazine layouts often have articles that are in separate text flows. In a PDF file, you can thread articles by their text flow. When you reach the bottom of the article in flow A on page 1, the continued article at the bottom of page 2 is displayed.

Threaded by Text Flow

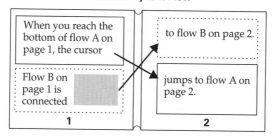

Threaded by Text Frame

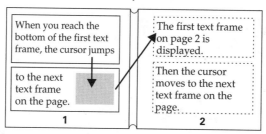

In a single-column document, articles are usually threaded by text frame, so the cursor moves from text frame to text frame instead of from flow to flow. This is the default value in the PDF setup.

To indicate how the articles will be threaded, follow these steps:

1. Display the print dialog box, then click the PDF Setup button. The PDF Setup dialog box is displayed (Figure 18-5 on page 470).

2. Click the Bookmarks sheet, then do one of the following:

   ■ To read the articles in a multicolumn document, click Thread by Column in the Articles drop-down list.

   ■ To read the articles in a single-column document, click Thread by Text Frame in the Articles drop-down list.

Specifying the Default Zoom Level and First Displayed Page

When the reader opens a PDF file, the first page from the FrameMaker file is usually displayed. You might want another page displayed first if, for example, the reader probably won't care about viewing the title page or front matter. You can also control the zoom level at which the PDF file is displayed. This zoom level overrides the default magnification in the reader's Acrobat settings.

To specify the default zoom level and first displayed page, follow these steps:

1. Display the print dialog box, then click the PDF Setup button. The PDF Setup dialog box is displayed (Figure 18-5 on page 470).

2. Click the Settings sheet, or click Settings in the drop-down list. The Settings sheet is displayed (Figure 18-5 on page 470).

3. To change the first displayed page, type the page number in the Open PDF Document on Page field.

4. To change the zoom level, click an item in the Zoom drop-down list:

   - **Default:** Uses the reader's Acrobat settings.
   - **Fit Page:** Displays the entire page in Acrobat.
   - **Fit Width:** Displays the width of the page.
   - **Fit Height:** Displays the height of the page.
   - **10% to 400%:** Specifies the magnification level.

Setting Up Registration Marks in a PDF File

When you convert a document to PDF, Acrobat Distiller *crops* the document, or removes extra space outside the boundaries of the page. To prevent this, you must increase the page size in the PDF setup and uncheck the Generate Acrobat Data option in the print dialog box.

To set up registration marks in a PDF file, follow these steps:

1. Display the print dialog box, then click Western or Tombo in the Registration Marks drop-down list (see Figure 18-1 on page 442).

2. Click the PDF Setup button. The PDF Setup dialog box is displayed (Figure 18-5 on page 470).

3. Click the Settings sheet, then click the type of registration marks in the Registration Marks drop-down list.

4. Add 1 inch to the width and height in the Page Size section.

If the registration marks for the PDF and PostScript files are different, those selected in the PDF Setup dialog box are converted to PDF.

Generating Tagged PDF Files

Tagged PDF files display a logical structure of the document so you can repurpose the PDF file for alternate displays, such as screen readers and small devices, and accurately export PDF as RTF from Acrobat 5. The tree structure shows paragraphs or elements in the document. The contents of anchored frames may be displayed if you assigned text attributes to the anchored frame object properties. You can create tagged PDF files with Acrobat Distiller 5.05 or later. In UNIX, the distillation process installed with FrameMaker 7 supports tagged PDF.

To set up a tagged PDF file, follow these steps:

1. Display the print dialog box, then click the PDF Setup button. The PDF Setup dialog box is displayed (Figure 18-5 on page 470).

2. Click the Tags sheet, or click Tags in the drop-down list. The Tags sheet is displayed.

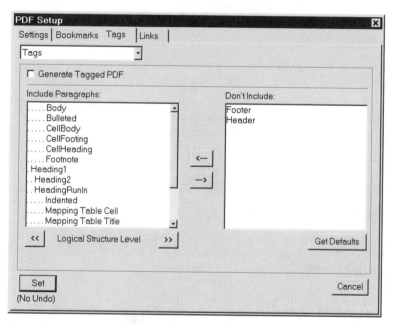

3. Indicate the tags you want to include in the logical structure by doing the following:

   ■ To include a paragraph tag in the logical structure, click a tag in the Don't Include section, then click the left arrow button.

   ■ To exclude a paragraph tag from the logical structure, click a tag in the Include Paragraphs section, then click the right arrow button.

4. Change the hierarchy of the tags by clicking a tag in the Include Paragraphs section, and then clicking the Logical Structure Level buttons (<< and >>) until the tag is indented logically in relation to the other tags. See "Generating Bookmarks" on page 469 for details.

Tip *To promote or demote all tags one level, SHIFT-click the left arrow or right arrow button.*

For information on describing the contents of anchored frames in tagged PDF files, see "Setting Anchored Frame Object Properties" on page 314.

Creating Hyperlinks to Other PDF Files

You can hyperlink elements or paragraphs from one PDF file to another by creating the PDF files with *named destinations*. For example, this option lets you add cross-references or hypertext links from one FrameMaker document to another without resaving the documents as PDF. Keep in mind that named destinations increase PDF size, so you should avoid this feature if you always re-create PDF files after adding hyperlinks to other documents.

To generate named destinations, follow these steps:

1. Display the print dialog box, then click the PDF Setup button. The PDF Setup dialog box is displayed (Figure 18-5 on page 470).

2. Click the Links sheet or Links in the drop-down list, then click the Create Named Destinations for All Elements and Paragraphs check box. FrameMaker will generate named destinations when you create the PDF file.

Printing and Converting Structured Documents to PDF Files

Print and PDF conversion work the same in unstructured and structured documents except for two features—hiding element boundaries and converting elements to bookmarks in the PDF file.

Hiding Element Boundaries

In a structured document, you can hide *element boundaries* before printing the document or converting it to PDF. Element boundaries show where each element begins and ends and make it easier to insert the cursor on the page. If you try to print a document with the boundaries showing, you must confirm that you do want to print boundaries or cancel printing and turn them off.

To hide element boundaries, select View, then uncheck Element Boundaries or Element Boundaries (as tags), depending on which type of boundary is displayed. See "Displaying Tags in the Document Window" on page 671 for more information on element boundaries.

Converting Elements to Bookmarks in a PDF File

In structured documents, bookmarks are based on elements rather than paragraphs. The bookmark hierarchy depends on the structure of the document, not levels indicated in the bookmark setup.

To create PDF bookmarks in structured documents, follow these steps:

1. Follow step 1 through step 3 on page 471.
2. Specify the elements you want to bookmark by doing the following:

   - In the Bookmark Source drop-down list, make sure Elements is displayed.
   - To include an element, click the item in the Don't Include column, then click the left arrow button. The element is displayed in the Include Paragraphs column.
   - To exclude an element, click the item in the Include column, then click the right arrow button. The element is displayed in the Don't Include Paragraphs column.

Tip *To quickly move all tags from one column to the other, press* SHIFT *while clicking the left arrow or right arrow button.*

3. To include the element tag name in the bookmark, check the Include Element Tags in Bookmark Text check box. This option helps you identify elements in draft PDF files.
4. To expand or collapse bookmarks in the PDF file, do one of the following in the Bookmarks Expanded through Level drop-down list:

   - Click None to collapse all bookmarks.
   - Click All to expand all bookmarks. A maximum of 25 bookmarks can be expanded.
   - Type a number to indicate the number of levels to expand. For example, to expand three levels of bookmarks, type **3**.

The Complete
Reference

FrameMaker 7

Chapter 19

Creating HTML and XML Output

479

You have a number of different ways to create HTML, XML, or online help from FrameMaker files. Some options give you "quick-and-dirty" conversions—easy to set up but with limited control over the output. Other choices are more difficult to configure but provide better customization options.

FrameMaker provides a Save As feature. In unstructured documents, this feature uses mapping tables stored on the reference pages; you can Save As HTML or XML. In structured documents, the Save As feature can use the same reference pages as the unstructured files, or you can define a structured application and use the parser to convert files. The parser and structured applications provide very powerful options. The reference pages, by contrast, provide simple, entry-level customization features. The Save As feature associated with structured applications is explained in Chapter 31, "Importing and Exporting XML/SGML Markup Files." This chapter discusses the Save As function that's used when you do not have a structured application.

Instead of using the Save As feature, you can use WebWorks Publisher Standard Edition, which is shipped with FrameMaker. The software can handle both structured and unstructured files.

In addition to the options included with FrameMaker, two powerful third-party tools are available. WebWorks Publisher Professional Edition and MIF2GO must be purchased separately (refer to Appendix A, "Resources," for company links); only a brief overview of those tools is provided in this chapter.

Choosing a Conversion Method

Before you begin converting your files, you need to decide which conversion technique to use. Here is a summary of your options:

- **Save as HTML/XML** works reasonably well for quick, one-time conversions of short files. You will not, however, be able to control exactly what the output looks like. As a result, this option is unsuitable for longer files or for environments where you need to convert lots of files frequently. The Save As feature can be useful for converting short files, if you don't mind editing the generated output files manually.

- **WebWorks Publisher Standard Edition** is a third-party application that's included when you buy FrameMaker. It offers some useful options, such as the ability to create Microsoft Reader files, but WebWorks Publisher Standard Edition provides only limited control over the generated output. Like the built-in Save As option, WebWorks Publisher Standard Edition is best used for short, one-time conversions, not for ongoing conversion requirements or large file sets.

- **WebWorks Publisher Professional Edition** is the heavy-duty sibling of WebWorks Publisher Standard Edition. It provides conversion templates for online help formats, such as JavaHelp, WinHelp, and HTML Help. You can customize the generated output extensively. Basic customization is relatively easy in the graphical interface; more advanced customizations require you to learn a complex macro language that's unique to WebWorks Publisher.

■ **MIF2GO** offers many of the same customization features as WebWorks Publisher but in a completely different product. MIF2GO provides a graphical interface for basic changes; more advanced changes require you to manipulate settings in a configuration file. You can process both structured and unstructured files out of FrameMaker 7. MIF2GO is significantly less expensive than WebWorks Publisher Professional Edition. The product provides an improved RTF export filter that is much better than FrameMaker's built-in filter; it also supports OracleHelp in addition to JavaHelp, WinHelp, and HTML Help.

■ **Structured applications** are available only for structured files. They are highly customizable, but they require more initial configuration than any of the other choices.

Saving as HTML or XML

You can use the Save As command to create HTML and XML files from both structured and unstructured files. However, the mechanism that creates the files is completely different depending on whether a structured application is available:

■ For unstructured files and for structured files that do not have an application in place for the output you want, FrameMaker uses mapping settings that are stored on the reference pages.

■ For structured files with an application, FrameMaker uses the parser.

This section discusses the first option—conversion that's performed using settings on the reference pages. For information about conversion of structured files through an application, see Chapter 31, "Importing and Exporting XML/SGML Markup Files."

The Save As HTML or XML feature lets you customize mappings and output to some degree. The conversion settings are saved on the reference pages; for HTML, the reference pages are called HTML and HTML(cont). Similarly, the XML settings are saved on reference pages called XML and XML(cont). If these pages are not included in the original document, FrameMaker creates the needed pages the first time you save to HTML or XML.

The Save As SGML option is available in the structured interface, but you can use it only for structured files (with an application). If you attempt to save an unstructured file as SGML, an error message is displayed.

Saving a File as HTML or XML

To save a file as HTML or XML, follow these steps:

1. Select File | Save As. The Save Document dialog box is displayed.

2. In the File name field, specify a name for the output file.

3. In the Save as type field, click HTML or XML.

4. Click the Save button to save the file in the specified format.

The first time you convert a file, FrameMaker creates several new reference pages, called either HTML or XML (depending on which format you chose). These reference pages store the conversion settings for your files.

Saving a Book as HTML or XML

To save a book file, you open the book file, select File | Save As, and choose HTML or XML format, just as you would in a document. FrameMaker processes each file in the book in turn and creates one (or more) HTML/XML output files for each FrameMaker file. The conversion settings for the book are stored on reference pages in the first file in the book called BookHTML and BookHeadings. To modify conversion settings, open the first file in the book, locate these reference pages, and change them just as you would file-level HTML and Headings reference pages.

If you have already set up file-level conversion and want to use those settings for a book conversion, copy the mapping tables from the HTML and Headings reference pages onto the BookHTML and BookHeadings reference pages of the first file in the book.

Modifying Conversion Settings Graphically

For HTML conversion, FrameMaker provides a graphical interface in which you can perform some basic mapping. The HTML Setup dialog box is somewhat useful in establishing initial conversion settings, but you will almost certainly need to fine-tune settings by modifying mapping tables on the HTML reference pages. For XML, an XML Setup dialog box is not available, so you must perform all customization on the XML reference pages.

 Do not attempt to make changes in the HTML Setup dialog box while displaying the HTML reference pages. This can cause file corruption.

You can customize the paragraph, character, and cross-reference mappings in the HTML Setup dialog box.

Paragraph Mappings

You can customize file conversion (but not book conversion) using the HTML Setup dialog box. This graphical setup is not available for XML conversion. To customize your paragraph mappings using the HTML Setup dialog box, follow these steps:

1. Open the file you want to convert. Make sure the reference pages are *not* displayed.

2. Select File | Utilities | HTML Setup. The HTML Setup dialog box is displayed.

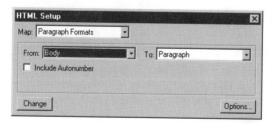

3. In the Map drop-down list, make sure that Paragraph Formats (the default) is selected.

4. The From drop-down list includes all of the paragraph tags in this document. For each paragraph tag, click the corresponding mapping in the To drop-down list. The options are as follows:

Mapping Style	Description
Heading (Auto Level)	Use for headings in your document. The heading level is determined by a mapping table on the reference pages. For details, see "Assigning Heading Levels" on page 488.
Paragraph	Use for body paragraphs in your document.
Preformatted Text	Use for monospaced paragraphs, such as code examples, in your text.
Address	Use for an address block.
Block Quote	Use for an indented quotation.
List Item	Use for bulleted and numbered lists.
List Item (Continued)	Use for paragraphs inside a bulleted or numbered list that do not have a bullet or number.
Data Term	Use for terms.
Data Definition	Use for definitions.
Data Definition (Continued)	Use for a continuation paragraph in a definition.
Throw Away	Use for paragraphs you want to eliminate from the HTML output.

Some mappings provide additional options. Headings, for example, include a Start New, Linked Web Page check box, which lets you specify whether a particular heading should cause a new HTML page to begin in the output. The options are as follows:

Available in...	Option	Description
All styles	Include Autonumber check box	If checked, the paragraph autonumber is included in the output. If unchecked, the paragraph autonumber is discarded.
Heading (Auto Level)	Start New, Linked Web Page check box	If checked, the specified paragraph tag starts a new web page.

Available in...	Option	Description
List Item List Item (Continued)	*Item will be in a bulleted/numbered list*	FrameMaker automatically sets either a bulleted or numbered list for list items.
List Item List Item (Continued)	Nest List at Depth...	Determines the indentation level of the list item.

5. When you are finished, click the Change button.

Character Mappings

You can set up initial character tag mappings in the HTML Setup dialog box. To map your character tags, follows these steps:

1. Open the file you want to convert. Make sure the reference pages are *not* displayed.

2. Select File | Utilities | HTML Setup. The HTML Setup dialog box is displayed.

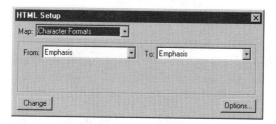

3. In the Map drop-down list, make sure that Character Formats is selected.

4. The From drop-down list includes all of the character tags in this document. For each character tag, click the corresponding mapping in the To drop-down list. The options are as follows:

Mapping Style	Description
Blink	Use to create blinking text.
Citation	Use for inline citations or quotes.
Code	Use for monospaced text, such as programming commands in text.
Definition	Use for inline definitions.

Mapping Style	Description
Emphasis	Use for emphasized text.
Keyboard	Use for text you type in (similar to Code).
Language (Intl.)	Specifies the language of the enclosed text.
Sample	Use for monospaced text.
Short Quotation (Intl.)	Use for inline quotes.
Span (CSS)	Use to reference formatting in a CSS file.
Strong Emphasis	Use for heavy emphasis.
Typewriter	Use to produce monospaced text; similar to Code.
Variable	Use for variables in programming code.
Plain Text	Use to output text with no additional formatting.
Throw Away	Use to delete text from the output.

Cross-Reference Mappings

You can set up initial cross-reference mappings in the HTML Setup dialog box. After this initial setup, you can further tweak these settings on the reference pages.

To set up cross-reference formats in the HTML Setup dialog box, follow these steps:

1. Make sure that the reference pages are *not* displayed.
2. Select File | Utilities | HTML Setup. The HTML Setup dialog box is displayed.

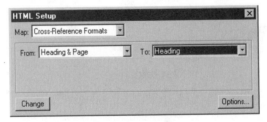

3. In the Map drop-down list, click Cross-Reference Formats. The dialog box now displays a list of cross-reference formats in the From drop-down list.
4. For each cross-reference format, assign a cross-reference mapping in the To list. Your options are as follows:

Mapping Style	Description
Heading	`<$paratext>` Displays the paragraph text only. Appropriate for most online references.
See Also	`See <$paratext>` Displays the paragraph text with "See."
Table All	`Table <$paranumonly>, <$paratext>` Displays the table number and title.
Table Number	`Table <$paranumonly>` Displays the table number only.
Original Cross-Reference Format	Processes the cross-reference without changing the format.
Throw Away	The cross-reference is deleted during conversion.

5. When you are finished, click the Change button.
6. Close the HTML Setup dialog box.

Setting the Format of Output Graphics

You can convert graphics into one of three formats: GIF, JPEG, or PNG. Or, if graphics were imported by reference in FrameMaker and the source files are in a web-ready format, you can copy the graphics instead of converting them.

To set your graphic conversion options, follow these steps:

1. Make sure that the reference pages are *not* displayed.
2. Select File | Utilities | HTML Setup. The HTML Setup dialog box is displayed.
3. Click the Options button. The HTML Options dialog box is displayed.

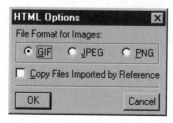

4. In the File Format for Images section, choose an output format for your graphics.

5. If you want to use source files instead of converting files for the items imported by reference, check the Copy Files Imported by Reference check box.

6. Click the OK button.

Modifying the Reference Pages

For better control over your output, you can make changes to the mapping tables on the reference pages.

Assigning Heading Levels

The heading levels in your output are determined by the Headings mapping table found on the Headings reference page. For a book conversion, this table is on the BookHeadings reference page:

Heading Level§	Paragraph Format§	Comments§
1§	**Title§**	§
2§	**Heading1§**	§
3§	**Heading2§**	§
4§	**HeadingRunIn§**	§
4§	**TableTitle§**	§

Headings Table§

The columns in this table are as follows:

- **Heading Level:** Determines the level of the output heading.
- **Paragraph Format:** Lists the heading paragraph tags in the document. In the preceding example, the paragraphs use the listed paragraph tags (for example, the Title listing is formatted using the Title paragraph tag), but this is not required.
- **Comments:** You can provide comments to explain the information in the table. By default, the Comments column is blank.

FrameMaker provides a default set of mappings, shown in the preceding example. If your document contains other paragraph tags, they are listed alphabetically by default. You can rearrange them in hierarchical order to make the table easier to maintain.

Setting Up Paragraph Mappings

The paragraph mappings are stored in the HTML Mapping Table on the reference pages:

§

HTML Mapping Table§

FrameMaker Source Item§	XML Item§		Include	Comments§
	Element§	New Web Page?§	Auto#§	
P:Body§	P§	N§	N§	§
P:Bulleted§	LI¶ Parent = UL¶ Depth = 0§	N§	N§	§
P:CellBody§	P§	N§	N§	§
P:CellHeading§	P§	N§	N§	§
P:Footnote§	P§	N§	N§	§
P:Heading1§	H*§	N§	N§	§
P:Heading2§	H*§	N§	N§	§
P:HeadingRunIn§	H*§	N§	N§	§
P:Indented§	P¶ Parent = UL¶ Depth = 0§	N§	N§	§
P:Mapping Table Cell§	P§	N§	N§	§
P:Mapping Table Title§	P§	N§	N§	§
P:Numbered§	LI¶ Parent = OL¶ Depth = 0§	N§	N§	§

You can modify settings here instead of working through the HTML Setup dialog box. Notice that the paragraph mappings start with a P: prefix.

FrameMaker creates an initial listing of tags in this table. If you add paragraph tags to your document, those tags are added into the table, but they may be added at the bottom of the table, not in the paragraph tag section. Keep in mind that paragraph tags, character tags, and cross-reference formats are all listed in this table, and that they are not always grouped together.

Mapping Character Tags

The HTML Mapping Table lists character tags with a C: prefix, as shown in the following example:

HTML Mapping Table§

FrameMaker Source Item§	XML Item§		Include	Comments§
	Element§	New Web Page?§	Auto#§	
C:Emphasis§	EM§	N§	N§	§
C:EquationVariables§	EM§	N§	N§	§

In this example, the Emphasis and EquationVariables character tags are both mapped to the EM element.

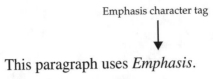

This paragraph uses *Emphasis*.

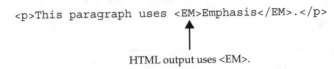

HTML output uses <EM>.

You could change the mapping table to produce different output. The code you enter is used to create opening <*xxx*> and closing </*xxx*> tags. Keep in mind that you must supply a tag that HTML can interpret.

Mapping Cross-Reference Formats

The mappings you establish in the HTML Setup dialog box are saved in the reference pages as part of the HTML Mapping Table. The cross-reference formats are listed with X: prefixes, as shown in the following example:

HTML Mapping Table§					
FrameMaker Source Item§	XML Item§		Include Auto#§	Comments§
	Element§	New Web Page?§		
X:Heading & Page§	Heading§	N§	N§	§
X:Page§	Heading§	N§	N§	§
X:See Heading & Page§	See Also§	N§	N§	§
X:Table All§	Table All§	N§	N§	§
X:Table Number & Page§	Table Number§	N§	N§	§

Unlike the paragraph and character tags, the elements listed for the cross-references (such as Heading and See Also in the preceding example) are not translated directly into HTML tags. Instead, the cross-reference formats use cross-reference macros. For example, Heading is defined as a macro in the Cross-Reference Macros table on the HTML reference pages, shown here:

Cross-Reference Macros§		
Macro Name§	Replace With§	Comments§
Heading§	<$paratext>§	§
See Also§	See <$paratext>.§	§
Table All§	Table <$paranumonly>, <$paratext>§	§
Table Number§	Table <$paranumonly>§	§

The Heading macro is defined as:

```
<$paratext>
```

The cross-reference macros are used to replace the original cross-reference format definition during conversion. FrameMaker automatically converts cross-references to HTML links, and that conversion is not reflected anywhere in the mapping tables.

Modifying Style Sheet Information

When you save to HTML, FrameMaker creates a cascading style sheet (CSS) file. This file controls the formatting of the items in the HTML file. You can make changes to the CSS file to control the look and feel of each item in the HTML output. The following example shows a CSS formatting specification:

```
P.Body {
    display: block;
    text-align: left;
    text-indent: 0.000000pt;
    margin-top: 0.000000pt;
    margin-bottom: 0.000000pt;
    margin-right: 0.000000pt;
    margin-left: 0.000000pt;
    font-size: 12.000000pt;
    font-weight: medium;
    font-style: Regular;
    color: #000000;
    text-decoration: none;
    vertical-align: baseline;
    text-transform: none;
    font-family: "Times New Roman";
}
EM.Emphasis {
    font-style: Italic;
}
```

By default, FrameMaker updates the CSS file every time you Save As HTML. If you make changes to the CSS file, be sure to make a copy of the file in another directory. After creating the output (and overwriting the CSS file), you can then copy your updated CSS file back into the HTML output directory.

Modifying Page Opening and Closing Code

The opening and closing tags in the output HTML are set by the System Macros table, shown here:

Macro Name§	Replace With§	Head§	Comments§
StartOfDoc§	§	`<TITLE>` `<$defaulttitle></TITLE>`§	§
EndOfDoc§	§	§	§
StartOfSubDoc§	§	`<TITLE>` `<$defaulttitle></TITLE>`§	§
EndOfSubDoc§	§	§	§
StartOfFirstSubDoc§	§	`<TITLE>` `<$defaulttitle></TITLE>`§	§
EndOfFirstSubDoc§	§	§	§
StartOfLastSubDoc§	§	`<TITLE>` `<$defaulttitle></TITLE>`§	§
EndOfLastSubDoc§	§	§	§

The available macros distinguish between documents (Docs) and subdocuments (SubDocs). If you break up a FrameMaker file into multiple output files, the first output file is considering the main document. The additional output files are subdocuments. The macros available to customize these output files are defined as follows:

- **StartOfDoc:** Beginning of the main document.
- **EndOfDoc:** End of the main document.
- **StartOfSubDoc:** Beginning of the subdocuments (except the first and last).
- **EndOfSubDoc:** End of the subdocuments (except the first and last).
- **StartOfFirstSubDoc:** Beginning of the first subdocument.
- **EndOfFirstSubDoc:** End of the first subdocument.
- **StartOfLastSubDoc:** Beginning of the last subdocument.
- **EndOfLastSubDoc:** End of the last subdocument.

Several building blocks are available for use in these macros to help you customize the output. You could, for instance, use the `<$nextsubdoc>` and `<$prevsubdoc>` macros to create a navigation bar. The following table lists the building blocks available to customize the system macros:

Building Block	Description
`<$paratext>`	The text of the current paragraph.
`<$paratag>`	The name of the current paragraph tag.
`<$paranum>`	The autonumber of the current paragraph tag.
`<$paranumonly>`	The numeric portion of the autonumber of the current paragraph tag.
`<$variable[`*variablename*`]>`	The definition of the *variablename* variable.
`<$defaulttitle>`	The text of the most recent paragraph tag that is tagged as a heading. (That is, it must be identified as a heading in the HTML Mapping Table.)
`<$nextsubdoc>`	The file name of the next document in the output.
`<$prevsubdoc>`	The file name of the previous document in the output.
`<$parentdoc>`	The file name of the document that is at the next higher level in the HTML output hierarchy.

Processing Special Characters

Special characters require special handling during conversion. The Character Macros table lets you define how special characters are processed:

Character Macros§		
Character§	Replace With§	Comments§
¢§	`&#162;`§	§
©§	`&#169;`§	§
®§	`&#174;`§	§
°§	`&#176;`§	§
—§	--§	§
–§	-§	§
…§	…§	§

For characters that don't work in the HTML/XML files, you need to set up a replacement by adding a line to this table. For instance, the trademark symbol, ™, doesn't translate properly, so you would add a line to the mapping table, as shown in the following example:

Character	Replace With	Comments
TM	&trade;	

Defining Macros

During conversion, you can further customize your output with macros. A *general macro* lets you define HTML code, which you can then use for mappings. You set up these macros in the General Macros table, shown in the following example:

General Macros§			
Macro Name§	Replace With§	Head§	Comments§
BodyBold§	<p><b>§	§	§

Once you define a general macro, you can reference it in the HTML or XML Mapping Table:

§

HTML Mapping Table§					
FrameMaker Source Item§	XML Item§			Include Auto#§	Comments§
	Element§	New Web Page?§			
P:Body§	P§	N§		N§	§
P:BodyBold§	BodyBold§	§		§	general macro§

Instead of assigning the general macro to a particular mapping, you can also insert arbitrary HTML/XML code in your document. To do so, define the code as a general macro, then insert a custom marker called HTML Macro in your document where you want the code to appear. In the marker, insert the name of the macro as the marker text.

Converting Structured Documents

When you convert structured documents through the Save As/reference page feature, FrameMaker ignores paragraph tags, character tags, and cross-reference. Instead, the mapping table lets you define mappings for elements and attributes, as shown in the following example:

HTML Mapping Table

FrameMaker Source Item	XML Item		Include	Comments
	Element	New Web Page?	Auto#	
E:Appendix	DIV	N	N	
E:Book	DIV	N	N	
E:Caption	P	N	N	
E:Chapter	DIV	N	N	
E:CodeExample	P	N	N	
E:Emphasis	SPAN	N	N	
E:FrontMatter	DIV	N	N	
E:Graphic	DIV	N	N	
E:GUIItem	SPAN	N	N	
E:Intro	P	N	N	
E:ListItem	P	N	N	
E:MiniTOC	DIV	N	N	
E:MiniTOCItem	P	N	N	
E:MiniTOCTitle	P	N	N	
E:Note	P	N	N	
E:OrderedList	DIV	N	N	
E:Para	P	N	N	
E:Section	DIV	N	N	
E:Title	P	N	N	

Converting with WebWorks Publisher Standard Edition

WebWorks Publisher uses a template-based approach to conversion. You use templates to set up conversion projects. A project consists of the following items:

- A list of files to be converted
- WebWorks Publisher styles
- A mapping list that links the FrameMaker tags to WebWorks Publisher styles

WebWorks Publisher Standard Edition includes the following templates:

- **Portable HTML.** Produces basic HTML files suitable for publishing on the Internet or your company's intranet. Cross-reference formats and other links in your FrameMaker file are automatically converted to hyperlinks. Netscape Navigator version 2 or higher and Internet Explorer version 3 or higher can display the output of this template.

- **Dynamic HTML.** Produces dynamic HTML, which stores formatting information in a CSS file. The Dynamic HTML template provides you with more control over the formatting of the output files. The output of this template is displayed by a version 4 or later web browser.

- **XML+CSS.** Creates XML files plus a CSS file for formatting.
- **XML+XSL.** Creates XML files plus an XSL file for formatting.
- **Microsoft Reader.** Creates a .lit file, an eBook format from Microsoft.
- **Palm Reader.** Creates a .pdb file, an eBook format for Palm OS. To create the final file, you must download a utility. Refer to the readme file included in the template for details.

For any template, the basic conversion process works as follows:

1. You create a WebWorks Publisher project that contains the files you want to convert.
2. WebWorks Publisher converts the FrameMaker files to Maker Interchange Format (MIF). See Chapter 24, "Maker Interchange Format," for more information.
3. WebWorks Publisher scans the MIF files and creates a list of the tags that are used in the files, including paragraph tags, character tags, and table tags.
4. You map the FrameMaker tags to Publisher styles.
5. Publisher generates the output files.

Planning

Before you begin processing your FrameMaker files with WebWorks Publisher Standard Edition, you should plan your conversion:

- If you want to convert related files, such as all the chapters in a book, put those files in a FrameMaker book file.

If you want to convert just one file or many unrelated files, you can use a separate project for each file.

- Update the FrameMaker book so that the cross-references and generated files are current. Be sure that the Create Hyperlinks option is checked for the index and the table of contents files.
- Determine what kind of output you require.
- Locate the files for any company logos or other graphics that you want to use in the header or footer of the output files. The files need to be compatible with the output you are producing (for example, use GIF or JPEG files for HTML output).

Setting Up a Project

In WebWorks Publisher, files are grouped into projects for conversion. A project is somewhat similar to a book in that deleting a file from the project removes it from the listing in WebWorks Publisher but does not delete the file from your system. When you create a project, you can start with a single file or a book.

To create a project, follow these steps:

1. In FrameMaker, select File | WebWorks Publisher Standard Edition to start the application. WebWorks Publisher starts and displays the Project Launcher.

Choose a template here. ⟶

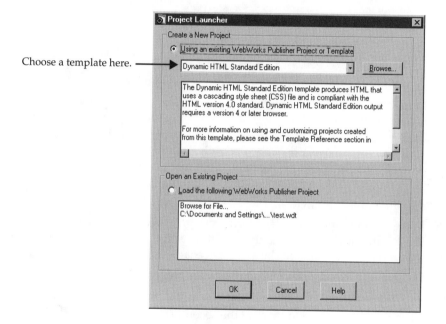

2. In the Create a New Project section, click a template in the Using an Existing WebWorks Publisher Project or Template drop-down list.

3. Click the OK button to begin creating your project. The first screen of the New Project Wizard is displayed.

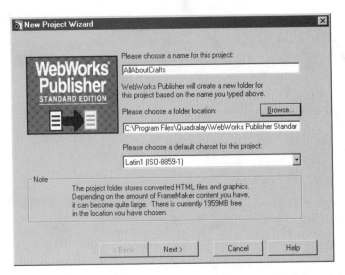

4. In the top field, type a name for the project. Keep in mind that this name will become part of a file name and also a folder name, so use only characters that are permitted for file or folder names on your system. Do not use spaces.

5. In the middle field, type a folder location, or click the Browse button to navigate to the folder where you want to store the project files. WebWorks Publisher will create a subfolder in the folder you specify. The subfolder uses the project name specified in the top field.

6. In the bottom drop-down list, click a character set. For English, French, German, Italian, and other languages that use the Latin character set, click Latin1. Otherwise, choose one of the available character sets:

   ■ Japanese, Korean, and Simplified Chinese for the corresponding languages.

   ■ Unicode for all other languages.

7. Click the Next button to display the second screen of the New Project Wizard.

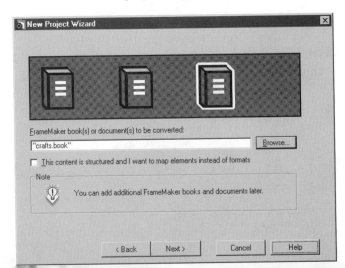

8. Click the Browse button, locate a file or book you want to convert, and click it.

9. If the document is structured, you can choose to map elements and not paragraph and character formats. Click the check box to map elements.

10. Click the Next button to display the third screen of the New Project Wizard.

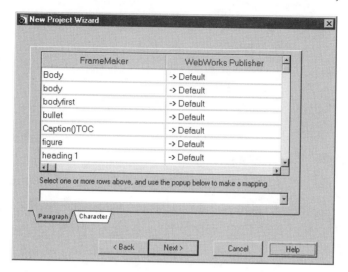

WebWorks Publisher displays a list of paragraph tags (or elements) on the left side of the window. On the right side, it displays the corresponding WebWorks Publisher style.

11. Map the styles as appropriate. Table 19-1 lists the available styles. A few are available only in a specific template, so the list you see will be shorter than this.

Style Name	Description
Default	Used for styles that are not mapped.
Body	For regular body text.
BodyRelative	For body text that needs to be indented the same amount as the preceding paragraph. Often used for paragraphs that continue a bulleted or numbered list.
CellBody	For table text.
CellHeading	For table headings (not table titles; use TableTitle).

Table 19-1. *WebWorks Publisher Paragraph Styles*

Style Name	Description
GroupTitlesIX	Automaps to the GroupTitleIX paragraph style used for headings in the index.
Heading1–4	For first- through fourth-level headings on the page.
Indented1–5	For first- through fifth-level indented text.
IndentedRelative	For text that should be indented one level more than the preceding paragraph.
Level1–5IX	For first- through fifth-level index entries.
NewChapter	For headings that should begin a new section (Palm Reader template).
NewHTMLPage	For headings that should begin a new output page.
NewSubChapter1–4	For headings that should begin new subsections (Palm Reader template).
NoOutput	For paragraph tags that should not appear in the output.
PreformattedRelative	For code and other text that you want to display in Courier with multiple spaces preserved. (Most other HTML styles strip out multiple spaces.)
SmartList1–5	For first- through fifth-level bulleted and numbered lists.
TableTitle	For table titles.
Title	For document titles.
TOC1–5	For first- through fifth-level table of contents entries.

Table 19-1.   *WebWorks Publisher Paragraph Styles (Continued)*

12. Click the Character tab and map the character tags as needed. Table 19-2 lists the available character styles.

Style	Description
Default	For most character tags. The Default style attempts to match the formatting from the FrameMaker file.
IgnoreFormatting	For character tags you want to remove in the output. IgnoreFormatting strips the character formatting.
WebJump	For URLs. Use this style for a FrameMaker tag that's applied only to URLs.

Table 19-2. *WebWorks Publisher Character Styles*

13. Click the Next button to display the last window in the New Project Wizard.

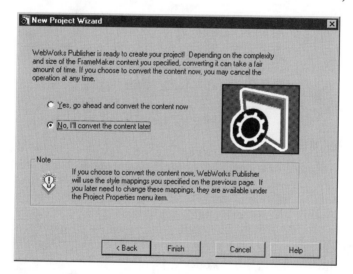

14. You can convert the project now or wait until later. Click the appropriate button, then click the Finish button.

Your project is displayed in the main WebWorks Publisher window.

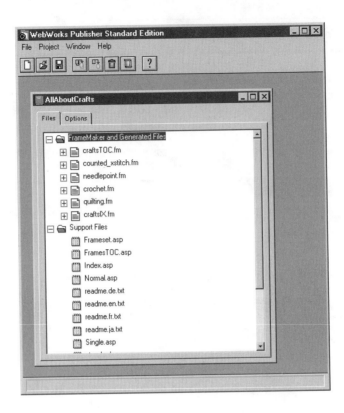

Generating Output

You can generate output for a single file or for the entire project. Generating for a single file is helpful when you want to test the results of a new mapping and don't want to wait for the entire project to generate.

To generate output, do one of the following:

- **For a single file:** Click the file, then select Project | Generate Selected.
- **For the entire project:** Select Project | Generate All.

Customizing Your Project

WebWorks Publisher Standard Edition offers some customization options. The inability to create new styles severely limits your ability to control the output, but you do have some choices. To customize the output, you can do the following:

- Change the mappings
- Change your conditional text settings

- Modify the user macros
- Customize the page templates

The following sections explain each of these options.

Changing the Mappings

You can change the mappings at any time. In addition to the paragraph and character mappings you set when you created the project, you can map table tags and cross-references.

To display and change the mappings, follow these steps:

1. Click the FrameMaker and Generated Files folder.
2. Select Project | Properties. The File Properties window is displayed.

   By default, the paragraph mappings are displayed, but you can click on a tab or subtab to display other mappings.

Click here to map cross-reference formats.

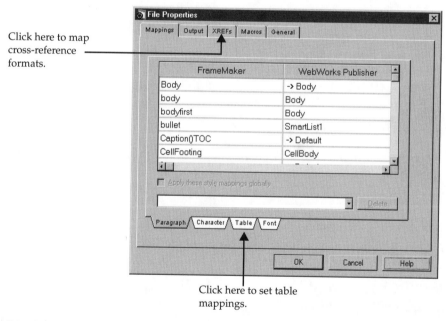

Click here to set table mappings.

Mapping Cross-Reference Formats   Cross-reference formats in print documents often contain page-specific references (for example, *see "Something Important" on page 897*). In online formats, you generally want to keep the link but not the page information. You can eliminate these page references during conversion.

To modify the cross-reference formats, follow these steps:

1. Click the FrameMaker and Generated Files folder.
2. Select Project | Properties. The File Properties dialog box is displayed.

3. Click the XREFs tab to display a list of cross-reference formats used in the files.

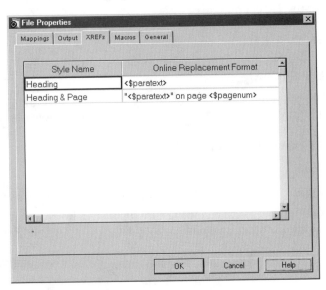

4. For each cross-reference, modify the Online Replacement Format column to produce the online output you want. The building blocks displayed here are FrameMaker building blocks. For example, a Heading & Page cross-reference format might have this initial format:

```
"<$paratext>" on page <$pagenum>
```

To produce a more appropriate format for online use, you could replace this text with the following code:

```
<$paratext>
```

5. Click the OK button to save your changes.
6. Select Project | Generate All to regenerate the files.

Changing Your Conditional Text Settings

You can use conditional text to include or exclude information from the output you generate in HTML. WebWorks Publisher will include any conditional text that's shown in FrameMaker in the output. Hidden conditional text is not included. Therefore, you should set up your FrameMaker files to display all the information needed for the online version and hide all the information that should be excluded from the online version.

Modifying the User Macros

WebWorks Publisher provides several user macros that let you control project settings. The available macros are as follows:

- **UMGraphicDPI:** Sets the resolution of the generated graphics in the output.
- **UMGraphicInterlaced:** Sets the graphics to be interlaced (1) or not interlaced (0).
- **UMGraphicTransparent:** Sets the graphics to be transparent (1) or not transparent (0).
- **UMGraphicJPEGQuality:** Sets the quality of generated JPEG files. Values range from 0 to 100. Higher-quality graphics look better, but result in larger files.
- **UMGraphicLayout:** Controls the alignment and spacing of the graphic.
- **UMGraphicPNGColors:** Controls the color depth of generated PNG files.
- **UMTOCFilter:** Controls the formatting of the table of contents entries. UMTOCFilter is used to strip off page numbers from table of contents entries.

To change the value of a user macro, follow these steps:

1. Click the FrameMaker and Generated Files folder to select it.
2. Select Project | Properties. The File Properties window is displayed.
3. Click the Macros tab.
4. In the Macro Name and Value drop-down list, click the macro you want to change.

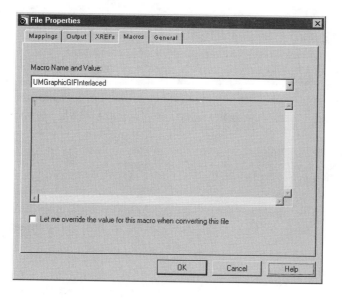

5. Check the Let me override the value for this macro when converting this file check box. The macro value is now editable:

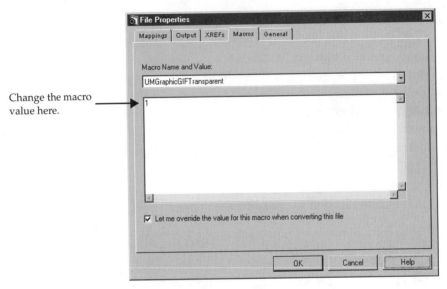

Change the macro value here.

6. Change the macro value as needed in the big field.
7. Click the OK button to save your changes.
8. Select Project | Generate All to regenerate the output.

Customizing the Page Templates

Page templates let you define the "wrapper" that goes around the generated output. Although HTML and other online formats don't technically have headers and footers, you can create repeated information shown at the top and bottom of each output file.

You can use any HTML editor or text editor to customize the templates. Although some of the page templates use .asp extensions, they are HTML files, *not* Active Server Pages.

To modify a page template, follow these steps:

1. Open the page template in your favorite HTML or text editor.
2. Modify the HTML as necessary. Be careful to preserve the $DATA; command, which is where the content of the generated output will be inserted. In the following example, the section in which page content is inserted is shown in boldface.

```
<!DOCTYPE HTML PUBLIC "-//W3C//DTD HTML 4.0 Transitional//EN" "http:/
/www.w3.org/TR/REC-html40/loose.dtd">
<html>
```

```
<head>
<meta http-equiv="Content-Type" content="text/html;
charset=$CHARSET;">
<meta name="GENERATOR" content="$VERSION;">
<meta name="TEMPLATEBASE" content="$TEMPLATENAME;">
<meta name="LASTUPDATED" content="$DATE(c);">
<link rel="StyleSheet" href="standard.css" type="text/css"
media="screen">
<title>$GET_ATTR($PAGE;, title);</title>
</head>


<body background="images/backgrnd.gif">


<table width="331" border="0" align="right" cellpadding="0"
cellspacing="0">
  <tr>
    <td><a href="$PAGEFIRST(html, name, $CHARSET;);"><img
src="images/navtoc.gif" width="84" height="23"
    border="0" alt="TOC"> </a></td>
    <td><a href="$PAGEPREV(html, name, $CHARSET;);"><img src="images/
navprev.gif" width="81" height="23"
    border="0" alt="PREV"> </a></td>
    <td><a href="$PAGENEXT(html, name, $CHARSET;);"><img src="images/
navnext.gif" width="81" height="23"
    border="0" alt="NEXT"> </a></td>
    <td><a href="$PAGELAST(html, name, $CHARSET;);"><img src="images/
navidx.gif" width="85" height="23"
    border="0" alt="INDEX"> </a></td>
  </tr>
</table>


<p><img src="images/wwplogo.gif" width="122" height="63" alt="Put
your logo here!"></p>
<hr align="left">


<blockquote>
<!--BeginHiddenExpansion
  $DATA;
  $NOTES;
EndHiddenExpansion-->
</blockquote>


<hr>
```

```html
<table align="right" border="0" cellspacing="0" cellpadding="0">
  <tr>
    <td align="right"><font size="1">
    <a href="http://www.webworks.com"><img src="images/webworks.gif"
width="150" height="20" border="0"></a><br>
    Quadralay Corporation<br>
    http://www.webworks.com<br>
    Voice: (512) 719-3399<br>
    Fax: (512) 719-3606<br>
    <a href="mailto:sales@webworks.com">sales@webworks.com</a><br>
    </font></td>
  </tr>
</table>

<table width="331" border="0" cellpadding="0" cellspacing="0">
  <tr>
    <td><a href="$PAGEFIRST(html, name, $CHARSET;);"><img
src="images/navtoc.gif" width="84" height="23" border="0"
    alt="TOC"> </a></td>
    <td><a href="$PAGEPREV(html, name, $CHARSET;);"><img src="images/
navprev.gif" width="81" height="23" border="0"
    alt="PREV"> </a></td>
    <td><a href="$PAGENEXT(html, name, $CHARSET;);"><img src="images/
navnext.gif" width="81" height="23" border="0"
    alt="NEXT"> </a></td>
    <td><a href="$PAGELAST(html, name, $CHARSET;);"><img src="images/
navidx.gif" width="85" height="23" border="0"
    alt="INDEX"> </a></td>
  </tr>
</table>

</body>
</html>
```

Converting Graphics

You can convert graphics in one of two ways:

- By copying the referenced graphic over to the output directory
- By processing the anchored frame to create a new graphic

If your FrameMaker document uses graphics that are usable on the web, such as GIF, PNG, or SVG, it makes sense to copy the graphics over to the output folder. This copy action is very fast, and the image quality is better than the result of processing.

If, however, your FrameMaker files use graphic formats that are not usable on the web, such as EPS or TIFF, or if your graphics are copied into the document (not imported by reference), you must convert the graphics. WebWorks Publisher accomplishes this by "printing" the contents of the anchored frame to PostScript and then processing the PostScript to produce GIF, JPEG, or PNG.

Like most other mappings, WebWorks Publisher provides styles for graphics. They are found in the Output tab's Graphics subtab.

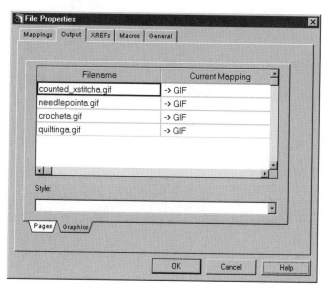

The graphic styles are as follows:

- **GIF:** Creates a GIF file from the contents of the anchored frame.
- **GIFImportedByReference:** Passes through a source GIF file unchanged.
- **GIFWithThumbnail:** Creates a GIF file from the content of the anchored frame and a thumbnail preview.
- **JPEG:** Creates a JPEG file from the contents of the anchored frame.
- **JPEGImportedByReference:** Passes through a source JPEG file unchanged.
- **PNG:** Creates a PNG file from the contents of the anchored frame.
- **PNGImportedByReference:** Passes through a source PNG file unchanged.
- **SVGImported:** Passes through a source SVG file unchanged.

Going Beyond Basic Customization

It's likely that your HTML and XML conversion requirements will go beyond what the Save As feature and WebWorks Publisher Standard Edition can provide. In that case, you need to consider other options:

- For structured files, you can create a structured application. Only structured applications allow you to export and import documents. See Chapter 31, "Importing and Exporting XML/SGML Markup Files," for details.
- Third-party converters give you much more flexibility.
- Scripting utilities (such as Perl) could allow you to write code that post-processes your output to produce exactly what you need.

Each option requires a significant amount of setup time and some scripting expertise. Alternatively, many consultants are available who can help set up "push-button" conversion environments.

Chapter 20

Color Output

FrameMaker lets you create full-color documentation using a rich set of tools. The available colors are stored in a color catalog, which is available through the Paragraph Designer, Character Designer, and many other dialog boxes. You assign color to text or objects by applying tags that contain references to color definitions. For example, to create a purple first-level heading, you assign purple to the Heading1 paragraph tag.

My Purple Paragraph

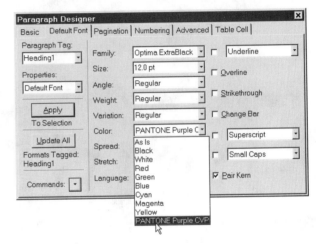

To create blue, underlined cross-references that stand out in PDF files, you create a character tag that applies blue and underlining, then insert the character tag in your cross-reference formats. In the PDF, the hyperlink will be underlined and displayed as blue text.

See "Life and How to Live It" on page 1200.

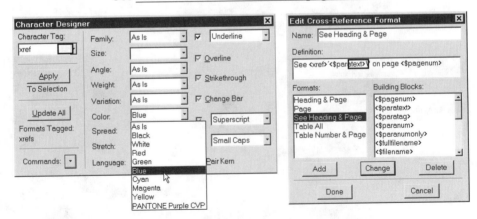

You assign color to some items, such as borders or FrameMaker drawings, by choosing a color in the Tools palette or object properties.

You assign color to objects in the object properties or the Tools palette.

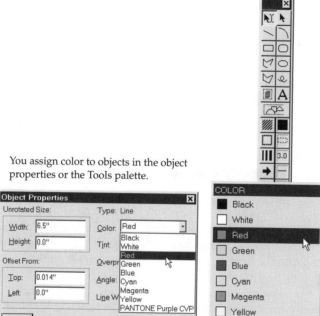

In structured documents, you apply color as you do in unstructured documents, or you can override formatting in an element definition if, for example, a paragraph tag is used in multiple elements, but one element needs a different color.

Understanding Types of Color

In FrameMaker, color definitions are based on one of three color models:

- **RGB.** Defines colors in percentages of red, green, and blue; usually for on-screen display. Colors are displayed in PDFs as RGB colors, and when you convert a FrameMaker document to an online format, images are converted to RGB images.

- **CMYK.** Defines colors in percentages of cyan, magenta, yellow, and black inks (black is the *key* color, thus the "K"). CMYK is for color printing. The four colors are used to print *color separations*—individual pages that describe how to mix cyan, magenta, yellow, and black for four-color printing. Because your computer monitor uses RGB to display colors, the colors you see onscreen do not match colors in print. Ask your print vendor to run a test document or get a swatch book to ensure that you pick the right colors.

■ **HLS.** Defines colors by their location on a color wheel (hue), lightness, and saturation. The amount of red, green, yellow, and blue determines the hue. The intensity of the color determines the lightness. The amount of gray determines the saturation. HLS color should be used only for documents that you plan to convert to online formats, though the color is translated to RGB upon conversion.

RGB, CMYK, and HLS colors are available in *color libraries*. If you plan to print the document, your print vendor typically recommends a color library based on paper quality and texture, ink color accuracy, lamination, and other printing factors. Most color libraries provide CMYK color; however, a few consist only of RGB or HLS color. See "Managing Color Definitions" on page 518 for details.

Understanding Process Color

When you send a document to be printed on a printing press (called *offset printing*), you can use two types of color: *process color* and *spot color*. Process color, or four-color printing, is mixed on the press from cyan, magenta, yellow, and black (CMYK) inks; spot color (described in the next section) is mixed before going to press. Using process color lets you combine the inks on the press to create a wide variety of colors. Process color works well for printing photographs and gradiated images.

To print process color, you create color separations. Each separation describes how to print a single color on the page. For a four-color document, you need four separations for each page:

■ The cyan separation shows only cyan portions of the page.

■ The magenta separation shows only magenta portions of the page.

■ The yellow separation shows only yellow portions of the page.

■ The black separation shows only black portions of the page.

For more economical four-color printing, leave blank pages out of your color separations. See "Skipping Blank Pages" on page 447 for details.

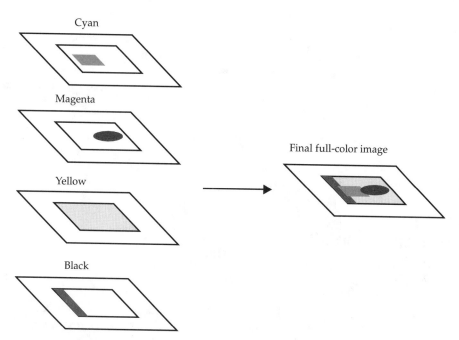

Cyan

Magenta

Yellow

Black

Final full-color image

Separations are burned onto individual plates. Each plate is used to print a single color onto a page. Registration marks allow the print technician to line up the separations correctly. Slight deviations in alignment can cause the color to print in the wrong place, and if the separations aren't aligned, the color combinations do not produce the colors you need. See "Modifying Existing Colors" on page 518 for information on preventing registration errors.

Separations were accurately aligned.

Separations were misaligned, so there is a gap between the overlapping objects.

Separations also define *halftones*—the overlapping grids of dots by which process color is printed. The more dots you include in the halftone, the darker the color. You also specify the angle of the grids, which helps print color smoothly instead of in a checkerboard pattern. Your print vendor might prefer to set up the halftones before going to press, so consult with them before changing halftone screens in FrameMaker.

FrameMaker can create separations only for imported EPS line art, CMYK TIFFs, and Desktop Color Separation (DCS) images. If you have a CMYK bitmap in an EPS file, FrameMaker can create separations if the EPS can also be separated in Adobe Illustrator.

To make sure your colors print correctly before going through the expense of printing to plate, ask the print vendor to print a color proof from a color laser printer. The colors won't be exact, but they'll be close.

Understanding Spot Color

In contrast to process color, spot color is mixed before your job goes to press. Instead of filling the ink wells on the press with CMYK, you use the premixed spot colors on the press. For print jobs that use only two or three colors, using spot colors cuts the cost of printing (because printing three colors is less expensive than printing four colors— fewer separations, fewer plates, fewer layers to keep in registration). If you use process color to produce those same two or three colors, you must set up plates for all four CMYK colors, even though you're mixing them to produce just a few colors.

Spot colors are also useful for printing colors that are outside the CMYK *gamut*; that is, colors that you cannot create by mixing CMYK inks. Metallic or fluorescent inks (neon colors) usually require a spot color because they are outside the CMYK gamut.

If you are using one spot color (plus black) to reduce costs, you can create the impression of additional colors by using *tints*, or lighter versions of a base spot color. Instead of printing a color at full strength, you only print a percentage of the color. For example, 50 percent of a deep blue produces a light slate blue. Because tints use the same base color as the spot color, they are set up on the same separation.

If you're printing images with solid patches of color and can create the necessary color with a few inks, consider using spot color. If your document contains color photographs, though, you'll need to use process color. See "Understanding Process Color" on page 514 for more information.

Applying Color to Text and Objects

You format text and objects with color by deciding on a color in the color catalog and assigning the color in one of the following items:

- Paragraph tags
- Character tags
- Table tags
- Condition tags

- Custom table ruling and shading
- Change bars
- Object properties
- Tools palette

You apply the appropriate tag, edit the object properties, or select the color in the Tools palette. If you modify a color in the color catalog, each item that uses that color is automatically updated. Suppose you create a custom color but decide to reduce the amount of red in the color. You update the color definition, and the color is updated globally—in existing text and objects and those you create later.

Table 20-1 summarizes assigning color to text. Table 20-2 summarizes assigning color to objects.

Item	How to Assign Color	More Information
Paragraph	Select the color in a paragraph tag.	"Modifying Paragraph Tags" on page 112
One or more words	Select the color in a character tag.	"Modifying Character Tags" on page 146
Conditional text	Select the color in the conditional tag definition.	"Creating and Modifying Conditional Tags" on page 547
Variable (all instances)	Type the character tag in the variable definition.	"Creating User Variables" on page 232
Cross-reference style (all instances)	Type the character tag in the cross-reference format definition.	"Formatting Cross-References" on page 200

Table 20-1. *Assigning Color to Text*

Caution   *Don't assign magenta to condition tags. Any time you apply two condition tags to the same text, you get magenta. If you assign magenta to a single condition tag, you won't be able to tell whether the magenta color results from your tag or from two overlapping condition tags, unless you look in the status bar, where the names of the applied condition tags are displayed.*

CREATING OUTPUT

Item	How to Assign Color	More Information
One object	Select the color in the object properties.	"Modifying Objects" on page 336
One or more objects	Select the color in the Tools palette.	"Modifying Objects" on page 336
Table border	Select the color in the custom ruling style definition.	"Changing Ruling Options" on page 177
Change bars	Select the color in the change bar properties, or select the change bar in a character tag.	"Using Change Bars" on page 90 and "Modifying Character Tags" on page 146

Table 20-2.   *Assigning Color to Objects*

Managing Color Definitions

FrameMaker documents contain eight basic colors by default. The color catalog lists them in the following order: black, white, red, green, blue, cyan, magenta, and yellow. You add more colors by doing one of the following:

- Modifying existing colors
- Creating custom colors
- Adding colors from a color library
- Renaming colors

When you paste an object from one document to another, the color of the object is added to the color definitions if it doesn't already exist. Colors defined in imported EPS files are also added to the color catalog. In addition, colors are imported when you open a Word document in FrameMaker. The new colors are named "Color n," where "n" equals the location in the color catalog. You can give the colors descriptive names. See "Renaming Colors" on page 526 for details.

Modifying Existing Colors

To modify an existing color, you move the sliders in the color definition or type a specific value until the color you want is displayed, as shown in Figure 20-1. You can experiment with values and update the color definition when you get the right color. This updates the color throughout the document.

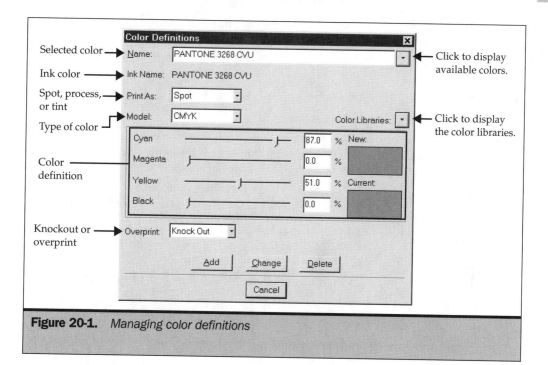

Figure 20-1.   *Managing color definitions*

To modify a color definition, follow these steps:

1. Select View | Color | Definitions. The Color Definitions dialog box is displayed (Figure 20-1).

2. In the Name drop-down list, click the color you want to modify. You cannot modify a default color—the sliders are grayed out, and the color value fields aren't displayed.

3. To change how the color will be printed, click one of the following in the Print As drop-down list:

   - **Spot:** Premixes the color.

   - **Process:** Mixes the color on the press. (Print CMYK colors as process for the best results.)

   - **Tint:** Prints a percentage of the selected color. (Be sure to test the tint. Those lighter than 10 percent don't display accurately and might not print correctly.)

   - **Don't Print:** Prevents colors such as white from printing.

4. To change the type of color, click one of the following in the Model drop-down list:

    ■ **CMYK:** Prints each color in percentages of cyan, magenta, yellow, and black.

    ■ **RGB:** Prints the color in percentages of red, green, and blue.

    ■ **HLS:** Prints the color in terms of the hue, lightness, and saturation.

5. To adjust the color values, do one of the following:

    ■ Click a slider and drag it to the right or left until the color you need is displayed in the New section. Remember that the color will look different in print, so refer to a swatch book.

    ■ Type a specific value in the fields. Most values are percentages, but in the HLS color model, the Hue represents the angle of the color on a color wheel.

Click the slider and drag it to the right or left to change color values.

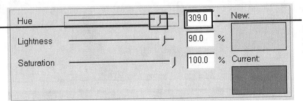

Type the degree at which the hue is displayed on the color wheel.

6. To indicate how FrameMaker prints the overlapping color of two objects, click one of the following in the Overprint drop-down list:

    ■ **Knock Out:** The overlapped portion looks white and doesn't print. Helps prevent the colors of a light object on top and a dark object on bottom from mixing, though the separations must be lined up correctly, or the knocked out piece may appear in the print copy.

The color of the top object is set to "knock out."

The overlapped portion of the square is cut out so that it looks white and won't print.

If separations aren't lined up correctly, the knocked out piece might print.

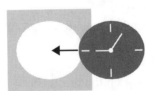

    ■ **Overprint:** Both colors from the overlapped portion of the objects are printed. Helps prevent a gap from printing between objects; however, if the top object is lighter than the bottom object, the two colors might mix.

The color of the
top object is set
to "overprint."

The overlapping portion
of the two objects prints.

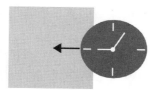

If the object on top is lighter
than the bottom object, the two
colors may appear mixed on
the overlapped piece.

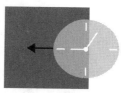

7. Click the Change button. The color definition is updated, and all items formatted with the color are reformatted. (If you modified the definition of a library color, a warning is displayed. Unless you intended to change the library color, click the Cancel button, then click the color in the Name drop-down list to restore the definition.)

Caution

Unless you use a library color as a basis for a new color, you shouldn't modify the definition of a library color. This changes the composition of the ink, so the color won't match the color you chose from the library. If you accidentally change a library color but don't save your changes, you can restore the original definition by clicking the color in the Name drop-down list. The original color definition and ink name are displayed.

Naming Colors

When you add new colors, you need to name the colors consistently. Most colors you choose from a library have an official ink name, but the name doesn't indicate that Pantone 252 CVU, for example, is a shade of pink. You can rename the color before adding it to your color definitions, and the ink name is still displayed in the color definitions.

Colors are easier to manage if you name them based on their function, not their color. Your company's logo color is a good example. Instead of naming the color "Aqua," name it "Logo." If the color changes from aqua to teal, you can update the Logo color definition, import the new color definition into all your files, and the Logo color is instantly updated throughout your documents. If you had named the color "Aqua," you would need to rename the color after changing the definition. See "Renaming Colors" on page 526 for details.

Creating Custom Colors

Instead of choosing a predefined color, you can create your own colors. To do so, follow these steps:

1. Select View | Color | Definitions. The Color Definitions dialog box is displayed (Figure 20-1 on page 519).

2. Do one of the following:

   ■ To base the color on an existing color, click the color in the Name drop-down list.

   ■ To create a unique color, click New Color in the Name drop-down list. "New Color" is displayed in the Name field, followed by a number. The number increments with each new color if you don't change this default name; however, you should name the color something descriptive.

   ■ To type specific RGB values in Windows and Mac OS, click the Color Libraries pop-up menu, click Common Color Picker (Windows) or Apple Color Picker (Mac). On the Mac, click the RGB Picker to display RGB colors. Type the values in the RGB percentage fields, or click and drag the slider, then click the Done button (Windows) or OK button (Mac).

Windows color picker   **Apple color picker**

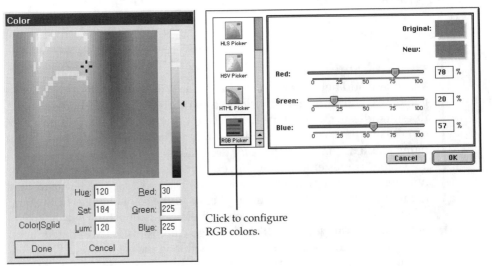

Click to configure RGB colors.

Note   *There is no operating system color picker in UNIX.*

3. Type the name of the new color in the Name field. If you based the color on a default color, the Add button is no longer grayed out.

4. Click the Add button. The new color is added to the document's color catalog.

Do not click the Change button (which is displayed only if you based the color on an existing nondefault color), or you'll rename the existing color definition. See "Renaming Colors" on page 526 for details.

Adding Colors from a Color Library

The color libraries provide predefined colors. Table 20-3 describes the color libraries available in FrameMaker.

Color Library	Description
RGB Color	
Common Color Picker (Windows) or Apple Color Picker (Mac)	Lets you select a color using the operating system's color picker. You can also type specific RGB or HLS values. (UNIX doesn't have a color picker.)
Crayon	Developed by Adobe to provide access to common RGB colors using everyday names in alphabetical order. Do not use Crayon colors as spot colors.
MUNSELL High Chroma Colors and Book of Color	Provides RGB colors in terms of hue, value, and chroma. ■ **Hue:** Shades of red, yellow, green, blue, and purple in ten hue sectors: R, YR, Y, GY, G, BG, B, PB, P and RP (red, yellow-red, yellow, green-yellow, and so on). ■ **Value:** Lightness of the color from 0 (for pure black) to 10 (for pure white). ■ **Chroma:** Saturation level, or the degree of gray in the color, from 0 to infinity.

Table 20-3. *Color Libraries in FrameMaker*

Color Library	Description
Online	Provides 216 "web-safe" colors that have a consistent appearance on all platforms when viewed with a web browser. The colors have a sequential number and a hexadecimal code.
CMYK Color	
DIC COLOR GUIDE SPOT	Provides spot colors; used mostly in Japan.
FOCOLTONE	Provides 860 process colors; helps prevent trapping and registration problems by showing the overprints that make up the colors.
Greys	Developed by Adobe; provides both process and spot shades of gray in 1-percent increments.
PANTONE Coated, PANTONE Uncoated, PANTONE ProSim, PANTONE ProSim EURO, PANTONE Process CSG, and PANTONE Process Euro	Define ink colors in CMYK equivalents. ■ **PANTONE Coated:** For printing on coated paper. The paper coating affects how you perceive the color—color on coated paper looks lighter than color on uncoated paper. ■ **PANTONE Uncoated:** For printing on uncoated paper. ■ **PANTONE ProSim** and **PANTONE ProSim EURO:** For simulating Pantone spot colors onscreen. (ProSim stands for "process simulation.") Use the Euro library for documents printed in Europe. ■ **PANTONE Process CSG** and **PANTONE Process Euro:** For printing process colors. Use the Euro library for documents printed in Europe.

Table 20-3. *Color Libraries in FrameMaker (Continued)*

Color Library	Description
TOYO COLOR FINDER	Provides more than 1,000 colors based on the most common printing inks in Japan.
TRUMATCH 4-Color Selector	Provides more than 2,000 computer-generated colors that predictably match the CMYK color spectrum.

Table 20-3. *Color Libraries in FrameMaker (Continued)*

 You can add a color library to FrameMaker if the library file is formatted in ASCII Color Format (.acf) version 2.1 or earlier, or in Binary Color Format (.bcf) version 2.0. Place the file in the frame7\fminit\color (Windows), $FMHOME/fminit/color (UNIX), or modules:color (Mac) directory, and restart FrameMaker. The library will be displayed with the default color libraries.

To add a color from a color library, follow these steps:

1. Select View | Color | Definitions. The Color Definitions dialog box is displayed (Figure 20-1 on page 519).
2. Click the Color Libraries button. The Color Pickers pop-up menu is displayed. The Windows, Mac, and UNIX color pickers look similar.

3. Click the library you want to display, then do one of the following:
   - Type the first few characters of the color name or number in the Find field.
   - Click and drag the slider.
4. Click the color you need. The name or number of the color is displayed in the top field.

Name of the color library

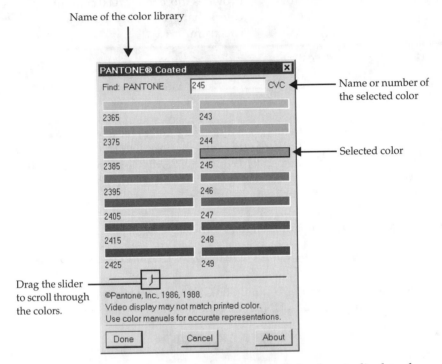

Name or number of the selected color

Selected color

Drag the slider
to scroll through
the colors.

5. Click the Done button. The Color Definitions dialog box is displayed.
6. Click the Add button. The new color is added to the document's color catalog.

Unless you use a library color as a basis for a new color, you shouldn't modify the definition of a library color. This changes the composition of the ink, so the color won't match the color you chose from the library. If you accidentally change a library color but don't save your changes, you can restore the original definition by clicking the color in the Name drop-down list. The original color definition and ink name are displayed.

Renaming Colors

When you rename a color, the name is updated throughout the document. For example, if you rename "Ocean Blue" to "Ocean Green," the new name is displayed instead of the original name where you can assign color—paragraph tags, object properties, and the like.

You cannot rename the eight basic colors; however, color names are case-sensitive, so you can create "green" in addition to the default "Green."

To rename a color, follow these steps:

1. Select View | Color | Definitions. The Color Definitions dialog box is displayed (Figure 20-1 on page 519).

2. In the Name drop-down list, click the color you want to rename.

3. Type a new name in the Name field, then click the Change button. A confirmation dialog box is displayed.

4. Click the OK button. The color is renamed throughout the document.

Note   *If you tried to rename the color using the name of an existing color, that color is displayed. Redisplay the original color and then assign a name that's not in use.*

Viewing Colors

You can configure up to six color views that show and hide specific colors in your document. View 1, the default color view, displays all colors used in the document. You should not modify this view. Each of the remaining views displays specific colors and hides others. For example, you can preview color separations before printing them by creating color views that each display only one color. In the following illustration, a different color view is displayed in each document:

View 1: All colors are displayed in this document.

View 2: The process color of the curtain is displayed in this document.

View 3: The spot color of the windowpane is displayed in this document.

You also set up color views to customize overlapping objects, such as those in the following example. In View 1 on the left, the text color is set to Normal, so the color of the dark object mixes with the lighter overlapping text. In View 2 on the right, the text color is set to Cutout, so the color is displayed accurately. Because View 1 is displayed most of the time, you could set the color of the text to Cutout in View 1.

View 1   View 2

The overlapping text looks slightly   When the text color is set to Cutout,
darker than the true color in the   the color is displayed accurately.
Normal view.

Selecting a Color View

To select a color view, follow these steps:

1. Select View | Color | Views. The Define Color Views dialog box is displayed (Figure 20-2).

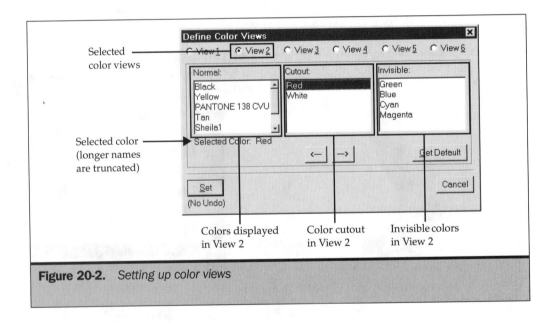

Figure 20-2.   *Setting up color views*

2. Click the radio button for the view you want to display, then click the Set button. The correct colors are displayed, cutout, or hidden in your document.

Setting up Color Views

To set up color views, follow these steps:

1. Select View | Color | Views. The Define Color Views dialog box is displayed (Figure 20-2).

2. Click the radio button for the view you want to modify.

3. Click the color you want to move, then click the left arrow or right arrow button until the color is displayed in the correct section. Your choices are as follows:

   ■ **Normal:** The color prints as normal.

   ■ **Cutout:** The color prints as white on overlapping objects.

   ■ **Invisible:** The color doesn't print.

 Tip   *Press SHIFT while clicking an arrow to move all colors from one section to the other.*

4. Click the Set button. The color view is updated.

Deleting Colors

You can delete any color except the eight default colors. If the color has been assigned in the document and you delete the color, a warning is displayed. You must substitute black for the deleted color or cancel the action.

To delete a color, follow these steps:

1. Select View | Color | Definitions. The Color Definitions dialog box is displayed (Figure 20-1 on page 519).

2. In the Name drop-down list, click the color you want to delete.

3. Click the Delete button. Do one of the following:

   ■ If the color is in use, a warning is displayed. Click the OK button to delete the color and reassign black to the items, or click the Cancel button if you don't want to delete the color.

   ■ Click the OK button to delete the color.

Color for Online Output

Many FrameMaker documents are converted to an online format, such as PDF, HTML, or HTML Help. Conversion often changes the color you chose in FrameMaker—aqua may look more teal onscreen, for example. To avoid this problem, make sure you choose RGB or HLS color for online documentation. If you need to print color separations *and* create online documentation, you can use RGB colors for most FrameMaker graphics and use CMYK only when necessary. You'll need to test the conversion to see if you like the onscreen color. See "Understanding Types of Color" on page 513 for more information.

| **Note** | *All default FrameMaker colors are RGB colors, and the Online, Crayon, MUNSELL, and Common Color Picker libraries also provide RGB colors.* |

The colors you specify in FrameMaker might not convert correctly. Some conversion processes alter color or replace it with a completely different color. Table 20-4 describes how to prevent color conversion problems.

Problem	Solution
Windows converts CMYK color to RGB when converted or printed.	■ Apply CMYK colors in EPS graphics only, which preserve the original colors. ■ Use a Mac. ■ Check converted colors; if unacceptable, convert the color to RGB in FrameMaker.
Distiller might alter color during PDF conversion (for example, it can convert RGB color to sRGB, the RGB color standard optimized for on-screen display.	Create your own Distiller job option profile that leaves the color unchanged. Refer to the Distiller documentation for more information.
Colors in Internet Explorer and Netscape don't match.	Apply colors from the Online color library. They're designed to display uniformly in web browsers.
Colored text is reformatted during WebWorks Publisher conversion.	Match the color in the FrameMaker paragraph tag and the WebWorks Publisher paragraph style mapped to the paragraph tag. See Chapter 19, "Creating HTML and XML Output," for details.

Table 20-4. *Common Online Color Problems*

Color in Structured Documents

Color is a part of paragraph tags, character tags, table tags, custom table formatting, conditions, and drawn objects. You select color in these items, but you can also write element definitions to override the paragraph formatting. This lets the designer create fewer paragraph tags and reuse them throughout the element definition document (EDD), while providing a degree of formatting flexibility. The designer may also specify format change lists, which modifies formatting throughout a document. For example, suppose you apply the BodyIndent element to several paragraphs, but in some rare instances, the text needs to be formatted as green instead of black. The format change list can provide that option.

Objects themselves have no structure, so you can apply any color defined in the document using the Tools palette or object properties. See Table 20-2 on page 518 for details.

For additional information on formatting your document, see Chapter 29, "Understanding the Element Definition Document."

The
Complete
Reference

FrameMaker **7**

Part VI

Advanced Techniques

533

Chapter 21

Setting Up
Conditional Text

Conditional text lets you identify sections as belonging to a particular version of a document. By assigning condition tags to various sections, and then showing and hiding the condition tags in different combinations, you change the information that is displayed. You can maintain two or more versions of the same document in a single file. For example, an instructor developing an exam could set up a file that includes both the exam questions and the answers to the questions. In this scenario, the condition tag ExamAnswers is applied to the answers. The instructor hides the ExamAnswers information to print out the exam for students and then displays ExamAnswers to print out the answer key.

Exam

Question 1: What is Avogadro's number? What is it for?

Question 2: What is the Pythagorean theorem?

Answer Key

Question 1: What is Avogadro's number? What is it for?

Answer: 6.023×10^{23}
Extra credit for describing its use in chemistry. Extra extra credit for using the word "mole."

Question 2: What is the Pythagorean theorem?

Answer: In a right triangle, the square of the hypotenuse is equal to the sum of the square of the other sides.

How Conditional Text Works

When you show and hide conditional text, FrameMaker automatically repaginates the document. Hidden conditional text is collapsed into a single (nonprinting) marker, and the text that follows automatically moves up into the space that the hidden conditional text occupied. When you show hidden conditional text, the text that follows automatically moves down to make room for the newly displayed information.

Conditional text
is showing.

> ### Building Your First Jet¶
>
> Building a jet is fun and easy. You buy the kit for a few million dollars, then spend sev-
> eral years assembling it. This is much cheaper than purchasing those "ready-to-fly" jets
> from aircraft manufacturers.¶
> Joe, I think you might want to be a little more specific here. - Fred¶
> Begin by identifying the model you want to build. Then, you'll need some basic tools.
> Keep in mind that hydraulic work is a little more challenging.¶

Conditional text
is hidden.

> ### Building Your First Jet¶
>
> Building a jet is fun and easy. You buy the kit for a few million dollars, then spend sev-
> eral years assembling it. This is much cheaper than purchasing those "ready-to-fly" jets
> from aircraft manufacturers.¶
> Begin by identifying the model you want to build. Then, you'll need some basic tools.
> Keep in mind that hydraulic work is a little more challenging.¶

Conditional text marker
indicates hidden text.

Do not delete the conditional text marker; this will delete the entire section of hidden conditional text! Fortunately, FrameMaker warns you when you are about to delete a conditional text marker:

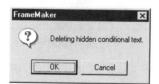

Some Conditional Text Examples

To create two versions of a document, you need two condition tags—one for information that's unique to version A and one for information that's unique to version B. Any information that's common to both versions is not tagged (that is, you leave it unconditional).

A common mistake is to apply all available condition tags to information that's used in all versions. If the information is "global," it does not need a condition tag.

If you're creating FrameMaker documents for print and online delivery, you could create two condition tags: PrintOnly and OnlineOnly. Conceptual information and graphics could be tagged PrintOnly; lists of related topics could be OnlineOnly. The

PrintOnly and OnlineOnly conditions are mutually exclusive—you would not apply both tags to the same information.

When you create additional condition tags, the complexity of managing the versions increases. Consider a situation where you need to document two versions of a single product—a light version and a professional version. The two products are used by different people, so you've decided to create two books: Widget Light User's Guide and Widget Professional User's Guide. The content of the two books is quite similar; the professional guide just contains more information than the light version. For this, you could create a single ProVersion condition tag. But in addition to that, you need to manage the printed and online information, so you also need PrintOnly and OnlineOnly condition tags.

The trouble in this situation arises when you need to tag information with multiple condition tags. When you use multiple conditional text tags on some text, FrameMaker displays the information when *one* (or more) of those tags is set to show. Consider the example shown in Figure 21-1. Some of the ProVersion information is also PrintOnly information. This will cause a problem when you try to deliver the online version of the professional user's guide. You set PrintOnly to be hidden and ProVersion to show. The result? FrameMaker shows the information that's tagged with both tags, even though you do not want this to happen.

The usual solution to this problem is to ensure that you never have multiple conditions applied to a single chunk of text. Instead, you create additional, more specific condition tags. In the example, you would need the following:

Tag	Used for...
ProVersionAll	Professional guide, printed and online versions
ProPrintOnly	Professional guide, printed version only
ProOnlineOnly	Professional guide, online version only
PrintOnly	Professional and light guides, print version only
OnlineOnly	Professional and light guides, online version only

You can use conditional text inside structured documents, but the condition tags are not part of the structure. If you export your document to SGML or XML, shown information is included, and hidden information is excluded. The condition tagging, however, is not exported. If you want to preserve the versioning information, use element attributes to flag information for a particular type of document. See Chapter 29, "Understanding the Element Definition Document," for details about setting up attributes.

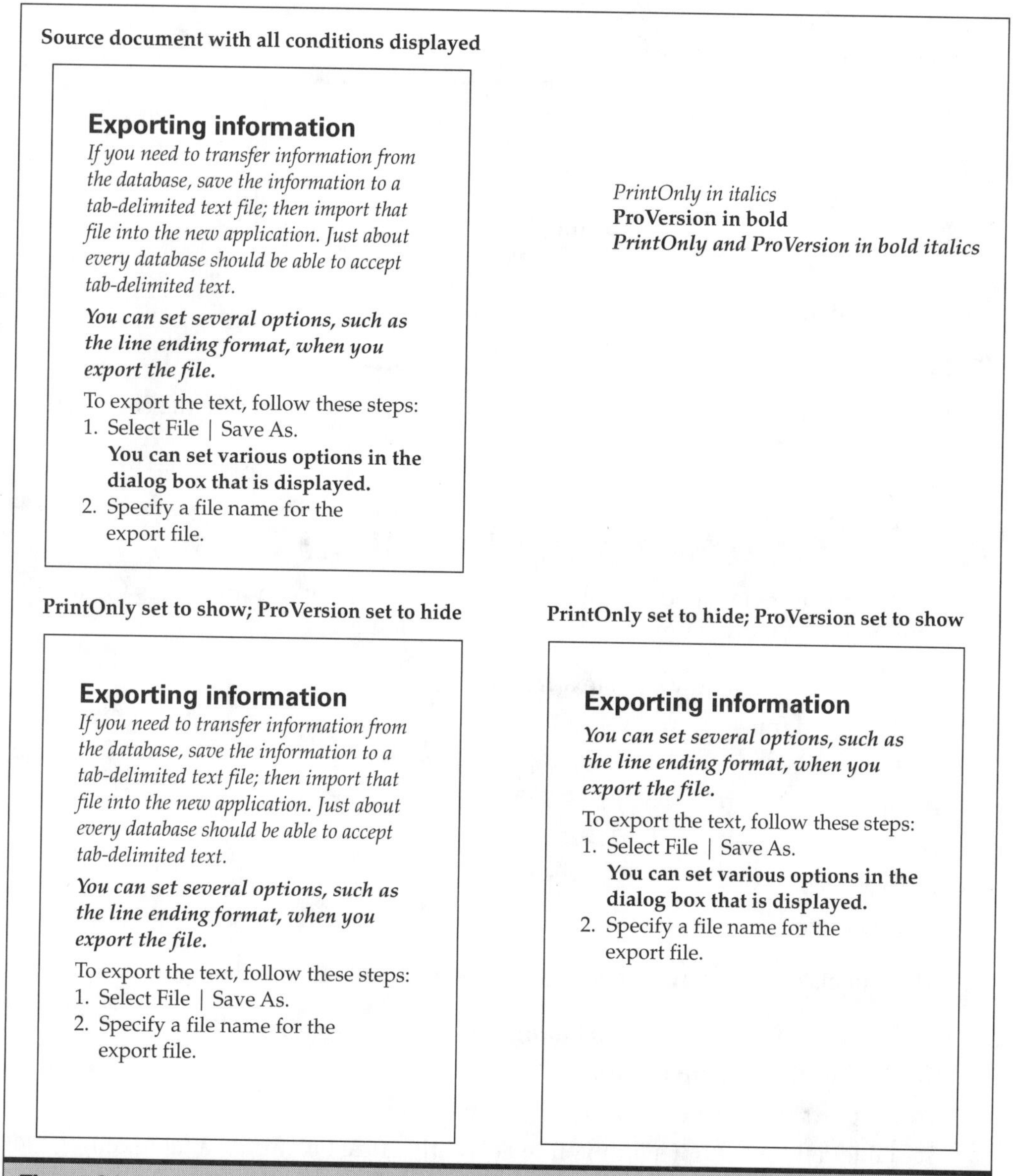

Source document with all conditions displayed

Exporting information

If you need to transfer information from the database, save the information to a tab-delimited text file; then import that file into the new application. Just about every database should be able to accept tab-delimited text.

You can set several options, such as the line ending format, when you export the file.

To export the text, follow these steps:
1. Select File | Save As.
   You can set various options in the dialog box that is displayed.
2. Specify a file name for the export file.

PrintOnly in italics
ProVersion in bold
PrintOnly and ProVersion in bold italics

PrintOnly set to show; ProVersion set to hide

Exporting information

If you need to transfer information from the database, save the information to a tab-delimited text file; then import that file into the new application. Just about every database should be able to accept tab-delimited text.

You can set several options, such as the line ending format, when you export the file.

To export the text, follow these steps:
1. Select File | Save As.
2. Specify a file name for the export file.

PrintOnly set to hide; ProVersion set to show

Exporting information

You can set several options, such as the line ending format, when you export the file.

To export the text, follow these steps:
1. Select File | Save As.
   You can set various options in the dialog box that is displayed.
2. Specify a file name for the export file.

Figure 21-1.   *Problems with overlapping condition tags*

If you are working in structured documents, you will probably use attributes instead of condition tagging. Attributes allow you to classify information. For example, you could set up the following attributes for each section in a document:

Attribute	Values
Platform	Windows Mac UNIX
Output	Print Online
VersionLevel	Professional Light

Each section has a single value for each attribute, which eliminates the complex conditional text setup needed to manage the combinations.

Applying and Removing Condition Tags

Although the feature is called conditional *text*, you can apply condition tags to many different items in your documents, including the following:

- Text in the main flow or in text frames
- Anchored frames
- Table rows
- Markers
- Cross-references
- Variables
- Equations

A few items *cannot* be made conditional. They include the following:

- Text lines or text inside a text line
- Graphic (unanchored) frames
- Graphics that are not in frames
- Table cells or columns (but you *can* conditionalize text inside a table cell)

To apply a condition tag, follow these steps:

1. Select the information that you want to make conditional.
2. Select Special | Conditional Text. The Conditional Text dialog box is displayed (Figure 21-2).

   All of the condition tags that are defined in the document are listed in the Not In list, indicating that the selected text does not have a condition tag applied to it.

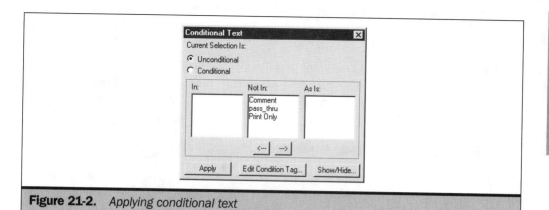

Figure 21-2.   *Applying conditional text*

3. Click the condition tag you want to apply to the selected items, then click the left arrow button to move it to the In list.

4. Make sure that all other condition tags are in the Not In list—unless you want to apply multiple conditions.

5. Click the Apply button. The selected information is now tagged with the condition you chose. You can verify this in two ways:

   ■ Many conditional text tags have colors or special formatting (such as an underline or a strikethrough) associated with them (see page 547). If the formatting of the selected text changes, you know that you applied the conditional text successfully. Keep in mind, though, that this formatting change occurs only if your condition indicators (discussed on page 549) are turned on.

   ■ The status bar indicates the condition tag for the selected text.

In this example, conditional text is red and underlined.

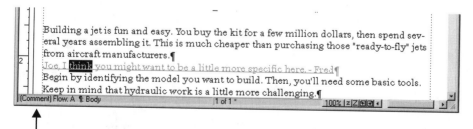

The status bar shows the current condition tag in parentheses.

Using the Keyboard Shortcuts

You can use keyboard shortcuts to apply conditional text. To do so, follow these steps:

1. Select the items that you want to make conditional.
2. Press CTRL-4. The lower left of the status bar displays a ? : prompt.
3. Type in the first few letters of the condition tag, or use the arrow keys to scroll through the list of condition tags.

4. When the tag you want is displayed in the status bar, press ENTER to apply it to the selected text.

Removing a Condition Tag

If you change your mind about a condition tag assignment, you can remove it. This process removes a single condition tag from the selected content. If you have several condition tags applied to the selected content and want to remove all of them at once, it's faster to remove all conditions from the text, as described in the next section.

To remove a condition tag, follow these steps:

1. Select the item from which you want to remove the condition tag.
2. Select Special | Conditional Text. The Conditional Text dialog box is displayed (Figure 21-2 on page 541).
3. Move the condition tag that you want to remove into the Not In list.
4. Click the Apply button.

You can accomplish the same thing using keyboard shortcuts. Follow these steps:

1. Select the item from which you want to remove the condition tag.
2. Press CTRL-5. The lower left of the status bar displays an upside-down question mark.
3. Type in the first few letters of the condition tag, or use the arrow keys to scroll through the list of condition tags.
4. When the tag you want to remove is displayed in the status bar, press ENTER.

Removing All Conditions from Text

To remove all conditions from text, follow these steps:

1. Select the text you want to make unconditional.
2. Select Special | Conditional Text. The Conditional Text dialog box is displayed.

Applying Conditional Text to Tables and Graphics

In tables, you can use conditional text to tag entire rows, or you can apply conditional text to text inside a table cell. You *cannot* apply conditional text to any of the following:

- A column in a table
- A cell or a group of cells in a table

For graphics, you can apply a condition tag to the anchored frame, which makes the entire graphic conditional, and to text inside the anchored frame, provided that the text is in a text frame. You *cannot* apply conditional text to any of the following graphic elements:

- An actual graphic—you must apply the condition tag to the anchored frame that surrounds the graphic. If the graphic is not inside an anchored frame, you cannot make it conditional.
- A text line or part of a text line.
- An unanchored frame.

3. Click the Unconditional radio button.
4. Click the Apply button.

There is also a keyboard shortcut available. Follow these steps:

1. Select the text you want to make unconditional.
2. Press CTRL-6.

*If you want to remove **all** condition tagging throughout a document, show all of the conditional text, and then select the entire document and press CTRL-6. If you do not display all of the conditions, pressing CTRL-6 removes conditions from all of the currently shown text but does not change the hidden conditional text.*

Showing and Hiding Conditional Text

Once you have assigned condition tags in your document, you can show and hide each condition tag individually. FrameMaker dynamically repaginates your document whenever you show or hide information.

To show or hide all conditional text in a book, go to your book file, select all of the files in the book, and follow these steps.

To show or hide conditional text, follow these steps:

1. Select Special | Conditional Text. The Conditional Text dialog box is displayed (Figure 21-2 on page 541).

2. Click the Show/Hide button. The Show/Hide Conditional Text dialog box is displayed.

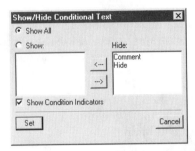

3. To change which conditions are displayed, do any of the following:

   - To show a condition, select it, then click the left arrow button to move it to the Show list on the left.

   - To hide a condition, select it, then click the right arrow button to move it to the Hide list on the right.

   - To display all conditions, regardless of their position in the Show and Hide lists, click the Show All radio button.

Tip   *Showing all conditions is useful when you are revising a document and want to be sure you don't miss anything.*

4. Click the Set button. The document displays the conditions you've specified.

5. *(optional)* Update the book that the file belongs to so that pagination and cross-references are updated.

Caution   *If you hide a cross-reference marker, and the cross-reference that uses the marker is still shown, the cross-reference becomes unresolved. To prevent this problem, be sure that the cross-reference and the cross-reference marker always have the same condition settings. After changing show/hide settings, we highly recommend that you update the book so that the generated files are correct.*

Planning Conditional Text

Before you create condition tags and start making your document conditional, some planning is advisable:

- **Analyze the information and identify the versions that are needed.** Determine which information is common to all versions (unconditional) and what information is needed in a specific version. Set a up condition tag for each version.

- **Use distinct condition tag names.** Using names that are easily distinguished alphabetically makes maintenance easier. For example, instead of using "revision 3" and "revision 4," try "3 revision" and "4 revision." The latter two tags are much easier to distinguish in an alphabetical list. Even better would be something like "April 2003 release" and "December 2003 release."

- **Limit the number of condition tags to the bare minimum.** FrameMaker can handle any number of tags, but the number of styles available as indicators makes smaller numbers more convenient. You can also use custom colors as indicators. See Chapter 20, "Color Output." The limiting factor in creating conditions is not FrameMaker, it's the user's ability to manage and apply the conditions correctly.

Tip   *In a department or workgroup, avoid "tag creep" by ensuring that condition tags are set up and maintained as part of the template. You do not want personal tags—such as JoesFirstDraft—in your documents.*

- **Avoid assigning multiple condition tags to the same information.** Multiple condition tags are very difficult to maintain.

When you begin assigning conditional text, try to keep the tagging as simple as possible. Here are two recommendations:

- **If possible, tag entire paragraphs as conditional.** Conditional paragraphs are much easier to maintain than conditional sentences or words.

- **Tag spaces consistently.** If you are tagging sentences or words, be consistent in whether you tag the space before and after the conditional part. If you are not consistent, when you hide the conditional text, you will have difficulties with missing spaces or two spaces in a row in your document.

If you need to transfer information from the database, save the information to a tab-delimited text file; then import that file into the new application. You can set several options, such as the line ending format, when you export the file. Just about every database should be able to accept tab-delimited text.

When tagging sentences, you must consistently apply condition tags to either the space before or the space after the sentence (but not both) to prevent spacing problems. The same is true when tagging individual words or phrases.

Common Condition Tags

The most difficult part of implementing conditional text is figuring out how to organize your information and set up the condition tags. Here are a few common uses for condition tags:

- **Different product levels.** If your product has entry-level and professional versions, you can break out the differences with conditional text. See page 538 for a detailed example.
- **Information that's under development.** Use conditional text to hide information that isn't appropriate for the current release of the documentation but needs to be included in the next version.
- **Review comments.** You can embed queries to reviewers or comments from reviewers using conditional text. This lets you hide the information and print out a clean draft. (Another alternative is to use a paragraph tag that's hard to miss—we use 14-point bold italic blue text.)
- **Platform differences.** Use Windows, Mac, and UNIX condition tags to manage platform-specific information.
- **Audience levels.** For a training manual, you might need Student and Instructor versions. Use condition tags to manage that information.
- **Delivery medium.** Conditional text is an important component of any single-sourcing effort. Use it to identify information that is delivered in a particular medium; you might have PrintOnly, PDFOnly, and OnlineOnly condition tags.

Alternatives to Conditional Text

In addition to conditional text, a few other techniques are available that let you set up different versions of information inside a document. Consider using these instead of—or in addition to—conditional text:

- **Variables.** For company names, product names, and other short pieces of text that are repeated throughout the document, consider using a variable. See Chapter 9, "Storing Content in Variables," for details.

■ **Marker types.** You can use custom marker types for different types of indexed information. You can then include or exclude those markers when you generate the index. For example, you could use the Index marker type for most index entries and then use a custom RangeIndex marker for ranges (which you want to exclude from the online version of the index).

If you hide a marker inside conditional text, the information in that marker is not available. This means, for example, that an index entry is not generated for a hidden marker.

■ **Graphics.** If you need to create two different versions of each graphic, one approach is to create two anchored frames and make them conditional. Perhaps a more efficient idea is to set up two sets of source graphic files and swap out the directories as needed. To make this work, you must have the same file names and three graphics directories—the directory in use, the directory for version A and the directory for version B. To swap files, you overwrite the content of the "in use" directory with the files from version A or version B.

Creating and Modifying Conditional Tags

Once you have analyzed your content and figured out what conditional tags you need, you're ready to create those tags.

To create a conditional tag, follow these steps:

1. Select Special | Conditional Text. The Conditional Text dialog box is displayed (Figure 21-2 on page 541).

2. To modify an existing tag, click on that tag (it doesn't matter which list it's in at the moment). To create a new tag, do nothing.

3. Click the Edit Condition Tag button.

   The Edit Condition Tag dialog box is displayed with the settings for the selected tag. If you did not select a tag, it displays the default ConditionName tag.

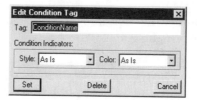

4. In the Tag field, type a name for the condition tag.

5. Set the condition indicators. You can set this conditional text to use a style, such as an underline, a color, or both.

  a. In the Style drop-down list, select a style for this condition tag. If you do not want to use a style, select As Is.

  b. In the Color drop-down list, select a color for this condition tag. If you do not want to use a color, select As Is.

FrameMaker uses magenta to indicate text that has multiple conditions applied. We recommend that you reserve magenta for this purpose—do not use it as the color indicator for a single condition tag.

The colors listed are taken from the color catalog. If the color you want isn't available, add it to the color catalog, and it will show up in this list. For details about adding colors to the document, see Chapter 20, "Color Output."

The colors and styles you assign to your condition tags can be hidden before you print the document. See "Using Conditional Indicators" on page 549.

6. Click the Set button to create (or modify) the condition tag.

Once you create the condition tag, it is listed in the Conditional Text dialog box, and you can apply it to content in your document.

Deleting a Condition Tag

You can delete condition tags from your document. If some text has one condition tag applied to it and you delete that condition tag, you can either delete that text (along with the condition tag itself) or make the text unconditional. If a particular piece of text uses more than one condition tag, the deleted tag is removed from your file, but the text stays in your file with the remaining condition tags still applied.

To delete a condition tag, follow these steps:

1. Select Special | Conditional Text. The Conditional Text dialog box is displayed (Figure 21-2 on page 541).

2. Select the tag that you want to delete.

3. Click the Edit Condition Tag button. The Edit Condition Tag dialog box is displayed and shows that tag's settings.

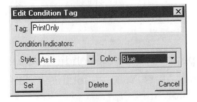

4. Click the Delete button. If the specified tag is the only tag applied to some text in your document, a dialog box is displayed:

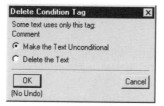

5. To delete the text that uses only this condition tag, click the Delete the Text radio button. To remove the condition tag and make the text unconditional, click the Make the Text Unconditional radio button.

6. Click the OK button to delete the condition tag.

Using Conditional Indicators

The style and colors that your condition tags use are called *condition indicators*. When editing a file on screen, they make it easy to see which information uses which condition tag. When you finalize your materials, though, you probably want conditional text to blend into the surrounding text.

You can turn off condition indicators, which control whether the condition tags provide color and style cues. Turning off condition indicators *does not* change, remove, show, or hide conditional text.

To turn the condition indicators on or off, follow these steps:

1. Select Special | Conditional Text. The Conditional Text dialog box is displayed (Figure 21-2 on page 541).

2. Click the Show/Hide button. The Show/Hide Conditional Text dialog box is displayed.

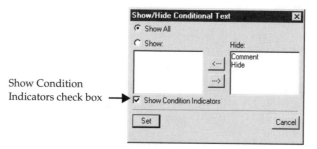

3. Check the Show Condition Indicators check box to display your condition tag indicators. Check the check box again to remove the condition indicators.

4. Click the Set button to apply your changes. Notice that although the text looks like regular text, the status bar still indicates that the text is conditional.

The Complete Reference

Chapter 22

Creating Interactive Documents with Hypertext

Hypertext refers to online documents that are connected with links. In a printed document, you can supply links by instructing readers to "see page 88." The reader then turns to page 164 to find the relevant information. In online documents, hypertext lets you create a live link; to go from one topic to another, the reader clicks on the link and immediately jumps to the new information.

The term *hypertext* is also used for the features that make documents interactive (such as links). FrameMaker provides hypertext commands—for items such as links, pop-up alerts, and image maps—that let you create interactive online documents.

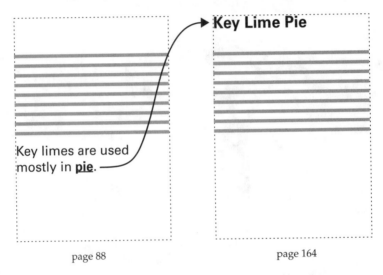

Key Lime Pie

Key limes are used mostly in **pie**.

page 88   page 164

Initially, FrameMaker hypertext was developed for use in view-only FrameMaker documents. The FrameViewer and FrameReader products allow others to read FrameMaker documents and use hypertext features. (The FrameMaker online help in versions 5.5 and earlier uses view-only FrameMaker files with hypertext commands for the links, index, and so on.)

These document readers never really took off, though. Today, most online documents are distributed as PDF (Portable Document Format, also called Adobe Acrobat format) or HTML files.

Hypertext is irrelevant in print but available when you convert FrameMaker files to PDF or HTML. Several of the FrameMaker hypertext commands, however, are only available in native FrameMaker documents. The FrameMaker-only commands are generally refinements of commands that work in other media; for example, the "jump to link" command works in all media but the "jump to link and open in a new window" works only in native FrameMaker files.

FrameMaker hypertext has become a critical part of a single-sourcing strategy because you can embed commands that are ignored in the print version but make the online files interactive.

Hypertext uses hypertext markers extensively. First, you insert a marker to identify a target, or *named destination*, with a keyword. To create a jump to that location, you insert a second marker that points to the named destination.

Link

Key limes are used
mostly in **pie**.

gotolink keylime

The link includes a
reference to a keyword
(in this case, keylime).

Link target

KeyLime Pie

newlink keylime

A marker identifies the
destination with a
unique keyword.

Cross-References vs. Hypertext

Cross-references are a specialized form of hypertext. When you create cross-references, FrameMaker automatically creates links for you, and these are also preserved in PDF or HTML. In many cases, you can use both cross-references and hypertext to accomplish the same goal, and you can use both features in the same document. Here are some things to consider when you decide which feature to use for a particular link:

- You can automatically format cross-references by embedding character formats in the cross-reference definitions. For hypertext, you must apply character formats separately.

- Hypertext lets you make any area of text (or a graphic) a link. With cross-references, you generally need to use the text of the destination or a page reference.

- It's easier and faster to create cross-references. Hyperlinks are more time consuming.

As a general rule, it's a good idea to use cross-references whenever you can and to reserve hyperlinks for those situations where cross-references aren't flexible enough for the job. For example, assume that you have some information about rowing a boat. You can easily create cross-references that look like this:

- see "Rowing a boat" on page 77
- see page 77
- Rowing a boat

You need hypertext commands to create links with wording that doesn't exactly match the text of the heading:

- Before you begin, make sure you know how to row.
- Learn all about rowing.

When creating documents for online distribution, a very common requirement is for a navigation bar. Users click a button in the bar to go to the next page in the document. You can set up hypertext links on the master pages of your document—like page numbers, their result changes for each body page. For example, you can set up a hyperlink with the nextpage command on a master page. On the body pages, the result is a link that takes the reader to the next page. When clicked on page 4, the link goes to page 5; from page 88, it goes to page 89.

This chapter describes how to create interactive hypertext features in your documents.

Setting Up a Basic Hypertext Link

A hypertext link lets the reader click an item and jump to another document or a different part of the current document. To create a hypertext link in FrameMaker, you need to complete three steps (described in detail in the sections that follow):

- Identify the target of the link
- Create a link to the target
- Create the link's active area

Identifying the Target of a Link

To identify a target, you must insert a hypertext marker that creates a *named destination*. A named destination serves as a unique label or identifier for a location in the document.

The named destination is equivalent to the cross-reference marker (with a unique numeric identifier) automatically inserted when you create a cross-reference.

To create a named destination for a link, follow these steps:

1. Click at the location where you want the target. That is, you need to set up a named destination where you want the link to end up.
2. Select Special | Hypertext. The Hypertext dialog box is displayed (Figure 22-1).

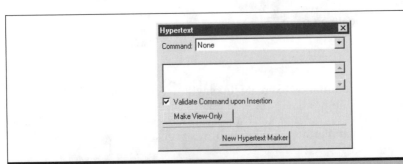

Figure 22-1. *Creating a new hypertext marker*

3. In the Command drop-down list, click Specify Named Destination. This inserts the newlink command into the text field.

*You can type **newlink** into the text field instead of selecting the command.*

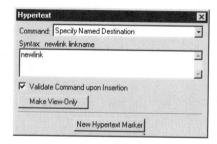

4. Type a name for this destination after newlink. To make maintenance easier, use alphanumeric, lowercase characters. We recommend avoiding spaces and keeping the names as short as possible; however, each named destination within a FrameMaker file must have a unique name. The marker text should look like this:

```
newlink linkname
```

5. By default, the Validate Command Upon Insertion check box is checked. We recommend leaving it checked; FrameMaker will check the syntax of your hypertext command when you create the marker. (If you want to create the gotolink command before the newlink command, validation fails because the destination doesn't exist yet. In that case, you might want to uncheck the validation check box.

Clicking the Make View-Only button changes the entire document to view-only. This could be useful if you want to check hypertext links, but to change the document back to an editable state, you must type ESC SHIFT-F L K.

6. Click the New Hypertext Marker button to insert the new named destination. A new hypertext marker is created at the cursor location. The marker stores the named destination information for you.

Creating a Link to the Target

After identifying the link's destination, you create the link itself. You can create links within a single file or from one file to another.

If you create cross-file links, you must deliver all of the files to the customer. If FileA links to FileB, you must ship FileA and FileB to your readers. If you forget to send FileB, readers will encounter a broken link.

To create a hypertext link, follow these steps:

1. Position your cursor in the text where you want the link to occur. If the files are going to be sent out for translation, the translators will appreciate markers at the beginning or end of a word instead of in the middle of words.

2. Select Special | Hypertext. The Hypertext dialog box is displayed (Figure 22-1 on page 554).

3. In the Command drop-down list, click Jump to Named Destination. This inserts the gotolink command into the text field.

*You can type **gotolink** into the text field instead of selecting the command.*

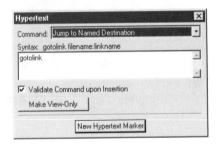

4. Type in the destination after gotolink. The *linkname* corresponds to the keyword you set up in the preceding section with the newlink command.

   For links within a file, use this syntax:

   ```
   gotolink linkname
   ```

   For links to another file in the same directory, use this syntax:

   ```
   gotolink file.fm:linkname
   ```

   For links to a file in a different directory, use this syntax (be sure to use forward slashes and not backward slashes in the path name):

   ```
   gotolink path/file.fm:linkname
   ```

5. Click the New Hypertext Marker button to insert the hypertext marker.

Creating the Active Area in Text

The active area is the "clickable" section of text that lets you use the hypertext link.

Key limes are used mostly in pie.

The word "pie" is the active area.

When you create a hypertext link, FrameMaker creates an active area in the paragraph where the link occurs. By default, the active area is the entire paragraph, but if you have any character tag formatting inside the paragraph, the active area stops where the character tag changes. If you want an entire paragraph to be active, the paragraph cannot contain any character tags or formatting overrides.

If you're delivering your files as PDFs for online viewing, consider setting up a special Hyperlink character tag, which sets the text to blue and underlined.

Tip *If you want to create active areas on a graphic, see "Creating Image Maps."*

To specify an active area, follow these steps:

1. Select the text you want to make active. The selected area must contain the hypertext marker you set up in the preceding section.

2. Apply a character format to the text. If you do not want the appearance of the text to change, create a character format in which every attribute is set to As Is and apply that.

Testing Links

To verify that links are working, you can test them. Do one of the following:

- **Windows.** Press and hold CTRL-ALT and move the cursor over the link. The cursor turns into a hand. Click on the link.

- **Mac.** Press and hold COMMAND-OPTION and move the cursor over the link. The cursor turns into a hand. Click on the link.

- **UNIX.** Press and hold CTRL and move the cursor over the link. The cursor turns into a hand. Right-click on the link.

If you need to test a large number of links, you may want to convert the document to a view-only document. In view-only documents, you click on links without holding down additional keys. To convert a document from editable to view-only, press ESC SHIFT-F L K. Repeat the key sequence to convert from view-only back to a regular, editable document.

Creating Image Maps

An image map is a graphic that links you to different locations based on where the reader clicks on the image. One very common use for image maps is a navigation bar with graphic elements that link to the next, previous, first, and last pages in the document.

Each section of the graphic provides a link: to the first page, previous page, next page, and last page.

FrameMaker provides two ways of creating image maps:

- If you need to divide the image into a grid with equally sized boxes, you can use a button matrix.
- If the active areas you want to create on the image are different sizes, you use text frames to identify each active area and insert a hypertext marker in the text frame.

These techniques are described in the sections that follow.

Unfortunately, button matrices are not supported in PDF. When you convert to HTML, the button matrix is converted only if the referenced flow is inside an anchored frame that's part of the main flow (which you wouldn't usually do because the referenced flow would be output as a graphic). For PDF and HTML, you would generally create active areas on the graphic using the second procedure.

Setting Up a Button Matrix

A button matrix is a grid that overlays the graphic. This feature is used most often for a group of evenly sized buttons with different options, such as a navigation bar.

To create a button matrix, follow these steps:

1. Select View | Reference Pages to go to the reference pages.

2. Create a new text frame on any reference page by clicking the Text Frame icon on the Graphic toolbar and drawing a frame on the page. The frame needs to be large enough to hold some hypertext commands, but doesn't have to match the graphic or be any particular size.

3. Select the frame (CTRL-click for Windows and UNIX, OPTION-click for Mac), then select Graphics | Object Properties. The Customize Text Frame dialog box is displayed (Figure 22-2).

4. In the Flow Tag field, type a name for the flow. The flow name cannot have any spaces. For example, for a collection of buttons that provide navigation, you could use NavBar.

5. Click the Set button to save the flow name and close the Customize Text Frame dialog box.

6. In the newly named text frame, type a hypertext command for each section of the matrix, one per line. The commands listed here correspond to the buttons row by row, column by column.

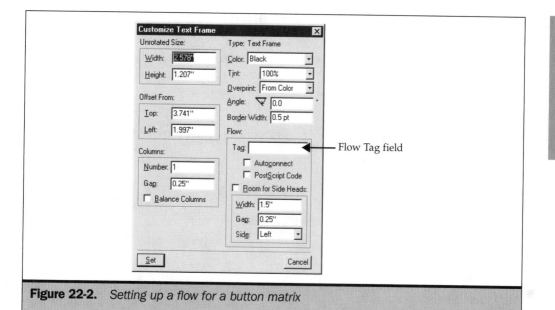

Figure 22-2. *Setting up a flow for a button matrix*

For a navigation bar, you might use the following commands:

```
firstpage
previouspage
nextpage
lastpage
```

7. Now, return to the body or master pages and locate your graphic. Draw a text frame on top of the graphic that's the same size as the graphic. FrameMaker will use this text frame to create a grid of link areas.

8. Position your cursor inside the text frame.

9. Select Special | Hypertext. The Hypertext dialog box is displayed (Figure 22-1 on page 554).

10. In the Command drop-down list, click Button Matrix. FrameMaker inserts the matrix command in the marker text field.

11. Specify the number of rows, number of columns, and the name of the flow you set up for the button matrix. For example, to create a button matrix with one row and four columns that uses the NavBar flow, type in:

```
matrix 1 4 NavBar
```

12. Click the New Hypertext Marker button to insert the marker.

The button matrix now provides different links for different parts of your graphic.

Creating Active Areas on a Graphic

Instead of creating a regular grid of active areas, you can set up a rectangular active area. To set up this type of active area, you must set up the destination with a newlink command as described on page 554. Then, you activate the graphic (or a portion of the graphic) with a text frame that contains the corresponding gotolink command.

To create an active area on a graphic, follow these steps:

1. Draw a text frame on top of the graphic. The dimensions of the text frame will become the active area on the graphic.

2. Position your cursor inside the text frame.
3. Create a hypertext marker in the text frame as described in "Creating a Link to the Target" on page 555.

   When you create an active area on a graphic, you insert only the hypertext marker in the text frame. You do not need any text in the frame.

Creating a Link to a Web Address

You can create links that point to a web address. When the link is displayed in FrameMaker, clicking it launches the default web browser. In PDF files, web links require that the Acrobat Reader be configured to handle web links. If the Reader is configured properly, clicking a web link displays the web page.

To create a web link, follow these steps:

1. Create an active area for the link, either with character tagging or by creating a text frame on top of a graphic.
2. Position your cursor in the active area.
3. Select Special | Hypertext. The Hypertext dialog box is displayed (Figure 22-1 on page 554).
4. In the Command drop-down list, click Go to URL. This inserts the message URL command into the text field.

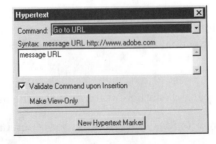

5. Type in the web address after message URL. For example:

```
message URL http://www.scriptorium.com
```

6. Click the New Hypertext Marker button to insert the marker.

Creating Pop-Up Alert Messages

FrameMaker provides two hypertext commands that let you create alert messages. Alert messages are not supported in HTML, and they are displayed in PDF as notes. You could, for example, include alert messages in a draft document where information is not yet available.

An alert message without a title. FrameMaker automatically puts "FrameMaker" in the title bar.

An alert message with a title. You can specify a title for the title bar in the hypertext command.

To create an alert message, follow these steps:

1. Create an active area for the link, either with character tagging or by creating a text frame on top of a graphic.

2. Position your cursor inside the active area.

3. Select Special | Hypertext. The Hypertext dialog box is displayed (Figure 22-1 on page 554).

4. In the Command drop-down list, select one of the Alert commands:

   ■ To create a pop-up message with no title, choose Alert. This inserts the alert command into the text field.

   ■ To create a pop-up message with a title in the title bar, choose Alert with Title. This inserts the alerttitle command into the text field.

5. Type the alert message in the marker text field. The limit is 255 characters. For example, to create a plain alert with the message "Not yet available", use this syntax:

```
alert Not yet available
```

To create an alert with a title, type in the title, then a colon, and then the alert text:

```
alerttitle Beta Software:Not yet available
```

6. Click the New Hypertext Marker button to insert the hypertext marker.

Creating Pop-Up Menus

Use the popup hypertext command to create a pop-up menu with a series of choices. Each choice is linked to a particular hypertext command. Pop-up menus are not supported in PDF or HTML output; they work only in FrameMaker files.

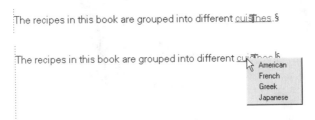

Like the button matrix command, the popup command uses a flow on the reference pages for the list of commands.

To create a pop-up menu, follow these steps:

1. On the reference pages, create a special reference page flow for the pop-up menu commands. For detailed instructions, see the information in the button matrix section: steps 1–5 on page 558.

2. Position your cursor in the new text frame.

3. For each pop-up menu item, insert the menu name and the corresponding hypertext command.

Reference page flow   Hypertext marker for the American entry.

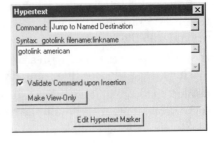

The pop-up menu choices can themselves contain submenus. To set this up, use the popup command in the hypertext commands. You cannot nest more than two levels of menus.

4. At the location where you want to create the pop-up menu, create an active area in text or on a graphic.

5. Position your cursor inside the active area.

6. Select Special | Hypertext. The Hypertext dialog box is displayed (Figure 22-1 on page 554).

7. In the Command drop-down list, click Popup Menu. FrameMaker inserts the popup command in the marker text field.

8. Specify the name of the flow you set up for the pop-up menu. For example, if you labeled the flow Links, insert the following:

```
popup Links
```

9. Click the New Hypertext Marker button to insert the marker.

Hypertext Links in Generated Files

When you set up indexes, tables of contents, and other generated files, you can specify that entries in the file be hypertext links by checking the Create Hypertext Links check box when you set up the generated file. (For complete instructions, see "Setting Up the Table of Contents File" on page 390.) After the generated file is created, the reader can jump from a page number in the file to the referenced item like any other hypertext link.

Creating Read-only Hypertext FrameMaker Documents

Most hypertext development is intended for PDF and HTML files that you produce from FrameMaker, but another hypertext option is to create read-only FrameMaker documents. As in standard FrameMaker documents, cross-references and page numbers in generated documents are hypertext links, but all the other hypertext commands are also "live." FrameMaker read-only documents support all of the hypertext commands, whereas PDF and HTML only support some.

To view these files, end users must have a copy of FrameMaker. Any fonts in the documents must also be installed on the end user's machine. For these reasons, read-only FrameMaker documents are not as popular as PDF.

Note   *In earlier versions of FrameMaker, view-only "reader" products were available (FrameViewer and FrameReader). These are no longer supported for version 7.*

To create a read-only file, you first insert all the cross-references and hypertext commands you want and then follow these steps:

1. Using the View menu, turn off all the non-printing symbols, such as Borders, Text Symbols, and Element Boundaries.

2. Select File | Save As. The Save dialog box is displayed.

3. In the Format drop-down list, click View Only.

4. Click the Save button to save the document in View Only format.

To toggle between view-only and editable formats in an open document, press ESC SHIFT-F L K.

Implementing Additional Interactive Features in PDF

If you plan to deliver your document as a PDF, then interactivity is not limited to creating cross-references and hypertext commands. You can also use pdfmark commands to further customize your documents. Detailed information about pdfmark is available in Adobe's online user documentation (installed in the help directory of your Adobe Acrobat folder).

Briefly, pdfmark is a special command for embedding information in PostScript files. When Acrobat Distiller processes the PostScript files, it reads the pdfmark commands and adds special features to the resulting PDF files. Using pdfmark, you can implement movies, sounds, annotations, forms, and much more.

You can embed pdfmark commands in FrameMaker using PostScript text frames. Follow these steps:

1. On the page where you want the pdfmark command to occur, draw a text frame.
2. Insert the pdfmark code into the text frame. Refer to Adobe's documentation for details about pdfmark commands.
3. CTRL-click (Windows or UNIX) or OPTION-click (Mac) to select the text frame.
4. Select Graphics | Object Properties. The Customize Text Frame dialog box is displayed.
5. In the Flow section, check the PostScript code check box. This tells FrameMaker to interpret the contents of the frame as PostScript code.

After setting up the PostScript text frame, you cannot edit the contents. Uncheck the PostScript code check box to make any changes.

For more details about advanced FrameMaker-to-Acrobat conversion techniques, we recommend that you consult www.microtype.com.

Hypertext Command Reference

Table 22-1 lists the hypertext commands you can use to create active areas. All of these commands work in read-only FrameMaker documents, and most work in HTML and PDF format, as noted in the table.

In addition to the gotolink command, which lets you jump to a specific named destination, an openlink command is available. In FrameMaker documents, openlink displays the link target in a new window, but in documents converted to PDF and HTML, openlink and gotolink have the same effect—the new information replaces the information in the current window. If you use hypertext only for PDF and HTML documents, you can safely ignore all of the openlink commands.

Feature	Works in...	Description and Syntax
Alert	FrameMaker; displayed as a note in PDF	Displays an alert box. `alert message of up to 255 characters`
Alert with Title	FrameMaker; displayed as a note in PDF; title is ignored	Displays an alert box with a title. `alerttitle message of up to 255 characters`

Specify Named Destination	All output	Defines a name used to create a link to the marker location.
		`newlink linkname`
		`newlink filename:linkname`

Jump to Named Destination	All output	Displays content that contains the named link.
		`gotolink linkname`
		`gotolink filename:linkname`

Jump to Named Destination & Fit to Page	All output; doesn't fit to page for PDF or HTML	Displays destination and fits to page.
		`gotolinkfitwin linkname`
		`gotolinkfitwin filename:linkname`

Jump to First Page	FrameMaker; PDF	Displays first page of specified document.
		`gotolink firstpage`
		`gotolink filename:firstpage`

Jump to Last Page	FrameMaker; PDF	Displays last page of specified document.
		`gotolink lastpage`
		`gotolink filename:lastpage`

Jump to Page Number	FrameMaker; PDF	Displays specified page.
		`gotolink pagenumber`
		`gotopage filename:pagenumber`

Jump to Previous Page	FrameMaker; PDF	Displays previous page reader viewed. `previouspage`
Jump to Next Page	FrameMaker; PDF	Displays next page of current document. `nextpage`

Table 22-1. *Hypertext Commands*

Feature	Works in...	Description and Syntax
Jump Back	FrameMaker	Displays location last viewed. `previouslink`
Jump Back and Fit to Page	FrameMaker	Displays location last viewed and fits to page. `previouslinkfitwin`

Open Document	All output	Displays another page of current or different document.
		`openlink linkname`
		`openlink filename:linkname`

Open Document & Fit to Page	All output; doesn't fit to page for HTML or PDF	Displays another page of current or different document and fits to page.
		`openlinkfitwin linkname`
		`openlinkfitwin filename:linkname`

Open Document at First Page	All output; doesn't open new window for PDF or HTML	Displays first page of current or different document.
		`openlink firstpage`
		`openlink filename:firstpage`

Open Document at Last Page	All output; doesn't open new window for PDF or HTML	Displays last page of current or different document.
		`openlink lastpage`
		`openlink filename:lastpage`

Open Document at Page Number	All output; doesn't open new window for PDF or HTML	Displays specific page number of current or different document.
		`openpage pagenumber`
		`openpage filename pagenumber`

Open Document as New	All output; doesn't open new window for PDF or HTML	Opens file as untitled document. `opennew filename`

Table 22-1. *Hypertext Commands (Continued)*

Feature	Works in...	Description and Syntax
Popup Menu	FrameMaker	Displays a pop-up menu containing hypertext links as choices. `popup flowname` See "Creating Pop-Up Menus" on page 562 for details.

Button Matrix	FrameMaker; HTML only if the flow is in an anchored frame in the main text flow	Allows reader to select from a matrix to run hypertext commands.
		`matrix number_of_rows`
		`number_of_columns flowname`

Go to URL	All output	Opens a web address. `message URL web_address`
Message Client	FrameMaker	Communicates with other applications. `message clientname parameters`
Close Current Window	FrameMaker	Closes current viewer window. `quit`
Close All Hypertext Windows	FrameMaker	Closes all viewer windows. `quitall`
Exit Application	FrameMaker	Exits application. `exit`

Table 22-1. *Hypertext Commands (Continued)*

Chapter 23

Writing Equations

I n FrameMaker, you can write complex equations, such as those found in scientific or mathematical documents. Equations consist of operators, alphanumeric characters, symbols, text strings, and other math elements.

$$(x \times y)^2 = y \qquad area = \pi r(\ )^2 \qquad \frac{(9+3)}{6}$$

To write an equation, you type the math elements or use the Equations palette to insert the items. For example, consider the following equation:

$$\log_a \Delta = \frac{\ln \Delta}{\ln a}$$

To write this equation, you first create a high-level approximation of the equation, as shown here:

$$? = \frac{?}{?}$$

You then replace the question marks with symbols, functions, and other math elements.

Equations are displayed in anchored or graphic frames. You can move an equation inside the frame by selecting the equation and using keyboard shortcuts or commands in the Equations palette. You can also shrink-wrap anchored frames to remove extra space between the frame and equation.

In a structured document, you write equations by inserting an equation element. FrameMaker inserts an anchored frame on the page, and you write the equation. The equation element is displayed in the structure view as a child of the element to which it's anchored.

In this chapter, the term "math element" describes math symbols and characters in general, not an element in a structured document.

Understanding the Equations Palette

Symbols, operators, delimiters, and other math elements are displayed in the Equations palette (Figure 23-1). Select Special | Equations or click the Equations icon in the upper-right corner of the FrameMaker window to display the Equations palette. The palette is divided into nine pages for each type of math element or command. You click one of the buttons to display the appropriate page, and then you click a button in the palette.

Table 23-1 describes each page in the Equations palette.

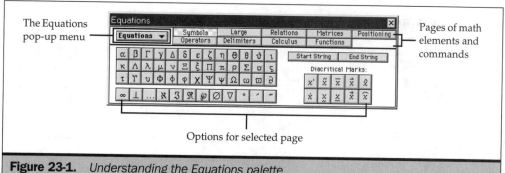

Figure 23-1. *Understanding the Equations palette*

Category	Description	Page
Symbols	Greek characters, atomic symbols, diacritical marks, and strings	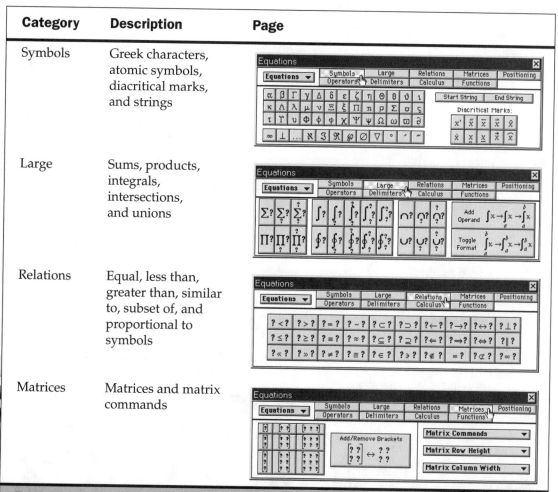
Large	Sums, products, integrals, intersections, and unions	
Relations	Equal, less than, greater than, similar to, subset of, and proportional to symbols	
Matrices	Matrices and matrix commands	

Table 23-1. *Equations Palette Pages*

Category	Description	Page
Positioning	Micropositioning, alignment, line breaks, and spacing options	
Operators	Roots, powers, signs, subscripts, superscripts, and logic symbols	
Delimiters	Parentheses, brackets, braces, and substitution symbols	
Calculus	Integrals, derivatives, partial derivatives, gradients, and limit symbols	
Functions	Trigonometric, hyperbolic, and logarithm functions; commands for evaluating expressions and for creating and applying rules	

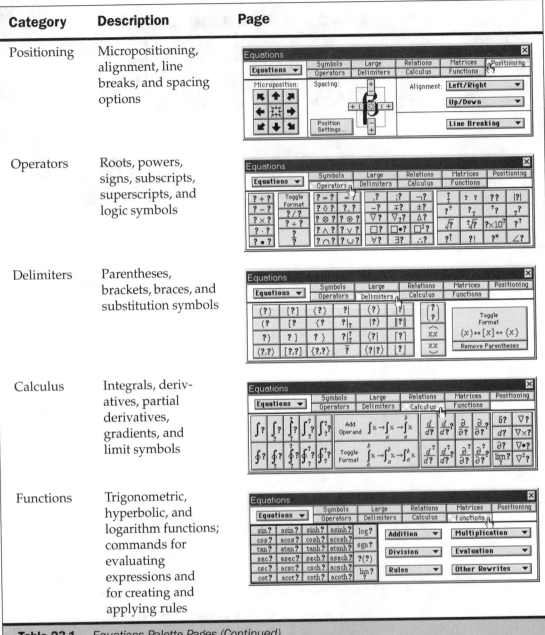

Table 23-1. *Equations Palette Pages (Continued)*

ADVANCED TECHNIQUES

Inserting Equations

Equations inserted in empty paragraphs, as shown in the following example, are called *display equations*.

Figure the square footage by solving the following equation:

$$l \times w = h$$

When inserted in sentences, as shown in the following example, equations are called *inline equations*.

Figure the square footage by calculating $l \times w = h$.

To insert an equation, follow these steps:

1. Do one of the following:

   ■ To create a display equation, position your cursor in an empty paragraph:

   Cursor ⟶ Figure the square footage by solving the following equation:

   ■ To create an inline equation, position your cursor where the equation should begin:

   Figure the square footage by calculating

   ↑
   Cursor

    ■ To create an equation in a graphic frame, select Graphics | Tools to display the Tools palette, click the Graphic Frame icon, then draw a frame on the page. Select the frame before proceeding.

2. Select Special | Equations, or click the Equations icon in the upper-right corner of the FrameMaker window. The Equations palette is displayed (Figure 23-1 on page 571).

3. In the Equations drop-down list, click the size of the equation you want to insert. The equation size is determined by the default font size and spread in the Equations Sizes dialog box. See "Changing Equation Font Sizes" on page 583 for details. Choices are as follows:

   ■ New Small Equation
   ■ New Medium Equation
   ■ New Large Equation

Note   *You can change the size of the equation later in the object properties if you don't like the size you selected. See "Changing the Equation Size" on page 585 for details.*

An *equation object* is displayed as a highlighted question mark. (The outline in the next example shows the location of the anchored frame.)

$$\boxed{\qquad\qquad ?\qquad\qquad}$$

4. Do one of the following:

   ■ Click math elements and commands in the Equations palette to replace the equation object with your equation.

   ■ Type the equation in place of the equation object.

   The next sections show how to write the following equation using each method:

$$? \longrightarrow \frac{8}{2} + \frac{10}{5} = 6$$

Using the Equations Palette

To use the Equations palette to write the preceding equation, follow these steps:

1. CTRL-click (Windows and UNIX) or click (Mac) the equation object, or press the SPACEBAR. The equation object is selected.

$$?$$

2. Click the Operators button in the Equations palette, then click the ⬛?-?⬛ button. The object is updated.

$$? = ?$$

3. With the question mark on the far left selected, click the ⬛?+?⬛ button. The object is updated.

$$? + ? = ?$$

4. With the question mark on the far left selected, click the ⬛?/?⬛ button. The object is updated.

$$\frac{?}{?} + ? = ?$$

5. Press the TAB key until the next single question mark is selected, then click the ⬛?/?⬛ button. The object is updated, and the final structure of the equation object is displayed.

$$\frac{?}{?} + \frac{?}{?} = ?$$

6. Type the numbers in the equation; press the TAB key to move between objects.

$$\frac{8}{2} + \frac{10}{5} = 6$$

Note *Though you must calculate equations, FrameMaker can transform selected expressions to alternate formats. See "Evaluating Equations" on page 585 for details.*

7. For equations in anchored frames, remove extra space between the frame and equation by selecting Shrink-Wrap Equation in the Equations pop-up menu or by pressing ESC M P. If you change the size of the equation fonts, the shrink-wrapped equations are automatically shrink-wrapped again to fit the new font sizes.

$$\frac{8}{2} + \frac{10}{5} = 6 \qquad \longrightarrow \qquad \frac{8}{2} + \frac{10}{5} = 6$$

Note *When you shrink-wrap an anchored frame, the anchoring position changes to At Insertion Point. You might need to reposition the frame based on where you want the equation displayed. See "Anchoring Graphics" on page 300 for details.*

Typing an Equation

If you're writing a simple equation or know the keystrokes, you might want to type the equation instead of using the Equations palette. To do so, follow these steps:

1. CTRL-click (Windows and UNIX) or OPTION-click (Mac) the equation object. The equation object is highlighted.

2. Type **8/2**. The fraction is displayed.

$$\frac{8}{2}$$

3. Press the SPACEBAR twice to select the equation, then type **+10/5**. The object is updated.

$$\frac{8}{2} + \frac{10}{5} = ?$$

4. Press the SPACEBAR twice to select the equation, then type =6. The final equation is displayed.

$$\frac{8}{2} + \frac{10}{5} = 6$$

To type text in an equation, click the Symbols page in the Equations palette, and then click the Start String button. Quotes are displayed, and when you type text, the text replaces the quotes. Click the End String button to close the text string.

Selecting Equations and Math Elements

You can select an entire equation as you do other objects, or you can select specific math elements. In individual equations, the location of the insertion point determines which characters are selected. For example, if a fraction is selected, and you press the DOWN ARROW key, the numerator in the equation is selected.

$$\frac{10}{2} + \frac{6}{3} = 7 \qquad \frac{10}{2} + \frac{6}{3} = 7$$

To select one or more characters in an equation, do one of the following:

■ To select an equation, CTRL-click (Windows and UNIX) or OPTION-click (Mac) the equation. The selection handles are displayed around the object.

$$\log_a \Delta = \frac{\ln \Delta}{\ln a}$$

■ To select part of an equation, drag the cursor across the text, or use one of the shortcuts in Table 23-2.

You must use your cursor to select a text string; the keyboard shortcuts don't work.

ADVANCED TECHNIQUES

Keystroke	Description
UP ARROW or SPACEBAR	Expands the selection. $\dfrac{10}{2}+\dfrac{6}{3}=7 \qquad \dfrac{10}{2}+\dfrac{6}{3}=7 \qquad \dfrac{10}{2}+\dfrac{6}{3}=7$
LEFT ARROW	Selects the next character on the left. $\dfrac{10}{2}+\dfrac{6}{3}=7 \qquad \dfrac{10}{2}+\dfrac{6}{3}=7 \qquad \dfrac{10}{2}+\dfrac{6}{3}=7 \qquad \dfrac{10}{2}+\dfrac{6}{3}=7$
RIGHT ARROW	Selects the next character on the right. $\dfrac{10}{2}+\dfrac{6}{3}=7 \qquad \dfrac{10}{2}+\dfrac{6}{3}=7 \qquad \dfrac{10}{2}+\dfrac{6}{3}=7 \qquad \dfrac{10}{2}+\dfrac{6}{3}=7$
DOWN ARROW	Selects the numerator in a fraction when the whole fraction is selected. $\dfrac{10}{2}+\dfrac{6}{3}=7 \qquad \dfrac{10}{2}+\dfrac{6}{3}=7$
CTRL-A (Windows, UNIX) COMMAND-A (Mac)	Selects all objects in an anchored or graphic frame. Before using this shortcut, you must select the frame or click an item inside the frame; otherwise, you'll insert a new equation object above the insertion point.

Table 23-2. *Selecting Items in Equations*

Navigating Through Equations

To move the cursor between math elements in an equation, you use the arrow keys. Table 23-3 shows how the insertion point moves when you press the arrow keys.

Key	Description
LEFT ARROW	Moves the cursor to the left.
	$\frac{10}{2} + \frac{6}{3} = 7|$ $\quad$ $\frac{10}{2} + \frac{6}{3} = |7$ $\quad$ $\frac{10}{2} + \frac{6|}{3} = 7$ $\quad$ $\frac{10}{2} + \frac{|6}{3} = 7$ $\quad$ $\frac{10}{2|} + \frac{6}{3} = 7$
RIGHT ARROW	Moves the cursor to the right.
	$|\frac{10}{2} + \frac{6}{3} = 7$ $\quad$ $\frac{10}{2|} + \frac{6}{3} = 7$ $\quad$ $\frac{10}{2} + \frac{|6}{3} = 7$ $\quad$ $\frac{10}{2} + \frac{6}{3} |= 7$
DOWN ARROW	Moves the cursor from the side of a fraction to its numerator.
	$\frac{|10}{2} + \frac{6}{3} = 7$ $\qquad$ $\frac{|10}{2} + \frac{6}{3} = 7$
UP ARROW	Moves the cursor from the numerator to the entire fraction.
	$\frac{|10}{2} + \frac{6}{3} = 7$ $\qquad$ $|\frac{10}{2} + \frac{6}{3} = 7$

Table 23-3. *Moving the Cursor Through Equations*

Moving Equations

Once you select an equation, you can move it on the page by one of three methods. To move an equation, select the equation, and then do one of the following:

- Drag the selected equation to a new location.
- Press ALT (Windows and UNIX) or OPTION (Mac) while pressing one of the arrow keys.
- Right-click the equation, then select Graphics | Object Properties. The Object Properties dialog box is displayed (Figure 23-2). Type new left or top offsets, then click the Set button.

For more information on modifying the position and alignment of objects, see "Rearranging Objects" on page 350.

Caution *You can move the equation outside the anchored frame; however, the equation is no longer linked to the paragraph, and text added or deleted above the equation may be displayed over the equation.*

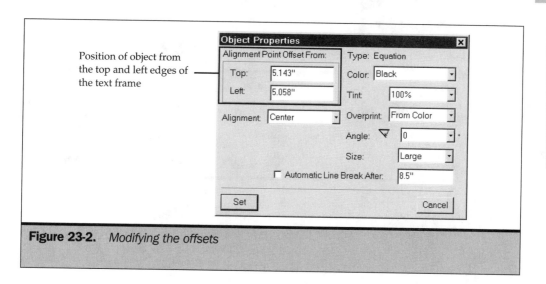

Figure 23-2. *Modifying the offsets*

Modifying Equations

After you write an equation, you can modify the spacing and alignment in several ways. For example, you can tighten the spacing or add a line break. You should wait to modify spacing and alignment until the equation is final, or you might need to make additional adjustments.

Moving Text Using Keyboard Shortcuts

You can move selected text up and down, left-to-right, and diagonally using keyboard shortcuts. To do so, select the text you want to move, and use keyboard shortcuts in the following table to microposition the text. (The point values apply to documents displayed at 100 percent.)

Direction	Windows/UNIX Shortcut	Mac Shortcut
Left one point	ALT-LEFT ARROW	OPTION-LEFT ARROW
Right one point	ALT-RIGHT ARROW	OPTION-RIGHT ARROW
Up one point	ALT-UP ARROW	OPTION-UP ARROW
Down one point	ALT-DOWN ARROW	OPTION-DOWN ARROW

Direction	Windows/UNIX Shortcut	Mac Shortcut
Left six points	ALT-SHIFT-LEFT ARROW	OPTION-SHIFT-LEFT ARROW
Right six points	ALT-SHIFT-RIGHT ARROW	OPTION-SHIFT-RIGHT ARROW
Up six points	ALT-SHIFT-UP ARROW	OPTION-SHIFT-UP ARROW
Down six points	ALT-SHIFT-DOWN ARROW	OPTION-SHIFT-DOWN ARROW

 Note   *Some of the keys on your computer may be specially programmed. If so, one or more keyboard shortcuts may not work as described. Consult your system documentation for help.*

Moving Text Using the Equations Palette

In addition to using keyboard shortcuts, you can reposition an equation using commands in the Positioning page.

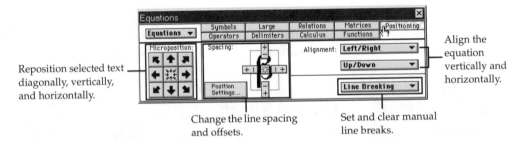

Reposition selected text diagonally, vertically, and horizontally.

Align the equation vertically and horizontally.

Change the line spacing and offsets.

Set and clear manual line breaks.

The following list describes some of the most common ways to modify equations using the Equations palette:

- **Adjusting the spread.** Add or remove space between characters in an equation by selecting the characters and clicking the appropriate Spacing arrow. (The middle button resets the alignment.)

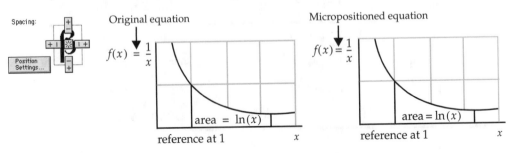

■ **Adjusting the line spacing.** Add or remove space between lines of a multiline equation by editing spacing in the Position Settings dialog box.

Original equation

0.35 picas was added
to the line spacing.

$$(10 - 2) + 6 + x^4 + 2y$$
$$+ y^2 + 3 + 10 + 2$$

$$(10 - 2) + 6 + x^4 + 2y$$
$$+ y^2 + 3 + 10 + 2$$

■ **Repositioning text.** Move selected text up and down, side-to-side, and diagonally by clicking one of the Microposition arrows. (The middle button resets the alignment.)

$$\log_a \Delta = \frac{\ln \Delta}{\ln_a}$$

Caution *If you add math elements after using the Microposition commands, the repositioned text will move back to its original location.*

■ **Aligning.** Line up equations at specific points (for example, along the equal signs or centers of the equations).

$$a(x)\frac{dy}{dx} + b(x)y = c(x)$$
$$\frac{dy}{dx} + p(x)y = q(x)$$

$$a(x)\frac{dy}{dx} + b(x)y = c(x)$$
$$\frac{dy}{dx} + p(x)y = q(x)$$

Manual alignment point is set
to the right of the equal signs.

Equations are
centered.

■ **Adding a line break.** Sets a manual line break in an equation. (You can set up an automatic line break in the equation's object properties.)

$$x - 3y + (10 \times 350) + 9 - 2 \longrightarrow$$
$$x - 3y + (10 \times 350)$$
$$+ 9 - 2$$

For more information on modifying the spacing and alignment of equations, see the FrameMaker documentation.

Deleting Equations

You can delete specific math elements in an equation or the entire equation. When you delete a math element, a question mark is displayed in place of the element. You can insert another item in place of the question mark or continue to delete more of the equation.

To delete items in an equation, follow these steps:

1. Do one of the following:

   ■ Select the item you want to delete.

   ■ Position the cursor on the right side of the item.

2. Press the BACKSPACE key. The item is deleted, and the question mark is displayed in its place.

3. Repeat to delete additional items.

To delete an entire equation, select the equation, then press the DELETE key.

Formatting Equations

FrameMaker lets you set the global font properties for equations. You customize equation fonts by assigning a character format. For example, you might create a character format with a sans-serif typeface and assign the format in the Equations palette. You can also modify the font sizes in small, medium, and large equations and adjust the default spread of each equation. When you modify global font settings, new and existing equations are updated, and shrink-wrapped equations are rewrapped, if necessary.

You reformat individual equations in the equation's object properties. In addition to modifying the typical object properties—color, tint, overprint, and angle—you set up automatic line breaks or change the size of the equation. To reformat certain characters in an equation, you must use character tags.

Changing Equation Fonts

In equations, alphanumeric characters, including functions, are formatted with the Times or Times New Roman typeface. You change the font properties by assigning a character tag. The five types of equation characters—math symbols, functions, numbers, strings, and variables—may use different character tags.

To modify default equation fonts, follow these steps:

1. Create a character tag for each kind of formatting. For example, you can create a separate tag for functions and numbers. See "Creating Character Tags" on page 149 for details.

2. Display the Equations palette, then click Equation Fonts in the Equations drop-down list. The Equation Fonts dialog box is displayed.

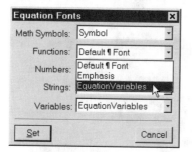

3. To change the math symbol font, click a font in the Math Symbols drop-down list. Only math fonts are displayed.

4. To apply a character tag to other math elements, click the character tag in the appropriate drop-down list.

The EquationVariables character tag is assigned to variables to italicize the characters. Don't delete this character tag from your template if you insert equations in your document.

5. Click the Set button. The default font properties in new and existing equations are updated.

Changing Equation Font Sizes

When you insert an equation, you choose a small, medium, or large equation. The default font sizes determine the size of the equation. Certain types of characters within each equation also differ in size. For example, integral and sigma symbols are larger than other characters, and there are three font sizes for different levels of alphanumeric characters. You can change the default font sizes for equations, and all existing equations are also updated.

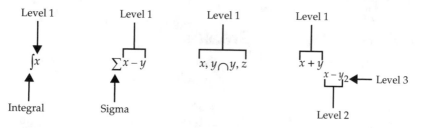

In addition to editing font sizes, you can change the equation's vertical or horizontal spread. The spread setting functions the same as spread in a paragraph tag. See "Default Font Sheet" on page 117 for more information.

To change the default font sizes and spreads, follow these steps:

1. Display the Equations palette, then click Equation Sizes in the Equations drop-down list. The Equation Sizes dialog box is displayed.

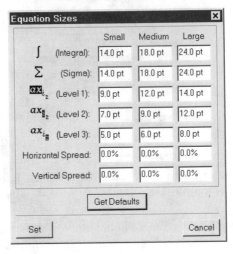

2. To change the font sizes for equations, type new values in the Small, Medium, and Large fields.

3. To change the spacing between characters, do any of the following:
   - To modify space horizontally, type new values in the Horizontal Spread values.
   - To modify space vertically, type new values in the Vertical Spread values.

To restore the default font sizes, click the Get Defaults button. (The defaults are displayed in the previous graphic.)

4. Click the Set button. The default font sizes in new and existing equations are updated.

Inserting Automatic Line Breaks

You can set up automatic line breaks in individual equations. When an equation reaches a certain length, the equation wraps to the next line. To insert an automatic line break, follow these steps:

1. Select the equation, then select Graphics | Object Properties. The Object Properties dialog box is displayed (Figure 23-2 on page 579).

2. Check the Automatic Line Break After check box, type the length at which the line break occurs, then click the Set button. The equation properties are updated.

Changing the Equation Size

After you insert an equation, you can change the size. For example, you might insert a small equation and decide the font is too small. Instead of modifying the size of the font globally, you can assign a different size to the equation. To change the equation size, follow these steps:

1. Select the equation, then select Graphics | Object Properties. The Object Properties dialog box is displayed (Figure 23-2 on page 579).
2. Click a size in the Size drop-down list, then click the Set button. The equation size is updated.

For details on changing equation sizes globally, see "Changing Equation Font Sizes" on page 583.

Applying Character Tags

You can reformat specific characters in an equation by applying character tags. This overrides the global character formatting specified in the Equation Fonts dialog box. For details, see "Changing Equation Fonts" on page 582.

To apply a character tag, select the text, and click a tag in the character catalog. You cannot use the keyboard shortcut for applying character tags because the shortcut is mapped to one of the operators in the Equations palette. For more information, see "Applying Character Tags" on page 144.

Evaluating Equations

FrameMaker can evaluate a selected expression and either display an alternate format or correct the syntax. The following example shows an expression before and after evaluation. In the numerator of the first expression, the parenthetical values were transformed to display the values in the correct order. The denominator was converted to its simplest expression. The second expression was also converted to its simplest value.

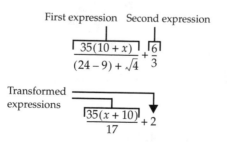

To evaluate an equation, follow these steps:

1. Display the Equations palette, then click the Functions button. The Functions page is displayed.

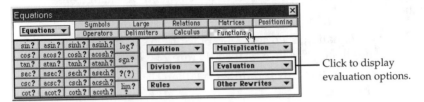

— Click to display evaluation options.

2. Select the expression you want to evaluate.
3. Click the Evaluation drop-down list, then click the appropriate command for your expression. Your equation is evaluated, and the alternate values are displayed.

For more information on evaluating equations, see the FrameMaker documentation.

Equations in Structured Documents

To write an equation in a structured document, you insert an equation element. This places an anchored frame on the page with an equation object in the middle of the frame. You then replace the equation object with your equation. If you're typing a simple equation or you know the keystrokes for math symbols and expressions, you can type in the structure view. However, to use the Equations palette to build your equation, you need to type in the document. For more information, see "Equation Elements" on page 712.

Chapter 24

Maker Interchange Format

Normally, FrameMaker files are stored in a binary format. In some cases, though, it's useful to have a text version of FrameMaker files. For this, an alternate Maker Interchange Format (MIF) is available. A MIF file contains the same information as a regular, binary FrameMaker file, but it's encoded in a plain text file instead of a binary file.

Editing MIF files directly provides an alternative to working in FrameMaker's graphical interface. For some issues, this is the most efficient way to work. For example, you can use MIF files to perform global search-and-replace operations on fonts. This is much faster than editing each tag in the paragraph catalog—even the global update options aren't as fast as editing MIF.

A MIF file contains all of the information that your FrameMaker file does in a markup format. The following MIF fragment shows one short paragraph of text:

What's displayed in FrameMaker

> Cross-stitching is easy to learn, fun, and relaxing. Best of all, it doesn't require a computer!

Corresponding MIF markup

Paragraph tag BodyFirst is assigned to the paragraph.

```
<Para
  <Unique 1035992>
  <PgfTag `BodyFirst'>
  <ParaLine
   <String `Cross-stitching is easy to learn,
fun, and relaxing. Best of all, it '>
   > # end of ParaLine
  <ParaLine
   <String `doesn\xd5 t require a computer!'>
   > # end of ParaLine
  > # end of Para
```

In addition to the text, graphics, markers, elements, and so on, the MIF file also contains a complete listing of your formatting catalogs. The following code excerpt shows the definition for the BodyFirst paragraph tag referenced in the preceding example. Notice that each item available in the Paragraph Designer has its own entry in the list.

```
<Pgf
  <PgfTag `BodyFirst'>
  <PgfUseNextTag No>
  <PgfNextTag `'>
  <PgfAlignment Left>
  <PgfFIndent  0.0">
  <PgfLIndent  0.0">
```

```
<PgfRIndent   0.0">
<PgfFIndentRelative No>
<PgfFIndentOffset   0.0">
<PgfTopSeparator `BodyFirst'>
<PgfTopSepAtIndent No>
<PgfTopSepOffset   0.0">
<PgfBotSeparator `'>
<PgfBotSepAtIndent No>
<PgfBotSepOffset   0.0">
<PgfPlacement Anywhere>
<PgfPlacementStyle Normal>
<PgfRunInDefaultPunct `. '>
<PgfSpBefore   4.0 pt>
<PgfSpAfter   4.0 pt>
<PgfWithPrev No>
<PgfWithNext No>
<PgfBlockSize 2>
<PgfFont
 <FTag `'>
 <FPlatformName `W.Veljovic.R.400'>
 <FFamily `Veljovic'>
 <FVar `Regular'>
 <FWeight `Regular'>
 <FAngle `Regular'>
 <FPostScriptName `Veljovic-Book'>
 <FEncoding `FrameRoman'>
 <FSize   11.0 pt>
 <FUnderlining FNoUnderlining>
 <FOverline No>
 <FStrike No>
 <FChangeBar No>
 <FOutline No>
 <FShadow No>
 <FPairKern Yes>
 <FTsume No>
 <FCase FAsTyped>
 <FPosition FNormal>
 <FDX   0.0%>
 <FDY   0.0%>
 <FDW   0.0%>
 <FStretch   100.0%>
 <FLanguage USEnglish>
 <FLocked No>
 <FSeparation 0>
```

```
  <FColor `Black'>
> # end of PgfFont
<PgfLineSpacing Fixed>
<PgfLeading  3.0 pt>
<PgfAutoNum No>
<PgfNumTabs 0>
<PgfHyphenate Yes>
<HyphenMaxLines 1>
<HyphenMinPrefix 4>
<HyphenMinSuffix 3>
<HyphenMinWord 5>
<PgfLetterSpace No>
<PgfMinWordSpace 90>
<PgfOptWordSpace 100>
<PgfMaxWordSpace 110>
<PgfMinJRomanLetterSpace 0>
<PgfOptJRomanLetterSpace 25>
<PgfMaxJRomanLetterSpace 50>
<PgfMinJLetterSpace 0>
<PgfOptJLetterSpace 0>
<PgfMaxJLetterSpace 10>
<PgfYakumonoType Floating>
<PgfAcrobatLevel 0>
<PgfPDFStructureLevel 3>
<PgfLanguage USEnglish>
<PgfCellAlignment Top>
<PgfCellMargins  0.0 pt 0.0 pt 0.0 pt 0.0 pt>
<PgfCellLMarginFixed No>
<PgfCellTMarginFixed No>
<PgfCellRMarginFixed No>
<PgfCellBMarginFixed No>
<PgfLocked No>
> # end of Pgf
```

After reviewing this, it's probably no surprise to find out that MIF files are generally larger than FrameMaker files. On average, MIF files are about 10 times larger than the corresponding FrameMaker file, so saving a 100KB FrameMaker file to MIF results in a 1MB MIF file.

Almost every third-party utility that can read or write FrameMaker files uses MIF as an intermediate format. HTML converters such as WebWorks Publisher and MIF2GO save FrameMaker files to MIF, and then process the resulting MIF files to produce HTML or other markup. Most database publishing applications generate MIF markup files, which can then be opened in FrameMaker.

Note *In addition to MIF format, a second markup format, Maker Markup Language (MML), is also available. MML is no longer being developed, so it's not nearly as rich as MIF. MML, however, is much easier to create than MIF. For this reason, MML is used for some applications because creating a complete MIF file would be too much work. For details on MML, refer to the MML Reference, found in the OnlineManuals folder in your FrameMaker installation directory.*

FrameMaker comes with the *MIF Reference*, found in the OnlineManuals folder in your FrameMaker installation directory. The *MIF Reference* describes MIF syntax and options in great detail. We strongly recommend that you consult this manual for detailed information about MIF syntax. At the highest level, the MIF file is organized into the following sections (shown in MIFBrowse in the example):

- **MIFFile:** Identifies the file as a MIF file and provides the FrameMaker version from which the file was created. Every MIF file must start with this statement.

- **Units** and **CharUnits:** Specify measurement units for this file.

- **ColorCatalog:** Lists the color definitions.

- **ConditionCatalog:** Lists the conditional text tag definitions.

- **CombinedFontCatalog:** Lists combined fonts (used in double-byte languages such as Japanese).

- **PgfCatalog:** Lists the paragraph tag definitions.

- **ElementDefCatalog:** Lists the element definitions for a structured file.

- **FmtChangeListCatalog:** Lists format change lists for structured documents.

- **FontCatalog:** Lists character tag definitions.

- **Ruling Catalog:** Lists table rule definitions.

- **TblCatalog:** Lists table definitions.

- **KumihanCatalog:** Provides line composition rules for Japanese text.

- **Views:** Lists color view definitions.

- **VariableFormats:** Lists variable definitions.

- **MarkerTypeCatalog:** Lists available custom marker types.

- **XRefFormats:** Lists cross-reference format definitions.

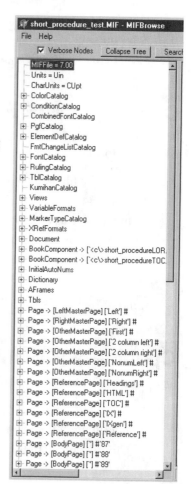

- **Document:** Lists document defaults, including volume, chapter, page, paragraph, and footnote numbering; document window size and location; text options; change bar properties; and view options.
- **BookComponent:** Lists settings for generated files.
- **InitialAutoNums:** Lists default starting numbers for autonumbered paragraphs.
- **Dictionary:** Lists words not in the dictionary but allowed in this document (added when you click the Allow in Document button in the spell-checker).
- **AFrames:** Lists the anchored frames that occur in this document. The frames' unique identifiers are used to reference the frames in the text flow where they are anchored.
- **Tbls:** Lists the tables that occur in this document. The tables' identifiers are used to reference the tables in the text flow where they are anchored.
- **Page:** Lists the master pages, reference pages, and body pages that occur in this document.
- **Text Flow:** Lists the text flows that occur in this document and their contents.

Creating a MIF File

To create a MIF file from a regular FrameMaker file, you need to save the FrameMaker file to MIF format. Follow these steps:

1. Open the file you want to save as MIF.
2. Select File | Save As. The Save dialog box is displayed.
3. In the Save as type drop-down list, click MIF Document.
4. In the File name field, specify a name for the file. Be sure to change the file extension to MIF; FrameMaker doesn't always do this automatically.
5. Click the Save button.

FrameMaker creates the MIF file.

Opening a MIF File in FrameMaker

To open a MIF file and convert it back to regular FrameMaker format, follow these steps:

1. Select File | Open. The Open dialog box is displayed.
2. Locate the MIF file on your system and select it.
3. Click the Open button to open the file.

FrameMaker reads the MIF file and displays it as a FrameMaker file. During conversion, a console window may display error messages. FrameMaker will skip any information it cannot process in the MIF file. For example, if you save a FrameMaker 7 file to MIF and then open that MIF file in version 6 (or earlier), error messages will be displayed.

Viewing a MIF File

You can view a MIF file in any decent text editor. If you don't have a good text editor available, you can use FrameMaker as a text editor.

To open a MIF file as text in FrameMaker, follow these steps:

1. Select File | Open. The Open dialog box is displayed.
2. Locate the MIF file you want to open, hold down the CTRL key (Windows and UNIX) or the OPTION key (Mac), and double-click the file.

FrameMaker reads the file as a text file instead of interpreting the MIF commands.

Caution   *Do not save the text file as a FrameMaker file. You could inadvertently overwrite your source FrameMaker file with text.*

A dedicated MIF browsing utility is available. If you plan to do a lot of working in MIF files, MIFBrowse may be helpful. It displays the MIF file and an accompanying tree view:

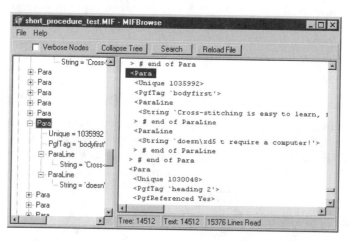

Refer to Appendix A, "Resources," for information on where you can download MIFBrowse (it's free!).

Cool Stuff You Can Do with MIF

There are numerous scenarios in which a MIF file can be helpful. Before you begin working in a file, assemble your arsenal; you will need the following items:

- A text editor that can handle MIF files. (Notepad and SimpleText cannot open most MIF files because they are too long.)

- A powerful search-and-replace engine. Some text editors offer advanced search-and-replace options; you can also use a scripting language such as Perl.

- A basic understanding of MIF syntax and the items you need to modify. If, for example, you want to work with index markers and aren't sure how the index markers look in MIF format, create a small sample file, insert an index marker with some unique text, save the file to MIF, and search for your sample text.

- Access to hex code references (Windows). FrameMaker provides a *Character Set Reference* in the OnlineManuals folder in your installation directory. This manual describes how extended ASCII characters are encoded. An em dash, for example, shows in a MIF file as "\xd1".

- A backup of your file, just in case.

The following sections describe a few common uses for MIF files.

Eliminating File Corruption Problems

FrameMaker files are usually quite stable. Every now and then, though, a file goes haywire for no apparent reason. One technique that can sometimes eliminate the problem is to save the file to MIF, open the MIF in FrameMaker, and save it back to FrameMaker format. You're not making any changes in the MIF file, so this operation is relatively safe.

Making a File Available to an Older Version of FrameMaker

Older versions of FrameMaker cannot open files created in newer versions. For example, a file created in FrameMaker 6 cannot be opened in any release of FrameMaker 5. In version 7, Adobe did include a "save as FrameMaker 6" option, so that you can write FrameMaker 7 files to a format that's compatible with FrameMaker 6. If, however, you need to transfer files back to an older version, you must go through MIF format.

Save your file to MIF format, open the older version of FrameMaker, and open the MIF file there. You will see a number of error messages in the console, but this technique should allow you to open files all the way back to FrameMaker version 3.

Keep in mind that any features that aren't available in the earlier version will be stripped from your file, which can cause formatting problems, especially if you are going back to a very old version of FrameMaker.

ADVANCED TECHNIQUES

Creating a Character Tag for a Vertical Baseline Shift

Some settings are available as MIF file settings but are not accessible through the graphical interface. Vertical baseline shift is one of those items. In the Character Designer, you can set up a character tag that uses a superscript, but you cannot use multiple vertical offsets in a single file—you only have superscripts available, and they always use the same vertical offset.

There is, however, a vertical offset setting available in FrameMaker. In a MIF file, you can assign this offset using the <FDY> token. You can create a character tag definition in a MIF file. You can then use that file as a template and import the tag into a document.

To create a character format with a vertical baseline shift, follow these steps:

1. Create a text file and insert the following text:

```
<MIFFile 7.00>
<FontCatalog
<Font
 <FTag `VerticalOffset'>
 <FDY -60>
 <FLocked No>
 > # end of Font
 > # end of FontCatalog
```

The offset value can range from -100 to 100; negative values move the text up, and positive values move the text down. The quotes surrounding the words VerticalOffset are the backtick character for the opening quote and a straight single quote for the closing quote.

2. Save the file with a .MIF extension.

3. In FrameMaker, open the MIF file and display the document that you want to import the character tag into.

4. Select File | Import | Formats. The Import Formats dialog box is displayed.

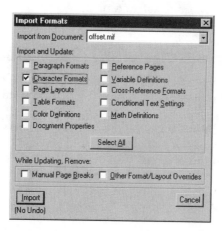

5. In the Import from Document drop-down list, click the MIF file to select it.

6. In the Import and Update section, check the Character Formats check box; make sure all other items are unchecked.

7. Click the Import button. The VerticalOffset character tag is displayed in the character catalog. When you apply it, a vertical offset results.

You cannot access the vertical offset setting from the Character Designer. However, if you make changes to the VerticalOffset character tag in the Character Designer and click the Update All button, the baseline offset setting will be deleted.

Using MIF Fragments to Update Catalog Settings

You can use the technique described in the previous section to add information to other catalogs. You might, for example, create a list of user variable definitions:

```
<MIFFile 7.00>
<VariableFormats
<VariableFormat
  <VariableName `book_title'>
  <VariableDef `Troubleshooting My Document'>
 > # end of VariableFormat
<VariableFormat
  <VariableName `version_number'>
  <VariableDef `6.2.5beta'>
 > # end of VariableFormat
 > # end of VariableFormats
```

You can import this MIF fragment into a FrameMaker file to add the listed variable definitions.

Once you import the variable definitions, they are available in the Variables dialog box. You can edit them just like any other variable.

Performing Global Search-and-Replace Operations

Inside FrameMaker, you have a significant number of Find/Change options available, but sometimes, you'll run across a problem that can't be automated in the Find/Change dialog box.

For example, you might have a situation where you were working on an index. After several hours of work, you realize that you inadvertently inserted markers with a Subject type instead of an Index type.

Here's how to fix this using the find/change feature in FrameMaker:

1. Select Edit | Find/Change. The Find/Change dialog box is displayed:

2. In the Find drop-down list, click Marker of Type; in the field to the right of Marker Type, type in **Subject**.

3. Click the Find button. FrameMaker locates the first Subject marker.

4. Select Special | Marker. The Marker dialog box is displayed.

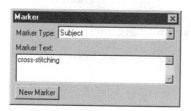

5. In the Marker Type drop-down list, click Index.

6. Click the Edit Marker button.

7. Repeat steps 3–6 for each problem marker.

The MIF alternative is much more appealing:

1. Save the problem files to MIF format.

2. Write a script that locates the Subject markers, or just use search and replace. The items that are the same for each marker are shown in boldface in the following example:

```
<Marker
 <MType 4>
 <MTypeName `Subject'>
 <MText `cross-stitching'>
 <MCurrPage `87'>
 <Unique 1075663>
 > # end of Marker
```

3. Globally change the <MType> to 2 and the <MTypeName> to Index, as shown in the following example:

```
<Marker
 <MType 2>
 <MTypeName `Index'>
 <MText `cross-stitching'>
 <MCurrPage `87'>
 <Unique 1075663>
 > # end of Marker
```

4. Save your modified MIF files.

5. Open the files in FrameMaker, and save them back to regular FrameMaker format.

These types of global search-and-replace operations can save you hours of work.

Writing Your Own Conversion Tools

If you are required to convert information in FrameMaker to other formats and third-party converters are not doing the job, you may want to consider writing your own conversion tool. With some Perl scripting knowledge, you could, for example, write a converter that takes a MIF file as input and creates man pages.

The MIF file contains all of the information needed to display and print a file, so converting it to online markup formats, such as man pages, troff, HTML, or XML, almost always involves throwing away large amounts of information.

Using MIF in Configuration Management Environments

Many configuration management or source control systems are designed for software development environments. Their support for text files is very good and includes the ability to "diff" files—that is, to compare two versions of a file side by side and see what changes were made.

FrameMaker's binary files can be stored under source control, but you will not be able to use many of the features that make source control so useful—the source control software cannot run a useful comparison on binary files. (A few source control systems, such as Documentum, do have direct support for FrameMaker.)

MIF provides one way to work around this problem. Instead of storing FrameMaker files, store MIF files under source control. There are, however, a number of problems with this technique:

■ **File size.** MIF files are much larger than FrameMaker files, so file storage requirements are increased. However, storing 10 versions of a binary file may require just as much space as storing one copy of a MIF file and a list of changes for each version.

■ **Workflow.** A MIF-based storage scheme requires that authors save files out to MIF before checking them in to the storage system. This can be automated with scripts, but it still adds an extra step to your workflow.

MIF files offer you a powerful alternative to working in the FrameMaker interface. The next time you face hours of manual reformatting or other tedious, repetitive work in FrameMaker, consider whether editing the MIF files might be quicker.

The Complete Reference

FrameMaker 7

Chapter 25

Creating Modules with Text Insets

Most desktop publishing applications let you link graphics—you set up a pointer from a document to a particular graphic file. If that file is updated, the graphic in the document is updated automatically. FrameMaker supports linked graphics (they are discussed in Chapter 12, "Importing Graphics"), but in addition to graphics, FrameMaker also lets you link text into a document. Instead of importing a graphic, you import a file that contains text. If you update the file, its content is also updated where it is linked.

The imported-by-reference text fragments are called *text insets*. A development process based on assembling text fragments into larger documents is referred to as creating *modular documentation* or modular text—your final document is made up of smaller text chunks or *modules*. The composite document that's assembled from modules is called a *container document*.

Text insets are used most commonly to import one FrameMaker file into another, but you can also import other supported file formats, such as Word files as text insets. This works best if the file is relatively simple and if the styles used in Word match paragraph tags in the FrameMaker file.

Breaking up documents into modules lets you create small, reusable topics. This modular approach makes sense if you must write documentation for several related products. By dividing information in small chunks, you can maximize reuse of common information and write separate modules where the products differ.

Consider the example shown in Figure 25-1. You have two installation documents, one for Product A and one for Product B. The two products have identical system requirements and licensing agreements, but other information in the installation instructions is different. To take advantage of reuse, you created a system requirements document (reqs.fm) and a licensing agreement document (license.fm) and imported these as text insets. Any updates to the inset files will be reflected in both installation documents. Because you only have one copy of the license.fm and reqs.fm files, it doesn't make sense to put them in a specific book file; instead, many authors set up a shared directory, as shown in the following example:

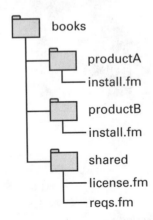

ADVANCED TECHNIQUES

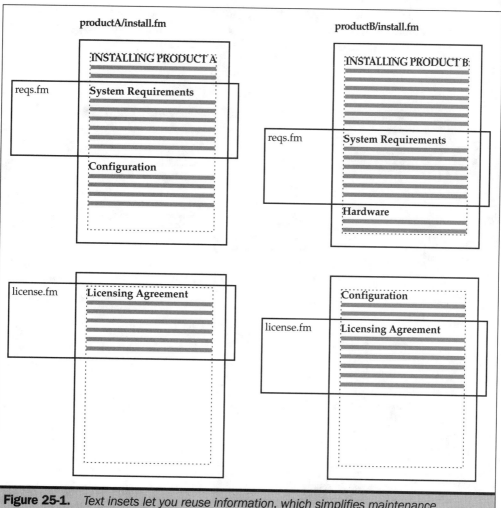

Figure 25-1.   *Text insets let you reuse information, which simplifies maintenance.*

A Text Inset Example

Although FrameMaker refers to text insets as importing files, that isn't completely accurate. When you create a text inset, you import a specific *flow* from a file; most often, the main body flow (flow A). However, in some cases, you might set up a document that contains several different flows that you might want to import. This would be especially useful if you have a series of standard warnings that you need to repeat throughout a book. Instead of copying and pasting, you could create text insets in the book so that you don't have to worry about consistency. In the following example, the author has set up separate text flows for each standard warning:

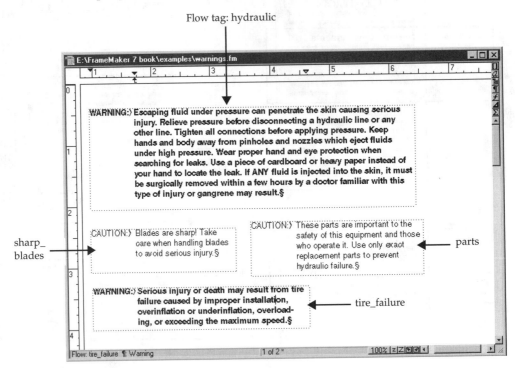

When you specify that you want to import text from the warnings file, you are prompted to choose a flow:

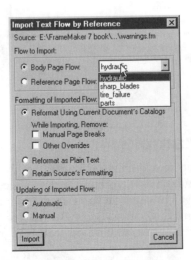

After selecting a flow, that information is included in the container document.

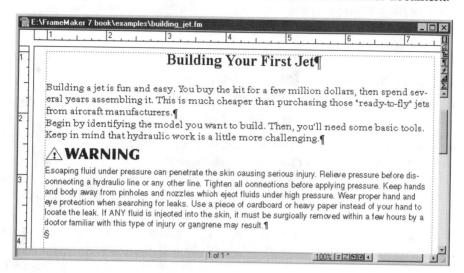

In the example shown here, formatting of the warning paragraph is quite different in the source (warnings.fm) than it is when used in a container. The paragraph tag definition in the container document is overriding the information provided in the source document. You can control this with the Formatting of Imported Flow section when you import the text flow.

You cannot edit text insets in the container document. Selecting them results in the entire text inset being selected, just like a cross-reference or a variable (except that the text inset could be many pages long).

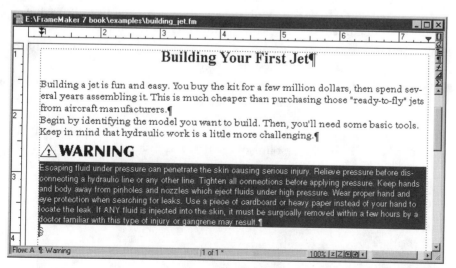

Instead, you must open the source document and make any changes there. After you save the file and update your text insets, the new information is displayed wherever that text inset is used.

Working with Text in Insets

For some features, content inside a text inset behaves like regular text. In some cases, though, there are differences between regular text and text in a text inset:

- **Finding unresolved cross-references.** Text insets are checked for unresolved cross-references when you open the container file.

- **Finding and replacing information.** The Find/Change command does not work inside text insets when searching a container file. To search inside a text inset, you must open the text inset file.

- **Spell-checking.** When you spell-check a container file, text insets are not spell-checked. You must open the text inset file to spell-check it.

- **Variable definitions.** If you use a variable inside a text inset, the container file may display the variable definition from the text inset or the variable definition from the container file, depending on your settings. If you specify that you want to retain the formatting from the source file, the variable definition from the text inset file is used. If you specify that the text inset should be reformatted using the container document's settings, the variable definition from the container document is used, *provided that the variable is defined in the container document.* If it is not, the original value from the inset file is used.

- **Conditional text settings.** Show/Hide settings and conditional text definitions (color and style settings) are handled the same way that variable definitions are. If you retain formatting from the source document, settings from the text inset are used. If you reformatted with the container document's settings, the container document overrides tags with matching names.

- **Generated lists.** When you create a generated list from the container file, information from the inset file is included.

- **Separating stacked text insets.** After a text inset, make sure you insert a blank paragraph (as regular text in the container document) with a space in it before beginning the next text inset. Stacking text insets without the "separator" paragraph causes formatting problems. The second text inset takes on the formatting used by the first line of the first text inset. (You can define the separator paragraph with a two-point font size and negative space above or below so that it doesn't take up any space on the page.)

- **Converting text with insets to HTML.** When you convert to HTML, text insets are treated like regular text.

Alternatives to Text Insets

Text insets are not the only way you can reuse information. As you begin to plan your physical file structure, consider using any or all of the following techniques:

- **Cross-references.** With cross-references, you can link to a paragraph of text. This works well for standard, repeated information, such as a copyright statement or standard warnings. However, you cannot create a cross-reference that picks up more than a paragraph of text at one time, so if you need to insert more than one paragraph of text, cross-references won't work.

- **Conditional text.** Conditional text lets you label information as belonging to a particular version of a document. You can use conditional text to embed two (or more) versions of the same document in a single file. Text insets, by contrast, let you reuse information in multiple files.

- **Multiple books.** You can create two versions of a document by creating two book files. You include the files that the two versions have in common in both files; the specific files are in only one book or another. The main disadvantage to this approach is that each file must start on a new page. If your product differences are at the chapter level, this approach usually works quite well. Text insets do not have to start a new page.

- **XML output with attributes.** Instead of using conditional text or text insets, you can use attributes to identify a particular section of text as belonging to one type of document or another. After exporting to XML, you can use the attributes to process the information in different ways. For example, you could label information with a Platform attribute (which might have values of Mac, Windows, UNIX, and so on), and then process the resulting XML to include and exclude text with certain Platform attribute values.

- **Text insets.** Lets you embed chunks of text from one file in another. Chunks can include any type of content—paragraphs, character tags, anchored frames, equations, and so on—and can be a paragraph or several pages long. When you create a text inset, the information is integrated into the container file without requiring a page break. To create different versions of content, you must create two or more container files and import different sets of text modules into those files.

Planning Modular Text

Like conditional text, text insets are much easier to create than to plan. Assigning a condition or importing a text inset is the easy part; deciding what conditions to use and what information should go in which text inset is much more difficult. Without careful planning, you're likely to encounter serious frustration with text insets.

Breaking Text Down into Modules

Breaking down information into modules can be a bit of a black art. Headings are a logical starting place. Some highly structured documents are easy to break up. For example, an alphabetical list of programming commands is easy to break into modules where each module contains one command, its explanation, code example, and the like. For task-oriented user's guides, a logical starting point for creating modules would be procedures. The most difficult part in creating modular procedures is the transition information from one procedure to the next. Instead of trying to write generic transitions in the text inset, consider inserting that content in the container document as you assemble the documents.

File Storage

File storage requirements will depend on the number of modules. If you are sharing just a few modules—such as a copyright page, system requirements list, and document conventions—across a few books, you may be able to create a simple file structure with a shared folder for the modules.

As the number of modules increases, however, it becomes more difficult to manage the module files. If you have hundreds or thousands of module files, you will probably need to set up a version control system, which lets you check in and check out files.

Information Retrieval

Setting up a storage system for files can be complicated, but establishing a system that ensures you can find relevant modules is an even bigger challenge. To locate files, you need to track some or all of the following information about each module:

- Main topic/title
- Keywords
- File location
- Author
- Last revision date
- Used in which books

For a small group of modules, a simple table or spreadsheet could suffice:

Topic	Keywords	File	Author	Revised
copyright	copyright, legal statements, trademarks	shared/ copyright.fm	SSO	6/5/02
system requirements	system requirements, hardware, software, RAM, memory	shared/ reqs.fm	SAL	5/20/02
document conventions	boldface, italic, conventions, menu selection	shared/ conventions.fm	ASP	1/16/02

If you have hundreds or thousands of modules, consider setting up a database to keep track of them.

Controlling Formatting and Structure in Text Insets

Like any other FrameMaker file, a file used as a text inset contains tagging information and—for structured documents—elements. The text inset file also includes formatting information that specifies how an element or a paragraph tag should be displayed.

When you import a file as a text inset, you can use the formatting specified in the text inset file. But more often, you specify that the container file's formatting should override the information in the text inset. This results in a situation where the appearance of information in the text inset file may be significantly different from the appearance in the text inset because the formatting templates are different.

The following example shows a warning in the original file. Notice the word "WARNING:" and the hanging indent.

> WARNING: Escaping fluid under pressure can penetrate the skin causing serious injury. Relieve pressure before disconnecting a hydraulic line or any other line. Tighten all connections before applying pressure. Keep hands and body away from pinholes and nozzles which eject fluids under high pressure. Wear proper hand and eye protection when searching for leaks. Use a piece of cardboard or heavy paper instead of your hand to locate the leak. If ANY fluid is injected into the skin, it must be surgically removed within a few hours by a doctor familiar with this type of injury or gangrene may result.§

After that text flow is imported into a container document, the appearance of the warning changes significantly. The warning paragraph tag in the container document uses a frame above the paragraph (see page 126) to insert the exclamation mark icon and the word warning. The font is different, and there is no hanging indent.

⚠ WARNING

Escaping fluid under pressure can penetrate the skin causing serious injury. Relieve pressure before disconnecting a hydraulic line or any other line. Tighten all connections before applying pressure. Keep hands and body away from pinholes and nozzles which eject fluids under high pressure. Wear proper hand and eye protection when searching for leaks. Use a piece of cardboard or heavy paper instead of your hand to locate the leak. If ANY fluid is injected into the skin, it must be surgically removed within a few hours by a doctor familiar with this type of injury or gangrene may result.¶

In addition to modifying paragraph styles, the inset items also inherit other settings, such as variable definitions and conditional text settings. That means you can set a variable for a product name in the text inset, and display different product names depending on the variable definition in each container document. You do not have to update the text inset's variable definition. The inset is displayed in different containers with different values for the variable.

If you are overriding formatting in the source files, the actual paragraph tag settings in the source files are irrelevant. It is important, though, to ensure that each text inset uses the correct set of tags or elements. When you update your template or your EDD, you must import those formats into each text inset file. To help make this task easier, consider creating a book to manage text insets. The book contains a link to each of the text inset files, so you can update formats or element definitions for each text inset by importing formats to all of the files in the book.

Using a dummy book also lets you perform global search-and-replace operations across text insets—remember that search and replace on a container file does *not* look inside the inset files.

Creating a Text Inset

To create a text inset, you need at least two documents: the module file and the container file into which you plan to import the module.

To set up the text inset, follow these steps:

1. Open the container document.
2. Position your cursor where you want the text inset to start.

Use a blank paragraph before the inset to ensure that the text inset doesn't get mashed into the previous paragraph.

3. Select File | Import | File, just as though you were getting ready to import a graphic. This displays the Import dialog box.

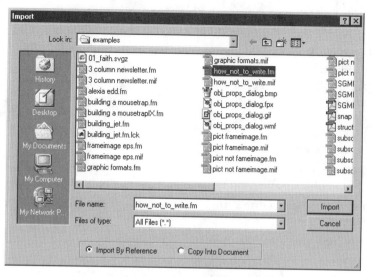

4. In the Import dialog box, locate and select the file you want to use.

5. Make sure that the Import by Reference radio button is selected, then click the Import button. The Import Text Flow by Reference dialog box is displayed (Figure 25-2).

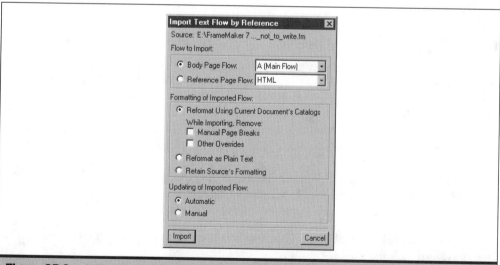

Figure 25-2.   *When importing, you can choose a particular flow and how the inset should be formatted.*

6. Select a flow to import. The main body page flow is usually A.

7. In the Formatting of Imported Flow section, specify whether you want to apply the current document's template and structure. Your choices are as follows:

■ **Reformat Using Current Document's Catalogs:** Inserts the content and applies the paragraph and other tags from the current document. Any matching tags are overwritten, so if the text inset uses a Body tag that's defined with Helvetica, and the container document has a Body tag that's defined with Garamond, all of the Body tags in the text inset will be displayed with the Garamond tag.

■ **Reformat as Plain Text:** The entire imported text flow is formatted using the format of the paragraph tag into which you are inserting the text.

■ **Retain Source's Formatting:** The inset retains the formatting specified in the inset document.

8. Specify how you want the imported flow updated:

■ **Automatic:** The text inset is updated when you open or print the container document, and when a book that includes the container document is updated with an update for text insets specified.

■ **Manual:** The text inset is updated only when you select Edit | References and specify that you want to update text insets set for manual updates or when you update the book and specify that you want to update text insets.

9. Click the Import button. The specified flow is imported into the container file.

Managing Text Insets

Text insets are updated differently from imported graphics. When you change a graphic file that's imported by reference, FrameMaker immediately picks up the change in the graphic and updates the version displayed in the FrameMaker file. With text insets, updating is similar to cross-references; it occurs when you open a file, update the book, and the like. However, unlike cross-references, you can set text insets for two different types of updates—manual or automatic. This setting determines when the text insets are updated.

When you first import a text inset, you are prompted to specify whether the inset should be updated manually or automatically (see step 8 in the preceding section).

To change a text inset's update status, follow these steps:

1. Double-click the text inset. This displays the Text Inset Properties dialog box (Figure 25-3).

2. Click the Settings button. This displays the Import Text Flow by Reference dialog box (Figure 25-2 on page 609).

3. In the Updating of Imported Flow section, choose Automatic or Manual.

4. Click the Import button to update the text inset's settings.

ADVANCED TECHNIQUES

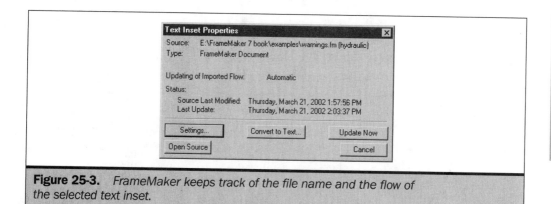

Figure 25-3. *FrameMaker keeps track of the file name and the flow of the selected text inset.*

FrameMaker provides several different ways to update text insets. Some update only the insets set up for automatic updates; some update both.

Text insets set for manual updates are refreshed only when you explicitly request an update.

To update a single text inset, double-click it to display the Text Inset Properties dialog box (shown in Figure 25-3), then click the Update Now button. To update all the text insets in a file, complete the next procedure.

To update text insets, follow these steps:

1. In the container document, select Edit | Update References. The Update References dialog box is displayed.

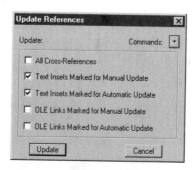

2. Check the items you want to update. To update all text insets, make sure that both the Text Insets Marked for Manual Update and the Text Insets Marked for Automatic Update check boxes are checked.

3. Click the Update button to update the specified items.

There are a number of other ways to update text insets; they are shown in the following table.

Action	Automatic Updates	Manual Updates
Open file	Yes	No
Edit | Update References	Yes, if Text Insets Marked for Automatic Update check box is checked	Yes, if Text Insets Marked for Manual Update check box is checked
Update book	Yes, if Update All Text Insets is selected	Yes, if Update All Text Insets is selected
Print file	Yes	No
Save file	Yes	No
Double-click text inset, then click Update Now button	Yes	Yes

Opening the Source File

You can open the text inset source file by selecting File | Open, locating the text inset, and opening it just like any other FrameMaker file. To edit a text inset that's displayed in the document window, double-click it, and then click the Open Source button in the Text Inset Properties dialog box (Figure 25-3 on page 611).

Converting Text Insets to Text

If necessary, you can convert text insets to regular text. Doing so destroys the link from the container file to the text inset file.

To convert text insets to text, follow these steps:

1. Double-click a text inset to display the Text Inset Properties dialog box (Figure 25-3 on page 611).

2. Click the Convert to Text button. This displays the Convert Text Insets to Text dialog box.

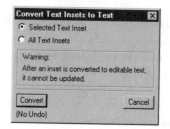

3. Do one of the following:

   ■ To convert only the current text inset, click the Selected Text Inset radio
     button.

   ■ To convert all text insets in this file to text, click the All Text Insets radio
     button.

*Converting text insets to text destroys the links. The information is no longer linked to
the source file, so updating the source file doesn't change anything in the files.*

4. Click the Convert button. The specified text insets are converted to text.

Structured Text Insets

Text insets work with structured and unstructured files. If your container document is
structured, you can create a text inset from a structured file. The inset file must use
elements that are defined in the container document; otherwise, the structure of the
container document will become invalid because of invalid structure in the text inset.
The text inset's structure is included in the structure view for the container document.

The text inset file might contain a structure fragment that's not valid on its own
(perhaps because the top-level element is not valid as the highest element), but when
imported into the container, the structure is merged into the container document's
larger structure and becomes valid. Like unstructured text insets, structured insets
cannot be edited in the container document. In the structure view, there is no indication
whether a particular element is part of a text inset or part of the container document.

Creating Cross-References to a Text Inset

If you want to create a cross-reference to some information that's inside a text inset (whether from a container file or from another text inset), you're going to run into a problem. You can create the cross-reference, but every time you update the inset, the cross-reference becomes unresolved. The problem is that two features collide in this scenario: cross-references, which must insert a cross-reference marker at the target location, and text insets, which you cannot change inside a container document.

To prevent this problem from happening, you must create a cross-reference marker inside the text inset.

To create a cross-reference to a text inset, follow these steps:

1. Open the text inset document (not the container).

2. In the paragraph you want to cross-reference, insert a Cross-Ref marker with a unique identifier. (For detailed instructions, refer to "Creating Spot Cross-References" on page 195.) You can also create a cross-reference to the heading paragraph, then delete the cross-reference, which will leave a cross-reference marker in the heading.

3. Save the text inset.

4. Open the container document.

5. Open the document in which you want to create the cross-reference.

6. Create the cross-reference by pointing to the container document and the cross-reference marker you created in the text inset.

Chapter 26

Templates

FrameMaker workflow relies on style sheets. By importing formats from a template file, different authors can create documents with consistent formatting and structure. FrameMaker files do not refer to an external template file; instead, once the template is set up, you must import formatting and structure information from the template file into the document files. Doing so creates a complete copy of all of the template information in the document files. Any document can theoretically be used as a template, but it's a very good idea to create a single, official template file and keep it in a safe place. All style sheet changes or additions should be made in that file. Without an official template, documents will eventually start to diverge as you or others add tags to individual files. (This phenomenon is known as "tag creep.")

Setting up FrameMaker templates requires much more detailed knowledge about the product than using templates after they are developed. Many organizations employ specialists or hire an outside consultant to set up their templates. Generally, the responsibilities in a writing group are divided into a number of different roles:

- **Template designer:** The template designer needs advanced FrameMaker skills. The designer creates FrameMaker templates and, for structured FrameMaker, the *element definition document* (EDD) that defines the structure of the documents.

- **Content creator (author):** The author needs basic-to-intermediate FrameMaker skills. Authors use established FrameMaker templates to create and edit information. In unstructured FrameMaker, authors need to know how to apply style sheets and create special entities, such as cross-references.

- **Production editor:** The production editor needs advanced FrameMaker skills. The production editor prepares documents for printing or other final output. Production editors check formatting, ensure that pages and lines break in appropriate places, and usually create the final version of tables of contents and indexes.

A larger publications group may also include technical editors, indexers, and the like; their level of FrameMaker knowledge needs to be similar to that of the authors. In a small publications group, one person often performs all of these roles.

In structured FrameMaker, the knowledge required of the template designer increases dramatically because the template designer must know how to analyze and define structure for a document. In some cases, two different people may perform document analysis and page design; they would work together to develop the structured templates.

This chapter describes some of the issues you must consider as a template designer. The information here focuses on creating formatting templates, which underpin structured FrameMaker but are mostly hidden from the user there. In unstructured FrameMaker, the formatting template is visible to the authors.

Why You Should Care About Templates

A well-designed template increases productivity greatly because it supports the authors, editors, and production editors in creating a document that's formatted correctly. Table tags, for example, let you define ruling and shading properties in a table so that when an author inserts a table, the table automatically uses the correct settings. Without a table tag, authors or production editors would have to spend time formatting each table manually. Running headers and footers save a lot of work by picking up information from the main body text, such as the current first-level heading, and automatically displaying it at the top or bottom of the page.

Reference page definitions control how generated tables of contents and indexes are formatted. Predefined cross-reference formats anticipate references that the author might need to insert and provide various options for the cross-reference text.

It's *possible* to create consistent documents without templates, but it's not efficient. In an environment where you are producing hundreds or thousands of pages of documents every year, working without an established template is a lot like walking a tightrope without a safety net—and wearing clown shoes.

Getting Started with Templates

The easiest way to begin creating templates is to start with an existing template and modify it to suit your requirements. When you install FrameMaker, several templates are put in your installation directory in the templates folder. These templates are also available when you select File | New | Document.

Adobe has also created a number of additional templates, which you can download from their web site. As this book goes to press, the templates are located at this URL:

```
www.adobe.com/products/framemaker/tempseries/
```

If that link doesn't work, try searching adobe.com for "framemaker templates." If you don't have the time to create your own templates, many FrameMaker consultants offer template design services.

Importing Settings from a Template File

When you import formats from a template file to a document, you can specify which catalogs you want to update. In each catalog, FrameMaker performs an additive merge—that is, tags with matching names are updated, and any tags that exist in the template but not in the document are added to the document.

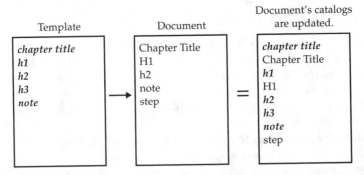

How you apply templates depends on whether you are working in structured or unstructured documents.

Unstructured Documents

To apply a template, follow these steps:

1. Open the template file.
2. Open your working file (the file you want to apply the template to).

To import formats into several files in a book file, open the book, then select the files you want to update.

3. Select File | Import | Formats. The Import Formats dialog box is displayed (Figure 26-1).

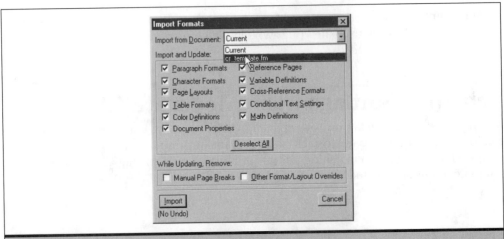

Figure 26-1. *Importing formats from one file to another*

4. In the Import from Document drop-down list, click the template file. Only open files are shown in this list.

Tip — *One quick way to remove overrides from a document is to import formats from the current file and check everything.*

---

5. In the Import and Update section, check all of the items you want to update from the template. Generally, you will want to update everything, but you can also perform selective updates. Click the Deselect All button to uncheck every option; click the Select All button (which replaces the Deselect All button) to check every option.

6. *(optional)* To remove page breaks that were set with overrides, check the Manual Page Breaks check box.

7. *(optional)* To remove overrides other than page breaks, check the Other Format/Layout Overrides check box.

8. Click the Import button to import the specified items from the template.

What's Imported?

Each check box in the Import and Update section of the Import Formats dialog box (Figure 26-1) controls a specific set of formatting catalogs. They are as follows:

- **Paragraph Formats:** Imports the contents of the paragraph catalog.
- **Character Formats:** Imports the contents of the character catalog.
- **Page Layouts:** Imports the master pages.
- **Table Formats:** Imports the table catalog; the list is in the Table Designer.
- **Color Definitions:** Imports the color catalog.
- **Document Properties:** Imports several miscellaneous settings. They include custom marker definitions, change bar settings, numbering properties, text options, and PDF settings.
- **Reference Pages:** Imports the reference pages.
- **Variable Definitions:** Imports the variables and their definitions.
- **Cross-Reference Formats:** Imports cross-reference formats.
- **Conditional Text Settings:** Imports conditional text tags and show/hide settings.
- **Math Definitions:** Imports custom math element definitions (used in equations).

Structured Documents

For structured documents, applying templates may involve one or two files. In some environments, the formatting and structure information are embedded in the same file. In others, you will have two separate template files: a formatting template and a structure template. The formatting template is a regular FrameMaker file; the structured template is the EDD.

To apply a template to a structured file, first check with your template guru to find out whether you're using one file or two. Then, follow these steps:

1. Open the template file(s) and the document you want to update.

2. Make sure that the document you want to update is the current document.

3. If you are using a separate formatting template, import its formats as you would for an unstructured document (see page 618).

4. Select File | Import | Element Definitions. The Import Element Definitions dialog box is displayed.

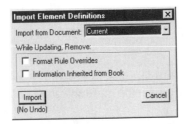

5. In the Import from Document drop-down list, click the EDD file you want to import from. Only open files are available in this list.

6. *(optional)* To strip all formatting overrides while importing elements, check the Format Rule Overrides check box.

7. *(optional)* Book files can also contain structure information. By default, that information is applied to the files in the book as well as the book file itself. To prevent the current file from inheriting information from the book file's structure template, check the Information Inherited from Book check box.

8. Click the Import button to import element definitions from the EDD.

The document now contains the formatting and structure information from your templates.

What Makes a "Good" Template?

Because templates involve making design decisions, beauty may well be in the eye of the beholder. There are, however, features that can make some templates more functional than others. The purpose of a template is to enable authors to create documents that have a consistent look and feel. A good template will assist in this process and help automate some tasks.

Consider, for example, the use of paragraph tags. It's possible to create two pages that look the same without using paragraph tags—the author could use the Format menu's Font selections and create two identical pages. It is, however, a tedious, manual, and time-consuming process. It would be much more efficient to create a couple of paragraph tags to format the items on the page. The paragraph tags, however, are useful only if the authors choose to use them.

Designing a good template requires more than just implementing paragraph tags. It also requires you, the template designer, to balance complexity and completeness. A *complete* template is a file that contains all of the tags needed to format documents consistently. But if that template is too *complex,* authors will face a steep learning curve in figuring out all the available tags and how to use them. Authors generally respond to an overly complex template by ignoring it.

Perhaps the best definition of a good template is any template that authors are willing and able to follow consistently, and can use to produce consistent results.

Structured FrameMaker simplifies formatting for the authors by hiding the paragraph tags and instead providing elements. The structure template controls which paragraph tag is applied in what context. Some authors prefer this environment because formatting is done automatically based on elements; other authors loathe it for the exact same reason.

Understanding Template Interactions

There is no single correct way to build a template. Some template designers start with master pages and page settings, and then they add paragraph tags to get the overall page design set up. Others insist that you must start with character tags because they are used by other features (such as paragraph autonumbering, variables, and cross-references). Still another approach is to create lots of different items as needed—if a paragraph tag needs a character tag for autonumber formatting, the designer jumps over to the Character Designer, creates the character tag, and returns to the Paragraph Designer to complete the paragraph definition.

We do recommend that you make a list of all of the needed formats and check them off as you build them so that you can keep track of what's needed and what's been created.

As you create your template, keep in mind that most of the template features are interdependent. Variables use character tags for formatting. Paragraph tags use the color catalog for available colors. Cross-references can call elements or paragraphs. The configuration of master pages affects how paragraph tags appear on the page. Master pages use system variables for headers and footers. All of these interactions can make designing a template a rather disconcerting experience because it's impossible to design in a linear process. See Figure 26-2.

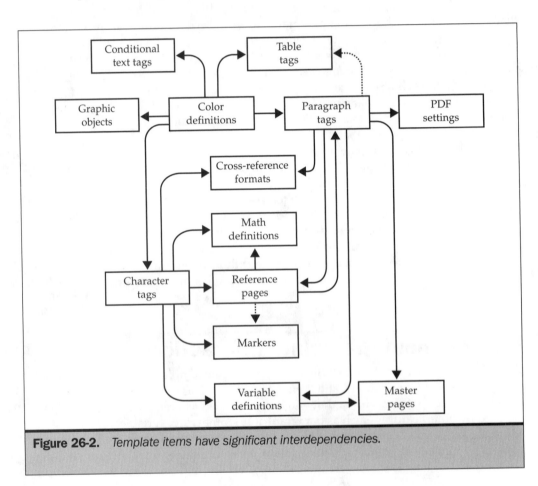

Figure 26-2. *Template items have significant interdependencies.*

The following sections explain how the template components interact.

Color Definitions

The color catalog is rarely the first item created in a template, but perhaps it should be. The color definitions are accessible to a number of other items, but color definitions do not have any dependencies on other template items. By default, eight colors are provided.

Character Tags

Character tags have only one dependency; the colors available in the Color drop-down list are taken from the color catalog. To assign a custom color to a character tag, you must first define the color in the color definitions.

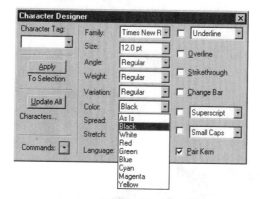

Character tags are widely used in other template components, including paragraph tags, variables, cross-references, and reference pages. They are also used in markers to assign formatting.

Graphic Objects

When you create various graphic objects using FrameMaker's drawing tools, the colors you can assign are determined by the color catalog.

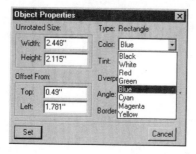

If your drawing includes text lines, they are formatted with character tags. Text in text frames is formatted with paragraph tags. Because not every graphic includes text, these relationships are not shown in Figure 26-2.

Conditional Text Tags

The colors available for conditional text tags are determined by the color catalog. Conditional text tags do not have any other dependencies.

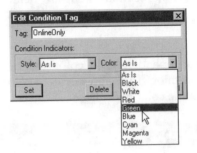

Paragraph Tags

Settings in the Paragraph Designer have three dependencies: color, reference pages, and character tags. For color, the situation is identical to the Character Designer; you can only assign colors that are defined in the color catalog. Character tags are available to format autonumbering. On the Advanced properties sheet, the reference pages are involved because the options available in the Frame Above and Frame Below drop-down lists correspond to the named graphic frames defined in the reference pages.

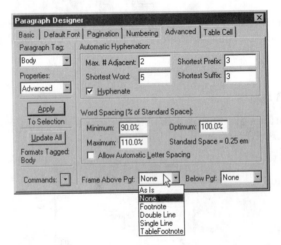

Paragraph tags are used by several other template components. Master pages use paragraph tags to determine which tag should be assigned to which page, variables call paragraph tags and use their text for running headers and footers, and so on.

Table Tags

Table tags use the color catalog and, under the covers, paragraph tags. The color definitions are available in several locations.

When you define shading colors, the Table Designer uses the color catalog:

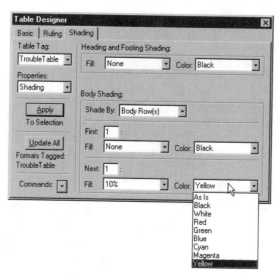

If you apply custom ruling and shading (Table | Custom Ruling & Shading), the color catalog is also accessed. Finally, if you edit a ruling style (click the Edit Ruling Style button on the Custom Ruling and Shading dialog box), you again have to use information from the color catalog.

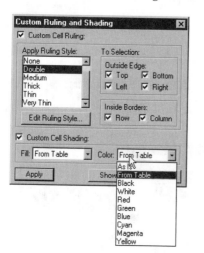

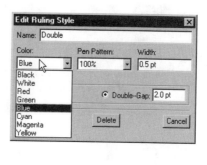

The relationship between table tags and paragraph tags is more subtle. The table definition stores a list of default paragraph tags used when you create new tables. For details, see "Applying Paragraph Tags" on page 174.

Cross-Reference Formats

Cross-references use character tags for formatting and paragraph tags (or elements) to get information. When you set up a cross-reference definition, character tags are available in the list of building blocks. The items available are taken from the document's character catalog.

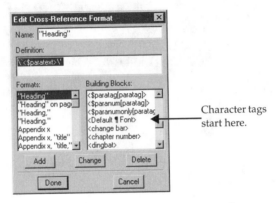

Character tags start here.

Several of the building blocks, such as <$paratext>, can be set up to refer to a specific paragraph tag.

Variable Definitions

Variable definitions, like cross-reference formats, use character tags for formatting and paragraph tags to determine what information to display. When you edit a system or user variable definition, you can assign character tags:

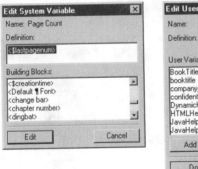
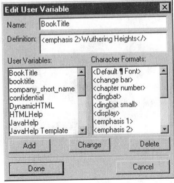

The </> building block is equivalent to <Default Para Font>, but takes up much less space.

Some variables, such as running headers and footers, let you reference specific paragraph tags with syntax such as:

```
<$paratext[ChapterTitle]>
```

Reference Pages

Reference pages use information from the character tags and paragraph tags, and in turn are used by paragraph tags. There is also a relationship between reference pages and markers. When you set up flows for generated files, you work on the reference pages. These flows use character tags for formatting and refer to paragraph tags and sometimes markers.

The Paragraph Designer uses reference page information for Frame Above and Frame Below settings.

Markers

When you create marker text, such as index entries, you can use character tags to control the formatting of the file generated with the marker information. The appearance of the marker text is further governed by the information set on the reference pages in the generated file.

Math Definitions

Math definitions are custom components for equations. For the most part, equations stand on their own separately from other document objects. Equations do, however, use character tags for formatting.

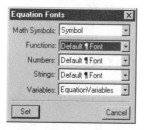

Equations can also use information from reference pages. You can define a custom equation object on a FrameMath reference page. This object is then available in the Equations Palette.

Master Pages

When you create master page definitions, you almost always use variables. The Current Page # system variable, for example, is on almost every master page definition. Running header and footer variables are also common.

You can assign master pages based on paragraph tags or elements that occur on the body pages. This makes the master pages dependent on paragraph tags.

The mapping table that establishes these links is stored on the reference pages.

PDF Settings

When you configure the PDF Setup dialog box (Format | Document | PDF Setup), the bookmarks and tags are set based on available paragraph tags or elements. PDF Setup is probably one of the last items you'll configure in your template.

The Bookmarks sheet lets you specify which FrameMaker paragraph tags or elements should be displayed as bookmarks in the PDF file; you also specify their hierarchy.

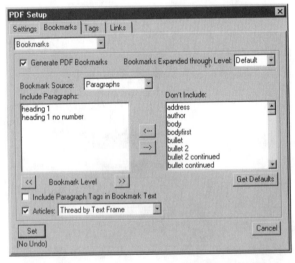

The Tags sheet lets you specify which FrameMaker paragraphs to include to create tagged (structured) PDF files.

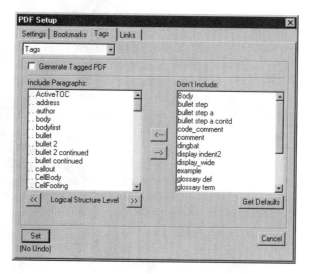

Tips and Tricks

This section describes some design tricks that automate certain features and make templates easier to use.

Paragraph Tags

When creating paragraph tags, pay close attention to naming conventions. Users spend more time using paragraph tags than any other item in the template.

Here are some issues to consider as you create paragraph tags:

- How many heading levels does the document need?
- How many types of body text does the document need?
- How many levels of indent?
- What kind of numbered lists?
- What kind of bulleted (unordered) lists?
- Do you need to set up header and footer styles? Are they different on left and right master pages?
- Does the document require an overall numbering scheme? Will you use <$volnum> and <$chapnum>? How will these integrate into the autonumbering you need to define?
- Do you need notes, cautions, warnings, tips, and other asides?
- Do you need formats for sidebars?
- What about table, figure, or example captions?

The following items will make your tags more useful:

■ **Use Keep with Next (Pagination properties) to avoid awkward page breaks.** Headings usually belong with the paragraph beneath them, so set heading formats to keep with the next paragraph. This eliminates unsightly headings hanging at the bottom of a page. Consider whether other paragraph tags have similar requirements.

■ **Control spell-checking with the Language setting (Default Font properties).** A language of None causes a paragraph to be skipped by the spell-checker, which is useful for code. If you have multiple languages in a single document, create paragraph tags for each language and set the Language attribute for each one. FrameMaker will use the dictionary and hyphenation settings of the specified language as it spell-checks each paragraph.

■ **Set Widow/Orphan Lines (Pagination properties) to reduce awkward page breaks.** Use a widow/orphan setting of at least 2 throughout the paragraph tags to prevent solitary lines at the beginning or end of a page. If you want to keep an entire paragraph on the same page, use a very high number (for example, 99 or 999).

■ **Use autonumbering for bullets, steps, notes, cautions, and any other repeated text.** Autonumbering is wonderful for numbered headings, figure captions, and tables, but don't forget the "text-based" autonumbering, which can also save significant amounts of time.

■ **Use the Start setting (Pagination properties) to set up paragraph tags that should always start at the top of a page or column.** Most often, this will be your chapter title (Start Top of Right Page) and your first-level headings (Start Top of Page).

■ **Use the Next Pgf Tag setting (Basic properties) where you can predict a likely paragraph tag.** Most heading paragraphs are followed by a body or firstbody paragraph. Most step 1 paragraphs are followed by step 2. By setting the default, you'll save your users a step—they won't have to assign the tag manually.

Character Tags

In addition to providing character-level formatting in regular text, character tags are referenced by several other features. Refer to this preliminary checklist as you build your list of required character tags:

■ Character-level formatting

■ Variables

■ Formatting for autonumbers

■ Cross-references

■ Generated files

- Markers, especially index markers
- Math definitions
- Reference pages
- Text lines

As you create your character tags, keep in mind the following issues:

- In general, it's best to use the As Is setting throughout the character tag and assign specific settings only to the items you want to change.
- The Language attribute in the character tag overrides the Language attribute assigned by the paragraph tag.
- Consider creating special one-letter character tags that make inserting formatting in markers faster. For example, you could italicize a word in an index entry with this syntax:

```
cross-stitching needle: <Emphasis>see<Default Para
Font> tapestry needle<$nopage>
```

But if you define an "i" character tag, you could use this syntax for the same result:

```
cross-stitching needle: <i>see<Default Para Font>tapestry
needle<$nopage>
```

These shorter tags will also be very helpful on the reference pages. (Notice that these tags do break the rule against naming tags by their formatting.)

Table Tags

In addition to the ruling and shading attributes, keep in mind that you can set several properties as defaults (although not in the Table Designer). The defaults are saved based on the settings in the selected table when you click the Update All button in the Table Designer. The settings saved as defaults are the number of rows and columns, the column widths, and the default paragraph tags for the heading rows, body rows, and footing rows.

Reference Pages

When you create a graphic frame on the reference pages, you must assign a name to the graphic frame. The graphic frames are not, however, labeled by default, so to figure out which frame has which name, you must click each graphic frame so see its name. To avoid this, add a text label next to each graphic frame as you create it.

Conditional Text Tags

If multiple conditional text tags are applied to an item, that item is shown in magenta. For this reason, avoid using magenta as a color indicator for a single condition tag; you won't be able to distinguish between that tag and a situation where two or more conditions have been applied.

Naming Conventions

The names you assign to tags can make your template significantly more or less usable. A carefully chosen set of tag names will be easy to understand and lend themselves to using keyboard shortcuts.

Capitalization

For the most part, the capitalization you choose for tags can be left to your personal preference. There are, however, a few things to consider:

- FrameMaker's default tags have an initial capital letter (Heading1, Body, and so on). If you plan to use the default tags, you may want to match other tags to use similar capitalization.

- If you do not plan to use FrameMaker's default tags, consider creating only lowercase tag names in your template so that you can easily distinguish your tags from any "renegade" tags.

- Default Word template styles use initial capital letters. When you convert Word files to FrameMaker, the style names are converted to paragraph tag names, and similar considerations apply as for the default FrameMaker templates.

Special Characters

FrameMaker *will* generally allow you to use special characters, such as asterisks (*), question marks (?), and pound signs (#), as part of your tag names. These characters can cause major problems, though, when you attempt to reference the tags (for example, in an EDD). We strongly recommend that you use only alphanumeric characters (a–z, A–Z, and 0–9), underscores, and spaces.

Taking Keyboard Shortcuts into Account

Authors can apply many tags using keyboard shortcuts. In general, you press a key sequence to display the tag list in the status bar, and press a letter to jump to that part of the list. To accommodate authors who use this shortcut, it's very helpful to create tag names whose first few letters are unique. A good example of how *not* to do this are the default heading names in FrameMaker: Heading1, Heading2, and HeadingRunIn. Instead, you might use 1Head, 2Head, and 3Head. Some template designers start each tag name with a short, unique prefix, as shown in the following example:

Format vs. Function Names

Most tag names are based on the format or function of the tag. For example, an Italics character tag is a format-based name; a PrintOnline conditional text tag is a function-based name.

Template designers generally recommend that you use names that describe functionality. There are a couple of reasons for this:

- **Tags named by function are easier for an author to learn.** For example, if a book title occurs in a document, the author has an easier time remembering to apply the BookTitle character tag than remembering that italics are required and then locating the Italics character tag.

- **You can change formatting associated with functional tags without making the tag name obsolete.** Consider a character tag that indicates menu selection. In the past, your style guide indicated that the menu choice must be boldface; the new standard is to make the menu choice italic. You can change a MenuItem character tag from boldface to italics; if your tag was named Bold, changing it to actually apply italics would cause great confusion.

- **Functional names are better suited to outputting structured documents.** A paragraph tag labeled Helv10pt would need to be mapped to an XML tag of <para> or something similar. Using functional names in both FrameMaker and XML makes it easier to understand the relationship between the two formats.

There are a few occasions where a combination of functional and formatting names might be useful. For example, you might create a Body paragraph tag (functional) and a second BodyBold paragraph tag (functional and formatting). BodyBold tells the author very quickly what the difference is between the two paragraph tags. A more functional name, such as BodyImportant, might not deliver the message as quickly.

When implementing functional names, keep in mind that tag duplication can become a problem. You might, for example, have several different functional items that need to be italicized:

- BookTitle
- ForeignWord
- Emphasis
- FileName
- URL

Some authors will learn quickly that BookTitle creates italics, and will use BookTitle any time they need italics, even though other tags are more appropriate. Again, the key is to balance the need for functional labels against the overall usability of the template.

Separating Out "Housekeeping" Tags

Every template will have a number of tags that are intended for use "under the covers" and should not be applied by authors. These might include paragraph tags for the header and footer paragraphs and other information that occurs on the master pages. Consider using a special prefix for those tags. For example, naming them with a z_ prefix ensures that these tags are sorted to the bottom of the paragraph catalog, which makes it less likely that an author will accidentally use one of those tags.

Documenting Your Template

Please document your templates. Documentation doesn't have to be elaborate, but a basic list of tags and how they are used will be extremely helpful to authors. It also helps to enforce consistency.

The best place to provide documentation for the template is in the template file itself. You can list paragraph tags in one table, character tags in another, conditional text settings in a third, and so on. Providing an example of each tag to show what it looks like is helpful.

Template documentation is a good place to list autonumbering streams. This helps you keep track of which series labels have been used and avoid collisions. For example, you might have something like the following table:

Tag	Autonumbering Definition
ChapterTitle	H:<$chapnum>
Heading1	H:<$chapnum>.<n+>
Heading2	H:<$chapnum>.<n>.<n+>
Figure	F:Figure <$chapnum>-<n+>
Table	T:Table <$chapnum>-<n+>
Step1	S:Step <n=1>
Step2	S:Step <n+>
SubStepA	U:<a=1>.
SubStepB	U:<a+>.

We recommend providing a list of tags for each type of formatting element. You may also want to provide additional documentation, such as standard settings for graphics (what resolution should be used when importing bitmaps?), instructions for creating books, tables of contents, and indexes, and perhaps even some basic style guidelines.

When you add new tags to the template, don't forget to update the template documentation.

Using Single-Purpose Templates

Some publishing applications have special documents that manage settings called *control files*. When you make a change in the control file, it is automatically applied to all of the files in the book.

FrameMaker does not have actual control files. You can, however, mimic this feature by using a single-purpose template, a document that contains a limited number of settings. You might, for example, create a document that contains no paragraph tags, character tags, or cross-references but has a full set of variable definitions. When you create a new book, all of the component files use the default settings for variables.

When you are ready to set the variables to the values needed for this book, you follow these steps:

1. Open the variable control file and set the variables to the values needed for this book.

2. Open the book file.

3. Select all of the files in the book.

4. Select File | Import | Formats. The Import Formats dialog box is displayed.

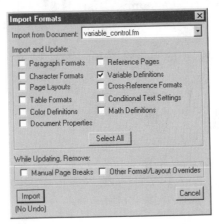

5. In the Import from Document drop-down list, click your variable control file.

6. In the Import and Update section, click the Deselect All button to uncheck all the boxes. (The button label toggles between Deselect All and Select All.)

7. Check only the Variable Definitions check box only.

8. Click the Import button to import variable definitions from the selected file into all of the files in the book.

You could accomplish the same thing by modifying the variables in a chapter file and importing the formats from that file to the others in the book. Maintaining a separate variable-only file makes it easier, though, to segregate the changes you want to make (variable definitions) from any other changes that might have crept into the other chapter files.

If you want to be extra-cautious (paranoid?) about accidentally copying in settings you don't want, you can create a MIF fragment that contains only the variable definitions instead of using a full-blown FrameMaker file. For details, see Chapter 24, "Maker Interchange Format."

The Complete Reference

FrameMaker 7

Chapter 27

Sharing and Managing Files Using WebDAV

W eb-based Distributed Authoring and Versioning, or *WebDAV*, is a technology that lets you share and manage documents over the Internet. Using WebDAV, you can take advantage of basic content management features without buying a separate software package. The documents you want FrameMaker to manage are stored on a Windows, UNIX, or Mac OS X server running the WebDAV protocol. To access the files, you set up a *workgroup* in FrameMaker that points to the WebDAV server. To edit files, you *check out* the files, which means working copies of the files are copied to a folder on your hard drive. FrameMaker also locks files to prevent users from modifying the same documents simultaneously. Other users can open the files you checked out and download the last version saved on the server, but they can't modify the files. When you're finished, you *check in* the files.

Note *Though WebDAV can run on UNIX clients and servers, FrameMaker 7 for UNIX doesn't include workgroup functionality.*

Both structured and unstructured FrameMaker files can be managed in a workgroup along with non-FrameMaker files, such as imported graphics or PDF files. Applications other than FrameMaker also support WebDAV, so you can open a managed graphic in Adobe Illustrator 10, for example, or open a managed PDF file in Adobe Acrobat 5.

Note *You can turn off the workgroup feature if you're not working with files on the WebDAV server. As a result, the WebDAVLinks palette isn't displayed when you open FrameMaker. However, if you open a managed document when workgroup functionality is off, the document is opened in read-only mode. See "Modifying Workgroup Preferences" on page 642 for details.*

Managing Workgroups

Before you begin sharing files, a WebDAV server must be installed and configured. Many WebDAV servers are available for free from www.webdav.org. Typically, your system administrator (or an eager coworker) handles the installation. The server can be difficult to configure, and security policies must be set up to provide for secure transfers over the Internet. You'll probably have a user name and password to download and upload files.

To create a workgroup in FrameMaker after the WebDAV server is installed, follow these steps:

1. Click in the text flow of a FrameMaker document
2. Select File | Workgroup | Workgroup Servers. The Workgroup Servers dialog box is displayed (Figure 27-1).

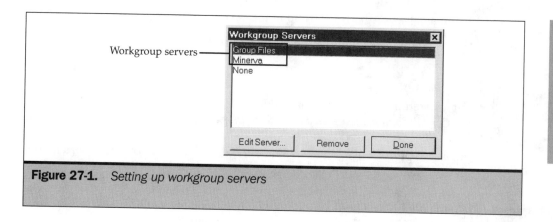

Workgroup servers

Figure 27-1. Setting up workgroup servers

Note *If your cursor isn't in the text flow, the Workgroup menu options are grayed out.*

3. If a server is selected, click None in the list of workgroup servers. (The New Server button reads "Edit Server" when you click an item in the list.)

4. Click the New Server button. The Server Setup dialog box is displayed (Figure 27-2).

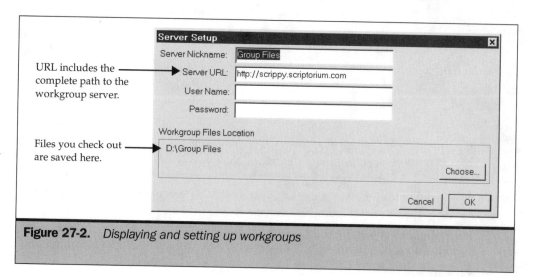

URL includes the complete path to the workgroup server.

Files you check out are saved here.

Figure 27-2. Displaying and setting up workgroups

5. Type in a name for the workgroup in the Server Nickname field.

6. Type the Uniform Resource Locator (URL) for the workgroup in the Server URL field.

Include the full URL for the workgroup server. After you click the OK button to save the workgroup settings, an error is displayed if you leave out "http://" or type an invalid URL. Consult with your system administrator for the correct information.

7. *(optional)* Type your user name in the User Name field and your password in the Password field. This gives you access to files on the WebDAV server.

Typically, you shouldn't add your user name and password. If you do, anyone who uses your computer will have access to files on the workgroup server.

8. To choose the folder to which you'll download files, follow these steps:

   a. Click the Choose button. The Browse for Folder dialog box is displayed.

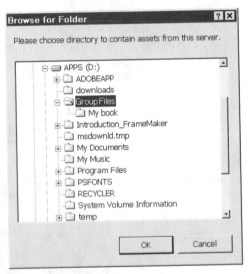

   b. Click the folder, then click the OK button. The Server Setup dialog box is displayed again (Figure 27-2 on page 639).

9. Click the OK button, then click the Done button. You've configured your workgroup server. If an error is displayed, verify that the server is working and you have the correct URL.

Editing a Workgroup

Once you create a workgroup, you can edit your workgroup settings. For example, you can change your local workgroup directory. After you change the directory, files you download and check out are saved to the new directory, and files in the old directory remain in the same location. To edit the workgroup settings, follow these steps:

1. Select File | Workgroup | Workgroup Servers. The Workgroup Servers dialog box is displayed (Figure 27-1 on page 639).
2. Click the server you want to modify, then click the Edit Server button. (The New Server button reads "Edit Server" when you click a workgroup.)
3. Modify the settings, then click the OK button. The Workgroup Servers dialog box is displayed again.

 Caution *Typically, you shouldn't add your user name and password. If you do, anyone who uses your computer will have access to files on the workgroup server.*

4. Click the Done button. Your changes are saved.

Deleting a Workgroup

When you delete a workgroup, FrameMaker removes the workgroup from your list of configured servers; the files on the server or in your local directory are not deleted. You need to delete obsolete workgroups—servers that no longer exist or to which you don't have access. If you don't delete them, a warning is displayed each time you display the list of workgroups. You can click the OK button to ignore the warning, but this gets tedious.

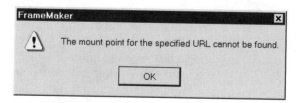

To delete a workgroup, follow these steps:

1. Select File | Workgroup | Workgroup Servers. The Workgroup Servers dialog box is displayed (Figure 27-1 on page 639).
2. Click the workgroup you want to delete, then click the Remove button. A confirmation dialog box is displayed.
3. Click the Yes button to delete the server. The server is removed from your workgroup setup in FrameMaker.

Modifying Workgroup Preferences

The workgroup preferences provide options for managing documents and links. You can also turn off the workgroup feature. Table 27-1 describes the preferences.

To modify the preferences, follow these steps:

1. Select File | Preferences | Workgroup. The Workgroup Preferences dialog box is displayed.

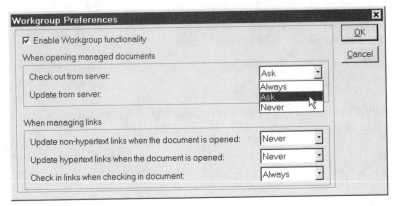

2. In each drop-down list, click Always, Ask, or Never. See Table 27-1 for details.
3. Click the OK button. The preferences are updated.

Option	Description
Enable Workgroup functionality	Turns the workgroup feature on or off. When turned off, the Workgroup menus are grayed out, and the WebDAVLinks palette isn't displayed when you open FrameMaker. Turning the feature off doesn't affect your managed files. When you turn the feature on again, the Workgroup menus are displayed, and the WebDAVLinks palette is displayed when you open FrameMaker.

Table 27-1. *Modifying Workgroup Preferences*

Option	Description
When opening managed documents	
Check out from server	**Always:** Checks out a file automatically when you open it. **Ask:** Asks if you want to check out the file. If you click the No button, a read-only version is displayed. **Never:** Never checks out the file. A read-only version is displayed. Because you might want to open a file only for reading (not for modifying), it's usually best to select Ask or Never. Never is the default setting. See "Checking Out Files" on page 650 for details.
Update from server (only affects documents that are checked in)	**Always:** Opens the latest version from the server instead of from your local directory. **Ask:** Asks if you want to open an updated version from the server. If you click the No button, your local copy is displayed. **Never:** Opens your local copy. To make sure you're always working from the most up-to-date file, keep the default setting, Always. See "Updating Local Documents" on page 652 for details.
When managing links	
Update non-hypertext links when the document is opened	**Always:** Automatically downloads the latest imported graphics, text insets, links to files in a book, and other non-hypertext links from the server when you open the file. **Ask:** Asks if you want to download the latest non-hypertext links from the server. **Never:** Never downloads the latest non-hypertext links. The links saved in your local copy of the document are displayed. See "Updating Managed Links" on page 659 for details.

Table 27-1.   *Modifying Workgroup Preferences (Continued)*

Option	Description
Update hypertext links when the document is opened	**Always:** Automatically downloads the latest cross-references, table of contents entries, index entries, and other hypertext links from the server when you open the file. **Ask:** Asks if you want to download the latest hypertext links from the server. **Never:** Never updates hypertext links. The links saved in your local copy of the document are displayed. See "Updating Managed Links" on page 659 for details.
Check in links when checking in document	**Always:** Automatically checks in links when checking in a document. **Ask:** Asks if you want to check in links. **Never:** Never checks in links. You have to check them in manually. See "Checking In Links" on page 659 for details.

Table 27-1. *Modifying Workgroup Preferences (Continued)*

Keep in mind that if a document is large or has many links, updating the links every time you open the file might cause your file to open slowly. In addition, the imported items don't need to be updated every time if they aren't modified frequently. You can later update the links all at once after opening the document. See "Updating Managed Links" on page 659 for details.

Working with Managed Documents

Files on the workgroup server are *managed* documents. You create managed documents by saving them from FrameMaker to the workgroup server. From there, you can work with the managed documents. Features include the following:

- **Saving a file on the workgroup server.** When you save a FrameMaker file onto the workgroup server for the first time, you create a managed document. A working copy is saved to your local workgroup directory, and you choose whether to check out the file. If you don't check out the file, a read-only version is displayed.

- **Opening a managed file.** When you open a file from the workgroup server, a read-only copy is displayed. You must check out the file to gain write access.

- **Checking out a file.** To modify a managed document, you check out the file. A copy is saved to your local workgroup directory. Others can't modify the file until you check it in. They can, however, open the file in read-only mode or update their local copy.

- **Saving a file.** To give others access to your changes while you have the document checked out, you can save the document to the workgroup server. Both your local copy and the server versions are updated.

- **Canceling a check out.** After checking out a document, you might decide that you don't need to modify it. To release the lock on the file and let others check it out, you cancel your check out.

- **Checking in a file.** To let others modify a managed document, you check in the file. You can also check in the managed links so that others may modify the linked items (such as imported graphics). When you check in a file, your local copy is displayed in read-only mode.

- **Updating your local copy.** While someone has a document checked out, you can update your local copy to view the latest version.

- **Reverting to the last saved copy.** To discard your changes to a file, you can revert to the last saved version.

- **Renaming a file.** You can rename files on the workgroup server; however, the file still exists under the original name until you delete it.

- **Uploading and downloading non-FrameMaker files.** FrameMaker lets you manage non-FrameMaker files on the workgroup server.

Adding Files to the Server

To add a file to the server, follow these steps:

1. Select File | Open, then open the file you want to upload.
2. Select File | Workgroup | Save As. The Save To Server dialog box is displayed.

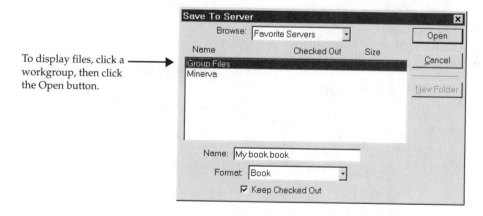

To display files, click a workgroup, then click the Open button.

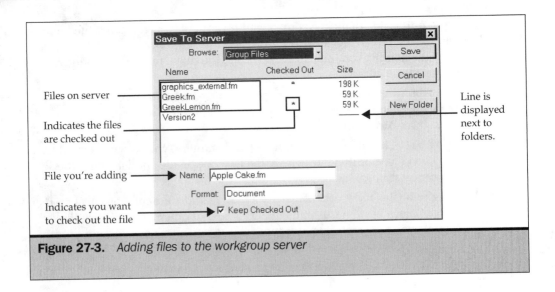

Files on server

Indicates the files
are checked out

File you're adding

Indicates you want
to check out the file

Line is
displayed
next to
folders.

Figure 27-3. *Adding files to the workgroup server*

3. To display the correct folder on the server, do one of the following:
   - Click a workgroup or folder, then click the Open button.
   - Click the workgroup or folder in the Browse drop-down list.

   The contents of the server or folder are displayed (Figure 27-3).

4. *(optional)* To create a new folder on the server, follow these steps:
   a. Click the New Folder button. The New Folder dialog box is displayed.

   b. Type the name of the folder, then click the Create button. The new folder is added to the drop-down list, and the Save To Server dialog box is displayed.

New folder (The new folder isn't
always displayed after you create
it, so you might need to select the
folder in the drop-down list.)

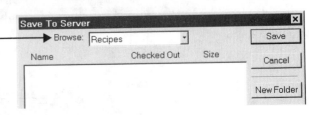

c. Click the new folder (scroll down if necessary), then click the Open button. The name of the new folder is displayed in the Browse field.

5. *(optional)* To save the file with a different name, type the name in the Name field. For example, you might need to add the .fm extension to a document in Macintosh so that other platforms can recognize the file format.

6. *(optional)* To save the file as a Maker Interchange Format (MIF) file, click MIF in the Format drop-down list. The file can then be opened in previous versions of FrameMaker, but unsupported features will not be available. For example, new FrameMaker 7 features aren't supported in FrameMaker 6.

7. *(optional)* To check out the file, check the Keep Checked Out check box. This means that others cannot modify the file until you check it in.

8. Click the Save button. A confirmation dialog box is displayed.

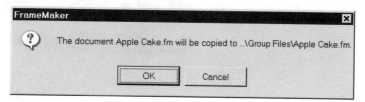

9. Click the OK button. If your user name and password are not specified for the server, the Authentication dialog box is displayed.

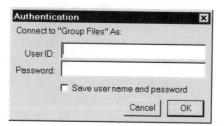

10. Type your user name and password, then click the OK button. The file is copied to your local directory and the workgroup server. One of the following might occur:

   ■ If the file is already in your local directory, a confirmation dialog box is displayed. To replace the existing file, click the Yes button.

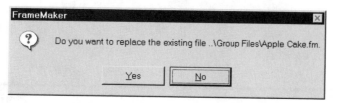

■ If the file is already in the workgroup directory, a confirmation dialog box is displayed. To replace the existing file, click the Yes button.

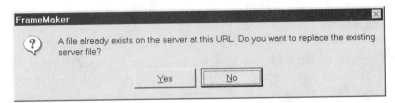

If you didn't check out the file, the file reverts to a read-only version, only the file name is displayed in the title bar, and the menus change. You need to check out the file to modify it. See "Checking Out Files" on page 650 for details.

In a read-only file, the menus change. ⟶

The full path is not displayed. ⟶

Opening Files

You can open a file on the server and check it out, or if it's already checked out, just view the document. To open a file, follow these steps:

1. Select File | Workgroup | Open. The Open From Server dialog box is displayed (Figure 27-4).

Files marked with stars are already checked out. A warning is displayed if you try to check them out.

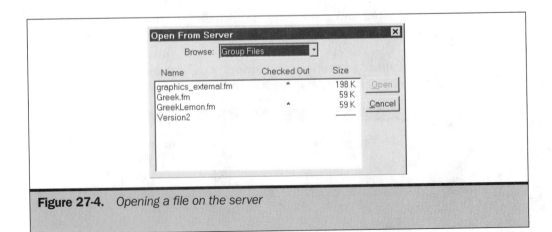

Figure 27-4. *Opening a file on the server*

2. To display the folder that contains the file, click the folder in the Browse drop-down list.

3. If you need to enter your user name and password, the Authentication dialog box is displayed. Type the information, then click the OK button. The Open From Server dialog box is displayed again (Figure 27-4).

4. Click the file, then click the Open button. One of the following occurs:

   ■ If your preferences are set up to update hyperlinks automatically, the links are updated.

   ■ If your preferences are set up to ask if you want to update hyperlinks, dialog boxes are displayed for updating hypertext links and non-hypertext links. Click the Yes buttons in both boxes to update links or the No buttons to avoid updating them. In a document with many links, the update may take some time. You can update the links later if you want to. See "Updating Managed Links" on page 659 for details.

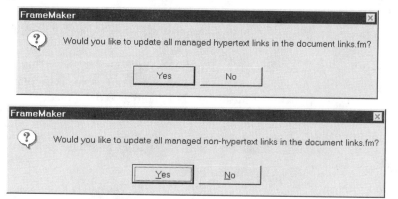

5. Next, one of the following occurs:

   ■ If your preferences are set up to check out files automatically when you open them, the file is copied to your local directory, and the file on the server is locked to prevent others from making changes.

   ■ If your preferences are set up to ask if you want to check out a file when you open it, a confirmation dialog box is displayed. Click the Yes button to check out the file and copy it to your local directory or the No button to display the file in read-only mode.

   ■ If your preferences are set up to never check out files automatically, the file is displayed in read-only mode.

Checking Out Files

After you open a file, you can check it out to make changes. FrameMaker locks the file and saves a copy to your local directory in the same directory structure as the server. For example, files are usually stored in subdirectories on the server. If the file is in the "Group Files/Recipes" subdirectory, FrameMaker creates the "Group Files/Recipes" folder in your local directory and copies the file into the new structure.

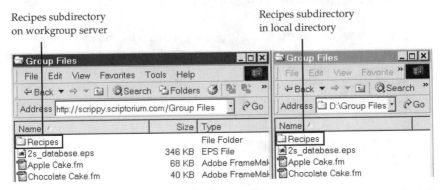

In the Open From Server dialog box (Figure 27-4 on page 648), the Checked Out column indicates which files are checked out. If checked out, a star is displayed next to the file name. You can open one of these files, but an error is displayed if you try to check out the file.

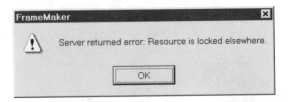

By default, FrameMaker prompts for a confirmation when you try to check out a file. You can configure the workgroup preferences to check out files automatically or never check out files when you open them. See "Modifying Workgroup Preferences" on page 642 for details.

To check out one or more open files, do one of the following:

- **Check out one open file.** Select File | Workgroup | Check Out.
- **Check out all open files.** Press SHIFT and select File | Workgroup | Check Out All Open Files.

The files are checked out, copied to your local workgroup directory, and locked.

Saving Managed Documents

You can save managed files in your local directory or on the server. If you save documents in your local directory, other users can't see your changes or update their local copies until you save the file on the server or check in the file. However, by saving the file on the server, you give others access to your changes without releasing your lock on the file.

Saving Files Locally

To save one or more files on your hard drive, save them as you do unmanaged documents. You can also save a file in a different directory as you normally do. See "Opening, Saving, Closing, and Printing Documents" on page 41 for details.

Saving Files on the Server

To save files on the server, do one of the following:

- **Save one open file.** Select File | Workgroup | Save.
- **Save all open files.** Press SHIFT and select File | Workgroup | Save All Open Documents.
- **Save an open file to another folder.** Select File | Workgroup | Save As. The Save To Server dialog box is displayed (Figure 27-3 on page 646). Browse to find the correct folder, then click the Save button.

 Note *When you check in files, FrameMaker saves the files on the server before checking them in.*

Canceling Check Outs

You can decide you only want to view a file after you check it out. If so, you cancel the check out. FrameMaker unlocks the file and discards your changes.

To cancel check outs, do one of the following:

- **Cancel check out on one file.** Select File | Workgroup | Cancel Check Out. A confirmation dialog box is displayed. Click the Yes button.

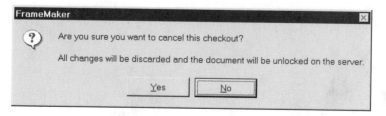

- **Cancel check out on all open files.** Press SHIFT and select File | Workgroup | Cancel Checkout of All Open Documents. A confirmation dialog box is displayed for each document. Click the Yes button for each document.

The files are unlocked, and read-only versions are displayed.

Checking In Files

After you modify a managed file, you check in the file. FrameMaker lets you check in all managed links and unlocks the file. To check in files, do one of the following:

- **Check in one open file.** Select File | Workgroup | Check In.
- **Check in all open files.** Press SHIFT and select File | Workgroup | Check In All Open Files.

If the document contains managed links, a confirmation dialog box is displayed. Click the Yes button to check in all managed links. The files are saved, unlocked, and read-only versions are displayed. See "Managing Links" on page 656 for more information on updating links.

Updating Local Documents

You can update your local copy of a managed document while another user has the file checked out. This lets you read the latest version of the document. To update local documents, do one of the following:

- **Update one open document.** Select File | Workgroup | Update.
- **Update all open documents.** Press SHIFT and select File | Workgroup | Update All Open Documents.

Reverting to the Last Saved Document

Before you save changes to a document, you have the option of reverting to the last saved copy on the server. When you revert, the changes you made are discarded (whether or not you saved them to your local workgroup), but the file remains checked out. To revert to the last saved copy of a document, do one of the following:

- **Revert one document.** Select File | Workgroup | Revert. A confirmation dialog box is displayed. Click the Yes button.

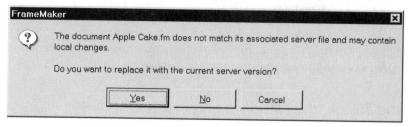

- ■ **Revert all open documents.** Press SHIFT and select File | Workgroup | Revert All Open Documents. A confirmation dialog box is displayed for each file that doesn't match the server version. Click the Yes button for each document.

Your changes are discarded, and the last-saved version of the document is displayed.

Renaming Files

You can rename a managed document, and the contents of the document are copied into a new document. If another user opens the document with the old name, FrameMaker does not display a warning, so you'll need to delete the old file or notify other users that you've changed the name.

To rename an open file, follow these steps:

1. Select File | Workgroup | Save As. The Save To Server dialog box is displayed (Figure 27-3 on page 646).

2. Type a new name in the Name field, then click the Save button. A confirmation dialog box is displayed.

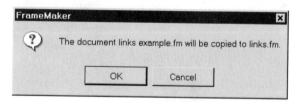

3. Click the OK button. The contents of the document are copied into a new file.

Closing Files

You close managed files just as you do unmanaged files—by selecting File | Close or pressing SHIFT and selecting File | Close All Open Files. Make sure you save or check in the file before closing it, because your changes will be discarded. If you don't check in the file, the file is still checked out to you, and other users will be unable to modify the file. See "Saving Managed Documents" on page 651 and "Checking In Files" on page 652 for details.

Uploading and Downloading Files

FrameMaker lets you download and upload files to the server without opening the files. For example, you can upload a graphic or spreadsheet. These files can be imported into managed files or opened in another program that supports WebDAV.

Uploading Files

To upload a file, follow these steps:

1. Select File | Workgroup | Put File on Server. The Please select a file to be uploaded dialog box is displayed.

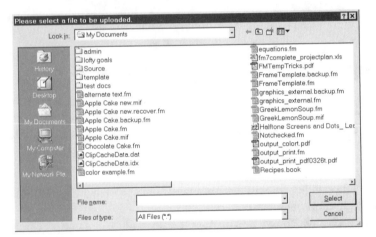

2. Click the file (you can only choose one at a time), then click the Select button. The Save To Server dialog box is displayed (Figure 27-3 on page 646).

3. *(optional)* To rename the file, type a new name in the Name field.

4. *(optional)* To prevent others from modifying the file, check the Keep Checked Out check box.

5. Click the Save button. A confirmation dialog box is displayed, stating that the file will be copied to your local directory.

6. Click the OK button. The file is uploaded to the server.

Downloading Files

To download a file to your local directory, follow these steps:

1. Select File | Workgroup | Get File from Server. The Open From Server dialog box is displayed (Figure 27-4 on page 648).

2. Click the Open button. The file is copied to your local directory.

Adding and Managing Links

In addition to managing documents, FrameMaker can manage the links in a document. Both hypertext and non-hypertext links are supported. Hypertext links include items such as cross-references, table of contents entries, and index entries. Non-hypertext include items such as imported graphics, text insets, and links to files in a book.

Link management options are similar to document management options. You can check in and out, save, cancel check outs, update, and revert hyperlinks to the last saved versions on the server.

Importing Files

You can import files into a managed document from your local directory or the server, either by creating a link to the file or copying the file into the document. When you check out a document that has imported files, those files aren't automatically checked out. You must check them out separately. See "Managing Links" on page 656 for details.

Importing Unmanaged Files

To import a file from your computer, import them as you do in an unmanaged document. See "Importing a Graphic" on page 304 for details. If you decide later that you want to manage the file, you can save the link to the server from the WebDAVLinks palette. See "Saving Unmanaged Links" on page 656 for details.

Importing Managed Files

To import a managed file into an open document, follow these steps:

1. Select File | Workgroup | Import. The Import From Server dialog box is displayed.

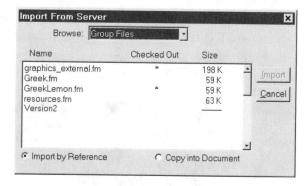

Import From Server				
Browse:	Group Files			
Name		Checked Out	Size	
graphics_external.fm		*	198 K	Import
Greek.fm			59 K	
GreekLemon.fm		*	59 K	Cancel
resources.fm			63 K	
Version2				

○ Import by Reference   ○ Copy into Document

2. Click the file, then click one of the following:

   ■ To create a link to the file, click the Import by Reference radio button.

   ■ To copy the file into the document, click the Copy into Document radio button.

3. Click the Import button. The file is displayed in the document and copied into your local directory.

Managing Links

After you import files into a document or add files to a book file, you manage their links in the WebDAVLinks palette. Select File | Links to display the palette. Basic information about links in the document is displayed, such as whether links are unmanaged, checked in, or checked out. The name and location of a selected link is also displayed.

In the Links drop-down list, you select options to manage your links. For example, you can save links to the server, check links in and out, revert to the last saved link on the server, updating links that are checked in, and cancel checked-out links.

Saving Unmanaged Links

You save unmanaged links on the server to begin managing them. FrameMaker prompts you to name each link and gives you the option of checking them out. To save links in a file you've checked out, follow these steps:

1. Select File | Links. The WebDAVLinks palette is displayed (Figure 27-5).

2. Indicate which links you want to save, then click an item in the Links drop-down list. The choices are as follows:

   ■ **Save one link.** Select the link, then click Save Link As.

   ■ **Save several links.** Select the links, then click Save Selected Link As.

   ■ **Save all links:** Deselect all links, then click Save All Links As.

   The Save To Server dialog box is displayed (Figure 27-3 on page 646).

3. *(optional)* To rename the file, type a new name in the Name field.

4. *(optional)* To check out the file, check the Keep File Checked Out check box.

5. Click the Save button. A confirmation dialog box is displayed.

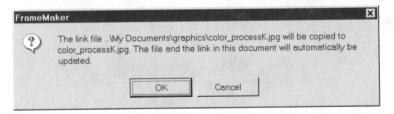

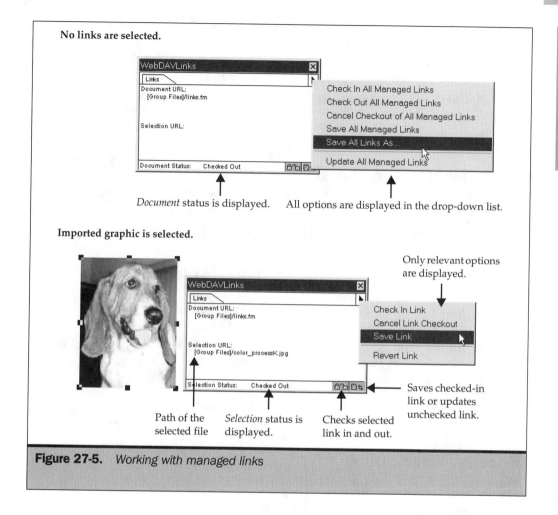

Figure 27-5. *Working with managed links*

6. Click the OK button. The file is saved and checked out (if chosen).

If there are additional unmanaged links, the Save To Server dialog box is displayed again. Repeat the procedure.

Checking Out Links

You check out links to prevent others from making changes while you're working with them. To check out links, follow these steps:

1. Select File | Links. The WebDAVLinks palette is displayed (Figure 27-5).

2. Indicate which links you want to check out, then click an item in the Links drop-down list. The choices are as follows:

- **Check out one link.** Select the link, then click Check Out Link or click the ▢▦ button in the lower-right corner of the Links palette.
- **Check out several links.** Select the links, then click Check Out Selected Links or click the ▢▦ button in the lower-right corner of the Links palette.
- **Check out all managed links.** Deselect all links, then click Check Out All Managed Links.

The links are checked out.

Saving Checked-Out Links

You save checked-out links to give other users access to your changes without checking in the links. To save checked-out links, follow these steps:

1. Select File | Links. The WebDAVLinks palette is displayed (Figure 27-5 on page 657).
2. Indicate which links you want to check out, then click an item in the Links drop-down list. The choices are as follows:
   - **Save one checked-out link.** Select the link, then click Save Link, or click the ▢▣ button in the lower-right corner of the Links palette.
   - **Save several checked-out links.** Select the links, then click Save Selected Links, or click the ▢▣ button in the lower-right corner of the Links palette.
   - **Save all checked-out links.** Deselect all links, then click Save All Managed Links.

The checked-out links are saved.

Canceling Check Outs

To cancel links you checked out and discard your changes, follow these steps:

1. Select File | Links. The WebDAVLinks palette is displayed (Figure 27-5 on page 657).
2. Indicate which checked-out links you want to cancel, then click an item in the Links drop-down list. The choices are as follows:
   - **Cancel link checkout.** Select the link, then click Cancel Link Checkout.
   - **Cancel checkout of several links.** Select the links, then click Cancel Checkout of Selected Links.
   - **Cancel checkout of all managed links.** Deselect all links, then click Cancel Checkout of All Managed Links.

The check outs are canceled, and your changes are discarded.

Checking In Links

To save and check in links, follow these steps:

1. Select File | Links. The WebDAVLinks palette is displayed (Figure 27-5 on page 657).

2. Indicate which links you want to check in, then click an item in the Links drop-down list. The choices are as follows:
   - **Check in one link.** Select the link, then click Check In Link or click the button in the lower-right corner of the Links palette.
   - **Check in several links.** Select the links, then click Check In Selected Links or click the button in the lower-right corner of the Links palette.
   - **Check in all managed links.** Deselect all links, then click Check In All Managed Links.

   The links are saved and checked in.

Updating Managed Links

To update the links in a local copy of a checked-in document, follow these steps:

1. Select File | Links. The WebDAVLinks palette is displayed (Figure 27-5 on page 657).

2. Click Update all Managed Links. The links are updated in your local document.

Note

You can't select or modify a link until you check out the document.

Reverting to the Last Saved Version

To revert to the server version of a link and discard your changes, follow these steps:

1. Select File | Links. The WebDAVLinks palette is displayed (Figure 27-5 on page 657).

2. Select the link on the page, then click Revert Link in the drop-down list. A confirmation dialog box is displayed.

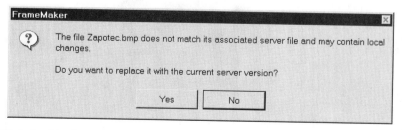

3. Click the Yes button. The latest version of the link is displayed.

The Complete Reference

FrameMaker 7

Part VII

Structured FrameMaker

Chapter 28

Working with Structured Documents

S tructured documents are made up of *elements.* An element can contain a paragraph, a text range, a marker, a cross-reference, or other FrameMaker items. You can also create elements that contain other elements. For example, for a cookbook, you might have an element called Recipe. The Recipe element consists of three elements: Name, IngredientList, and Instructions. The IngredientList, in turn, contains several Ingredient elements, and each Ingredient element contains Quantity, Item, and perhaps a PrepMethod element. The resulting structure for a simple recipe is shown in Figure 28-1.

Unlike paragraph tags in an unstructured document, elements have hierarchical relationships. For example, in Figure 28-1, the IngredientList element contains several Ingredient elements. If you move the IngredientList, all of the subordinate elements move with it. The relationships are described using terms that you might apply to a family tree—parent, child, and sibling.

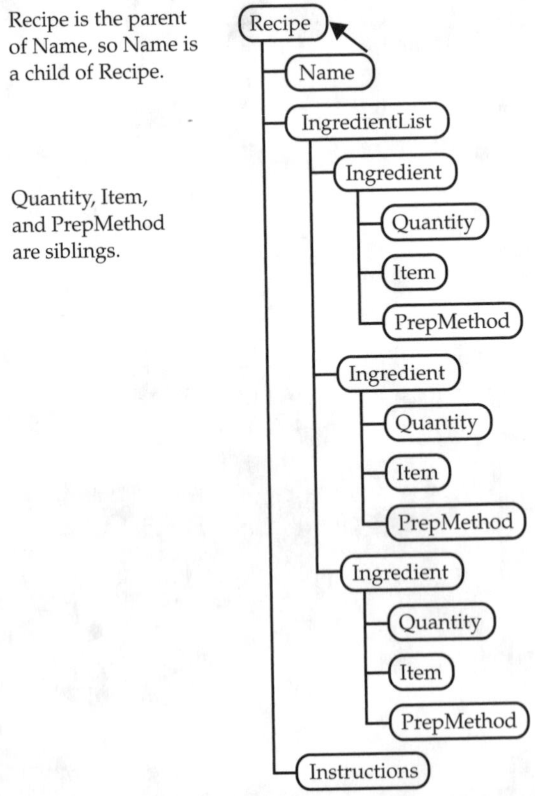

Recipe is the parent of Name, so Name is a child of Recipe.

Quantity, Item, and PrepMethod are siblings.

- Recipe
  - Name
  - IngredientList
    - Ingredient
      - Quantity
      - Item
      - PrepMethod
    - Ingredient
      - Quantity
      - Item
      - PrepMethod
    - Ingredient
      - Quantity
      - Item
      - PrepMethod
  - Instructions

Figure 28-1. *Understanding document structure*

A *parent* element is an element that is one level above the current element in the hierarchy. In Figure 28-1, Recipe is the parent of Name, IngredientList, and Instructions. IngredientList is the parent of the Ingredient elements. Ingredient is the parent of Quantity, Item, and PrepMethod.

A *child* element is an element that is one level below the current element. Name, for example, is a child of Recipe.

A *sibling* element is an element that's at the same level as the current element. Name, IngredientList, and Instructions are all siblings. Quantity, Item, and PrepMethod are also siblings.

A *descendant* element is an element that is one or more levels below the current element. A child element is a descendant that's just one level below the current element, but you can have descendants that are several levels down. In Figure 28-1, Recipe is the highest-level element, so all of the other elements are descendants of Recipe.

An *ancestor* element is an element that's one or more levels above the current element. A parent element is an ancestor that's one level above the current element, but the term ancestor is more general and allows you to go up several levels in the hierarchy. The Recipe element is an ancestor of all of the other elements in the hierarchy.

Note *In XML or SGML, the relationship among the various elements is defined in a document type definition, or DTD. In structured FrameMaker, you define the relationships in an element definition document, or EDD. See Chapter 29, "Understanding the Element Definition Document," for details.*

Understanding the Structure View

In structured FrameMaker, you work with your document in two views. The first is the familiar word-processing environment, where you can see how text is positioned on the page and where graphics fall. The second view is called the structure view. It shows you the relationship of all the elements you're working with.

The document window in structured FrameMaker (Figure 28-2) looks just like a regular FrameMaker document window with a few additions:

- An Element menu is now available.
- A few new buttons are available on the right side of the interface with the buttons for the paragraph catalog, character catalog, graphics toolbar, and equation editor.
- In some menus, new choices are added.

The title bar indicates you're working in structured FrameMaker.

The Element menu appears only in structured FrameMaker.

More buttons are added here.

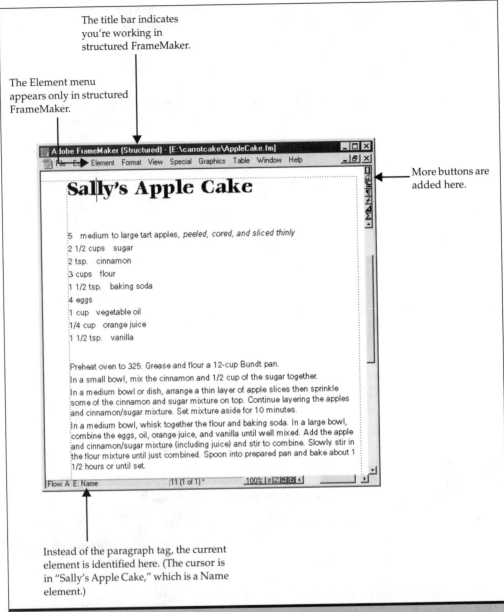

Instead of the paragraph tag, the current element is identified here. (The cursor is in "Sally's Apple Cake," which is a Name element.)

Figure 28-2. *A structured document in the document window*

The corresponding structure view (Figure 28-3) shows you how elements are arranged in a document. To display the structure view, click the Structure View button in the top-right corner of the document window.

Displays the
structure view ⟶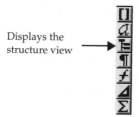

In the structure view, you can see each element and the first few words of that element's text. The structure view gives you a visual representation of the document structure and lets you manipulate the structure.

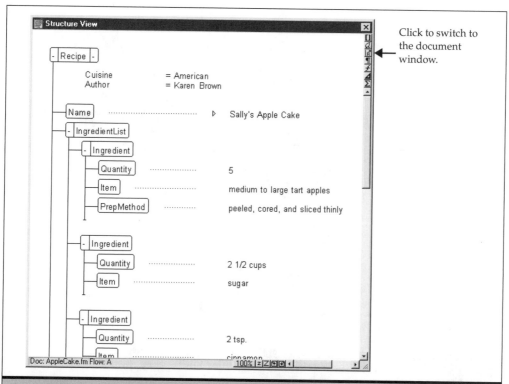

Figure 28-3.   *The structure view lets you see the element hierarchy.*

The following sections explain how to work with existing elements. For information about creating new elements, see page 684.

Collapsing and Expanding Elements

An element with children (also called a *container* element) has a minus sign or plus sign to its left. A minus sign indicates that all of the element's children are displayed; click it to collapse the bubble and hide the child elements. A plus sign and a "shadowed" bubble indicates that the element's children are hidden; click the plus sign to expand the hierarchy and display the child elements. This affects only the structure view, not the document window.

When you collapse an element, you cannot see the text for the collapsed elements in the structure view.

Note   *To collapse an element and all of its siblings, SHIFT-click the minus sign to the left of the element. To expand an element and all of its siblings, SHIFT-click the plus sign.*

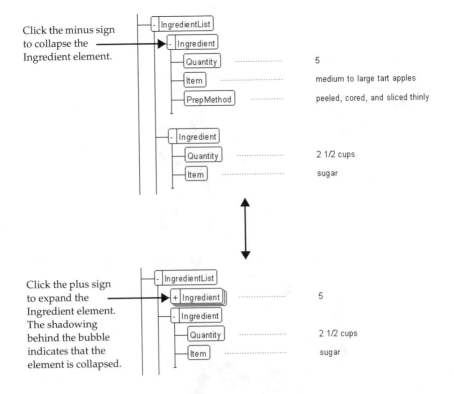

Click the minus sign to collapse the Ingredient element.

IngredientList
Ingredient
Quantity 5
Item .... medium to large tart apples
PrepMethod .... peeled, cored, and sliced thinly
Ingredient
Quantity .... 2 1/2 cups
Item .... sugar

Click the plus sign to expand the Ingredient element. The shadowing behind the bubble indicates that the element is collapsed.

IngredientList
Ingredient 5
Ingredient
Quantity .... 2 1/2 cups
Item .... sugar

Selecting and Moving Elements

You can use the structure view to move elements around. When you select an element in the structure view, the corresponding content in the document window is also selected.

Clicking on PrepMethod also selects content in the document window.

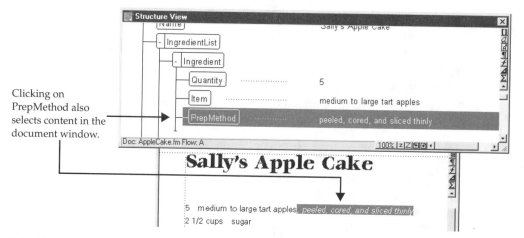

Selecting an element also selects its children and lower-level descendants.

Note *Although you can still use regular cut-and-paste operations in the document window, moving large sections is usually more efficient in the structure view. If you just need to copy and paste a few words, though, you'll probably want to use the document window.*

Clicking Ingredient selects its children: Quantity, Item, and PrepMethod. The content in the document window is also selected.

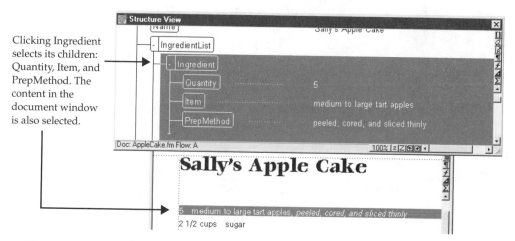

You can move an element by selecting it in the structure view and then dragging and dropping it at its new location.

To move an element, follow these steps:

1. *(optional)* If the element you are moving has a lot of descendants, click it to collapse the element to a single, shadowed bubble.

2. Select the element, and then drag it to the new location. Some symbols are displayed:

   - An up-and-down arrowhead is shown as you drag the element.
   - An arrow to the left of the element points to where the element will go when you drop.
   - A check mark in the element bubble indicates that the currently selected location creates a valid structure.

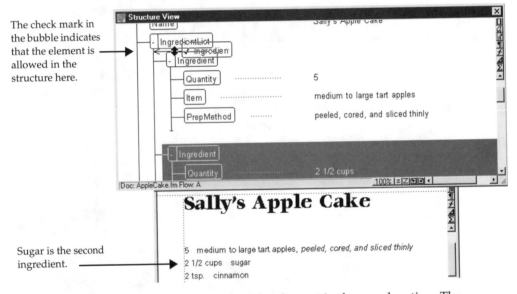

The check mark in the bubble indicates that the element is allowed in the structure here.

Sugar is the second ingredient.

3. Release the mouse button to place the element in the new location. The information in the document window is also rearranged to reflect the new organization.

Note *In structured FrameMaker, formatting is associated with the structure, so rearranging information by moving elements can result in formatting changes. For example, moving a Heading element so that it is nested three levels deep instead of two usually results in a smaller font size for the heading text.*

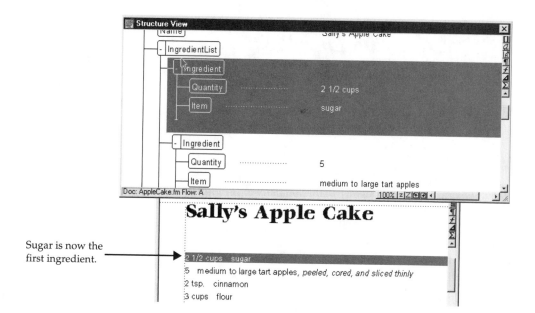

Sugar is now the
first ingredient.

Displaying Tags in the Document Window

Most users like working in the structure view because you can easily see the hierarchy of the various elements. You can, however, set the document window to display structure information. In the document window, you can display the element boundaries as brackets, or you can display the tag names inline. The element boundary defines where the element begins and ends; it's similar to opening and closing tags in HTML (for example, <h1>...</h1>).

To toggle display of the element boundaries, select View | Element Boundaries or View | Element Boundaries (as Tags). Figure 28-4 shows the results.

The symbols used for element boundaries will print, so we recommend that you turn off element boundaries before printing. If you forget, FrameMaker displays a reminder that element boundaries are on when you try to print.

Understanding Attributes

An *attribute* is a piece of information that's associated with a specific element. Each attribute has a name and a value. Attributes are very useful for tracking information about the document (sometimes called *metainformation*), such as authors, revision dates, version numbers, and the like.

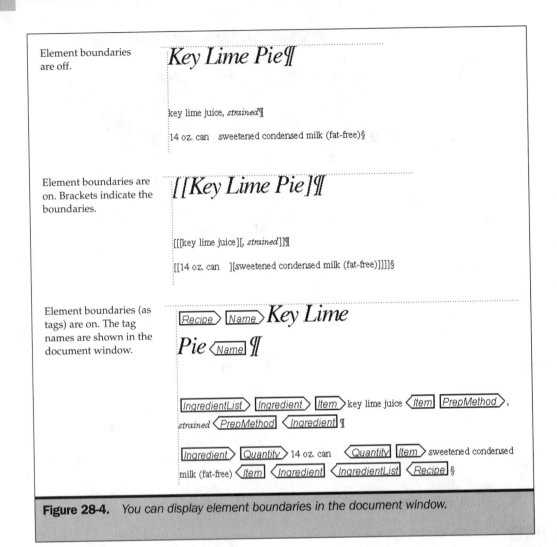

Figure 28-4.   *You can display element boundaries in the document window.*

You can also use attributes to assign unique identifiers to each element. These unique identifiers can be used to keep track of cross-reference links and are often important when converting to SGML or XML. In the cookbook example, the Recipe element has attributes for the author and the type of cuisine.

Element attributes are shown underneath the element they belong to. If an element has attributes, the right side of the element bubble has a minus or plus sign. Click the right side of the element bubble to collapse or expand the attributes list. Attributes are listed under the element bubble in the structure view; they are not displayed in the document window. You can add, delete, and modify attributes in your document. For details, see "Working with Attributes" on page 692.

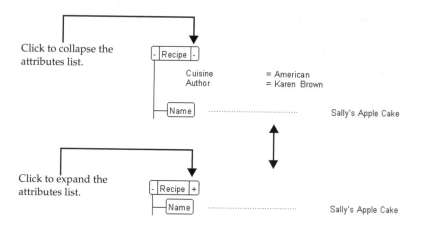

Click to collapse the attributes list.

Click to expand the attributes list.

Creating New Structured Content

To insert new information into a structured document, you insert elements and then any associated content for that element. Some elements serve only as parents for other elements; they do not have any content of their own. Other elements have both content and child elements.

When you create a new structured document, the structure view is blank, and you need to insert new elements using the element catalog. To open the element catalog, select the element catalog icon (in the top right of the document window), or select Element | Element Catalog.

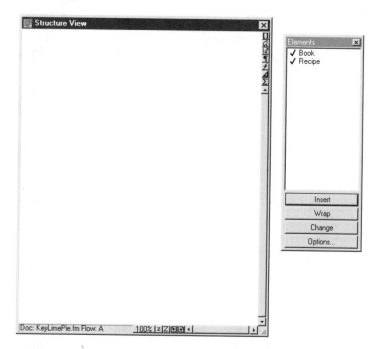

STRUCTURED FRAMEMAKER

The list of elements in the element catalog changes depending on where your cursor is located. By default, you see only those elements that are allowed (valid) at the current location in the document. As you move your cursor to different places in the document, the list of elements displayed in the element catalog changes.

To insert an element, follow these steps:

1. Position your cursor where you want to insert the element.

2. In the element catalog, click the element, then click the Insert button (or double-click on the element) to insert it. If the element you're inserting requires attributes, FrameMaker prompts you to insert them. See "Working with Attributes" on page 692 for details.

The new element is displayed in the structure view.

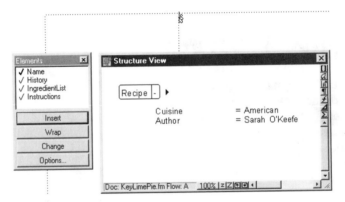

The element catalog now lists additional elements that are available. The boldface check mark next to an element (Name in the preceding example) indicates the element that's required next in the structure. (The other symbols are described in Table 28-1 on page 676.) Double-click an element to insert it.

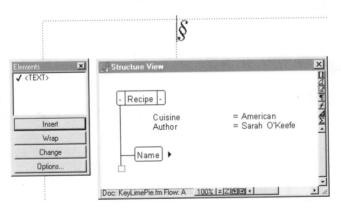

When the element catalog lists <TEXT>, it indicates that you need to insert text for the element. Type the information next to the element, and it is displayed in the document window with the correct formatting applied.

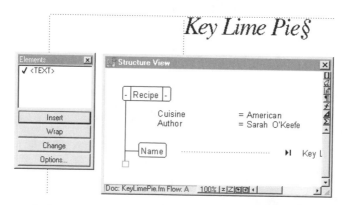

The red box at the bottom of the current structure indicates that a required element is missing. Click to the right of the red box and below the Name element to position your cursor to insert the next element, as shown here:

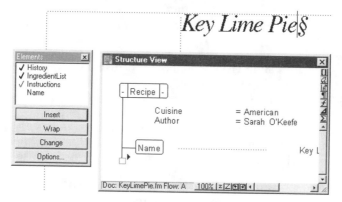

You can now continue by inserting one of the boldface elements listed in the element catalog and inserting text as necessary.

  See "Details About Inserting Different Element Types" on page 684 for information about how to work with specific element types (paragraphs, graphics, and so on).

Understanding the Element Catalog Symbols

In addition to listing the available elements, the element catalog provides some additional information about each element using symbols that appear to the left of an element.

Table 28-1 explains the symbols in the element catalog.

Symbol	Meaning
✓	**Heavy check:** The element is valid at this location.
✓	**Light check:** The element is valid later in the current element (for example, another child element must precede this element in the structure).
✓₊	**Plus sign:** The element is an inclusion in the current element. An *inclusion* is valid at any point within a particular element or within its descendants. The plus sign is always displayed with the heavy check.
?	**Question mark:** The element could be a replacement for the selected element or the element following the insertion point.
\<INVALID\>	**\<INVALID\>:** The contents of the element are not valid. This symbol is not displayed in the element catalog when you set it to display all elements.
\<TEXT\>	**\<TEXT\>:** You must type text at this location.
\<UNDEFINED\>	**\<UNDEFINED\>:** The element is undefined in the document (for example, the element was part of a section that was cut and pasted from another document that has a different structure). This symbol is not displayed in the element catalog when you set it to display all elements.
No symbol	The element is not valid at the current location.

Table 28-1. *Element Catalog Symbols*

Using Keyboard Shortcuts to Insert Elements

Instead of double-clicking items in the element catalog to insert them, you can use keyboard shortcuts. When you press ENTER to begin a new paragraph, FrameMaker assumes that you want to insert a new element, so it provides a list of elements in the status bar. Use the arrow keys to scroll to the element you want, and press ENTER to insert it.

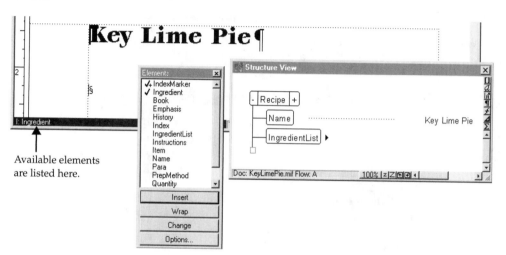

Available elements
are listed here.

Another keyboard shortcut lets you insert new elements among existing text. To do so, follow these steps:

1. In the text, position the cursor where you want the new element.
2. Press CTRL-1. Notice that the left side of the status bar changes color.
3. Display the element name you want by doing any of the following:
   - Use the arrow keys to scroll through the list of available tags.
   - Type a letter to jump to that section of the element catalog.
   - Type the first few letters of the tag name.
4. Press ENTER. The selected element is inserted as a child of the current element.

Positioning the Cursor in the Structure View

In the structure view, triangular symbols indicate where you've inserted the cursor.

Cursor Location	Symbol		
Beginning of element text	⊣Name	▷	Key Lime Pie
End of element text	⊣Name	▷|	Key Lime Pie

Cursor Location	Symbol
Inside element text	Name .... ▷ Key Lime Pie
Ready to insert element	Name .... Key Lime Pie ▶ IngredientList

When you're attempting to position the cursor to insert an element, use the structure view or turn on the element boundaries to work in the document view.

Locating Missing and Invalid Elements

Structured documents require that elements be inserted in a certain sequence. When the document does not conform to the required structure, the problems are shown in the structure view.

Missing and invalid elements are displayed in red. The indicators are as follows:

■ A missing element is indicated by a red square. In the following example, several required elements (IngredientList, Instructions, and their child elements) are missing.

The square (which is red on screen) indicates required elements are missing. ──▶

■ Invalid structure is indicated by a dashed line. In the following example, two required parent elements (IngredientList and Ingredient) are missing between Name and Quantity.

The dashed red line indicates incorrect structure. ──▶

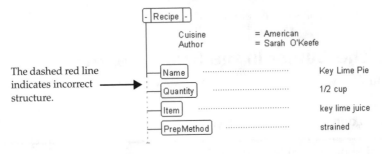

■ A required attribute that has no assigned value is indicated by a red box next to the attribute and <no value> in red. A required attribute that's missing entirely is shown in red with an x next to it.

The red square indicates the
attribute requires a value
and doesn't have one.

To correct these problems, you need to rearrange the elements in the document to match the required structure. In many cases, you can insert a required element, or change the name of one element to resolve the problem quickly.

Changing Elements

You can change an element from one item to another. If, for example, you accidentally insert a History element when you meant to insert an IngredientList element, you can correct the problem.

To change an element, follow these steps:

1. In the structure view, click the element you want to change.

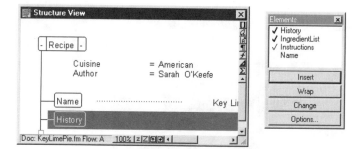

2. In the element catalog, click the new element name, then click the Change button.

The new element name is assigned to the selected element.

The keyboard shortcut for changing an element is CTRL-3.

STRUCTURED FRAMEMAKER

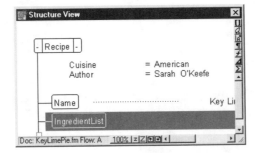

Wrapping Elements

When you wrap elements, you insert a new element and turn the current elements into children of the new element. In other words, you create a new parent element for the current element. To wrap elements, follow these steps:

1. In the structure view, click the elements you want to wrap.

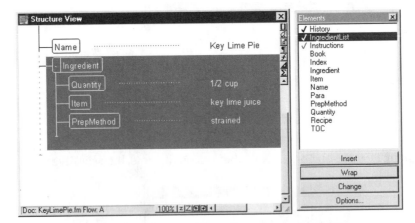

2. In the element catalog, click the new parent element.

3. Click the Wrap button. The element is inserted as a parent of the selected elements.

The keyboard shortcut for wrapping an element is CTRL-2.

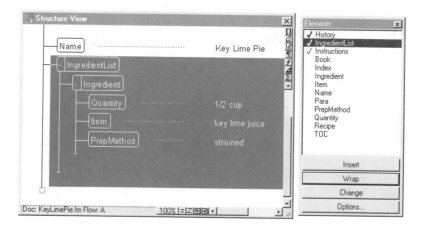

Unwrapping Elements

Unwrapping elements lets you remove a parent element and promote the child elements up one level. Unwrapping is very useful for correcting errors in the structure. To unwrap elements, follow these steps:

1. In the structure view, select the elements you want to unwrap. The top element in the selection will be removed.

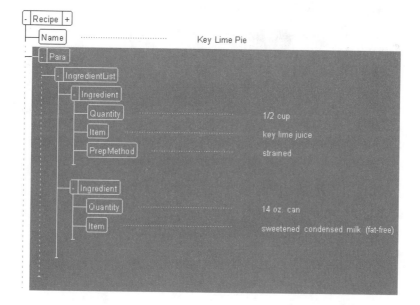

2. Select Element | Unwrap.

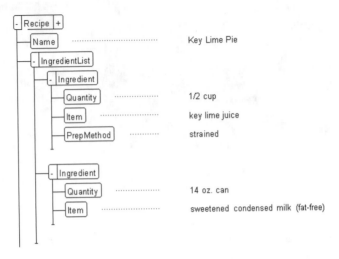

Merging Elements

Merging elements lets you combine two or more sibling elements into a single element. The resulting element will use the first element's name.

To merge elements, follow these steps:

1. In the structure view, select the elements you want to merge.

2. Select Element | Merge to merge the selected elements. The selected elements are combined into just one element. That new element now contains two paragraphs.

Splitting Elements

Splitting elements lets you insert another instance of the current parent element in the structure.

To split, follow these steps:

1. In the structure, click where you need to insert another instance of the current parent element. In the following example, two ingredients are accidentally listed in a single Ingredient element.

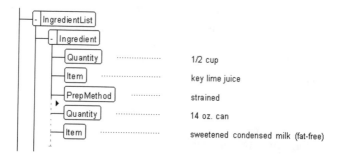

2. Select Element | Split. At the cursor location, another parent element is inserted. The child elements underneath the split location are now children of the new element.

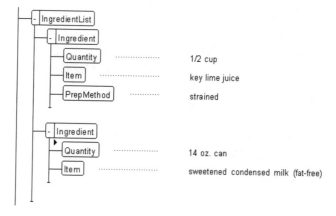

Notice that unlike most of the other commands, you do not select an element for splitting; the parent element is always used. You can change the element after the split, if you need to.

Details About Inserting Different Element Types

As explained in "Creating New Structured Content" on page 673, the basic procedure for inserting a new element is as follows:

1. Make sure that your cursor is positioned correctly in the structure view—the cursor should be the solid triangle indicating you can insert an element (▶).

2. In the element catalog, click the element, then click the Insert button.

The element is inserted into the structure view. If the EDD requires an attribute for the element you inserted, you'll be prompted by a dialog box to specify the value for attribute. See "Working with Attributes" on page 692 for information about specifying attributes.

In addition to specifying required attributes, you will need to complete some other tasks based on the type of element you inserted.

Paragraphs

If you insert an element for text, you need to type the text for that element. For example, insertion of a Head element requires text for the heading, as demonstrated by the display of the <TEXT> indicator in the element catalog. You can type the text for the heading in the document window or the structure view. The structure view only displays the first few characters of each element, so if you're typing a lot of text, working in the document window will be easier.

Text Ranges (Character Tags)

You can use elements to set character tagging attributes, such as boldface or italic type for emphasis. In structured documents, the elements that create character-level formatting are called *text ranges*. The text range can have a character tag associated with it.

As you type in content, you can insert a text range element for emphasis. When you are finished, you must position your cursor in the parent element (but underneath the text range) so that you can continue with the regular text formatting.

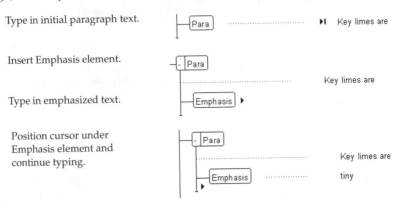

Instead of this rather painstaking process, we recommend that you type in all of the paragraph first, and then apply the emphasis formatting.

After typing the entire paragraph, select the text you want to emphasize.

In the element catalog, click the Emphasis element, and then click the Wrap button. This applies the Emphasis element to the selected text.

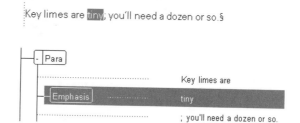

Graphics

Graphic elements automatically prompt you either to set up an anchored frame or to import a file, depending on how the element was defined by the template designer. When you insert an anchored frame graphic element, the Anchored Frame dialog box is displayed, which prompts you to insert an anchored frame into the document window. You can make all the same changes to anchored frames that are allowed in unstructured documents. See "Anchoring Graphics" on page 300 for details.

If you insert a graphic element that's set up to import a file, FrameMaker automatically displays the Import File dialog box. You specify the file you want to import, and it is inserted in an anchored frame for you. See "Importing a Graphic" on page 304 for details.

Once you insert a graphic element of either type, it is shown as a square bubble in the structure view. The text <GRAPHIC> is displayed next to the bubble.

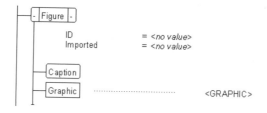

Tables

When you insert a table element, the Insert Table dialog box is displayed.

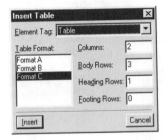

Specify the table format and the number of columns and rows, and then click the Insert button to create the table. The structure view shows the inserted table element and its descendants, which can include elements such as TableTitle (for the table caption) and TableCell (for cell text).

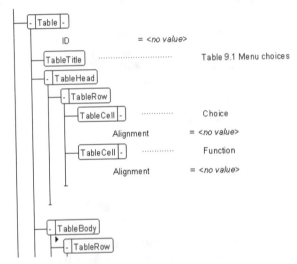

You may find it easier to type the text for the table in the document window (in the table itself). For details about working with tables, refer to Chapter 7, "Understanding Table Design."

Cross-References

When you insert a cross-reference element, FrameMaker displays the Cross-Reference dialog box. For details about creating element-based cross-references, see Chapter 8, "Cross-References."

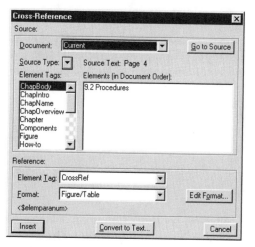

Once you insert the cross-reference, it is displayed in the structure view with a square bubble.

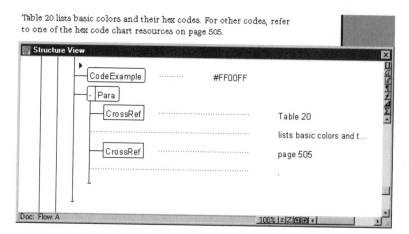

Equations

Insert an equation element to create an equation. The information inside the equation is not structured—this is similar to how anchored frames are treated. In the structure view, the equation is indicated by <EQUATION> where element text is normally displayed.

Footnotes

To create a footnote, insert a footnote element. FrameMaker automatically puts the footnote information at the bottom of the page, but the text also appears in the structure view at the location where you inserted the footnote. For details about footnotes, see "Working with Footnotes" on page 95.

Marker

Insert a marker element to create a structured marker. The template designer can assign a default marker type; for example, IndexMarker elements always default to the Index marker type.

Marker elements are displayed as square bubbles in the structure view. For details on inserting marker text, see "Creating Index Entries" on page 408 or Chapter 22, "Creating Interactive Documents with Hypertext."

Variables

You can have elements for system variables but not for user variables. For details, see "Using Variables in Structured Documents" on page 236.

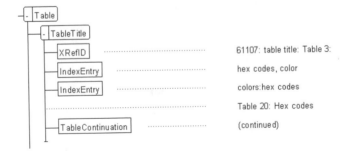

Controlling What's Displayed in the Element Catalog

By default, the element catalog displays only the elements that are valid at the cursor location. This feature reduces the number of elements you have to read through to find the one you want. In some cases, though, you might want to list all of the elements, especially if you're creating pieces of a document and aren't yet ready to structure everything just right. You can change what's displayed in the element catalog.

To change which elements are displayed in the element catalog, follow these steps:

1. Display the element catalog.

2. Click the Options button. The Set Available Elements dialog box is displayed (Figure 28-5).

3. Click one of the following radio buttons:

   - **Valid Elements for Working Start to Finish:** Displays only elements that are valid at the cursor location. This is the default, and most restrictive, option.

   - **Valid Elements for Working in Any Order:** Displays elements that are valid at the current location or later in the element. This gives you a bit more flexibility than the first option.

   - **Elements Allowed Anywhere in Parent:** Displays all valid elements for the current parent element. This option is useful when you're creating a document section by section and can't (or don't want to) build the document in order.

   - **All Elements:** Displays all elements. This option is very useful when you're wrapping, merging, or changing existing content. It also lets you insert elements and worry about making the structure valid later.

   - **Customized List:** Lets you create your own list of elements. See "Creating a Customized List of Elements" on page 691 for details.

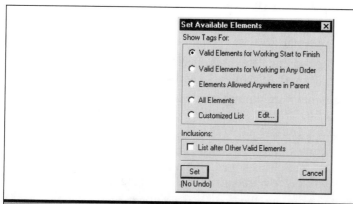

Figure 28-5.   *Changing which elements are displayed*

4. Normally, elements that are allowed because of an inclusion (an element that's valid anywhere) are listed as valid elements. To list them separately underneath the valid elements, check the List after Other Valid Elements check box. If you rarely use the included elements, this can reduce the number of options available at each point in the document.

Validating Structure

As described in "Locating Missing and Invalid Elements" on page 678, the structure view tells you when you've created invalid structure with dotted red lines and red boxes.

In addition to seeing the structure view's indicators of invalid structure, you can use FrameMaker's validation feature to check the validity of your document. Validating a document is a bit like spell-checking. Instead of looking for spelling errors, the validator looks for structure errors; specifically, required elements that are missing or structures that are not allowed by the EDD.

When you validate a document, structured FrameMaker shows you each instance where the structure is invalid and gives you a chance to correct it.

To begin validating a document, follow these steps:

1. Select Element | Validate. The Element Validation dialog box is displayed.

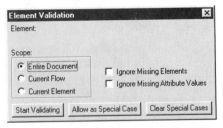

2. Specify the scope of validation by clicking one of the following radio buttons:

   ■ **Entire Document:** The information in the entire file is validated.

   ■ **Current Flow:** The information in the current flow tag is validated.

   ■ **Current Element:** The current element is checked to ensure that its children are valid, but any children of the child elements are *not* checked.

3. To exclude missing elements from the validation's search, check the Ignore Missing Elements check box. If your document is not yet complete, you may want to ignore missing elements.

4. To exclude missing attribute values from the validation's search, check the Ignore Missing Attribute Values check box. This means that FrameMaker does not check to ensure that all the required attributes are present.

5. Click the Start Validating button to begin validating the document.

Creating a Customized List of Elements

You can set up the element catalog so that it always displays a specific list of elements. However, doing so disables the context-sensitive display of elements. Furthermore, any elements that you hide will be hidden permanently—you won't be able to use them until you go back and change the settings to redisplay them.

To set up a customized list of elements, follow these steps:

1. Display the element catalog and click the Options button. The Set Available Elements dialog box is displayed (Figure 28-5 on page 689).

2. Next to the Customized List radio button, click the Edit button. The Customize List of Available Elements dialog box is displayed.

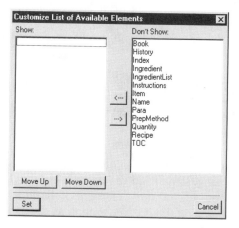

3. Move the elements you want displayed in the element catalog to the Show list on the left. To move an element, click it, then click the left arrow in the middle of the dialog box.

4. Adjust the order of the elements in the list:

   ■ To move an element up in the list, click it, then click the Move Up button.

   ■ To move an element down in the list, click it, then click the Move Down button.

5. Click the Set button to save your changes and return to the Set Available Elements dialog box.

6. Click the Set button. The element catalog now displays your customized list of elements.

FrameMaker searches the document for invalid structure. When it finds an error, it highlights the problem in the document window and the structure view. A message about the invalid structure is displayed in the upper-left corner of the Element Validation dialog box.

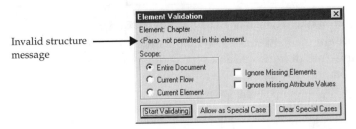

Invalid structure message

6. Correct the error, or mark it as a special case by clicking the Allow as Special Case button. (This is equivalent to the Learn button in the spell-checker.)

When you allow a special case, you are overriding the structure that's normally required for the document. The next time you validate this document, the error is ignored. To remove the special cases, click the Clear Special Cases button. Allowing a special case is similar to allowing a word not found in the dictionary while spell-checking.

Correcting an error in your document's structure can involve one of many actions, such as the following:

- **Moving an element.** If validation indicates that an element is in an invalid location, you need to move the element. See "Selecting and Moving Elements" on page 669 for details.

- **Adding a required element.** When validation finds a location where an element is missing, structured FrameMaker places the insertion point where the element should go, and the elements valid at that point are displayed in the element catalog. Insert an element, as described in "Creating New Structured Content" on page 673.

- **Correcting an invalid attribute value.** Validation identifies incorrect attribute values. For information on how to change attribute values, see "Changing an Attribute Value" on page 694.

- **Attribute undefined for element.** The specified element's definition doesn't include the attribute. You need to remove the attribute or change the element.

- **Element undefined.** The specified element is not defined in the document; you may have copied the element from another file. You need to change the element to another element.

7. Click the Start Validating button to continue validating.

Once you eliminate all the structure problems, FrameMaker tells you that the document is valid.

Working with Attributes

Attributes are additional information about elements that you can see in the structure view but not in the document window. The EDD determines whether an element requires an attribute, and if you insert an element with a required attribute, you're prompted to insert a value. Even if an attribute is optional for an element you're inserting, you can insert attribute values when you place the element.

When you insert an element that requires attributes, you are prompted to insert the attribute values in the Attributes for New Element dialog box.

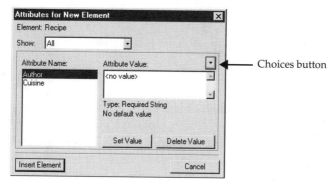

To insert the attributes, follow these steps:

1. In the Attribute Name list, click an attribute.

2. In the Attribute Value field, type in a value. For attributes with choices provided (an attribute with a Choice type), click the Choices button and select an option from the pop-up menu.

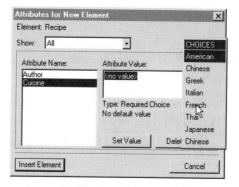

3. Click the Set Value button to save the attribute with the new value.

4. When you have set all of the attributes, click the Insert Element button.

Prompting for Attribute Values

By default, you are prompted to insert attributes when you create new elements. You can, however, change this setting.

To set prompting for attribute values, follow these steps:

1. Select Element | New Element Options. The New Element Options dialog box is displayed.

STRUCTURED
FRAMEMAKER

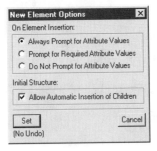

2. Choose one of the following options:

   ■ **Always Prompt for Attribute Values** (default setting): Whenever you insert an element that calls for attributes, you are reminded to insert those attributes.

   ■ **Prompt for Required Attribute Values:** If you insert an element that has required attributes, you are reminded to insert them. If the element has only optional attributes, you are not reminded to insert them.

   ■ **Do Not Prompt for Attribute Values:** When you insert elements, you are never reminded to insert attributes. If the attributes are required, your structure will be invalid until you go back and add the required attributes.

3. To disable automatic element insertion, uncheck the Allow Automatic Insertion of Children check box.

   Some structured documents are defined with automatic insertions, which are intended to help you by inserting child elements automatically. For example, when you first create a Chapter element, automatic insertion might insert a Section child and then a Heading child for you. By default, this feature is turned on (it makes your authoring more efficient), but you can disable it here.

4. Click the Set button to save your changes.

Changing an Attribute Value

To change the value of an existing attribute, double-click the attribute's name in the structure view. The Attributes dialog box is displayed.

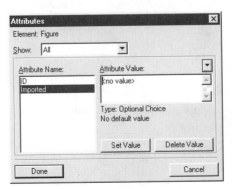

Follow the instructions in "Working with Attributes" on page 692 to change the attribute values.

 If an attribute is set to be read-only, you cannot change it.

Copying Attribute Values

Instead of setting attributes one by one, you can copy the values from one element to another.

To copy attributes, follow these steps:

1. In the structure view, select the element with the attributes you want to copy.
2. Select Edit | Copy Special | Attribute Values.
3. Select the element you want to add the attribute values to.
4. Select Edit | Paste. The attribute values are added to the element.

 Both elements must use the same attributes. If they do not, the structure will become invalid.

Setting Attribute Display Options

By default, all attributes (except for hidden attributes, which you cannot access) are displayed in the structure view. You can, however, limit or even eliminate the attributes.

To change which attributes are displayed, follow these steps:

1. Select View | Options | Attribute Display Options. The Attribute Display Options dialog box is displayed.

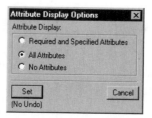

2. Select one of the following radio buttons:

   - **Required and Specified Attributes:** Displays attributes that have a value set and required attributes.
   - **All Attributes:** Displays all attributes.
   - **No Attributes:** Displays no attributes.
3. Click the Set button to save your changes.

The Complete Reference

FrameMaker 7

Understanding the Element Definition Document

An *element definition document (EDD)* provides the template for a structured FrameMaker file. A regular, unstructured template contains catalogs of paragraph tags, character tags, and other formatting instructions. The EDD describes an element catalog, the relationship of the elements to each other, and how to format them. In some cases, the EDD references paragraph or other formatting tags, but you can also embed formatting instructions directly in the EDD without using tags. The EDD is equivalent to the document type definition (DTD) used in SGML and XML, except that DTDs do not include formatting information.

You can use any document as an unstructured template. When you import formats, FrameMaker grabs the information defined in the various formatting catalogs and copies it to the new document. In structured FrameMaker, document structure is controlled by the element catalog, but you cannot edit the element catalog in a regular file. Instead, you define the element catalog in an EDD, which displays a text-based specification for each element.

The EDD lists element definitions. Each element definition has a name; when you apply the EDD to a structured document, the element names become the items listed in the element catalog (Figure 29-1).

How Elements Correspond to FrameMaker Features

Each element definition has an element type, many of which correspond to FrameMaker features. For example, element types are available for equations, cross-references, graphics, and markers. These are called *object elements*; they contain one instance of the specified item. The most common element, though, is a *container* element. Container elements hold text and other elements. This lets you create a hierarchy of elements within your structure. Container elements are used for both paragraphs and text ranges (a few words or characters within a paragraph).

Remember *Container elements are not related to container files for text insets.*

In Figure 29-1, all of the element definitions shown are for container elements. The Name element has a general rule of <TEXT>, which indicates that it contains text. Other elements have a list of element names in their general rule, which defines the allowed child elements.

An unstructured file always has a flat hierarchy; it consists of a series of paragraphs with formatting applied to them. The document doesn't describe the relationship between paragraphs. In structured documents, the hierarchy of the elements provides that additional information (Figure 29-2 on page 700).

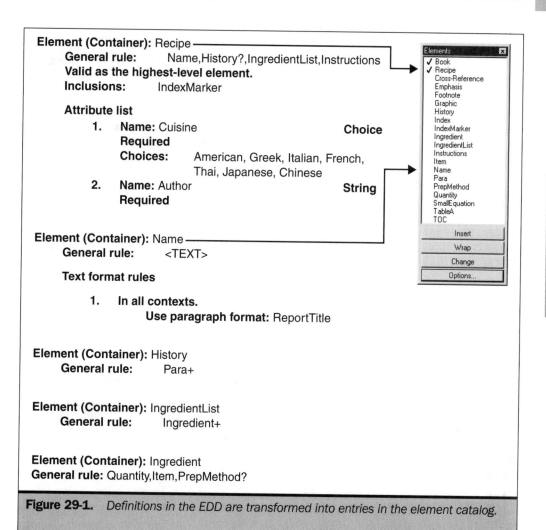

Figure 29-1.   *Definitions in the EDD are transformed into entries in the element catalog.*

When you set up a container element, you describe which elements are allowed inside the container. The child elements, in turn, can also be containers. In a structured document, containers provide the document hierarchy. Container elements are the most complex to define. Each container element must have a *general rule*, which describes the elements that are permitted as children of the container element. Writing general rules requires you to learn how to describe element structure as a pattern. If you're already familiar with regular expressions (a feature found in most programming languages), writing general rules won't present any difficulty. If you're new to pattern matching, learning the general rule syntax can be a little challenging.

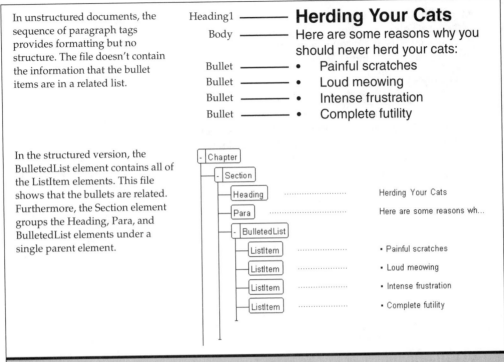

In unstructured documents, the sequence of paragraph tags provides formatting but no structure. The file doesn't contain the information that the bullet items are in a related list.

In the structured version, the BulletedList element contains all of the ListItem elements. This file shows that the bullets are related. Furthermore, the Section element groups the Heading, Para, and BulletedList elements under a single parent element.

Figure 29-2. *Comparing unstructured and structured documents*

In addition to the element name and type, most element definitions include additional information. For certain object elements, you can define an initial format. For example, you can set the initial default cross-reference format for a cross-reference element and the marker type for a marker element.

Any element can have associated attributes. Attributes let you embed additional (nonprinting) information about an element in the structured document. (This information about the document is also called *metainformation*.) To make attributes available to authors, you must define the attributes in an attribute list as part of the EDD. Attributes often identify the author, version, and security level of an element.

After defining the structural information, you can add formatting specifications to some elements. As part of the element definition, you can specify a paragraph tag, character tag, table tag, cross-reference format, and other information depending on the type of element that's being inserted. Because a single element can have several different formatting settings depending on its position in the document's hierarchy, the formatting information can become quite complex. It's quite common, for example, to define a single Head element and then format it differently based on whether it's a first-level, second-level, or third-level Head.

To make the EDD easier to read, you can add Section and Comment elements. These do not affect the structure you're defining; they provide ways to group elements inside the EDD and insert explanatory information about the elements.

Opening an EDD or Exporting the EDD from a Structured File

The EDD is a FrameMaker file, so you open EDD files by selecting File | Open, just like any other file. If you have a structured file, but not a copy of the EDD that it's based on, you can extract the EDD from the structured file. The exported EDD is slightly different from the original EDD:

- The elements are listed in alphabetical order, not in the order that the EDD developer chose.
- Section titles are lost when you export.
- Any special formatting used in the original EDD is lost. For example, if the original EDD uses text insets or user variables to make maintenance easier, those are not preserved when you export the EDD from a structured document.

For these reasons, it's preferable to open the original EDD. If you do not have access to the source EDD, exporting from a structured document based on that EDD is a reasonable alternative.

To export an EDD from a structured document, follow these steps:

1. Open the structured document.
2. Select File | Structure Tools | Export Element Catalog as EDD.

FrameMaker creates the EDD in an untitled document and displays that document.

Reading the EDD

The element definitions in the EDD are themselves structured text. For example, the following illustration shows the definition for the Recipe element in a cookbook EDD:

Element (Container): Recipe
> **General rule:**   Name,History?,IngredientList,Instructions
> **Valid as the highest-level element.**
> **Inclusions:**   IndexMarker
>
> **Attribute list**
>> 1.   **Name:** Cuisine   **Choice**   **Required**
>>   **Choices:**   American, Chinese, Greek, Italian, French, Thai, Japanese
>> 2.   **Name:** Author   **String**   **Required**

This information is also available in the document's structure view:

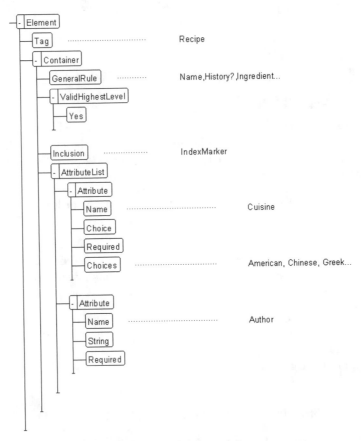

The Recipe element definition provides the following information:

- The element is defined as a container element, which means that text or additional elements occur inside this element.
- The general rule describes which elements are allowed inside this element and in what order.
- The statement "Valid as the highest-level element" (inserted by the ValidHighestLevel element) indicates that this element can be used as the top-level element in a document. When authors start a new document, only elements with this setting are available by default.
- The Inclusions section lists elements (in this case, IndexMarker) that can be used anywhere inside this element, including anywhere in the element's children.
- The Attribute List describes the attributes attached to this element. The Recipe element has two required attributes: Cuisine and Author. The Cuisine attribute is a choice attribute, which means the available options are defined in the EDD. The authors choose from that list to set the attribute value. The Author attribute is a string attribute, which means the authors type in the appropriate information.

To make changes to the EDD, you can work either in the structure view or in the document window.

Analyzing Document Structure

To create an EDD, you need to understand the structure of the documents it describes. If you already have an SGML or XML DTD, you can import the DTD into FrameMaker and use the resulting EDD as a starting point (see Chapter 31, "Importing and Exporting XML/SGML Markup Files," for details). If you do not have an existing DTD, detailed document analysis is probably required.

To begin, identify the high-level pieces of a document. For example, typical user documentation consists of front matter (title, table of contents, preface), an introduction, a series of chapters, perhaps some appendices, and then back matter, such as an index and perhaps a glossary. You can create elements for each of these major pieces. Keep in mind that you want to have a top-level element available for each FrameMaker file, so you'll probably want to create elements such as Chapter, Appendix, Preface, Glossary, Index, and so on.

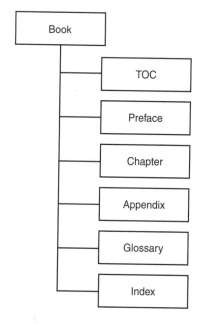

Next, you need to work out the structure that's needed inside these high-level elements. The glossary file, for example, is usually highly structured; it consists of pairs of glossary terms and definitions.

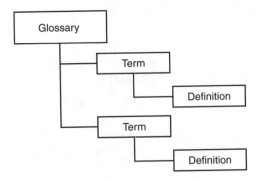

For more complex information, such as what's found in chapters, you'll probably need to define several layers of structure. You might decide that chapters consist of an introduction followed by one or more sections. Sections, in turn, have a heading, body, and sometimes procedures, and can themselves contain more sections. Procedures consist of introductions followed by steps. They might also include notes, graphics, and index markers.

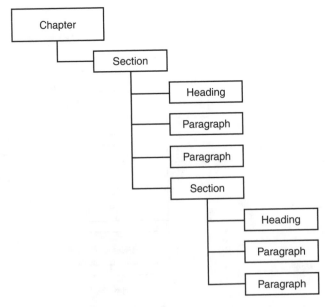

Your finished analysis provides the information you need to define the structure in the EDD.

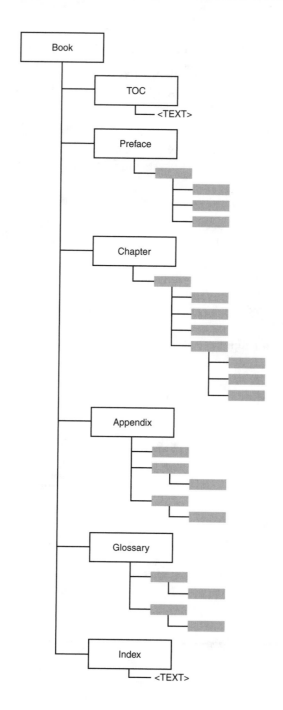

Creating a New EDD

You can create an EDD as a new document, or you can start by converting an existing DTD to an EDD. Converting an existing DTD is discussed in Chapter 31, "Importing and Exporting XML/SGML Markup Files."

To create a new EDD, follow these steps:

1. Select File | Structure Tools | New EDD. FrameMaker creates a blank, untitled document and automatically inserts the first few elements in the EDD (Figure 29-3).

   The following elements are inserted automatically:

   - **Version:** You cannot change the version information. The version corresponds to the FrameMaker version in which the EDD was created.

   - **CreateFormats:** When you import this EDD, FrameMaker automatically creates any tags (paragraph, character, and so on) that are specified in the EDD but don't exist in the document. If you do not want to create formats on import, change the CreateFormats element to the DoNotCreateFormats element.

   - **Element and Tag:** FrameMaker inserts the first Element/Tag combination so that you can begin adding element definitions immediately.

2. You're now ready to create element definitions in the EDD. This process is discussed in detail in the next section.

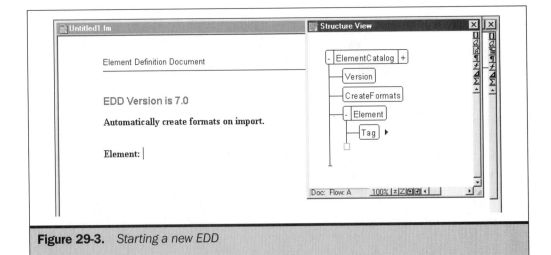

Figure 29-3. *Starting a new EDD*

Organizing Your EDD

For a relatively short EDD, you can probably get away with just creating element definitions as they occur to you. However, as the EDD gets more complex, you'll probably want to group information for easier maintenance. Here are some of the things you can do to help keep track of all the elements:

- Use the Section element to create section labels for different parts of your EDD, and group related information in sections. For example, you could create a Table Definitions section and define the table elements there.

- Use the Comment element to insert explanatory information in the EDD. For example, you might note that the ListItem element is used for several different types of lists.

- Create informative names for your elements, but try to keep them as short as possible so that they fit in the element bubbles.

- If you are planning to export information to SGML or XML, keep in mind that SGML and XML have much more restrictive rules for naming elements than FrameMaker does. You may want to conform to the more limited SGML/XML rules to simplify conversion. For example, SGML and XML do not allow spaces in element names; FrameMaker does.

- The order in which elements are listed in the EDD does not affect the order in which they are presented in the element catalog. Consider alphabetizing elements within a section to make them easier to find.

- Some EDD developers like to put elements in order from most used to least used.

Creating New Elements in the EDD

An EDD is itself a structured document (and has its own EDD!), so when you make changes to your EDD, you work as you would in any other structured document. The element catalog lists which items are available at every step in EDD development.

To create a new element, follow these steps (working mostly in the structure view):

1. Position your cursor at the highest level in the document and insert the Element element. (FrameMaker does this automatically for the first element in the EDD, as you can see in Figure 29-3.)

2. Underneath the Element element, insert a Tag element. (This is also done automatically for the first element in a new EDD.)

3. Type a name for the new element. This name will be displayed in the element catalog for authors.

4. Choose the element type. The EDD's element catalog lists the available choices.

Some of the available element types are object elements, which means that they contain one instance of the specified element and no children. Cross-references, equations, graphics, markers, rubi, and system variables are all object elements. Each of these element types are discussed in detail starting on page 709.

5. Add the elements required for that element type. Table 29-1 on page 710 lists which elements are available for each element type. The following is a complete list of possible elements (listed with a reference to more detailed information on setting up each element):

- **AttributeList:** Defines attributes for the element. This element is available for all element types. See "Defining Attributes (AttributeList)" on page 722.

- **AutoInsertions:** Specifies that child elements will be inserted automatically when you insert this element. See "Setting Up Elements with Automatic Insertion of Children (AutoInsertion)" on page 725.

- **Exclusion:** Defines elements that are not allowed as children of the current element. See "Including and Excluding Elements (Inclusion, Exclusion)" on page 730.

- **FirstParagraphRules:** Sets formatting rules for the first paragraph in this element. See "Adding Formatting Information to the EDD" on page 732.

- **GeneralRule:** Defines which child elements and text are available for this element. Used for container elements, footnotes, and table elements. See "Writing General Rules (GeneralRule)" on page 726.

- **Inclusion:** Defines elements that are allowed in any of the current element's descendant elements. See "Including and Excluding Elements (Inclusion, Exclusion)" on page 730.

- **InitialObjectFormat:** Specifies the default cross-reference format or marker type used when the author inserts this element. See "Cross-Reference Elements" on page 711 or "Marker Elements" on page 716.

- **InitialStructurePattern:** Defines an initial structure that's inserted automatically for the table. See "Table Elements" on page 718.

- **InitialTableFormat:** Defines the default table tag used when a table element is inserted. See "Table Elements" on page 718.
- **LastParagraphRules:** Sets formatting rules for the last paragraph in this element. See "Adding Formatting Information to the EDD" on page 732.
- **PrefixRules:** Specifies a prefix to be added before this element's content is inserted. See "Inserting Prefixes and Suffixes for Elements (PrefixRules, SuffixRules)" on page 740.
- **SuffixRules:** Specifies a suffix to be added after this element's content is inserted. See "Inserting Prefixes and Suffixes for Elements (PrefixRules, SuffixRules)" on page 740.
- **SystemVariableFormat:** Specifies which system variable is inserted. The system variable is assigned by the element, not by the author. See "System Variable Elements" on page 717.
- **TextFormatRules:** Controls the formatting of this element's text. See "Adding Formatting Information to the EDD" on page 732.
- **ValidHighestLevel:** Specifies whether the element can be used as the top-level element in a book or document.

6. Repeat these steps for each element you need to add. You can use the Comments element in the EDD to add explanatory information to the document, and you can use the Section element if you want to organize your list of elements.

STRUCTURED FRAMEMAKER

Creating Container Elements

A *container element* is an element that can include text and other elements, and is usually the most common type of element in a document. Container elements are also the most difficult to set up because of the many options available to define them.

When you create a container element, you must specify what content is permitted inside the element with a general rule. The *general rule* describes the element structure by listing the elements that are allowed as children of the current element. If the container has child elements but no text of its own, the element definition can be quite short—it just needs an element name, a Container element, and a general rule.

Element (Container): Book
    General rule: TOC,Preface,Chapter+,Appendix*,Glossary?,Index
    Valid as the highest-level element.

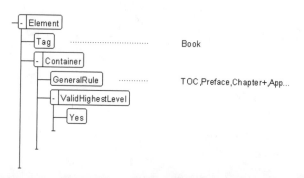

Element Types

EDD Element	Container	Cross-Reference	Equation	Footnote	Graphic	Marker	Rubi	RubiGroup	SystemVariable	Table	TableBody	TableCell	TableFooting	TableHeading	TableRow	TableTitle
AttributeList	✔	✔	✔	✔	✔	✔	✔	✔	✔	✔	✔	✔	✔	✔	✔	✔
AutoInsertions	✔											✔				
GeneralRule	✔		✔				✔	✔		✔	✔	✔	✔	✔	✔	✔
Exclusion	✔		✔				✔	✔		✔	✔	✔	✔	✔	✔	✔
FirstParagraphRules	✔															
Inclusion	✔			✔			✔	✔		✔	✔	✔	✔	✔	✔	✔
InitialObjectFormat		✔	✔		✔	✔										
InitialStructure Pattern									✔	✔	✔		✔	✔	✔	
InitialTableFormat										✔						
LastParagraphRules	✔															
PrefixRules	✔															
SuffixRules	✔															
SystemVariable Format									✔							
TextFormatRules	✔		✔				✔	✔		✔	✔	✔	✔	✔	✔	✔
ValidHighestLevel	✔															

Table 29-1.   *Different Element Types Require Different Elements in the EDD.*

In addition to child elements, you can specify in the general rule that a container element has text content.

The general rule for an element that contains either a paragraph or a text range is the same:

```
<TEXT>
```

You can also write more complicated rules that allow both text and child elements. For a detailed discussion of general rules, see "Writing General Rules (GeneralRule)" on page 726.

In addition to the general rule and attributes (which are available for every element), the following items are available for container elements:

- **Automatic insertion:** Specifies child elements that are inserted automatically when the author inserts this element. See "Setting Up Elements with Automatic Insertion of Children (AutoInsertion)" on page 725.

- **Inclusions and exclusions:** Defines elements that are not allowed as children of the current element. See "Including and Excluding Elements (Inclusion, Exclusion)" on page 730.

- **Formatting rules:** A number of different formatting options are available for elements that contain text, including rules for text, first paragraphs, and last paragraphs. These are discussed in "Adding Formatting Information to the EDD" on page 732.

- **Prefixes and suffixes:** Specifies text that appears before and after the element's text. See "Inserting Prefixes and Suffixes for Elements (PrefixRules, SuffixRules)" on page 740.

- **Valid at the highest level:** Specifies whether the container element can be used as the top-level element for a file or a book. Only elements with this setting are displayed at the beginning of a document or as available elements for a structured book.

Cross-Reference Elements

Cross-reference elements are object elements, so they cannot have any children in the document structure. When you define a cross-reference element in the EDD, you can set up attributes (see page 722) and an initial object format; both are optional. Use the InitialObjectFormat element to specify the cross-reference format that is chosen by default when the author inserts a cross-reference element. For example, you could define a cross-reference element that looks like this:

Element (CrossReference): PageReference
    Initial cross-reference format
        1.   **In all contexts.**
               Use cross-reference format: Page

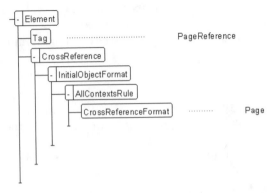

When the author inserts this cross-reference element, the cross-reference format defaults to the Page format. Note, however, that the EDD only specifies the default or initial cross-reference format. The author can change the cross-reference to a different format; the EDD does not enforce a particular cross-reference format.

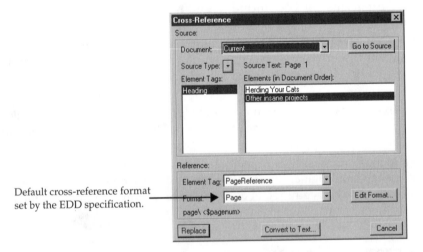

Default cross-reference format set by the EDD specification.

Equation Elements

Equation elements are object elements, so they cannot have any children in the document structure. As with cross-reference elements, you can set up two options: attributes (see page 722) and an initial object format. The initial object format lets you specify whether you want a small, medium, or large equation.

Element (Equation): SmallEquation
    Initial equation size
        1.   **In all contexts.**
               Insert small equation.

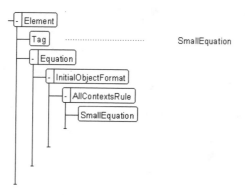

When the author inserts an equation element, FrameMaker inserts an anchor and the anchored frame for the equation:

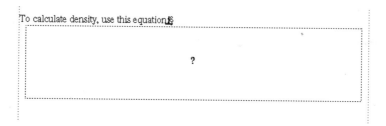

In the structure view, the equation appears as a child of the element in which it is anchored:

Footnote Elements

The footnote element is a container element; it can hold child elements (for example, text range and system variable elements). There are some restrictions, though. You cannot, for example, insert a footnote inside a footnote. If an author attempts to do this, FrameMaker displays an error message. To help prevent these error messages from being displayed, it's a good idea to exclude the elements that aren't permitted inside the footnote. For details, see "Including and Excluding Elements (Inclusion, Exclusion)" on page 730.

The footnote's element definition normally includes a general rule and a text formatting specification.

Element (Footnote): Footnote
    General rule: <TEXT>

Exclusions: SmallEquation,Footnote
Text format rules
      Element paragraph format: Footnote

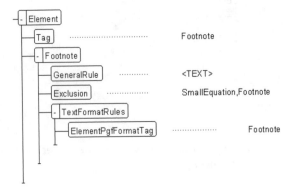

The footnote element creates a footnote at the bottom of the page, but the element is displayed in the structure view where the footnote reference is in the main body text.

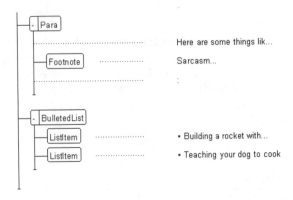

Graphic Elements

In a structured document, inserting a graphic element inserts an anchored frame. In the EDD, the graphic element's definition can include an initial object format. For the initial format, you have two choices:

- **AnchoredFrame:** When the author inserts a graphic element, the Anchored Frame dialog box is displayed. The author sets options for the anchored frame and inserts it. After inserting the empty anchored frame, the author can put graphics or other content into the anchored frame.

- **ImportedGraphicFile:** When the author inserts a graphic element, the Import dialog box is displayed. The author chooses a graphic file to import, and FrameMaker automatically creates an anchored frame (centered, the default setting) and puts the graphic inside this frame.

Element (Graphic): Graphic
    Initial graphic element format
        1.   **In all contexts.**
        Insert imported graphic file.

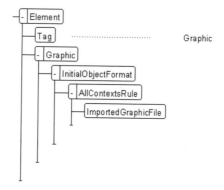

The information inside the anchored frame is not part of the current structure. You can, however, have structured information inside any text flow in a document, so if the anchored frame contains a text frame, that text frame can contain structured information in a separate flow.

You can define attributes for a graphic object. This is not at all the same thing as the object attributes available for graphics (in structured and unstructured FrameMaker) by selecting an anchored frame, then Graphics | Object Properties and then clicking the Object Attributes button. The two types of attributes are not related. For details on graphic object attributes, see page 314.

STRUCTURED
FRAMEMAKER

Marker Elements

You can specify an attribute list (see page 722) and an initial object format for a marker element. The InitialObjectFormat element lets you set the default marker type. For example, you can set an IndexEntry element to use the Index marker type by default. In unstructured FrameMaker, the marker type defaults to whatever type was last used, which frequently causes authors to make mistakes—they forget to reset the marker type while indexing, for example. Correcting these problems is tedious, so the ability to default to the correct marker type is quite helpful.

You can use context rules to create different marker types. For example, many authors use a special IndexFront marker to accommodate the Roman numerals in the front matter. (See "Eliminating Unwanted Chapter Numbers" on page 422 for a detailed discussion.) You can create a single IndexEntry element that automatically defaults to the correct marker type by checking to see whether the marker is inside the preface or not:

Element (Marker): IndexEntry
    Initial marker type
        1.   **If context is:** * < Preface
                Use marker type: IndexFront
        Else
                Use marker type: Index

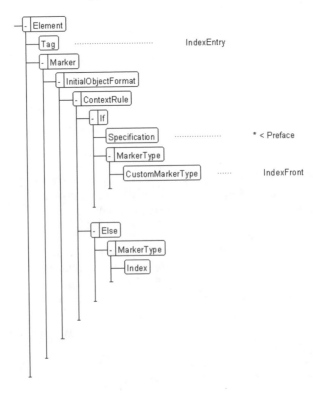

Remember to define the custom marker type in your formatting template; if the custom marker is not defined in the document, attempting to insert the element results in an error message.

Inside a Preface element, inserting the IndexEntry marker results in this:

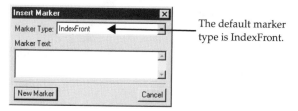

The default marker type is IndexFront.

After inserting the marker, the IndexEntry element and its associated text are shown in the structure. Notice that the marker type does not appear anywhere in the structure.

Rubi and RubiGroup Elements

The Rubi and RubiGroup elements are used only in Japanese text. A rubi is a phonetic pronunciation guide that's printed above a character. You group the character (kanji) with its rubi in a rubi group. Refer to the online *Structured FrameMaker Developer's Guide* (found in the OnlineManuals directory) for details on setting up these elements.

System Variable Elements

You can define elements for system variables (but not user variables). If needed, you can define attributes as part of the system variable element. The system variable format rule lets you specify which variable you want to use in the element.

Element (System Variable): Filename
    System variable format rule
        1.   In all contexts.
                Use system variable: Filename (Long)

When the author inserts a system variable element, FrameMaker automatically inserts the specified system variable. The author does not have to choose a variable; the Variable dialog box is not even displayed.

Keep in mind that you can create structured or unstructured system variables. User variables are always unstructured.

Authors cannot double-click the structured system variable to edit it. Instead, they must explicitly select Special | Variable to display the Variable dialog box.

Table Elements

Tables have a detailed structure, and when you create an EDD, you must define elements for each part of the table. The available element types for tables are as follows:

- Table
- TableBody
- TableCell
- TableFooting
- TableHeading
- TableRow
- TableTitle

You must use these element types in a specific hierarchy to create a valid table. Consider, for example, the following simple table:

Table 1: Troubleshooting

Problem	Solution
Can't open the file.	Install the reader software.
Fonts are missing.	Make sure you embed fonts.
Colors don't print properly.	Check printer driver settings.

The table is displayed as usual in the document window. In the structure view, the table items are written out row by row. As a result, the structure view for a table takes up a lot of space.

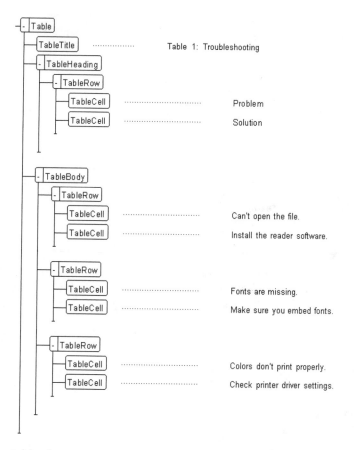

Each of the table element types must contain certain structures to create a valid table. The rules are as follows:

Element	Structure	General Rule Example
Table	Must contain a TableBody element. The TableTitle, TableHeading, and TableFooting elements are optional; you can have zero or one of each.	`TableTitle?,` `TableHeading?,` `TableBody,` `TableFooting?`
TableHeading	Must contain at least one TableRow element.	`TableRow+`
TableBody	Must contain at least one TableRow element.	`TableRow+`

Element	Structure	General Rule Example
TableFooting	Must contain at least one TableRow element.	`TableRow+`
TableRow	Must contain at least one TableCell element.	`TableCell+`
TableCell	Contains paragraphs and other text elements, but never another table element.	`<TEXT>`
TableTitle	Contains paragraphs and other text elements, but never another table element.	`<TEXT>`

If you want to allow tables in your documents, you'll need to define each of these elements at least once. The following shows a sample set of table definitions (the structure view is omitted in this example):

Table Definitions

Element (Table): Table
  General rule: TableTitle,TableHeading,TableBody,TableFooting?
  Initial structure pattern for table: TableTitle,TableHeading,TableBody
  Initial table format
    1. **In all contexts.**
      Table format: Format A

Element (Table Title): TableTitle
  General rule: `<TEXT>`
  Text format rules
    Element paragraph format: TableTitle

Element (Table Heading): TableHeading
  General rule: TableRow+
  Text format rules
    Element paragraph format: CellHeading

Element (Table Body): TableBody
  General rule: TableRow+
  Text format rules
    Element paragraph format: CellBody

Element (Table Row): TableRow
  General rule: TableCell+

Element (Table Cell): TableCell
  General rule: `<TEXT>`

Element (Table Footing): TableFooting
General rule: TableRow+

Instead of defining generic table elements (such as TableRow), you can create table definitions that reflect the purpose of the table. For example, the troubleshooting table shown in the preceding example uses generic tags (Table, TableRow, TableCell, and so on). If your documents have many troubleshooting tables, you might instead set up a table that uses elements such as Troubleshooting, Problem, and Solution:

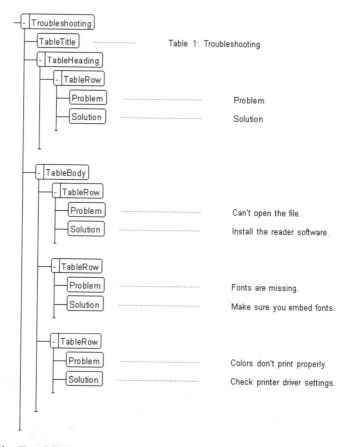

To create the Troubleshooting table element, just rename the table definition:

Element (Table): Troubleshooting
    General rule: TableTitle,TableHeading,TableBody,TableFooting?
    Initial structure pattern for table: TableTitle,TableHeading,TableBody
    Initial table format
        1. **In all contexts.**
                Table format: TroubleTable

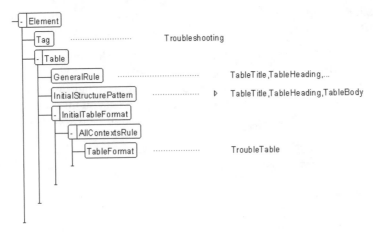

When the authors first insert a table, FrameMaker automatically creates the entire structure for the table. Inside the table rows, there are two cells, a Problem element and a Solution element. The InitialStructurePattern element lets you specify that you want FrameMaker to insert these elements automatically when the author first creates the table:

Element (Table Row): TableRow
    General rule: Problem,Solution
  Initial structure pattern for table row: (Problem,Solution)

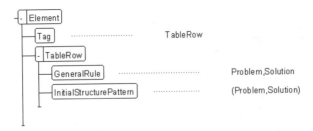

The information in parentheses is repeated as necessary to create the structure within the table row. If you do not provide the parentheses, FrameMaker uses the last element in the general rule to "fill in" any additional rows.

Defining Attributes (AttributeList)

You can define attributes for any element by inserting the AttributeList element in the EDD. When you set up the AttributeList element, you are prompted to provide the following specifications for each attribute:

- **Name:** The attribute's label, such as Revision or Author.
- **Attribute type:** Among other options, you can specify that the author must choose the value of the attribute from a list (Choice attribute), or that the

attribute's value must be unique in this document (UniqueID). UniqueID attributes help to manage links from one section of a document to another.

- **Optional or required:** If the attribute is optional, the document author is not required to insert it. If the attribute is required, the document is invalid until the author supplies a value for the attribute.

- **Attribute controls:** You can set an attribute to be hidden or read-only. Hidden attributes are stored in the document but not displayed to the author. Read-only attributes are displayed, but the authors cannot modify them. These attributes are useful for attribute values that are being imported from SGML/XML source documents and that you do not want changed.

- **List of values:** If you specify the Choice attribute type, you must provide a list of values (which become the list of choices for the authors).

Creating an Attribute Definition

To define an attribute for an element definition, follow these steps:

1. Insert the AttributeList element at the appropriate location inside the element definition. FrameMaker automatically inserts the Name element as a child of AttributeList.

2. Specify a name for the attribute.

3. Specify the attribute type. Your choices are as follows:

   - **Choice:** The author will choose from a list of options to specify the value for the attribute. You define the list of choices later in the attribute definition.

   - **IDReference:** The attribute references another element's UniqueID attribute. Most often, you'll use this attribute type to create cross-references that point to a UniqueID attribute.

   - **IDReferences:** Same as IDReference, except that the attribute can have multiple values.

   - **Integer:** The value of the attribute must be a whole number, such as 4 or -214. Decimals are not allowed.

   - **Integers:** Same as Integer, except that the attribute can have multiple values.

   - **Real:** The value of the attribute is a number, such as 3.2 or -777.4.

   - **Reals:** Same as Real, except that the attribute can have multiple values.

   - **String:** The value of the attribute is a text string.

   - **Strings:** Same as String, except that the attribute can have more than one string as a value.

   - **UniqueID:** The value of the attribute is a unique text string.

4. Specify whether the attribute is required or optional by inserting the appropriate element.

STRUCTURED
FRAMEMAKER

5. If you created a Choice attribute, you must specify the choices available. Insert the Choices element, then type in the options, separated by commas.

6. If needed, you can make the attribute hidden or read-only. To do so, insert the SpecialAttributeControls element, then insert the Hidden or ReadOnly child. Most often, hidden attributes are used when you are importing information from SGML or XML. You can preserve information that's needed, but that isn't useful to the authors working in FrameMaker. Read-only attributes are handy for attributes that are set automatically, such as IDReference attributes.

Setting Up a Choice Attribute

When you set up a choice attribute, you must provide a name for the attribute and a list of choices, as shown in the following example:

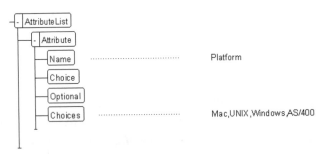

When the author inserts the element that includes this attribute definition (in the preceding example, it's Section), the Attributes for New Element dialog box is displayed automatically. The items listed in the Choices element in the EDD become the pop-up Choices list in this dialog box.

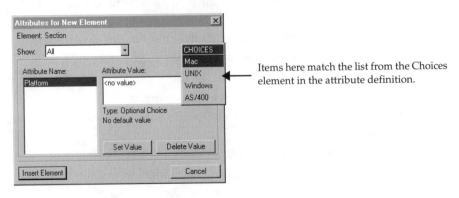

Items here match the list from the Choices element in the attribute definition.

Setting Up Elements with Automatic Insertion of Children (AutoInsertion)

In some cases, you can predict the structure that needs to be created. For example, it's very common to have a Section element that requires Heading as a child. You can set up your EDD to insert child elements automatically for some elements. This saves the authors some time.

 Tip *For tables, you need to insert quite a few children before beginning to insert content. The table elements provide a special InitialStructurePattern element, which lets FrameMaker insert the complex table structure automatically. Automatic insertion of children is less flexible, so use the InitialStructurePattern for table elements.*

Unfortunately, you cannot use automatic insertion to create several sibling elements under one parent. You can, however, specify a child element, and additional nested children. For example, if the Chapter element generally starts with a Section element, and the Section has a Heading child, you could define the Chapter element to insert these elements automatically:

Element (Container): Chapter
> **General rule:**   Section,Section+
> **Valid as the highest-level element.**
> **Inclusions:**   Footnote,Note
>
> **Automatic insertions**
>> **Automatically insert child:**   Section
>> **and nested child:**   Heading

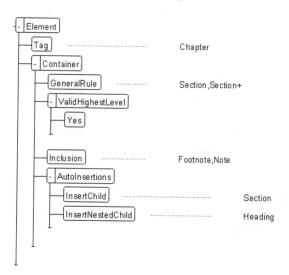

The author inserts the Chapter element and immediately gets the two child elements in the structure:

The insertion point is positioned under the Heading element, so the author can immediately begin typing in the heading text.

Writing General Rules (GeneralRule)

General rules have their own syntax. For each element, you write out a command that defines all of the children and content allowed in that element. For some elements, this can result in lengthy, complicated rules. For most elements, you list the elements that occur in sequence and separate them with commas. The simplest general rule specifies that the element requires content:

```
<TEXT>
```

When you use <TEXT>, any elements defined as inclusions are also available for that element. If you want to allow text, but not any elements—not even inclusions—you use the following general rule:

```
<TEXTONLY>
```

Keep in mind that <TEXTONLY> only prohibits elements; you cannot prevent the authors from inserting *unstructured* information, such as nonelement cross-references, markers, and the like.

The <EMPTY> general rule lets you create container elements that do not have any child elements or content. You might use this command for an element that uses a paragraph tag with an autonumber but no text in the paragraph itself. An element that requires a marker of a particular type but no marker text could also use this syntax.

The <ANY> general rule permits text or any element defined in the EDD. Using <ANY> creates a very loose element definition because you cannot control what elements will be inserted underneath the element. Use it sparingly, if at all.

Many of your container elements will need explicit references to child elements. To create these, you list the elements you want to allow (or require) in the general rule. To indicate a particular sequence, you separate the elements with commas. For example, the general rule for a Chapter element could be as follows:

```
Section+
```

This means that underneath the Chapter element, a Section element is required. The plus sign indicates one or more Section elements are required, so any of the following examples would be legal structures:

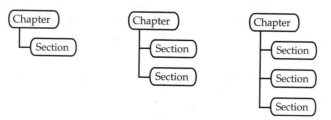

If you want to require a minimum of *two* Section elements in a Chapter, use this general rule:

```
Section,Section+
```

The plus sign is called a *quantifier*; it sets the quantity of the preceding element (that is, the element immediately to the left of the quantifier). Other quantifiers are the question mark (?) for zero or one elements and the asterisk (*) for zero or more elements. Table 29-2 lists all the commands.

Most element definitions list the elements in the order in which they must occur. For example, the Section element could be defined as follows:

```
Heading,Overview,Para+
```

Heading, Overview, and Para are elements. The commas indicate that the elements must occur in the order specified. If you want to allow elements in any order, you use an ampersand (&), as in this Para definition:

```
<TEXT> & Emphasis & Graphic & Equation
```

This definition, however, requires one Emphasis, one Graphic, and one Equation in the Para element along with text. Instead of the preceding example, you would probably use the pipe symbol (|) and parentheses to group the optional elements:

```
<TEXT>, (Emphasis|Graphic|Equation) *
```

This indicates that the element contains text and any number of the Emphasis, Graphic, and Equation elements. Text is allowed before and after the Emphasis, Graphic, or Equation elements.

The <TEXT> specification does not support quantifiers; all the following have the same result:

```
<TEXT>
<TEXT>+
<TEXT>?
<TEXT>*
```

In other words, the <TEXT> specification is always "optional and repeatable" (Adobe's phrase).

Command	Example	Meaning
	`Element1`	One instance of Element1
? (question mark)	`Element1?`	Zero or one instances of Element1
+ (plus sign)	`Element1+`	One or more instances of Element1
* (asterisk)	`Element1*`	Zero or more instances of Element1
, (comma)	`Element1,Element2`	One Element1 followed by one Element2
& (ampersand)	`Element1&Element2`	One Element1 and one Element2 in any order
| (pipe symbol)	`Element1|Element2`	Element1 or Element2
	`(Element1|Element2)+`	One or more Element1 or Element2 (in any order)
	`<TEXT>`	This element requires text. Authors can also insert elements that are available as inclusions.
	`<EMPTY>`	The element is empty.
	`<ANY>`	The element can contain text or any elements defined in the EDD.
	`<TEXTONLY>`	The element requires text. It cannot have any child elements, not even elements defined as inclusions.

Table 29-2. *General Rule Syntax*

As you define general rules, you will likely start with the highest-level element and work down through the document structure. In the cookbook EDD, for example, the general rule for Recipe is as follows:

```
Name,History?,IngredientList,Instructions
```

It requires one Name element, followed by zero or one History elements, followed by one IngredientList element, followed by one Instructions element.

Several of these elements, in turn, also contain elements. The IngredientList element, for example, has this general rule:

```
Ingredient+
```

And the Ingredient element, in turn, has this rule:

```
Quantity, Item, PrepMethod?
```

An author who uses the cookbook EDD is guided into producing a structured document that looks something like this at the top level:

Note   *The History element is optional in the general rule for Recipe; it does not occur in the preceding example. The structure would also be valid if a History element occurred between Name and IngredientList.*

The IngredientList structure looks like this:

```
- IngredientList
    + Ingredient  ..............      1
    + Ingredient  ..............      1
    + Ingredient  ..............      1
    + Ingredient  ..............      1
    + Ingredient  ..............      1 cup
    + Ingredient  ..............      3
    + Ingredient  ..............      1.5
```

The general rule for IngredientList is as follows:

```
Ingredient+
```

It requires at least one Ingredient element. If you wanted to require at least two Ingredient elements, you could write this general rule:

```
Ingredient, Ingredient+
```

The Ingredient elements, in turn, are as follows:

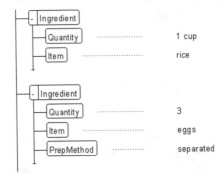

The first Ingredient element has the required Quantity and Item elements but not the optional PrepMethod element. In the second Ingredient element, PrepMethod does occur. The Instructions look like this:

If your container element has only other elements as its contents, specifying the general rule (and perhaps some attributes, described on page 722) is enough to fully define the container element. If the element contains text, however, you must provide details about how to format that text. See "Adding Formatting Information to the EDD" on page 732.

Including and Excluding Elements (Inclusion, Exclusion)

Some elements are permitted almost anywhere in the document. Instead of adding those elements to nearly every general rule throughout the EDD, consider using inclusions and exclusions to make these elements available to authors. For example, the Footnote element might be available in any part of your text. Instead of including the Footnote element in every element definition for the main body text, you can set up your Chapter element to allow the Footnote element as an inclusion. When you create an inclusion, the element is allowed anywhere inside the specified element—that is, in the element and all of its child elements.

You cannot insert any child elements inside object elements (marker, graphic, equation, cross-reference, and system variable). A general rule of <TEXTONLY> or <EMPTY> also disallows included elements (or any children).

Element (Container): Chapter
    General rule: Section,Section+
    Valid as the highest-level element.
    Inclusions: Footnote

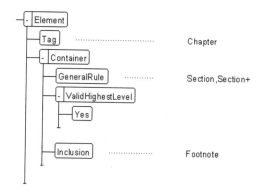

If you need to allow the element everywhere with a few exceptions, set up the inclusion (for example, for the Chapter) and then exclude the element from the items where it's not allowed. You might, for example, have a style guideline that footnotes are not permitted inside notes. In that case, you would still set up an inclusion for the Chapter element but then create an exclusion for the Note element:

Element (Container): Note
    General rule: <TEXT>
    Exclusions: Footnote

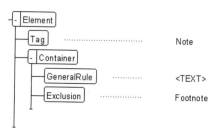

Inclusions appear in the element catalog with a check mark and a plus sign. In the following example, Footnote, IndexEntry, Note, and Table are available because of inclusions:

To display inclusions after other valid elements, change your element display options (click the Options button in the element catalog).

Adding Formatting Information to the EDD

In unstructured FrameMaker, the distinction between paragraph tags and character tags is clear. You apply paragraph tags to entire paragraphs; you apply character tags to chunks of text within a paragraph. In structured FrameMaker, some of that separation is lost. Depending on how you define formatting for an element, the element can become either a paragraph or a text range (a section of a paragraph). FrameMaker will automatically add an end-of-paragraph carriage return if you define an element with paragraph formatting; if you change the definition to set up a text range, FrameMaker automatically removes the carriage return at the end of the text.

A further difference between structured and unstructured FrameMaker is in how "unformatted" elements are handled. In regular FrameMaker, it's not possible to create a paragraph without a paragraph tag. The paragraph may use the default Body tag, but you cannot insert a paragraph without some sort of tag applied to it. In structured FrameMaker, text elements create paragraphs by default (you must explicitly define text ranges), but you are not required to include a paragraph tag or any formatting information in the element definition. If you omit formatting information from the element, the element will inherit formatting instructions from its ancestors. If no instructions are provided for any ancestor element, FrameMaker uses the default Body tag.

Specifically, formatting instructions are handled this way:

- **Elements in tables.** FrameMaker searches up to the top-level table element, but does not go any further up the hierarchy.
- **Elements in footnotes.** FrameMaker searches only up to the footnote element. If no formatting instructions are found, FrameMaker uses the Footnote or TableFootnote default paragraph tags.
- **Books.** If a document is in a book, an element can inherit information from book-level elements. The search automatically goes all the way up to the top level.

Formatting Choices

In the EDD, there are several ways to provide formatting information for text. If you are working with elements that correspond to paragraphs, you can associate paragraph tags with the elements. You can also associate character tags with text range elements. Instead of using paragraph or character tagging, you can embed the formatting specifications in the EDD using either format change lists (a named list of formatting specifications) or formatting overrides. Finally, you can omit a specification and allow the element to inherit formatting from a parent or ancestor element. Some EDDs use a combination of formatting commands—an element references a paragraph tag (or inherits one) and then overrides portions of that paragraph tag's formatting with EDD-based formatting information.

Before deciding on which approach to use, consider these issues:

- If you define one paragraph tag per element (more or less), your content will be formatted even if the EDD is not available. That makes it easier to use the paragraph template in unstructured documents. If you use format change lists or formatting overrides, you cannot match the look of your structured documents in unstructured FrameMaker. Furthermore, opening a structured document in an unstructured environment will result in a loss of most of your formatting in addition to the structure information.

- Defining formatting in the EDD lets you set up inheritance relationships. This lets you make a single formatting change in one location, which then cascades through several elements. This is impossible with paragraph tags.

- If you set up the EDD to reference paragraph tags, you can create a separate formatting template with the various paragraph definitions. You can then update the formatting template without making changes to the EDD. This could be useful if you have different people responsible for EDD creation and format creation.

- Defining formatting in the EDD means that users can import element definitions from the EDD and start working. If you define formatting in a separate formatting template, users must import twice: once to import formats and once to import element definitions. You can work around this by storing the formatting information in the EDD, but your template designer must work directly in the EDD instead of a separate formatting template. Perhaps the best alternative is to import the element definitions into the formatting template and provide that file to authors.

For any of these options, you can set up context-sensitive formatting, which means that the formatting of the element depends on the element's position in the structure. To do so, you write context rules, which provide the logic to determine which formatting to use. This section addresses only how to format elements globally ("in all contexts"); refer to "Controlling Formatting with Element Context" on page 742 for details about context rules.

Associating Paragraph Tags with Elements

To associate a paragraph tag with an element, you insert the TextFormatRules element with the ElementPgfFormatTag child. In the second element, you specify the paragraph tag you want to use. The result looks something like this:

Element (Container): Para
    General rule: <TEXT>
    Inclusions: Cross-Reference,Footnote,SmallEquation

    Text format rules
Element paragraph format: Body

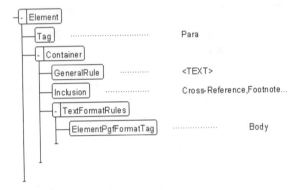

To set up an element that uses paragraph formatting, follow these steps:

1. Create a container element and specify <TEXT> as part of the general rule.
2. Underneath the general rule, insert the TextFormatRules element.
3. Underneath the TextFormatRules element, insert the ElementPgfFormatTag element.
4. In the ElementPgfFormatTag element, type in the name of the paragraph tag you want to use for this element.

Associating Character Tags with Elements

If you specify that a particular element is a text range, you can associate a character tag with the text range. The resulting definition looks like the following illustration:

Element (Container): Emphasis
    General rule: <TEXT>
    Text format rules
       1.   **In all contexts.**
             Text range.
               Use character format: Emphasis

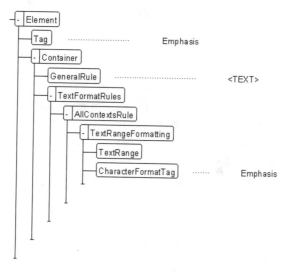

To set up an element that uses character tag formatting, follow these steps:

1. Create a container element, and specify <TEXT> as part of the general rule.
2. Underneath the general rule, insert the TextFormatRules element.
3. Underneath the TextFormatRules element, insert the AllContextsRule element.
4. Underneath the AllContextsRule element, insert the TextRangeFormatting element. FrameMaker automatically inserts the TextRange element as a child.
5. Insert the CharacterFormatTag element as a sibling of the TextRange element.
6. In the CharacterFormatTag element, type in the name of the character tag you want to use for this element.

Using Format Change Lists

A *format change list* is a named collection of style specifications, which sounds a lot like a paragraph tag definition. In paragraph tags, though, you must provide a setting for every one of the paragraph options. Format change lists can contain just one or two settings instead of a full-blown paragraph definition. This lets you use the format change list to override portions of the underlying paragraph definition. Format change lists are stored as part of the EDD.

Inside a format change list, you can supply some or all of the settings that are available in the Paragraph Designer. In a few cases, the format change list is actually more flexible than the Paragraph Designer. You can, for instance, set a relative tab (a tab that is indented from the starting point of the paragraph). In the Paragraph Designer, tabs are always absolute.

To create a format change list, follow these steps:

1. Insert a FormatChangeList element. This element is valid after the CreateFormats or DoNotCreateFormats element anywhere at the top level of the EDD structure. You can also position it inside a Section element anywhere after the Head element. FrameMaker automatically inserts the Tag element as a child.

2. Specify a name for the format change list. For example, you could create a format change list for a bulleted list called Bullet.

3. *(optional)* To specify a base paragraph tag, insert the ParagraphFormatTag element and supply the name of the paragraph tag you want to start with. If you do not provide a ParagraphFormatTag element, the format change list is applied to whatever paragraph tag the element has inherited.

4. An element is available for each of the Paragraph Designer's property sheets. To create a new setting, select the relevant element name, then specify the setting you want to change. For instance, to set an autonumber in the format change list, insert the PropertiesNumbering element, then use the available child elements to create the autonumbering settings, as shown in the following example:

Format change list: Bullet
  Numbering properties
      Autonumber format: \b\t
      Position: Start of paragraph

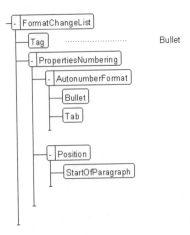

Once you define the format change list, you can reference it in element definitions:

Element (Container): ListItem
      General rule: <TEXT>

Text format rules
    1.   **In all contexts.**
        Use format change list: Bullet

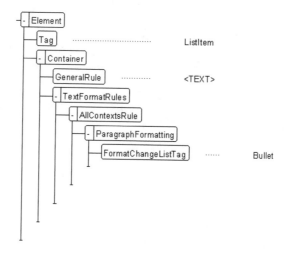

Using Formatting Overrides in the EDD

Instead of tag specifications and format change lists, you can embed formatting overrides directly into the EDD. Just as formatting overrides are usually discouraged in unstructured documents, we recommend against using them in structured documents. They can make maintaining the document difficult.

However, if you decide to use formatting overrides (perhaps because it allows you to see the formatting settings in the element definition), the EDD gives you all of the options from the Paragraph Designer or the Character Designer depending on whether you're formatting a paragraph or a text range. For example, in a text range, you can insert a PropertiesFont element and then specify the font properties with the available elements:

Element (Container): Link
    General rule: <TEXT>
    Text format rules
        1.   **In all contexts.**
            Text range.
            Font properties
                Color: Blue
                Underline: Single

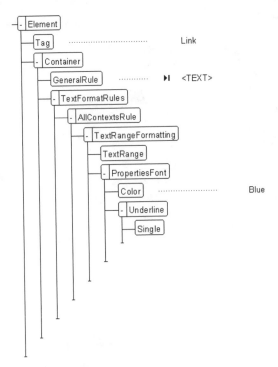

In a paragraph-based text element, you can choose from the properties available in the Paragraph Designer and then provide the specifications for any settings you want:

Element (Footnote): Footnote
>   **General rule:**   <TEXT>
>   **Exclusions:**   SmallEquation,Footnote
>   **Text format rules**
>>   1.   **In all contexts.**
>>>   **Basic properties**
>>>>   **Tab Stops**
>>>>>   **Tab stop position:** 1 pc
>>>>   **Indents**
>>>>>   **Left indent:** 1 pc
>>>>   **Numbering properties**
>>>>>   **Autonumber format:** <n+>.\t
>>>>   **Default font properties**
>>>>>   **Family:** Helvetica
>>>>>   **Size:** 8 pt

This structure excerpt shows only the text formatting rules. The PropertiesBasic and PropertiesFont elements have been collapsed.

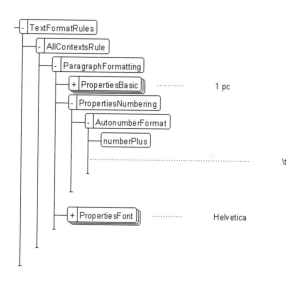

Setting Minimum and Maximum Values for Formatting Properties

You can set up minimum and maximum values for certain formatting properties as part of the EDD. By default, your font size can range between 2 points and 400 points. If you want to limit that range further, use the FormatChangeListLimits element in your EDD.

Note   *You cannot use this element to create less restrictive limits.*

The FormatChangeListLimits element must be the last element in your EDD, so it comes after all the element definitions and format change lists. For each item, you can specify a new minimum, a new maximum, or both.

Limit values for format change list properties
    Font size
        Minimum: 4 pt

Inserting Prefixes and Suffixes for Elements (PrefixRules, SuffixRules)

As part of an element definition, you can specify prefixes and suffixes for a text-based element. At first glance, these look almost identical to autonumbering—you can insert text before or after the element's text and can format that text differently from the main body text of the element. There are, however, several differences between setting paragraph autonumbering and defining prefixes and suffixes:

- With paragraph autonumbering, you can set an autonumber at the beginning or the end of the paragraph, but not both. You can assign both a prefix and a suffix to the same element.

- You can use prefixes and suffixes with text range elements. Autonumbering is available only for paragraphs, not for text ranges.

- You can use attribute values in prefixes and suffixes but not in autonumbers.

Use prefixes and suffixes to format information when you do not want to add the text to the element itself. For example, assume that you have a directory listing:

```
Smith, Joe (Dr.)
411 Info Highway
Teeceepee, IP 19281
```

The title, Dr., is enclosed in parentheses, but these parentheses are just formatting information; they aren't really part of the title itself. Using a prefix and a suffix to insert these parentheses lets you ignore them when you export content to SGML or XML.

To set a prefix or suffix, insert the appropriate PrefixRules or SuffixRules element. A sample Title element would look something like the following example.

The prefix for the Title element is defined as a space followed by an open parenthesis; the suffix is a closing parenthesis. The prefix and suffix are included only if the Title element occurs. If the element isn't used, the prefix and suffix aren't used, either.

 When you use spaces or special characters (such as tabs) in the prefix definitions, they are impossible to see in the EDD. We highly recommend that you provide a comment for the element that describes the prefix and suffix settings whenever they contain whitespace characters. This is especially useful if you use "invisible" characters such as em spaces, en spaces, or thin spaces.

```
Element (Container): Title
    General rule:        <TEXT>
    Prefix rules
        1.    In all contexts.
                Prefix:  (
```

Text format rules
1.   **In all contexts.**
             Text range.
Suffix rules
1.   **In all contexts.**
             Suffix:)
The prefix is space (, the suffix is).

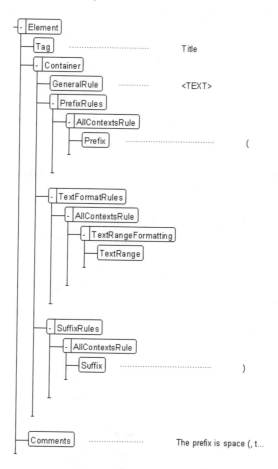

Using Attributes in Prefixes and Suffixes

You can use attributes, either from the current element or an ancestor element, in prefixes and suffixes. To reference an attribute, use the following syntax:

```
<$attribute[attribute_name] >
```

When you insert this command into a prefix or suffix, FrameMaker looks for the specified attribute in the current element and inserts the value of the attribute as the text. If the attribute has multiple values, the first value is used.

If you need to pick up an attribute that's part of an ancestor element, specify the element after the attribute name:

```
<$attribute[attribute_name:element_name]>
```

You can also specify that FrameMaker should look for the attribute in one of several elements. It will then use the attribute value from the closest element it finds:

```
<$attribute[attribute_name:element_name,element_name2,...]>
```

Controlling Formatting with Element Context

In a simple element definition, formatting is set by specifying a tag, format change list, or formatting override. The element always uses the same formatting. You can also create context-dependent formatting—the formatting varies depending on the element's position in the hierarchy.

For production editors and others responsible for creating finished documentation, context-dependent formatting is one of structured FrameMaker's most powerful and useful features because you can write EDDs that automatically enforce certain formatting rules.

One of the most common examples of this is in lists. In unstructured FrameMaker, you might create three paragraph tags—BulletFirst, Bullet, and BulletLast—so that you can put some extra space above the first bullet and some extra space below the last bullet. The author, however, must remember to apply the paragraph tags correctly. If a bullet moves from the middle of the list to the beginning, the tags must be changed accordingly.

Heading1 ——— **Herding Your Cats**

Body ——— Here are some reasons why you should never herd your cats:

BulletFirst ——— • Painful scratches

Bullet ——— • Loud meowing

Bullet ——— • Intense frustration

BulletLast ——— • Complete futility

If you insist on trying this, we recommend our popular padded jacket.

In structured FrameMaker, you can use context-dependent formatting to accomplish this automatically. Formatting changes are made automatically when the author moves bullets around.

While writing your EDD, you can use the following techniques to create context-dependent formatting:

- **Counting ancestors.** You can write a rule that counts from the current element up through the hierarchy and counts the number of a certain element. You can, for example, count ancestor Section elements to determine whether a Heading element should use a Heading1 (one Section ancestor), a Heading2 (two Section ancestors), or a Heading3 (three Section ancestors).

- **First and last paragraph rules.** You can assign special formatting to the first and last paragraphs under a particular element.

- **Context rules.** You can write short if-then statements to test your element's context. You can actually use context rules to count ancestors or set first and last paragraph rules, but the special-purpose elements provided for this are usually easier to set up. Context rules give you a tool for testing context and then implementing formatting based on the result.

The first two alternatives are generally easier to set up. Context rules, however, give you the most flexibility.

These three choices are not mutually exclusive. You can write a first paragraph rule that uses a context rule, a context rule that counts ancestors, or a level rule that contains a context rule, so all three features can interact with each other.

Counting Ancestor Elements (LevelRules)

Counting ancestor elements lets you determine how deeply an element is nested and then apply formatting based on that information. You specify the ancestor element you want counted, and provide formatting instructions based on the number of ancestors:

Element (Container): Heading
    General rule: <TEXT>
    Text format rules
        1.   **Count ancestors named:**   Section
           If level is: 3
               Use paragraph format: Heading3
           Else, if level is: 2
               Use paragraph format: Heading2
           Else, if level is: 1
               Use paragraph format: Heading1

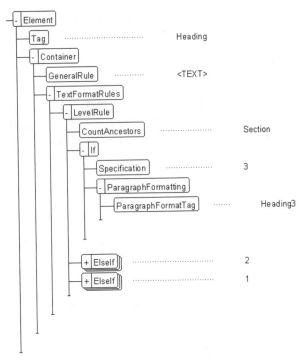

You can list the counts in any order; FrameMaker first counts the total number of ancestors, and then uses the level rule that matches exactly. In other words, a Heading nested in three Sections (count = 3) will *not* match counts of 1 or 2—only 3.

There are a few other features you can use when counting ancestors:

■ Instead of listing a single element to be counted, you can list several. For example:

1. **Count ancestors named:**   Section,Chapter,Preface

In this case, FrameMaker counts every ancestor that matches the list and generates a single total ancestor count.

■ If you leave out the CountAncestors element, FrameMaker uses the current element name and counts ancestors that match that name.

■ The StopCountingAt element lets you specify an element that halts counting of ancestors.

Formatting First and Last Paragraphs

The FirstParagraphRules and LastParagraphRules are applied to children of the current element, not to the current element. Furthermore, any formatting specifications inside the child element will override the first or last paragraph rule being inherited from the parent. To format a bulleted list with a special paragraph format for the first item in the list and the last item in the list, you could use something like the following example:

Element (Container): BulletedList
    General rule: ListItem,ListItem+
    Format rules for first paragraph in element
        1.   **In all contexts.**
               Use paragraph format: BulletFirst
    Format rules for last paragraph in element
        1.   **In all contexts.**
               Use paragraph format: BulletLast
    Text format rules
        Element paragraph format: Bullet

Element (Container): ListItem
    General rule: <TEXT>

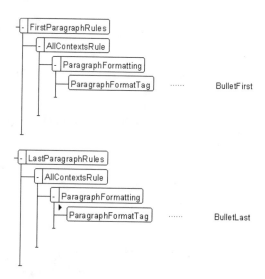

Here are some interesting notes about this example:

- You could use format change lists or formatting overrides instead of calling a specific paragraph tag. If you use a paragraph tag, make sure that it's defined in the formatting template.

- The ListItem element definition doesn't contain any formatting information because that would override the definitions provided in the parent element. Instead, the BulletedList element includes specifications for a default format (Bullet), the first paragraph, and the last paragraph.

- You could accomplish the same thing using context rules inside the ListItem element. The context rules check for BulletedList as the parent and then for the element's position (first or last) in the list.

- You can write context rules inside the first/last paragraph formatting rules, if necessary.

Writing Context Rules

Context rules provide you with the most powerful way to customize formatting. When you insert a context rule, you must provide a *specification* for each context rule. The specification is the if part of the context rule; the formatting information provides the then result. Context rules are useful for elements you want to use in multiple locations with different formatting.

Context rules are also available for other parts of the element definition. For example, you can set the initial marker type based on the element context; an example of this is shown in "Marker Elements" on page 716.

For example, a note that occurs inside a table cell is often formatted differently from a note in regular text. In unstructured FrameMaker, you use two paragraph tags, such as Note and TableNote. Because both notes are structurally the same thing, they should really use a single element. You can write a context rule to check whether the Note element is inside a table. If it is, you use the TableNote paragraph format; if it isn't, you use the regular Note format, as shown in the following example:

Element (Container): Note
> **General rule:**   \<TEXT\>
> **Exclusions:**   Footnote
> **Text format rules**
>> 1.   **If context is:** * \< Table
>>> **Use paragraph format:** TableNote
>> **Else**
>>> **Use paragraph format:** Note

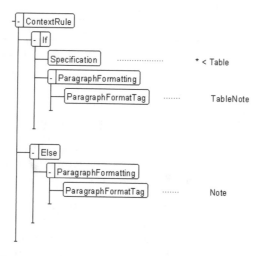

Table 29-3 shows the context rule syntax options.

When you provide multiple context rules for a single element, FrameMaker tests each in turn and applies those where the if condition (the specification) is true. That means that the third context rule could override the first context rule if you're not careful. To prevent this problem, put your rules in order from specific to generic. For example, consider a more complex set of requirements for a Note element:

- A note in a table uses the TableNote format.
- A note in a list must be indented from a regular note.
- If you have multiple notes, they should start with "NOTES:" instead of "NOTE:" and the second, third, and subsequent notes should be indented without a Note label.

To accomplish this in unstructured FrameMaker, you would need several paragraph tags, as shown in Figure 29-4 on page 750.

Rule	True if...
ElementName	ElementName is the parent of the current element.
ElementName < Section	ElementName is the parent, and ElementName's parent is Section.
ElementName < * < Preface	ElementName is the parent, and Preface is an ancestor.
* < (ElementName | ElementName2)	ElementName or ElementName2 is an ancestor of the current element.
{first}	The current element is the first element of its parent. Setting a context rule with {first} is equivalent to setting a first paragraph rule on the parent element. Keep in mind that the context rule takes precedence over formatting that's inherited from the parent element.
{last}	The current element is the last element of its parent.
{only}	The current element is the only child element of its parent.
{middle}	The current element is neither the first nor the last element of its parent.
{notfirst}	The current element is *not* the first element of its parent.
{notlast}	The current element is *not* the last element of its parent.
{before ElementName}	The current element occurs before ElementName; that is, ElementName is the next sibling.
{after ElementName}	The current element occurs after ElementName; that is, ElementName is the preceding sibling.
{any}	Anything. Specifying {any} is equivalent to no context rule at all. This command is useful in making complex context rules easier to read.

Table 29-3. *Context Rule Syntax*

Rule	True if...
`{between ElementName, ElementName2}`	The current element occurs after ElementName and before ElementName2.
`ElementName [name= "value"]`	The current element is a child of ElementName, and ElementName has an attribute called *name* set to *value*.

Table 29-3.   *Context Rule Syntax (Continued)*

In structured FrameMaker, the document uses a single Note element for all of these items:

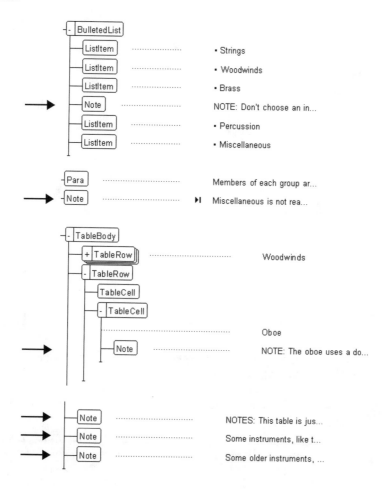

Orchestras

An orchestra is made up of several types of instruments:

- Strings
- Woodwinds
- Brass

NoteIndent tag ———→ **NOTE:**   Don't choose an instrument in this group unless you like loud noises.

- Percussion
- Miscellaneous

Members of each group are described in the table that follows.

Note tag ———→ **NOTE:**   Miscellaneous is not really a grouping, but it's helpful to keep track of unusual instruments, such as harps, that aren't used in every piece.

Instruments

Group	Instruments
Woodwinds	Clarinet
	Oboe **NOTE:** The oboe uses a double reed; other woodwinds use a single reed.
Brass	Trumpet
	French horn
	Trombone
Strings	Violin
	Viola
	Cello
	Double bass

TableNote tag ———→ (points to the Oboe NOTE row)

Notes tag ———→ **NOTES:**   This table lists some instruments; it is not complete.

NoteCont tag ———→ Some instruments, like the piano, are most often used in an orchestra only when a soloist is playing.

NoteCont tag ———→ Some older instruments, such as the viola da gamba, are not listed here.

Figure 29-4.   *Multiple Note formats are required in unstructured FrameMaker.*

The context rules to make this work are as follows:

Element (Container): Note

    General rule: \<TEXT\>

    Exclusions: Footnote

    Text format rules

        1.   **If context is:** * < Table

                Use paragraph format: TableNote

        2.   **If context is:** {after Note}

                Use paragraph format: NoteCont

            Else, if context is: {before Note}

                Use paragraph format: Notes

        3.   **If context is:** BulletedList

                Use paragraph format: NoteIndent

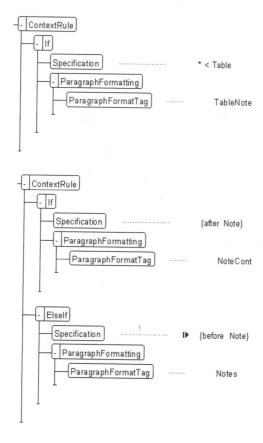

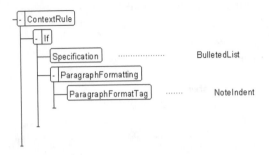

Setting and Using Context Labels

As part of a context rule, you can set a context label. Context labels are not shown in the element catalog, but they do appear in dialog boxes where there are lists of elements. This makes it possible to select only some elements based on the context labels. For example, when you create a table of contents, it's likely that you want to include just the first few levels of headings, not all of them. For this, a context label is handy because you can see the level of each heading at a glance:

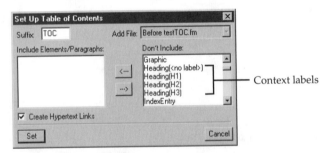

Context labels

The context label is set up inside the context rules:

Element (Container): Heading
    General rule: <TEXT>
    Text format rules
        1.   **Count ancestors named:**   Section
            If level is: 3
                Context label: H3
                Use paragraph format: Heading3

Else, if level is: 2
    Context label: H2
    Use paragraph format: Heading2
Else, if level is: 1
    Context label: H1
    Use paragraph format: Heading1

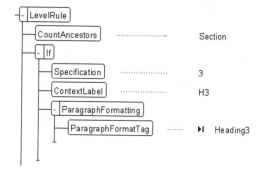

Testing the EDD

As you develop the EDD, the structure of the EDD itself helps you to ensure you insert all required information. The EDD must be valid for the EDD to function. Most of the errors that occur in EDD development, however, are not structure problems. Because you cannot see a graphical representation of the elements and their dependencies, it's common to define an element and then forget to name that element in a general rule. When you import the element definitions into a file, FrameMaker checks those relationships. If it finds any errors, the Element Catalog Manager Report is displayed:

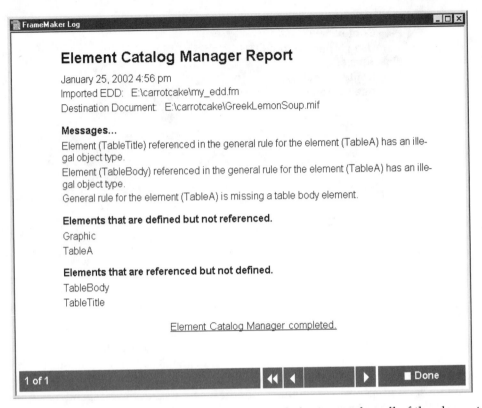

This report gives you additional information to help tie together all of the elements needed in the EDD.

Testing context rules can be particularly challenging. To help with this, you can display the context of an element in a test document. To display the element context, follow these steps:

1. Click in the element whose context you want to display.
2. Select File | Structure Tools | Show Element Context. The Show Element Context dialog box is displayed.

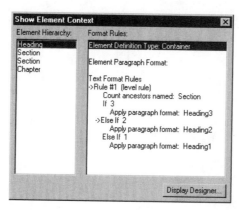

The Element Hierarchy section shows the selected element's ancestors, from parent to most distant ancestor. The Format Rules section on the right displays the formatting rules from the EDD. An arrow to the left of a rule indicates that rule is being used on the current element.

Chapter 30

Adding Structure to Unstructured Documents

ontent developed in unstructured FrameMaker can be converted over to structured FrameMaker. In theory, you could just open the unstructured file in structured FrameMaker, import the element definitions from your EDD, and then assign elements to content. However, wrapping each chunk of content individually would take a *very* long time. FrameMaker provides a way to automate most of this process, although you probably will need to do some manual touching up at the end of the process.

To add structure to an unstructured document, you use a conversion table, which lists how unstructured items, such as paragraph tags, character tags, and markers, are converted to elements. In general, you structure from the bottom of the hierarchy to the top; for example, you assign elements to character tags and paragraph tags, and then add the parent elements that group the paragraphs into sections.

Generating a Conversion Table

When you generate a conversion table for a document, FrameMaker makes a list of items that could be turned into elements.

To generate an initial conversion table, follow these steps:

1. Make sure that you are working in structured FrameMaker.

2. Open an unstructured file you need to convert.

3. Select File | Structure Tools | Generate Conversion Table. The Generate Conversion Table dialog box is displayed.

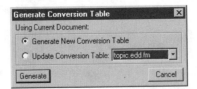

4. Click the Generate New Conversion Table radio button.

5. Click the Generate button.

FrameMaker creates a new, untitled document that contains the generated conversion table.

Understanding the Conversion Table

The conversion table is a regular FrameMaker table. It has three columns, as shown in the following example:

E:\FrameMaker 7 book\examples\initial_mapping.fm		
Wrap this object or objects	**In this element**	**With this qualifier**
P:heading 1	heading1	
P:What's in	What'sin	
P:Whatisbullet	Whatisbullet	
P:bodyfirst	bodyfirst	
P:tiny	tiny	
P:heading 2	heading2	
P:body	body	
P:note	note	
P:heading 3	heading3	
P:step 1	step1	
P:figure	figure	
P:step cont.	stepcont.	
P:warning	warning	
P:step 2	step2	

Flow: A ¶ CellBody   1 of 2   100%

STRUCTURED
FRAMEMAKER

FrameMaker creates a list of paragraph tags, character tags, and several other items in the left column. The list of items is generated from the information in the original document. The middle column specifies what element will be used for the specified object; FrameMaker supplies a default element name that matches the tag name on the left. The third column can contain a *qualifier*, which is a temporary identifier used when you process items into different elements.

The list of objects in the left column includes prefixes; P: indicates a paragraph tag, C: indicates a character tag, and so on.

Prefix	Object Type
C:	Character tag
E:	Element (needed when you create complex wrapping rules later)
F:	Footnote
G:	Graphic (anchored frame)
M:	Marker
P:	Paragraph tag
Q:	Equation
RG:	Rubi group (used in Japanese text only)

Prefix	Object Type
R:	Rubi text (used in Japanese text only)
SV:	System variable
T:	Table
TB:	Table body section (all body rows)
TC:	Table cell
TF:	Table footing section (all footing rows)
TH:	Table heading section (all table heading rows)
TI:	Text inset
TR:	Table row
TT:	Table title
UV:	User variable
X:	Cross-reference

We strongly recommend that you add a fourth column to the conversion table for comments. The extra column is ignored during processing but lets you insert explanations of the conversion rules.

E:\FrameMaker 7 book\examples\initial_mapping.fm

Wrap this object or objects	In this element	With this qualifier	Comments
P:heading 1	heading1		chapter title
P:What's in	What'sin		title for list of topics at the beginning of the chapter
P:Whatisbullet	Whatisbullet		
P:bodyfirst	bodyfirst		
P:tiny	tiny		
P:heading 2	heading2		
P:body	body		
P:note	note		
P:heading 3	heading3		
P:step 1	step1		
P:figure	figure		
P:step cont.	stepcont.		

Flow: A ¶ CellBody |1 of 2 *   100% |z|Z|⊕|⊡| ◄|

If you prefer to create your own conversion table, create a blank document and insert a table. Then, fill in the table as appropriate with the wrapping information. The conversion table must have a minimum of three columns; any additional columns are ignored during processing.

Creating Conversion Rules

For the most part, an unstructured document has a flat hierarchy. Paragraph tags have a sequence but do not have hierarchical relationships. In structured FrameMaker, an element hierarchy does exist. Adding the hierarchy information to the document is by far the most difficult part of conversion.

When you begin setting up a conversion table, we recommend that you start by mapping the lowest-level items: character tags, markers, anchored frames, and cross-references. These objects usually don't have child elements, so you don't need to worry about establishing the hierarchy.

After mapping these elements, you can set up basic mappings for your paragraph tags. Then, you can further wrap the elements you just created in parent elements. The following sections describe how to convert each type of object.

Converting Character Tags

When you begin setting up structure rules, it's best to work your way from bottom to top. Character tags are a good place to start. Locate the list of character tags, which have the C: prefix. In the following example, the emphasis 2 character tag applies italic formatting and is usually used to emphasize a word. The emphasis 1 character tag assigns boldface and is most commonly used for menu choices, button names, and other interface items that the reader must select. The EDD contains an Emphasis element for italics and a GUIItem element for boldface interface objects, so you map the character tags accordingly.

Wrap this object or objects	In this element	With this qualifier	Comments
C:emphasis 2	Emphasis		italics
C:emphasis 1	GUIItem		boldface

Converting Markers

Depending on your EDD, markers may or may not be structured. If they are, you need to map them. If not, you can delete them from the conversion table. The most common requirement is to map an index marker.

Wrap this object or objects	In this element	With this qualifier	Comments
M:Index	IndexEntry		

If you want cross-references to be structured, you need to create elements for any existing cross-references and cross-reference markers. An example is shown in "Converting Cross-References" on page 763. To create unstructured cross-references, delete the M:Cross-Ref mapping line and all of the cross-reference mappings (which start with X:).

Converting Footnotes

In the mapping table, FrameMaker identifies footnotes as being Table footnotes or Flow footnotes, so you can map the two types of footnotes to different footnote elements if needed. In the following example, both table footnotes and regular footnotes are assigned the Footnote element:

Wrap this object or objects	In this element	With this qualifier	Comments
F:Flow	Footnote		
F:Table	Footnote		

Converting Anchored Frames

FrameMaker provides a special graphic element type in EDDs. Only anchored frames can use this element type, and they cannot have any children. Because anchored frames do not have names or catalog types, they are listed simply as "G:" in the conversion table. The following rule wraps all anchored frames in the AnchoredFrame element:

Wrap this object or objects	In this element	With this qualifier	Comments
G:	AnchoredFrame		

Converting Cross-References

Cross-reference wrapping is based on the cross-reference format, so you can wrap cross-references in different elements based on their format. In the following example, the Heading cross-reference format is used exclusively for a list of topics at the beginning of the chapter, so it gets a special element name, MiniTOCXref. The other cross-references are all assigned to the generic CrossRef element.

Wrap this object or objects	In this element	With this qualifier	Comments
X:Heading	MiniTOCXref		Heading is only for the topic list at the beginning of each chapter.
X:Chapter x	CrossRef		
X:Figure #	CrossRef		
X:Figure x-x on page x-x	CrossRef		
X:Table Number \& Page	CrossRef		
X:Page	CrossRef		
X:Heading \& Page	CrossRef		
X:Table #	CrossRef		
X:Table x-x	CrossRef		
X:Chapter x\, "title\,"	CrossRef		
M:Cross-Ref	Cross-Ref		

Converting Tables

Tables have required components in unstructured FrameMaker, such as a table body section, which contains rows, which in turn contain cells. Those components are translated into table structure elements when you convert to structured FrameMaker. The default table structure uses elements such as BODY, CELL, and ROW. These elements correspond to items in the mapping table.

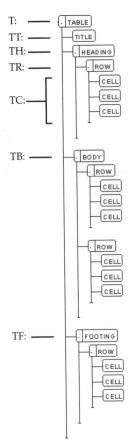

FrameMaker provides generic table structure elements, such as CELL and ROW, but you can define your own table elements, too. You must provide a mapping for each of the table "pieces," so a typical table mapping would look something like the following:

Wrap this object or objects	In this element	With this qualifier	Comments
T:basics	Table		You can wrap each table tag in a different element.
TT:	TableTitle		

Wrap this object or objects	In this element	With this qualifier	Comments
TH:	TableHeading		
TB:	TableBody		
TF:	TableFooting		
TR:	TableRow		
TC:	TableCell		

Converting Paragraph Tags

Most of the items in the conversion table will probably be paragraph tags. You need to wrap each one in the corresponding element. In many cases, several paragraphs might use the same element; in the following example, heading 1, heading 2, heading 3, and heading 4 all use the Title element.

Note

See page 767 for an explanation of qualifiers, used in the following table for P:bullet, P:heading 1, P:step 1, and P:step 2.

Wrap this object or objects	In this element	With this qualifier	Comments
P:body	Para		
P:bodyfirst	Intro		
P:bullet	ListItem	unordered	
P:display	CodeExample		
P:figure	Caption		
P:heading 1	Title	TopLevel	chapter title
P:heading 2	Title		
P:heading 3	Title		
P:heading 4	Title		
P:heading 4	Title		

Wrap this object or objects	In this element	With this qualifier	Comments
P:indent	Para		
P:note	Note		
P:note indent	Note		
P:step 1	ListItem	ordered	
P:step 2	ListItem	ordered	
P:step cont.	Para		
P:table body	Para		
P:table heading	Title		
P:warning	Warning		

Creating Hierarchy with Parent Elements

Once you have wrapped the paragraph tags in elements, you need to add in the parent elements that do not have a paragraph equivalent. For example, your structured ListItem elements probably have a parent element—either UnorderedList or OrderedList. There's not a paragraph available from which you can create UnorderedList or OrderedList, so instead, you create another wrapping rule.

Wrap this object or objects	In this element	With this qualifier	Comments
E:ListItem+	UnorderedList		

The result would be that all collections of ListItem elements would be wrapped into a parent UnorderedList item. There are two problems with this scenario:

- FrameMaker will wrap all lists in UnorderedList, but some of them should be wrapped in OrderedList instead.
- Some lists might have additional elements, such as graphics, cross-references, and markers, in the list. The description previously provided doesn't allow any other items in the list, so many lists would be missed. Instead, your definition would probably need to be more complicated:

```
ListItem, (ListItem |Para|Graphic|Note|CodeExample|Warning)+
```

This definition, however, still does not allow you to distinguish between list items for unordered lists and list items for ordered lists. For that, you need qualifiers, which are discussed in the following section.

> *The definitions you create for wrapping use the same syntax as general rules in the EDD. In fact, the definitions are quite often identical to the element's general rule, so try cribbing general rules for use in writing definitions. See Chapter 29, "Understanding the Element Definition Document," for details.*

Creating Temporary Qualifiers

To address the problem of separating the ListItem elements intended for ordered lists from the ListItem elements intended for unordered lists, you can use a qualifier when you first create the ListItem element. The qualifier lets you provide a temporary label to identify items. For instance, when you wrap a bullet paragraph tag, you know that it should become part of an unordered list, and a step paragraph tag should become part of an ordered list. You can wrap accordingly with a qualifier, then use the qualifier to specify which lists get which parent. Here is the revised conversion table:

Wrap this object or objects	In this element	With this qualifier	Comments
P:step 1	ListItem	ordered	
P:step 2	ListItem	ordered	
P:bullet	ListItem	unordered	
E:ListItem[ordered]+	OrderedList		
E:ListItem[unordered]+	UnorderedList		

The qualifier does not appear anywhere in the new, structured file; it is only used temporarily to identify different types of elements.

The conversion table is read in order, so it's important to put the lower-level wrapping (the step and bullet tags) before the higher-level wrapping (the ListItem rules).

Notice that the ListItem wrapping rules use the E: prefix (for element). If you do not supply a prefix, E: is assumed.

> *In general, it's a good idea to use prefixes for labeling, even though they are not required for elements. If, however, you have two objects with identical names, you must use prefixes to differentiate them. For example, if you have an element called Para and a paragraph tag called Para, you must identify the objects explicitly with E:Para or P:Para.*

Identifying Formatting Overrides

While structuring the document, you can identify paragraph and character overrides. You can also identify character formatting that was applied without using a character tag. To do so, you add special "override-hunting" commands, shown in the following table:

Wrap this object or objects	In this element	With this qualifier	Comments
flag paragraph format overrides			
flag character format overrides			
untagged character formatting	FixOverride		

The two "flag" commands search paragraphs and characters, respectively, for overrides. Where overrides occur, FrameMaker adds an Override attribute with a value of "yes" to the element being created, as shown in the following example:

The "untagged character formatting" command assigns an element to untagged formatting. You can search for that element and remove or change it as necessary. In the example conversion table, overrides are to be wrapped in the FixOverride element. For example, you might start out with the following text:

- Thread (stitchers call it *floss*) in the various colors needed for the project

If the word "floss" was italicized using the button on the Formatting Bar (or by selecting Format | Style | Italic), the result after running the conversion table would be as follows:

You would need to change the FixOverride element to correct the structure:

Correcting one or two of these overrides is no big deal, but the process of several per page over hundreds or thousands of pages would quickly lose its charm. Once again, untagged formatting and formatting overrides cause problems—better to prevent them by convincing authors to follow the templates and tag consistently.

Promoting Elements

By default, items that occur inside paragraphs are listed as children of that paragraph. For example, a paragraph that contains markers will result in a structure where the marker is a child of the container paragraph element.

This works well for some element types—markers, cross-references, footnotes, and character tags. In the case of other element types, especially tables and graphics, you may want to create sibling elements, not child elements. To accomplish this, you can move up elements one level as they are wrapped. Insert "(promote)" after the element you want to move up.

Wrap this object or objects	In this element	With this qualifier	Comments
T:basics	Table(promote)		
G:	AnchoredFrame (promote)		

Without the promotion command, the result for an anchored frame would look something like this:

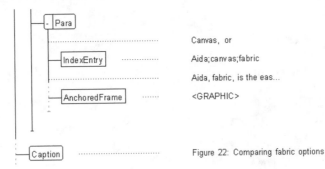

Notice that the AnchoredFrame element is a child of Para, which leads to invalid structure. Also, the Caption element, which belongs with the graphic, is one level above and not connected to the graphic. The structure you want looks like this:

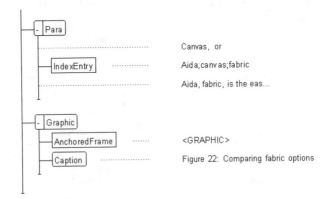

The mappings you need to accomplish this are as follows:

Wrap this object or objects	In this element	With this qualifier	Comments
P:figure	Caption		
G:	AnchoredFrame (promote)		
E:AnchoredFrame, E:Caption	Graphic		

Assigning Attribute Values

As you are wrapping elements, you can assign attribute values. To do so, include the name of the attribute and the value after the element name, as shown in the following example:

Wrap this object or objects	In this element	With this qualifier	Comments
P:heading 1	ChapterTitle [Platform="All"]		

Applying a Structure Rules Table to One Document

As you develop the conversion table, you'll probably want to run a test conversion to ensure that the rules you are writing are working as expected. The initial wrapping is usually relatively trouble-free; it's getting the hierarchy in order that causes problems. You probably will not be able to develop a conversion table that performs an error-free, perfect conversion, but a 95–99 percent accuracy rate is feasible. You can then identify the last few troublesome items and clean those up manually.

Here's how to apply a structure rules table:

1. In structured FrameMaker, open the document with your conversion table.
2. Open the unstructured document.
3. From the unstructured document, select File | Utilities | Structure Current Document. The Structure Current Document dialog box is displayed.

4. In the Conversion Table Document drop-down list, select the file that contains the conversion table. Notice that only open documents are available in the list.
5. Click the Add Structure button.

FrameMaker now applies the conversion table to your document. If there are any syntax errors in the conversion table, an error message dialog box is displayed.

Batch Processing Documents

If you need to convert a large number of documents, you can process them as a group. To do so, you need to put all of the documents that need conversion in a single folder or directory on your system. Then, you run the conversion table against every document in that folder.

To convert a group of documents, follow these steps:

1. Make sure that the conversion table document is open in structured FrameMaker.

2. Select File | Utilities | Structure Documents. The Structure Documents dialog box is displayed.

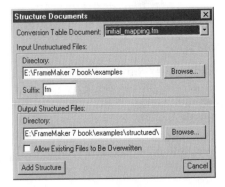

3. In the Conversion Table Document drop-down list, select the file that contains your conversion table.

4. In the Input Unstructured Files section, specify the directory in which the unstructured files reside and a suffix for those files. In the preceding example, FrameMaker will process all files ending with .fm in the specified directory.

5. In the Output Structured Files section, specify the directory in which you want FrameMaker to create the new, structured files.

Do not use the same directory as the input directory. This overwrites your unstructured files.

If you already have earlier versions of the structured files in the output directory, check the Allow Existing Files to Be Overwritten check box so that FrameMaker can create new files for you.

6. Click the Add Structure button to process the files in the specified directory.

Some Closing Notes on Naming Conventions

When you develop a conversion table, it's likely that you're working with existing information and thus have little or no control over how the tags were named in the original document. However, here are some points to keep in mind that will make conversion a little easier:

- **Avoid duplicate names.** Try to avoid creating element, paragraph, and character tag names that are identical. They are more difficult to keep track of in the conversion table. We use lowercase for all tag names and an initial capital letter for element names. You might also consider tag prefixes, such as pCode and cCode to differentiate between paragraph and character tags.

- **Avoid special characters.** Special characters, such as quotes, ampersands, and the like, must be escaped out in the conversion table. The following characters must be escaped out with a backslash if they occur as part of the tag name:

  ```
  ( ) & | , * + ? % [ ] : \
  ```

  Several of these characters are used for commands.

  Apostrophes and quotes also present a problem because you must match the straight quote to a straight quote and the curly quote to a curly quote.

Note

When you generate a conversion table from an existing document, FrameMaker automatically escapes out the special characters for you. However, if you add additional rules to the table, you must remember to escape the characters as necessary.

STRUCTURED FRAMEMAKER

Chapter 31

Importing and Exporting XML/SGML Markup Files

S tructured FrameMaker can read and create XML and SGML (markup) files. You set up an authoring environment in which you can open a markup file, save it as a FrameMaker file, make changes, and save the file back to markup. You could then modify the markup file and later reimport the updated file into FrameMaker. This workflow, in which you transfer information back and forth and make changes in either environment, is known as *round-tripping*.

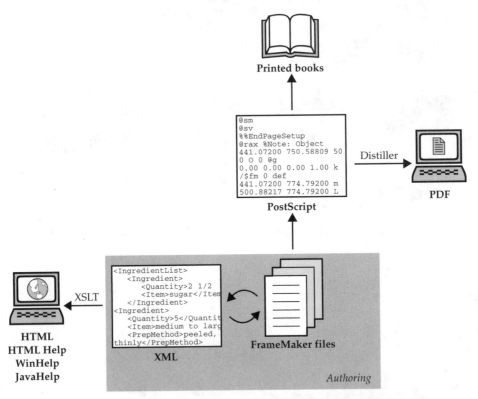

Like template design and EDD creation, setting up the environment that allows you to import and export markup files is usually done by one FrameMaker expert. Once the environment is set up, importing and exporting is done via the Open and Save As commands. This chapter describes the basics of setting up an import/export or round-tripping environment. Adobe provides hundreds of additional pages in documentation in the *Structured FrameMaker Developer's Guide,* found in the OnlineManuals folder in your FrameMaker installation directory. If you are not responsible for setting up the environment, you may want to skim this chapter to get an idea of what's involved. You will, however, need to peruse the information about setting applications and opening and closing files.

How Import and Export Work

In some environments, you may only need one-way conversion. For example, you might be required to deliver XML documents in addition to the print and PDF you create from FrameMaker, but those XML documents are not modified, and you don't have to worry about reimporting them back into FrameMaker later. One-way conversion is much easier to implement than round-tripping because you can throw away information. If, for example, you don't need index markers in XML, you could simply skip them during conversion.

When information needs to make a round-trip from XML to FrameMaker and back (or vice versa), you cannot discard any information—you'll need it to complete the round-trip process.

To allow for importing, exporting, or round-tripping of markup files, you need to set up a structured application (shown in the following illustration). An *application* describes how the structured FrameMaker files relate to the XML/SGML markup files. A structured application, however, is not a software program; it's just a collection of files that define how the XML/SGML translates to and from FrameMaker.

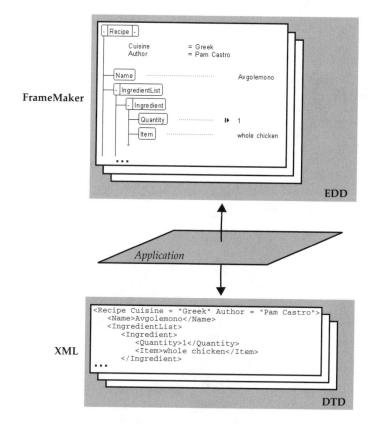

On the FrameMaker side, a structured document has elements. Their relationships are defined by the element definition document (EDD). On the XML/SGML side, a document has elements. Their relationships are defined by the document type definition (DTD). When converting files from one format to another, FrameMaker uses a built-in parser to interpret the files. The application lets you control how the parser works.

Adobe recommends that you build your structured application and customize as much as possible. If you reach a dead end and require further customization that the structured application cannot supply, you can implement more complex customizations using the FrameMaker Developer's Kit (FDK). Programming in the FDK is not exactly a trivial matter; it requires writing C code. The FDK is free and available from Adobe. The programming talent is usually not free.

The application settings are stored in a structured FrameMaker file, structapps.fm. By default, this file resides in the FrameMaker installation directory at this location:

```
structure/structapps.fm
```

On the UNIX platform, the file can reside in one of three locations (which are searched in the order shown):

```
startdir/fminit/language/structured
userhome/fminit/language/structured
fmhome/fminit/language/structured
```

where the directories are as follows:

- *startdir* is the directory from which the user launched FrameMaker.
- *userhome* is the user's home directory.
- *fmhome* is the FrameMaker installation directory.
- *language* is the user interface language; for example, usenglish.

The applications listed in structapps.fm are available as application choices. For example, when the user selects File | Set Structured Application, the list of applications is shown in a drop-down list. Figure 31-1 shows the default applications; any application you add would also be displayed.

Figure 31-1. *Setting the structure application lets you specify how files are converted.*

Once the application definition is set up, the process of converting files is transparent to users. They open XML/SGML files in FrameMaker to display them as structured files, and they can save FrameMaker files out to XML or SGML.

Understanding the Application File

To set up importing, exporting, or round-tripping, you need to define an application for your structured files. Among other things, the application specifies the location of the following items:

- **EDD.** Describes structure and associated formatting of the elements in a FrameMaker file.
- **DTD.** Describes structure of the elements in a markup file.
- **Read/write rules.** Describes how elements are translated during conversion between FrameMaker elements and markup elements.

FrameMaker provides several default applications, and if you are new to working with structured documents, you may want to start by experimenting with those files. The *XML Cookbook* is also somewhat helpful. The tutorial is installed with FrameMaker; its location depends on your operating system:

- Windows and Mac: In the FrameMaker installation directory in the XMLCookbook folder
- UNIX: *fmhome*/fminit/*language*/XMLCookbook

Setting up a structure application requires knowledge of FrameMaker, structured authoring, and EDDs, in addition to an understanding of markup languages, DTDs, entities, and many other XML and SGML concepts. If you are not familiar with these concepts, you will need some additional reference materials.

Most XML books and classes are geared toward using XML for data exchange (for example, creating invoice information and delivering it electronically). Look for references that focus on structuring content rather than data processing. SGML references tend to be more content-oriented.

To display the structapps.fm application definition file, select File | Structure Tools | Edit Application Definitions. The following excerpt shows the XHTML application definition:

```
Application name:                    XHTML
     DOCTYPE:          html
     File Extension Override:htm
     DTD:              $STRUCTDIR\xml\xhtml\app\dtd
     Template:         $STRUCTDIR\xml\xhtml\app\template
```

Read/write rules: $STRUCTDIR\xml\xhtml\app\rules
CSS2 Preferences:
Generate CSS2: Disable
Add Fm CSS Attribute To XML: Disable
Retain Stylesheet Information: Disable
XML Stylesheet
Type: css
URI: /$STRUCTDIR/xml/xhtml/app/xhtml.css
Use API client: Xhtml
Namespace: Enable
XML character encoding: UTF-8
Entity locations
Public ID: -//W3C//ENTITIES Latin 1 for XHTML//EN
Filename: $STRUCTDIR\xml\xhtml\app\xhtml-lat1.ent
Public ID: -//W3C//ENTITIES Special for XHTML//EN
Filename: $STRUCTDIR\xml\xhtml\app\xhtml-special.ent
Public ID: -//W3C//ENTITIES Symbols for XHTML//EN
Filename: $STRUCTDIR\xml\xhtml\app\xhtml-symbol.ent
Public ID: -//W3C//DTD XHTML 1.0 Transitional//EN
Filename: $STRUCTDIR\xml\xhtml\app\dtd

The structapps.fm file shipped with FrameMaker includes a defaults section. The information specified in that section is used for all application definitions in this file, unless an application definition specifies a different value, in which case that value overrides the default. The default information is as follows:

Default API client: FmTranslator
SGML character encoding: ISO Latin1
XML character encoding: UTF-8
Namespace: Enable
CSS2 Preferences:
Generate CSS2: Disable
Add Fm CSS Attribute To XML: Disable
Retain Stylesheet Information: Disable
Entity locations
Entity search paths
   1. $HOME

Setting Up a New Structured Application

Setting up a structured application requires you to create an application definition in the application file. You must provide a FrameMaker template for formatting and structure (that is, a formatting template with the EDD imported into it), a DTD for markup structure, and read/write rules that link the two files together. The application definition also provides several configuration settings.

Creating a New Application Definition

To begin setting up a new structured application, you need to add the application definition to the structapps.fm file.

To add the application, follow these steps:

1. Select File | Structure Tools | Edit Application Definitions to open the application definition file. The file itself is structured, as shown in the following excerpt:

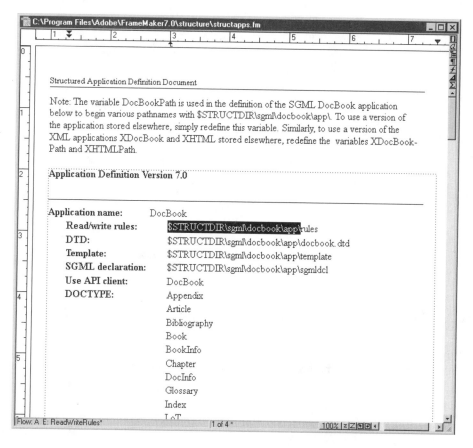

Structured Application Definition Document

Note: The variable DocBookPath is used in the definition of the SGML DocBook application below to begin various pathnames with $STRUCTDIR\sgml\docbook\app\. To use a version of the application stored elsewhere, simply redefine this variable. Similarly, to use a version of the XML applications XDocBook and XHTML stored elsewhere, redefine the variables XDocBook-Path and XHTMLPath.

Application Definition Version 7.0

Application name: DocBook
   Read/write rules: $STRUCTDIR\sgml\docbook\app\rules
   DTD: $STRUCTDIR\sgml\docbook\app\docbook.dtd
   Template: $STRUCTDIR\sgml\docbook\app\template
   SGML declaration: $STRUCTDIR\sgml\docbook\app\sgmldcl
   Use API client: DocBook
   DOCTYPE: Appendix
                        Article
                        Bibliography
                        Book
                        BookInfo
                        Chapter
                        DocInfo
                        Glossary
                        Index
                        LoT

Flow: A E: ReadWriteRules*   1 of 4 *   100%

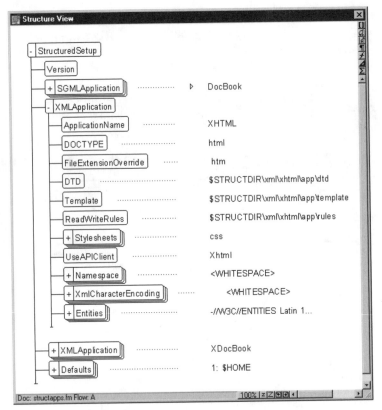

2. Add an XMLApplication or SGMLApplication element as a sibling of the existing application elements, then insert the needed elements to specify where the files that go with this application belong. (You could also copy an existing application and modify the elements as needed.) For details on the elements, refer to the following sections.

3. When you are finished, save the structapps.fm file.

4. To make the new application available immediately, make sure structapps.fm is the current file, then select File | Structure Tools | Read Application Definitions. You can also close and reopen FrameMaker to force FrameMaker to scan the file for application definitions. Each of the applications that's defined is now available in the application list.

Specifying Application Settings

For each application you define, you must provide a number of settings. Except for the application name, which occurs at the top of the definition, the elements can be inserted in any order. They are as follows:

- **Application name.** The application name is a label for the application; for example GeneralTechDoc. The name you specify here appears in the Set Structured Application and Use Structured Application dialog boxes when you are prompted to choose an application.

- **DOCTYPE.** Specifies the document type that appears at the top of a markup file. When you import a markup file, FrameMaker checks the DOCTYPE specified there against the list in the application definitions and uses the application that provides the specified DOCTYPE. (If a particular DOCTYPE is listed in more than one application, you will be prompted to choose an application.)

- **File Extension Override.** By default, all SGML applications use the .sgm extension; all XML files use .xml. If you want your application to use a different extension, specify it here. For example, if you're using an application to export XHTML, you might want to use the .html or .htm extension.

- **DTD.** Specifies the location of the DTD file. You must have a matching EDD and DTD to create a working application.

- **Template.** Specifies the location of the empty FrameMaker template file, which contains all formatting information and the structure information. You must import the EDD into the formatting template and use the resulting file as the template here. We strongly recommend that you keep a separate EDD for maintenance purposes.

Caution

The template file cannot contain any information; it must be a blank file.

- **Read/write rules.** The location of the read/write rules file. The read/write rules control how elements are translated from markup to FrameMaker and back.

- **CSS2 Preferences.** Specifies whether a cascading style sheet (CSS) file is generated and how. You can generate a CSS file for formatting information based on the information provided in the EDD. Most often, you would probably disable this feature because you already have a CSS file available for formatting. Some of the context-dependent formatting that EDDs support cannot be duplicated in a CSS file. As a work-around, FrameMaker provides the fmcssattr attribute. Where necessary, this attribute is inserted into the XML output to provide a way to deliver the formatting information whose context rules don't work in CSS. If you use fmcssattr, keep in mind that your DTD must allow for it in XML. Also, if you import the files back into FrameMaker, you must either allow these attributes or drop them using a read/write rule.

- **Use API client.** If you have written a special application programming interface (API) client to customize output, specify it in this element. The XHTML application, for example, refers to the XHTML client. If you need to create an API client, refer to the programmer documentation set.

- **Namespace.** Enabled or disabled. If enabled, namespaces are supported in the FrameMaker authoring environment. See page 790 for an explanation of namespaces.
- **XML character encoding.** Specifies the encoding used by the XML files. Normally, this is UTF-8.
- **Entity locations.** Specifies where entity files are stored.

Creating EDDs and DTDs

The FrameMaker EDD and XML/SGML DTD have the same purpose: to define permitted structure in a document. To transfer information back and forth, you need a matching EDD and DTD. Specifically, the two documents need to describe the same elements and the same relationships among those elements.

If you plan to author using the EDD and then export to XML, you could create an EDD that's stricter than the DTD. When you export, the more permissive DTD would certainly allow any structure you could create in the stricter EDD. Of course, the reverse would also work—authoring in a strict DTD and then importing content into FrameMaker where you have a looser EDD. However, you cannot author in the permissive structure document and expect the structure to be valid in the stricter environment.

FrameMaker provides tools to help you create an EDD from a DTD and vice versa. We recommend that you finalize one before creating the other.

Creating a DTD from an EDD

The process of creating EDDs is discussed in Chapter 29. To create a DTD from an existing EDD, follow these steps:

1. Open the EDD.
2. Select File | Structure Tools | Save As DTD. The Save dialog box is displayed.
3. Specify a name and location for the DTD file.
4. Click the Save button.
5. If the Set Structure Application dialog box is displayed, choose <No Application> to use the default parser settings. The Select Type dialog box is displayed.

6. Specify whether you want to create an SGML or XML DTD.

7. Click the OK button. As the DTD is created, any errors are displayed in an error log.

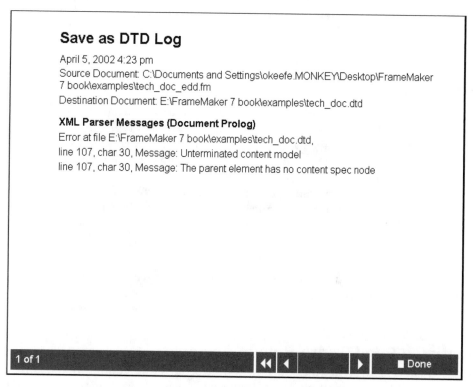

Save as DTD Log

April 5, 2002 4:23 pm
Source Document: C:\Documents and Settings\okeefe.MONKEY\Desktop\FrameMaker
7 book\examples\tech_doc_edd.fm
Destination Document: E:\FrameMaker 7 book\examples\tech_doc.dtd

XML Parser Messages (Document Prolog)
Error at file E:\FrameMaker 7 book\examples\tech_doc.dtd,
line 107, char 30, Message: Unterminated content model
line 107, char 30, Message: The parent element has no content spec node

1 of 1   ◀◀ ◀   ▶   ■ Done

8. Once the DTD has been created, you will need to open the DTD in an external editor, correct any errors, and customize it as necessary.

Creating an EDD from a DTD

If you have an existing DTD, you can use it to create the initial EDD. Because a DTD does not provide any formatting information, the resulting EDD will lack any formatting specifications. You will need to add those to the generated EDD.

To create an EDD from a DTD, follow these steps:

1. Select File | Structure Tools | Open DTD. The Open DTD dialog box is displayed.

2. Locate the DTD you want to use, select it, and then click the Open button.

3. If the Use Structure Application dialog box is displayed, select <No Application>, then click the Set button. The Select Type dialog box is displayed.

4. Specify whether you want to create an EDD for SGML or XML. FrameMaker processes the DTD and displays the new EDD. This can take some time.

The structure rules transferred from the DTD do not use inclusions or exclusions; instead, each available element is explicitly defined in the general rules. You may want to modify the EDD by setting up inclusions and exclusions to make the EDD easier to read and maintain.

Creating Read/Write Rules

The read/write rules file controls how elements are converted from FrameMaker to markup and back. In structured FrameMaker, special element types are available; in addition to container, you have graphic elements, marker elements, and so on. However, XML and SGML make no distinction regarding element types. You need to create read/write rules that process these element types correctly.

Another common use for read/write rules is to connect two elements with different names. For example, you can write a rule that links the XML element named "li" with the FrameMaker element ListItem:

```
element "li" is fm element "ListItem";
```

Keep in mind that read/write rules are not needed for every mapping. If the FrameMaker element name and the markup element names match, you probably do not need a read/write rule unless you need to specify a special element type.

Creating a Read/Write Rules Document

You can create a read/write rules document from scratch by creating a new, blank FrameMaker file. Another alternative is to select File | Structure Tools | New Read/Write Rules. This creates a new, untitled document with the following content:

```
fm version is "7.0";

/*
 * Include all ISO entity mapping rules.
 */

#include "isoall.rw"
```

Each read/write command is inserted after this header information.

Syntax

The read/write rules govern both markup-to-FrameMaker and FrameMaker-to-markup conversion. In its simplest form, a rule has the following syntax:

```
element "a" is fm element "b"
```

Based on this rule, the following information from XML/SGML

```
<a>This is a test.</a>
```

would be converted to the following FrameMaker structure:

To ensure that cross-references are translated correctly, you need to specify their element type during conversion:

```
element "link" is fm cross-reference element "Cross-Ref";
```

A similar syntax is required for markers and footnotes:

```
element "FNote" is fm footnote element "FNote";
element "IndexItem" is fm marker element "IndexEntry";
```

You can delete an element during translation, either on import or export. Use one of the following commands:

```
element "x" drop;
fm element "y" drop;
```

The online manual *Structured FrameMaker Developer's Guide* contains more than 100 pages of reference information listing all of the read/write rule commands. We strongly recommend that you consult this reference for detailed examples, syntax, and an alphabetical list of available commands.

Setting the Structured Application

Before you can import and export information using the application you have set up, you need to set the application. To do so, follow these steps:

1. Select File | Set Structured Application. The Set Structured Application dialog box is displayed (Figure 31-1 on page 778).
2. In the Set Structured Application drop-down list, select an application.
3. Click the Set button.

The selected application is now used for importing and exporting markup files. The application you select is used until you specify another, even after closing and reopening FrameMaker.

If you have not set an application, FrameMaker prompts you to specify one when you import or export files, or perform other actions that normally use an application.

Caution   *You can specify an application in an EDD.*

STRUCTURED
FRAMEMAKER

Exporting to XML/SGML Markup Files

You can export a single file or batch-process an entire directory. The following sections explain each process.

Exporting the Current File

To export the file you are working on to XML/SGML, follow these steps:

1. Select File | Save As. The Save Document dialog box is displayed.
2. In the Save As Type drop-down list, click either XML or SGML.
3. In the File Name field, specify a name for the exported file.
4. Click the Save button.
5. If you have not yet set a structured application, the Set Structured Application dialog box is displayed (Figure 31-1 on page 778). In the Set Structured Application drop-down list, choose your structured application, then click the Set button to save the file.

Exporting a Batch of Files

Instead of exporting files one by one, you can export all the FrameMaker files in a particular directory. To do so, follow these steps:

1. Select File | Utilities | Convert Documents to Structured Format. The Convert Documents to Structured Format dialog box is displayed.

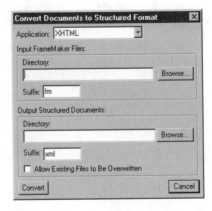

2. In the Application drop-down list, select the structure application you want to use for conversion.

3. In the Input FrameMaker Files section, specify the directory in which the FrameMaker files are located, then specify their file name suffix.

4. In the Output Structured Documents section, specify the directory to which you want to write the new XML/SGML files, then specify their suffix.

5. If you already have files in the output directory and want to replace them, check the Allow Existing Files to Be Overwritten check box.

6. Click the Convert button.

The files in the selected directory are converted, and the output is written to the specified output directory.

Opening XML/SGML Markup Files

Once the structure application is established, you can open XML/SGML files in FrameMaker. The files are translated from XML/SGML into structured FrameMaker, and you can edit them just like any other file. You can open a single file or batch-process a directory of files.

Opening a Single XML/SGML File

You can open an XML file using the usual File | Open command.
To open an XML/SGML file, follow these steps:

1. Select File | Open. The Open dialog box is displayed.

2. Select the XML or SGML file, then click the Open button.

3. If you have not yet set a structured application, the Set Structured Application dialog box is displayed (Figure 31-1 on page 778). In the Set Structured Application drop-down list, choose your structured application, then click the Set button to save the file.

4. Click the Set button to open the file.

The file is displayed as a structured FrameMaker file.

Converting a Directory of XML/SGML Files to FrameMaker Format

Instead of opening files one by one, you can convert the contents of a directory all at once. To do so, follow these steps:

1. Select File | Utilities | Convert Structured Documents. The Convert Structured Documents dialog box is displayed.

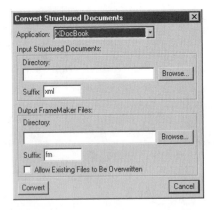

2. In the Application drop-down list, select the structure application you want to use for conversion.

3. In the Input Structured Documents section, specify the directory in which the structured files are located, then specify their file name suffix.

4. In the Output FrameMaker Files section, specify the directory to which you want to write the new FrameMaker files, then specify their file name suffix.

5. If you already have files in the output directory and want to replace them, check the Allow Existing Files to Be Overwritten check box.

6. Click the Convert button.

Using Namespaces

Namespace is an XML concept. A *namespace* provides a way of labeling elements. For example, consider the temperature element. In a medical document, temperature might refer to a patient's vital sign. In a meteorological context, temperature might refer to climate. In a cooking application, temperature would be the correct setting for the oven. To distinguish among each of these elements, you could use a namespace, which uses a prefix in front of the element name:

```
<medical:temperature>
<weather:temperature>
<cookbook:temperature>
```

For more information about namespaces, consult the World Wide Web Consortium:

```
www.w3.org/TR/REC-xml-names/
```

If an XML structure application allows for namespaces, then you can manage namespaces inside FrameMaker. Inside FrameMaker, namespaces are treated somewhat like attributes. You can view and edit the namespace setting, but the namespace does not affect the information displayed in FrameMaker.

If an element has a namespace defined, the element is displayed with an asterisk to the right of the name in the structure view.

To view the namespace settings, select Element | Namespaces. The Namespaces dialog box is displayed.

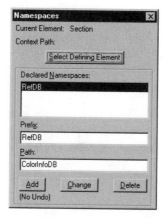

To remove a namespace, click the Delete button. The namespace is removed immediately. Note that you cannot undo this action.

To change a namespace, modify the Prefix and Path fields, and click the Change button.

To add a namespace, modify the Prefix and Path fields, and click the Add button.

The
Complete
Reference

Part VIII

Appendixes

Appendix A

Resources

his appendix lists FrameMaker-related resources, including add-on software, web sites, and mailing lists. Please keep in mind that web sites do change; we have verified all of these sites at the time of printing, but web site addresses become obsolete very quickly.

FrameMaker-Related Web Sites

www.adobe.com   Adobe Systems makes FrameMaker software. The web site contains product information, support information, printer drivers, and more.

www.frameusers.com   An unofficial FrameMaker resource site. It contains information about FrameMaker service providers, add-on software, and more.

www.frame-user.de   Another unofficial FrameMaker resource site. If you speak German, this is the site for you. Even if you don't speak any German, check it out. The web site creator designed the site to look like a FrameMaker document; it's quite a unique look for a web site!

www.scriptorium.com   Scriptorium Publishing offers FrameMaker and WebWorks Publisher template design, training, and consulting. The web site contains useful white papers and a collection of links to other FrameMaker resources.

Other Helpful Web Sites

www.fxtrans.com/resources   Resources and links from Foreign Exchange Translations, Inc.

www.rpbourret.com/xml/NamespacesFAQ.htm   XML Namespaces FAQ.

www.stg.brown.edu/service/xmlvalid   The Scholarly Technology Group's XML Validation Form lets you validate your XML by uploading the file or typing the URL.

www.w3.org/International   The World Wide Web Consortium (W3C) internationalization web site.

www.w3.org/MarkUp/SGML   This site lists several SGML resources, including web sites and mailing lists.

www.w3.org/TR/REC-xml   The W3C Recommendation on XML 1.0.

www.w3.org/TR/REC-xml-names   The W3C Recommendation on namespaces.

xml.coverpages.org/xml.html   Offers an extensive XML reference that lists publications, software, events, support, and more.

http://www.adobe.com/type/opentype/main.html   Provides an excellent introduction to OpenType fonts along with a complete list of Adobe OpenType fonts.

Mailing Lists

framers@frameusers.com A mailing list for FrameMaker users. The framers list has been around for at least seven years; its membership includes both new FrameMaker users and experts, some of whom have subscribed to the list for many years. List traffic is heavy but generally fairly well-focused on issues related to FrameMaker. To subscribe, send email to:

```
majordomo@frameusers.com
```

In the body of the message, type:

```
subscribe framers
```

framers@omsys.com Similar to the framers list based at frameusers.com. Many topics are posted to both lists. The framers@omsys.com list tends to be more focused on power user issues than the other list. The framers@omsys.com list also has less traffic than framers@frameusers.com. To subscribe, send email to:

```
majordomo@omsys.com
```

In the body of the message, type:

```
subscribe framers
```

HATT (groups.yahoo.com/group/hatt) A high-volume list for help authoring tools and technology.

techwr-l (www.raycomm.com/techwhirl/index.php3) A high-volume list for technical writers.

XML-L (listserv.heanet.ie/lists/xml-l.html) A general discussion of XML.

xml-doc (groups.yahoo.com/group/xml-doc) A mailing list for technical authors interested in XML.

wwp-users (groups.yahoo.com/group/wwp-users) A mailing list for WebWorks Publisher users. Discussions are usually highly focused on WebWorks Publisher–specific topics.

APPENDIXES

Plug-Ins, Add-On Software, and Third-Party Tools

FrameMaker offers lots of features, but every now and then you run across something you really wish it had. In many cases, a third-party plug-in or add-on software is available to accomplish what you want. This section lists some of the more popular software that extends FrameMaker's features.

AutoText (www.frameexpert.com/plugins/brucefoster.html)   Lets you associate keystrokes with text or graphics; very similar to Word's AutoText feature.

CrossFont (www.asy.com)   Converts both TrueType and PostScript Type1 fonts between the PC and Macintosh platforms.

CudSpan Tools (www.telecable.es/personales/cud)   Generates a list of paragraph overrides, lets you delete unused paragraph tags, runs batch processes on documents or book files, provides bookwide searches, remembers page and line breaks in generated files, and associates icons with paragraphs.

Enhance (www.sandybrook.com)   Provides outlining similar to Microsoft Word inside FrameMaker. You can collapse the content of a file so that it shows just the heading paragraphs, and then you can expand just the section you want to edit.

Filtrix (www.blueberry.com)   Converts files from one format to another; has bidirectional MIF filtering capability.

FrameScript (www.framescript.com)   Lets you automate tasks inside FrameMaker. Writing in FrameScript can be daunting, but many scripts are available for download.

Ghostscript (www.ghostscript.com)   Interprets the PostScript printer language, so you can display a PostScript file without printing it. It's helpful for printing a PostScript file to a non-PostScript printer.

ImpGraph (www.frameexpert.com/plugins/brucefoster.html)   Using the ImpGraph plug-in, you can specify the default settings for the anchored frames around inserted figures.

Index Tools Professional (www.siliconprairiesoftware.com)   Lets you embed index markers and format entries outside the FrameMaker Marker window, add continuation lines, and generate a master index for a set of books.

IXgen (home.pacifier.com/~franks/ixmid.html)   Places all of the index markers across a book file's documents in one list, where you can edit them. An indispensable add-on that makes indexing much faster and more efficient.

MIFBrowse (www.wideman-one.com/gw/tech/framemaker/mifbrowse.htm)
A MIF file editor; especially useful when troubleshooting a file.

MIF2GO (www.omsys.com) Provides industrial-strength conversion for creating HTML and online help from FrameMaker files.

Miramo (www.miramo.com) Lets you bring database content into FrameMaker.

PatternStream (www.fml.com) Lets you bring database content into FrameMaker.

Tagged PDF (www.adobe.com/products/acrobat/adobepdf.html) Acrobat 5.0 lets you implement logical structures in PDF files.

TableCleaner (www.frameexpert.com) TableCleaner removes overrides to formatting in tables imported from Word documents.

Toolbox (www.systec-gmbh.com/tdsolution/en/index.html) Provides a range of useful utilities, such as removing all unused formats in a file and generating lists of formats and their properties.

WebWorks Publisher (www.webworks.com) Provides industrial-strength conversion for creating HTML and online help from FrameMaker files. A stripped-down version of the Professional Edition, WebWorks Publisher Standard Edition, is bundled with FrameMaker 7.

Online Manuals

FrameMaker comes with several helpful manuals in PDF format, which are in the OnlineManuals folder in the FrameMaker 7 installation directory. The online manuals include the *Structured FrameMaker Developer's Guide, FrameMaker Character Sets,* and the *MIF Reference Online Manual.*

APPENDIXES

Appendix B

Managing Fonts Across Platforms

F onts can cause problems when FrameMaker documents are opened on different platforms—unless you anticipate and plan for common issues. Some font names vary among platforms. For example, Optima Medium in Windows is called Optima on other platforms, and the Medium weight is a separate property. This can cause font substitutions when you open a FrameMaker document you created in Windows on other platforms. To prevent the problem, you map Optima-Medium to Optima in FrameMaker for Windows.

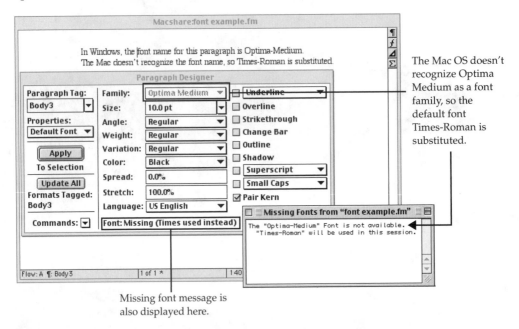

The Mac OS doesn't recognize Optima Medium as a font family, so the default font Times-Roman is substituted.

Missing font message is also displayed here.

In addition, some fonts exist only on certain platforms. For example, Chicago and Geneva are Mac system fonts and are unavailable in Windows and UNIX. If you must use these fonts, make sure that Windows and UNIX users map them to an available font on their systems.

The way FrameMaker locates and displays fonts also varies. On the Windows and Mac platforms, font management is integrated into the operating system. FrameMaker does not directly manage any fonts; you must manage fonts using the operating system tools and possibly add-on software such as Adobe Type Manager (ATM), which comes with FrameMaker. In UNIX, FrameMaker recognizes fonts only in certain directories.

This appendix discusses how to install fonts in Windows, Mac, and UNIX environments and how to transfer files from one platform to another without losing font settings.

Installing Fonts

Some fonts are installed along with FrameMaker, but they vary according to the platform. The fonts are as follows:

- **Windows.** Euro fonts—Euro Mono, Euro Sans, and Euro Serif—when you run eurofont.exe in the FrameMaker root directory
- **Mac.** TimesNewRoman, Arial, and the Euro fonts
- **UNIX.** Arial, Arial Narrow, AvantGarde, BookAntiqua, Bookman, Century-Schoolbook, Euro fonts, Symbol, TimesNewRoman, ZapfChancery, and ZapfDingbats

In Windows and Mac OS, you install fonts using the operating system instructions. For example, in Windows 2000, the Fonts Control Panel manages all fonts. A font management program, such as ATM, isn't necessary unless you're using a Multiple Master font (a customizable PostScript font from which you can create different weights, variations, and other properties). In Mac OS, fonts are usually stored in the System Folder:Fonts directory. See your operating system documentation for details on installing new fonts.

In UNIX, there are two ways to install fonts:

- Copy the fonts into the $FMHOME/fminit/fontdir (for fonts available to all users) or the $HOME/fminit/fontdir directory (for fonts available only to your login). Bitmap fonts must be copied to the $FMHOME/fminit/fontdir/bitmaps or $HOME/fminit/fontdir/bitmaps directory.
- Use the Display PostScript tools to help FrameMaker find fonts in other directories. Programs that support Display PostScript often install fonts in the usr/psres or $HOME/psres directories. You can edit the PSRESOURCEPATH environment variable to point FrameMaker to the default psres directories. See your UNIX documentation for more information.
  Display PostScript requires Adobe Font Metrics (AFM) and PostScript Font ASCII (PFA) files. Many font foundries provide AFM files with UNIX fonts, or you can convert PFM files to AFM using third-party tools, such as Ghostscript or CrossFont. For more information, see Appendix A, "Resources."

Note *If you use Display PostScript tools, make sure the <PostScript Resources> statement is in the fontlist file. See "Mapping Fonts in UNIX" on page 809 for details.*

In UNIX, you might prefer to copy new fonts to the fontdir directory for simplicity's sake; however, if you have fonts in other directories and don't want to duplicate them in the fontdir directory, you should use the Display PostScript tools.

Installing Asian Fonts

In Windows and Mac OS, you install Asian fonts as you do other fonts—according to the operating system instructions. In UNIX, you install Asian fonts into the $FMHOME/fminit/fontdir or $HOME/fminit/fontdir directory in language-specific subdirectories—for example, /ko for Korean, /ja for Japanese, /zh for Simplified Chinese, and /zh_TW for Traditional Chinese. The Asian characters are displayed in FrameMaker; however, to modify the text, you'll need to copy the character-to-glyph mapping (CMAP) files into the /cmap subdirectory. For more information, refer to the *Unix_Fonts* online manual located in $FMHOME/fminit/ *language*/OnlineManuals.

Managing Your Fonts

When FrameMaker can't find the fonts specified in a document, other fonts are displayed. If Remember Missing Fonts is selected in the FrameMaker preferences, FrameMaker saves the names of the original fonts and displays other fonts until you close the file. If the Remember Missing Fonts option isn't selected, FrameMaker permanently substitutes the default FrameMaker fonts for the original fonts.

The simplest way to prevent font substitutions is to use fonts available on all platforms. For example, FrameMaker installs Arial in UNIX and Mac platforms, and several programs (such as Adobe Acrobat) install Arial in Windows. Times or TimesNewRoman is also available on most platforms. *OpenType,* a new font format developed by Adobe and Microsoft, is also compatible with Windows, UNIX, and Mac OS.

Much of the time, you'd probably rather use more attractive fonts. This section describes how you can map fonts in FrameMaker to avoid permanent substitutions.

Mapping Fonts in Windows

In Windows, the *maker.ini* file tells FrameMaker how to display fonts by mapping them to other fonts. For example, non-Windows font properties (such as the name, weight, and angle) are mapped to Windows font properties, and the default font properties are specified. The maker.ini file includes many font mappings, but you can modify them or create your own.

To map fonts in Windows, follow these steps:

1. Close FrameMaker, then find the maker.ini file in one of the following directories:

   - If all users on your computer have the same FrameMaker preferences, go to the \Program Files\Adobe\FrameMaker 7 directory.

   - If users have different FrameMaker preferences, go to \Documents and Settings*username* (Windows 2000 and XP), \Windows\Profiles*username* (Windows Millennium Edition (Me) and 98, or \WinNT\Profiles*username* (Windows NT 4.0.)

2. Create a backup file, then open the original maker.ini file in a text editor.

3. Scroll down until the Font Options section is displayed.

```
;================================================================
;                          Font Options
;================================================================
```

4. Do any of the following:

   - To find the default fonts that are substituted for missing fonts, go to the unknown fonts section (shown in "Changing the Default Fonts"). For example, you can change the default font from Times New Roman to Veljovic.

   - To find the non-Windows font weight or angles that are mapped to Windows equivalents, go to the font weight and angle alias section (shown in "Mapping Non-Windows Weights and Angles" on page 806). For example, FrameMaker maps the non-Windows Bolded weight to Bold so that Windows can recognize the weight.

   - To find mappings for non-Windows fonts, go to the non-Windows platforms section (shown in "Mapping Unknown Fonts" on page 807). For example, FrameMaker maps system fonts, such as the Mac Geneva font, to Windows fonts.

   - To find mappings for Windows font names, go to the Windows font alias section (shown in "Mapping Windows Fonts to FrameMaker Fonts" on page 807). For example, FrameMaker maps the Windows font Helvetica-Narrow to the FrameMaker font Helvetica with a Narrow variation so that non-Windows platforms recognize the font correctly.

5. Edit the text, then save the maker.ini file. Your changes are saved and applied the next time you open FrameMaker.

Changing the Default Fonts

The default fonts defined in the maker.ini file are substituted for missing fonts unless you create a different mapping. For example, you might open a document that uses the Veljovic font. If your system doesn't have the font, FrameMaker substitutes the default font, which is Times New Roman or Times Roman. If you know ahead of time that a document uses a font you don't have, you can map the font to a more appropriate font using techniques described later in this section.

The default font properties are shown in the following mappings:

```
; Default used to map unknown fonts:
;
DefaultFamily=Times New Roman, Tms Rmn
DefaultAngle=Regular
DefaultVariation=Regular
DefaultWeight=Regular
DefaultSize=12
```

The maker.ini file also lists the available font angles, weights, and width variations. You use these terms when mapping fonts, and you can add your own. Just make sure that you don't delete a property that's used in a mapping.

```
; Definition of the font vocabulary:
;   Angles, Variations: a list of the words.
;   Weight: the list of words and the associated weight for Windows,
if any.
;
Angles=Regular, Kursiv, Slanted, Oblique, Italic, Obliqued

Variations=UltraCompressed, ExtraCompressed, Compressed, Condensed,
Narrow, Regular, Wide, Poster, Expanded

Weights=Thin 100, ExtraLight 200, SemiLight 250, Light 300, Book 300,
Regular 400, SemiBold 600, DemiBold 600, Bold 700, ExtraBold 800,
Heavy 900, Bolded 700
```

When you create a new FrameMaker document using one of the predefined FrameMaker templates, the default fonts defined in the maker.ini file are selected in paragraph and character tags.

Mapping Non-Windows Weights and Angles

The weight and angle font properties are slightly different among the platforms. For example, the Mac font weight Demi is called DemiBold in Windows. When you create a document on a Mac that uses the Demi weight and then open the document in Windows, the default weight is displayed. In Windows, FrameMaker maps these and other properties to the FrameMaker equivalents shown in the next example:

```
; Angle/Weight aliases used when reading documents from other
platforms (basically synonyms used when reading a document):

[FontAngleAliases]
Obliqued=Oblique

[FontWeightAliases]
Medium=Regular
Roman=Regular
Semi=SemiBold
Demi=DemiBold
Bolded=Bold
```

In the absence of angle and weight aliases, the default angle or weight is displayed.

Mapping Unknown Fonts

In the maker.ini file, you can map non-Windows fonts to similar Windows fonts. For example, the Mac font Chicago is mapped to Helvetica by default. The code that substitutes Helvetica says, "When the Chicago font name is found, substitute Helvetica." Asterisks (or *wildcards*) are inserted for the properties you don't want to change, as shown in the following example.

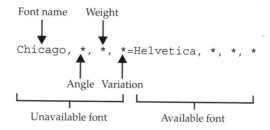

When FrameMaker substitutes Helvetica for Chicago, the original font is grayed out in the paragraph tag, and the FrameMaker Console displays the font substitution.

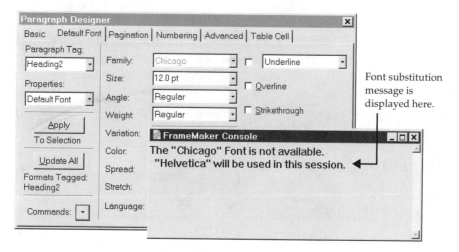

Font substitution message is displayed here.

Notice that the font family (or name), angle, weight, and variation are listed in the same order in the maker.ini file and the Paragraph Designer.

Mapping Windows Fonts to FrameMaker Fonts

In Windows fonts, the angle, weight, and variation are sometimes part of the font name, as in Helvetica-Narrow. On other platforms, these properties are independent from the font—Narrow is a variation of Helvetica. If you map the Windows font name to the FrameMaker font name in the maker.ini file, the font properties are displayed correctly in Windows, UNIX, and Mac OS.

Before the font is mapped, the Narrow variation is displayed as part of the font name.

In the Windows font name, the Narrow variation is part of the font name.

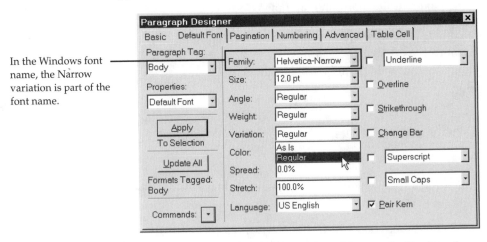

After mapping the Windows font to the FrameMaker font, Narrow is displayed as an option in the Variation drop-down list, and the font name is just Helvetica.

In the FrameMaker font name, Narrow is displayed as the Variation.

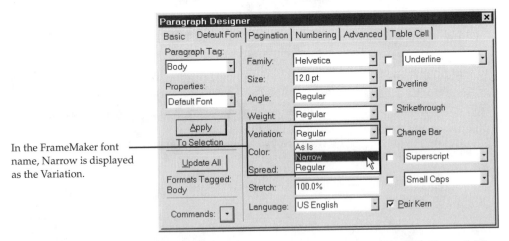

Helvetica-Narrow and many other Windows fonts are mapped to their FrameMaker equivalents in the maker.ini file that is installed with FrameMaker. The following example shows the mapping for Helvetica-Narrow:

```
[WindowsToFrameFontAliases]
Helvetica-Narrow, Regular, *=Helvetica, Regular, *, Narrow
```

Mapping Fonts in UNIX

In UNIX, fonts are mapped in the fontlist file. The default font properties, variations, weights, angles, and font substitutions are defined in the fontlist file. You can also set an option to ignore foundry abbreviations in font names.

Typically, your font mappings are located in the fontlist file in the $FMHOME/fminit/fontdir directory. These mappings are available to all users. You may also create a fontdir folder in your $HOME/fminit directory, create your own fontlist file, and then specify settings that are only displayed when you're logged in. For example, you might want to change the default font to Arial but not change the setting for other users.

FrameMaker searches for the fontlist file in the $FMHOME/fminit/fontdir directory first and then searches your home directory.

Note   *Asian fonts are defined in separate fontlist files—fontlist.ja for Japanese fonts, fontlist.ko for Korean fonts, fontlist.zh for Simplified Chinese, and fontlist.zh_TW for Traditional Chinese. See "Installing Fonts" on page 803 for details on installing Asian fonts.*

To map fonts, follow these steps:

1. Close FrameMaker, then locate the fontlist file in one of the following directories:

   ■ **$FMHOME/fminit/fontdir.** For editing settings for all users. Only users with administrative privileges can edit this file, so consult your system administrator.

   ■ **$HOME/fminit/fontdir.** For editing just your settings.

2. Create a backup of the file, then open the original fontlist file in a text editor.

3. Do any of the following:

   ■ To find the default fonts that are substituted for missing fonts, go to the <DefaultFamily> section (shown in "Changing the Default Fonts" on page 810). For example, you can change the default font from TimesNewRoman to Arial.

   ■ To find the non-UNIX font angles, weights, and variations that are mapped to UNIX equivalents, go to the <Angle>, <Weight>, or <Variation> section (shown in "Mapping Non-UNIX Weights, Angles, and Variations" on page 810). For example, the non-UNIX Roman weight is mapped to Regular.

   ■ To find mappings for non-UNIX fonts, go to the <MapFont> section (shown in "Mapping Unknown Fonts" on page 811). For example, the Mac Chicago font is mapped to Arial.

   ■ To find mappings for UNIX fonts, go to the <FamilyAlias> section (shown in "Mapping Non-UNIX Fonts to UNIX Fonts" on page 811). For example, the TmsRmn font is mapped to Times.

4. Edit the text, then save the file. Your changes are saved and applied the next time you open FrameMaker.

Changing the Default Fonts

The <DefaultFamily> statement specifies which font family to substitute for unknown fonts. The defaults are shown in the following example:

```
<DefaultFamily TimesNewRoman >
<NonText Symbol >
<NonText ZapfDingbats >
<NonText EuroMono >
<NonText EuroSans >
<NonText EuroSerif >
<MathFamily Symbol >
<FrameFamily Frame >
```

When FrameMaker can't find a font, these defaults are used unless you've mapped the font in another statement.

Mapping Non-UNIX Weights, Angles, and Variations

You define the default font weight, angle, and variation in the <Weight>, <Angle>, and <Variation> statements. For example, the following statement makes the Narrow variation available in FrameMaker:

```
<Variation Narrow>
```

The weight, angle, and variation statements end with the corresponding default property, such as the following default variation:

```
<DefaultVariation Regular>
```

You can also map non-UNIX weights, angles, and variations so the properties will be displayed correctly in UNIX. For example, the Roman and Medium weights are unavailable in UNIX, so they're mapped to Regular using the following mapping:

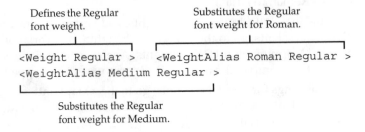

Defines the Regular font weight.   Substitutes the Regular font weight for Roman.

```
<Weight Regular >    <WeightAlias Roman Regular >
<WeightAlias Medium Regular >
```

Substitutes the Regular font weight for Medium.

You can use the same syntax to map width variations and angles.

Mapping Unknown Fonts

As mentioned previously, the default fonts specified in the fontlist file are substituted for fonts that FrameMaker cannot find. Instead of using the default fonts, you can map the missing fonts to fonts you like. The <MapFont> section of the fontlist file specifies the font mappings. For example, the Mac font Chicago is mapped to Arial. Another font—Book Antiqua—is mapped to Adobe Garamond.

```
<MapFont <Chicago> <Arial>>
<MapFont <Book Antiqua> <AGaramond>>
```

If you plan to swap files with other UNIX users, make sure everyone has a copy of the same fontlist file. Then, you don't have to worry about font substitutions.

Mapping Non-UNIX Fonts to UNIX Fonts

As mentioned previously, font names often differ among platforms. You can map non-UNIX fonts in the <FamilyAlias> section of the fontlist file, and the UNIX font is displayed instead of the original font. The following alias is included by default:

```
<FamilyAlias TmsRmn Times >
```

You can map additional non-UNIX fonts using the same syntax.

Hiding Font Foundry Names

Some font foundries add their abbreviations to font family names. The abbreviation is displayed along with the font family in FrameMaker. The following are examples of font foundries and sample fonts:

- **ITC.** International Typeface Corporation (ITC Franklin Gothic)
- **MT.** Monotype (Arial MT)
- **PS.** PostScript (TimesNewRomanPS)
- **MS.** Microsoft (Trebuchet MS)
- **ICG.** Image Club Graphics (BodoniHighlightICG)

UNIX ignores the foundry abbreviation using the following statement:

```
<IgnoreToken ICG>
```

You don't need to map the ITC, PS, and MT abbreviations because FrameMaker ignores them by default in UNIX; however, you can turn off the setting by adding the following statement:

```
<ClearIgnoreTokens>
```

This statement prompts UNIX to display the foundry abbreviations in FrameMaker. Because some fonts are made by several foundries, you may want the foundry displayed in FrameMaker so you know which font you're choosing.

APPENDIXES

Mapping Fonts in Mac OS

The Mac OS manages fonts, so FrameMaker doesn't need a font configuration file to display fonts. You should avoid using system fonts, such as Chicago, Geneva, and New York, because these fonts aren't available on other platforms. If you do need a system font, make sure that Windows and UNIX users map the font to a similar font on their computer. See "Mapping Fonts in Windows" on page 804 and "Mapping Fonts in UNIX" on page 809 for details.

Appendix C

Building Blocks

Building blocks are placeholders in FrameMaker. When FrameMaker encounters a building block, it replaces the building block with the real value. Building blocks are used in cross-reference formats, variables, autonumbered paragraph tags, reference pages, and master pages. For example, the cross-reference format called "See Heading & Page" displays the heading and page of the referenced paragraph tag as: See "Managing Color Definitions" on page 518.

The cross-reference definition is:

```
See "<$paratext>" on page <$pagenum>.
```

When the document is opened or saved, the heading and page number are updated automatically. If the heading changed to "Editing Color Definitions," the cross-reference would include the updated heading.

Building blocks are enclosed by angle brackets and are often preceded by a dollar sign (<$year>, for example). The following table describes all FrameMaker building blocks and indicates where each building block is valid. The table is sorted by symbols and then alphabetical entries, so you'll find building blocks beginning with "$" toward the top and building blocks such as "<R>" at the end.

FrameMaker provides Japanese building blocks for sorting symbols and generated lists and displaying the date and time, however, they're not covered here. Refer to the FrameMaker documentation for details.

> **Note**
> *Some building blocks don't do anything when used alone; instead, they work with other building blocks to display information. For example, <$creationtime> doesn't display the creation time; it causes the building blocks that follow (such as <$hour>:<$minute> <$AMPM>) to display the creation time. Building blocks that don't produce output have "(undisplayed)" in the description.*

Used In

Building Block	Displays	Autonumber	Cross-Reference	Index Marker	Variable	HTML Reference Page	Other Reference Pages
:	Separates levels in an index marker			✔			
;	Separates entries in an index marker			✔			
[ ]	Indicates sort order for an index entry			✔			
\b	Bullet	✔					

		Used In					
Building Block	**Displays**	Autonumber	Cross-Reference	Index Marker	Variable	HTML Reference Page	Other Reference Pages
\t	Tab	✔					
< =0>	Resets value to zero or another specified number (undisplayed)	✔					
< >	Keeps value of first counter (undisplayed)	✔					
<$alphabetics>	Sort order for alphabetic entries						✔
<$ampm>	Lowercase morning or evening designation (am)				✔		
<$AMPM>	Uppercase morning or evening designation (AM)				✔		
<$attribute[attrname]>	Value of the specified attribute for the linked element		✔		✔		
<$autorange>	Automatic page ranges						✔
<$chapnum>	Chapter number	✔	✔		✔	✔	✔
<$condtag[condtag]>	Specified condition tag				✔		
<$creationtime>	Causes any following time building block to display the creation time (only in running h/f and non-time system variables; undisplayed)				✔		
<$curpagenum>	Page number (used only on master pages)						✔
<$currenttime>	Causes any following time building block to display the current time (only in running h/f and non-time system variables; undisplayed)				✔		
<$dayname>	Name of the day (Monday)				✔		
<$daynum>	Number of the day (1)				✔		
<$daynum01>	Number of the day with leading 0 (01)				✔		

Used In

Building Block	Displays	Autonumber	Cross-Reference	Index Marker	Variable	HTML Reference Page	Other Reference Pages
`<$defaulttitle>`	Text of the first document heading					✔	
`<$elempagenum [elemtag] >`	Page number on which the specified element occurs	✔			✔	✔	✔
`<$elempagenum>`	Page number of the linked element	✔			✔	✔	✔
`<$elemparanum [elemtag] >`	Element's autonumber, including text (1.1 Introduction)	✔			✔	✔	✔
`<$elemparanum>`	Displays the autonumber of the linked element	✔			✔	✔	✔
`<$elemparanumonly [elemtag] >`	Element's autonumber, excluding text	✔			✔	✔	✔
`<$elemparanumonly>`	Autonumber of linked element, excluding text	✔			✔	✔	✔
`<$elemtag [elemtag] >`	Name of the specified element	✔			✔	✔	✔
`<$elemtag>`	Name of the linked element	✔			✔	✔	✔
`<$elemtext [elemtag] >`	Text of first element on page matching the tag	✔			✔	✔	✔
`<$elemtext>`	Text of first linked element on page, including autonumber	✔			✔	✔	✔
`<$elemtextonly [elemtag] >`	Text of first element on page matching the tag, excluding autonumber	✔			✔	✔	✔
`<$elemtextonly>`	Text of first linked element on page, excluding autonumber	✔			✔	✔	✔
`<$endrange>`	End of a page range			✔			
`<$filename>`	Name of the file ■ widget.fm *(Windows)* ■ widget *(Mac)* ■ widget.fm *(UNIX)*	✔			✔	✔	

Used In

Building Block	Displays	Autonumber	Cross-Reference	Index Marker	Variable	HTML Reference Page	Other Reference Pages
`<$fullfilename>`	Name of the path and file ■ c:\Book\widget.fm *(Windows)* ■ Book:widget *(Mac)* ■ $HOME/Book/widget.fm *(UNIX)*		✔		✔	✔	
`<$highchoice [attrname]>`	Highest value of the attribute on the page				✔		
`<$hour>`	Hours (1)				✔		
`<$hour01>`	Hours with leading 0 (01)				✔		
`<$hour24>`	Hours in 0–24 military format (13)				✔		
`<$lastpagenum>`	Last page number in document				✔		
`<$lowchoice [attrname]>`	Lowest value of the attribute on the page				✔		
`<$marker1>`	Header/Footer $1 marker text				✔		
`<$marker2>`	Header/Footer $2 marker text				✔		
`<$minute>`	Minutes (1)				✔		
`<$minute00>`	Minutes with leading 0 (01)				✔		
`<$modificationtime>`	Causes any following time building block to display the time the file was last opened or saved (only in running h/f and non-time system variables; undisplayed)				✔		
`<$monthname>`	Name of the month (January)				✔		
`<$monthnum>`	Number of the month (1)				✔		
`<$monthnum01>`	Number of the month with leading 0 (01)				✔		
`<$nextsubdoc>`	URL of the next document					✔	
`<$nopage>`	Suppresses the page number			✔			

Building Block	Displays	Used In					
		Autonumber	Cross-Reference	Index Marker	Variable	HTML Reference Page	Other Reference Pages
`<$numerics>`	Sort order for numeric entries						✔
`<$ObjectId>`	Numeric identifier assigned to the linked object						✔
`<$ObjectType>`	Numeric identifier indicating the type of link						✔
`<$pagenum>`	Page number of the linked paragraph	✔	✔				✔
`<$paranum[paratag]>`	Autonumber of first matching paragraph tag on page, including text (Chapter 1)	✔	✔	✔			✔
`<$paranum>`	Autonumber of the linked paragraph, including text	✔	✔				✔
`<$paranumonly [paratag]>`	Autonumber of first matching paragraph tag on page, excluding text (1)	✔	✔	✔			✔
`<$paratag[paratag]>`	Name of first matching paragraph tag on page (ChapterTitle)	✔	✔	✔			✔
`<$paratext[+,paratag]>`	Text of last paragraph on page matching the tag	✔	✔	✔			✔
`<$paratext[paratag1, paratag2,paratag3]>`	Text of first paragraph on page matching the tag	✔	✔	✔			✔
`<$paratext>`	Text from the source paragraph	✔	✔	✔			✔
`<$parentdoc>`	URL of the first document					✔	
`<$prevsubdoc>`	URL of the previous document					✔	
`<$relfilename>`	Relative path to linked file ■ Book\widget.fm (Windows) ■ Book:widget (Mac) ■ Book/widget.fm (UNIX)					✔	✔

		Used In					
Building Block	**Displays**	Autonumber	Cross-Reference	Index Marker	Variable	HTML Reference Page	Other Reference Pages
<$second>	Seconds (1)				✔		
<$second00>	Seconds with leading 0 (01)				✔		
<$shortdayname>	Name of the day (Mon)				✔		
<$shortmonthname>	Name of the month (Jan)				✔		
<$shortyear>	Year (30)				✔		
<$singlepage>	Designates single page number after <$nopage>			✔			
<$startrange>	Beginning of page range			✔			
<$symbols>	Sort order for symbolic entries						✔
<$tblsheetcount>	Total number of table sheets				✔		
<$tblsheetnum>	Number of current table sheet				✔		
<$variable[*varname*]>	Text of the variable					✔	
<$volnum>	Volume number	✔	✔		✔	✔	✔
<$year>	Year (2030)				✔		
<a+>	Lowercase alphabetic numbering; value increased by 1	✔					
<A+>	Uppercase alphabetic numbering; value increased by 1	✔					
<a=1>	Lowercase alphabetic numbering; value set to 1 (or another number)	✔					
<A=1>	Uppercase alphabetic numbering; value set to 1 (or another number)	✔					
<a>	Lowercase alphabetic numbering; value unchanged	✔					

Used In

Building Block	Displays	Autonumber	Cross-Reference	Index Marker	Variable	HTML Reference Page	Other Reference Pages
`<A>`	Uppercase alphabetic numbering; value unchanged	✔					
`<char_tag>`	Applies the specified character tag to the items that follow in the cross-reference definition	✔	✔	✔	✔	✔	✔
`<Default Para Font>`	Removes any character formatting and returns to the regular paragraph formatting of the parent paragraph	✔	✔	✔	✔	✔	✔
`<n+>`	Numeric numbering; value increased by 1	✔					
`<n=1>`	Numeric numbering; value set to 1 (or another number)	✔					
`<n>`	Numeric numbering; value unchanged	✔					
`<r+>`	Lowercase Roman numeral numbering; value increased by 1	✔					
`<R+>`	Uppercase Roman numeral numbering; value increased by 1	✔					
`<r=1>`	Lowercase Roman numeral numbering; value set to 1 (or another number)	✔					
`<R=1>`	Uppercase Roman numeral numbering; value set to 1 (or another number)	✔					
`<r>`	Lowercase Roman numeral numbering; value unchanged	✔					
`<R>`	Uppercase Roman numeral numbering; value unchanged	✔					

Index

INTERNATIONAL CONTACT INFORMATION

AUSTRALIA
McGraw-Hill Book Company Australia Pty. Ltd.
TEL +61-2-9417-9899
FAX +61-2-9417-5687
http://www.mcgraw-hill.com.au
books-it_sydney@mcgraw-hill.com

CANADA
McGraw-Hill Ryerson Ltd.
TEL +905-430-5000
FAX +905-430-5020
http://www.mcgrawhill.ca

GREECE, MIDDLE EAST, NORTHERN AFRICA
McGraw-Hill Hellas
TEL +30-1-656-0990-3-4
FAX +30-1-654-5525

MEXICO (Also serving Latin America)
McGraw-Hill Interamericana Editores S.A. de C.V.
TEL +525-117-1583
FAX +525-117-1589
http://www.mcgraw-hill.com.mx
fernando_castellanos@mcgraw-hill.com

SINGAPORE (Serving Asia)
McGraw-Hill Book Company
TEL +65-863-1580
FAX +65-862-3354
http://www.mcgraw-hill.com.sg
mghasia@mcgraw-hill.com

SOUTH AFRICA
McGraw-Hill South Africa
TEL +27-11-622-7512
FAX +27-11-622-9045
robyn_swanepoel@mcgraw-hill.com

UNITED KINGDOM & EUROPE (Excluding Southern Europe)
McGraw-Hill Education Europe
TEL +44-1-628-502500
FAX +44-1-628-770224
http://www.mcgraw-hill.co.uk
computing_neurope@mcgraw-hill.com

ALL OTHER INQUIRIES Contact:
Osborne/McGraw-Hill
TEL +1-510-549-6600
FAX +1-510-883-7600
http://www.osborne.com
omg_international@mcgraw-hill.com